Locke's Metaphysics

Locke's Metaphysics

Matthew Stuart

CLARENDON PRESS · OXFORD

OXFORD
UNIVERSITY PRESS

Great Clarendon Street, Oxford, OX2 6DP,
United Kingdom

Oxford University Press is a department of the University of Oxford.
It furthers the University's objective of excellence in research, scholarship,
and education by publishing worldwide. Oxford is a registered trade mark of
Oxford University Press in the UK and in certain other countries

British Library Cataloguing in Publication Data
Data available

ISBN 978-0-19-964511-4

Printed and bound in Great Britain by
CPI Group (UK) Ltd, Croydon, CR0 4YY

For my father,
Floyd C. Stuart

Preface

This book attempts to survey, to interpret, and to analyze what Locke has to say about some questions that belong to the province of metaphysics. These include questions about the ultimate categories to which things belong, the most general features of minds and bodies, the distinction between essence and accident, the individuation of bodies and persons, and the nature and scope of volition. They include such questions as whether God exists, whether bodies have colors in the dark, whether any material things have the power of thought, and whether our wills are free. Though I have tried to make this survey of Locke's metaphysics reasonably comprehensive, I have not tried to make it perfectly so. I devote my attention proportionally to the topics to which Locke devotes his. There is a point of diminishing returns in efforts to unearth or to reconstruct a philosopher's views about matters that he or she does not address directly and at some length. Such efforts may display impressive learning about the books a philosopher is likely to have read, about the ideas that were in the air when he or she wrote, but they generate conclusions that must be regarded as highly tentative. That is because the philosophers who demand our attention are precisely those who do not simply absorb influences and transmit them to posterity.

When I told my friend Alison that I was writing a book about Locke's metaphysics, she quipped: "Short book?" She made me laugh, but the notion does persist that Locke is not to be taken quite seriously as a metaphysician. One reason for this may be his own characterization of his goals in the *Essay*. Locke says that he aims "to enquire into the Original, Certainty, and Extent of humane Knowledge; together, with the Grounds and Degrees of Belief, Opinion, and Assent" (I.i.2). I am content to take this at face value, and to say that Locke wrote the book to answer epistemological questions, not metaphysical ones. Still, it cannot be said that he pursued that goal hurriedly, or single-mindedly. He is a brilliant polymath, and his *Essay* is a sprawling, discursive work. When he finds himself in the neighborhood of a metaphysical question, he can rarely resist saying something about it. What he says is nearly always interesting, frequently instructive, and sometimes profound.

Perhaps another reason that some take Locke less seriously as a metaphysician is that they see his theorizing as curtailed by his empiricism. It is true that the *Essay* does not give us untethered speculation. For some of us, that is a point in its favor. On the other hand, it is a mistake to see Locke as a sort of seventeenth-century logical positivist. He does hold that knowledge must ultimately be grounded in simple ideas received through sensation and introspection. Yet he also allows that we have the ideas of quality and essence, of man and person, of will and action—and that we can explore their contents and their relations with one another. I do think that there are serious problems with Locke's theory of ideas, and that he may not have the resources to explain how we get some of the ideas that he thinks we have (Stuart 2008, 2010). The conclusion that I draw from this is that although we laud him as the founder of modern empiricism, there may be more to admire in his metaphysics than in his epistemology.

There may also be those who underrate Locke as a metaphysician because they accept the common image of him as an insightful but unsystematic thinker whose work is rife with inconsistencies. While I do not claim that he can be acquitted on every charge of sloppiness or inconsistency, I do hope to show that Locke's writings on metaphysical topics are freer of inconsistency than many have supposed. He has been accused of bungling the definition of 'quality,' of waffling about secondary qualities, and of offering more than one story about the requirements for free action. Some find tensions in his remarks about solidity, in his thoughts about natural kinds, and in his attitude toward mechanism. In these cases, and more besides, I try to show that Locke can be successfully defended against the charges.

Many of the topics dealt with in the following pages have been discussed by commentators repeatedly, and expansively. Much of this secondary literature is of high quality, and I have learned a great deal from it. Nevertheless, like all of the commentators before me, I add to the pile because I have not been entirely satisfied with the interpretations of others, and because I hope to do better myself. In the pages that follow, I defend new readings of many familiar passages, and try to untangle knots that others have worked on. I have tried to keep the discussion and criticism of other authors to a minimum; but when I have found it useful or necessary to engage with other readings, I have focused my energies on interpretations and arguments that struck me as having a lot going for them. So it is in this business: the colleagues whose work we most admire become our targets!

One benefit of surveying a large swathe of Locke's metaphysics is that this allows us to see connections between the positions he takes, giving us a richer picture of him as a systematic thinker. Thus we will see that Locke's denial that bodies can be co-located (§43) explains why he holds a "chock full" conception of matter on which the empty spaces within a body are not parts of it (§10); that his rejection of essentialism (§23) leads him to embrace relativism about identity (§46); that his relativism about identity equips him to respond to objections to his account of personal identity (§54). Seeing such connections is important. At the same time, I would not exaggerate the degree to which Locke is a systematic metaphysician. Elaborating upon a fragment by the Greek poet Archilochus, Sir Isaiah Berlin distinguished two basic intellectual and artistic types: the hedgehogs, who relate everything to a single organizing principle; and the foxes, who seize upon a great many ideas and objects without attempting to unite them (Berlin, 1953). Berlin calls Plato and Dostoevsky hedgehogs, Aristotle and Shakespeare foxes. As I read him, Locke is more fox than hedgehog.

There are other benefits to taking a broad look at Locke's metaphysics. We learn that certain interpretive avenues that one might have thought were open are in fact closed. So the recognition that Locke repudiates relations (§5) constrains the interpretations that might be given to his suggestion that God is responsible for laws of motion (§36); the recognition that he uses 'real essence' in a nominal-essence-relative sense (§21) helps to undermine the suggestion that he is committed to a Leibnizian view of the relationship between a substance and its features (§34); the recognition that he thinks that a person's past can shrink (§48) shows that he cannot be conceiving of persons as four-dimensional things (§54).

The attempt to take in the whole sweep of Locke's metaphysics also focuses our attention on some chapters in the *Essay* that have received less of it than they deserve. One such chapter is IV.x, whose primary business is to argue for the existence of God. The main argument involves a step so patently fallacious that commentators have been understandably reluctant to dwell long upon it. However, the chapter also contains a number of curious sub-arguments that are well worth sorting out. These include arguments about panpsychism, about the relation between motion and thought, and about the sort of self-regulation required for freedom and rationality. Another chapter that has received less than its due is II.xxi, "*Of Power.*" Scholars have paid some attention to Locke's discussions of volition, voluntariness, freedom, and motivation, but not enough to the evolution of his views over the *Essay*'s several editions. Scholarship has tended to focus on later versions of the chapter; and when the changes have been discussed, the focus has been on the addition of Locke's so-called "doctrine of suspension." I devote a whole chapter to Locke's first edition account, detailing its confusion about the nature of volition, and exploring a difficulty with his account of forbearance. In a separate chapter, I examine the changes he makes in later editions. These include an improved treatment of volition, a new account of motivation, some remarks about suspending desire that amount to commonplace observations rather than a "doctrine," and a muddying of the waters about whether it is possible to forbear willing on an action once it is proposed.

I have undertaken this survey with the primary goal of coming to understand what Locke's metaphysical positions are, and how he supports them with arguments. A secondary objective is to learn some philosophy in the pursuit of the first goal. I do not believe that these two goals are incompatible. We can learn from both the successes and the failures of a great philosopher, but we cannot know what those successes and failures are until we know what the philosopher is saying. I have tried to be charitable in my reading of Locke. I have enough respect for his powers, and enough hard-earned modesty about my own, to think that this is the best way to discover what his views are, and so the best way to learn from his arguments. Still, I have not shied from saying when I find his views untenable, or his arguments unpersuasive. On occasion, I make a suggestion about how a position of his, or an argument of his, might be improved. In these cases, my ambition is to describe a view that is recognizably Lockean in spirit, but that evades a difficulty that I have identified. I have tried to make it very clear when I mean to be offering an interpretation of his words, and when I am describing a line of thought that might be regarded as a friendly amendment.

Locke's writings present us with many interpretive challenges. At times his meaning is unclear. At times he seems to contradict himself. At times he makes claims to which there would seem to be obvious objections. We would like to understand what he means by the words that he chooses to commit to print, and the most important thing that we can do toward that end is to read them closely. When that is not enough, we must draw upon the other things that we know, and work to articulate and defend an interpretation that is better than the others that appear available. Other things being equal, we should prefer an interpretation that accommodates more of what Locke says, one that assigns to his words meanings that it is more reasonable to think he might have given them, and one that ascribes to him views and arguments that are freer of defects. I have tried to develop interpretations with these desiderata. Of course, I am aware that other things are not always equal, that the desiderata will sometimes pull in different directions, and that such cases are occasions for judgment calls about which reasonable people might disagree.

Brunswick, Maine

Acknowledgments

Work on this book was generously supported by several paid leaves from Bowdoin College, and by a Fellowship from the National Endowment for the Humanities. I'm very grateful to both institutions.

Thanks to the friends and colleagues whose comments and conversation have helped me to better understand Locke's metaphysics: Jenny Ashworth, Jonathan Bennett, Justin Broackes, Vere Chappell, Jill Dieterle, Michael Della Rocca, Don Garrett, Michael Jacovides, Nicholas Jolley, Samuel Levey, Stephen Naculich, Robert Pasnau, Stephen Perkinson, Lewis Powell, David Robb, Todd Ryan, Alison Simmons, Kenneth Winkler, and Douglas Young. I must especially single out Vere Chappell, who has been the ideal senior colleague: friendly, generous, wise, critical, and encouraging. My sincere thanks to Mike Jacovides and Walter Ott, who read the manuscript for Oxford University Press and gave me very helpful comments. Peter Momtchiloff, my editor at OUP, has been remarkably patient and encouraging. Thanks also to John Rogers, who shared his typescript of portions of Draft C of the *Essay*.

My colleagues in the philosophy department at Bowdoin College— Denis Corish, Sarah Conly, Scott Sehon, and Larry Simon—have been unflaggingly supportive throughout the long period of this book's germination. I've also received help from four philosophy department coordinators: Gerlinde Rickel, who set the gold standard, and Kevin Johnson, Emily Briley, and Jean Harrison, who lived up to it admirably. John Bunke combed through the entire manuscript looking for misquotations and incorrect citations, and saved me from many errors.

Some material incorporated here appeared previously in "Locke's Colors," *Philosophical Review* 112 (2003), 57–97 (copyright Cornell University, all rights reserved and reprinted by permission of the publisher, Duke University Press), and in "Revisiting People and Substances," in *Debates in Modern Philosophy*, Antonia Lolordo and Stewart Duncan, eds., London: Routledge, 2012, 186–96. My family and friends have been living with this book for a long time, and I am grateful to them all for their support and encouragement. My daughters, Franny Stuart and Pearl Stuart, deserve special thanks for their patience and their love.

Contents

Abbreviations and Other Conventions

I have adopted the practise of using single quotation marks when *referring* to a word, phrase, or symbol rather than *using* it. I use double quotation marks when using a word or phrase that names an idea or nominal essence. So 'gold' names gold, and the nominal essence "gold"—which for Locke is the same thing as the abstract idea associated with 'gold'—might be "yellow, malleable metal soluble in *aqua regia*."

Except when it appears in quotations, the symbol '§' refers to sections of this book. I use it in the synopsis that I give at the beginning of each chapter, hoping to equip the reader with signposts to the road ahead. I use it in the text and notes to refer the reader back to earlier discussions or results, or to indicate where a topic will be discussed more fully.

Throughout the text, I use the somewhat awkward 'persons' as the plural for 'person' in the specifically Lockean sense, that is, the sense in which there is a distinction between a person and a man or a human being.

In the case of articles and single volume works, all references are to page number, unless otherwise specified. In the case of multi-volume works, all references are to volume number and page number, unless otherwise specified.

References to Locke's *Essay Concerning Human Understanding* are, unless otherwise specified, to the OUP edition edited by P. H. Nidditch, and are given by book, chapter, section, and (when necessary) line.

References to specific early editions of the *Essay* take the form of a book, chapter, and section citation followed by the number of the edition in brackets, e.g., "II.xxi.5 [1st]" for book II, chapter xxi, section 5 in the first (1690) edition.

References to the following works employ these abbreviations:

Works   *The Works of John Locke, A New Edition Corrected*, 10 vols., London: Printed for Thomas Tegg, 1823. References are to volume number and page number.

Drafts   *Drafts for the* Essay Concerning Human Understanding *and Other Philosophical Writings*, Volume 1: Drafts A and B. P. Nidditch and G. A. J. Rogers (eds), Oxford: Clarendon Press, 1990.

Draft C   A typescript of Draft C prepared by Professor G. A. J. Rogers for future publication in the Clarendon Edition of the Works of John Locke.

Corresp.   *The Correspondence of John Locke*, 8 vols., E. S. DeBeer (ed.), Oxford: Clarendon Press, 1976–1989. References are to volume number, letter number, and page number.

CSM   *The Philosophical Writings of Descartes*, 2 vols., J. Cottingham, R. Stoothoff, D. Murdoch (eds), Cambridge: Cambridge University Press, 1985.

CSMK   *The Philosophical Writings of Descartes*, vol. 3: *The Correspondence*, J. Cottingham, R. Stoothoff, D. Murdoch, and A. Kenny (eds), Cambridge: Cambridge University Press, 1991.

I

Categories

§1. The fundamental categories of Locke's ontology are the familiar ones of substance and mode. We must look carefully at how he defines and uses these terms if we are to understand what he means by them. This task is made more difficult because of Locke's carelessness about the distinction between ideas and their objects. §2. His conception of mode is a non-standard one, for it includes events as well as features of things. §3. He conceives of substances as things or stuffs that enjoy ontological independence. Modes are dependent upon substances either because they are ways that substances are, or because they are events that feature substances as constituents. Substances include not only natural things and stuffs, but also artifacts. §4. Locke defines a class of ideas that he calls ideas of "mixed modes." These are complex ideas that represent features or events, and that have more than one type of simple idea as a constituent. Ideas of mixed modes include the ideas of beauty, of theft, and of a rainbow. Locke draws several contrasts between ideas of substances and ideas of mixed modes, and one of these seems to imply that the world does not contain beauty, theft, or rainbows. What he means is not that, but that our ideas of mixed modes do not count as defective if there happens to be nothing in the world answering to them. §5. Locke says that all of our complex ideas can be "reduced under these three Heads. 1. Modes 2. Substances. 3. Relations." He also notes that many features of things depend upon their relations. This suggests that he endorses a three-category ontology. However, though his remarks about relations are spare, he is best understood as denying their existence.

§1 Introduction

One of the tasks of metaphysics is to give an account of the most basic constituents of reality. Philosophers have long approached this task by trying to describe the broadest categories into which things fall. In this endeavor, economy and completeness are the cardinal virtues, the object being to describe the smallest set of categories that suffices to accommodate all there is. Not surprisingly, philosophers have quarreled about the details. They have offered different lists of categories, and different accounts of the features that earn a thing its place in one or another category. Yet as a matter of historical fact, these differences have frequently been worked out within a common framework, an inheritance from Aristotle. This framework involves a commitment to at least two most fundamental categories, substance and accident. A substance is understood to be a particular that is the subject of accidents, and that is characterized by some sort of independence. A substance's accidents are supposed to depend on it for their existence. In the seventeenth century, the ontological framework of substance and accident was an ancient tradition, but still a living one. It found expression in the writings of a diverse array of philosophers and theologians: the Scholastics and Spinoza, the Cartesians and the Cambridge Platonists, Edward Stillingfleet and John Locke.

Though Locke's metaphysics is framed in traditional terms, it would be unwise to suppose that he simply relies upon tradition to supply the meanings for these terms. Few of the best philosophers in the tradition did that. That is one reason why the tradition does not speak with one voice about what are the criteria that something must meet to be counted as a substance, an accident or an essence. While it is surely helpful to have some awareness of historical antecedents, there is no substitute for looking at what a philosopher actually says about what he means by terms of art. It can be just as important to look at the way that he uses them in his reasoning about the basic character of reality—to look at the premises he accepts, the examples he offers, the inferences he makes, the conclusions he draws.

One potential source of trouble as we turn to what Locke actually says is that often he is careless about distinguishing between ideas and their objects. This is particularly true when the topic is modes or ideas of modes, qualities or ideas of qualities. Sometimes this carelessness is merely a matter of his writing 'idea' when he means "quality." He confesses to that habit at II.viii.8, and it has been widely noted by commentators. There are straightforward instances of this in his discussions of substance, as when he says that we do not imagine that "simple *Ideas*" can subsist by themselves, and so "accustom our selves, to suppose some *Substratum*, wherein they do subsist" (II.xxiii.1). Surely what he means is that we do not imagine that *the qualities in bodies* that give rise to our simple ideas can subsist by themselves, and thus we come to think of these qualities as subsisting in a substratum.

As Jonathan Bennett has shown, Locke is also guilty of more substantive conflations (Bennett 1996). The very passage in which he confesses to sometimes saying "idea" when he means "quality" is muddled in a way that substituting 'quality' back for 'idea' will not straighten out: he talks about the "*Ideas*" of white, cold, and round "as they are in the Snow-ball" and "as they are Sensations, or Perceptions, in our Understandings" (II.viii.8). He cannot really want to say either that ideas are *both* in the snowball and in our understandings, or that qualities are. Locke also sometimes speaks of modes as though they were ideas. So, for example, he says: "*Modes* I call such complex *Ideas*, which however compounded, contain not in them the supposition of subsisting by themselves, but are considered as Dependences on, or Affections of Substances" (II.xii.4). Here modes are called ideas, but they are also said to be considered as "Dependences on" substances. While he may in fact hold that ideas are "Dependences on" substances—that ideas are dependences upon the minds having those ideas—it seems plain that he means to be telling us that *all* "Dependences on" substances are modes. We might imagine that this is a case of his saying "*Ideas*" where he means "qualities," except that it is *ideas* that are simple or complex for Locke, not qualities. Thus we have a conflation of modes and ideas of modes rather than a clean ambiguity involving 'idea.' Locke's conflation of qualities and ideas is a minor annoyance in some cases, and a real obstacle to understanding his position in others.

Another challenge is that it can be difficult to tell when Locke's claims about the nature and content of our ideas are *just* claims about how we think of things, and when they are supposed to convey something about how things are. Consider his announcement at II.xii.3 that all of our complex ideas can be "reduced under these three Heads. 1. *Modes* 2. *Substances*. 3. *Relations.*" Strictly speaking, this is a claim about the classification of our ideas, not a claim about the ultimate categories of being. Yet it is tempting to suppose that he takes our ideas to be reflective of reality in this case—to suppose that mode, substance, and relation are the three fundamental categories of his ontology. To establish whether this is really so will take some work. We will turn to part of that task shortly. For the moment, let us simply note this as one instance of a more general difficulty: it can be hard to tell when Locke is making a claim about our ideas of things, and when he is trying to say something about how things are.

An examination of the fundamental categories of Locke's ontology does not take us immediately to his most important contributions, but it is a good place to start. It allows us to locate him within a philosophical tradition to which he does belong, and to appreciate when he is reacting against elements of that tradition. So we begin by considering Locke's views about which things count as modes and substances, and why they do. Later in the chapter, we will turn to some questions about the status of mixed modes and relations.

§2 Modes

Locke uses a number of general terms to refer to the ways that substances are: 'mode,' 'accident,' 'quality,' 'affection,' 'property,' 'attribute,' and their plurals. We have already seen that he characterizes modes as "Dependences on, or Affections of Substances" (II.xii.4). Even if we set aside the fact that Locke sometimes uses 'mode' to mean "idea of a mode," he gives 'mode' a wider scope than it has in the writings of many philosophers. Modes for him include not only features of substances, but also events. A triumph— that is, a parade celebrating a military victory—counts as a mode for Locke (II.xxii.8), as does a resurrection (III.v.5) and a stabbing (III.v.6).

Locke holds that "all things that exist are only particulars" (III.iii.6), and so is committed to the view that all modes are non-repeatable particulars.[1] That is of course what one should expect of the modes that are events. The second showing of a movie may resemble the first in many respects; but since it occurs at a different time, it is a different event. The same goes for triumphs, resurrections, and stabbings. Simultaneous showings, triumphs, resurrections, or stabbings can also be distinguished by place or participants rather than time of occurrence. Yet Locke also conceives of the modes that are not events as non-repeatable individuals, rather than abstract entities.[2] Lockean modes that are not events are what are now sometimes called "tropes."[3] They are particular instances of features. An example would be the redness of Massachusetts Hall, where this is understood not as a shade

---

[1] For other statements of the view that only particulars exist, see III.iii.1, 11 and *Works* X, 250.

[2] This point is made by Armstrong 1997, 25.

[3] The term 'trope' was introduced by Donald C. Williams (1953). It has been widely, but not universally, adopted. Keith Campbell favors 'abstract particular' (Campbell 1990), and other authors have invoked such phrases as "concrete properties" or "individual accidents."

that might characterize other brick buildings, but as something peculiar to Massachusetts Hall however similar any other buildings may be in respect of color. Though tropes are particulars, they are distinct from the things they characterize. In the context of Locke's ontology, they figure as ways that substances are rather than as substances themselves.

Locke offers no argument against the existence of abstract objects, but he does make some attempt to show how we can do without them. At II.xi.9 and III.iii, he gives an account of the semantics of general terms that is broadly nominalist in spirit. On that account, a general term is one that can represent more than one particular. A general term can do this because it stands for an abstract idea. For an idea to be abstract is not for it to be a non-particular, but rather for it to be the product of abstraction, a mental operation. In abstraction one selectively attends to one component of a complex idea, removing or leaving out the other components of it (Stuart 2008). The product of abstraction is an idea that is able to represent more than one particular because it represents features common to several particulars without representing those that distinguish them.

When he first introduces the idea of a mode, Locke offers as examples "*Triangle, Gratitude, Murther, etc.*" (II.xii.4). This is an odd list, even after we have made allowance for the conflation of modes and ideas of modes. There is not much difficulty about gratitude and murder being on the list. A murder is a kind of event. '*Gratitude*' might refer either to the property characterizing the mind of a person while she is feeling grateful, or to a mental event, an episode of feeling grateful. It is less clear why '*Triangle*' belongs on the list. To make sense of this, we must observe that '*Gratitude*,' and '*Murther*' are general terms. What Locke has offered us is really a list of kinds of modes, rather than a list of particular modes. Yet it is the members belonging to those kinds that Locke wants to say are dependences on, or affections of, substances. To preserve the parallel, '*Triangle*' should name a kind whose members are dependences on, or affections of, substances. It does this if it refers to the kind whose members are the instances of triangularity in the world (if there are any). It is not beyond the pale that one might use 'triangle' to name that kind, though one would have expected 'triangularity' or 'triangular' to fill that role. Curiously, Locke never uses those terms, despite the fact that he mentions triangles, and discusses our knowledge of them, on dozens of occasions.

Of the terms that Locke uses to refer to the ways that substances are, 'quality' is another that figures particularly prominently in his metaphysical theorizing. Locke's definition of 'quality' and his classification of qualities will occupy us for the next two chapters. As for his handling of other terms that designate ways that substances are—'attribute,' 'property,' 'affection,' and 'accident,' a quicker survey will suffice.

Locke does not use 'attribute' as a noun very often. He makes no attempt at defining this term, and does not say that he means to use it in a specialized sense. In practice, however, he reserves it for only the most basic features of substances, features that are so basic that they are not liable to change.[4] Locke recognizes three basic kinds of substances: bodies, finite intelligences, and God (II.xxvii.2). He calls extension an attribute of matter (II.xv.4), and he suggests that the power to act may be the "proper attribute" of spirits (II.xxiii.28). Most intriguing is the fact that although he uses 'attribute' so rarely, he almost always uses it when he is referring to a feature of God, presumably because none of the features of God are liable to change.[5]

Today we tend to use 'property' as a generic, catch-all term for ways that things are. However, there is a long tradition—reaching back to Aristotle through Porphyry—of sometimes reserving 'property' (and the terms we translate as 'property') for an aspect of a substance that is not essential, but that is possessed by all and only that substance's conspecifics. At other times, Aristotle uses 'property' in a slightly less narrow sense, one on which properties also include essential features.[6] On either of these narrower senses, the ability to learn grammar is a property of man (*Topics* 102a20), as is the ability to laugh (Porphyry 2003, 12). Locke may sometimes use 'property' and 'properties' in our wide sense; at other times, he clearly uses it in one or the other of Aristotle's narrower senses. He may be using it in our wide sense on

---

[4] This makes Locke's use of 'attribute' similar in some respects to Descartes's use of 'principal attribute' (*Principles* I, 53 in Descartes 1985, vol.1, 210) and to Spinoza's use of 'attribute' (*Ethics* 1d4 in Spinoza 1985, vol. 1, 408, but also see the discussion in Bennett 1984, 60–6). However, we should not make too much of this. For both Descartes and Spinoza, 'attribute' is explicitly introduced in a specialized sense, and the corresponding concept is an important nexus in an elaborate attempt to answer basic questions of ontology. It is not so for Locke.

[5] See I.iv.15; II.xvii.1; IV.x.6, 12. In this Locke follows Descartes (see *Principles* I, 56, in Descartes 1985, 1:211).

[6] The transliteration of the Greek term rendered as 'property' in these contexts is *'idion.'* Terence Irwin and Gail Fine explain: "Aristotle uses *idion* as a technical term (Latin 'proprium') for a nonESSENTIAL but necessary property F, belonging to all and only Fs, *Catg.*3a21, 4a10, *Top.* 102a18–30 (discussed fully in *Top.* v). He also uses the term less strictly, so that it includes essential properties, *APo* 73a7, 75b18, 76a17, *DA* 402a9, *Met.* 1004b11, *EN* 1097b34" (Aristotle 1995, 578). For the same use in Porphyry, see Porphyry 2003, 11–12.

those occasions when he seems to speak of indifferently of a thing's modes, qualities, or properties.[7] He may also be using 'Properties' in its widest sense when he calls color, weight, and fusibility "Properties" of the parcel of Matter that makes the ring on his finger (III.iii.18). For in that passage the point of characterizing the ring as a parcel of matter is precisely to avoid considering it in relation to an essence that might serve to distinguish its essential from its non-essential features. Yet Locke is clearly using 'Properties' in one of the narrower senses at III.vi.6, where he says that "Properties [belong] only to *Species*, and not to Individuals."[8] He cannot mean to deny that individuals have qualities. Rather, he is saying that it is only in relation to some species that a quality counts as a property in one of the narrow senses. Locke does not call attention to the fact that he uses 'Properties' in different senses, so naturally he does not tell us when he is employing which. Often it does not much matter which sense he intends. When it does matter, we can only look to the context to discover what it is.

Locke does not use 'affection' or 'accident' very often. When he does use these terms, he does not seem to mean anything different than what he means by 'quality.' He calls extension a quality (II.viii.9) and an affection (II.xiii.24). He calls heat and cold sensible qualities (II.i.3; II.xxiii.7), but also affections (II.xxvii.11, 24). He refers to the color white as a "Quality or Accident" (IV.xi.2). One could say such things and yet take the extensions of 'quality,' 'affection,' and 'accident' to be systematically overlapping but non-equivalent. I have found no evidence that Locke is doing that.

§3 *Substances*

Complex ideas can, we are told, be reduced under three heads. The first was "*Modes*," and the second is "*Substances*":

The *Ideas* of *Substances* are such combinations of simple *Ideas*, as are taken to represent distinct particular things subsisting by themselves; in which the supposed, or confused *Idea* of Substance, such as it is, is always the first and chief. Thus if to Substance be joined the simple *Idea* of a certain dull whitish colour, with certain degrees of Weight, Hardness, Ductility, and Fusibility, we have the *Idea* of *Lead*; and a combination of the *Ideas* of a certain sort of Figure, with the powers of Motion, Thought, and Reasoning, joined to Substance, make the ordinary *Idea* of a *Man*. (II.xii.6)

[7] See, for example, II.xxiii.6, 30.
[8] Another place that Locke uses 'properties' in this special sense is two sections later, at III.vi.8.

Locke says that ideas of substances are ones that are taken to represent distinct particular things, but his examples suggest a less tidy picture. A man is not a surprising candidate for being a distinct particular thing, but "*Lead*" ought to give us pause. Lead would seem to be a stuff, or a kind of stuff, rather than a distinct particular thing. This is not a singular slip: Locke refers to gold, water, vitriol, bread, and iron as substances.[9] We could accommodate "*Lead*" as a distinct particular thing by supposing that Locke regards the totality of any kind of stuff as composing a distinct particular thing, and that '*Lead*' refers to such a thing. Another possibility is that when Locke calls lead a substance, what he really means is that each individual, cohering bit of lead is a substance (Odegard 1969).

R. S. Woolhouse goes so far as to suggest that Locke's ideas of substances are usually not ideas of distinct particular things. He points out that the complex ideas of substances that Locke is most concerned about—the ones that are the focus of his attention in such chapters as "*Of our Complex* Ideas *of Substances*" (II.xxiii) and "*Of the Names of Substances*" (III.vi)—are ideas of kinds of things. They are general ideas such as "man," rather than the ideas of particular men. These are ideas of the items that Aristotle in the *Categories* had called secondary substances, rather than ideas of such primary substances as an individual man or an individual horse.[10] Woolhouse concludes that Locke's "substance-ideas are, in the end, not to be understood as ideas of Aristotelian first substances" (Woolhouse 1983, 98).

Woolhouse is right to point out that Locke is sometimes more concerned with general ideas of kinds of substances than with the ideas of particular continuants. Yet he goes too far when he suggests that Lockean ideas of substances are not ideas of distinct particular things. Locke's repudiation of abstract objects means that if the idea "man" is to represent anything in the world, it can only represent one or more particulars. What makes it a general idea is just that it represents several particular men, rather than one particular man. So there is still a perfectly straightforward sense in which ideas of kinds of substances "represent distinct particular things subsisting by themselves" (II.xii.6). It is just that in these cases the relation of idea to thing is not one-to-one.

The idea of a man is an idea of a substance, Locke tells us. If 'Caesar' names a man, then Caesar is a substance on his view, and the idea of Caesar is the

[9] II.xxiii.3, 6, 9.
[10] Aristotle 1984, *Categories* 2a15–16.

idea of a substance. Let us assume that Locke would also count Cleopatra as a substance, and the idea of Cleopatra as an idea of a substance. His examples of modes include a triumph and beauty. Thus the idea of Caesar's quadruple triumph in 46 BC is the idea of a mode, as is the idea of Cleopatra's beauty. The defining feature of ideas of substances for Locke is that they are ideas whose objects are conceived as subsisting by themselves. The defining feature of ideas of modes, by contrast, is that they are conceived as being dependences on, or affections of, substances. Thus Locke holds that Caesar and Cleopatra do, in some important sense, subsist by themselves. He also holds that Ceasar's triumph and Cleopatra's beauty do, in some important sense, depend on substances.

What sort of independence is it that Caesar and Cleopatra are supposed to enjoy, and what sort does Locke mean to deny of Caesar's triumph and Cleopatra's beauty? One candidate for the sort of dependence that modes have on substances is causal dependence. It is not unreasonable to suppose that Locke would regard Caesar's triumph and Cleopatra's beauty as depending on substances that cause them to exist. It is, however, unlikely that he has causal *independence* in mind when he says that such things as Caesar and Cleopatra subsist by themselves. The familiar facts of generation and corruption would seem to entail that men and women are not causally independent, and there is no reason to suppose that Locke thinks otherwise.[11]

Perhaps it will be suggested that Locke has causal dependence in mind when he says that modes are dependences on substance, but some other, non-causal sort of independence in mind when he says that substances subsist by themselves. There are good reasons for resisting this. One is that it makes a hash of the contrast that Locke draws between modes and substances.

---

[11] One might object that Locke would have taken Caesar and Cleopatra to be at least partly constituted by immaterial souls that were naturally indestructible and hence causally independent. To this, several points of reply are in order, all of which look forward to issues that we will take up in Chapter 8. First, it is "a man" that is said to be a substance, and on the usage that Locke introduces at II.xxvii.6, a man is an organism, and thus the sort of thing that might perish naturally. Second, Locke is officially agnostic about whether or not any human person is even partly constituted by an immaterial soul. Therefore, even if "a Man" in II.xii means "a person" he should not be helping himself to the presumption that such things are causally independent because they are partly or wholly constituted by immaterial souls. Third, even if it is Caesar the *person* we are talking about and even if we assume that persons are wholly constituted by immaterial souls, it would not be right to say that Locke would regard Caesar as being causally independent because Caesar is constituted by an unperishable soul. For on the view of personhood that Locke defends in II.xxvii, a person can be destroyed by means that need not involve the destruction of an immaterial soul that constitutes the person.

The suggestion is that at II.xii.4 he is telling us that modes are causally depend-ent, while at II.xii.6 he is denying that substances are dependent in some non-causal sense. That is like the waiter at an Indian restaurant telling you that the difference between two dishes is that one is hot and the other not, when he means that the first dish is spicy and that the other one is not heated. A second problem for the reading under consideration is that because they are causally dependent on substances, Caesar and Cleopatra would count as modes on this reading even if they also qualify as substances in virtue of some non-causal variety of self-subsistence. Yet it seems clear that Locke means for the categories of substance and mode to be mutually exclusive.

If it is not causal dependence that Locke has in mind when he portrays modes as dependent on substances, and substances as independent, then what sort of dependence is it? The obvious answer—and I think the cor-rect one—is ontological dependence. Modes depend on substances for their existence because their manner of existence requires—not causally, but log-ically or metaphysically—the existence of certain other things. These other things enjoy a manner of existence that does similarly require the existence of still other things. This conception of the relation between modes or acci-dents and substances is as old as Aristotle, and in the seventeenth century it was the common property of scholastics and Cartesians, of Spinoza and Robert Boyle.[12] On this conception, a mode is a way that something is, or possibly a way that some things are. The characterization of modes as onto-logically dependent derives from the insight that it is impossible for there to be ways things are without there being things that are those ways. From the idea that not everything is a way that something else is, we get the idea that there must be some things that are ontologically independent.

This way of drawing the distinction between substance and mode is schematic, but even so it raises difficulties that Locke ignores. For instance, it seems reasonable to say that features can have features—that the ways things are can themselves be different ways. This means that if the categories of substance and mode are supposed to be mutually exclusive, a substance cannot be understood simply as a bearer of features. One might define sub-stances as things that are not ways of being other things. Modes could be

---

[12] See Aristotle's *Categories* 1a20–28, 2a13–15 (1984 v.1, 3–4); Eustachius a Sancto Paulo's *Compendium* I.1 (Ariew, Cottingham, and Sorrell 1998, 72); Descartes's *Second Replies* (1985, 2:114) and *Principles* I:56 (CSM, 1:211); Malebranche's *Dialogues on Metaphysics*, Dialogue 1 (1980b, 27); Spinoza's *Ethics* 1d3, 1d5, 1p1 (1985, 408–10); Boyle's *Origin of Forms and Qualities* (1991, 21–2, 57).

said to include ways substances are, but also whatever stands in the ancestral of that relation to a substance.

Another, and possibly more serious, problem with using ontological dependence to distinguish modes and substances concerns the idea that things are more basic than the ways things are. This assumption crops up again and again in the history of philosophy, but it seems vulnerable to a simple objection. Though it is true that a way of being cannot exist without some thing or other being that way, it is just as true that a thing cannot exist without being some way or other. On the face of it, the dependence relations between things and the ways they are would seem to be perfectly symmetrical. A possible response to this would be to say that we need to take greater care in cashing out the notion of ontological dependence. Rather than conceiving of it as mere existential dependence, we should conceive of it as some other non-causal relation, but one that is necessarily asymmetrical. So instead of saying that x is ontologically dependent upon y just in case the existence of x entails the existence of y, we might say that x is ontologically dependent upon y just in case the existence of y explains the existence of x. Or we might say that x is ontologically dependent upon y just in case x depends for its identity upon y.[13] These are interesting possibilities, though they raise difficulties of their own, including the challenge of explicating the relevant notion of explanatory dependence, or identity dependence, in a satisfactory way. How exactly to characterize the ontological dependence of modes upon substances is something that Locke does not discuss, and it would take us too far afield were we to explore all of the options that might be available to him.

That Locke is thinking of the dependence of modes on substances as ontological, rather than causal, may already be implied by his characterization of modes as "Dependences on, or Affections of Substances" (II.xii.4). An affection of a substance is a way the substance is. One way to read "Dependences on, or Affections of Substances" is as suggesting an equivalence between being a "dependence on" a substance and being an "affection of" a substance. On this reading, all modes are ways substances are. In that case, Locke is saying that even events are ways substances are. This raises a problem: Caesar's triumph is certainly not a way that Caesar is. Perhaps the suggestion is that Caesar's triumph is an affection of Caesar and

---

[13] These are two possibilities explored in Lowe 2009.

a number of other substances. Yet one might worry that Caesar's triumph could be an affection of a collection of substances only if the collection constitutes a substance, which in the case of Caesar and his retinue seems implausible.[14] Another problem is that events seem to have temporal parts whereas, on the usual way of thinking about them, substances do not. How could a four-dimensional event be a feature of a three-dimensional collective substance?

A better way of understanding the claim that modes are "Dependences on, or Affections of Substances" is to read the two clauses as non-equivalent, but as having overlapping extensions. One can see Locke as attempting to make room for events as dependences on substances without treating events as affections. Being an affection of a substance is one way of being a dependence on a substance, but being an event that has the substance as a constituent is another. This reading avoids both of the difficulties that face the previous one: it is unproblematic that a triumph is a mode, and the category of modes is broad enough to include things with temporal parts. On this reading, the dependence of modes on substances is still ontological dependence. Just as there cannot be ways a thing is without a thing that is those ways, so there cannot be events involving things without there being those things. As the redness of a brick could not exist without the brick, so the brick's breaking a window could not exist without the brick. Caesar's triumph is a dependence on Caesar, and on various other men and horses, because that particular parade could not have occurred without those substances existing then.

On the reading that we have been developing, anything that exhibits the right sort of ontological independence—anything that is a subject of properties without being an event or a property of something else—counts as a substance. In an influential paper, Martha Bolton contends that Locke counts only natural things or stuffs as substances (Bolton 1976, 488). Locke's

---

[14] One might try to mount a reply on Locke's behalf by pointing to his talk of "*Collective* Ideas *of Substances*" (II.xxiv), and to the fact that he offers the idea of an army as one of these (II.xii.6). If an army is a substance, then Caesar's triumph could be an affection of Caesar's army. The question is whether Locke counts an army as a substance. Most of the time, he seems to think of collective ideas of substances as ideas of groups of substances, but not as ideas of substances composed of groups of substances. The section heading for II.xii.6—which reads "*Substances Single or Collective*"—could be offered as evidence that armies and flocks of sheep are supposed to be collective *substances*, and not just collective ideas of substances. However, given Locke's carelessness about ideas and their objects, and given his failure to talk of collective substances elsewhere, one cannot have much confidence that "*Substances ... Collective*" is supposed to denote a class of complex ideas rather than a class of items in the world.

substances, according to her, are things or stuffs that figure in laws of nature (Bolton 1976, 511–12). It is true that the examples of substances that Locke offers are nearly always examples of naturally occurring things or stuffs. They are men, horses, stones, gold, lead, and so on. It is also true that though he frequently speaks of "natural Substances," he tends to speak of artificial *things* rather than of artificial substances.[15] On the other hand, there are several reasons for thinking that artifacts count as substances for Locke. First, there is the fact that not *all* of Locke's examples of substances belong to natural kinds: at II.xxiii.6 he characterizes bread as a substance. Second, his discussion of "*Collective* Ideas *of Substances*" seems to imply that artifacts are substances. Collective ideas of substances are so called, Locke says, "because such *Ideas* are made up of many particular Substances considered together" (II.xxiv.1). This is one of the relatively rare occasions on which he conflates substances and ideas of substances. He means, surely, that collective ideas of substances are made up of *ideas* of many particular substances considered together.

Locke's examples of collective ideas of substances include the idea of an army, the idea of a city, and the idea of a fleet (II.xxiv.2). This is trouble for Bolton's reading, because although an army may consist solely of men (an unequipped army being perhaps still an army of sorts), collections of men do not make a city, or a fleet. Even a collection of *sailors* does not make a fleet. If the idea of a fleet is a collective idea of substances, then it would seem that a ship must be a substance. If the idea of a city is a collective idea of substances, then some man-made structures are substances. One might resist these conclusions by arguing that an idea counts as a collective idea of substances so long as it includes the ideas of a number of substances, even if it also includes the ideas of a number of non-substantial items. Thus one might contend that the idea of a city is a collective idea of substances because it includes the idea of a number of human inhabitants, even though it also includes the ideas of (allegedly) non-substantial man-made structures. However, this line of argument will succeed only if Locke thinks that it is true by definition that cities and fleets include people. If he thinks that an abandoned city is still a city, and an unmanned fleet still a fleet, then he must be thinking of buildings and ships as substances.

[15] For "natural Substances," see II.xxi.2; III.iv.1, 3; III.vi.2, 11, 41. For "artificial things," see II.xxvi.2 and III.vi.40, 41.

A third reason for thinking that artifacts count as substances for Locke—and surely the most important one—is that they seem to satisfy his account of what a substance is. A substance, he tells us at II.xii.6, is something that subsists by itself. We are left to understand what this means by understanding what a substance is not. A substance is not dependent in the way that a mode is. This means that a substance is not related to something else as an affection; it is not a way that something else is. It also means that a substance is not an event that depends for its existence on its constituents. Caesar, his horses, and his soldiers are substances because none of them is either an affection of something else, or an event that has some other thing as a constituent. By this reasoning, houses, ships, and typewriters should qualify as substances.

Bolton denies that artifacts subsist by themselves in the sense that Locke has in mind. According to Bolton, when Locke says that a substance "subsists by itself" he means that "the existence of a substance requires nothing but what is dictated by laws of nature" (Bolton 1976, 511). Substances are self-subsistent because "everything required for their existence is determined by the laws of nature about them" (Bolton 1976, 511). The idea seems to be that a substance's self-subsistence involves causal independence, but causal independence of a very restricted and unusual sort—a sort that is compatible with an enormous amount of causal dependence. If something is self-subsistent, on Bolton's reading, then it is free from "extra-legal" causal dependencies: any causal dependency that it does have is captured by some law of nature or other.[16] A typewriter fails to qualify as self-subsistent in the relevant sense because typewriters depend for their existence on typewriter factories and typewriter repairmen, and such things do not figure in any laws of nature. The biggest problem with this reading is that it strays so far from any ordinary understanding of Locke's phrase 'subsists by itself' as to defy credibility, and does so in the absence of direct textual evidence. When Locke talks about things being capable or incapable of subsisting by themselves, he makes no mention of laws of nature. In fact, he has very little to say about laws of nature in any context. A further problem is that since

---

[16] Bolton seems to think that Lockean self-subsistence also involves ontological independence. At one point she says, "Substances 'subsist by themselves,' because they do not require modes or entities of another category in order to exist (although the laws of nature make them dependent on other substances)" (Bolton 1976, 511). Presumably the idea is that both artifacts and natural substances satisfy this requirement, but that artifacts are excluded from the category of substance because of their extra-legal causal dependencies.

presumably God does not figure in any laws of nature, Bolton's reading threatens to exclude from the category of substance anything that depends causally on God for its existence. It thus threatens to yield the result that there are no substances.

At the end of his short chapter on collective ideas of substances, Locke makes a curious observation about the nature of artifacts. He says, "Amongst such kind of collective *Ideas*, are to be counted most part of artificial Things, at least such of them as are made up of distinct Substances" (II.xxiv.3). Strictly speaking, this is a tautology. A collective idea of substances is, by definition, the idea of a number of substances considered together. So in the passage just quoted, Locke is saying that if an artifact is "made up of distinct Substances," then the idea of it is a collective idea of substances. The same could be said of an organism, or of a stone. It is true of anything that *if* it is a conglomeration of substances, then the idea of it is the idea of a number of substances considered together. Yet in singling out artifacts for special mention, Locke seems to intend some contrast between artifacts and other things. The contrast seems to be this: we are more apt to think of the parts of artifacts as being substances—distinct particular things capable of subsisting by themselves—than we are the parts of natural substances. Why might this be? One reason is that in many cases the parts of artifacts are coherent chunks of stuff with their own well defined boundaries; that is less often true of the parts of natural substances. Think of the gears, springs, screws, and so forth that make up a clock, and compare these with the tissues of an animal body. Another, not unrelated, reason that the parts of an artifact might seem more like distinct particular things is that in many cases artifacts can be disassembled and reassembled, whereas—at least in Locke's day—natural substances could not be.

What it is for a substance to subsist by itself is for it not to be ontologically dependent in the ways that modes are. However, the sort of ontological dependence that Locke takes to be definitive of modes is not the only sort of ontological dependence that one might conceive. There is also the dependence of a composite thing on its parts, and (perhaps) the dependence of an ordinary object on the matter out of which it is composed. If freedom from these sorts of ontological dependence were required of substances, then only simple, immaterial things could be substances. Such a conclusion would be too profoundly revisionist for Locke's taste: he would be more apt to look around for another characterization of substance rather than abandon the notion that ordinary physical objects are substances.

§4 *Mixed Modes*

We have seen that Locke departs from tradition in taking the category of modes to include not only features of things, but also events. This is far from being the only complication in his treatment of modes. Another wrinkle is that although he offers ideas of modes, substances, and relations as the three fundamental kinds of complex ideas—and although he evidently takes all ideas of substances[17] and of relations[18] to be complex ideas—he does not think that all ideas of modes are complex ideas. Indeed, it seems that for Locke all—or nearly all—simple ideas are ideas of modes.

At II.iii.1, Locke marks a "*Division of simple* Ideas"[19] into four sorts: those that enter through one sense only, those that enter through more than one sense, those that come from reflection only, and those that are "suggested to the mind *by all the ways of Sensation and Reflection.*" His examples of ideas in the first class include ideas of colors, noises, tastes, and smells, and also the ideas of heat, cold, and solidity (II.iii.1). Ideas in the second class include the ideas of space, extension, figure, rest, and motion (II.v). Those in the third include the ideas of perception and of willing (II.vi.2). Those in the fourth include the ideas of pleasure, pain, power, existence, and unity (II.vii.1). Nearly all of these seem to be ideas of modes. That is, they seem to be ideas

---

[17] It seems clear that Locke takes all ideas of substances to be complex ideas, but it is hard to find a place where he comes right out and says this. He frequently refers to our "complex ideas of substances," and takes each of these to be an idea whose parts include several simple ideas plus the "confused *Idea* of *something* to which they belong" (II.xxiii.3). Yet there being many complex ideas of substances is, strictly speaking, compatible with there also being one or more simple ideas of substances. Perhaps the nearest Locke comes to explicitly ruling that out is at II.xxiii.14, where he says that "*our specifick* Ideas *of Substances* are ...complex and compounded." Yet even this is an observation about ideas of *kinds* of substances, and leaves open the possibility that the idea of some particular substance is a simple idea. The most likely candidate would be the idea of God, and Locke explicitly ranks that among the complex ideas (see II.xxiii.33–35).

[18] Locke says that ideas of relations are another of the three kinds of complex ideas (II.xii.3, 7 and II.xxxi.14), and again it seems fairly obvious that this means that all ideas of relations are complex ideas. Yet again he does not seem to explicitly rule out the possibility that some ideas of relations are, or might be, simple. He might seem to do so at II.xxv.11, where he says that "all the *Ideas* we have of *Relation*, are made up, as the others are, only of simple *Ideas.*" Yet even this can be disputed. It is not clear what are the "others" to which he refers in this passage. If they are other complex ideas, then the whole remark could be taken as being yet another comment about just those ideas of relations that are complex. If the "others" are *all* other ideas, then Locke must hold that even simple ideas are "made up ...of simple *Ideas*" (namely, themselves), again leaving the door open for simple ideas of relations. Further complicating matters is the fact that some commentators see Locke as backing away from his compositionalism in later editions of the *Essay*, and as coming to hold that ideas of relations are neither simple nor complex. For criticism of this, see Stuart 2008.

[19] Marginal heading.

whose objects qualify as affections of, or dependences upon, the things that Locke counts as substances (bodies, minds, people). A possible exception is the idea of space. At II.xiii.17, Locke tells us that he cannot say whether space is substance or accident, which seems to leave open the possibility that the idea of space is the idea of a substance. There is also a general reason for thinking that simple ideas must be ideas of modes. They cannot be ideas of substances or relations, since those are all complex ideas. So if simple ideas are ideas of items in Locke's ontology, and if substance, mode, and relation are the three fundamental categories of his ontology, it would seem that simple ideas must be ideas of modes.

Making matters more complicated is Locke's distinction between what he calls ideas of "simple modes" and what he usually calls ideas of "mixed modes" (but occasionally calls ideas of "complex modes"[20]). This is not, as one might think, a distinction between mode-ideas that do not have parts and those that do. Ideas of simple modes and ideas of mixed modes are all complex ideas. For ideas of simple modes are not simple ideas, but instead ideas that are "only variations, or different combinations of the same simple *Idea*, without the mixture of any other, as a dozen, or score" (II.xii.5). We might say that these are complex ideas that are homogenous. The idea of dozen is the idea of a simple mode because it is a complex idea whose parts are twelve instances of the idea of a unit. The idea of a mixed (or complex) mode, by contrast, is a complex idea whose parts are tokens of different types of simple ideas. As an example of an idea of a mixed mode, Locke offers the idea of beauty, "consisting of a certain composition of Colour and Figure, causing delight in the Beholder" (II.xii.5).

The simple/mixed distinction is one that applies in the first instance to ideas, sorting them by reference to their constituent ideas. If it applies at all to the objects of those ideas—if Locke means to speak of simple modes and of mixed modes as two classes of properties and events—then it applies to

---

[20] See II.xxii.5, 7, 10 and III.vi.45. On one occasion, Locke seems to depart from this usage, and to use the phrase 'complex modes' not to talk about mixed modes but to talk about what he usually calls "simple modes." This comes at II.xv.9. Speaking about the infinitely divisible parts of duration and of space, he says, "But the least Portions of either of them, whereof we have clear and distinct *Ideas*, may perhaps be fittest to be considered by us, as the simple *Ideas* of that kind, out of which our complex modes of Space, Extension, and Duration, are made up, and into which they can again be distinctly resolved." This seems to mean that though space is infinitely divisible, we can (and should) treat our idea of the smallest space of which we have a clear and distinct idea as a simple out of which our ideas of larger spaces are constructed. The implication seems to be that the idea of a large space is made up of a number of tokens of the idea of the smallest space of which we have a clear and distinct idea.

these items in a derivative or secondary way. Whether he uses the simple/ mixed distinction in this secondary way is rendered somewhat obscure by his failure to always carefully distinguish ideas and their objects. Very often one can read apparent references to modes as careless talk about ideas of modes. Even if Locke does employ the simple/mixed distinction in this secondary way to non-ideas, it is an epistemological distinction rather than a metaphysical one: it sorts into two classes items that are on the same metaphysical footing.

A further complication involves the locutions 'mode of' and 'modification of.' Locke uses these phrases in two different ways, without announcing this or even betraying any particular awareness of it. If a mode (or a modification) is an affection of, or dependence upon, a substance, one would expect the claim that something is a mode of x (or a modification of x) to indicate that it is an affection of, or a dependence upon, a thing or substance x. Locke does sometimes use 'modification of' this way. Thus at II.xiii.18 he speaks of the possibility that God, spirits, and matter might agree in the "same common nature of *Substance*" and differ only in "a bare different modification of that *Substance*."[21] Surprisingly, he never uses 'mode of' (or 'modes of') this way in the *Essay*. When he says that something is a mode of x, he means that it is a determinate of the determinable x. When the something in question is an idea, what this comes to is that the idea in question is less general than the idea x, and its object is something that falls under that more general idea. Thus at II.xiii.4 Locke says that "[e]ach different distance is a different Modification of Space, and *each* Idea *of any different distance, or Space, is a simple Mode of this* Idea." What the first clause amounts to is unclear. It depends upon whether 'Space' refers to space or to the idea of space, and it may also depend upon Locke's conception of space. What the rest of the passage means is that the idea of any particular distance is less general than the idea "a space," and the former idea represents something that falls under the latter. Locke sometimes uses 'modification of' (and 'modifications of') in this way too.[22]

Locke's examples of ideas of mixed modes include the ideas of beauty (II.xii.5), theft (II.xii.5), rainbow (II.xviii.4), parricide (II.xxii.4), a triumph (II.xxii.8), fencing (II.xxii.9), drunkenness (II.xxviii.15), courage (II.xxx.4),

---

[21] For other examples where 'modification of x' means "affection of x," see II.xiii.18; II.xxi.14, ll.27–28; and IV.iii.6.

[22] See, for example, II.xiii.1, 5, 9; II.xviii.3; II.xix.1; III.x.11.

and adultery (III.v.5). There is no difficulty about why these count as ideas of mixed modes: each term in the list can be plausibly construed as standing for a kind of property or event, and the ideas of these are not likely candidates for being what Locke calls simple modes. What is worrisome is a strand of argument in the *Essay* that seems to imply that nothing *in rerum natura* answers to these ideas.

Locke draws several contrasts between ideas of substances and ideas of mixed modes. He says that ideas of substances are intended to copy nature in a way that ideas of mixed modes are not (II.xxxi.3). He tells us that ideas of mixed modes are arbitrary in a way that ideas of substances are not (III. iv.17; III.v.3; III.vi.28); that they are the workmanship of the human understanding in a way that ideas of substances are not (III.v.13). He says that real and nominal essences are distinct in the case of substances, but identical in the case of mixed modes (III.x.19). Most important, for our purposes, is the intimation of a further contrast. At times, it looks as though Locke is saying that the world does contain things that answer to our ideas of substances, but that it does not contain anything that answers to our ideas of mixed modes. He says that "*Mixed Modes and Relations* [have] no other *reality*, but what they have in the Minds of Men" (II.xxx.4), and that they have "nothing to represent but themselves" (II.xxxi.3).[23] He observes that ideas of substances "carry with them the Supposition of some real Being, from which they are taken," and he suggests that ideas of mixed modes do not (III.v.3). He claims that the names of mixed modes "*lead our Thoughts to the Mind, and no farther*" (III.v.12), and he says that they "for the most part, *want Standards* in Nature" (III.ix.7). At least one commentator has read these passages and concluded that Locke holds that "there is nothing, in reality, which corresponds to our ideas of modes" (Conn 2003, 6). To deny that anything *in rerum natura* answers to our ideas of mixed modes would be to deny that there are instances of beauty in the world, that there is drunkenness, that there are cases of parricide. These would be strange and implausible things to say. Fortunately, Locke is not saying them. Although he holds that the reality and the adequacy of ideas of mixed modes is independent of whether anything corresponds to them, he does not hold this because he thinks that nothing corresponds to them.

---

[23] This is probably a case of his saying "mixed modes" when he means "ideas of mixed modes." At IV.iv.5, it is clearly the *idea* of a mixed mode that is "not designed to represent anything but it self."

Locke thinks that what an idea is *for*—and in particular, whether it is supposed to model something external to it—depends upon its maker's intent. This determines the conditions that are necessary for it to be "real" or "adequate." He calls ideas "real" if they have a "Foundation in Nature" and a "Conformity with the real Being, and Existence of Things, or with their Archetypes"; otherwise they are *"Fantastical or Chimerical"* (II.xxx.1). He calls ideas adequate only if they perfectly represent "those Archetypes, which the Mind supposes them taken from; which it intends them to stand for, and to which it refers them" (II.xxxi.1); otherwise, they are inadequate. Simple ideas are made not by us, but by the operation of external things on us in ways ordained by God. God means for these ideas to allow us to "distinguish the sorts of particular Substances, to discern the states they are in, and so to take them for our Necessities, and apply them to our Uses" (IV. iv.4). To serve this purpose, these ideas need only "answer and agree to those Powers of things, which produce them in our Minds" (II.xxx.2), something that (because of God's power) they cannot fail to do. Simple ideas are therefore incapable of being fantastical or inadequate. Complex ideas, on the other hand, are made by us, and so the conditions that govern their reality and adequacy depend upon our purposes.[24] Locke is chiefly concerned with abstract ideas and general names, rather than the ideas and names of particular things or events. He thinks that when we make general ideas of substances, we take external things as their archetypes; but that when we make ideas of mixed modes, we do not. Ideas of mixed modes *are* their own archetypes (II.xxx.4), and they are archetypes "to rank and denominate Things by" (II.xxxi.3).

According to Locke, general ideas of substances are modeled upon external things, and are defective if nothing in the world corresponds to them. If a careless naturalist observes a new species, puts together an abstract idea meant to capture its features, but forms an idea to which no actual living thing corresponds, then his idea is faulty. By contrast, if nothing in the world answers to our ideas of mixed modes, this does not imply that they are defective. If nothing in the world is perfectly triangular, this does not mean that there is anything wrong with our idea of a triangle. If all married people were faithful, this would not mean that there was a problem with our idea of adultery. When Locke says that ideas of mixed modes have "nothing

---

[24] Locke says that we make complex ideas at II.xii.1 and *Works* IV, 11.

to represent but themselves" (II.xxxi.3), and that they *"want Standards* in Nature" (III.ix.7), he means that extra-mental facts are irrelevant to the reality and the adequacy of these ideas. When he says that mixed modes have "no other *reality*, but what they have in the Minds of Men" (II.xxx.4), he is making a claim about *ideas* of mixed modes, and again it is that their reality and adequacy does not depend upon anything extra-mental.[25]

Far from thinking that there are no things of the sorts that ideas of mixed modes represent, Locke thinks that in a certain sense there are too many of them. The number of different kinds of features and events that we could frame ideas of, and then name, vastly outstrips the number that we have any reason to talk about. That is why he says that it is to a certain extent arbitrary which ones we do frame general ideas of, and invent names for.[26] The choices we make in that regard are relative to, and reflect, our interests. These interests make it worthwhile for us to be able to communicate readily about the killing of a father by his child, and so we have the idea of parricide and the word 'parricide'; they have not led us to fashion an idea of, and designate a term for, the killing of a sheep (III.v.6). Different peoples will have different interests because of their differing circumstances; so different linguistic communities employ not only different words, but to a certain extent different categories. That, Locke says, is why we find that between any two languages there are always some untranslatable terms.[27]

Why do we not model ideas of mixed modes upon external archetypes as we do ideas of substances? Locke's answer may have to do with the nature of events and features themselves. He says repeatedly that ideas of mixed modes are not modeled upon patterns.[28] Occasionally, he expresses himself a bit more fully, saying that they are not modeled upon *standing* patterns.[29] He may think that we do not model ideas of mixed modes upon standing patterns because the objects of these ideas are not, in the relevant sense, standing. Locke's substances are continuants that endure through time and that change in orderly ways. They exhibit a stability and a unity that seems independent of

[25] That Locke's subject is *ideas* of mixed modes becomes clear when one considers the entire sentence in which the quoted remark appears. It reads: "*Secondly, Mixed Modes and Relations,* having no other *reality*, but what they have in the Minds of Men, there is nothing more required to those kind of *Ideas*, to make them *real,* but that they be so framed, that there be a possibility of existing conformable to them." Here "*Mixed Modes and Relations*" are plainly called kinds of ideas.

[26] II.xxii.4; III.v.3, 6, 15.

[27] II.xxii.6 and III.v.8.

[28] II.xxii.2; III.iv.17; III.v.3, 5, 6.

[29] II.xxxi.3; III.xi.15.

us. They can be observed for long stretches, and re-encountered after periods of absence. This allows us to refine and improve our ideas of them, modifying those ideas to more accurately reflect the collections of qualities we find repeatedly and stably co-instantiated. The case of items represented by ideas of mixed modes is different. Locke says that triumphs and apotheoses cannot "exist altogether any where in the things themselves, being Actions that required time to their performance, and so could never all exist together" (II. xxii.8). They cannot "exist altogether any where in the things themselves" because it is their nature to unfold over time—that is, because they have temporal parts that cannot co-exist. Later he makes the point in more picturesque language, saying that actions "perish in their Birth" (III.vi.42). The fleeting nature of events makes them poorly suited to serve as archetypes for ideas. We cannot observe them for sustained periods, cannot re-identify them after periods of absence, and so have little chance to refine our ideas of them.[30]

In emphasizing the degree to which ideas of mixed modes are supposed to be independent of external models, Locke may seem to overplay his hand. Consider II.xxii.9, where he describes these three ways in which we get complex ideas of mixed modes:

1. By Experience and *Observation* of things themselves. Thus by seeing two Men wrestle, or fence, we get the *Idea* of wrestling or fencing. 2. By *Invention*, or voluntarily putting together of several simple *Ideas* in our own Minds: So he that first invented Printing, or Etching, had an *Idea* of it in his Mind, before it ever existed. 3. Which is the most usual way, by *explaining the names* of Actions we never saw, or Notions we cannot see; and by enumerating, and thereby, as it were, setting up before our Imaginations all those *Ideas* which go to the making them up, and are constituent parts of them.

Here Locke does concede that we can acquire ideas of mixed modes by observing the events they represent; but he also says that we more frequently get them without having observed what they represent. This would seem to sit poorly with the fact that our interests in communicating with one another are dominated by the practical business of negotiating our way

---

[30] Events lack a certain kind of stability and unity because they are not continuants. What of the other items that are represented by ideas of mixed modes, namely property instances? Locke may think that they lack stability and unity for the same reason as events do. He might think that the redness of an apple or the beauty of a woman is not something that literally persists through time. It is hard to see how there could be a fact of the matter concerning whether today's beauty is *the very same* token of beauty as yesterday's, or else a different token of exactly the same type.

through the world, a fact that seems to ensure that most of the mode-ideas that we make represent features and events that frequently recur in our experience.

The solution here is that there are different senses in which an idea might be said to be newly made. An idea is in one sense newly made when it is half of an idea/term pair making its first entrance into a language; it is in another sense newly made when it is half of an idea/term pair that is a fresh addition to some particular speaker's repertoire. At II.xxii.9, Locke is concerned with the expansion of an individual's conceptual and linguistic repertoire. He is making the point that such expansions usually (but not always) happen when others explain to us what ideas are associated with terms that are already being used by other members of our linguistic community. This is clear from a discussion earlier in the chapter, where he says that we commonly get ideas of mixed modes by hearing others explain the meanings of terms already in circulation. "Thus," he says, "a Man may come to have the *Idea* of *Sacrilege*, or *Murther*, by enumerating to him the simple *Ideas* which these words stand for, without ever seeing either of them committed" (II.xxii.3).

Though individuals may acquire ideas of events and properties of which they lack personal experience, we should expect new idea/term pairs to be introduced to a language only when people have reason to think and talk about what the idea/term pairs represent. This is just what we find Locke saying about the expansion of a language. At III.v.7 he tells us that "[t]hough these complex *Ideas* [of mixed modes] be not always copied from Nature, yet they are always...made for the convenience of Communication, which is the chief end of Language." He goes on to note that in making ideas of mixed modes, men have regard only to those combinations of qualities that they have occasion to mention to one another. One chapter later, he goes on to explain that when an individual acquires new ideas of mixed modes by learning more of a language, there is a real sense in which those ideas *do* take other things as their archetypes. They take as their archetypes not events or features in the world, but ideas in the minds of competent speakers of the language. Thus Adam's children, wanting to learn the meanings of words that Adam had introduced to the language, "were obliged to conform the *Ideas*, in their Minds, signified by these Names, to the *Ideas*, that they stood for in other Men's Minds, as to their Patterns and *Archetypes*" (III.vi.45).

§5 *Relations*

We have seen that Locke thinks that all of our complex ideas can be "reduced under these three Heads. 1. *Modes*. 2. *Substances*. 3. *Relations*" (II.xii.3). It is tempting to infer that mode, substance, and relation are also the three basic categories of his ontology. Locke certainly believes that there are substances, and it is equally certain that substance constitutes an ultimate category for him. We have also seen that we need not saddle him with the view that nothing answers to our ideas of modes. Indeed, there is every reason to think that modes constitute another ultimate category for him. Do relations constitute a third? Locke says relatively little about relations. Even in the chapter "*Of Relation*" (II.xxv), he is more interested in discussing the nature and origin of *ideas* of relations, and the role of relative *terms* in language, than he is in discussing the nature of relations themselves.[31] Still, it is worthwhile to consider what he does say about relations, especially as the topic has received so little attention from commentators.

Locke sometimes lumps ideas of relations in with ideas of mixed modes. This makes for a number of places in which he seems to be denying that there are relations. However, we are now in a position to see that these passages do not really demand such a reading. It is not just mixed modes, but also relations, that are said to have "no other *reality*, but what they have in the Minds of Men" (II.xxx.4). It is not just mixed modes, but also relations, that are said to be "Archetypes without Patterns," and so to have "nothing to represent but themselves" (II.xxxi.3). Mixed modes and relations are also discussed together in III.v ("*Of the Names of mixed Modes and Relations*"). After telling us that ideas of mixed modes are made by the understanding (III.v.2), that they are made arbitrarily and without patterns (III.v.3), that they can be made prior to the existence of what they represent (III.v.5), and that their names "*lead our Thoughts to the Mind, and no farther*" (III.v.12), Locke observes that what "has been said here of mixed Modes, is with very little difference applicable also to Relations" (III.v.16). These passages do not show that Locke thinks that there are

---

[31] When it comes to relations, even those topics that get more of his attention get less of it than we might wish. His explanations of how we make ideas of relations, of what their constituents are, and of how they are related to ideas of relata, are underdeveloped and inadequate. For discussion, see Stuart 2008.

no relations. They show that he thinks that the conditions that govern the adequacy and reality of ideas of relations are like those that govern the adequacy and reality of ideas of mixed modes. He thinks that neither ideas of mixed modes nor ideas of relations are made with the purpose of modeling stable and unified items in the world. Neither ideas of mixed modes nor ideas of relations are reckoned defective if there happens to be nothing answering them.

The question of the ontological status of relations is raised most conspicuously by something that Locke says in the course of explaining how ideas of relations are sometimes clearer than ideas of relata:

> *Secondly,* This farther may be considered concerning *Relation,* That though it be not contained in the real existence of Things, but something extraneous, and superinduced: yet the *Ideas* which relative Words stand for, are often clearer, and more distinct, than of those Substances to which they do belong. (II.xxv.8)

Commentators do not agree about what is being said here. T. H. Green and James Gibson take Locke to be denying that relations are real, although both also say that he finds himself unable to consistently adhere to this view (Green 1885, 35; Gibson 1917, 193–5).[32] Jonathan Bennett suggests in passing (in the midst of a discussion about Hume) that Locke may mean that all relations are reducible in a certain sense (Bennett 1971, 253–4). Rae Langton says that Locke is endorsing the view that relations are irreducible in a certain sense (Langton 2000).

If we are to extract from II.xxv.8 a view about the ontology of relations, we must understand what Locke means by 'contained in the real existence of Things,' and by 'extraneous, and superinduced.' Of the commentators mentioned in the previous paragraph, Langton makes the most serious attempt at explicating these phrases. She looks to Locke's characterization of primary qualities as "real," and says that for him "real" qualities—and "real" things generally—are ones that are independent of perceivers and other things (Langton 2000, 79–80). She then declares that she takes Locke's spatial metaphor—his talk of what is "contained in" the real existence of things—to convey the idea

---

[32] As Green puts it, "Locke was not the man ... to become speechless out of sheer consistency" (Green 1885, 36). Green and Gibson do not agree about Locke's reasons for denying that relations are real. See Gibson 1917, 193–4.

of supervenience.[33] Putting these together, she concludes that Locke's remark about relations not being "contained in the real existence of Things" means that relations do not supervene on the intrinsic features of things.

Langton's reading is almost directly at odds with the one suggested by Bennett. His suggestion is that when Locke tells us that relations are not "contained in the real existence of Things," he means that they are reducible to the non-relational features of things.[34] Bennett does not explain the connection between Locke's language and the view ascribed to him. Perhaps the idea is that if relations are reducible then they would not be "contained in the real existence of Things" because they need not be mentioned in an account of the most basic constituents of reality. An inventory of the world could be complete even if the names of relations do not appear on it. Yet this still makes the connection rather tenuous. Suppose we grant that one who held that relations are reducible might be led to deny that relations are "contained in the real existence of Things." Even so, this does not show that someone who denies that relations are "contained in the real existence of Things" is trying to express the view that relations are reducible.

A sensible way to explore the question of what Locke means when he says that relations are not "contained in the real existence of Things"

---

[33] The idea of supervenience that she seems to have in mind is what Jaegwon Kim has termed "strong supervenience" (Langton 2000, 78n6). This is a relation between families of properties, A and B:A *strongly supervenes* on B just in case, necessarily, for each x and each property F in A, if x has F, then there is a property G in B such that x has G, and *necessarily* if any y has G, it has F (Kim 1984, 165).

[34] The notion of reduction that Bennett has in mind is also close to Kim's notion of strong supervenience. He says that a relation, R, is reducible to non-relational properties of relata just in case:For all x and y, there are non-relational properties F and G such that $(Fx \& Gy) \rightarrow xRy$ (Bennett 1971, 253)There is a difference between (i) the claim that relations are reducible to non-relational properties in Bennett's sense of 'reducible' and (ii) the claim the relations strongly supervene on non-relational properties in Kim's sense of 'strongly supervene.' Kim's notion has a modal requirement built into it. For relations to strongly supervene on the non-relational properties of things, it must be true not only that things having the non-relational properties they do suffices for their standing in the relations they do; it must be true that their having the non-relational properties they do *necessarily* suffices for their standing in the relations they do. Thus if it were a contingent matter that things having the non-relational properties they do sufficed for their standing in the relations they do, relations would be reducible to non-relational properties but would not strongly supervene upon them. It is hard to see how this difference between (i) and (ii) could matter, since it is hard to see how it could be a contingent matter that things having the non-relational properties they do sufficed for their standing in the relations they do.

is to look at how he uses language like this in other contexts, and then to extrapolate. The phrase 'the real existence of things' occurs quite a number of times in the *Essay*, and in each case it seems to refer simply to what there is in the world. The phrase crops up several times in discussions about ideas of mixed modes. When Locke describes one as putting together ideas of mixed modes without first witnessing the events they represent, he says that one is putting together ideas that "were never offered to his Mind by the real existence of things" (II. xxii.3). When he says that ideas of mixed modes are not modeled upon items in the world, he says that we do not "examine them by the real Existence of Things" (III.v.3).[35] He also refers to the real existence of things when speaking of the truth and falsity of ideas. Locke distinguishes two senses in which ideas can be true or false, one having to do with "*the Conformity they have to the* Ideas *which other Men have, and commonly signify by the same Name*" (II.xxxii.9), and the other being truth or falsehood "*in reference* to the *real Existence* of Things" (II.xxxii.13). Several sections later, he says that ideas of substances are false when "they put together simple *Ideas*, which in the real Existence of Things, have no union: as when to the Shape, and Size, that exist together in a Horse, is joined, in the same complex *Idea*, the power of Barking like a Dog" (II.xxxii.18).[36] It is not only ideas, but also propositions, that can be true or false. In IV.v ("*Of Truth in general*"), Locke distinguishes mere verbal truth from "real" or "metaphysical" truth, and says that the latter is "nothing but the real Existence of Things, conformable to the *Ideas* to which we have annexed their names" (IV.v.11). Finally, he characterizes external world skepticism as the worry that our experiences happen "without the real Existence of Things affecting us from abroad" (IV.xi.6).

On all of these occasions, Locke seems to be using the expression 'the real existence of things' in a most ordinary, straightforward sense. He seems to be referring simply to what exists, or to what exists independently of us. If what belongs to the real existence of things is what exists, or what exists independently of us, then Locke's claim that

---

[35] See also III.v.6, 14.

[36] Locke also says that "he that hath *Ideas* of Substances, disagreeing with the real Existence of Things...hath...*Chimæras*" (III.x.31); and that knowledge of substances is real only if the ideas of those substances are "taken from the real existence of things" (IV.iv.12).

relations do not belong to the real existence of things means that relations do not exist, or that they do not exist independently of us. That this is what he does mean is perhaps most strongly suggested by the linguistic parallel between II.xxv.8 and this passage from the chapter on general terms:

> To return to general Words, it is plain, by what has been said, That *General and Universal*, belong not to the real existence of Things; but *are the Inventions and Creatures of the Understanding*, made by it for its own use, *and concern only Signs*, whether Words, or *Ideas* (III.iii.11).

Commentators who discuss this passage are unanimous in taking it to express Locke's repudiation of abstract objects.[37] They all take the claim that "*General and Universal*, belong not to the real existence of Things" to mean that there are no general or universal things, or at least that there are none outside the mind. If they are right about that, then surely the claim that relations do not belong to the real existence of things must mean that there are no relations, or at least that there are none independent of our mental activities.

If II.xxv.8 is telling us that there are no relations, or that relations do not belong to the mind-independent world, then neither Langton's reading nor Bennett's speaks to the issue that Locke is addressing there. One could deny that relations supervene upon non-relational features because one thinks that there are no relations; or one could do so because one thinks that relations constitute a separate and ontologically basic category. Langton does not distinguish these two stances, but our reading of II.xxv.8 rules out the second. One could say that relations are reducible to non-relational features as a way of trying to accommodate relations and to give an account of what they are, or else as a way of eliminating them. It is not clear which Bennett has in mind, but our reading of II.xxv.8 rules out the first. Neither Langton's reading nor Bennett's has Locke denying that relations exist, or denying that they belong to the mind-independent world. In this instance, it is the older commentators—Green and Gibson—who have understood Locke better.

---

[37] See, for example, O'Connor 1952, 138–9; Alexander 1985, 257; Guyer 1994, 126; Lowe 1995, 154; Bennett 2001, vol. 2, 17.

There is a reading of Locke on which he holds that relations exist, but that they do not belong to the world as it is independent of us. This is a reading on which he holds that our mental activities bring relations into being. Locke does sometimes suggest that relations obtain because of acts of comparison on our part. He says that "*The nature . . . of Relation*, consists in the referring, or comparing two things" (II.xxv.5), and that "*Relation* is a way of comparing, or considering two things together" (II.xxv.7). This might lead one to conclude that he thinks that a relation between two things is "extraneous" to them, and "superinduced" upon them, because it depends for its existence on some subject comparing them. Walter Ott reads Locke this way. He attributes to Locke a view that he calls "foundational conceptualism," according to which "relations are fully mind-dependent and have no real being," though "the mind-independent world provides a foundation (and a justification) for us to form the ideas of relations that we do" (Ott 2009, 167). According to Ott, Locke takes relations to be mind-dependent because he holds that relations *are* comparisons (Ott 2009, 167).[38] On this view, there are no relations whenever we are not comparing things, though even then things will have the intrinsic features that ground the comparisons we make when we do make comparisons.

If relations were something other than acts of comparing, it would be an utter mystery how acts of comparing could give rise to relations. Ott's reading avoids saddling Locke with that mystery, but faces difficulties of its own. Here on the desk where I write there is a photograph in which I am standing next to my mother with my arm around her. I am five inches taller than she is. Or at least, that is how I would ordinarily put it. On the view that Ott ascribes to Locke, it would seem that we should say that though

---

[38] Ott also describes Locke as holding a reductionist view of relations according to which "when a proposition of the form *aRb* is true, it is true *only* in virtue of the non-relational, intrinsic properties of *a* and *b*" (Ott 2009, 149, 159). On the face of it, there is an inconsistency here. If relations are acts of comparing, then propositions asserting that relations hold must be made true by facts about what thinkers do, and not just by other things having the intrinsic features they do. Ott resolves the inconsistency by pulling back on the commitment to Locke being a reductionist. Though he *says* that Locke holds the reductionist view just described, what he seems to mean by this is only that Locke holds that the intrinsic features of relata ground the comparisons we would make if we were to make comparisons (Ott 2009, 165–7).

my mother is five feet six inches tall, and I am five eleven, I am taller than her only when some observer compares us in respect of height. For when there *is* no such relation as the relation "taller than," I can hardly stand to my mother in that relation. This is a strange result, though admittedly no stranger than the situation we face if we deny that there are relations at all. Indeed, the real difficulty for Ott's reading is to say how it amounts to anything but a notational variant of the view that Locke does away with relations altogether.

What could it possibly mean to say that relations *are* acts of comparing things? One who denies that relations have any reality (including mind-dependent reality) can say that my mother has the intrinsic feature of being five six, and that I have the intrinsic feature of being five eleven, and that these are the only facts that are needed to ground the truth of anybody's judgment that I am taller than her. What more is added to this by saying that such a judgment—or the act of comparing that prompts one to make it—*is* the relation "taller than"? In both cases we have two human beings with their intrinsic features, and an observer who compares them in regard to some of those features. In both cases, the intrinsic features of the human beings are all that is needed to account for the truth of the observer's judgment. The only difference seems to be that on the view Ott ascribes to Locke the name 'relation' is bestowed upon a mental event in the life of the observer. What makes this any sort of realism about relations, rather than anti-realism about relations paired with a peculiar use of language?

It is more charitable, but also more plausible, to suppose that when Locke says that "*The nature...of Relation*, consists in the referring, or comparing two things," he is again being careless about the distinction between ideas and their objects. He does not mean that relations are, or arise from, acts of comparing; he means that *ideas* of relations are, or arise from, acts of comparing. His view is that there are ideas of relations, but no relations.

If there are no relations, what can it mean to say that relations are "extraneous, and superinduced"? 'Extraneous' makes only two appearances in the *Essay* besides the one at II.xxv.8, and in both cases what is "extraneous" to something seems to be what is distinct from it or independent of it.[39] Locke speaks of the relative notion "*Father*" being superinduced to a substance or a man (II.xxv.4), and he also speaks of various perfections that God bestows upon matter as being "superinduced" by Him (*Works* IV, 462). In both cases what is "superinduced" seems to be something extra that is added, though it seems likely that different senses of addition are at work. We make ideas of relations through acts of comparison, and we are prone to thinking that items in the world answer these ideas, just as we are prone to thinking that there are abstract objects answering to our abstract ideas. Relations are "extraneous" to and "superinduced" upon the things we compare, because we project our ideas of relations on to the world rather than copying them from it.

Locke's repudiation of relations is, like his repudiation of abstract objects, a statement of his ontological predilection rather than part of a fully worked-out theory. He does not show how we can get by without the supposition that there are relations in the world, just as he does not show how we can get by without the supposition that there are abstract objects. The want of a Lockean theory of relations is to be felt all the more keenly because on several other occasions he suggests that ideas of relations are more ubiquitous, and relations more important, than we commonly suppose. The chapter on power includes this observation: "*Power includes in it some kind of relation*...as indeed which of our *Ideas*, of what kind soever, when attentively considered, does not?" (II.xxi.3). Locke goes on to list other ideas that have ideas of relations as parts. They include ideas of extension, duration, and number ("do they not all contain in them a secret relation of the Parts?"), and perhaps also ideas of such sensible qualities as colors and smells ("what are they but the *Powers* of different Bodies, in relation to our Perception?").[40]

---

[39] In the chapter on true and false ideas, Locke says that "When-ever the Mind refers any of its *Ideas* to any thing extraneous to them, they are then *capable to be called true or false*" (II.xxxii.4). His point is that ideas can be true or false so long as they represent something other than themselves. Then as Locke is explaining the defining feature of merely probable judgment or belief, as opposed to certain knowledge, he says this: "That which makes me believe, is something extraneous to the thing I believe; something not evidently joined on both sides to, and so not manifestly shewing the Agreement, or Disagreement of those *Ideas*, that are under consideration" (IV.xv.3). His point is that propositions are known with less than perfect certainty whenever our reasons for believing them depend upon something other than our grasp of the propositions themselves.

[40] A difficulty is that many of these ideas that are supposed to include in them some kind of relation are ones that he elsewhere calls simple (see II.iii.1, marginal heading and II.v).

Two chapters later, he says that "most of the simple *Ideas*, that make up our complex *Ideas* of Substances, when truly considered, are only Powers" (II.xxiii.37).[41] Putting this together with the observation at II.xxi.3, we get the result that most of the constituents of our ideas of substances are ideas that "include" some kind of relation. Then at IV.vi.11 Locke says that we are "wont to consider the Substances we meet with, each of them, as an entire thing by it self," and that we fail to notice how many of their features depend on their relations to other things. We fail to notice how the color and weight of a sample of gold depend upon its relations to ourselves and to other objects, how animals depend for their lives and motions upon "extrinsecal Causes and Qualities of other Bodies." For all we know, says Locke, the "great Parts and Wheels" of planetary phenomena may depend upon "Stars, or great Bodies incomprehensibly remote from us."

We can only presume that Locke does not mean his talk about the ubiquity of ideas of relations to entail the ubiquity of relations; and that when he does seem to highlight the importance and ubiquity of relations or relational features, he is not doing ground-floor metaphysics. Locke must think that whatever truth there is in his own claims about the ubiquity of relations could in principle be captured by claims about substances, events, and instances of monadic features. Locke's observation that "*Relation*...is not contained in the real existence of Things" tells us something about the austere ontology that he finds appealing. Nothing in his writings tells us how to effect the translation from his unrestrained talk of relations and relational features to a more rigorous language befitting that austere ontology.

---

[41] Again, it is a problem that Locke tells us that many simple ideas are ideas of powers, because at II.xxi.3 he says that ideas of powers contain ideas of relations and he seems to hold that ideas of relations are complex.

2
Qualities

§6. Locke is usually taken to have defined 'quality' so that all qualities are pow-ers to produce ideas in us. However, he is better understood as telling us only that powers are among the qualities of bodies. §7. It has been suggested that the drafts of the Essay *show Locke working toward the view that all qualities are powers of a certain sort, but a closer look at the drafts does not bear this out. §8. For Locke, the "primary" qualities of bodies are the ones a thing must have in order to qualify as a body. For him it is a conceptual truth that the primary qualities are inseparable from any body, though there are empirical factors that explain why we have the idea of body that we do. §9. Extension is one feature that something must have if it is to qualify as a body. Locke grants that every extended thing has infinitely many proper spatial parts, but as he understands it, this does not settle the question of whether atomism is true. §10. Solidity is another primary quality, one that confers impenetrability. Locke distinguishes solidity from hardness, and holds that all bodies are equally solid. He can say this because he holds the "chock-full" conception of matter, on which spaces within the confines of bodies are not parts of them. The impenetrability that Locke takes to be a consequence of solidity is not imperviousness to piercing or channeling, but to co-location. §11. There are various sorts of untidiness relating to the other features he includes on lists of primary qualities. There is overlap in the mean-ings of 'extension,' 'bulk,' and 'size.' "Mobility" is a better candidate for being a primary quality than either motion or "motion or rest." Number seems to be a primary quality because every body is* one *thing (and perhaps many things too). Contrary to what some have suggested, Locke also holds that all bodies—even atoms—possess texture.*

§6 Qualities and Powers

Locke usually reserves the term 'quality' for features of *bodies*. At one point, he tells us that "the general term *Quality*, in its ordinary acception" stands only for those features we learn about through a single sensory modality (III.iv.16).[1] On that use of the term, colors, sounds, odors, and flavors would be qualities, but not "Extension, Number, Motion, Pleasure, and Pain, which make impressions on the Mind, and introduce their *Ideas* by more Senses than one." Clearly that is not how Locke himself uses the term 'quality,' since he explicitly includes extension, number, and motion among the qualities of bodies. There is a passage in which he offers what looks like a definition of 'quality' as he means to use the term. This is II.viii.8, where he also tries to explain what he means by 'idea':

Whatsoever the Mind perceives in it self, or is the immediate object of Perception, Thought, or Understanding, that I call *Idea*; and the Power to produce any *Idea* in our mind, I call *Quality* of the Subject wherein that Power is.

This passage has almost universally been read as saying that all qualities are powers to produce ideas in us. This is problematic, both because this view of qualities is enormously implausible in its own right, and also because it fits poorly with the rest of Locke's philosophy.

It is natural to think of a body's powers as dispositional features that might be exercised or not. If that is right, and if all qualities are powers, then it is a mistake to think of dispositional qualities as ultimately grounded in categorical ones. An object might have certain powers because it has certain other powers, or because its parts have certain other powers. The possession of these other powers might in turn be a consequence of the possession of still further powers (and so on), but nowhere along the line are powers grounded in categorical or non-dispositional qualities. This view of things has its modern defenders (Shoemaker 1980; Blackburn 1990), and it may even be one that is imposed upon us by contemporary physics. The trouble with II.viii.8 is that Locke seems to be saying not only that all qualities are powers but that all qualities are *powers to produce ideas*. This makes for a

---

[1] The distinction goes back to Aristotle, who calls features detected by just one sense "special sensibles," and those detected by more than one sense "common sensibles" (*De Anima* II 6, 418a7–19). The suggestion that 'quality' is ordinarily reserved for special sensibles could either be meant as a claim about ordinary linguistic usage, or as a claim about general philosophical usage. Either way it seems doubtful.

strange and anthropocentric metaphysics, one on which each substance's features are exhausted by its capacities to appear to us one way or another. It also renders enormously implausible any attempt to explain why any body has the powers it does. It is one thing to say that a substance has a capacity that it does because it or its parts have certain other capacities. It is quite another to say that a substance has a capacity to produce certain ideas in us because it or its parts have the capacity to produce other ideas in us. Suppose one wants to explain an object's capacity to trigger the idea of yellow in us. One might hope to do this by citing certain facts about the arrangement of its smaller parts. However, if all qualities are powers to produce sensory ideas in us, then even a body's extension is just its capacity to produce certain visual or tactile impressions in us. The prospects of explaining an object's capacity to produce ideas of colors by citing the capacities of its smaller parts to produce tactile impressions of resistance are dim indeed.

The suggestion that all qualities are powers to produce ideas also fits poorly with other things that Locke says. It makes it difficult to see what is supposed to be the distinction between qualities in general and secondary qualities in particular. For Locke distinguishes secondary qualities as "nothing in the Objects themselves, but Powers to produce various Sensations in us by their *primary Qualities*" (II.viii.10). He singles out secondary qualities as "mere powers" (II.viii.24), "powers barely" (II.viii.24) and "bare powers" (II.xxiii.8). It is hard to see what the contrast is supposed to be if all qualities are powers. There is also at least one passage where Locke explicitly allows that figure and bulk are not powers. At II.xxxi.8 he says, "The simple *Ideas* whereof we make our complex ones of Substances, are all of them (bating only the Figure and Bulk of some sorts) Powers."[2] Moreover, since he holds that bodies produce ideas in us by causing us to have sensations, the view that all qualities are powers to produce ideas in us seems to entail that particles so small as to be insensible cannot by themselves possess any qualities. Yet Locke quite clearly holds that individually insensible particles do have primary qualities. At II.viii.9, where the notion of primary qualities is introduced, he says that reducing a body to insensible parts by a mill, or pestle, cannot deprive those parts of their primary qualities. Later, he speaks of the

---

[2] The *OED* defines 'bating' as meaning "excepting." Locke adds the qualification "of some sorts" because not all sorts of substances have figure and bulk: immaterial substances lack bulk, and God lacks figure.

"primary Qualities of the insensible Parts of Bodies" (IV.iii.12) and even of "insensible *primary* Qualities" (II.viii.23).[3]

As we have seen, Locke says: "the Power to produce any *Idea* in our mind, I call *Quality* of the Subject wherein that Power is" (II.viii.8). Let us call this the Power/*Quality* passage. Many commentators take this passage to be a gaffe. Reginald Jackson (1929, 71), J. L. Mackie (1976, 12) and Jonathan Bennett (2001, vol. 2, 79) all take this passage to be saying that all qualities are powers, and so dismiss it as not reflecting Locke's considered position. Other commentators try to save the Power/*Quality* passage, arguing that one or another of the terms in it is being used in a non-standard sense. For example, Martha Bolton and Michael Jacovides argue that primary and secondary qualities are both powers for Locke, but "powers" in different senses (Bolton 2001, 111; Jacovides 2007, 111–13). When Locke calls secondary qualities "powers," he means that they are dispositions to produce certain sensory ideas in us; but when he calls primary qualities "powers," he means only that they are the causes of certain sensory ideas in us. On their reading, Locke is not saying that all qualities are dispositions to trigger sensory ideas in us. His mistake in the Power/*Quality* passage is just that of giving the impression that he identifies qualities with powers on some single understanding of 'power.'[4]

The Power/*Quality* passage might seem to commit Locke to the following pair of propositions:

(2.1)   For all x, if x is a quality, then x is a power to produce an idea in us.

(2.2)   For all x, if x is a power to produce an idea in us, then x is a quality.

John Campbell argues that when Locke says 'idea' in II.viii, he should be understood to mean "simple idea" (Campbell 1980, 573). He concludes that the Power/*Quality* passage commits Locke not to (2.1) and (2.2), but to these two propositions:

(2.3)   For all x, if x is a quality, then x is a power to produce a simple idea in us.

(2.4)   For all x, if x is a power to produce a simple idea in us, then x is a quality.

---

[3] The many other passages committing Locke to insensible bodies having qualities include II.viii.10, 15, 24; II.xxi.73, and IV.iii.11.

[4] Other commentators who attempt to save the Power/*Quality* passage by claiming that he uses one or another of the terms in it in some special sense are John Campbell (1980, 572) and Peter Alexander (1985, 165–6).

Campbell's case for thinking that 'idea' always means "simple idea" in II.viii is not a strong one.[5] However, there is a conclusive reason why Locke must identify qualities with powers to produce *simple* ideas if he identifies them with any powers to produce ideas. He thinks that simple ideas are the only ideas that bodies produce in us. Locke says that ideas "enter by the Senses simple and unmixed" (II.ii.1), that sensation does not give us any complex ideas (II.xii.1), and that *we* make all of the complex ideas we have (*Works* IV, 11).

The commentators mentioned above agree that the surface meaning of the Power/*Quality* passage entails (2.1) or (2.3) on some reading of (2.1) and (2.3). They do not all think that Locke expresses himself clearly, or that what he says reflects his considered position, but they agree that in this one passage he says that all qualities are powers. I submit that the passage admits of another reading. When Locke says that "the Power to produce any *Idea* in our mind, I call *Quality* of the Subject wherein that Power is" (II.viii.8), this might be an expression of (2.1), or of (2.1) and (2.2), or of (2.3), or of (2.3) and (2.4). Yet it could also be read as an expression either of (2.2) alone, or of (2.4) alone. Since I have already argued that Locke is committed to (2.4) if he is committed to (2.2), let me simplify matters by focusing on the possibility that it is (2.4) alone that captures Locke's meaning. My suggestion is that the Power/*Quality* passage can be read as saying that a thing's powers to produce simple ideas in us are among its qualities. To be sure, if it is (2.4) that he is trying to express, then he might have done a better job of it. He might have said something like "Powers to produce *Ideas* in our mind, I reckon among the *Qualities* of the Subjects wherein they are." On the other hand, it is equally true that if he is trying to say that all qualities are powers, he might have done a better job of that. He might have said something like "by *Quality* I mean the Power any thing has to produce an *Idea* in our mind."

The Power/*Quality* passage is often characterized as one in which Locke defines 'quality.'[6] If one takes it as an expression of (2.1) and (2.2), or of (2.3) and (2.4), this seems apt. For in that case it spells out necessary and sufficient conditions for something's counting as a quality. On the other hand, if one

---

[5] He calls attention to the title of II.viii ("*Some farther Considerations concerning our simple* Ideas"), and adds that in that chapter "the distinction between simple and complex ideas is never once invoked" (Campbell 1980, 573). It is not even clear that these two points are compatible. Locke's references to simple ideas in the title of II.viii and in II.viii.1 seem to me to qualify as invocations of the distinction between simple and complex ideas. In any case, these points hardly seem decisive. It is easy to imagine Locke wanting to make some general claims about ideas in a chapter that is primarily about simple ideas.

[6] Jackson 1929, 71; Curley 1972 444; Campbell 1980, 568; Alexander 1985, 165; Jacovides 2007, 110.

takes it to express (2.4), one should be reluctant to characterize it as a definition of 'quality,' even if one concedes that it is a passage in which Locke tells us something about the meaning he gives that term. If there were independent reason to think that Locke intends the Power/*Quality* passage as a proper definition of 'quality,' this would count against my reading, on which it is an expression of (2.4) only. This may look like trouble for my reading, because in the index to the *Essay*—which was apparently compiled by Locke himself[7]—II.viii.8 is cited in the entry "QUALITY...What." However, the case for thinking that Locke means to be giving us a proper definition of 'quality' in the Power/*Quality* passage is inconclusive.

The index to the *Essay* includes many entries of the form "SO-AND-SO...What." Some of these cite passages that are plausibly regarded as Locke's definitions of so-and-so; others cite passages that merely tell us something important about so-and-so. The entry "PERSON...What" points us to II.xxvii.9, where Locke defines 'person' as he understands the term. Similar things might be said about the passages he cites in the entries "BODY...What," "LIBERTY...What," and "VOLUNTARY...What." On the other hand, the entry "ABSTRACTION...What" cites IV.ix.1, where Locke makes the point that when we reflect upon abstractions, we do not know whether anything real corresponds to them. This is an important fact about abstraction, but not a definition of 'abstraction.' The entry "SUBTLETY...What" cites a passage (III.x.8) in which Locke does not define 'subtlety,' but instead remarks that affected obscurity is what passes for subtlety and acuteness among the Schoolmen. The entry "REMEMBRANCE...What" cites two passages: one (I.iv.20) that might be taken for a definition of 'remember,' but another (II.x.7) where he makes the point that remembering is often a mental activity, something that we can will to do.

The index entry "QUALITY...What" cites II.viii.8 and III.iv.16. Both of these passages tell us something important about how Locke uses the term 'quality.' Neither must be read as offering the necessary and sufficient conditions for something's counting as a quality. The Power/*Quality* passage tells us that Locke, unlike some other philosophers, does not hesitate to count mere powers as genuine qualities. The relevant portion of III.iv.16 is where

---

[7] The evidence that the index is Locke's work comes from a letter to Clarke, dated 19 March, 1694, in which he says, "I intend to make an alphabetical index to the book" (*Corresp.*, 5, #1723, 36). One could take this to mean only that he would supervise the making of the index, but it seems unlikely that he would entrust the job to anyone else, or that anybody but him could have done such a good job.

he tells us that 'quality' is ordinarily reserved for features detectable by one sense only. Note that II.viii.8 is also cited in the index entry "IDEA…What," and yet there is reason to doubt that he takes himself to be defining 'idea' there, either. To be sure, the passage tells us something important about how he uses that term. However, when his contemporary John Norris complains that he ought "to have Defined what he meant by Ideas" (Norris 1690, 3), Locke does not reply that he has done so at II.viii.8. Instead, he remarks on the futility of attempting to define such a term (*Works* X, 248). He says that if we are after knowledge of our own ideas, we would do better to look within ourselves. If we want to know "their causes and manner of production in the mind, i.e. in what alteration of the mind this perception consists," then we are bound to be disappointed. Experience shows this to be so, he says, and then he offers a reason why: "no man can give any account of any alteration made in any simple substance whatsoever; all the alteration we can conceive, being only of the alteration of compounded substances; and that only by a transposition of parts." If II.viii.8 does not contain proper definitions of 'quality' and 'idea,' this should not surprise us. Locke's main business there is not to define his terms, but to apologize for the habit of speaking of ideas as though they were in things—to make it clear that his considered position is that "Ideas [are] *in the Mind, Qualities in Bodies*" (II.viii.8, marginal heading).

§7 *Qualities in the Drafts*

Edwin Curley has argued that the drafts of the *Essay* show Locke working his way toward the identification of qualities with powers of a certain sort (Curley 1972, 444–45). He concedes that Locke's definition of 'quality' "may not be successful," and points to Locke's failure to distinguish certain of a body's powers from the categorical bases of those powers (Curley 1972, 445, 447–50). Still, Curley says that the drafts show that Locke really does mean to claim that all qualities are powers. If he were right about this, it would undermine my reading of the Power/*Quality* passage. However, I believe that a close look at the drafts does not bear Curley out. It does show Locke making a more straightforward attempt at defining 'quality' than any we find in the *Essay*. It also shows him keen to make the point that a body's powers are among its qualities, and somewhat careless about distinguishing powers, causes, and constitutions. Though there is a moment at which Locke does seem to identify qualities with powers, this comes just after he seems to have given an altogether different account of qualities. At most, we see Locke briefly flirting with the identification of qualities with powers, rather than working his way toward that view. If a comparison of the drafts with the published *Essay* shows us anything, it may be that the published *Essay* benefitted from the process of revision.

In 1671, Locke produced two manuscripts that prefigure the *Essay*. These are commonly referred to as Draft A and Draft B. Another manuscript, called Draft C, dates to 1685. This is incomplete, with surviving portions corresponding only to the first two books of the published *Essay*. Draft A contains two passages that look forward to II.viii.8. The first is this sentence, written in the margins early in the draft: "by qualitys I would be understood to meane that which is the cause of any simple Ideas in my minde" (*Drafts*, 9). This looks like a definition of 'quality,' but one on which qualities are identified with causes of simple ideas, rather than with powers to produce ideas. The second passage in Draft A that anticipates II.viii.8 is a two-paragraph "Memorandum" that comes at end of the draft. The second paragraph of the memorandum begins this way:

> [A] When I speak of simple Ideas as existing in things I would be understood to mean. such a constitution of that thing which produces that Idea in our mindes. soe that Idea when it is spoken of as being in our understanding is the very perception or thought we have there, when it is spoken of as existing without is the cause of that perception. & is supposed to be resembled by it. [B] & this also I call quality. whereby I meane anything existing without us which affecting any of our senses produces any simple Idea in us. [C]& because the powers or capacitys of things which too are all conversant about simple Ideas, are considered in the nature of the thing & make up a part of that complex Idea we have of them therefor I call those also qualitys & distinguish qualities into actuall & potential ... (*Drafts*, 82–3).[8]

In [A] we have a terminological clarification similar to the one that we find in II.viii.8. Locke says that when he speaks of "ideas" as being outside the mind, he is referring not to ideas strictly so-called, but to the causes of those ideas.[9] In [B], we are told that he also calls these causes "qualities." He then repeats the definition of 'quality' that he had given in the earlier marginal interpolation:

---

[8]   The bracketed letters are my additions.

[9]   Michael Jacovides suggests that we think of this passage as "an early description of primary qualities" (Jacovides 2007, 112). However, Locke seems to be speaking about qualities generally, and not just about what he will later call primary qualities. He does say that these qualities, the causes of ideas in us, are "supposed" to resemble the ideas they cause in us. Yet even in the *Essay*, he thinks that we are prone to the mistaken supposition that secondary qualities resemble ideas of secondary qualities.

qualities are causes of simple ideas. In [C], Locke makes the point that he counts powers or capacities as qualities too. His wording—the 'also' in "I call those also qualitys"—implies that powers or capacities are qualities, but that some of the causes that are qualities are *not* powers or capacities.

Putting [B] and [C] together, we get the result that a thing's "powers or capacitys"—or at least those of its powers and capacities that are "conversant about simple Ideas"—are causes of simple ideas. For "powers or capacitys" are said to be qualities, and qualities are identified with the causes of simple ideas. It is rather strained, but perhaps not exactly wrong, to say that a body's power to produce a certain idea in us is the cause of that idea in us. This is like saying that a vase's fragility is the cause of its breaking on some occasion. One can imagine circumstances in which one might explain that a vase broke during transit because it was very fragile. However, a thorough accounting of the vase's breaking would presumably cite other factors, including whatever features of the vase explain its having the capacity to break easily, and whatever triggering event or condition explains why that capacity was exercised on a particular occasion. Either of these might be better reckoned "the cause" of the breaking. Similarly, it is not necessarily wrong, but also not very enlightening, to say that a body's power to produce an idea in us is the cause of its producing an idea in us.

In Draft B, Locke continues to identify qualities with the causes of simple ideas.[10] He also continues to hold that powers are qualities, and to imply that not all qualities are powers. He again says of powers "I call those also qualitys…" (*Drafts*, 164), and so again suggests that some qualities are not powers. He also says more about the contrast between powers and other qualities:

For he hath the perfectest Idea most of any particular substance, who hath gatherd & put togeather most of those simple Ideas, or rather qualitys which are causes of these simple Ideas which doe exist in it, among which are to be recond its active powers & passive capacitys i e not only those qualitys which doe actualy exist in it, but such as are apt to be alterd in it, or that thing is apt to alter in any other subject upon due application of them togeather. Thus it is a property of the sun by shineing long on a fair face to make it swarthy on a green apple to make it red, & on yellow wax to make it white; A load stone hath the power of drawing Iron & Iron a capacity to be drawne by the loadstone. (*Drafts*, 163)

[10] Locke says: "Soe that, by Idea…when it is spoken of as existing without us I meane the cause of that perception & is vulgarly supposd to be resembled by it & this cause I call also quality, whereby I meane any thing which produces or causes in us any sensible simple Ideas these all I say I call qualitys" (*Drafts*, 164).

Here we have a contrast between the qualities that "doe actualy exist in" a thing, and its "active powers & passive capacitys." All of these are said to be "causes of simple Ideas" and so "qualitys." This means that the qualities that "doe actualy exist in" a thing are just some of the qualities it has. Later in the same section, Locke offers "the taste colour smell & tangible qualitys of all the component parts of a cherry" as examples of the "actuall qualitys" that are in a thing (*Drafts*, 164–5). It seems reasonable to presume that the qualities that "doe actualy exist in" a thing are its "actuall qualitys," and Locke seems to be identifying these with a thing's occurrent sensible qualities. His remarks about the sun and the loadstone suggest that he conceives of active powers as powers to alter the sensible qualities of other things, and of passive powers as a thing's powers to have its own sensible qualities altered.

In Draft C there are two chapters that speak to the issue of Locke's conception of quality. One is II.vii, which includes much of the material located in II.viii in the *Essay*. This chapter in Draft C contains the first appearance of Locke's distinction between primary and secondary qualities. It also contains this sentence: "And the power to produce any Idea in the minde I call a *quality* of the subject wherein the power is."[11] The differences between this and the Power/*Quality* passage are insignificant. Both sentences are susceptible to the same variety of readings.

The other chapter in Draft C that bears on Locke's conception of quality is II.xxvii, which contains much that appears in the *Essay's* II.xxiii. At II.xxvii.7 in Draft C, we again find the admonition that when he speaks of ideas as being in things, he is to be understood as referring to the qualities in things that cause ideas in us. Here, as in both of the earlier drafts, qualities are identified with the causes of simple ideas. In this case however, the causes of simple ideas are further characterized as constitutions that have powers to produce those ideas:

When I speak of simple Ideas as Existing in things v.g. heat in the fire & red in a cherry I would be understood to meane such a Constitution of that thing as has power by our senses to produce that Idea in our mindes soe that by Idea when it is spoken of as being in our understandings I meane the very thought & perception we have there when it is spoken of as Existing without us I meane the

---

[11] Draft C, II.vii.10.

cause of that perception...& this cause as I have said I call also quality whereby I meane anything which produces or causes any simple Idea in us...(Draft C, II.xxvii.7).[12]

We are not told exactly what a "constitution" is, but it seems reasonable to suppose that it is an intrinsic, structural feature of a thing—a property that a thing has in virtue of the arrangement of its smaller parts.

As he had done in the earlier drafts, Locke goes on to say that some powers and capacities are qualities:

Farther because all the powers & capacitys which we can conceive in things are conversant only about simple Ideas & are Considerd as belonging to & makeing up part of the Complex Idea of that thing they are in I call these also qualitys & destinguish qualitys into actual & potential...(Draft C, II.xxvii.8).

Here "powers & capacitys" are said to be qualities, but once again the 'also' in "I call these also qualities" implies that not all qualities are powers.

There is at least the appearance of conflict between II.xxvii.7 and II.xxvii.8 in Draft C. The later passage tells us that powers to produce simple ideas are qualities; the earlier seems to say that qualities are constitutions that *have* powers to produce simple ideas. Perhaps a careful reading of II.xxvii.7 offers a way out. What Locke says at II.xxvii.7 is not that *all* qualities are constitutions with powers to produce simple ideas, but that the qualities he calls "ideas" are constitutions with powers to produce ideas. He might be thinking that such qualities as heat and red are constitutions, but that some other qualities are not. In fact, this may be his distinction between actual qualities and potential qualities. He explains that actual qualities are causes of simple ideas "that are in anything v. g. the taste, Colour, smell, & tangeible qualitys of all the component parts of a cherry" (Draft C, II.xxvii.8). Potential qualities are of two sorts: active and passive. The active ones are powers to change the "simple Ideas" (sensible qualities) of other things. The passive ones are a thing's susceptibilities to having its own "simple Ideas" (sensible qualities) changed. Locke does imply that all qualities are causes of simple ideas, but if his conception of cause is sufficiently elastic, he can say that the causes of simple ideas include some constitutions and also some powers.

[12] A lightly edited version of II.xxvii.7–10 from Draft C can be found in Aaron 1971, 69.

On the face of it, there is a problem about how potential qualities count as qualities at all. Qualities are supposed to be causes of simple ideas, and these potential qualities are powers to interact with other bodies, not powers to produce ideas in minds. A solution is suggested by a corresponding passage in Draft B, where Locke says of these powers that they "doe mediately affect our senses" (*Drafts*, 164). If an object exercises its power to change the sensible qualities of another thing, then it is indirectly responsible for the simple ideas produced in us when we sense the other thing. Locke does not shrink from calling powers "causes," so we should not be surprised that he counts a thing's powers to change the sensible qualities of other things as indirect causes of the simple ideas we might have when we sense those other things.

The most vexing Draft C passage relating to Locke's conception of quality comes just after he has explained the distinction between active and passive potential qualities:

all that I desire is to be understood what I meane by the word quality when I use it & if it be used by me some thing differently from the Common acception I hope I shall be pardoned being lead to it by the Considerations of the things this being the nearest word in its common use to those notions I have applied to it By the word then quality I would here & else where be understood to meane a power in any thing to produce in us any simple Idea & the power of altering any of the qualitys of any other body. (Draft C, II.xxvii.8)

The last half of this passage seems to tell us that all qualities are powers after all. It seems to tell us that every quality is either a power to produce a simple idea, or else a power to alter the sensible qualities of other bodies. We have considered the possibility that Locke takes the latter sort of power to be a power to produce a simple idea indirectly. The claim that all qualities are powers to produce simple ideas does not fit with the other things he has said in II.xxvii.7–8. In II.xxvii.7, he told us that at least some qualities are constitutions that *have* powers to produce simple ideas. In II.xxvii.8, he implied that not all qualities are powers, and suggested that we call the ones that are not powers "actual qualitys." We might try to resolve the apparent inconsistency by reading 'here & else where' in the above passage as meaning not "here and everywhere" but "here and in some other places." In that case, he would be telling us not that all qualities are powers, but only that some are. Otherwise, we must say that in this place at least he conflates powers to produce simple ideas with the constitutions in virtue of which things have those powers.

Curley has this to say about Locke's attempts, in the drafts, to say what he means by 'quality':

Anyone who compares his successive attempts at a definition will see that the definition of II, 8, 8 is the result of a long process of reflection and that Locke was quite conscious of being controversial. (Curley 1972, 444)

Curley is right to say that the *Essay*'s II.viii.8 was the product of long reflection. Locke's attempts to explain what he means by 'quality' date back to 1671. Curley is also right to say that Locke was aware that his conception of quality might be viewed as non-standard. In both Draft B and Draft C, he concedes that he may be using the term "differently from the common acceptation" (*Drafts*, 165). However, we need not suppose that he makes this concession because he endorses the view that all qualities are powers. He treats mere "powers & capacities" as genuine qualities, and this makes his conception of quality more inclusive than some philosophers'. This is enough to explain his remarks about using 'quality' differently than others do.

Let us take stock. In all of the drafts, Locke says that some qualities are powers, but implies that some qualities are not powers. In all of the drafts, he identifies qualities with the causes of simple ideas. Draft C contains a passage very similar to the Power/*Quality* passage, one that could be read as saying that all qualities are powers, but that can also be read as saying only that a body's powers are among its qualities. Draft C also has Locke seeming to identify qualities both with constitutions, and with powers to produce ideas in us. It is not obvious how either of these identifications fits with the concurrent story about powers being some, and only some, of a body's qualities. Perhaps they can be made to do so. If Locke wrestles with different definitions of 'quality,' nearly all of the wrestling seems to go on in Draft C, and there no clear winner emerges. Also notice what we do not find in the drafts. We do not find Locke first taking up, and then casting off, various alternatives to the view that all qualities are powers. We do not find anything that requires us to see the Power/*Quality* passage as offering a definition of 'quality' that he has settled upon after careful reflection. It is compatible with all that we do see that, as he prepared the *Essay* for publication, he abandoned the attempt to define 'quality' at all and settled instead for indicating that his use of 'quality' is broad enough to include powers.

§8 Defining Primary Qualities

In the *Essay*, Locke introduces primary qualities at II.viii.9.[13] The section begins this way:

Qualities thus considered in Bodies are, First [1] such as are utterly inseparable from the Body, in what estate soever it be; [2] such as in all the alterations and changes it suffers, all the force can be used upon it, it constantly keeps; and [3] such as Sense constantly finds in every particle of Matter, which has bulk enough to be perceived, and [4] the Mind finds inseparable from every particle of Matter, though less than to make it self singly be perceived by our Senses.[14]

Toward the end of II.viii.9, Locke calls the properties in the class that he is describing the "*original* or *primary Qualities* of Body." If we can sort out this passage, we will be well on our way to understanding what Locke's primary qualities are, and how he arrives at his list of them. Robert Wilson describes two broadly divergent readings of the passage (Wilson 2002). On what he calls the "conceptual point interpretation" of this passage, Locke is making a point about the meaning of 'body.' Clause [1] is making a claim about the content of our commonsense concept of body, and [2] and [4] are redundant.[15] Clause [3], which tells us that all observable bodies are observed to have the qualities that belong to our concept "body," is a supplementary empirical claim that sits uneasily with the others. On what Wilson calls the "transdictive inference interpretation" of the passage, clauses [3] and [4] offer "a two-step rule for determining what the primary qualities are" (Wilson 2002, 210). Clause [3] tells us to identify the qualities that are found in all sensible bodies, and [4] tells us to infer that these qualities are to be found in all bodies whatsoever. Together, clauses [3] and [4] play a crucial role in justifying the claim ([1]) that primary qualities are inseparable from bodies (Wilson 2002, 207).

---

[13] I refer here to the fourth edition of the *Essay*, which is the basic text for P. H. Nidditch's Clarendon edition. In the first three editions of the *Essay*, II.viii.9–10 correspond pretty closely with what became II.viii.9 in the fourth edition. In the first three editions, there is nothing that corresponds very closely with the passage on secondary qualities that we find at II.viii.10 in the fourth edition.

[14] The bracketed numbers are not Locke's, but ones that I (following Robert Wilson) have introduced for ease of reference.

[15] Wilson says that on the conceptual point interpretation [4] is "simply re-expressing clause [1]" (Wilson 2002, 207). He also says that on the conceptual point interpretation [4] "provides a crucial test case for thinking about what the primary qualities are" (Wilson 2002, 210). These can be reconciled if, as I presume, he means that [4] says essentially the same thing as [1], and [1] gives expression to a crucial conceptual requirement for something's counting as a body.

Wilson favors the transdictive inference interpretation. He describes two versions of it, without choosing between them. On the basic version, [1] and [2] say that primary qualities are possessed by all bodies. These claims are justified by [4], which itself is an hypothesis supported by the "transdictive inference" from [3] (Wilson 2002, 210). Wilson shies from saying so, but on this reading [4] justifies [1] and [2] only because [1] and [2] add little of substance to what is conveyed by [4]. They all boil down to the claim that primary qualities are possessed by all bodies. On the more radical version of the transdictive inference interpretation, [1] and [2] are to be seen as making claims only about everyday observable bodies (Wilson 2002, 209). On this reading, it is [2] and [3] that add little of substance to [1], and the focus is on the "transdictive inference" from these three to [4]. This is the inference from the fact that certain qualities are found in all observable bodies to the conclusion that they are possessed by all bodies.

How plausible is it to read [1] and [2] as having to do only with *observable* bodies? Wilson tries to motivate this reading with the following:

Take Locke's talk of the inseparability and constancy of the primary qualities of *a given body* in clauses [1] and [2] not so much as an expository convenience but, rather, as indicating that he has in mind here *only* everyday observable bodies, not postulated bodies too small to see with the naked eye: these observable objects have primary qualities inseparably and constantly (Wilson 2002, 208–9).

One can see how talk of "a given body" could be construed as talk about a body that is given to us by our sensory experiences of it. The trouble is that Locke does not talk about "a given body" in [1] or [2], or anywhere else. He simply talks of bodies and of the qualities utterly inseparable from them. Wilson also tries to smooth the way for his reading by claiming that a number of Locke's references to bodies in II.viii make sense only if 'body' is being used in a sense that excludes insensible corpuscles. He cites passages where Locke attributes primary qualities to the "solid parts" of bodies (II. viii.23, 26), and he argues that we cannot make sense of these if we take "bodies" to include corpuscles, since corpuscles are partless (Wilson 2002, 209). The problem with this is that far from taking corpuscles to be partless, Locke explicitly commits himself to at least some corpuscles having parts. Even indivisible atoms he conceives of as having surfaces, and hence spatial parts in some sense (§9). As for corpuscles, Locke responds to the suggestion that cohesion is the effect of "pressure of the Æther" by pointing out that this theory "leaves us in the dark, concerning the cohesion of the parts of the Corpuscles of the Æther it self: which we can neither conceive without parts, they being Bodies, and divisible; nor yet how their parts cohere" (II.xxiii.23). If the corpuscles of the æther have parts, then presumably other corpuscles might have parts too. When Locke enumerates the qualities that are "utterly inseparable from Body," there is no reason to think that he is speaking only of bodies big enough to see.

Let me present—in language slightly clearer than Locke's, but with a minimum of interpretation—what I take to be the surface meaning of the first sentence in II.viii.9:

> There is a class of properties such that if x is a member of this class and B is a body, then (i) B cannot exist without x, (ii) B is never without x, (iii) every particle of matter that is observed is observed to have x, and (iv) the mind finds that even insensibly small particles of matter cannot exist without x.

The main difference between [1] and [2] is that [1] tells us that there is a class of properties that bodies *cannot* be without, while [2] tells us that the members of this class are properties that bodies *are not* without. It does seem that [2] is redundant. Clause [3] conveys the empirical claim that the properties belonging to the class that Locke is describing are ones that we always observe bodies to have. Since he has already told us that they are properties that bodies do have, this is what we should expect if our senses are reliable detectors of the features of observable bodies. Clause [4] tells us that the mind finds even insensibly small bodies to have the properties that belong to the class that he is characterizing. Wilson takes this to mean that we hypothesize that even insensibly small bodies have these properties. I will suggest a different reading of [4] in a moment.

Wilson invites us to choose between seeing [1] as making a conceptual point about the contents of our idea of body, and seeing [3] as making an empirical claim that plays a role in justifying our beliefs about which qualities are primary qualities. This is a false dichotomy. We can and should do both. Suppose that [1] is making a conceptual point about bodies. What point might that be? It is not that *solidity, extension, motion or rest, number and figure* are inseparable from bodies. Locke does not mention any specific qualities until later in the section. Nor is it that *primary qualities* are inseparable from qualities. He does not introduce talk of primary qualities until the end of the section. If [1] is making a conceptual point, it is just that there are *some qualities* that are inseparable from bodies. This point follows almost immediately from Locke's account of abstraction. On that account, the necessary features of an *x* are just those included in our abstract idea "*x*." So if the abstract idea "body" has any content at all, there must be some qualities inseparable from bodies.

If [1] is making the conceptual point that some qualities are inseparable from bodies, then [2] is making the redundant point that there are some qualities that bodies never lack. This brings us to [3], the claim that every particle of matter that is observed is seen to have the qualities that are inseparable from body. This empirical claim does not justify the conceptual point made by [1], but that does not make [3] secondary or anomalous. Given Locke's empiricism and his account of abstraction, the fact conveyed by [3] is absolutely central to his view about why our abstract idea "body" has the contents that it does have. Locke takes it to be a deliverance of experience that "a certain number of these simple *Ideas* go constantly together" (II.xxiii.1). Sense reveals to us that certain clusters of qualities are repeatedly and somewhat stably co-instantiated. Noticing that a number of individuals possess certain qualities in common, we can make an abstract idea of a sort that comprehends them. We encounter many things that occupy space, that move about, and that resist the impingement of other moving, extended things. We make an abstract idea by starting with the complex idea of one of these things, and then removing from it those of its constituent simple ideas corresponding to features not shared by other of these things.[16] For we do find that some of them have colors, sounds, flavors and smells, but that others lack one or more of these qualities. At the end of this process, we are left with the idea of "something that is solid, and extended, whose parts are separable and movable different ways" (II.xiii.11), and it is this idea that we associate with the term 'body.' Thus does it become for us a conceptual truth that extension, mobility, and solidity are inseparable from body.[17]

Clause [4] tells us that we cannot conceive of bodies as lacking the properties definitive of this class that is being described. This is what we should expect. We are supposing that the reason that primary qualities are "inseparable" from bodies is that we associate 'body' with an abstract idea whose

---

[16] See II.xi.9 and III.iii.11. For a defense of this characterization of Lockean abstraction, see Stuart 2008.

[17] At II.xiii.11, Locke entertains the possibility that Cartesians who "would persuade us, that *Body and Extension are the same thing*" mean something different by 'body' than other people do.

constituents include the ideas of those qualities. If we try to conceive of a particle of matter that is not solid, or that is not mobile, or that is not extended, we find that we cannot do it. We cannot do it because anything that is not solid, or that is not mobile, or that is not extended, simply does not answer to our idea "body." In that case, there are important relations between [1], [3], and [4], but they are not the ones that Wilson suggests. The inseparability referred to in [1] obtains because we associate a certain idea with 'body.' Clause [3] describes a kind of empirical fact that figures prominently in the explanation of how we came to associate that idea with 'body.' Clause [4] describes the process by which we assure ourselves about the contents of the idea that we have come to associate with 'body.' We try to conceive of a body as lacking certain qualities, find that we cannot do it, and so are assured that our idea of body includes the ideas of those qualities.

This reading has [1] making a conceptual point about body, but it is not vulnerable to the objections that Wilson raises against the conceptual point interpretation. His first complaint is that the conceptual point interpretation gives ordinary experience too limited a role to play in our understanding of primary qualities, and that it gives experimental inquiry none at all (Wilson 2002, 205). This would be worrisome because of Locke's empiricism and his corpuscularian sympathies. On the reading I have suggested, ordinary experience plays a central role in shaping our judgments about which are the primary qualities of bodies. It is largely because we have the ordinary experiences we do that we have the idea of body that we do, and it is because we have the idea of body that we do that we take certain qualities and not others to be necessary features of bodies. Experimental inquiry may also play a role in explaining why we have the idea of body that we do. There may be qualities that casual observation always shows to be present in solid, mobile and extended things, but that experimental inquiry shows is sometimes absent in such things. Or there may be qualities that are always present in solid, mobile, and extended things, but that we learn about only through experimental inquiry. In either case, experimental inquiry could lead us to revise our concept of body, and so to change our views about the necessary features of bodies.

Wilson's second objection to the conceptual point interpretation is that if the claim about the inseparability of primary qualities were a conceptual point, we should expect Locke to explain how the concept of body implies his full list of primary qualities. As Wilson notes, Locke does not do that.

One might reply to this by pointing out that Locke also fails to provide a detailed accounting of the empirical evidence supporting hypotheses about the particular qualities that insensible particles have. However, let us not rest too much weight on the significance of what Locke does *not* do. If we read [1]–[4] as I have suggested, there is a more direct reply available. Although Locke does not deduce each primary quality from the idea of body, he does, in clause [4], allude to the test by means of which we determine whether a particular quality belongs to our idea of body. By this means we could arrive at the full list of Locke's primary qualities. This reading of [4] gets support from what comes next. One way to imagine a body as lacking a particular quality is to imagine some process by which it loses that quality. Locke illustrates his point in [4] by asking us to think about the changes that can and cannot be wrought upon a grain of wheat by division:

Take a grain of Wheat, divide it into two parts, each part has still *Solidity*, *Extension*, *Figure*, and *Mobility*; divide it again, and it retains still the same qualities; and so divide it on, till the parts become insensible, they must retain still each of them all those qualities. (II.viii.9)

Locke's conclusion here shows that he is not reporting the results of an actual experiment, but inviting us to conduct a thought experiment. His conclusion is not that grains of wheat have been observed to retain solidity, extension, figure, and mobility after successive division. His conclusion is that bodies *must* retain these qualities, even when division yields insensible parts: "division...can never take away either Solidity, Extension, Figure, or Mobility from any Body" (II.viii.9). Like most thought experiments, this one gets its traction from familiar experience, but it aims to tell us not just about what is observed but about what is possible or necessary.

Wilson also objects to the conceptual point interpretation on the grounds that the conceptual derivation of primary qualities would be "out of keeping with Locke's general scepticism about mere appeals to words," and would invite just the sort of verbal dispute he so often criticizes (Wilson 2002, 206). However, Locke does not have any general objection to arguments that appeal to the contents of our ideas or to the meanings of words. What he objects to are arguments vitiated by the imperfections of language, or by the abuse of words. These include disputes in which a term is unwittingly used to stand for different ideas (III.ix.15–17), and arguments in which words are not associated with any clear ideas at all (III.x.2, 3).

There is no particular reason to think that our efforts to unpack the contents of the idea that we associate with 'body' will involve us in such transgressions.

Michael Jacovides raises another difficulty for the view that II.viii.9 is spelling out the contents of our idea of body. He says that this "doesn't fit with the brevity of Locke's descriptions of the constituents of the abstract idea of body" (Jacovides 2007, 115). One of the descriptions he cites is at II.xiii.11, where Locke says that 'body' stands for "something that is solid, and extended, whose parts are separable and moveable different ways." Another is at II.xxiii.22, where he says that our idea of body is "an extended solid Substance, capable of communicating Motion by impulse." In these passages, Locke does not mention bulk, size, figure, number, situation, texture, and some of the other primary qualities that appear on his lists in II.viii. Jacovides offers this as a reason for thinking that the primary qualities listed in II.viii are not all ones that Locke arrives at by analyzing his idea of body.

As a first response, note that Locke does not give exactly the same analysis of "body" even in the passages cited by Jacovides. In one case he mentions the possession of separable parts, but in the others he does not. In one case he mentions the ability to communicate motion, and in the others he does not. We might say that he is simply inconsistent in his analyses of the idea of body, but it would be more charitable to note that some of his remarks about our idea of body are offered almost in passing, in the service of other points. It should not come as a surprise if they fall short of a full-dress analysis of the idea of body. What we get at II.viii.9 is closer to a full-dress analysis of the idea of body, though even in that one section we find two different lists of primary qualities. Locke's prose style is looser than we would like: but before we condemn him too harshly we should also consider that he may sometimes be using different terms to say much the same thing. If there is conceptual overlap between some of the items on his lists, then some of those lists may be longer than they need to be—longer than they would be if succinctness were his goal. Fleshing this out may diminish the contrast between the longer lists of primary qualities in II.viii and the briefer analyses of "body" elsewhere in the *Essay*. This will require digging deeper into Locke's lists, and exploring the relations between the qualities on them. These are the tasks we turn to next.

§9 *Extension*

Locke says that it is part of the meaning of 'body' that bodies are extended (II.xiii.11). He takes the idea of extension to be a simple idea given to us both by visual experience and by tactile experience (II.v). Simple ideas are indefinable (III.iv.4), and those who attempt to define 'extension' find themselves making use of the very idea they are supposed to be explaining:

> For to say, as is usually done, That Extension is to have *partes extra partes*, is to say only, That *Extension* is *Extension*....As if one asking, What a Fibre was; I should answer him, That it was a thing made up of several Fibres ...(II.xiii.15).

At times, Locke treats 'space' and 'extension' as different names for the same simple idea (II.v). At other times, he uses 'space' as the name for something that has extension as one of its features, something that has inseparable, unmovable parts (II.iv.5). Though he does sometimes speak of space as extended, he suggests that we might do better to reserve 'extension' for the relevant feature of bodies, and to use 'expansion' as a more general term applicable to both bodies and space (II.xiii.26; II.xv.1).

Locke suggests that there is something deeply mysterious about the extension of bodies. While making his case that we are equally in the dark about body and spirit, he considers the complaint that we do not know how we think. To the one making this complaint, he replies: "Neither knows he how he is extended; how the solid parts of Body are united, or cohere together to make Extension" (II.xxiii.23). Later he repeats this formulation about the cohesion of solid parts "making" the extension of body (II.xxiii.26, 27). If we took him to be suggesting that it is the cohesion of a body's parts that accounts for the fact that the body is extended, this would be deeply puzzling. Extension is such a basic feature that it is hard to imagine how the possession of any other feature could explain why a thing is extended. Moreover, if Locke meant to be explaining the fact of a body's being extended in terms of the cohesion of its parts, then his explanation would plainly be unhelpful and circular. For the cohering parts would themselves be extended things whose extendedness would call for explanation. These passages make better sense if we take the relevant *explanandum* to be not a body's being extended, but its having the particular extension that it does. When he speaks of the cohesion of solid parts as making a body's extension, Locke is thinking that a body has the particular spatial features that it does because a certain number of smaller bodies—its parts—cohere together. He is saying that we are unable to explain how any body has the particular spatial features that it does because we are unable to explain the coherence of its parts.

Although Locke does not really think it mysterious that bodies are extended, he does think that there is a mystery about the extension of bodies:

For I would fain have instanced any thing in our notion of Spirit more perplexed, or nearer a Contradiction, than the very notion of Body includes in it; the divisibility *in infinitum* of any finite Extension, involving us, whether we grant or deny it, in consequences impossible to be explicated, or made in our apprehensions consistent…(II.xxiii.31).

Locke grants that the idea of body entails its infinite divisibility, but he also says that this commits us to consequences that we cannot explain or render consistent. What those consequences are, or in what the alleged inconsistency is supposed to lie, he does not tell us. When he discusses the infinite divisibility of matter elsewhere, it is not to raise paradoxes, but to point to the inadequacy and obscurity of our ideas. At times he suggests that it is a liability that we cannot form the idea of "a Body infinitely little" (II.xvii.12), or those of "actual, infinite Parts" (II.xxix.16). Not having any idea of "the least Extension of Matter," he says, "we are at a loss about the Divisibility of Matter" (IV.xvii.10).

For Locke, to ask whether matter is infinitely divisible is not the same as asking whether atomism is true. His discussions of infinite divisibility, with their references to least extensions and to infinitely small bodies, show that in those passages he is concerned with what might be termed "conceptual" divisibility. He takes the question of whether body is infinitely divisible to be that of whether every body has proper spatial parts. By contrast, he defines an atom as "a continued body under one immutable Superficies" (II.xxvii.3). A superficies is a boundary that forms an outer surface but that itself has no depth. So for Locke, an atom is a body that does have spatial dimensions, but whose outer boundary cannot be changed. An atom has a left half and a right half, but it cannot be physically divided or bent, stretched, or dented. He is noncommittal about whether there are atoms. One might think it unlikely that he would bother to offer the definition if he thought that nothing satisfied it. On the other hand, whether there are atoms in his sense would seem to be an empirical question about which he could have no evidence. Though Locke does not say whether or not there are atoms, he is clearly committed to corpuscularianism, whose central thesis is that many of the observable properties of bodies are ultimately consequences of the properties of, and relations between, the smaller "corpuscles" or particles that compose them. Locke nowhere suggests that the bodies that count as corpuscles or particles for the purpose of scientific explanation are atoms in his sense.

Locke does, on at least one occasion, use 'atom' in a looser sense, meaning just a very small body. Ironically, he does this in the course of discussing the divisibility of matter. Voicing skepticism about our ability to fashion clear and distinct ideas of bodies much smaller than those we can sense, he asks the reader "[w]hether taking the smallest Atom of Dust he ever saw, he has any distinct *Idea*, (bating still the Number which concerns not Extension,) betwixt the 100 000, and the 1000 000 part of it" (II.xxix.16). Locke is denying that we can fashion distinct ideas of very small extensions, though he grants that we can form clear ideas of the corresponding numbers. If he means that we cannot conjure up distinct mental images of the two tiny parts, and if he presumes that having ideas is always a matter of having mental images, this would explain his pessimism about our ability to fathom the infinite divisibility of matter. It still does not tell us what inconsistencies are supposed to be involved in the idea of matter as infinitely divisible. In any case, the "atom" whose parts he is talking about is a visible mote, and presumably the smallest visible bits of dust are not atoms in the strict sense of physically indivisible particles.[18]

§10 *Solidity*

Although Locke holds that the idea of body includes the idea of extension, he repudiates the Cartesian doctrine that the idea of body just *is* the idea of extension. He takes solidity to be another essential component of our idea of body. Indeed, he says that the idea of solidity seems to be the one *most* "intimately connected with, and essential to Body"; for not only is all matter solid, but solidity is "found or imagin'd" only as a feature of matter (II.iv.1). "By this *Idea* of Solidity," Locke explains, "is the Extension of

---

[18] There are other places as well where Locke speaks of atoms and may be speaking loosely. See II.i.15; II.xxiv.2; IV.x.15–17; *Works* IV, p.168.

Body distinguished from the Extension of Space" (II.iv.5). The solidity of bodies accounts for the fact that bodies not only have spatial dimensions but *fill* space. It accounts for their "*mutual Impulse, Resistance, and Protrusion.*" Locke says that we receive this idea by touch almost constantly, whatever our posture and whether we are moving or at rest. We get it when we feel something that is supporting us, or hindering the approach of our body parts toward one another (II.iv.1).

Were someone to ask him what solidity is, Locke says that he would "send him to his Senses to inform him," instructing him to put a flint or a football between his hands and then push his hands together (II. iv.6). Yet Locke also offers what looks very much like a definition of 'solidity':

That which thus hinders the approach of two Bodies, when they are moving one towards another, I call *Solidity*. (II.iv.1)

He adds that others might prefer the term 'impenetrability' where he uses 'solidity.' Though he makes no strenuous objection to that, he suggests that 'solidity' is more fitting because it has a positive ring to it, while impenetrability "is negative, and is, perhaps, more a consequence of *Solidity*, than *Solidity* it self."

Locke distinguishes solidity not only from impenetrability, but also from hardness. Whereas solidity consists in "repletion, and so an utter Exclusion of other Bodies out of the space it possesses," hardness is a matter of a thing's not easily changing its figure (II.iv.4). Hardness and softness come in degrees, and are typically judged in relation to the constitution of our own bodies. Locke counts quantities of air and of water as solid. For him, the difference between fluids and non-fluids has to do not with solidity or unsolidity, but with hardness or softness. All bodies are equally solid, and a body's "Resistance, whereby it keeps other Bodies out of the space which it possesses, is so great, That no force, how great soever, can surmount it" (II. iv.3). Diamonds are harder than water because the relative situation of the parts of a diamond are less easily changed than those of a quantity of water. If the parts of a quantity of water were somehow prevented from moving relative to one another, the solidity of those parts would prevent the coming together of two pieces of marble as effectively as the diamond would (II.iv.4). Indeed, that is an understatement, since diamonds too fall short of perfect hardness.

Suppose we call any body whose parts are prevented from moving relative to one another a "Frozen" body. We have already seen that Locke takes an atom, in the strict sense, to be a body whose outer surface at least is Frozen. If any Frozen body of sufficient bulk were between two other advancing bodies, those advancing bodies could touch one another only if the Frozen body were first moved out of the way. Locke comes close to making this point with a thought experiment:

All the Bodies in the World, pressing a drop of Water on all sides, will never be able to overcome the Resistance, which it will make, as soft as it is, to their approaching one another, till it be removed out of their way...(II.iv.3).

The supposition that the drop is being pressed on all sides is meant to limit the changes in relative situation that are possible for the drop's parts. For those parts to change their situation, there must be some place for them to go. On the scenario he imagines, none of the drop's parts can move outside the drop's original boundaries unless some of the encroaching bodies give way. The drop is not Frozen, however. For all Locke has said, there might be spaces between its parts, and some compression of the drop might be possible. At some point, it would become so tightly packed that all the world's bodies could advance no further.

Locke also describes an actual experiment, one reportedly carried out in Florence. A globe of gold was filled with water and then compressed until "the water made it self way through the pores of that very close metal, and finding no room for a nearer approach of its Particles within, got to the outside, where it rose like a dew and so fell in drops" (II.iv.4). Here we have a quantity of water passing through a metal wall, so in one sense we have one material thing passing through another. Locke invokes this experiment as an illustration of "the solidity of so soft a body as Water" (II.iv.4). Presumably the thought is that if water were not solid, it could not penetrate something so hard as metal.

Locke's remarks about solidity have seemed to many fraught with tension. On the one hand, he treats solidity as all-or-nothing, says that all bodies have it, and that it entails impenetrability. On the other hand, he suggests that we are constantly receiving the idea of solidity from our tactile experiences of ordinary bodies, and these are experiences of things that do not all seem to us to be equally or perfectly solid and impenetrable. His examples include such things such as quantities of water and footballs. If the water's passage through close metal in the Florentine experiment seems to count toward its solidity, it also seems to speaks against the absolute solidity and impenetrability of the globe. A football between the hands may convey an idea of solidity, but it would seem to be a different idea than that conveyed by a flint. For even a properly inflated football feels somewhat compressible.

The apparent tension in Locke's remarks about solidity leads some commentators to offer fixes. Peter Alexander says that he draws a distinction between absolute solidity and relative solidity, and that he means to ascribe absolute solidity only to individual corpuscles (Alexander 1985, 139–40; 1994, 145). Alexander says that sensible bodies are always more or less hard, more or less penetrable, and that for Locke absolute solidity is a theoretical idea arrived at by extrapolation from the experience of bodies whose corpuscles are tightly packed. Robert Wilson's account is similar (Wilson 2002, 217–18). He suggests a distinction between what he calls experiential solidity (or relative incompressibility) and absolute solidity (which involves something completely filling the space of its boundaries). Wilson claims that it is the idea of experiential solidity that Locke means to say that we get from our sense of touch, and that the idea of absolute solidity is an abstraction that he may well regard with suspicion.

The problem with both of these readings is the almost total lack of textual support for them. It may be that Locke should have recognized two different senses of 'solidity,' but there is very little basis for claiming that he did do so. Moreover, these readings run directly afoul of the explicit claims that Locke does make. Alexander and Wilson have Locke saying that the idea of solidity that we receive from sensible bodies is that of hardness or relative incompressibility. Locke explicitly distinguishes the idea of solidity from that of hardness. Alexander and Wilson have him saying that the idea of solidity that we receive from sensible bodies is a matter of degree. Locke is explicit that hardness is a matter of degree, but that solidity is not. He denies that "an Adamant [is] one jot more solid than Water" (II.iv.4).

When thinking about solidity, penetrability, and compressibility, we do well to take account of some distinctions. First, consider that there are two ways of thinking about a material object. On one way of thinking about a material object, any voids that are circumscribed by its matter are contained in it and so are in some sense parts of it. On this view, the holes in a Swiss cheese are regions belonging to the Swiss cheese. Call this the holes-and-all conception. On another way of thinking about a material object, every part of a material object is material, and every space within its boundaries is an occupied space. Strictly speaking, the holes are not parts of a Swiss cheese, but lie outside its boundaries. This is so even if the boundaries of those holes are wholly defined by those of the cheese. On this second way of thinking about material objects, atomism may well entail that all ordinary physical things are scattered objects. For on this view, the spaces that lie between a body's constituent atoms do not belong to it. Call this the chock-full conception of a material thing.

There are also at least three senses in which we might speak of one thing as being penetrated by another, and so three senses in which we might speak of bodies as impenetrable. One sense of penetration involves one material thing breaking through another. This is the sense in which a thorn might penetrate your skin, or in which a bullet might penetrate the door of a car. With this sort of penetration, there is a collision, and parts of the penetrated object move to make way for the penetrating object. Call this penetration by piercing. A second sort of penetration is illustrated by the Florentine experiment. The metal of the globe may be "very close," but still there are voids between its constituent corpuscles. The pressure of the screws force very small particles of the water to negotiate those voids, and so to spring forth on its outer surface. Thus does the water, in a sense, penetrate the globe. Call this penetration by channeling.[19] A third sort of penetration involves a part of one thing coming to occupy the same location as a part of another, without their sharing those parts. This is the sense in which a material object may penetrate a region of space. Call this penetration by co-location.

There is a relation between one's conception of material objects and what one says about the sorts of penetration to which material objects may be subject. On the holes-and-all conception, material objects can be penetrated by piercing and by channeling. On the chock-full conception, however, penetration by channeling is impossible. On the chock-full conception of material objects, no body can travel through passages in another because no body has any passages. There is also a relation between one's conception of material objects and what one says about the sort of compression to which a material object may be subjected. On the holes-and-all conception, a material object might be compressed in a sense that entails

[19] I use that term in the sense given by the third entry under 'channel, v.' in the *OED*: "To convey through (or as through) a channel."

its coming to occupy a smaller region of space. That is the natural way to think of what goes one when one packs a snowball, reducing its diameter and making it denser. On the chock-full conception, however, one might bring the scattered parts of a material object closer together, but one cannot make the total region that it occupies any smaller. One makes a material object more dense not only by moving its parts closer together, but also by reducing the unoccupied places within its boundaries. If no material object has any unoccupied places within its boundaries, then no material object can be made more dense.

Jacovides has suggested that Locke embraces the chock-full conception of material objects. He offers this as a way of explaining how Locke can say that all bodies are equally solid, while still accommodating the obvious fact that bodies vary in their degrees of penetrability and compressibility:

It is true that fluids and ordinary bodies aren't absolutely solid, if these are taken as agglomerations of matter and void. Locke, however, thinks of them as entirely material, with no part that is a void. That is, he thinks of them as divided, gappy objects, made only of matter, and only present where matter is present....Yes, the water starts on one side of the globe and ends up on the other. He makes it clear that he thinks that the water doesn't pass through the matter of the globe. Rather, it passes through the "pores" in the globe. (Jacovides 2008, 224)

That last remark will not quite do as it stands, as Jacovides is presumably aware. The water cannot pass through pores in the globe, because the globe does not have any pores. What we would ordinarily describe as water passing through a straw is, on the chock-full conception of matter, just water passing along part of its surface. Even to call that part the straw's *inner* surface is to invite misunderstanding. By the same token, what we loosely describe as the water's passage through pores in the globe is more accurately described as travel across portions of its irregular and variegated surface.[20]

If we see Locke as holding the chock-full conception of material objects, we can account for his claim that all bodies are equally solid. All bodies are equally solid because no body contains any empty space as a part of it. Can we also invoke his conception of material objects to account for his claim that solidity entails impenetrability? It is obvious that in calling

[20] Jacovides may reply that the globe can have pores without having them as parts. If 'The globe has pores' does not mean that pores are parts of the globe, then it would seem to be saying something about the irregularity of the globe's surface. In that case, talk of travel through the pores would again be equivalent to talk of travel across the globe's irregular surface.

bodies impenetrable Locke does not mean to deny that they are susceptible to penetration by piercing. His acceptance of the chock-full conception of material objects would explain why bodies are impervious to penetration by channeling, because it would entail that apparent cases of penetration by channeling are really something else. Yet even a brief survey of his remarks about solidity shows that the sort of impenetrability that he is concerned with—the sort that he is declaring to be conferred by solidity—is not imperviousness to penetration by channeling, but imperviousness to penetration by co-location:

The idea of solidity...arises from the resistance which we find in Body, to the entrance of any other Body into the Place it possesses, till it has left it. (II.iv.1)

The *Idea* of which filling of space, is, That where we imagine any space take up by a solid Substance, we conceive it so to possess it, that it excludes all other solid Substances...(II.iv.2)

Solidity consists in repletion, and so an utter Exclusion of other Bodies out of the space it possesses...(II.iv.4)

Locke's commitment to the chock-full conception of material objects is not what explains his view that all bodies are equally impervious to penetration by co-location. The view that two bodies cannot occupy the same place at the same time is one of his most basic metaphysical commitments (§§42–43). To imagine that two bodies could be at the same place at the same time "takes away the distinction of Identity and Diversity, of one and more, and renders it ridiculous" (II.xxvii.2).

Though Locke's commitment to the chock-full conception of material objects does not explain his view that bodies cannot be penetrated by co-location, his view that bodies cannot be penetrated by co-location may well explain his commitment to the chock-full conception of material objects. If the void regions whose boundaries are circumscribed by an object's matter did belong to it as parts of it, and if another material object could come to be co-located with one of those regions, then it would be possible after all for one material object to be co-located with part of another. It seems plain that material objects sometimes come to be co-located with regions whose boundaries are at least partially circumscribed by those of material objects. Cases of this include ones that we would ordinarily describe by saying that water passed through a straw, or that a knife passed through the holes in a block of Swiss cheese. Locke's view that there cannot be two material objects at the same place at the same time commits him to denying that such regions are, strictly speaking, parts of material objects.[21]

We have been attempting to resolve the apparent tensions between, on the one hand, Locke's pronouncements about the ideas of solidity, impenetrability, and hardness; and on the other, some facts about our experiences of bodies that he surely wants to accommodate. We have explained how he can say that all bodies are absolutely solid despite the fact that many seem to have empty spaces in them. He can say this because when the chips are down he denies that the empty spaces are really to be counted as parts of the objects. Given this, he can allow that many material objects are compressible in one sense (their scattered parts may be brought into closer proximity), though he will deny that they are compressible in another (they cannot be made more dense). We have also explained how Locke can say that all bodies are impenetrable. The impenetrability that he is ascribing to bodies is an imperviousness to penetration by co-location, which does not entail an imperviousness to penetration by piercing or channeling. We have yet to account for his claim that the idea of absolute solidity is constantly delivered to us by tactile experience.

Locke twice tells us that solidity consists in repletion, which is the fact or condition of being filled up (II.iv.4; *Works* IV, 392).[22] We need to make sense of two of his claims about the repletion or filledness of bodies: first, that it is proper to distinguish this from impenetrability; second, that it is perceivable. Let us take these in turn. Locke has told us that 'solidity' conveys something positive, and that impenetrability is negative and better regarded

---

[21] There may be another possibility. One could say that an empty space can be a part of a material object, but only if it is *completely* circumscribed by solid parts of that object. On this view, the half-moon-shaped holes visible in the side of a block of Swiss cheese are not parts of the block, but spherical voids within the block are. When a knife cuts into one of these spherical voids, the void ceases to be a part of the cheese and instead acquires the same status as the half-moon-shaped holes that one could see before the cut. On this view, there could be voids that are parts of material objects, and yet no other material object could come to be co-located with such a void by piercing it or cutting into it. One problem with this view is that its conception of material objects lacks independent motivation. Another is that it seems possible for a fully enclosed void within a material object to come to contain another material object that is not a part of the first. Picture God creating a small metal pellet inside the spherical void inside a block of Swiss cheese. The pellet comes to be co-located with a region that is part of the Swiss cheese, so we seem to have a material object co-located with part of another. If one replies that in creating the pellet God has annihilated one of the empty parts of the Swiss cheese, then one's conception of material parthood has gotten even stranger and its motivations even murkier.

[22] This is the second meaning listed for 'repletion' in the *OED*. The first is that of eating or drinking to excess.

as a consequence of solidity. This distinction between positive and negative terms or features would seem to be a grammatical or logical distinction, but it gestures at other differences between the two features. I suggest that he is thinking of the solidity of a body as an intrinsic, occurrent feature of it; and of impenetrability as an extrinsic, dispositional feature that it has because it is solid. He is conceiving of the relation between solidity and impenetrability as like that between a body's shape or figure[23] and the "negative" feature of its being unable to fit through certain openings. The figure of a square peg (or a rectangular prism, to be more exact) is an intrinsic, occurrent feature of it; the peg's inability to fit through some particular round hole is an extrinsic, dispositional feature of it that it has because it has the shape it does. Analogously, Locke thinks that any body is disposed to resist the impingement of another because it is replete. Were we to speak only of impenetrability—and not to distinguish impenetrability from solidity—we would be treating a dispositional and extrinsic feature of body as fundamental, rather than grounding it in body's intrinsic, non-dispositional features. It is the fact that solidity underlies impenetrability in this way that Locke is trying to get across in II.iv.1, when he seemed to be defining 'solidity.'

Locke says that the idea of solidity "arises from the resistance which we find in Body, to the entrance of any other Body into the place it possesses" (II.iv.1). It is experiences of resistance that cause us to have the idea of solidity. We may think of resistance not as another property of body, but rather as a feature of interactions between bodies. It is true that we would not experience resistance were bodies not impenetrable and somewhat hard, but this does not mean that the experience of resistance does not give rise to the idea of solidity as well. We would not perceive figure by sight if we did not perceive color, but it does not follow from this that we see only colors and not figures. Along the same lines, Locke points out that solidity cannot exist without extension, but that these are still distinct ideas given by sense experience. He avers that "[m]any *Ideas* require others as necessary to their Existence or Conception, which yet are very distinct *Ideas*" (II.xiii.11).

Locke says that we receive the idea of solidity from our experiences handling bodies and being supported by bodies. As we have seen, some

---

[23] Locke speaks of "figure" more often than he does of "shape," but he does use both terms. Most of the time, he seems to use them interchangeably. Occasionally he speaks of the figure *and* shape of a thing, suggesting that these terms stand for distinct qualities (II.xxxiii.17; III.ix.15; *Works* IV, 314). However, neither his use of the terms, nor the *OED*, suggests what the difference between them might be.

commentators are reluctant to take this at face value. They would have him deny that absolute solidity is something that we ever observe, seeing it instead as something only suggested by the relative hardness of some bodies. These commentators are misconstruing what it means for solidity to be absolute, and they are encouraged in this mistake by their failure to grasp the sense in which Locke takes all bodies to be impenetrable. Those who would have him deny that we experience absolute solidity are likely thinking of absolute solidity as the maximum amount of something that varies in degree. They are thinking of it as maximum incompressibility, impenetrability or hardness, and they are understandably reluctant to saddle Locke with the view that we experience any such thing. This is not how Locke thinks of solidity. He thinks of solidity as absolute just in the sense that it is all-or-nothing. He thinks that for a thing to have *any* degree of hardness or incompressibility—for a thing to be very soft even—it must be solid. The temptation to think of solidity as a matter of degree is fostered by the misunderstanding of his claim that solidity renders bodies impenetrable. Bodies *are* more or less susceptible to piercing. If one thinks of bodies on the holes-and-all model—as perhaps we all do when we are not doing metaphysics—they are also more or less susceptible to channeling. If one is thinking of the impenetrability conferred by solidity as imperviousness to piercing or channeling, then one will be tempted to think of solidity as something that might be a matter of degree. Yet as we have seen, the impenetrability that Locke takes to be a consequence of solidity is not imperviousness to piercing or channeling, but imperviousness to co-location, which is all-or-nothing.

The fact that all of the bodies that we handle fall short of being perfectly impervious to piercing, squashing, or denting is not a reason for Locke to deny that we receive the idea of solidity through tactile experience. Is there another, better reason? It may be urged that we experience solidity only by experiencing impenetrability and hardness, and that this makes solidity a theoretical posit, a feature inferred rather than directly perceived. Here again we may draw on the comparison with figure to develop a reply on Locke's behalf. Suppose that one is blindfolded and handling a square peg. It would be strange to say that one does not perceive the peg's figure, and that instead one merely infers that it has the figure it does from its abilities and inabilities to fit in various spaces. A body's figure is an intrinsic feature of it that we perceive by touch, and not one that we merely infer on the basis of other qualities that we perceive. Similarly, Locke can say that a body's solidity is an intrinsic feature of it that we perceive by touch, and not one whose presence we merely infer from our experiences of impenetrability and hardness. Indeed, he might even go further, turning the objection upon itself and raising questions about the directness of our perceptual awareness of such dispositional features as impenetrability and hardness. We seem to perceive dispositions either by perceiving occurrent features that indicate their presence, or else by perceiving episodes that are manifestations of them. One perceives the vase's fragility either by seeing that the vase is made of thin glass, or else by watching it break. Since the vase's fragility is not to be identified with the thin glass, the thinness of the glass, or with the breaking of the glass, it would seem that we perceive the fragility only by perceiving something other than the fragility. If we do not perceive dispositional properties directly, but instead perceive them only by perceiving non-dispositional markers of them or events that are manifestations of them, then perhaps we should say that we perceive impenetrability and hardness only by perceiving solidity.

§11 *Other Primary Qualities*

Locke's lists of primary qualities include, besides extension and solidity, bulk, figure, motion, motion or rest, mobility, number, situation, size, and texture. Figure is the quality that appears most frequently on these lists, and also the one that seems the most straightforward. There is the ambiguity of 'figure'—the fact that it can refer either to the quality or to something instantiating that quality—but this seems relatively harmless. Even Locke seems to regard figure as unproblematic. He notes that because our ideas of figures are so clear and distinct, their names are among those least liable to doubt or uncertainty (III.ix.19). He is thinking of relatively simple figures, perhaps. Elsewhere, he acknowledges that in the case of a Chiliaedron our idea of the number of its sides may be distinct, but our idea of its figure is likely to be confused (II.xxix.14). Locke says that figure is the consequence of finite extension (II.xxiii.17). The figure of body just is the termination of its extension and solidity (II.xxxi.2). He takes the idea of figure in general to be a simple idea delivered both by touch and by sight (II.v), and says that we detect the particular figures of bodies and spaces by touching or viewing their extremities (II.xiii.5). He adds that by repeating and manipulating the idea of space we can also manufacture the ideas of an inexhaustible range of figures that we have not seen or felt.

The meanings of 'extension,' 'bulk' and 'size' overlap. As the *Oxford English Dictionary* tells us, 'extension' can mean a thing's spatial magnitude; 'bulk' can mean its volume, or its magnitude in three dimensions; and 'size' can mean its bulk, or its magnitude in any dimension. Thus a finite extended thing must have some particular bulk, and talk of the "size" of a thing could refer either to that bulk or to the measure of one dimension of that bulk (length or height, for example). This explains why all of Locke's lists of primary qualities contain at least one of these three terms, and yet only one of them—at II.viii.26—contains two of them. All bodies are extended, and to be extended is to have bulk and size; so extension, bulk, or size should appear on any list of the qualities that are inseparable from body. On the other hand, though the three terms are not exactly equivalent, a list containing more than one of them is likely to involve some redundancy.

Wilson suggests, with some plausibility, that in Locke's hands 'bulk' and 'size' mean not just volume, but filled or solid volume (Wilson 2002, 213–14). As he points out, this would explain why 'solidity' is absent from the lists of primary qualities that include either 'bulk' or 'size.' They are absent, on this interpretation, because a thing's having bulk or size already entails its being solid. If Wilson is right, then of course we should not expect Locke to speak of the bulk or size of empty spaces. There are some passages where he does seem to be mindfully avoiding ascribing bulk to empty spaces. At II.xiii.22, he speaks of "a void Space equal to the bulk of a Mustard-seed." Though he is speaking about a void space that has the same dimensions as the mustard seed, he ascribes bulk only to the mustard seed. At II.xv.8, he says that "the Extension of any Body is so much of that infinite Space, as the bulk of that Body takes up." There he not only avoids speaking of the bulk of an empty region of space, but implies that the bulk of the body is what is filling the space.

There is, however, one passage that poses a problem for Wilson's reading. It comes as Locke is arguing for the actual existence of boundless space. Where there is matter, he reasons, there is occupied space. If at some distance from us the world's matter gives out, we can conceive of nothing beyond the last bodies that might prevent one of them from moving still further. In the service of this last point, he compares the empty spaces between bodies with those that might lie beyond them. He finds that neither can have anything to hinder a body from moving into it:

[T]he same possibility of a Body's moving into a void Space, beyond the utmost Bounds of Body, as well as into a void Space interspersed amongst Bodies, will always remain clear and evident, the *Idea* of empty pure Space, whether within, or beyond the confines of all Bodies, being exactly the same, differing not in Nature, though in Bulk...(II.xvii.4)

Locke's argument for the infinity of space is a failure. He does not consider the possibility that travel in a straight line might ultimately bring one back to where one started. What matters for our present purpose is Locke's observation that interstitial voids and those beyond the reach of all matter differ not in nature but in bulk. He seems to be saying that interstitial voids and those lying beyond matter differ not in nature but in volume. He might say this because he is thinking of the former regions as finite and of the latter infinite. Or he might only be making a point about the arrangement of interstitial volumes and of those lying beyond matter. He might be saying that the volumes of these spaces differ because one is homogeneous and the other punctuated by matter. In either case, he seems to be speaking of the bulk of empty space.

Motion, "motion or rest" and mobility all appear on Locke's lists of primary qualities, presenting us with something of a puzzle. He cannot mean that these are three distinct primary qualities, each of them inseparable from body. For one thing, it is quite clear that he does not think that motion is inseparable from body. At II.i.10, he characterizes the relation of motion to body as like that of perception to the mind: "not its Essence, but one of its Operations." At II.xiii.21 [*bis*], he makes it plain that he thinks that God can put an end to all motion in matter, leaving bodies in a state of rest. It is presumably to accommodate the fact that bodies need not be in motion that he sometimes offers "motion or rest" as a single quality. The trouble is that it seems arbitrary to count such an irreducibly disjunctive feature as a single quality. As Jacovides points out, the same kind of gerrymandering would allow us to generate other "inseparable" qualities that Locke would not really want to count as primary (Jacovides 2007, 102). If "motion or rest" is to count as a primary quality, then why not "colored or transparent" and "odorous or non-odorous"? Neither motion nor "motion and rest" will do as an inseparable, primary quality of body. However, mobility is a good candidate for that role. Mobility is a dispositional property, a capacity that a thing can possess equally whether or not it is moving.

Locke speaks of mobility as a primary quality of body when he is emphasizing that these are features that bodies cannot lose. Thus 'mobility' appears twice at II.viii.9, in lists of the qualities that bodies cannot lose as a result of division. It appears again at II.xxi.73, as one of the few primary, original ideas that we receive by sensation from bodies. There are also a few other occasions when Locke speaks of the capacity for motion as a defining feature of body. At II.iv.3, and again at II.xiii.14, he suggests that the capacity for motion is one of the things that distinguishes body from space. At II.xxiii.3, he says that "Body is a *thing* that is extended, figured, and capable of Motion." Finally, in the *Examination of P. Malebranche's Opinion of Seeing All Things in God*, he says, "The essence of matter, as much as I can see of it, is extension, solidity, divisibility and mobility" (*Works* IX, 253).

Since it is mobility that Locke should reckon among the inseparable qualities of bodies, it may seem a disappointment that 'motion' and 'motion or rest' appear far more often on his lists of primary qualities. However, a closer look at the contexts of these lists shows that he is often on firmer ground than one might think. As Wilson notes, many of Locke's lists of primary qualities come as he is citing the properties of bodies that explain certain other changes or effects. "In that context," Wilson explains, "it is not surprising to see motion alone appear on Locke's lists, since it is motion, and motion of the parts more particularly, that is typically the *efficient* cause here" (Wilson 2002, 223–4). If a body's mobility is to be causally relevant to the occurrence of some event or state, this can only be because the body moved in some way that helped to precipitate that event or state. It is mobility, rather than motion, that is the necessary feature of body; but whenever this feature is invoked to explain a particular event or state, it will be because of some manifestation of mobility, some motion. This will be true even when the state in question is the possession of a higher level disposition. If the mobility of the insensibly small parts of a body explain its possession of the power to produce an idea of red in us, this will only be because the motions of the insensibly small parts of that body play a role in causing the idea of red in us.

In a summary at the end of his most important discussion of primary and secondary qualities, Locke does include motion on a list of "those before mentioned *primary Qualities*" (II.viii.26). That is unfortunate, since the context there is not one that justifies the reference to a short-lived manifestation of mobility rather than to the "inseparable" disposition itself. Still, most of the lists of primary qualities that include 'motion' are lists of the features of insensibly small particles that are causally relevant to the production of the observable qualities and doings of larger bodies. Most of these are cases in which the motions of a body's insensibly small parts are cited as causes of our sensations of colors, sounds, or tastes (II.viii.10, 13–17; IV.iii.13). Locke also includes 'motion' in a list of the observable qualities of bodies that can be perceived at a distance by sight (II.viii.12), and in a list of the features of the insensibly small parts of manna responsible for producing pains in us (II.viii.18).[24] Other cases in which the appearance of 'motion' on a list of qualities seems justifiable include one in which Locke is listing the perceiver-independent features of bodies (II.xxiii.9), and others in which he is listing some of the features of bodies of which we are woefully ignorant (IV.iii.24, 25). It is true that bodies move independently of our perceiving their motions, and often without our perceiving their motions.

Locke's treatment of "motion or rest" as a single, primary quality is unfortunate, but not every case in which he uses the phrase 'motion or rest' needs to be seen as an instance of that. His claim, at II.viii.23, that the "*Motion, or Rest*" of the solid parts of bodies are perceiver-independent is unexceptionable. So is his implication, at IV.vi.14, that "Motion, and Rest" are among the "divers modifications" that give rise to the various effects of matter. It is not unreasonable for him to suppose that bodies rest whether or not we perceive them doing so, and that sometimes it is the stillness of certain of a thing's minute parts that explains its having some of the observable qualities it does. Less happy is Locke's suggestion, at II.viii.9, that "Motion, or Rest" are among the "*original* or *primary Qualities* of Body, which…produce simple *Ideas* in us." There he is pulled in two directions. Because he is listing qualities that trigger a sensory response in us, he reaches for a term that refers to the manifestation of mobility rather than to the disposition itself. On the other hand, because this is the very section in which he has introduced primary qualities as inseparable features of bodies, he vaguely realizes that 'motion' will not do. So he settles for 'motion or rest' instead. Another appearance of 'motion or rest' comes at II.viii.22, in a list of the qualities of

---

[24] According to the *OED*, manna is "a sweet pale yellow or whitish concrete juice obtained from incisions in the bark of the Manna ash, *Fraxinus Ornus*…used as a gentle laxative." Given Locke's remark, one suspects that it was not always that gentle.

bodies that are "always in them." Again, Locke was right not to use 'motion' there, but he would have done better to use 'mobility.'

Number appears on many, but not all, of the lists of primary qualities. It is not immediately clear what 'number' refers to in this context. Wilson (2002, 214n39) claims that it is to the determinate number of parts that each thing has. In support of this, we may point to the fact that "number of Parts" appears on one of Locke's lists of primary qualities later in the *Essay* (IV.iii.15). Against it, we may remind ourselves that number is among the affections that he says are common to bodies and spirits. Can he really mean to say that each spirit has a determinate numbers of parts? It may be suggested that he can, since—as we shall see later—he is committed to the view that spirits have spatial extent. On the other hand, if a body or a spirit has a number of parts just in virtue of having spatial extent, then it would seem that each one must have an infinite number of parts. If every body has an infinite number of parts, then it is hard to see what explanatory work can be done by number as a primary quality. If the number of a body's parts is supposed to be a primary quality of it, Locke needs some more restrictive way of counting a thing's parts, one on which finite bodies of different sizes or constitutions count as having different finite numbers of parts. He offers no such account. Were one to supply such an account on his behalf, one would again face the problem of whether that same account could be used to count the parts of spirits.

Another way to make sense of Locke's talk of number as an affection of body and spirit is to see it in light of his claim, at the beginning of his short chapter "*Of Number*," that each thing affords us the idea of "*Unity*, or One" (II.xvi.1). Every object of our senses, every thought in our minds, he says, brings that idea along with it. This leads to his observation that number applies itself to everything that we can imagine (II.xvi.1). Though each thing has number because it is one thing, nearly all things will have number in other ways too. A man is one man, but at any given moment he is also a large number of atoms (§§39–44). It is easy to see why to be possessed of number in this sense might be regarded as inseparable from body; but once again it is hard to see how this leaves room for the primary quality of number to do any explanatory work. That might explain why number is missing from many of Locke's lists of primary qualities. He may take number to be a basic and irreducible affection of each thing, and yet worth mentioning only for the sake of completeness.

Locke uses both 'texture' and 'situation' to refer to the arrangement of a body's smaller parts. Many commentators have pointed out that Locke's use of 'texture' is likely influenced by Boyle. Some claim that for Boyle it is only molecule-sized bodies, and not individual corpuscles, that can have textures (Alexander 1985, 78; Anstey 2000 47–8). Some then draw the conclusion that Locke too holds that it is only larger bodies, and not individual corpuscles, that have textures (Alexander 1985, 123; Smith 1990, 234; Wilson 2002, 215). This poses a problem if we take texture to be a primary quality and take the primary qualities to be ones that are inseparable from body.

The evidence that Boyle denies that individual corpuscles have textures is weak. There is even less reason to say that Locke does so. For starters, there is vagueness about what counts as a corpuscle for Boyle. In *The Origins of Forms and Qualities*, he says that he has "forborne to employ arguments that are either grounded on, or suppose, indivisible corpuscles called *atoms*" (Boyle 1991, 7). The smallest bodies with which he concerns himself—those he calls *minima naturalia*—are insensibly small bodies that are "entire or undivided" and yet "*mentally*, and by divine omnipotence, divisible" (Boyle 1991, 41). To call bodies "entire and undivided" is at least to say that they are not scattered things. It seems likely that Boyle also means his *minima naturalia* to be bodies that, in the ordinary course of nature, remain entire and undivided. Though they are not partless, and their division is not impossible, they will in the ordinary course of nature not be broken down into more basic constituents with their own chemical or physical properties. This makes his *minima* in one respect like atoms, but it leaves open the possibility that their chemical or physical properties result from the nature and arrangement of their parts— result, that is, from their texture. Boyle goes on to say that concretions of these *minima* may yet be singly insensible and so stable as to be rarely divided in the course of nature. He refers to these as "primitive concretions or clusters...of particles," but he also calls them corpuscles (Boyle 1991, 42).[25] These molecular corpuscles are clearly supposed to have textures.

---

[25] In his discussion of Boyle, Anstey introduces a distinction that Boyle himself does not make, between "atomic corpuscles" and "molecular corpuscles" (Anstey 2000, 63n28). This distinction is problematic both because its first term mistakenly suggests that Boyle is committed to atomism, and because it effectively closes the door on a possibility that Boyle's language leaves open. This is the possibility that Boyle applies 'corpuscle' univocally to *minima naturalia* and to concretions of those, and that he regards all corpuscles—even those that are indivisible in the ordinary course of nature—as being molecular in the sense of being composed of smaller parts whose properties and arrangements give rise to their own features.

Peter Anstey is one who argues that Boyle's *minima naturalia* at least cannot have textures. In support of this, he offers this passage from *The Origin of Forms and Qualities*:

[W]hen many corpuscles do so convene together as to compose any distinct body,...then from their other accidents (or modes)...there doth emerge a certain disposition or contrivance of parts in the whole, which we may call the *texture* of it. (Boyle 1991, 30)

Anstey says that Boyle is defining 'texture' here, and he concludes that for Boyle "[t]exture is not essential at the atomic level because, by definition, no atomic corpuscles have it" (Anstey 2000, 48). However, there is little reason to see this passage as offering necessary and sufficient conditions for the occurrence of a texture. Boyle says only that when many corpuscles form a concretion, the contrivance of that concretion's parts is what we may call a texture. He does not say that the *only* textures are those possessed by concretions of corpuscles.[26]

Though Boyle does not deny that the bodies he treats as *minima* have parts arranged in certain ways, one can understand why the textures that concern him are those of larger particles. He is interested in formulating and testing empirical hypotheses about the structures that give rise to observable phenomena. Even the molecular bodies that he calls "primitive concretions" are insensibly small, and how arrangements of them might give rise to the physical and chemical features of observable bodies is at best a subject for risky hypotheses. The bodies that he treats as *minima* are supposed to be still smaller, and so stable that they are not broken down into their parts in the ordinary course of nature. In all likelihood, he would regard speculation about the arrangement of their parts as quite idle.

As for Locke, we have already seen that he does not regard individual corpuscles as partless. To the contrary, he thinks that the very idea of body entails its infinite divisibility, and he sees the coherence of the parts of corpuscles as something standing in need of explanation. Even Locke's atoms are not partless. Atoms, if there are any such things, are just bodies whose outer parts are Frozen together. Any body that has parts must have those

---

[26] Anstey cites several other passages (Boyle 1991, 49, 51, and 142) in support of the view that "atomic corpuscles" lack texture (Anstey 2000, 64n43). Again, each shows only that Boyle regards concretions of physically indivisible *minima* as having textures, and not that he regards only such concretions as having textures.

parts arranged one way or another. That is all it takes for a body to have a texture or a situation of its parts. There is thus no difficulty with the suggestion that texture is a feature that Locke regards as inseparable from body.

Our tour of the affections that Locke counts as primary qualities of body is now complete but for a few outliers. Toward the end of II.xxiii, he summarizes his case for thinking that we are in roughly the same epistemic situation with regard to material and immaterial substances. After observing that the substance of spirit and that of body are equally unknown to us, he says:

Two primary Qualities, or Properties of Body, *viz.* solid coherent parts, and impulse, we have distinct clear *Ideas* of: So likewise we know, and have distinct clear *Ideas* of two primary Qualities, or Properties of Spirit, *viz.* Thinking, and a power of Action ... (II.xxiii.30)

Are we to take seriously the suggestion that 'solid coherent parts' and 'impulse' are primary qualities of body? I suggest not. First, neither of these phrases names a quality at all. The former stands for a number of substances, and the latter names a kind of event, a transfer of motion. Second, if we were to take seriously the suggestion that 'solid coherent parts' and 'impulse' name primary qualities, then the rhetorical context would require us to say that these are the only primary qualities of body. For Locke is repeating the point, made earlier in the chapter, that when it comes to material and immaterial substances we have only two "*primary* Ideas" peculiar to each kind of substance (II.xxiii.17–18). Yet it is clear that he thinks that there are more than two primary qualities of bodies. In this very passage, he goes on to say, "We have also the *Ideas* of several Qualities inherent in Bodies, and have the clear distinct *Ideas* of them: which Qualities, are but the various modifications of the Extension of cohering solid Parts, and their motion" (II.xxiii.30). This seems an obvious reference to our ideas of bulk, figure, texture, number, and the other primary qualities of bodies.

When Locke calls "solid coherent parts" and "impulse" the two "primary Qualities, or Properties of Body," he is not using the phrase 'primary Qualities' in its ordinary sense. One suspects that he does better for himself when, earlier in the chapter, he speaks instead of the two "*primary* Ideas" peculiar to body (II.xxiii.17). The main thing that he wants to convey is that these two ideas take us most of the way toward our understanding of what it is that material substances are. The rest is just filling in details. It would be nice to be able to say that Locke takes the ideas of solid coherent parts and of impulse to be the two primary ideas of body because he takes these to be the two most basic ideas peculiar to body. The suggestion would be that even though other, more basic, ideas apply to bodies (those of number and expansion come to mind), these other ideas also apply to things besides bodies. Yet this reasoning cannot justify Locke's actual candidates for the primary ideas of body. The simple idea of solidity is more basic than the complex idea of solid, cohering parts, and yet Locke thinks that the idea of solidity applies only to bodies. All in all, it seems best not to place much weight on Locke's reference, at II.xxiii.30, to two primary qualities of body. His counting of "*primary* Ideas" or "Properties" to demonstrate parity in our grasp of material and immaterial substances is a rhetorical maneuver in the service of a broad epistemological point; it is not a careful expression of his metaphysical views.

One other unusual appearance in a list of primary qualities comes as Locke is explaining what it would take for us to have a tolerable degree of knowledge about substances. For that, he says, we would have to know what changes the primary qualities of one body are able to produce in those of another, and also how the primary qualities of bodies cause sensations or ideas in us. He observes that "[t]his is in truth, no less than to know all the Effects of Matter, under its divers modifications of Bulk, Figure, Cohesion of Parts, Motion, and Rest" (IV.vi.14). The surprise here is the appearance of "Cohesion of Parts" alongside the primary qualities of bulk, figure, motion and rest.

Does this mean that cohesion is a primary quality for Locke? I do not think that it does. It could be argued that cohesion of some sort is inseparable from body, since even a scattered object will have constituents—perhaps atomic constituents—whose parts cohere. On the other hand, a thing's having parts that are individually cohering is not the same as *it* cohering. We have already seen reason to think that Locke embraces the chock-full conception of material objects. That conception of material objects, when paired with corpuscularianism, leads to the view that ordinary physical objects might be scattered things. If Locke allows even the possibility of scattered bodies, then bodies need not have parts all of which cohere with one another. Another reason to doubt that cohesion is a primary quality for Locke is that he treats it as a phenomenon that stands in need of a physical explanation (II.xxiii.23–24). That is not what we would expect if he is thinking of it as a universal feature of body, a feature that any thing must have if it is to count as a body. A final reason for thinking that Locke does not regard cohesion as a primary quality of body is that he does not include it in any of the lists that he explicitly presents as lists of primary qualities. His inclusion of it here, alongside some of the primary qualities of bodies, does not show that he takes it for a primary quality. Here his point is that to have a scientific understanding of how bodies interact with one another and with our minds, we would have to know what contributions are made by the different volumes, shapes, and motions of bodies, and by the different degrees of cohesion in and among them. It is reasonable of him to say this even if he is not thinking of cohesion as a primary quality.

I have suggested that Locke may use 'bulk' and 'size' to refer to the same feature—a body's volume—but that he may use it to refer to the measure of a body's volume along a single dimension. Either way, talk of a body's bulk makes talk of its size redundant. I have also argued that Locke expresses himself best when he speaks of mobility—rather than motion, or motion and rest—as a primary quality. Finally, I have said that he treats 'situation of parts' and 'texture' as synonymous. In light of these claims, and taking into consideration the arguments of the foregoing sections, we arrive at the following as a list of primary qualities that is exhaustive without being redundant: bulk, extension, figure, mobility, number, solidity, and texture. Locke tells us that the primary qualities of body are "utterly inseparable from the Body, in what estate soever it be" (II.viii.9). I have argued that he means that they are necessary features of bodies, features that any thing must possess if it is to count as a body. Each of the qualities on the list above passes the test. To qualify as a body, a thing must be extended in three dimensions, and so have a volume and a shape. It must be solid, and mobile. It must have extended parts that are arranged in a certain way. Finally, it must be one thing of some sort, and so possessed of number in a sense.

There is a good deal of variation across Locke's lists of primary qualities, but this does not mean that he vacillates about which are the primary qualities. Many of his lists are not offered as lists of the primary qualities, but instead as lists of qualities that have a certain feature, or that play a certain role. We saw this when considering why so many of the lists include 'motion' rather than 'mobility.' We saw that in most of those cases he is listing qualities that cause sensations of color or pain, or that can be perceived at a distance, or that are perceiver-independent. In those cases, he cites motions rather than mobility because particular motions play the relevant roles. Even if the qualities that have a certain feature or that play a certain role *are* primary qualities, the context may not require an exhaustive listing of the primary qualities for Locke to make his point. Thus at II.viii.13 he asks us to suppose that "the different Motions and Figures, Bulk, and Number" of very small particles affect our organs and thus produce sensations of colors and smells in us. This is in service of the point that it is conceivable that God could establish such connections despite there being no resemblance between those qualities and the ideas they cause in us. There is no need for him to list all of the primary qualities of bodies; his point stands whatever we imagine about whether other primary qualities—situation and texture, for instance—are relevant to the production of sensations of color and odor.

There are conceptual relations among some ideas of primary qualities, and these mean that sometimes a short list of qualities can entail a longer list. Locke draws attention to some of these connections himself, noting that solidity entails extension (II.xiii.11), that solidity entails figure (III.x.15), and that figure entails extension (IV.iii.14). We might just as well add that any finite solid thing must have bulk and figure; that any thing with bulk must have extension; that any solid, extended thing must have its parts arranged in some way or other, and so must have a texture. We have also seen that Locke holds that everything imaginable is characterized by number (II.xvi.1). Thus if one wanted to offer a compressed list of the necessary features of body, one could simply say that bodies are finite, solid, mobile substances. This would entail that each body must also be extended, that it must have a bulk, a figure, a texture, and number.

Earlier I defended the view that it is for Locke a conceptual truth that primary qualities are inseparable from body. The primary qualities of body are just those corresponding to the ideas that are components of our abstract idea "body." We considered several objections to this reading, and one—suggested by Jacovides—was that it squared poorly with some of Locke's brief analyses of the idea of body. Now we can see that Locke's brief descriptions of the contents of the idea of body are simply incomplete analyses. He says that a body is "something that is solid, and extended, whose parts are separable and movable different ways" (II.xiii.11). If we make the reasonable assumption that he is implicitly restricting the universe of discourse to finite things, then the extension and solidity of a body will entail that it also has number, bulk, figure, and texture. If we also make the assumption that anything composed entirely of mobile parts is mobile, then his claim that bodies have separable and movable parts will entail that bodies are mobile. Much the same can be said about Locke's claim at II.xxiii.22 that a body is "an extended solid Substance, capable of communicating Motion by impulse," though in that case we must say that he is assuming that something can communicate motion *by impulse* only if it can move and so strike the thing to which it communicates the motion.[27]

Richard Aaron long ago raised the question of whether it is determinable or determinate qualities that Locke is talking about when he declares that primary qualities are inseparable from body (Aaron 1937, 117). Since then many commentators have complained that Locke's use of inseparability as a criterion to distinguish primary qualities depends upon unfair comparisons of determinables and determinates (Mackie 1976, 20–1; Jolley 1999, 63; Jacovides 2007, 102). If figure qualifies as a primary quality of body because all bodies must have some figure or other, then why does color not count as a primary quality? A visible body can be deprived of its particular color, but must it not always have some color or other? In reply to this last question, one may say that a colored body can be deprived of color altogether by being divided into invisibly small parts. The rejoinder to this is that dividing a colored body into invisibly small parts is not depriving that body of color; it is destroying that body and leaving behind the tiny bodies that had formerly been its parts.

To ask whether Locke's primary qualities are determinables or determinates may already be to get off on the wrong foot. For one thing, the distinction between determinables and determinates does not apply to all of the qualities that Locke counts as primary. We can make sense of there being a variety of determinate extensions, volumes, figures, numbers, and textures, but we cannot make sense of there being a variety of determinate mobilities or solidities. Also notice that the distinction between determinable qualities and determinate ones is not exclusive. Many terms stand for qualities that are both determinable and determinate. Red is a determinate instance of the determinable color, but it is

---

[27] One other passage that Jacovides cites is III.vi.33, where Locke illustrates the fact that abstract ideas of substances are designed to facilitate the communication of our thoughts by observing that one who wanted to "make and discourse of Things, as they agreed in the complex *Idea* of Extension and Solidity, needed but use the word *Body*, to denote all such." It is true that we cannot extract mobility from extension and solidity alone. However, Locke's point is secure so long as everything that is solid and extended falls within the scope of 'body.' We need not understand him to be saying that "solid, extended thing" exhausts the meaning of 'body.'

also a determinable of which carmine and vermillion are determinate instances. When Locke says that extension, bulk, figure, and texture are inseparable from body, he certainly does not mean to deny that bodies can persist through changes in volume, or shape, or in the arrangement of their parts. If one wants to express this by saying that it is the determinable qualities of extension, bulk, figure, and texture that he takes to be inseparable from body, that may be harmless enough.

A further matter is whether Locke means to count as primary qualities the determinate instances of inseparable determinable qualities. So, for example, does he mean to count "cubical" as a primary quality, even though it not necessary that every body be cubical? Surely he does. Locke tells us over and over that it is the primary qualities of insensibly small particles that produce the observable features of the larger bodies they compose. Yet the primary qualities that play these productive roles cannot be the determinable qualities of bulk, figure, texture, etc. Locke does not think that a body looks red, or tastes like licorice, simply because its smaller particles have *some* size or other, *some* shape or other, *some* texture or other. The observable features of larger bodies are determinate features, and so the primary qualities that produce one set of determinate features rather than another can only be determinate qualities themselves. Locke defines determinable primary qualities in terms of inseparability, but takes it for granted that the determinates of those inseparable determinables are to be reckoned primary qualities, even though they are not themselves inseparable.

Those who complain that Locke unfairly compares determinables and determinates are in effect saying that he should regard color, odor, and sound as being just as inseparable as shape is. To this I make two replies. First, let us not be misled by the term 'inseparable,' which suggests the impossibility of taking a property away from its bearer. The point that Locke is making at II.viii.9 is not just that bodies that happen to be already possessed of extension, bulk, figure, etc. cannot then be deprived of them. His point is that extension, bulk, figure, etc. are features that all bodies must have. Color, on the other hand, is not a feature that all bodies must have. Even if dividing a body into invisibly small pieces is not depriving it of color (because it is simply destroying the body), the mere fact that we can conceive of invisibly small (and hence colorless) bodies shows that color does not meet Locke's inseparability requirement for being a primary quality. Second, Locke does in fact think that visible bodies can be deprived of their colors without those bodies being made to go out of existence. He thinks that bodies cease to be colored whenever we are not having sensations of their colors. To show this will be one of the main tasks of the next chapter.

3

Secondary Qualities

§12. Locke distinguishes two types of secondary qualities: secondary qualities immediately perceivable are powers that bodies have to produce various sensations in us, and secondary qualities mediately perceivable are powers they have to alter the perceivable qualities of other bodies. The first include colors, sounds, odors, etc., and Locke thinks that we are prone to mistake these for features resembling our ideas of them. The second include such features as the sun's power to color a fair face, and these we easily recognize as the bare powers they are. §13. Though he denies that ideas of secondary qualities resemble secondary qualities, Locke does say that ideas of primary qualities resemble primary qualities. It is hard to make good sense of this claim, and it may be an unreflective concession to philosophical tradition. Many of Locke's predecessors and contemporaries say that ideas resemble the items they represent, though there is little consensus among them about the nature of this resemblance. §14. There is an apparent tension in Locke's account of colors. He describes bodies as losing their colors when they are unobserved, which suggests a subjectivist account of color. Yet he also identifies colors with powers to produce ideas, which suggests a dispositionalist account. §15. The solution is to recognize that he takes colors to be relational but non-dispositional features that bodies have just in case they are causing observers to have color experiences. Colors are "powers" in a degenerate sense. This makes them mind-dependent, but not features of minds. §16. If being colored just is causing a color experience, then there are no merely apparent colors. Passages in which Locke seems to mark a distinction between apparent color and real color can be given other readings. §17. Locke's frequent assimilation of colors and pains might seem to suggest a subjectivist account of color, but a closer look at the relevant passages does not bear this out. §18. The view that objects lose their colors when we do not see them is more attractive than one might initially think. §19. There is evidence that Locke identifies other secondary qualities immediately

perceivable, and even secondary qualities mediately perceivable, with powers in the degenerate sense.

§12 *Two Kinds of Secondary Qualities*

At II.viii.9–10, Locke distinguishes three types of qualities. We have examined much of what he has to say about the first sort, those he calls primary qualities. The second sort he at first calls simply secondary qualities:

> 2*ndly*, such *Qualities*, which in truth are nothing in the Objects themselves, but Powers to produce various Sensations in us by their *primary Qualities, i.e.* by the Bulk, Figure, Texture, and Motion of their insensible parts, as Colours, Sounds, Tasts, *etc.* These I call *secondary Qualities*. (II.viii.10)

How are we to expand the '*etc.*'? Which qualities, besides colors, sounds and flavors, are secondary qualities? Locke mentions "Smells" (II.viii.13) and "tangible Qualities" (IV.vi.10). By "Smells" he of course means odors, but what he means by "tangible Qualities" is less clear.

In the *Essay*, Locke does not say what are all of the "tangible Qualities," or which of them are secondary qualities. He does frequently include warmth or heat in what seem to be lists of secondary qualities (II.i.3; II.viii.15–17, 24; II.xxxi.2). Yet there are also times when he identifies warmth or heat with the motion of insensibly small particles in our bodies (II.vii.4; II.viii.21, ll.25–27), which is to identify it with the manifestation of a primary quality. The terms 'warmth' and 'heat' are for Locke ambiguous. Sometimes they denote the motion of particles; and sometimes they denote a power that bodies have in virtue of the motion of their constituent particles—the power to produce an idea that he calls the idea of warmth or heat. This idea is not that of corpuscular motion, but rather the idea that one is having when one is feeling heat. At one point, Locke even seems to use 'heat' to stand for this idea (II.iii.1). The power to produce this idea is one of the secondary qualities that we perceive through touch. The idea of cold is a different idea than that of heat, but its cause is just the privation of the motion of constituent particles (II.viii.2). Thus 'cold' will be ambiguous in just the way that 'heat' is.

At one point Locke suggests that the sensation of heat and cold is "nothing but the increase or diminution of the motion of the minute Parts of our Bodies" (II.viii.21, ll.32–33). He does not really mean to be offering a materialist account of a mental event. He is suggesting that the ideas of heat and cold are triggered not by some absolute values of corpuscular agitation, but by the increase and decrease of corpuscular agitation in our body parts, respectively. This allows him to explain how one object can simultaneously trigger both ideas in us. For if two body parts have different degrees of corpuscular agitation to begin with, contact with the same object may increase the agitation in one while decreasing that in the other.

Though Locke sometimes speaks as though there are just two discrete ideas of heat and cold caused in us by all our experiences of touching bodies of various temperatures, it may well be that these two are meant to stand in for a range of subtly different ideas. For he seems to identify the having of a sensory experience with the having of a sensory idea (Stuart 2010, 38–9), and there is a range of similar but distinguishable experiences that one can have touching bodies of different degrees of warmth or coldness. Serving as the boundaries of this range are the experiences of pain that are caused by touching something that is very cold or very hot (II.vii.4). It is best to think of tactile experiences of temperature as perceptions of a single type of secondary quality, much as visual experience of all of the colors we see are perceptions of a single type of secondary quality. To treat the power to produce each distinguishable degree of heat or cold as a different secondary quality would make no more sense than treating each distinguishable speed of a moving object as the manifestation of a different primary quality. Let us therefore say that Locke recognizes heat/cold as being one of the tangible secondary qualities of body. His use of the plural "tangible Qualities" implies that there are others.

Sometime after 1697, Locke produced a short introduction to natural science titled *Elements of Natural Philosophy*. The *Elements* sheds some light on his knowledge of, and views about, the science of his day; it must also be treated with some caution, as it seems to have been dictated for the instruction of a boy, and not composed with an eye toward publication.[1] In the *Elements*, Locke describes heat as "a very brisk agitation of the insensible

---

[1] It is Pierre Desmaizeaux, editor of the 1720 collection in which the piece first appeared, who tells us that Locke "composed, or rather dictated these Elements for the use of a young Gentleman, whose education he had very much at heart" (Locke 1720, "Dedication"). Locke's nineteenth-century biographer H. R. Fox Bourne plausibly suggests that the young gentleman was Francis Masham, son of Sir William and Lady Damaris Masham, with whom Locke lived for the last decade of his life (Fox Bourne 1876, vol.2, 449n2). A reference in the *Elements* to Huygens's *Cosmothereos* dates it to 1698 or later. Francis Masham was twelve in 1698. Desmaizeaux warns us that "this small tract is far from being what Mr. Locke would have made it, had he written upon that matter professedly, and design'd to make it a complete work" (Locke 1720).

parts of the object, which produces in us that sensation from whence we denominate the object hot" (*Works* III, 327–8). He also offers this list of the tangible qualities of bodies: "hard, soft, smooth, rough, dry, wet, clammy, and the like" (*Works* III, 327). Are these tangible qualities that are secondary qualities? If they are, then we may need to say that each of these terms is ambiguous for Locke in the way that 'heat' is, standing in the first instance for a primary quality—or perhaps a complex affection ultimately reducible to certain primary qualities—and in the second instance for a power to produce a certain idea, a power that the thing has because it has the corresponding primary quality or complex affection. We have already seen that Locke identifies hardness with a firm cohesion of the parts of matter (II.iv.4). If "hard" were also to be a secondary quality, then the suggestion would be that there is some distinctive sensory idea triggered in us by bodies whose parts firmly cohere, and that 'hard' is sometimes used to denote the power to trigger that idea. Similarly, 'rough' presumably denotes a sort of texture, but one might say that it can also stand for a power to produce some distinctive idea triggered in us by our tactile experiences of things with that sort of texture.

On the other hand, in the *Elements* Locke offers "hard, soft, smooth, rough, dry, wet, clammy, and the like" not as tangible secondary qualities, but simply as qualities perceived only by the sense of touch. In the *Elements*, the distinction between primary and secondary qualities is not even mentioned. It is far from clear that all of the tangible qualities mentioned in the *Elements* are fundamental enough to belong on a list of secondary qualities. Should we not say that "rough" and "clammy" stand to tactile experience in something like the way that "polka-dotted" and "checked" do to visual experience? There is a case for saying that our experiences of hardness and softness, of roughness and smoothness, of dryness and wetness, are all experiences of different degrees and distributions of resistance or pressure on various parts of our bodies. Pressure on a body part may be a state of affairs describable in terms of primary qualities alone, but it strikes me as plausible to say that there is a distinctive phenomenology to the experience of such pressure. If this is right, then Locke could say that all experiences of pressure or resistance involve the having of a certain sensory idea. He could say that the solidity, texture, and motion of bodies and their smaller parts gives them powers to produce the ideas of different degrees and distributions of pressure on our peripheries, much as those same features give bodies powers to produce in us the ideas of different colored surfaces. In that case, Locke could make do with a very short list of tangible secondary qualities: heat/cold and pressure. This is speculative, however. He simply does not tell us what he takes to be the secondary qualities perceived through touch.

The third type of quality that Locke introduces at II.viii.9–10 is one to which he does not at first give a name. He says:

> To these might be added a third sort which are allowed to be barely Powers though they are as much real Qualities in the Subject, as those which I to comply with the common way of speaking call *Qualities*, but for distinction *secondary Qualities*. For the power in Fire to produce a new Colour, or consistency in Wax or Clay by its primary Qualities, is as much a quality in Fire, as the power it has to produce in me a new *Idea* or Sensation of warmth or burning, which I felt not before, by the same primary Qualities, *viz.* The Bulk, Texture, and Motion of its insensible parts. (II.viii.10)

Some commentators dub the third sort of quality "tertiary qualities" (Wilson 1979), but Locke eventually calls them "*Secondary Qualities, mediately perceivable*" (II.viii.26). The "Colours, Sounds, Tasts, *etc.*" that he had at first called simply "*secondary Qualities*," he comes to qualify as "*Secondary Qualities, immediately perceivable*" (II.viii.26).[2] In calling both of these types of qualities "secondary qualities," he means to convey that they have something important in common: both ultimately affect the ideas that are produced in us. Secondary qualities immediately perceivable are powers that bodies have to affect our sensations by acting upon us directly. Secondary qualities mediately perceivable are powers that bodies have to change the observable qualities of bodies, and so to affect our sensations indirectly. Further complicating matters is the fact that even after he has introduced the term '*Secondary Qualities, mediately perceivable*' (II.viii.26), Locke sometimes uses the term 'secondary qualities' to refer to powers the bodies have to produce ideas in us (II.xxiii.9; II.xxxi.2). On these occasions, he seems to have in mind just secondary qualities immediately perceivable, and not the broader class of secondary qualities that also includes secondary qualities mediately perceivable.

---

[2] When, in the *Essay*'s second edition (1694), Locke adds marginal headings, he reinforces the suggestion that his "third" sort of quality is one of two kinds of secondary qualities. For II.viii.26, he adds the heading: "*Secondary Qualities two-fold; First, immediately perceivable; Secondly, mediately perceivable.*"

Secondary qualities mediately perceivable are not limited to powers to alter bodies' secondary qualities. Thus Locke's examples of these qualities include not only the sun's power to blanche wax (II.viii.23) and to color a fair face (II.viii.25), but also the power that fire has to melt lead (II.viii.23) and to change the consistency of wood (II.xxiii.7). Melting a metal may involve changing its color, but it is at least conceivable that it should involve changing only its primary qualities (the relative situation of its parts, and so perhaps its hardness).

Locke initially characterizes secondary qualities mediately perceivable as powers that things have to affect the observable features of *other* bodies (II.viii.26). This makes them what he calls active powers (II.xxi.2). Yet when he comes to describe the ideas of qualities that make up our complex ideas of substances, he lists three sorts: (i) those of primary qualities, (ii) those of secondary qualities, and (iii) those of the "aptness we consider in any Substance, to give or receive such alterations of primary Qualities, as that the Substance so altered, should produce in us different *Ideas* from what it did before" (II.xxiii.9). Here the third category includes not only active powers, but also what he calls a body's passive powers—its powers to be acted upon in ways that make for observable changes in it. So (iii) includes not only the idea of a loadstone's power to draw iron (II.xxiii.7, 9), but also those of gold's power to be melted (II.xxiii.10), of its ductility and of its solubility in *Aqua Regia* (II.xxxi.9). If it is not absolutely clear that Locke means to number a body's passive powers to be altered in observable ways among its secondary qualities mediately perceivable, it is clear that he means to accord those two kinds of powers much the same status. Both are merely powers (II.xxxi.9), though they pass for "inherent Qualities" in bodies (II.xxiii.7). Both "terminate only in sensible simple *Ideas*" (II.xxiii.9), by which he means that our cognizance of them is grounded in our sensations. Both far outrun our cognizance of them, since we have not observed all of any body's possible interactions with other bodies (II.xxxi.13; II.xxxii.24; IV.iii.16).

Even if a body's passive powers to be altered in observable ways are numbered among its secondary qualities mediately perceivable, the three types of qualities that Locke distinguishes and names do not encompass all of the qualities there are. For bodies can have powers to interact with other bodies in ways that do not make for observable changes:

I doubt not, but there are a thousand Changes, that Bodies we daily handle, have a Power to cause in one another, which we never suspect, because they never appear in sensible effects. (II.xxiii.9)

One could insist that such changes will ultimately contribute to changes in one or the other body's dispositions to appear this way or that. This might lead us to contemplate different degrees of secondary qualities mediately perceivable, some being powers to change observable features, others being powers to change powers to change observable features, and so on. However, to say this is to go further than Locke takes us.

Locke suggests that the three types of qualities that he names do at least comprehend all those "whereby we take notice of Bodies, and distinguish them one from another" (II.viii.26). Yet even that is probably an overstatement. It will be closer to the truth if Locke does count such passive powers as ductility and solubility as secondary qualities mediately perceivable. Still, there are salient qualities of bodies that do not easily find a place within his three categories. For example, at II.xxiii.8 he mentions the "soporifick or anodyne Virtues" of opium. Where would we locate these qualities within his classification? They are not primary qualities. They are not secondary qualities immediately perceivable, since the powers to induce sleep or to inhibit pain are not powers to produce ideas in us. They are not secondary qualities mediately perceivable, because although they are "Powers…to produce different Operations, on different parts of our Bodies" (II.xxiii.8), they are not powers to alter the observable features of those body parts.

Locke's mention of opium comes as he is making a point about a difference in how we think about the two kinds of secondary qualities. He says that we tend to look upon secondary qualities immediately perceivable as "*real Qualities*" in bodies, as "something more than mere Powers" (II.viii.24). On the other hand, secondary qualities mediately perceivable are both "*call'd, and esteemed barely Powers*" (II.viii.24). Locke draws our attention to this difference because he thinks that it involves a mistake. In fact, the two kinds of secondary qualities "are all of them equally Powers" (II.viii.24). Locke mentions the capacities that opium has to induce sleep and to inhibit pain because he thinks that those are qualities that we have no temptation to think of as anything more than "meer Powers" (II.xxiii.8). He encourages us to take the same attitude toward opium's color and flavor.

Locke says that we mistakenly take secondary qualities immediately perceivable for "*real Qualities*." What does this mean? In denying that colors, sounds, and odors are real qualities, is he denying that there are colors, sounds, and odors? Or is he merely denying that colors, sounds, and odors enjoy a certain status? In the first sentence of II.viii.17, Locke comes as close as he ever comes to offering a definition of 'real Qualities':

The particular *Bulk, Number, Figure, and Motion of the parts of Fire*, or *Snow*, are really *in them*, whether any ones Senses perceive them or no: and therefore they may be called *real Qualities*, because they really exist in those Bodies.

One thing we learn from this passage is that primary qualities are "*real Qualities*." At various times Locke characterizes lists of primary qualities as lists of "*real Qualities*" (II.viii.17), of "*primary*, and *real Qualities*" (II.viii.22), of "*real Original*, or *primary Qualities*" (II.viii.23), and of "*original Qualities*" (II.viii.12, 13; II.x.6). The freedom with which he slides between these characterizations suggests that he may think not just that the primary qualities are among the real qualities, but that the two classes are coextensive. The first sentence of II.viii.17 also tells us that primary qualities are perceiver-independent. This is a point that he repeats later (II.viii.23, ll.21–22; II.xxiii.9). Most importantly, the 'therefore' in that sentence indicates that it is *because* primary qualities are perceiver-independent that they qualify as "*real Qualities*." This too is a point that Locke makes again later. At II.viii.23, after describing the three sorts of qualities in bodies, he says that the first sort are "properly called *real Original*, or *primary Qualities*, because they are in the things themselves, whether they are perceived or no." Perceiver-independence is thus at least a necessary condition for a quality's being "real."

Locke thinks that we mistake colors, sounds, and so forth for real qualities, but that we easily take secondary qualities mediately perceivable for the bare powers that they are. The passage in which he tries to explain why we do these things—II.viii.25—has got to be one of the most convoluted in the whole *Essay*. Yet it is worth working our way through it, because it brings us face to face with some important strands in Locke's account of qualities. He begins by telling us that we are not apt to recognize that ideas of colors, sounds, etc. are the effects of primary qualities in bodies. We are not apt to recognize this, because:

[T]he *Ideas* we have of distinct Colours, Sounds, *etc.* containing nothing at all in them, of Bulk, Figure, or Motion, we are not apt to think them the Effects of these primary Qualities, which appear not to our Senses to operate in their Production; and with which, they have not any apparent Congruity, or conceivable Connexion.

Here Locke does not explain why it is not apparent to our senses that primary qualities produce ideas of colors, sounds, etc., but surely part of the reason is that the relevant qualities are those of insensibly small particles. When he says that there is no conceivable connection between primary qualities and ideas of colors, sounds, etc., he does not mean that it is inconceivable that there be a causal connection between the two, but rather that reason cannot discover any necessary connection between particular primary qualities and the sensory responses they trigger in us. Even if we did know about the primary qualities of the insensibly small particles that compose different colored surfaces, reason could not tell us why one surface produces the idea of blue in us and another produces the idea of yellow.[3]

Secondary qualities mediately perceivable are powers that bodies have to alter the primary qualities of other bodies, and so to change their colors, flavors, odors, etc. They may or may not also include the powers that bodies have to be changed in observable ways by the primary qualities of other bodies. For the purposes of exposition, let us call a body that changes the colors, flavors, odors, etc. of another an "agent body," and the one receiving such changes the "patient body." We may speak still more broadly of things that give and receive change as "agents" and "patients" respectively, whether they be bodies or persons. As II.viii.25 continues, Locke explains that when secondary qualities mediately perceivable are manifested, we can see that there is no resemblance between the qualities produced in the patient body—the color, flavor, odor, etc.—and anything that is to be found in the agent body. Because of this, he says, we look upon the quality produced in the patient body as "a bare Effect of Power." He explains this in reference to the example of the sun's changing the colors of things:

[W]hen we see Wax, or a fair Face, receive change of Colour from the Sun, we cannot imagine, that to be the Reception or Resemblance of any thing in the Sun, because we find not those different Colours in the Sun it self. For our Senses, being able to observe a likeness, or unlikeness of sensible Qualities in two different external Objects, we forwardly enough conclude the Production of any sensible Quality in any Subject, to be an Effect of bare Power, and not the Communication of any Quality, which was really in the efficient, when we find no such sensible Quality in the thing that produced it.

---

[3] Locke elaborates upon both of these points—our ignorance of the relevant primary qualities, and the lack of any discoverable connection between primary qualities and ideas of colors, sounds, etc.—at IV.iii.10–13.

When we see the new color in a sunburned face, and know that it is the sun that caused the change, we are not tempted to conceive of this interaction as a matter of the sun's communicating its color to the face. For we can see the color of the sun (yellow), and it is different than that produced on the face (red). Because we are not tempted to think that the sun has communicated its color to the face, we readily conclude that the change in color in the face is merely an effect of some power in the sun.

Let us sum up. Locke thinks that when we reflect upon the changes wrought by the operation of secondary qualities immediately perceivable—that is, when we think about the production in us of ideas of colors, sounds, etc.—we are prone to making two mistakes. One mistake is to think that ideas of colors, sounds, etc. resemble features that really exist in external objects. A second is to think that the production of ideas of colors, sounds, etc. in us involves the communication to us of qualities that were really in external objects. By contrast, when we reflect upon changes wrought by the operation of secondary qualities mediately perceivable—when we think about the observable changes produced in bodies by the operation of other bodies—we do not make analogous mistakes. We do not think that the colors, sounds, etc. produced in patient bodies must resemble those in the agent bodies that elicit them, and we are not tempted to think that the production of colors, sounds, etc. in patient bodies involves the colors, sounds, etc. of agent bodies traveling to those patient bodies.

§13 Resemblances and Bare Powers

When he writes about the production of ideas of secondary qualities, Locke seems to consider two models of causal interaction. One we may call the transfer/resemblance model. It says that when an agent body produces an effect in a patient, this involves the transfer of a feature from the agent to the patient, with the result that the effect produced in the patient resembles a feature of the agent body. Let us call the two components of this model the transfer claim and the resemblance claim, respectively.

It is easy to see how the transfer/resemblance model might suggest itself. A hot body touches a cool body, warming it and getting cooler in the process. We say that some of the first body's heat has been transmitted to the second body. A moving body strikes a resting body, causing it to move while the first body slows down. We say that some of the first body's motion has been transferred to the second body. Locke's scholastic predecessors explained the communication of motion in more theoretical terms, but still in terms of a theory that incorporates a transfer claim and sometimes a resemblance claim. This is the theory of impetus, according to which the hurling of a javelin involves a hand impressing upon, or implanting in the javelin a force that accounts for its continued motion even after the javelin leaves the hand.[4] At least some scholastic philosophers held that the impetus conveyed by a mover to a resting body was a similitude or species of a force in the mover.[5]

The scholastics also use the transfer/resemblance model to explain the production of ideas. Drawing upon Aristotle's treatment of perception, many philosophers in the scholastic tradition hold that forms or species of objects travel through the air from bodies to our sense organs and then on to our intellects. They describe these forms as "similitudes" or "resemblances" of sensible objects, and take their travel to be a matter of the forms' successive reproduction at adjacent locations in the media and in our sense organs. Some scholastics also say that if the form of a thing travels to the mind of a perceiver, and the thing is perceived or thought about, this is a matter of the object itself existing in the mind in a certain way. Theories of sensible and intelligible species won wide acceptance in the thirteenth century, and remained standard fare through the seventeenth century.

A second model of causal interaction that Locke considers is what we may call the bare power model. On this model, bodies have powers to produce certain effects under certain conditions. The production of an effect shows that some body had the relevant power on that occasion, but it does not license the inference that the effect was transmitted from the body, or that it resembles any feature of the body. To call this a "model" of causation may seem a bit extravagant, since nearly all of its content is negative. Yet the

---

[4] This theory developed as an alternative to Aristotle's unsatisfactory treatment of "unnatural" motion, according to which the continued motion of the javelin required continued contact with some mover. Aristotle held that it was successive regions of air behind a projectile that moved one another and the projectile along with them (see *Phys.* VIII. 10., 266b.27–267a). Philoponus replies that if a projectile were being pushed along by the air behind it, then it should be possible for an army to perch its arrows on a parapet and to launch them with bellows. Yet if one were to try this, he says, "The arrow would not move even the distance of a cubit" (Sorabji 1988, 228). The impetus theory was revived by John Buridan in the fourteenth century, and was thence widely held until Newtonian mechanics and its concept of inertia prevailed in the eighteenth century. For an account of the development of impetus theory, see Clagett 1959, ch.8.

[5] The thirteenth-century philosopher Peter John Olivi discusses this view, though he probably did not hold it himself (Clagett 1959, 517–18).

negative claims are important. Locke expects that most of his readers will assume that the ideas in our minds are "exactly the Images and *Resemblances* of something inherent in the subject" (II.viii.7), and he wants to challenge this assumption. He speaks of *bare* powers not to distinguish one class of powers from another (*clothed* powers?), but to emphasize how little, in some cases, we can infer from ideas about their causes.

When it comes to the production of ideas in us, Locke does supplement the bare powers model with an account of why bodies have the powers they do. He cites three different factors. He says that when bodies have powers to produce ideas of colors, sounds, etc. in us, they do so in virtue of their primary qualities, or in virtue of the primary qualities of insensibly small particles that compose light or some other medium (II.viii.10,13,23,24). He says that bodies produce ideas in us "*by impulse*, the only way which we can conceive Bodies operate in" (II.viii.11). Finally, he says that it is God who gives bodies powers to produce ideas in us, and that He does so "by established Laws, and Ways" that are "suitable to his Wisdom and Goodness, though incomprehensible to us" (II.xxxii.14). These are not rival explanations of bodies' powers to produce ideas, but three components of a single account. On that account, the production of sensory ideas in us is triggered by the impact of bodies on our sense organs. The primary qualities of those bodies determine which ideas are triggered in us, and they do so in accordance with laws that God has established (§§35–36).

One lesson of II.viii.25 is that when it comes to explaining ideas of secondary qualities, Locke favors the bare powers model over the transfer/resemblance model. According to him, we fail to see that ideas of colors, sounds, etc. are produced by primary qualities, and so mistake them for resemblances of features really existing in bodies. When it comes to secondary qualities mediately perceivable, we see that the observable changes wrought by their operation are not resemblances transmitted between bodies, and so we recognize them as "the Effects of certain Powers, placed in the Modification of their primary Qualities, with which primary Qualities the *Ideas* produced in us have no resemblance." It is tempting to see Locke as simply rejecting an outdated scholastic account of sensible qualities in favor of a modern corpuscularian one.[6] Yet the big picture is more complicated than that.

[6] The commentators who have succumbed to this temptation include Woolhouse (1983, 161), McCann (1994, 63–4) and Heyd (1994).

Though he abjures the transfer/resemblance model when it comes to ideas of secondary qualities, Locke embraces at least part of it when it comes to ideas of primary qualities. After the sections in which he explains that bodies cause ideas in us by impulse, he offers this:

> From whence I think it is easie to draw this Observation, That the *Ideas of primary Qualities* of Bodies, *are Resemblances* of them, and their Patterns do really exist in the Bodies themselves; but the *Ideas, produced* in us *by* these *Secondary Qualities, have no resemblance* of them at all. (II.viii.15)

Ideas of secondary qualities do not resemble secondary qualities, but ideas of primary qualities do resemble primary qualities. These are what Michael Jacovides calls Locke's negative resemblance thesis and his positive resemblance thesis, respectively (Jacovides 1999). It is the negative thesis that gets more of Locke's attention; it is the positive thesis that deserves more of ours. Locke expects that most men will judge him "very extravagant" for denying that ideas of qualities all perfectly resemble their objects as images in mirrors do theirs (II.viii.16). We modern readers are vexed by his apparent concession that some ideas *are* like mirror images of the qualities they represent.

A number of sympathetic commentators have proposed recherché interpretations of Locke's positive resemblance thesis, interpretations on which he does not mean that any ideas resemble their objects as mirror images do theirs. Several suggest that what he means when he says that ideas of primary qualities resemble those qualities is that the terms used to characterize primary qualities also appear in the correct explanations of how ideas of primary qualities are caused (Bennett 1971, 106; Curley 1972, 452–3; Cummins 1975, 401–5). Others take him to be saying that all of the objects answering to any given primary quality idea share a certain "fine structure" or microphysical constitution (Campbell 1980, 582; Hill 2004). Kenneth Winkler suggests that when Locke speaks of an idea resembling something, this may sometimes mean that the idea resembles those sensory ideas we would have were we to view the thing under favorable circumstances (Winkler 1992, 155–6). What these recherché readings of Locke's plain language have going for them is just that on each of them his positive resemblance thesis turns out to mean something that we—his late twentieth-century and early twenty-first-century readers—are inclined to think is true. I think that this is not enough.

Locke is roundly critical of "Schoolmen and Metaphysicians" who too freely coin new terms (III.x.2). His *Essay* contains a long chapter on the abuses of words. In it, he says that among the most serious abuses are the inconstant use of terms (III.x.5) and "an *affected Obscurity*, by either applying old Words, to new and unusual Significations; or introducing new and ambiguous Terms, without defining either" (III.x.6). He concedes that linguistic innovation is sometimes necessary if we are to express new ideas, but he emphasizes the importance of declaring the meanings of words "where a Man uses them in a Sense any way peculiar to himself" (III.xi.12). Locke seems to heed his own advice. There are a great many cases in which he either introduces a new term, or uses an old term in a peculiar sense. He generally either explains how he is using the term, or issues a *pro forma* apology to draw attention to the innovation.[7] We have already come upon one notable case, in which Locke begs the reader's pardon for using '*Mode*' in "somewhat a different sence from its ordinary signification" (II.xii.4). There is nothing like this to suggest that when Locke speaks of ideas as resembling things, he is using 'resemblance' in a new, unusual, or technical sense.

There is another, particular reason for being skeptical about the recherché interpretations of Locke's positive resemblance thesis: he makes it abundantly clear that he believes that all of his readers *already accept the thesis*. Locke says that it is "usually" (II.viii.7) and "commonly" (II.viii.16) thought that *all* ideas of qualities are resemblances of them. He takes himself to be departing from common opinion only by advancing the negative resemblance thesis. That he sees the dialectical situation this way is also evident in the following passage, in which he does not speak of ideas resembling qualities, but instead employs the scholastic trope of qualities or objects existing in the mind:

A Circle or Square are the same, whether in *Idea* or Existence; in the Mind, or in the *Manna*: And this, both *Motion and Figure are really in the Manna*, whether we take notice of them or no: This every Body is ready to agree to...And yet Men are hardly to be brought to think, that *Sweetness and Whiteness are not really in Manna*; which are but the effects of the operations of *Manna*, by the motion, size, and figure of its Particles on the Eyes and Palate. (II.viii.18)

---

[7] For explanations of idiosyncratic or technical uses of terms, see for example I.i.8 ('*Idea*'), II.xxi.13 ('*Necessity*'), II.xxvii.9 ('*Person*'), II.xxxi.1 ('*Adequate Ideas*'), and III.vi.2 ('*nominal essence*,' '*real essence*'). For apologies in connection with neologisms, see II.xxi.73 ('*Perceptivity*,' '*Motivity*'), II.xxix.16 ('*Addibility*'), III.iii.15 ('*Sortal*'). For apologies in connection with new uses of old terms, see II.x.7 ('secondary Perception') and II.xxi.28 ('*Action*'). For more examples and discussion, see Hall 1975 and Hall 1996.

Locke thinks that his readers will agree with him about the relation between motion and the idea of motion, and about the relation between figure and the idea of figure. If they do, then surely it cannot be because they are already convinced that all of the objects answering to our ideas of a certain kind of motion or figure share a "fine structure," or because they think that our ideas of motions and figures resemble the sensible ideas we would have under some idealized conditions.

The fact that Locke takes only his negative resemblance thesis to be a departure from received opinion resolves a puzzle about II.viii.15, the passage in which he advances the two resemblance theses. Recall that he spends II.viii.11–14 telling us that it is the primary qualities of bodies striking our sense organs that determine not just which primary-quality ideas are produced in us, but also which secondary-quality ideas are produced in us. It is this, he says, that makes it "easie to draw" the observation that ideas of primary qualities are resemblances and that ideas of secondary qualities are not (II.viii.15). But why should a corpuscularian story about idea-production justify any conclusions about whether ideas resemble qualities? Why should the fact that ideas of primary and of secondary qualities are produced in the same way justify *different* conclusions about whether they resemble the qualities that determine them? The answer is that because Locke thinks that he and his reader already agree about the positive resemblance thesis, he thinks that it is only the negative thesis that he needs to support with argument. He believes that he will have shown that ideas of secondary qualities do not resemble secondary qualities if he has shown that they do not resemble the features in bodies that cause them. Having explained, in II.viii.13–14, that ideas of secondary qualities are caused by the operation of powers that bodies have in virtue of their primary qualities, he feels that he has done that.

Locke is a philosopher who takes pains to be understood by his readers. He can be maddeningly obscure, but he is not willfully so. His *Essay* is blessedly free of the oracularity that characterizes so many philosophers' works. The most obvious faults on display in his writing—the prolixity, the tendency toward repetition—are but more evidence of his desire to get his point across. For this reason, and for the others I have given, I think that we ought to take Locke's positive resemblance thesis at face value. This does not necessarily mean interpreting that thesis literally. The face value of a coin is not simply a matter of the symbols stamped on its surface, but of the way that those symbols are interpreted by those who use the coin in financial transactions. My suggestion is that we must confine ourselves to interpretations of Locke's words that he might possibly have expected his contemporary readers to give them. This includes the literal reading, but it includes other readings as well. Taking Locke's thesis at face value does not even commit us to saying that there is any one best way to make sense of it. A philosopher's words may be hopelessly vague, ambiguous, or obscure, and they might have seemed so even to his well-informed contemporaries.

Many of Locke's philosophical predecessors, contemporaries, and near contemporaries describe mental representations of bodies as resembling them, particularly in regard to primary qualities. By considering what some of these thinkers seem to have meant by such talk, we can perhaps gain insight into how Locke might have expected his readers to understand his positive resemblance thesis. I will describe five interpretations that were available to his readers, considering how each fares when taken in the light of Locke's other claims.

When a philosopher speaks of an idea or some other mental representation as resembling its object, one possibility is that we are to understand this metaphorically. What he is really saying is that the idea portrays the object as it is, that it renders the object intelligible to us. When Descartes and Malebranche speak of ideas as resembling bodies, there is some reason to read them this way (CSM 1, 223; Malebranche 1980a, 228). Both clearly deny that ideas of colors, sounds, and other secondary qualities resemble anything in bodies (CSM 1, 153, 218–219; Malebranche 1980a, 228). Descartes suggests that we perceive the geometrical qualities of bodies by a purely intellectual grasp of them that does not involve imagination (CSM 2, 20); Malebranche says that we do it by way of immutable, eternal, necessary, infinite, and uncreated ideas in God's mind (Malebranche 1980b, 33–9). In neither case does it sound as though our representations of primary qualities are themselves things with shapes, sizes, and motions.[8] Still it is Leibniz

---

[8] I do not mean to imply that it is clear that Descartes affords no role to mental images in explaining the perception of primary qualities. Some scholars do deny that he conceives of the representation of geometrical qualities as involving mental images or mental objects of any kind (Arbini 1983; Costa 1983). However, the majority favor a "representationalist" interpretation on which he holds that the perception of primary qualities involves acquaintance with mental objects of some sort, supplemented by judgment or intellect in some way (Maull 1978; Jolley 1990, 91–2; Wilson 1992; Simmons 2003). This renders very murky the question of what he thinks about whether or how any ideas of sensible bodies or primary qualities might resemble them. As for Malebranchean ideas, scholars disagree about what these are, but none of the plausible candidates are the sorts of things that might resemble sensible bodies or qualities in any straightforward sense. Radner suggests that for Malebranche the ideas in God's mind are "generative definitions" (Radner 1978, 117), Jolley that they are abstract entities (Jolley 1990, 57), Nadler that they are "pure concepts or definitions of things" (Nadler 1992, 51), and Pessin that they are "possible divine volitions" (Pessin 2004). Despite this, some scholars do continue to take Malebranche's talk of resemblance seriously (Radner 1978, 113–18; McCracken 1983 58–9).

who offers us the clearest example of metaphorical talk of ideas resembling objects. In the *New Essays*, he insists that "there is a resemblance of a kind" between ideas of sensible qualities and their causes, but he cashes out the metaphor immediately (Leibniz 1981, 131). He says that the resemblance of ideas and sensible qualities is "not a perfect one which holds all the way through, but a resemblance in which one thing expresses another through some orderly relationship between them." He gives the example of the relationship between an ellipse and the circle of which it is a projection on a plane. One thing resembles another in this sense just in case there is a one-to-one correspondence of some sort between their parts or features, a correspondence that allows us to understand the one by the other.

A number of commentators have suggested that Locke's talk of resem-blance is metaphorical, and has to do with accuracy of representation (Woozley 1964, 32–4; Mackie 1976, 13; Alexander 1985, 105; Ayers 2011, 152). They take his claim that ideas of primary qualities resemble primary quali-ties to mean that objects have the features that ideas of primary qualities represent. One problem with this gloss is that it portrays the positive resem-blance thesis as having to do with the relation between complex ideas and the bodies they represent, whereas Locke presents it as a thesis about the relation between simple ideas of primary qualities and those qualities. He seems to be committed to saying that the idea of cubicalness resembles cubicalness, even if that idea is a component of one's inaccurate idea of a cubical Earth. One might reply that the idea of a cubical Earth is accurate insofar as it presents the Earth as *shaped*. The lesson, one may say, is that for ideas of primary qualities to "resemble" primary qualities is for them to be ideas of determinable properties that bodies actually have. The trouble with this is that it turns Locke's negative resemblance thesis into the denial that bodies have secondary qualities. There are commentators who embrace this result, as we shall soon see. There are those who read Locke as a subjectiv-ist about secondary qualities. They face an uphill climb, for Locke tells us that secondary qualities are powers to produce certain ideas in us, and he seems to hold that bodies do sometimes have such powers. His distinction between primary and secondary qualities is, he says, a distinction between sorts of qualities "that are in *Bodies* rightly considered" (II.viii.23).

A second way to understand the suggestion that mental representations resemble sensible objects is to suppose that the representations are images of some sort, and to interpret the talk of resemblance literally. Here there would seem to be two possibilities: either the images in question are corporeal, or they are non-corporeal. That visual perception involves images formed on the retina was understood from Kepler's work at the beginning of the seventeenth century (Lindberg 1976, 178–208). Descartes is one of a number of seventeenth-century writers who hold that sense perception and imagination also involve corporeal images in the brain. He claims that the two optic nerves produce two images on the internal surfaces of the brain, and that these in turn lead to the production of a single image on the surface of the pineal gland (CSM 1, 105–106, 340–342). Descartes suggests that brain images resemble their objects in some respects, as engravings do theirs (CSM 1, 165–166; CSM 2, 265). In early writings, he calls the image on the "common sense" or pineal gland an "idea" (CSM 1, 41–42, 105–106). Though he later drops that usage (CSMK, 185), he was not the only writer familiar to Locke who called images in the brain "ideas" (MacIntosh 1983; Michael and Michael 1989). Even in the *Meditations*, where his references to "ideas" are to non-corporeal items, Descartes likens ideas to images:

Some of my thoughts are as it were the images of things, and it is only in these cases that the term 'idea' is strictly appropriate...(CSM 2, 25).[9]

In what respects Descartes takes ideas to be like images is a matter of conjecture and debate.

Locke too likens ideas to images or pictures.[10] Some commentators take all of his references to ideas to be references to mental images (Ayers 1991, vol.1, 44–51; Jolley 1999, 39–44). Many others say that at least some of them are (Ryle 1932/1971, 129; Aaron 1971, 99; Woolhouse 1971, 36–7; Jacovides 1999; Bennett 2001, vol. 2, 13). Whether ideas are corporeal or incorporeal Locke does not say, even after an early critic presses him on the point.[11] This is in keeping with his agnosticism about whether matter may think, and with his resolve at the outset of the *Essay* not to "meddle with the Physical Consideration of the Mind" (I.i.2). Jacovides argues for a literal interpretation of Locke's resemblance theses (Jacovides 1999). He portrays

---

[9] See also CSM 2, 29.

[10] See II.x.5,7; II.xxiv.1; II.xxv.6; II.xxix.8; III.iii.7; IV.vii.16.

[11] The critic is John Norris, who complains that Locke "ought *first* to have Defined what he meant by Ideas" (1690, 3). Norris asks whether Locke's "ideas" are substance or modification, and if substances whether they are material or immaterial. He suspects that Locke will say that they are material substances, and he repeats Malebranche's arguments against such a view (1690, 22–7). Locke publishes no response, but leaves behind drafts of replies in which he refuses to engage the question of whether ideas are corporeal or incorporeal (*Works* X, 248–9, 256; Acworth 1971, 10–11).

Locke as holding that the ideas by which we represent primary qualities are mental images that are the products of visual experience. He says that Locke might have conceived of these as having sizes, shapes, and motions whether they were corporeal or not. Mental images can resemble objects literally even if they do not have exactly the same primary qualities as the objects do.[12] Corporeal images would naturally be smaller than most of the things they represent. Incorporeal images might lack determinate, measurable lengths, and yet possess such spatial features as having certain shapes, taking up certain portions of one's visual field, and being bigger or smaller than one another. On this reading too, we face the problem that the sort of resemblance on offer is a relation between bodies and complex ideas, whereas Locke's positive resemblance thesis concerns qualities and simple ideas. Jacovides's solution is to say that a simple idea of F resembles a quality in a body if the idea is an aspect or component of a complex idea that resembles the body with respect to F (Jacovides 1999, 468).

Any interpretation that depends upon a claim about what Locke's "ideas" are labors under some difficulty. Locke seems very determined *not* to give an account of the nature of ideas, beyond saying that they are the immediate objects of our mental operations. He offers that vague, noncommittal formulation twice in the *Essay*,[13] and repeats it later in response to critics.[14] When the English Malebranchean John Norris complains that Locke ought

[12] Jacovides distinguishes between strict resemblance—which involves co-exemplification of *precisely* the same quality—and the looser notion of literal resemblance on which a small plastic Statue of Liberty may be said to resemble the copper and steel structure on Liberty Island (Jacovides 1999, 468). His suggestion is that Locke takes ideas of bodies to resemble bodies literally with respect to their primary qualities, but not strictly.

[13] At I.i.8, after apologizing for his frequent use of the term 'idea,' he says: "It being that Term, which, I think, serves best to stand for whatsoever is the Object of the Understanding when a Man thinks, I have used it to express whatever is meant by *Phantasm, Notion, Species*, or whatever it is, which the Mind can be employ'd about in thinking; and I could not avoid frequently using it." (I.i.8). The take-home message here is just that 'idea' refers to an object of thought. The claim that it also refers to whatever is meant by 'phantasm,' 'notion' or 'species' is not to be taken seriously, unless perhaps Locke is suggesting that the only salvageable meaning of *those* terms is "Object of the Understanding when a Man thinks." For Locke is surely aware that those who employ the terms 'phantasm,' 'notion' and 'species' do not typically regard them as equivalent; that different writers use these terms differently; and that for many of the meanings of these terms are inextricably linked to scholastic theories of mind and perception that Locke rejects. When, later in the *Essay*, he again attempts something like a definition of 'idea,' he says: "Whatsoever the Mind perceives in it self, or is the immediate object of Perception, Thought, or Understanding, that I call *Idea*" (II.viii.8).

[14] When John Sergeant, author of *Solid Philosophy Asserted*, complains of "Idiests" who ground discourses on "Similitudes or Resemblances," Locke writes in the margins of his own copy: "That is as Mr Locke expresses it the immediate objects of the mind in thinking" (Sergeant 1697/1984, "Preface"). In the correspondence with Stillingfleet, Locke quotes both I.i.8 and II.viii.8 to explain what "ideas, in my sense of the word, are," but leaves out the bit about phantasms, notions, and species (*Works* IV, 72).

to do more to acquaint us with the nature of ideas (Norris 1690, 3), Locke replies that nobody can say "in what alteration of the mind this perception consists" (*Works* X, 248). He numbers himself among those who at least "have the ingenuity to confess their ignorance" about the matter (*Works* X, 249). It is true that Locke does often liken ideas to images or pictures, but this may be breezy metaphor rather than serious theorizing. An "image" or a "picture" can be anything that represents or symbolizes something else, even if it does not do so visually or quasi-visually.[15] The suggestion that only *some* "ideas" are mental images is also problematic. Locke's commitment to empiricism is his commitment to the view that all complex ideas are composed of simple ones acquired through experience. We can make sense of this only if there is a single way of understanding his talk of simplicity, complexity, and parthood. This seems less likely if some ideas are images and some are not. To combine or to rearrange the parts of a picture is quite a different thing from combining or rearranging the parts of a definition or a concept. Finally, there is a problem with ascribing to Locke the view that we represent primary qualities solely by ideas received through sight. Jacovides defends this by saying that "Locke believes that sense organs other than the eyes produce mostly ideas of secondary qualities" (1999, 467). Yet Locke says that the ideas of space, extension, figure, rest, and motion are ones that can be conveyed to the mind either by sight or by touch (II.v). So either he thinks that we represent primary qualities by means of ideas that are not mental images, or else he holds that components of mental images can enter through touch.

A third way to understand the claim that certain ideas are resemblances of objects or their qualities is to see this as a holdover from scholastic accounts of sense perception. Locke's talk of ideas being received by the senses and conveyed to the mind may encourage such a reading.[16] In his *Theory of the Ideal World* (1703), Norris relates that he had at first been inclined to read Locke as holding "that sensible Objects do send or convey Ideas from themselves to our Minds by the Senses, as the most commonly receiv'd Opinion concerning their Origin supposes" (Norris 1703, 371). He means that he was at first inclined to take at face value Locke's characterization of ideas as items that travel from bodies to our sense organs and thence on to our understandings. He tells us that he read Locke this way

---

[15] *Oxford English Dictionary*: entries for 'image' and 'picture.'
[16] For examples of such talk, see II.i.3, II.iii.1, II.vii.1.

"because he expresses himself much after the same manner as the Schools do whose known meaning this is, according to that Maxim quoted by *Aquinas* from *Aristotle's* Metaphysicks, *Principium Nostre Cognitionis est à Sensu*." Locke's claim that items conveyed by the senses are resemblances of objects might be further encouragement to see him as falling back upon elements of a scholastic theory of perception. The view that sense perception involves the assimilation of the subject's mind to perceived objects goes back to Aristotle, and is a point of wide agreement among scholastic philosophers.

Even if we were to see Locke's positive resemblance thesis as a vestige of scholasticism, this would not necessarily tell us how to cash out the talk of ideas resembling bodies or qualities. For although most scholastics pay lip service to the claim that mental representations of bodies resemble them, different writers mean different things by this, and in many cases it is unclear what the supposed resemblance amounts to. A few of Locke's predecessors do take sensible or intelligible species to be "similitudes" or "resemblances" of bodies in the most straightforward sense. Roger Bacon and William Craythorn hold that a species of color is an instance of color, and that its reception involves the soul itself becoming colored (Pasnau 1997, 65–6, 89–100). Yet many other scholastics—from Thomas Aquinas in the thirteenth century to Antonio Rubio and Francisco Suarez in the seventeenth—understand the talk of resemblance quite differently (Hatfield 1994, 956–58; Simmons 1994; Pasnau 1997, 33–4, 111–17). They hold that when species exist in media and in us, they do so only "intentionally," not "naturally," and their resemblance to sensible things is mere "representational" resemblance. The notion of intentional existence is not fully explained, but intentionally existing things are supposed to represent things other than themselves, and to be material only in an incomplete or attenuated way. What representational resemblance comes to is also obscure, though it is clear that it is not supposed to require shared accidents or properties. There are still other scholastics who dispense with sensible species altogether, and yet speak of sense perception as involving mental states that resemble sensible objects. The thirteenth-century philosopher Peter John Olivi and the fourteenth-century philosopher William of Ockham repudiate sensible species, but say that acts of cognition or intellection are themselves likenesses of sensible objects (Pasnau 1997, 21–7, 121–4). How an act can resemble an object is something that they do not explain.

It is plain that Locke does not think that ideas of primary qualities are forms or species that travel from objects to our minds. At III.x.14 he offers talk of *"intentional Species"* as an example of the "Gibberish, which in the weakness of Humane Understanding, serves so well to palliate Men's Ignorance, and cover their Errours." In the posthumous *Examination of P. Malebranche's Opinion of Seeing All Things in God*, Locke is even more forthright: "I do not think any material species, carrying the resemblance of things by a continual flux from the body we perceive, bring the perception of them to our senses" (*Works* IX, 215). If Norris had read the *Essay* more carefully, he would have seen that Locke must be speaking loosely or metaphorically even when he describes ideas as being conveyed in to the mind by the senses. For as we have seen, Locke explicitly raises the question of how bodies produce ideas in us, and his answer is that they can do this only by impulse (II.viii.11–12). The interaction that takes place between bodies and our sense organs is ultimately a matter of the communication of motion through physical contact.

There are philosophers in the second half of the seventeenth century who retain elements of scholastic accounts of sense perception—including the view that perception involves an object's likeness being in the mind—and combine these with elements of corpuscularianism. Sir Kenelm Digby is a case in point, and Locke's early critic John Sergeant follows Digby closely on these matters. A fourth way to understand the suggestion that ideas resemble physical qualities would be to see it as a component of some hybrid theory such as theirs.

Sir Kenelm Digby rejects "intentionall specieses" and maintains that "bodies work upon our senses no other wayes then by a corporeall operation; and that such a one is sufficient for all the effects we see proceed from them" (Digby 1665a, 307). So far, he sounds like a corpuscularian. Yet his suggestion that "little parts or atomes" are squeezed or evaporated from sensible bodies in a perpetual flux is reminiscent of scholastic views according to which species emanate from bodies in all directions (Digby 1665a, 338; cf. Sergeant 1697, 65). Digby characterizes these material emanations as "likenesses or extracts of those substances" (Digby 1665a, 333; cf. Sergeant 1697, 69), and says that they pass through the senses and are conveyed by spirits to the brain (Digby 1665a, 338–40; cf. Sergeant 1697, 65). He holds that cognizing a thing involves having the thing's nature in oneself (Digby 1665b, 3; cf. Sergeant 1697, 37–8). Because he equates numerical identity with perfect qualitative similarity (Digby 1665b, 3–4; cf. Sergeant 1697, 35), Digby concludes that to apprehend an object is for *the object itself* to exist in one's mind, not corporeally, but "in an admirable and spirituall manner" (Digby 1665b, 51; cf. Sergeant 1697, 29–38, 59). This echoes the scholastic view that to cognize a thing is for the thing itself to be in one's mind intentionally (Pasnau 1997, 86).

Locke's positive resemblance thesis cannot be the result of his accepting Digby's theory of perception, or anything much like it. Digby's theory implies that *all* sensory ideas are resemblances of bodies or their qualities, because it says that all sense perception is the consequence of likenesses of them traveling to our brains and taking up residence there in a spiritual fashion. In Digby's theory, there is no distinction between primary qualities and secondary qualities, no commitment to explaining non-mechanical qualities in terms of more perspicuous mechanical ones.[17] Locke also cannot abide the suggestion that material objects might exist in minds, unless this is mere metaphor. He does occasionally resort to something like this metaphor when he speaks of shapes existing in the mind (II.viii.18; IV.iv.6). Yet he is sharply critical of the metaphysics of Digby and Sergeant's account. This is clear in the correspondence with Stillingfleet, where Locke has some fun at the Bishop's expense. He argues that Stillingfleet must admit that ideas are the immediate objects of his thoughts, unless he is so perfect a convert of "Mr. J. S.'s, that you are persuaded, that as often as you think of your cathedral church, or of Des Cartes's vortices, that the very cathedral church at Worcester, or the motion of those vortices, itself exists in your understanding; when one of them never existed but in that one place at Worcester, and the other never existed any where in *rerum natura*" (*Works* IV, 390–391).[18]

---

[17] Digby says that our sense of touch is affected by "little bodies of heat, or cold, or the like" (Digby 1665a, 338), and that light conveys "atomes of colour" from the surfaces of bodies (341).

He does concede that sound is nothing but a "motion of the ayre," but still insists that moving particles must leave the surface of the sounding body, enter through the ears, and travel all the way to the brain (339). Sergeant says that the "*Effluviums* sent out from Bodies, have the *very Natures* of those Bodies in them, or rather are themselves Lesser Bodies of the *Selfsame* Nature, (as the smallest imperceptible parts of Bread and Flesh, are truly Bread and Flesh)" (Sergeant 1697, 69).

[18] Locke's hostility to Sergeant's view is also on display in his marginalia to Sergeant's *Solid Philosophy*. When Sergeant says that knowledge involves the object itself existing in the knowing subject, Locke writes: "What is it for a material thing to exist spiritually?" and "What is it to be Corporeo-spiritual?" (Sergeant 1697/1984, 59, 66). When Sergeant speaks of the soul's ability to know God, Locke points out that this theory of perception may have untoward theological consequences: "It should here be inferred according to w^t J.S. says in this § by wch the soul becomes God" (Sergeant 1697/1984, 40).

One feature common to both the standard scholastic account of sense perception and Digby's hybrid theory is that the resemblance between a mental representation and its object is explained as a consequence of the transfer of something from object to perceiver: a sensible species in the first case, a physical likeness or extract in the second. There is some reason to think that Locke too would explain resemblance as a consequence of transfer. Consider again his reasoning in II.viii.25 about secondary qualities mediately perceivable. There the subject is not the production of ideas in us, but the production of observable qualities in bodies. He says that it is because we can see that a feature produced in the patient body (the red color of a sunburned face) does not resemble that in the agent (the yellow sun) that we dismiss the possibility that it was communicated to the patient from the agent. Because we can see that there is no resemblance, we infer that there is no transfer. Locke says that ideas of primary qualities are resemblances of them, and he holds that bodies produce ideas by impulse. Might he think that impulse results in a kind of transfer that explains the resemblance?

We have already seen that Locke does not think of impulse as involving the transfer of species or physical likenesses. Yet we have also seen that he is committed to the existence of tropes. Locke holds that everything that exists is a particular, and he includes qualities among the things there are, so his qualities are so many particular tokens rather than abstract objects. He seems to hold that the communication of motion by impulse is a matter of trope transfer:

For in the communication of Motion by impulse, wherein as much Motion is lost to one Body, as is got to the other, which is the ordinariest case, we can have no other conception, but of the passing of Motion out of one Body into another… (II.xxiii.28)[19]

---

[19] Leibniz evinces some doubt about whether Locke really conceives of impulse as involving trope transfer. His spokesman in the *New Essays*, Theophilus, says this about II.xxi.4, where Locke speaks of bodies communicating motion to one another: "I am not sure whether you are contending that motion passes from subject to subject, and that the numerically same motion is taken across….I doubt that this is your view, or that of your able friends, who usually stay well clear of such fantasies." (Leibniz 1981, 171–2). Theophilus sounds more resigned about the passage at II.xxiii.28, with its talk of motion passing from one body to another: "I am not surprised that you encounter insurmountable problems when you seem to be entertaining something as inconceivable as an accident's passing from one subject to another; but I see no reason why we have to suppose such a thing" (Leibniz 1981, 224).

If impulse involves the transfer of motion from bodies to our sense organs, might it also involve the transfer of other primary qualities? If primary qualities and not secondary qualities are transferred through impulse, might this explain why ideas of primary qualities do, and ideas of secondary qualities do not, resemble their objects?

There is little reason to see Locke as holding that shape tropes or size tropes are transferred by impulse. In cases of trope transfer, the donor has to lose the trope it donates, and a body does not typically lose its shape or size when it strikes another body.[20] On the other hand, when a signet is pressed into wax, we do speak of the wax as having gained a new shape. No quality token passes from one to the other, but the signet produces in the wax a new token of its own shape type. Metaphysically, this is as much a sort of transfer as that envisioned by many scholastics, who conceive of the "travel" of species as a matter of their serial reproduction at adjacent locations. If a relatively large spherical body strikes a sensitive organ, this communicates motion to a differently shaped or sized region of the organ than if a relatively small cube-shaped body does. We might think of this as the *mechanical* transfer of sizes and shapes—of ways of being extended—to our sense organs. The sizes and shapes communicated to a sense organ will not necessarily be those of the objects sensed,[21] but patterns of such transfers might be enough to account for literal resemblance between features of the affected regions of our organs and the parts of objects that we see and feel.[22]

[20] This seems to me a reason to resist Bennett's suggestion that the sensible species of the scholastics are tropes (Bennett 2001, vol. 1, 91–2).

[21] This is true even in the case of touch, where typically we feel only a part of the surface of an object at any one time. It is particularly clear in the case of vision, where the shape and size tropes communicated will be those of insensibly small particles (or collections of them), rather than those of the macroscopic objects seen.

[22] The other primary qualities, number and solidity, are less promising candidates for mechanical transfer. The case of number may be one in which no transfer is required to explain resemblance. Earlier I suggested that Locke counts number among the inseparable qualities of body because he thinks that each thing is a unity, and so is something numerable. Since every thing resembles every other thing in this respect, we get resemblance in this case for free as it were. Solidity is more worrisome. Because it is all-or-nothing, bodies cannot gain or lose ways of being solid as they gain or lose ways of being extended. Furthermore, it would seem that the idea of solidity could resemble that quality only if the idea itself were solid. Since Locke holds that solidity entails extension and figure, and that anything extended and solid is a body, this means that the idea of solidity could resemble that quality only if the idea is itself a body. Yet, as we shall see, Locke is agnostic about whether our mental states are the states of material or of immaterial substances, and accordingly about whether our ideas are corporeal. Jacovides suggests that Locke means to reserve judgment on whether the idea of solidity resembles that quality (Jacovides 1999, 480). If this is right, then we are spared the embarrassment of trying to ground that resemblance claim in a corresponding transfer claim.

The trouble is that even if these transfers make for similarities between the primary qualities of our sensory surfaces and those of the bodies we sense, this does not explain why or how *ideas* of primary qualities resemble them. Locke says almost nothing about how impulse produces ideas. This is not surprising, given his commitment to property dualism (§33) and his lean toward a substance dualist account of human beings (§32). His reticence about the nature of ideas, and his agnosticism about the nature of mind, make it unlikely that we can use the transfer of primary qualities to explain his view that ideas of primary qualities are resemblances of them. If the production of ideas of primary qualities were to involve trope transfer, then either Locke would be committed to saying that minds have moving parts, or he would have to countenance "unowned" tropes (e.g., instances of motion that are in the mind without this entailing the mind's moving).[23] To countenance "unowned" tropes is to allow physical qualities to have a special mode of existence no less puzzling than the scholastics' intentional existence or Digby's "spirituall" existence. The mechanical transfer of sizes and shapes also cannot explain why ideas of primary qualities are resemblances unless ideas are corporeal things.

We have considered five ways that Locke's readers might have understood his positive resemblance thesis. Some of these readings labor under heavier burdens than others, but there is no winner among them. We have failed to find a reading that takes Locke's words at face value, and that fits with what he does and does not say about ideas. I am inclined to conclude that he is, in this case, hopelessly vague. When he tells us that ideas of primary qualities are resemblances of them, his words do not have enough determinate content for us either to exonerate him or to convict him of any particular absurdity. Though it is not impossible that one of our interpretations does capture his meaning, it just as likely that he did not have any particular conception of resemblance in mind.

In the context of his day, Locke's claim that some ideas resemble their objects is wholly unremarkable. He is right to say that most of his readers take sensory ideas to be resemblances of bodies or their features. However, the consensus to which he points is a superficial one. His readers do not actually share a single view about what this resemblance comes to, or why it obtains. Many of them are no clearer than he is about these matters.

---

[23] On the problem of unowned tropes, see Bennett 2001, vol. 1, 92–3.

Some are speaking metaphorically. Some are speaking literally because they conceive of ideas as corporeal images in the brain. Some mean that mental representations are "representational" rather than "natural" likenesses of sensible things. Some mean that they are physical likenesses that exist in our minds in a spiritual way. Locke's commitment to the view that some simple ideas resemble their objects may be an unreflective concession to philosophical tradition—a case of letting one idol stand while he is busy taking down another. His attention is focused on showing that not *all* simple ideas resemble their objects, and this is a sufficiently large target. Despite Locke's considerable influence, the view that all ideas resemble their objects continues to be voiced by English philosophers well into the eighteenth century. In 1728, Zachary Mayne can still write that "the very Essence of an *Idea* (as is agreed on all hands) consists in that Relation it has to the original or primary *Object*, namely, in being its *Picture, Image* or *Resemblance*" (1728, 166).

§14 *Colors*

If we want to better understand Locke's views about the nature and status of secondary qualities, it makes sense to begin by examining in some detail his remarks about colors, as these are the secondary qualities about which he has far and away the most to say. He is sometimes portrayed as holding that colors are wholly subjective. More often he is thought to identify colors with dispositions—powers that bodies have to produce certain ideas in us. Many interpreters find two or more incompatible strands in Locke's account of color, and so are led to distinguish an "official," prevailing view from the conflicting remarks into which he occasionally lapses. Many who see him as officially holding that colors are dispositions concede that some of his remarks imply that colors are in us rather than in objects. After briefly considering some of the difficulties that these readings face, I will offer an alternative. I will argue that Locke takes colors to be relational, but not dispositional, properties of the objects around us. I will contend that, on his view, an object is red if and only if it is actually causing a certain sensation in some observer.

The philosophical problem of what colors are can be distinguished from various empirical questions about colors, though the answer to the former is sure to be greatly constrained by answers to the latter. It is the prerogative of science to investigate the physical and chemical properties of the surfaces of objects, the propagation of light, the triggering of rods and cones in our retinae, the transmission of signals up neural pathways, and the processing of this information in the brain. Physiologists and psychologists explore the color discriminations that different species—and different individuals within our own species—are able to make. Yet even if the whole empirical story were in, there would still be the question of which, if any, of the features quantified over by the scientific account are the referents of 'red,' 'yellow,' and so forth in our everyday color ascriptions. This is what the philosopher is asking when he asks whether there are colors, and if so what sorts of properties colors are. Before turning to Locke's answer, it will be useful to have in mind a rough taxonomy of possible answers to this philosophical question about color.

First, there is what we may call eliminativism about color. According to this view, no property in the scientific account of color has enough in common with colors as pre-scientifically conceived to permit their identification. According to the eliminativist, the correct conclusion to draw after carefully surveying the results of color science is that in reality nothing is colored. There is nothing that is the referent of 'red,' just as there is nothing that is the referent of 'phlogiston.'

A second view is what we may call subjectivism about color. The subjectivist agrees with the eliminativist that colors are not really features of the physical objects around us, or features of the intervening media. However, the subjectivist finds room for colors in his ontology: colors are features of our perceptual states. Whether the subjectivist's colors are physical properties or not will depend on whether our perceptual states are physical states.

The other answers to the philosophical question about color we may call various forms of realism about color. They have in common a commitment to color being a respectable physical property. One division within realist theories of color is that between theories on which colors are features of physical objects (where this category may be construed broadly enough to include apples, bodies of water, soap bubbles, and collections of airborne droplets), and theories on which colors are properties of light alone.[24] Realist theories on which colors are features of physical objects can be further classified by means of the familiar (but not entirely unproblematic) distinctions between intrinsic and extrinsic properties, and between

---

[24] The view that strictly speaking it is only light that is colored is one that Boyle was inclined toward (Boyle 1664, 90), and has recently been defended by Sinott-Armstrong and Sparrow (2002).

non-dispositional and dispositional properties. There may be: (i) theories on which colors are intrinsic, non-dispositional features of physical objects, (ii) theories on which colors are intrinsic dispositions, (iii) theories on which colors are extrinsic, non-dispositional properties, and (iv) theories on which colors are extrinsic dispositions. I will have more to say about some of these options below.

Locke is sometimes taken to have advanced a subjectivist account of color. Berkeley and Kant read Locke this way.[25] There are several strands in Locke's discussions of sensible qualities that encourage a subjectivist reading. These come together at II.viii.17:

> The particular *Bulk, Number, Figure, and Motion of the parts of Fire, or Snow, are really in them*, whether any ones Senses perceive them or no: and therefore they may be called *real Qualities*, because they really exist in those Bodies. But *Light, Heat, Whiteness*, or *Coldness, are no more really in them, than Sickness or Pain is in* Manna. Take away the Sensation of them; let not the Eyes see Light, or Colours, nor the Ears hear Sounds; let the Palate not Taste, nor the Nose Smell, and all Colours, Tastes, Odors, and Sounds, as they are such particular *Ideas*, vanish and cease, and are reduced to their Causes, *i.e.* Bulk, Figure, and Motion of Parts.

Here there are at least three factors encouraging us to read Locke as a subjectivist about color. There is (i) the claim that colors are not really in bodies, (ii) the comparison of colors and pains, and (iii) the suggestion that colors vanish when we do not see them. Each of these merits a closer look.

We saw earlier (§12) that II.viii.17 is one of the passages that shows us what it means, in Locke's idiom, for a quality to be "real" or "really in" a body. We saw that for a quality to be "real" or "really in" a body, it must be perceiver-independent. Locke also seems to slide easily between speaking of "real" qualities and of primary or original qualities. If 'real quality' is supposed to be equivalent to 'primary quality,' then inseparability is the criterion for something's being a real quality. In that case, a body's real qualities cannot depend upon its contingent relations to any other things, including perceivers. For if a quality did depend upon changeable relations, it would not meet the inseparability test. Real qualities will thus be not only perceiver-independent but intrinsic. If, on the other hand, 'real

---

[25] It seems safe to assume that Berkeley has Locke in mind at *Principles* 1.9–10. Kant gives his reading of Locke on color in "Remark II" in the First Part of the *Prolegomena*.

quality' is simply co-extensional with 'primary quality,' then there are at least two possibilities. One is that Locke takes perceiver-independence to be the defining criterion for a quality's being "real." Another is that he thinks that a quality must be both perceiver-independent and intrinsic to count as real. In either case, it may seem surprising that he should regard 'real quality' as co-extensional with 'primary quality,' since bodies seem to have intrinsic and perceiver-independent features (e.g. their particular shapes) that are not inseparable from them. However, we need to remind ourselves that the inseparability requirement is not meant to rule out bodies undergoing changes in shape or volume (§11). Locke counts non-permanent qualities as primary qualities so long as they are determinate instances of determinable qualities that bodies cannot be without. Whatever his understanding of the relation between 'real quality' and 'primary quality,' it is clear that Locke does not think that colors are inseparable, intrinsic, and perceiver-independent features of bodies. An obvious way to explain this is to say it is because he does not think that colors are features of bodies at all.

Locke compares the status of colors to the status of pains not just at II.viii.17, but in a number of places. At II.viii.16 he asks, "Why is Whiteness and Coldness in Snow, and Pain not, when it produces the one and the other *Idea* in us; and can do neither, but by the Bulk, Figure, Number, and Motion of its solid Parts?" Two sections later, he says that we "would need some Reason to explain" why sweetness and whiteness are in manna when "the Pain and Sickness, *Ideas* that are the effects of *Manna*, should be thought to be no-where, when they are not felt" (II.viii.18). At II.xxx.2, he seems to go even further, positively asserting that "Whiteness and Coldness are no more in Snow, than Pain is." Each of these passages can be seen as suggesting that color is no more an objective feature of the things that cause color experiences than pain is an objective feature of the things that cause painful experiences. We are all subjectivists about pain. If colors have the same status as pains, then bodies are no more colored than knife blades and hot stoves are "painy."

It is not obvious how we are to understand the last sentence of II.viii.17. At first blush, Locke seems to be following up on his suggestion that colors have the same status as pains. He seems to be saying that just as pains cease when we cease to feel them, so colors vanish when we stop seeing them. Yet notice that it is colors "as they are such particular *Ideas*" that are said to "vanish and cease" when we stop seeing colors. This could be interpreted in any of several ways. One possibility is that Locke is telling us that colors *are* particular ideas, and that these cease to exist when we cease to have visual experiences. This would make him a subjectivist about color, and would mean that he is speaking in a loose and popular sense when he refers to the eyes seeing colors. A second possibility is that Locke is a realist about colors, and he is saying that ideas of colors vanish when we cease to have visual experiences. This obliges us to say that the first occurrence of 'Colours' in the sentence refers to colors, while the second refers to ideas of colors. A third possibility is that Locke is a realist about colors, and he is saying that colors vanish when we are not seeing them. This fits with the immediately preceding claim that whiteness is not a "real" feature of bodies, for one who takes colors to be features of bodies need not take them to be "real" in Locke's sense (i.e. mind-independent). However, it requires us to say that the phrase "as they are such particular *Ideas*" is an instance of his unfortunate tendency to say "ideas" when he means "qualities" (§1).[26] Taking the sentence in isolation, no one of these readings is obviously superior to the others.

If the final sentence of II.viii.17 is sufficiently ambiguous to leave it unsettled whether Locke means to be saying that colors go out of existence when we stop having visual experiences, later passages show this to be his view. At II.viii.19, he says that if we "Hinder light but from striking on it," the red and white colors in porphyry will "Vanish." He asks whether anyone can think that "those *Ideas* of whiteness and redness, are really in *Porphyre* in the light, when 'tis plain *it has no colour in the dark*?" (II.viii.19). At II.xxxi.2, he suggests that whereas solidity, extension, figure, and motion "would be really in the World as they are, whether there were any sensible Being to perceive them, or no," it is not so with other sensible qualities. He mentions whiteness and sweetness as being in this latter category, but illustrates the point with reference to light and heat:

[W]ere there no fit Organs to receive the impressions Fire makes on the Sight and Touch; nor a Mind joined to those Organs to receive the *Ideas* of Light and Heat, by those impressions from the Fire, or the Sun, there would yet be no more Light, or Heat in the World, than there would be Pain if there were no sensible Creature to feel it, though the Sun should continue just as it is now, and Mount *Ætna* flame higher than ever it did.

---

[26] The final clause of II.viii.17 muddies the waters still further. Locke tells us that "Colours...as they are such particular *Ideas*" not only vanish and cease but "are reduced to their Causes, *i.e.* Bulk, Figure, and Motion of Parts." One might wonder how colors can both vanish *and* be reduced to their causes. The most plausible solution here is to say that he is using 'reduced' in a somewhat peculiar sense, and means that when "Colours...as they are such particular *Ideas*" vanish, they leave behind only their causes, the primary qualities of the bodies in question.

Still later, at IV.vi.11, Locke says that if a piece of gold were causally isolated, it would instantly lose its color.

Despite all of the seeming support for reading Locke as a color subjectivist, there is strong textual evidence that he means to endorse color realism. For one thing, he describes physical objects as colored even in II.viii, where we can presume that he is being as attentive as ever to the status of colors. He speaks of "*the cause* of that Colour in the external Object" (II.viii.3), of the "Colours and Smells of Bodies" (II.viii.13), of "the blue Colour, and sweet Scent" of a violet (II.viii.13), and of "the red and white colours in *Porphyre*" (II.viii.19). Even more compelling are the many passages in which he gives us his account of what colors are. Over and over again, Locke identifies colors and other secondary qualities with powers that bodies have to produce certain sensations in us. Here is a sampling:

What I have said concerning *Colours* and *Smells*, may be understood also of *Tastes* and *Sounds, and other the like sensible Qualities*; which, whatever reality we, by mistake, attribute to them, are in truth nothing in the Objects themselves, but Powers to produce various sensations in us, and *depend on those primary Qualities, viz.* Bulk, Figure, Texture, and Motion of parts; as I have said. (II.viii.14)
...those *secondary* and *imputed Qualities*, which are but the Powers of several Combinations of those primary ones, when they operate...(II.viii.22)
...we immediately by our Senses perceive in *Fire* its Heat and Colour; which are, if rightly considered, nothing but Powers in it, to produce those *Ideas* in us...(II.xxiii.7)
But these being nothing, in truth, but powers to excite such *Ideas* in us, I must, in that sense, be understood, when I speak of secondary *Qualities*, as being in Things...(II.xxxi.2).[27]

In these passages, and in many others like them, Locke's emphasis is on the negative: colors are not "real" qualities of bodies, they are nothing more than "bare" powers. He emphasizes these negative claims because he thinks that his readers are apt to imagine that colors and other secondary qualities enjoy a status that they do not. Despite its emphasis on the negative, Locke's oft-repeated account of what colors are includes some important positive theses. Colors are qualities, rather than ideas or features of ideas. Colors are in the bodies around us, rather than in us. Colors are powers of a certain sort.

---

[27] See also II.viii.10, II.viii.23–26, II.xxi.3, II.xxiii.8–10, II.xxxi.9, and III.viii.1.

In Locke's hands, the terms 'red' and 'idea of red' are ambiguous. This brings to mind the ambiguities of 'heat' and 'idea of heat,' but there is a difference. Locke uses 'heat' to refer both to the motion of corpuscles and to the simple idea that such motion produces in us. I can find no clear case in which he uses 'heat' to refer to the power of producing the simple idea that corpuscular motion produces in us. By contrast, Locke does not use 'red' (or the names of any other colors) to refer to any corpuscular motion or structure that might be thought to be common to the things that trigger visual sensations of redness (or another color) in us. He sometimes uses 'red' to refer to (i) the power to trigger a certain simple visual idea in us, and other times uses it to refer to (ii) the simple idea mentioned in (i). The phrase 'idea of red' Locke sometimes uses to refer to (ii), and other times to refer to (iii) the complex idea of the power mentioned in (i). The idea of the power mentioned in (i) must be a complex one, because it is the idea of a power, and "*Power includes in it some kind of relation*" (II.xxi.3). Power includes in it some kind of relation because to specify which power one is referring to inevitably requires mention of something that the power is a power to do,[28] and often some thing that the power is a power to change. Ideas of relations are, on Locke's view, complex ideas (II.xii.3,7; II.xxix.1). The simple idea of red is the common possession of everyone who has ever had a visual experience as of something red. The complex idea of red is one that a person might not acquire until she has read Locke's *Essay* and learned that for something to be red is for it to have the power of producing a certain idea in her.

Locke's claims that colors are in bodies and that they are powers of a certain sort look like strong evidence that he is a realist about color. Not without reason, they are often taken for a forthright and explicit endorsement of dispositionalism about color. On a dispositional account of color, a body's being colored is held to be, in important respects, like its being flammable, or soluble, or fragile. These are the philosopher's stock examples of dispositional properties. With each of these properties, there is a distinction to be drawn between a thing's merely having the property, and its manifesting or exercising that property. This is the difference between a thing's being flammable, and its being in flames; between its being soluble and its dissolving; between its being fragile and its breaking when struck

---

[28] All power relates to action, Locke tells us at II.xxi.4.

by no great force. A dispositional property that goes unmanifested is not to be confused with a property that is merely possible and not actual. An object may actually be soluble when it is not dissolving—indeed even if it never dissolves. The claim that an object possesses a dispositional property entails that certain conditional statements are true. These are the statements specifying the conditions under which the disposition would be manifested or exercised. Thus the claim that a piece of paper is flammable entails that it would ignite under certain conditions. Objects with different internal structures may possess the same dispositional property. One vase may be fragile because its constituent molecules have weak bonding relations at room temperature, while another of sturdier composition may be fragile only because it has been super-cooled.

Applying these general observations about dispositions to the case of color, we see that if color is a dispositional property, then there is a distinction to be drawn between an object's merely being colored, and its manifesting its color. An object's being colored is a matter of its being disposed to produce certain sorts of sensations in certain sorts of observers under certain conditions. For an object to manifest its color is for it to produce those sensations. The full story of what color is must involve the specification of standard observers to whom, and standard conditions under which, a colored object's color would be made manifest. The object remains colored even when there are no observers of that sort under those conditions. On the dispositional account of color, it must be possible for there to be a colored object that never manifests its color. It may also be possible for two objects of the same color to be so in virtue of different non-dispositional properties. Finally, on the dispositional account of color an object need not be the color that it appears to be. An object can appear red to some observer under some conditions even if it would not appear red to a standard observer under standard conditions.

Dispositions to interact with other things may be conceived either as intrinsic features or as extrinsic ones. Suppose that a key has the power to open a particular lock, such as the lock on my front door. Like dispositions generally, this is a power to bring about or undergo some change under certain specified conditions; it is a power to bring about a change in the internal arrangement of the lock when placed in the lock and turned. The key can be deprived of this power by altering the works of the lock on my front door, without effecting any change in the intrinsic features of the key. On the other hand, we cannot in this manner deprive the key of its power to open locks fitting the general physical description of the lock on my door as it was before we altered its works. To do that, we must alter the intrinsic features of the key itself, breaking it in two, or shaving off a part of it, or melting it, etc. The first sort of power has been called an "individual" or extrinsic power; the second, a "sortal" or intrinsic power.[29]

Colors may be conceived either as intrinsic dispositions or as extrinsic ones. The dispositionalist may identify colors with intrinsic features of bodies despite the fact that the specification of those dispositions involves reference to things other than the colored bodies (for example, observers and light sources). Just as it may be an intrinsic feature of a key that it can open any lock fitting a certain physical description, so it may be an intrinsic feature of the surface of an object that it will produce a certain sort of sensation in certain sorts of observers under certain sorts of conditions. It is important for the instrinsic dispositionalist that it is *types* of observers and *types* of light sources that are mentioned in specifying which dispositions colors are. If instead reference were made to particular observers, or to particular light bulbs, then a colored object could be deprived of its color by a change in something other than itself. If being colored were a matter of having the power to produce certain sensations in Chris and Susie, then one could deprive objects of their colors by altering the sense organs of Chris and Susie.

Building in reference to particular observers or light sources is one way of characterizing colors as extrinsic dispositions. Another is to identify colors with powers to produce certain sensations in certain types of observers under certain conditions, but then to specify circumstances in which changes in something other than the colored objects deprive the objects of their colors. One who holds that the laws of nature are contingent or mutable may be an extrinsic dispositionalist on the grounds that changes in the laws could deprive objects of their powers to produce ideas in us.[30] It is also possible to identify colors with powers to produce ideas in us, to

[29] The example of the key and the lock is Boyle's (Boyle 1991, 23). Curley 1972 draws the distinction between individual and sortal powers; Shoemaker 1990 calls them extrinsic and intrinsic powers.

[30] Perhaps someone who held that the laws of nature are contingent or mutable, but who wanted to endorse *intrinsic* dispositionalism, could do so by including among the conditions required for colors to be made manifest the condition that the laws of nature be what they are presently.

insist that colored objects remain colored under many circumstances that do not permit the manifestation of color (as when, for instance, all percipients within range have their eyes closed), but to deny that they remain colored under *all* such circumstances. Thus a dispositionalist about color might want to say that objects would lose their colors if there were no sentient creatures in the world.[31]

Talk of powers or capacities is often virtually synonymous with talk of dispositional properties. Fragility, solubility, and flammability can all be described as powers of objects, especially if we are willing to follow Locke in construing 'power' broadly enough so that there are not only powers to act but also powers to be acted on (II.xxi.2). An object is fragile if it has the power to break easily, soluble if it has the power to dissolve, flammable if it has the power to ignite. Thus Locke's identification of colors with powers to produce certain ideas in us would seem to be straightforward endorsement of a dispositionalism about color. However, he also says a good deal that does not fit well with dispositionalism.

Locke says that porphyry loses its color in the dark (II.viii.19). He says that gold would lose its color if it were "separate from the reach and influence of all other bodies" (IV.vi.11). These claims do not bespeak intrinsic dispositionalism about color. If Locke were an intrinsic dispositionalist, he should be saying that objects retain their colors in the dark, and when causally isolated, so long as they *would* produce the relevant sensations if they *were* observed by the right sorts of creatures under the right conditions. Perhaps then Locke is an extrinsic dispositionalist, holding that colors are dispositions to produce certain sensations in us, but that bodies lose these dispositions when it is dark, and when causally isolated?[32] There are difficulties with this reading too. If "real" qualities are qualities a body has whether it is being perceived or not, then both the intrinsic dispositionalist and the extrinsic dispositionalist should reckon color among the real qualities of bodies. Not to do so is to do away with the distinction between bodies

---

[31] Aristotle endorses something parallel to this when he says that air would cease to be breathable if there were no animals to breathe it (*Topics* 5.9, 138b30–37).

[32] Such a reading might be further refined in light of II.xxxi.2. There Locke explains the sense in which secondary qualities are "in" things by saying that if there were no "fit Organs" of sight and touch, or no minds united to such organs, there would be no light or heat. He says that we have reason to look upon solidity, extension, figure, and motion and rest as "the real modifications of Matter" because they are the ones that "would be really in the World as they are, whether there were any sensible Being to perceive them, or no." So it might be said that Locke's colors are dispositions that bodies lose in the dark, when causally isolated, and when there are no sensible beings with fit organs to perceive them.

having powers to produce certain ideas in us, and bodies exercising those powers.[33]

Most of those who hold that Locke is a dispositionalist about color concede that he says a good deal that is inconsistent with his "official" view. Thus E. M. Curley acknowledges that "Locke sometimes says that the secondary qualities are not *really* in external objects and do not exist at all whenever, for one reason or another, they are not being perceived," and concludes that these "are examples of those unfortunate inconsistencies for which Locke's work is so famous" (Curley 1972, 440). E. J. Lowe is another who reads Locke as a dispositionalist about color. He chalks up the offending passages to Locke's being "ambivalent about some of these matters, and perhaps even a little confused" (Lowe 1995, 52). Of the denial that objects are colored in the dark, Lowe says:

Locke seems to be confusing a repudiation of naive realism about colours (the thought that redness *as it characterizes our visual sensations* is literally "in" an external object) with a mistaken rejection of the stability of colour ascriptions (mistaken, that is, on the terms of his own theory of the latter). (Lowe 1995, 52)

Lowe sees the dispositional account of color as a tenable one, but says that Locke "does not always follow through its implications" (Lowe 1995, 53).

No honest and careful reader of the *Essay* will say that Locke can be defended against every charge of inconsistency or carelessness. We have already seen that he confesses to sometimes saying "ideas" when he means "qualities" (§1). He stumbles in other ways when he is handling the distinction between sensory ideas and the powers that bodies have to produce them. At II.viii.24, he says both that light and warmth are rightly considered as perceptions in us, and that they are powers in the sun. At II.xxiii.10, he tells us both that yellowness is not actually in gold, and that it is a power that is in gold. He follows this up by saying both that heat is not really in

---

[33] As we saw earlier (§14), it may be Locke's view that in order to be "real" a quality must be not only perceiver-independent, but intrinsic. This opens the possibility that he is an extrinsic dispositionalist of the sort described, and denies colors the status of being "real" not because they are perceiver-dependent but because they are extrinsic. I do not have an argument that shows conclusively that this reading is unworkable, but it does seem to me unmotivated. Why say that bodies retain their colors when there are no observers present, but that they lose them when it is dark? In both cases, what prevents a body from manifesting its color is something external to the body itself. One can understand the reluctance to say that bodies lose their colors when observers merely close their eyes. The reluctance seems to have its source in the fact that it is such an easy thing for the bodies to begin manifesting their colors again: we need only open our eyes. However, vanquishing the darkness is usually a simple matter too, a mere matter of lighting a lamp.

the sun, and that it is a power in the sun. In each of these cases, we can see pretty well how to untangle things on Locke's behalf. His confusions presumably stem from the fact that such terms as 'heat,' 'warmth,' and 'light' are multiply ambiguous. As we saw earlier (§12), he sometimes uses 'heat'"and 'warmth' to refer to primary qualities (the motion of particles), sometimes to secondary qualities (powers that bodies have in virtue of those motions to produce certain sensory ideas in us), and sometimes to sensory ideas (the ones he calls the ideas of heat and warmth). Similarly, in his hands 'light' sometimes names an idea (II.iii.1, II.iv.6), sometimes a quality possessed by a body (II.viii.16, II.xiii.13), sometimes a physical phenomenon or a collection of particles (II.xiv.20, III.iv.10).

Though we must concede that Locke is sometimes careless, we should nevertheless be troubled by the alleged inconsistencies in his account of color on the reading that takes his official position to be dispositionalism. We should be troubled because in this case the alleged "inconsistencies" seem to be systematic. Locke seems to think that there is one right answer to the question of whether bodies have colors in the dark, and that it is "no."[34] He consistently denies that colors are among the "real" properties of bodies, the ones they have independently of being perceived. He says almost nothing about the conceptions of "standard observers" and "standard observing conditions" that—if colors are dispositions—play such an important role in determining which dispositions colors are.[35] He does not seem to be handling colors the way that a dispositionalist about colors should. I suggest that this is because he is not thinking of these "powers to produce various Sensations in us" as dispositions.

---

[34] It is instructive to contrast Locke's handling of the color-in-the-dark issue with Boyle's. Boyle says that there is a sense in which bodies are colored in the dark and a sense in which they are not. In *Experiments and Considerations Touching Colours*, he writes that "Colour may be considered, either as it is a quality residing in the body that is said to be coloured, or to modifie the light after such and such a manner; or else as the Light itself, which so modifi'd, strikes upon the organ of sight" (Boyle 1664, 10). He expresses a preference for the latter way of speaking, but does not deny "but that Colour might in some sense be consider'd as a Quality residing in the body that is said to be Colour'd" (21). He goes on to say that the "famous Controversie" over whether objects are colored in the dark is largely "Nominal": "if Colour be indeed, but Light Modify'd, how can we conceive that it can Subsist in the Dark," and "if Colour be consider'd as a certain Constant Disposition of the Superficial parts of the Object to Trouble the Light they Reflect after such and such a Determinate manner...there seems no just reason to deny, but that in this Sense, Bodies retain their Colour as well in the Night as Day" (74–75).

[35] At II.xxiii.10 (a passage quoted above), he says that yellowness is a power in gold "to produce that *Idea* in us by our Eyes, when placed in a due Light." At III.viii.1, he characterizes whiteness as "a power to produce the *Idea* of Whiteness in one, whose Eyes can discover ordinary objects."

§15 Degenerate Powers

Expressions of the form "x can φ," "x is able to φ," and "x has the power to φ" can be used in various ways. Often when one says that x can φ or that x is able to φ, one is attributing to x a capacity that x retains even when x is not φing. One may truly say of a man who is speaking English that he can speak Chinese, or of a woman who is sleeping that she is able to play the violin. However, there are contexts in which the claim that x can φ, or is able to φ, is appropriate only if x has φed, is φing, or will φ. Suppose that you are looking out to sea when the friend by your side reports, "I see a two-masted schooner on the horizon," and then asks, "Can you see it?" In this context, the reply "Yes, I can see it" is called for only if you *do* see it. Similarly, there are contexts in which "Green Bay was able to regain the lead in the third quarter" means "Green Bay did regain the lead in the third quarter."

A. M. Honoré uses an example from J. L. Austin to distinguish two uses of 'can' (and related expressions):

Suppose a competent golfer must hole a short putt in order to win a game. No doubt there is a sense in which a competent golfer can hole a short putt: he has the ability to do so, and there is nothing to prevent him from exercising his ability on this occasion. But in another sense, with which we are now concerned, his competence as a golfer does not conclude the matter. In this sense, namely the *particular* sense of 'can,' it is proper to ask of even a competent golfer addressing himself to a short putt "can he sink the putt" and it is proper for him to assert "I can sink it" or "I ought to be able to sink it," or "I think I can sink it." In this sense, 'can' is almost equivalent to 'will' and has a predictive force. (Honoré 1964, 463–4)

If a competent golfer earnestly tries and fails to sink a putt, there is an ordinary use of language on which it is appropriate to say that he couldn't sink the putt. This is so even if the golfer's general capacity to make putts of equal or greater difficulty is not in doubt.[36] Honoré labels this use "'can' (particular)" because, he says, it is usually governed by success or failure on some particular occasion of trying: "If the agent tried and failed, he could

---

[36] Though the golf example is Austin's, he draws a different moral from it. Austin writes, "Nor does 'I can hole it this time' mean that I shall hole it this time if I try or if anything else: for I may try and miss, and yet not be convinced that I could not have done it" (Austin 1961, 166n1). I side with Honoré against Austin on this. "I can hole it this time" sounds to me like a prediction of imminent success, one that would be confuted by failure upon an earnest attempt.

not do the action…if he will succeed provided he tries, he can" (Honoré 1964, 464). The sense of 'can' used to ascribe a general competence to perform some kind of action—the sense that applies to the sleeping violinist—Honoré calls "'can' (general)" (Honoré 1964, 464–5).[37]

Honoré (1964, 466–7) suggests that there is a secondary use of 'can' (general), to talk about particular actions. I am not persuaded, but will not pursue that issue. It seems to me more nearly correct to say that there is a secondary application of 'can' (particular) to general types of actions. There is a sense of 'can' in which x can φ only when the conditions are such that x does φ. Let us broach this by considering situations in which we say that x can φ, but then we go on to delimit the claim by specifying some conditions under which x would not or will not φ. The most straightforward cases concern "doings" that are not actions in the strict sense, and so that do not involve us in questions about trying. Fortunately, these are also the cases that concern us. Consider this statement:

The boiler in my basement can heat the house on a cold winter day, but only if there is oil in the tank.

This is an ordinary use of 'can.' We might suppose that the 'can' involved is 'can' (general). In that case, what is being ascribed to the boiler is a general capacity to heat the house on cold winter days, a capacity that it retains in many circumstances when it is not actually heating the house, but one that it loses if the oil tank becomes empty. What is ascribed to the boiler is an extrinsic disposition.

Next consider:

The boiler in my basement can heat the house on a cold winter day, but only if there is oil in the tank, and only if there is water in the system, and only if the radiator valves are open, and only if the thermostat is turned up, and only if the windows are closed.

Are we still dealing with 'can' (general)? The expanded statement does concern what the furnace will do in a general type of circumstance (on cold winter days, rather than on some particular cold winter day, such as January 8, 2010), but the added conditions diminish those situations in which the boiler could be said to retain an unexercised capacity to heat the house. We could

---

[37] Daniel Dennett revives the 'can'(general)/'can'(particular) distinction in Dennett 1984, arguing that the failure to appreciate it accounts for the seeming plausibility of some arguments for incompatibilism (144–52; see also Dennett 2003, 75–7).

expand the statement indefinitely by adding further conditions ("…and only if the floors are not waist-deep in ice cubes, and only if temperatures outside do not plummet to 200 below zero," etc.); each brings us nearer to saying that the boiler *can* heat the house on a cold winter day in just those circumstances in which it *does* heat the house on a cold winter day. Make an extrinsic disposition extrinsic enough, and it ceases to be a disposition at all.

There is a use of 'can' on which x "can" φ (or x "is able to" φ) just in case x does φ. There is a corresponding use of 'cannot': if any condition obtains on which x does not φ, this may be cited as a reason that x "cannot" or "could not" φ, even if x retains the disposition to φ under other conditions. My brother's decision not to answer the phone means that I cannot talk with him; closing my eyes means that objects cannot produce visual sensations in me. Notice also that instead of saying that the boiler "can" heat the house only if there is oil in the tank, etc., we might just as well talk of the boiler "having the power to" heat the house only if there is oil in the tank, etc. Ordinarily, when we ascribe a power to an object, we are ascribing a disposition—a capacity that the object retains even when it is not exercising it. However, there is a degenerate, non-dispositional sense of 'power' in which something has a power to φ only in those circumstances in which it does φ.

Locke identifies colors with powers to produce certain sorts of sensations in us. It is usually supposed that he means to be identifying colors with dispositions—capacities that colored objects retain even when they are unperceived. We can make better sense of all that he says if we suppose that he is using 'powers' in a degenerate sense. To identify colors with powers in this sense is to identify them with relational but non-dispositional properties of objects. On this view, an object is colored just so long as it is standing in a certain causal relation to an observer of some sort, with a certain result obtaining. To be colored is to be contributing in a certain way to the production of a certain sort of sensation. The colored object need not be, and indeed never will be, the sole cause operating to bring about an observer's sensation.[38] Though the colored object is not causing a sensation all by itself, its being colored is a matter of its being among the causes of an occurring sensation. On this account, an object loses its color when it ceases to cause a color experience, even if the reason that it does so is that observers have closed their eyes or that the object is no longer illuminated.

---

[38] Locke recognizes this at IV.vi.11.

On the proposed reading—call it the "degenerate power reading"—colors are, in one legitimate sense, powers that belong to bodies. We can therefore accommodate Locke's repeated claims that colors are qualities, that they are in bodies, and that they are powers. However, unlike the reading on which he takes colors to be dispositions, we can also accommodate his repeated claims that colors, like pains, cease to exist when they cease to be experienced. If his "Powers to produce various Sensations" (II.viii.10) are powers in the degenerate sense, then he is right not to count colors as among the "real" qualities of bodies, given his use of that term. For on this view of color, the colors of bodies are not "*really in them*, whether any ones Senses perceive them or no" (II.viii.17). Locke's repeated denial that colors are mind-independent features of bodies is usually taken for support of subjectivism about color, but what should not be overlooked is that not all mind-dependent properties are properties of minds. The property of causing a sensation in a mind is mind-dependent, even if it is not the property of a mind.

The account of colors as powers in the degenerate sense fits nicely with Locke's characterization of colored bodies as "denominated from" our ideas of colors. He speaks of one thing as being denominated from, by, or in relation to, another whenever a name applies to the first thing in virtue of its relation to the second. Thus Cajus is denominated "Older" in relation to one person, and "Younger" in relation to another (II.xxv.5).[39] Locke several times speaks of bodies as denominated from ideas or sensations of colors (II.viii.15,16,22; *Works* III, 327–328). He means that color terms apply to the bodies they do only because those bodies stand in certain relations to our color sensations. At II.xxv.5, Locke says that the nature of relation consists in comparing one thing to another, with the result that one or the other "comes to be denominated." He then adds that "if either of those things be removed, or cease to be, the Relation ceases, and the Denomination consequent to it, though the other receive in it self no alteration at all." He gives the example of Cajus, who ceases to be a father—ceases to merit the denomination "father"—immediately upon the death of his son. By the same token, if color terms are "External Denominations" that apply to bodies because

---

[39] And thus Locke speaks of objects in general as denominated from or by the nominal essences that we associate with their names (II.xi.9, III.ix.11, III.x.33, and *Works* IV, 84), and of substances as denominated by the qualities in them of which we take notice (IV.vi.11, 585, l.34).

they cause our color sensations, we should expect those terms to cease to apply as soon as our sensations are "removed, or cease to be."

Let me be clear about what I am, and am not, proposing. I am saying that Locke takes colors to be powers to produce certain sensations in creatures like us, but "powers" in a peculiar, non-dispositional sense: objects are correctly said to have these powers only when they produce the sensations. I am saying that in the *Essay* he consistently maintains this view of color, and thus that he is not a dispositionalist about color and does not waffle between subjectivism about color and realism about color. I am not claiming that Locke never uses color terms to refer to ideas or features of ideas. He does do that. Since it does not seem likely that there is a univocal sense of 'color' that applies to both features of external objects and of our sensations, one or the other of these uses must presumably be to stand for something other than a color. I maintain that when Locke uses color terms to refer to ideas, he uses them to refer not to colors but to the standard effects of colors.

To decide whether the degenerate power reading is better than rival interpretations of Locke's remarks about color, one must decide (among other things) how to apply the principle of charity. When passing judgment on an interpretation, one must decide how to weigh such factors as the number of relevant texts it accommodates, its entailments about the author's consistency in applying terms and adhering to substantive positions (at least, when inconsistency is not openly avowed by the author), and the independent plausibility of the positions it attributes to the author. I regard the degenerate power reading as better than its rivals because it is consistent with nearly all of what Locke says about color, and it attributes to him a steadily held view of color that has considerable merits.

§16 Apparent Colors

If colors are powers in the degenerate sense, then a body's being colored is a matter of its actually causing a color experience in some perceiver. Because it is possible for an object to simultaneously cause different types of color experiences in different perceivers, one who identifies colors with powers in the degenerate sense faces a choice: either discriminate among the relations a colored object bears to different perceivers, singling out one of them as constitutive of its genuine color at that moment, or else grant that it has a color corresponding to each type of color experience that it causes.

The first approach has little to recommend it. Having abandoned the notion that an object's color is an intrinsic and relatively stable feature of its surface, there is scant reason to see some of its short-lived relations with perceivers as constitutive of genuine colors, and others of merely apparent colors. On the second approach, there is, in a sense, no such thing as mistaking a thing's color. If a perceiver judges an object to be a certain color on the grounds that the object is causing in him an idea of that color, then the object *is* that color (if it is in fact causing the experience).[40] If Locke's colors were dispositions, we should expect him to distinguish between genuine and apparent colors, and to hold that a thing's genuine color is the one that it would seem to have when viewed by normal observers under standard conditions. If his colors are features that things possess when, and only when, they are causing color experiences, then we should expect him to hold that appearing a color is sufficient for being that color. We might therefore look for evidence of whether he recognizes a distinction between genuine and apparent colors in hopes of confirming or confuting the degenerate power reading.

Support for the degenerate power reading can be found in Locke's claim that all simple ideas are "adequate," in the sense that they "perfectly represent those Archetypes, which the Mind supposes them taken from" (II.xxxi.1–2), and "true" in the sense that they conform to the "*real Existence of Things*" (II.xxxii.13). Ideas of colors are Locke's favorite examples of simple ideas. It seems reasonable to presume that a color idea perfectly represents its archetype, and conforms to the real existence of things, only when it presents something as being a color it is. If all of the color ideas produced in us do this, then there are no merely apparent colors. Locke justifies his claims about the adequacy and truth of simple ideas this way at II.xxxi.2:

[*A*]*ll our simple* Ideas *are adequate*. Because being nothing but the effects of certain Powers in Things, fitted and ordained by GOD, to produce such Sensations in us, they cannot but be correspondent, and adequate to those Powers: And we are sure they agree to the reality of Things. For if Sugar produce in us the *Ideas*, which we call Whiteness, and Sweetness, we are sure there is a power in Sugar to produce those *Ideas* in our Minds, or else they could not have been produced by it.[41]

---

[40] There is, of course, still the possibility of misreporting an object's color by using the wrong color term, and of mistakenly judging what color an object would be in different circumstances.

[41] See also II.xxxii.14 and IV.iv.4.

He seems to be saying that when sugar produces the idea of whiteness in me, I can be certain that the sugar is white, because whiteness just *is* the power to produce that idea. The production of the idea is unassailable evidence of the existence of something with the power to produce it. In that case, appearing white suffices for being white. Notice that if this is what Locke means, then he is using 'power' in the degenerate sense. If he were using 'power' in the dispositional sense, the knowledge that the sugar was white would require not only knowledge that a certain idea was produced in me, but also that I was a normal observer and that the conditions of observation were standard ones.

Perhaps the dispositionalist reading can accommodate Locke's claims about simple ideas being adequate and true by supposing that the scope of these claims is implicitly restricted to those ideas produced in normal observers under standard conditions. The passage just quoted could be read as saying that the regular production of ideas of whiteness (in normal observers under standard conditions) evinces over time the disposition that sugar has to produce that kind of idea. This would not entail that appearing white on some particular occasion is sufficient for being white then. As evidence that Locke *did* recognize a distinction between genuine and apparent color, the defender of the dispositionalist reading might then point to IV.iii.15, where Locke says that "no one Subject can have two Smells, or two Colours, at the same time." If one subject can simultaneously appear different colors to different observers, and yet none can *be* two colors at the same time, it would seem that there must be a difference between a thing's appearing a certain color and its being that color.

Locke's claim about colors excluding one another is not as straightforward as it might seem. To appreciate this, we must consider his response to the objection that an opal or an infusion of *Lignum Nephriticum*[42] may have two colors at the same time. In the section just mentioned, he says:

To which I answer, that these Bodies, to Eyes differently placed, may at the same time afford different Colours: But I take Liberty also to say, that to Eyes differently placed, 'tis different parts of the object, that reflect the Particles of Light: And therefore, 'tis not the same part of the Object, and so not the very same Subject, which at the same time appears both yellow and azure. For 'tis as impossible that the very same Particle of any Body, should at the same time differently modify, or reflect the Rays of Light, as that it should have two different Figures and Textures at the same time.

[42] "Two distinct woods were known as lignium nephriticum: (1) the small Mexican tree or shrub *Eysenhardtia polystacha* and the large Philippine tree *Pterocarpus indica*. In the sixteenth, seventeenth, and early eighteenth centuries, cups, powders, and dried extracts of this wood were thought to have a great medicinal powers. The infusion was fluorescent" (Eklund 1975, 30).

Locke seems about to concede that an opal can simultaneously be two colors "to Eyes differently placed," but then he denies that it is really the same object that is appearing different colors. He reasons that the eyes in question must be gathering light reflected from different regions of the opal's surface, since one "Particle" cannot differently modify rays of light. The inference is shaky: even if light reaching the eyes had been uniformly "modified" by the surface of the opal, it seems possible that the different locations of the eyes (and hence the different paths traveled by the light) could account for differences in the resulting appearances. Let us set that aside, and attend to the conclusion that Locke draws from the fact that one particle cannot modify light in different ways at the same time. It is that the opal does not, after all, present us with a case of one object *appearing* both yellow and azure. The opal was supposed to be a counterexample to the thesis that "no one Subject can have two...Colours." If the opal fails as a counterexample because it does not provide us with a case of one object *appearing* both yellow and azure, this suggests that Locke is treating "one subject can have two colors" as equivalent to "one subject can appear two colors." This supports the degenerate power reading rather than undermining it.

Though he denies that the same subject appears both yellow and azure, Locke certainly does not mean to deny that one half of a surface can appear yellow, and the other half azure. Nor does it seem likely that he means to deny that one object can appear different colors to differently constituted observers. Locke himself raises the possibility that the same surfaces might present systematically different appearances to observers because of differences in the observers' sense organs (II.xxxii.15). When he denies that the opal appears both yellow and azure, he means that the opal does not provide us with a case of one uniformly-colored surface simultaneously appearing both yellow and azure *to one observer*. (When he speaks of "Eyes differently placed," he is thinking of two eyes in the same head.) Combining this result with that of the previous paragraph, we see that Locke's claim that colors exclude one another should be understood in a way that is compatible with a thing's being different colors for different observers. When he says that no object can have two colors at the same time, he means that no uniformly colored surface can simultaneously appear different colors to one observer. He means that yellow and azure cannot be simultaneously and distinctly exhibited by one object in the way that yellow and round can be, or yellow and hot. This is not an exciting claim, but bear in mind its context: it is offered as an example of our knowledge of the incompatibility of certain qualities. In the same section he makes the equally unexciting observation that no object can have two different shapes at the same time.

Another passage that may seem to show that Locke does distinguish between real and apparent color is II.ix.8, where he claims that ideas of sensation are often changed by the faculty of judgment. Locke says:

> We are farther to consider concerning Perception, that the *Ideas we receive by sensation, are often* in grown People *alter'd by the Judgment*, without our taking notice of it. When we set before our Eyes a round Globe, of any uniform colour, *v.g.* Gold, Alabaster, or Jet, 'tis certain, that the *Idea* thereby imprinted in our Mind, is of a flat Circle variously shadow'd, with several degrees of Light and Brightness coming to our Eyes. But we having by use been accustomed to perceive, what kind of appearance convex Bodies are wont to make in us; what alterations are made in the reflections of Light, by the difference of the sensible Figures of Bodies, the Judgment presently, by an habitual custom, alters the Appearances into their Causes: So that from that, which truly is variety of shadow or colour, collecting the Figure, it makes it pass for a mark of Figure, and frames to it self the perception of a convex Figure, and an uniform Colour; when the *Idea* we receive from thence, is only a Plain variously colour'd, as is evident in Painting.

Here we are to imagine a subject looking at a uniformly-colored sphere placed before him. Locke claims that the ideas that will be imprinted on this subject's mind are, at least initially, those of a variously-colored, two-dimensional circle. Thus it may seem that he is asking us to imagine a scenario on which a sphere is actually uniformly-colored, but apparently variously-colored. In fact, Locke is not doing that. He is not claiming that to "grown People" uniformly-colored spheres look like variously-colored two-dimensional objects. Instead, he is saying something about the role that judgment plays in explaining how grown people come to see uniformly-colored spheres as uniformly-colored and spherical. To see just *what* he is saying about this takes a bit of sorting out.

Let us start with Locke's claim that "*the Judgment*" changes the ideas that we receive by sensation. One might take this to mean that a metamorphosis takes place in the mind of a grown person each time she sees a uniformly-colored sphere. Particles rebounding off the sphere initially cause in her an array of simple, visual ideas that together constitute the appearance of a two-dimensional, variously-colored circle. The faculty of judgment then quickly intervenes and causes her to have a different array of visual ideas, one that constitutes the appearance of a three-dimensional, uniformly-colored sphere. A moment's reflection shows that this is not what Locke means. Phenomenologically, it does not seem that each time one turns one's eyes in the direction of a uniformly-colored sphere one is first presented with one sort of appearance, only to find it quickly supplanted by another. Locke himself says that we do not notice the changes that judgment makes to the ideas that we receive by sensation, so perhaps it will be suggested that the switch happens so quickly that we never notice the first appearance that is presented to us. Yet in that case, what is the basis for claiming that the first appearance is presented at all? Locke rejects as incoherent the suggestion that we might have ideas without being aware of them: "to be in the Mind, and, never to be perceived, is all one, as to say, any thing is, and is not, in the Mind" (I.ii.5).

Another way to understand Locke's claim that judgment changes the ideas one receives by sensation is to suppose that he is talking about a one-time change that happens in infancy or early childhood. When a new-born infant turns her eyes in the direction of a uniformly-colored sphere, this produces in her an array of simple, visual ideas as of a variously-colored, two-dimensional circle. At some point, she has tactile experiences of a uniformly-colored sphere, and discovers its three dimensionality. She then proceeds to manipulate the sphere or to walk around it, and also discovers its uniform coloring. Judgment is involved in these discoveries. From this point on, when she turns her eyes in the direction of a uniformly-colored sphere, the array of simple, visual ideas produced in her is as of a uniformly-colored sphere. This cannot be Locke's meaning, either. He says that when we set before our eyes a uniformly-colored sphere, the ideas imprinted in our mind are those of a flat, variously-colored circle. This is an observation about the ideas produced in grown people, not speculation about those produced in the minds of infants.

Though Locke does speak of judgment altering or changing the ideas that sensation produces in us, he does not think that judgment causes a different array of visual ideas to be produced in us than would be produced otherwise. Judgment changes the ideas that sensation delivers not by making sensation deliver different ideas, or by transmuting the ideas that sensation delivers, but rather by changing how we interpret the ideas that sensation delivers. His point is that our visual representation of depth is not solely a function of our having the visual ideas that we do have. The array of visual ideas that is produced in us when we look at a uniformly-colored sphere is one that would—if our judgment were inert or untutored—lead us to believe that we were confronted with a variously-colored two-dimensional object. Because we have in the past experienced such arrays in conjunction with what proved to be uniformly-colored spheres, we take them for presentations of those. Thus we make what is "truly a variety of shadow or colour" pass for a mark of figure, and by means of this "Plain variously colour'd" judgment frames to itself the perception of a convex figure.[43] This reading is confirmed by his summation in the next section. At II.ix.9, he says that we have acquired a settled habit by means of which we "take that for the Perception of our Sensation, which is an *Idea* formed by our Judgment; so that one, *viz.* that of Sensation, serves only to excite the other, and is scarce taken notice of it self." [44] Our attention comes to be fixed not on the actual visual array produced by sensation, but on a different idea, one that represents our judgment about how things are.[45]

There is one more objection to the degenerate power reading that we ought to consider before turning to a closer examination of his assimilation of colors and pains. One passage that poses a problem for both the degenerate power reading and the dispositional reading is the close of II.viii.19, just

[43] Notice that what Locke here describes as being "variety of shadow or colour" is not the sphere, and must be the ideas themselves. Since he does not think that ideas are powers to produce ideas in us, or that they possess powers to produce ideas in us, he must be speaking loosely when he characterizes them as a colored plain. Perhaps he is thinking of them as mental images, and as "colored" in whatever derivative sense mental images might be colored. Or perhaps it is a shorthand way of saying that to perceive these ideas by themselves—absent the influence of judgment in light of our past experience— would be to have a visual experience as of a flat and variously-colored circle. In any case, Locke is not saying that either the sphere or the ideas appear to grown people to be colored one way while they are really colored another way.

[44] At II.ix.10, he repeats the point: "'tis not so strange, that our Mind should often change the *Idea* of its Sensation, in to that of its Judgment, and make one serve only to excite the other, without our taking notice of it."

[45] Perhaps it will be suggested that II.ix.8 commits Locke to saying that uniformly-colored spheres will seem *to infants* to be variously-colored. I reply that we can only speculate what he would have said about infants' perceptions of the spheres that we judge to be uniformly-colored, but that he is not committed to saying that such spheres appear to infants variously-colored while they are in fact uniformly-colored. He might say that to perceive something either as a uniformly-colored sphere or as a variously-colored flat circle requires the deployment of abstract ideas that infants do not have yet. To infants, the world might be one of separate, short-lived colors and sounds rather than one of enduring physical objects. Or he might say that what are uniformly-colored spheres to us *are* variously-colored things to infants. Here he might treat this case as he does that of spectrum inversion. Locke holds that if two people are spectrum-inverse with respect to each other, both have "true" ideas of objects' colors because the ideas in both answer to powers in the bodies that produce them, and because the differences would not give rise to any inter-personal confusion (II.xxxii.15). He could say much the same thing about the infants and us.

after Locke's claim that porphyry has no color in the dark. Still speaking of the porphyry, he adds:

It has, indeed, such a Configuration of Particles, both Night and Day, as are apt by the Rays of Light rebounding from some parts of that hard Stone, to produce in us the *Idea* of redness, and from others the *Idea* of whiteness: But whiteness or redness are not in it at any time, but such a texture, that hath the power to produce such a sensation in us.

The first part tells us that whether or not porphyry is illuminated, it has an aptness to reflect light in such a way as to produce the ideas of redness and whiteness in us. This is compatible with all of the interpretations that we have considered. What follows the colon is not quite grammatical, and on any reading something must be supplied to make sense of it. The question is not whether Locke stumbles, but how he stumbles and what he is trying to say. If we suppose that 'whiteness' and 'redness' refer to qualities, and that an 'is' was inadvertently dropped from the end of the sentence, then Locke will seem to be endorsing subjectivism: whiteness and redness are never in the porphyry, but a texture that has a power is. The clause could also be read as a clumsy endorsement of the view that porphyry's color is its texture—an intrinsic but non-dispositional feature of its surface. However, that would not accord with much else that Locke says about color. Those who favor the dispositionalist reading or the degenerate power reading can accommodate the clause by supplying the missing 'is' while supposing that 'whiteness' and 'redness' refer not to qualities, but to the ideas of those qualities. Or they can dismiss it as so muddled as not to support any inference about Locke's view of color.

§17 Colors and Pains

Perhaps the greatest challenge to the degenerate power reading is whether it can accommodate Locke's assimilation of colors and pains. The dispositional reading faces the same challenge. Whether each of these readings can meet the challenge depends on the respects in which Locke is alleging that colors and pains are similar. Colors might be said to be like pains in any of a number of ways, depending in part on one's views about the status of pains. Consider these claims:

(3.1)   Colors are like pains in that they are sensations or features of sensations.

(3.2)   Colors are like pains in that they exist only when perceived.

(3.3)   Colors are like pains in that they exist only in minds.

(3.4)   Colors are like pains in that ideas of them do not resemble the bodies or qualities that occasion them.

(3.5)   Colors are like pains in that they exist only in animate bodies.

If (3.1) or (3.3) is what Locke has in mind, then his assimilation of color and pain commits him to subjectivism about color and can be accommodated by neither the dispositional reading nor the degenerate power reading. On the other hand, although (3.2) is incompatible with the dispositional reading, it is a deliverance of the degenerate power reading. If (3.4) is the point of Locke's assimilation of colors with pains, this can be accommodated equally well by any of the readings that we are considering. As for (3.5), it would be very strange to say that colors have locations in our bodies in the way that pains do. This is a non-starter in any case, since Locke does not even think that pains are literally in our bodies. At one point he speaks somewhat poetically of God having scattered pains in the "*things that environ and affect us*" (II.vii.5). He sometimes speaks in a more ordinary fashion of pains as being of, or in, our bodies (II.xxi.31,38,41; *Works* IX, 218). Yet his considered opinion is that what we call pains of the body are truly "Constitutions of the Mind...occasioned by disorder in the Body" (II.xx.2).

Locke first compares colors to pains at II.viii.13. He invites us to suppose that a violet produces in us the ideas of its scent and its color by "the impulse of such insensible particles of matter of peculiar figures, and bulks, and in different degrees and modifications of their Motions." Then he adds:

It being no more impossible, to conceive, that God should annex such *Ideas* to such Motions, with which they have no similitude; than that he should annex the *Idea* of Pain to the motion of a piece of Steel dividing our Flesh, with which that *Idea* hath no resemblance.

God has made it so that the motion of a knife cutting our flesh causes us to have the idea of pain, though that idea does not resemble the motion. Similarly, God can make it the case that the motions of particles traveling from the surface of a violet trigger in us "the *Ideas* of the blue Colour, and sweet Scent of that Flower," though these ideas do not resemble those motions. The point of comparison here is captured by (3.4).

Locke next compares colors to pains at II.viii.16. The section begins with the observation that flame is denominated "hot," and snow "cold," from the ideas they produce in us. Locke points out that the same fire produces first sensations of warmth, and then of pain, in an approaching observer. He asks the reader what grounds there are for saying that his "*Idea of Warmth*" is in the fire, and that his "*Idea of Pain*" is not. He then asks a second question: "Why is Whiteness and Coldness in Snow, and Pain not?"

One might suppose that when Locke asks about the *idea* of warmth being in fire, this is another instance of his carelessness about ideas and qualities. One might take him to be insinuating that the quality warmth has the same status as pain. In that case, it would be natural to read his next question as challenging our grounds for locating the quality "whiteness" in snow. This would be a mistake. His real target in this passage is not realism about secondary qualities, but the particular brand of realism about secondary qualities that he believes is common to scholastic philosophers and naive realists. He describes it this way:

[Heat, light, white, cold, sweet] are commonly thought to be the same in those Bodies, that those *Ideas* are in us, the one the perfect resemblance of the other, as they are in a Mirror; and it would by most Men be judged very extravagant, if one should say otherwise.

Locke is attacking the view that the same item, or the same sort of item, is both in the colored (or hot, or sweet) object and in the perceiver's mind. Those who hold this view *do* think that the idea of warmth—or something very much like it—is in the fire. Locke sometimes uses 'whiteness' to refer to a quality, and sometimes to refer to the idea triggered by that quality.[46] Reading his second question as parallel to the first, we should see it as asking why the idea "whiteness" is in snow and pain not. Again, the challenge is directed not at everyone who thinks that snow is white and cold, but at scholastic philosophers and naive realists who think that the idea "whiteness" and the quality "whiteness" are the same kind of thing. So the assimilation of colors and pains in II.viii.16 is another expression of (3.4).

Locke compares color and pain again at II.viii.17, all of which was quoted above (§14). There he says that "*Light, Heat, Whiteness, or Coldness, are no more really in* [fire or snow], *than Sickness or Pain is in* Manna." Since sickness and pain are not in manna, it may seem that we are supposed to draw the conclusion that whiteness is not in snow. In that case, the comparison

[46] At III.iv.15, Locke says, "Whiteness is the Name of that Colour he has observed in Snow, or Milk." In the section heading to IV.xi.2, he refers to the "whiteness of this Paper" (Locke 1975, 630). On the other hand, he speaks of "the Sensation or *Idea* we name *Whiteness*" at IV.ii.11.

of color and pain would be regarded as an expression of (3.1) or (3.3). However, a closer look at the passage and its immediate context suggests another reading. What Locke says is that whiteness is not "really" in snow any more than pain is in manna. This comes immediately after his explanation that the bulk, number, figure, and motion of parts of fire and snow are "*really*" in them—are "*real Qualities*"—because they are in them whether they are perceived or not. Seen in light of this, the comparison of whiteness and pain in II.viii.17 looks more like an expression of (3.2) than of (3.1). Sickness and pain are not qualities of manna. Though snow is sometimes white, whiteness is no more a "real" (that is, mind-independent) quality of snow than pain is a quality of manna.

The next section, II.viii.18, contains two comparisons of colors and pains, distinguished below as [A] and [B]. Locke begins by saying that everybody will agree that "*Motion and Figure are really in the Manna*, whether we take notice of them or no." He also expects universal agreement that the "*Ideas of Sickness and Pain are not in the* Manna, but Effects of its Operations on us, and are no where when we feel them not." So far, so good. What comes next is this observation:

[A] And yet Men are hardly to be brought to think, that *Sweetness and Whiteness are not really in Manna*; which are but the effects of the operations of *Manna*, by the motion, size, and figure of its Particles on the Eyes and Palate; as the Pain and Sickness caused by *Manna*, are confessedly nothing, but the effects of its operations on the Stomach and Guts...

Toward the end of the section, whiteness and pain are again compared:

[B] [W]hy the Pain and Sickness, *Ideas* that are the effects of *Manna*, should be thought to be no-where, when they are not felt; and yet the Sweetness and Whiteness, effects of the same *Manna* on other parts of the Body, by ways equally as unknown, should be thought to exist in the *Manna*, when they are not seen nor tasted, would need some Reason to explain.

We can begin to appreciate the murkiness of these passages by noting that in both of them Locke identifies "whiteness" with the *effect* of manna's operation on us. By itself that does not show that Locke takes the color white to be an idea. Outside of II.viii there are both apparently straightforward cases of Locke using 'whiteness' to refer to a quality in bodies, and apparently straightforward cases of him using 'whiteness' to refer to an idea in us. So it could be that he regards 'whiteness' as ambiguous between an idea and a feature of the body that causes it, and that here he is talking about the former. But *why* is he talking about the idea "whiteness" here? What does he hope to show by comparing (i) the relation in which the *idea* "whiteness" stands to manna, and (ii) the relation in which pains stand to manna?

One answer is that Locke is arguing for, or endorsing, the view that the color white is an idea in us. In that case, these passages are expressions of (3.1) or (3.3), and cannot be accommodated by either the dispositional reading or the degenerate power reading. Passage [A] is easy enough to make sense of this way, but [B] becomes something of a mystery on this reading. If Locke is arguing for subjectivism about color, then [B] is directed against the realist about color. In that case, it is hard to see the force of the challenge that he issues at the end of the passage. For the realist will grant that "whiteness" is an effect of manna on the body only if he understands "whiteness" to be referring to the *idea* "whiteness"; and the realist about color will have no inclination to say that *this* is in the manna, or that *it* exists when no sensations are being had.

Once again it is (3.4) that captures the point that Locke is making. In II.viii.18 he is not arguing against color realism, but against the view that there is some one kind of thing that is both in the colored body, and then in us when we have a sensation of color. He presumably has uppermost in mind the scholastic doctrine of sensible species, but he does not think that it is only philosophers who are prone to making this sort of mistake. At II.xxxii.14, he argues that simple ideas are "true" so long as they "answer" the powers God has placed in bodies to cause them. He adds: "Nor do they become liable to any Imputation of *Falshood*, if the Mind (as in most Men I believe it does) judges these *Ideas* to be in the Things themselves." Nearly everybody, he suggests, succumbs to a kind of naive realism about color, one involving the assumption that the idea we are immediately acquainted with when we have a color experience is the same thing, or the same sort of thing, as is in the colored object. Locke rejects this naive realism. His point in II.viii.18 is that my idea of color is as distinct from its cause in the colored body as my pains are from any features of the bodies that cause them.[47] He does not expect either scholastic philosophers or ordinary folks to say that

---

[47] Locke is reminding us of this same point when, at II.xxx.2, he says, "But though Whiteness and Coldness are no more in Snow, than Pain is; yet those *Ideas* of Whiteness, and Coldness, Pain, *etc.* being in us the Effects of Powers in Things without us, ordained by our Maker, to produce in us such Sensations; they are real *Ideas* in us..." The beginning of this remark would seem to entail color subjectivism but for his immediately making it clear that he is denying that the *ideas* "whiteness" and "coldness" are in snow, and not that snow is white and cold.

there is an idea or form of pain in the manna, and so he challenges them to explain their different treatments of color and pain.

When Locke says that colors are like pains, it is natural to assume that he means that both colors and pains are in us rather than out there in objects. Our closer survey of these passages has shown that none of them entails that colors are wholly subjective.

§18 *Transient Colors*

I have argued that Locke takes colors to be powers that bodies have to produce certain ideas in us, but powers in a degenerate, non-dispositional sense. A body has one of these powers just in case it is actually producing an idea of the relevant sort in some perceiver. An object is the color it is not because of the experience it would produce in a normal observer under standard conditions, but because of the experience it is causing in some actual observer under actual conditions. Some may be reluctant to ascribe this view to Locke because it seems to them such an implausible account of color. I will not attempt a full-scale defense of the account here, but I will try to show that it is not so implausible that we should be reluctant to ascribe it to a good philosopher.

The aspect of Locke's theory that is most apt to trouble one is its entailment that objects lose their colors when they are not being observed. It does sound somewhat odd to say that the walls of my study lose, and then regain, their mossy green color when I am its sole occupant and I blink my eyes. It sounds somewhat less odd (at least to my ears) to say that objects lose their colors in the dark. I find this remark in Richard Feynman's *Lectures on Physics*: "If the intensity of the light is very low, the things that we see have *no color*" (Feynman, Leighton, and Sands 1989, 35–2).[48] Anyone who says that objects lose their colors in low-light situations should presumably also say that they lose them in the dark. Perhaps the best way to acclimatize oneself to the notion that objects lose their colors when unobserved is to contemplate the difficulties involved in trying to say what color an object is when it is unobserved.

---

[48] Italics in original. The claim that there is no color in low-light situations appears once more on the same page, but so does the remark that the colors of the ring nebula and the Crab nebula are "not artificial colors" despite the fact that nobody has ever seen them.

Consider the strangeness of saying that the color that an object is when it is unobserved is the color that it would appear to most human beings to be if it were seen against a neutral homogenous background under the illumination of a tungsten lamp at a certain temperature through a filter approved in 1931 by the International Commission on Illumination.[49] Why is *that* appearance privileged? Each object presents many different appearances when observed under different lighting conditions. Things that appear the same color in daylight may appear to be different colors in other situations. The apparent color of some objects depends on viewing distance and background colors. Some works of art were designed to be viewed in dim churches with stained glass windows. Different animals make different color discriminations, and even normally sighted human observers produce different results in color matching tasks. It seems highly arbitrary to select one lighting condition, one viewing distance, one sort of background, and one sort of observer as being those in relation to which an object presents its one *real* color, the one it has even when it is not being observed.

Any fair assessment of Locke's theory of color must consider it in relation to its rivals. Earlier I offered a taxonomy of philosophical positions on the nature of color. The rivals to Locke's theory include eliminativism, subjectivist theories, theories on which colors are features of light, theories on which colors are intrinsic non-dispositional property of objects, theories on which they are intrinsic dispositions, and theories on which they are extrinsic dispositions. Anyone who balks at the notion that objects lose their colors in the dark should presumably have even less patience for theories on which objects are never colored at all. This includes eliminativism, subjectivist theories, and theories on which colors are features of light. These theories entail that we are mistaken when we ascribe colors to objects on the basis of our perceptual experiences. The principle of charity should make us quite reluctant to embrace this result.

The view that colors are intrinsic, non-dispositional properties of objects does yield the result that objects are colored whether or not they are being perceived. In Locke's day, the hypothesis that all of the objects that appear a certain color (to a subject under certain conditions) share some intrinsic, micro-structural feature in common would have been a bold empirical speculation. Locke regards it as likely but not certain that objects with a number of observable qualities in common will share the same underlying

---

[49] See MacAdam 1985 for a clear account of standard illuminants.

corpuscular structure or real essence.[50] It is less clear that he would have regarded similarities in color alone as justifying any such inference. We now know that such an inference would be mistaken, unless one is willing to countenance highly disjunctive properties as the shared intrinsic features.[51]

A dispositionalist might identify the color of an object with its disposition to reflect light of a certain character. The supposition that all objects that appear the same color (to some observer under some particular conditions) reflect light of the same character would have been a risky empirical hypothesis in Locke's day, when the nature of light was poorly understood. Subsequent investigation has proven it false. Light samples of indefinitely many different wavelength profiles can produce color experiences of the same sort in the same person under fixed conditions (Hardin 1984, 494–5). The dispositionalist can get around this by identifying colors with dispositions to produce certain kinds of sensations in certain types of observers under certain types of conditions. This raises difficulties about what are to count as normal observers and normal viewing situations. Specifying what count as normal viewing conditions is especially problematic. One might try to get around the worry that the specification of any single illuminant is arbitrary by pointing to the fact that the evolution of our color language must have largely occurred outdoors in daylight. Yet there will still be the problem that the colors of stars, phosphorescent dyes and neon tubes should not be specified in terms of their appearances in daylight conditions.[52]

Much more would need to be said to show that the view of color that I have attributed to Locke is superior to its rivals. But it does have many virtues: it entails that objects have colors when they seem to, it permits us to say that both reflecting surfaces and light emitters are colored in the same sense, its truth does not hinge on risky speculations about commonalities in micro-structures or light samples, and it skirts all of the difficulties involved in specifying standard observers and standard observing conditions. If it is somewhat difficult to rid oneself of the feeling that objects are colored when unobserved, it is positively liberating to jettison the idea that there is such a thing as *the* real color each object has no matter what the viewing conditions or the conditions of the viewers.

---

[50] See III.vi.36 and *Works* IV, 91.

[51] See Nassau 1985 and chapter 1 of Hardin 1988.

[52] See Hardin 1983 for a discussion of the problems involved in specifying standard observing conditions.

§19 *Other Powers*

Locke says repeatedly that colors are powers to produce certain ideas in us, and he also says that bodies lose their colors when they are in the dark or causally isolated. I have argued that the way to reconcile these claims is to understand him as holding that colors are powers in a degenerate sense: they are extrinsic, non-dispositional features that bodies have only when they are actually causing perceivers to have the relevant sort of sensory ideas. If that is Locke's view about what colors are, then it must also be what he thinks that sounds, odors, flavors, and certain tactile qualities are.

A survey of the *Essay*'s pivotal chapter on sensible qualities (II.viii) makes it plain that Locke takes all secondary qualities immediately perceivable to have the same metaphysical status. When he introduces the category of secondary qualities, it is not just colors, but "Colours, Sounds, Tasts, *etc.*," that he characterizes as nothing but powers to produce various sensations in us (II.viii.10). Summarizing things later, he says much the same thing about "Colours, Sounds, Smells, Tasts, *etc.*" (II.viii.23). Locke treats ideas of secondary qualities together when giving his account of how bodies produce sensations (II.viii.13). He illustrates the account with reference to the color and smell of a violet, but adds that "[w]hat I have said concerning *Colours* and *Smells*, may be understood also of *Tastes* and *Sounds, and other the like sensible Qualities*" (II.viii.14). It is ideas of secondary qualities in general that are said not to resemble sensible qualities or bodies (II.viii.15). It is "all Colours, Tastes, Odors, and Sounds, as they are such particular *Ideas*," that are said to vanish and cease when one takes away the sensation of them (II.viii.17). Not only manna's whiteness, but also its sweetness, is denied the status of being "really in" it (II.viii.18). When he illustrates the dependence that some sensible qualities have upon a body's underlying texture, Locke notes that crushing an almond with a pestle alters both its color and its taste (II.viii.20). Finally, it is ideas of secondary qualities immediately perceivable—"Colours, Sounds, *etc.*"—that we are said to mistake for real qualities resembling something in the bodies that produce them (II.viii.24–25).

Like most philosophers writing about perception, Locke offers little detail about sensible qualities other than color. However, the little that he does say is compatible with the supposition that he takes sounds, odors, flavors, and certain tactile qualities to be degenerate powers to produce ideas in us. His most focused discussion of these other sensible qualities comes in *Elements of Natural Philosophy*. There Locke has this to say about sound:

That which is conveyed into the brain by the ear is called sound; though, in truth, till it come to reach and affect the perceptive part, it be nothing but motion.
The motion, which produces in us the perception of sound, is a vibration of the air, caused by an exceeding short, but quick, tremulous motion of the body from which it is propagated; and therefore we consider and denominate them as bodies sounding.
That sound is the effect of such a short, brisk, vibrating motion of bodies from which it is propagated, may be observed from what is known and felt in the strings of instruments…(*Works* III, 326).

In the first sentence, Locke speaks of sounds as being conveyed into the ear, much as he elsewhere describes ideas as being conveyed in by the senses. This is loose talk, as he makes clear in the second half of the sentence. What actually enters via the ears are motions, and it is not until these affect "the perceptive part" that there is sound. If affecting the perceptive part means producing the idea of the sound, then this passage lends positive support to my reading. For in that case, Locke is saying that sounds do not come into being until perceivers have auditory experiences. The second sentence tells us that perceptions of sounds are the effects of vibrations in the air, which in turn result from tremulous motions of the bodies that we describe as sounding. The third sentence is ambiguous, depending upon whether we take the antecedent of 'it' to be 'sound' or 'motion.' On the first reading, Locke is saying that sound is propagated from bodies, and is the effect of the motions of those bodies. In that case, he is speaking loosely of sound as traveling from bodies, and at the same time is calling it the effect of motions that travel from those bodies. On the second reading, he is saying that motion is propagated from bodies, and that sound is the effect of that motion. In that case, if 'sound' refers to the idea of sound—and it may[53]—this makes perfect sense. If 'sound' refers to a quality of the sounding body, then Locke is saying that this quality is the effect of motions that the sounding body transfers to the air around it. Initially, it may seem odd to say both (i) that sound is a quality of the body, and (ii) that sound is produced by motions that the sounding body transmits to other bodies. Yet this is not so odd if we are thinking of

[53] In Locke's hands, such terms as 'sound,' 'smell,' and 'taste' display the same sort of ambiguity that 'colour' and 'whiteness' do. Sometimes they name qualities (as 'Sounds' does at II.viii.10), and other times they name the ideas those qualities produce in us (as '*Sound*' does at II.viii.5).

sound as a relational quality that the body possesses when it causes motions that trigger auditory experiences in perceivers.

There is one passage in the *Essay* that may seem difficult to reconcile with the view that sounds are degenerate powers. At II.ix.4, Locke describes the phenomenon of a person so focused in contemplation that he does not hear what he otherwise would:

How often may a Man observe in himself, that whilst his Mind is intently employ'd in the contemplation of some Objects; and curiously surveying some *Ideas* that are there, it takes no notice of impressions of sounding Bodies, made upon the Organ of Hearing, with the same alteration, that uses to be for the producing the *Idea* of a Sound?

There is no problem with the suggestion that bodies might affect organs of hearing in the usual way without this leading to the production of ideas of sounds. However, Locke describes his case as one in which a man takes no notice of "impressions of sounding Bodies." The "impressions" in this case must be physical impressions—motions conveyed to our inner ears—if this is a case in which auditory perception does not occur. The difficulty for my reading is that these impressions are described as coming from "sounding Bodies," whereas on the degenerate power reading there ought to be no sounds if no ideas of sounds are produced. One solution would be to say that he is speaking loosely when he calls the sources of vibration "sounding Bodies": they are bodies that *would be* sounding if only the subject's attention were not focused so exclusively on something else. Another is to say that he is imagining a situation in which although one person is too focused to hear, the air vibrations around him do trigger auditory experiences in others.

We have already given some consideration to the tactile qualities that Locke numbers among the secondary qualities (§12). These include powers to produce in us the ideas of heat and cold. Exactly what other powers they include is unclear. We saw earlier that Locke uses 'heat' and 'cold' not only as the names of secondary qualities, but also as the names of the primary qualities in virtue of which bodies have those secondary qualities. Because of this, we should not necessarily expect to find him describing bodies as hot or cold only when we touch them. A body may be hot in one sense only when it is producing the idea of heat in somebody, but it can be hot in the other sense even when it is causally isolated.

Locke says little about odors and flavors except for the remarks in II.viii that we have already discussed. In the *Elements of Natural Philosophy*, he does mention that we detect odors at a distance, by means of effluvia that originate in the "smelling body" (*Works* III, 326). This last phrase suggests that he locates smells at their sources, rather than in the air near our faces. Flavors too he seems to locate in the bodies we taste. He notes that we cannot perceive flavors at a distance, but only by the immediate application of the bodies to our tongues (*Works* III, 327). Though Locke seems to locate odors and flavors at the bodies that occasion them, he also suggests that our ideas of them do not include the idea of extension (II.xiii.24). By this he may mean that odors and flavors do not seem to be spread out in space in the way that colors do. When a body is colored, the colored portion of it will be a surface whose area can be measured. It is not unnatural to speak of the color itself as having an area. Locke seems to hold that nothing like this is true in the case of odors and flavors.

I have suggested that Locke takes all secondary qualities immediately perceivable to have the same status that colors do. They are all degenerate powers to produce ideas in us. What about secondary qualities mediately perceivable? Are these too degenerate powers? There is some evidence to support this. Locke says that both kinds of secondary qualities are merely powers (II.viii.10,23). This would be an odd thing to say if in fact he thinks that they are "powers" in different senses; and yet arguably they would be powers in different senses if secondary qualities immediately perceivable are degenerate powers and secondary qualities mediately perceivable are non-degenerate powers. There are also a couple of passages suggesting that Locke may conceive of secondary qualities mediately perceivable as degenerate powers. One is II.xxiii.37, where he says :

[M]ost of the simple *Ideas*, that make up our complex *Ideas* of Substances, when truly considered, are only Powers, however we are apt to take them for positive Qualities; *v.g.* the greatest part of the *Ideas*, that make our complex *Idea* of *Gold*, are Yellowness, great Weight, Ductility, Fusibility, and Solubility, in *Aqua Regia, etc.* all united together in an unknown *Substratum*; all which *Ideas*, are nothing else, but so many relations to other Substances; and are not really in the Gold, considered barely in it self, though they depend on those real, and primary Qualities of its internal constitution, whereby it has a fitness, differently to operate, and be operated on by several other Substances.

Here we have the familiar conflation of ideas and qualities. We can presume that it is *ideas* of powers that are supposed to be among the components of ideas of substances such as gold. Locke then seems to be making several claims about the powers themselves: that they are often mistaken for positive qualities, that they are relations, that they are not intrinsic features of substances, and that they depend on underlying real, primary qualities. It is hard to see how yellowness, weight, ductility, *etc.* could be both powers of the gold and relations between the gold and something else. Presumably he means that they are relational features of the gold. The denial that they are "really in the Gold, considered barely in it self" rules out their being intrinsic dispositions. It leaves the door open for their being extrinsic dispositions, but also for their being powers only in the degenerate sense.

Another piece of evidence is IV.vi.11, where Locke makes the point that many of the salient features of bodies actually depend upon "*external, remote, and unperceived Causes.*"[54] He illustrates that point this way:

Put a piece of *Gold* any where by it self, separate from the reach and influence of all other bodies, it will immediately lose all its Colour and Weight, and perhaps Malleableness too; which, for ought I know, would be changed into a perfect Friability. *Water*, in which to us *Fluidity* is an essential Quality, left to it self, would cease to be fluid.

It seems plausible that Locke would count malleableness and fluidity as passive powers, and as secondary qualities mediately perceivable. For a body to be malleable is for it to be susceptible to being acted upon by other bodies in ways that would make for observable changes in it. The fluidity of water Locke seems to think of as a matter of "the Particles of *Water* [being] so perfectly loose one from another, that the least force sensibly separates them" (II.xxiii.26). This too would seem to be a susceptibility to being acted upon in ways that would make for observable changes. If Locke is thinking that water loses its fluidity when there is nothing that could splash into it or push through it, this would explain what is otherwise a quite puzzling remark. However, his remark about malleableness remains a puzzle. For though he suggests that gold may lose its malleableness when it is causally isolated, he does this by suggesting that it may become friable instead. To be friable is to be brittle or crumbly, which would seem to be just another sort of susceptibility to being acted upon in ways making for observable changes.

Even if Locke does take secondary qualities mediately perceivable to be degenerate powers, we should not ascribe to him the view that *all* powers are degenerate powers. We can see this by looking ahead to his view about what is required for agents to be free (§58). Locke holds that an agent is free with respect to φ-ing only if φ-ing and not-φ-ing are both equally in his power (II.xxi.8). Suppose that he were to think that an agent has the power to φ only when he is actually φ-ing. In that case, the agent could not simultaneously have both the power to φ and the power to not-φ. This would mean that by Locke's lights no agent ever acts freely. Yet he clearly holds that we do sometimes act freely. So he is not thinking of the powers that agents have to act as powers only in the degenerate sense.

---

[54] Marginal heading for IV.vi.11–12.

4

Essence

§20. Locke draws a distinction between real and nominal essences. A real essence is the inner constitution responsible for a thing's observable features; a nominal essence is an abstract idea associated with a general term. Locke distinguishes two opinions about real essences: one shared by scholastic defenders of substantial forms, the other a corpuscularian conception that he favors. §21. Locke himself uses 'real essence' in two senses: as standing for the totality of a thing's inner constitution, and in a nominal-essence-relative sense on which it refers to the part or aspect of a thing's inner constitution that is responsible for the thing's having certain observable features. It is sometimes unclear whether he is thinking of real essences as features or things, and sometimes it does matter which he has in mind. §22. Locke defends two theses about the boundaries between species. At times he defends the relatively bold thesis that nature does not divide things into kinds, and that only people can do that. His more modest, fall-back position is that even if nature did divide things into kinds, our kind terms reflect boundaries that we have drawn, rather than ones copied from nature. §23. Locke emphatically rejects essentialism, the doctrine that individuals have some features necessarily and others contingently, independent of anyone's linguistic or conceptual activity. This does not mean that he embraces accidentalism, the view that every feature of every thing is one that it could exist without. §24. Locke thinks that the individuals answering to a nominal essence are likely to share a relative real essence, though for all he says the shared features may be very general ones. §25. Locke thinks that we can and should try to improve upon the nominal essences that we have made. Nominal essences are better when they group together individuals that are more likely to have similar internal constitutions, and so more likely to share as-yet-undiscovered observable features.

§20 *Real and Nominal Essences*

Metaphysicians invoke the notion of essence for a number of different purposes. The essence of a thing is supposed to explain why the thing has the salient features it does, and what sort of a thing it is. If one knows the essence of a thing, one is supposed to be able to discriminate between the thing's necessary features and its contingent ones. Acquaintance with the essence of a thing is supposed to enable one to answer questions about its individuation at a moment, and its identity over time. Locke's discussions of essence touch on all of these roles. Perhaps the most distinctive feature of his account is that he distinguishes several different notions of essence, and distributes some of these traditionally recognized functions among them. It is at III.iii.15 that he undertakes to "consider the *several significations of the Word Essence.*" First, he says:

Essence may be taken for the very being of any thing, whereby it is, what it is. And thus the real internal, but generally in Substances, unknown Constitution of Things, whereon their discoverable Qualities depend, may be called their *Essence.*

Locke claims that this is the original sense of the word 'essence,' and he points to the fact that our English term derives from '*essentia*,' a Latin word for "being." That Latin word was invented by Aristotle's Roman translators to render some curious but important phrases in his writings (Cohen 2009). Aristotle spoke of the "what it was to be" of a thing, and of the "what it is" of a thing. Locke's definition of essence as the "very being of any thing, whereby it is, what it is" reaches back to these phrases in Aristotle.

How Locke understands his own definition of 'essence' is something that we can begin to see by considering his candidates for the things that satisfy it. We get a glimpse of this in the second sentence of the passage quoted above, but that glimpse may be somewhat misleading. He seems to say that essences in this sense are real, internal constitutions responsible for the discoverable qualities of things, and that in the case of substances these are generally unknown. Yet he will later apply the notion of real essence not only to corporeal substances, but to spirits, simple ideas, and mixed modes. Could he be invoking a broad notion of "internal constitution" that is supposed to apply not only to bodies but to such things as the idea of redness, beauty, and a military parade? More likely he is already narrowing his focus to the case of substances, and to corporeal substances in particular. It would be distinctly odd to speak of the real, internal constitutions of simple ideas, events, and complex features. We do not find Locke talking that way elsewhere in the *Essay*. Spirits presumably have something whereby they are what they are, something that explains or gives rise to their discoverable qualities. It might not be too much of a stretch to call that something the mind's "internal constitution," but Locke is little inclined to theorize about such things.

The second sense of 'essence' that Locke distinguishes at III.iii.15 is the one that he says has come to be the more familiar sense of the term. He introduces it this way:

> But it being evident, that Things are ranked under Names into sorts or *Species*, only as they agree to certain abstract *Ideas*, to which we have annexed those Names, the *Essence* of each *Genus*, or Sort, comes to be nothing but that abstract *Idea*, which the General, or *Sortal* (if I may have leave so to call it from *Sort*, as I do *General* from *Genus*,) Name stands for.

This passage makes at least two things clear. First, essence in this sense has to do with sorting and classification. Just before the quoted passage, Locke explains that this second sense of 'essence' has come to predominate over the original one because the "Learning and Disputes of the Schools [have] been much busied about *Genus* and *Species*." Second, Locke identifies essences in this sense with abstract ideas that are associated with general terms.

Jonathan Bennett has suggested that Locke does not really mean to identify essences in this second sense with *ideas*, but rather with the features represented by those ideas (Bennett 2001, vol. 2, 98). Bennett's proposal would locate these essences where philosophers have traditionally located essences: in the things whose essences they are. He reads the passage above as another instance of Locke's tendency to conflate ideas and qualities. Locke does have that foible, but Bennett's reading cannot stand. Locke is remarkably consistent about identifying essences in this sense with abstract ideas. He does so whether he is talking about the essences of substances, of mixed modes, or of simple ideas. To identify the sort of essences involved in classification with something *in us*, rather than in the objects whose essences they are, is a surprising move. Yet Locke makes this move self-consciously, and offers it as a philosophical innovation, an improvement upon the tradition he inherits. He is, as he explains later, using scholastic terminology for his own ends, and doing so because he thinks that the traditional concepts of essence and species cannot account for our possession of even the limited knowledge that he thinks we do have about the sorts of things there are (IV.vi.4).

At the end of III.iii.15, Locke gives names to the two senses of 'essence' that he has distinguished: "These two sorts of *Essences*, I suppose, may not unfitly be termed, the one the *Real*, the other the *Nominal Essence*." Let us start with nominal essences. These are ideas that constitute the meanings of general terms. Locke offers three reasons why language must have general terms if it is to serve our purposes. First, communication would be impossibly cumbersome if we could only refer to the birds in a flock, or the leaves on a tree, by employing proper names for each of them. Even if we could invent all the names we needed, we could not remember them (III.iii.2). Second, a language in which the only names were proper names would enable us to communicate only with people who had seen the same particular things we had, and only about those particular things (III.iii.3). Third, a language without general terms would be of little use in expanding our knowledge, which "though founded in particular Things, enlarges it self by general Views" (III.iii.4).

On Locke's view, the reference of a word is determined by the idea for which it stands. A general term is able to refer to more than one thing because it stands for an abstract idea. An abstract idea is itself just another particular, but one that is the product of abstraction. This is a mental operation that takes as its input the rich, fully detailed idea of some particular thing. The mind removes some of the constituents of that idea, or selectively attends to others, and this yields an idea that is not fully detailed (II.xi.9; III.iii.6–9). Often, the input is the idea of a thing that we have observed to be similar in some respects to one or more other things, and the output is an idea that represents just those features the things had in common. Such an idea, when married with a name, becomes a nominal essence. It is an idea to which more than one thing in the world might answer (III.vi.1), but it is not just the idea of the particulars whose similarities might have spurred us to make it.[1] It serves to distinguish those things, and perhaps indefinitely

---

[1] Locke seems not to have considered that if all it takes for an idea to be abstract is the bare possibility that more than one thing answers to it, this threatens to make every idea abstract. Let one's idea of some thing be as rich in detail as you like, and it is at least conceivable that there could be two things in the world answering to that idea. One response would be to say that a non-abstract idea is one that includes the representation of causal or historical features unique to a single thing. However, this would be difficult to reconcile with Locke's evident assumption that at least sometimes it is just the observable features of individuals that (together with the idea of substance in general) enter into our ideas of them. A better Lockean response would be to say that what makes an idea abstract is just that it is the product of abstraction. To say this is to concede that an abstract idea and a non-abstract idea could be intrinsically just alike. However, that is something that Locke must say anyway, since he holds that simple ideas are originally delivered to us by experience, and that they can also be arrived at by abstraction.

many others, as the members of a kind or species. On Locke's view, as we shall see, this is something that only a nominal essence can do.

The nominal essences that will most concern us are ideas of kinds of corporeal substances, ideas such as those associated with the names 'man,' 'gold,' and 'swan.' Locke holds that each of these is a complex idea whose constituents include (i) ideas of observable qualities that have been found to co-occur regularly, and (ii) the vexed idea of the substance or substratum in which those qualities are supposed to inhere. We shall have much more to say about (ii) in Chapter 5. As for (i), Locke thinks that these include ideas of primary qualities, and of both sorts of secondary qualities (II.xxiii.9). He sometimes speaks of *the* nominal essence of a kind such as gold (IV.vi.9) or man (IV.vi.15). Yet he is also committed to the view that each speaker's words can stand only for ideas in his own mind, and this only when he voluntarily makes them the signs of those ideas (III.ii.2). This means that we can talk about the nominal essence of a kind as a public possession only to the extent that various speakers associate the same idea with the name of that kind. In fact, Locke thinks that it is often the case that different people associate somewhat different ideas with the same general term (III.vi.26, 30, 31, 48). How much trouble this causes depends upon the context in which language is being used, and the demands that are being placed upon it. Locke distinguishes between the civil and the philosophical uses of language, and sees the latter as requiring a greater degree of exactness (III.ix.3–4). He thinks that there is enough overlap in the ideas that we associate with general terms to serve our everyday purposes in communicating with one another. Greater difficulties arise when we employ them in the course of philosophical or scientific research (III.ix.15; III.xi.10). How, and how far, we might overcome these difficulties are questions that we will take up below.

Usually when Locke speaks of the nominal essence *of* something, he is speaking of the nominal essence of a kind. That is to say, he is speaking of the abstract idea that defines that kind. However, he does also sometimes speak of the nominal essence of an individual thing—that of a particular parcel of matter for example (III.iii.18), or a sun (*Works* IV, 84). In such cases, he is speaking of the abstract idea to which that individual thing conforms. Again, we must not be misled by talk of *the* nominal essence of an individual. There will always be a great many abstract ideas to which any individual conforms. This is because each individual has a great many qualities, and for any subset of these one can fashion the abstract idea of a thing having the qualities belonging to that subset. An illustration can be found in Locke's account of how we make ideas of genera by leaving out constituents of richer ideas of lower species. He describes how one might make the idea "animal" by removing some of the constituents from one's idea "man"; and how, by further iterations, one might arrive at successively more general ideas: "*Vivens*," "*Body*," "*Substance*," and at last "*Being*" or "*Thing*" (III.iii.9). Each of these is a nominal essence to which each individual man conforms.

After introducing the distinction between real and nominal essence, Locke goes on to distinguish two opinions about the real essences of bodies:

> Concerning the real Essences of corporeal Substances, (to mention those only,) there are, if I mistake not, two Opinions. The one is of those, who using the Word *Essence*, for they know not what, suppose a certain number of those Essences, according to which, all natural things are made, and wherein they do exactly every one of them partake, and so become of this or that *Species*. The other, and more rational Opinion, is of those, who look on all natural Things to have a real, but unknown Constitution of their insensible Parts, from which flow those sensible Qualities, which serve us to distinguish them one from another, according as we have Occasion to rank them into Sorts, under common Denominations. (III.iii.17)

It can be a little hard to see what are supposed to be all of the points of difference separating those who hold these two opinions. Locke initially characterizes real essences—or at any rate, the real essences of bodies—as real, inner constitutions responsible for things' discoverable qualities. Here he is supposed to be describing two opinions about essences in that sense. So the fact that the second opinion involves the belief that natural things have real constitutions from which their sensible qualities flow is presumably not what is supposed to distinguish the second opinion from the first. On the other hand, it may well be that Locke means to allow that those who hold the two opinions use 'constitution' differently when they describe real essences as constitutions. Locke says that according to the second opinion the real essences of bodies are constitutions of their insensible *parts*. This seems to commit the holder of the second opinion to conceiving of real essences either as material things or as arrangements of material things. The holder of the first opinion need not have that commitment.

There are at least three claims that are made by those who hold the first opinion about real essences, and not by those who hold the second. The first is that there is a "certain number" of real essences, a "certain number of Forms or Molds, wherein all natural Things, that exist, are cast" (III.iii.17). That is to say, there is some fixed number of real essences to be found in nature. We may not know what that number is, but it does not change because of how we conceive things or name them. The second claim is that individuals partake in these real essences exactly. By this Locke means that whether or not an individual has such a real essence is an all-or-nothing affair. He makes this clear when he observes that "[t]he frequent Productions of Monsters, in all the Species of Animals, and of Changelings, and other strange Issues of humane Birth, carry with them difficulties, not possible to consist with this *Hypothesis*" (III.iii.17). The third claim is that partaking in a real essence suffices to make an individual belong to a species. Since it is supposed to be nature that fixes a certain number of real essences, this means that the existence of species is determined by nature, and not by us.

It is the scholastic doctrine of substantial forms that Locke seems to have uppermost in mind as he describes this first opinion about real essence. This is suggested by the work that essences do on the first opinion, by Locke's reference to "Forms or Molds" in III.iii.17, and by the fact that substantial forms are a primary target in his later discussions of species and classification (III.vi.10, 24–25, 33). The theory of substantial forms, which had its roots in Aristotle's physics, was widely embraced throughout the scholastic era, though it received its fullest defense only in the sixteenth century, when it began to be challenged (Pasnau 2011, 551–2). There were disagreements among the scholastics about the number of substantial forms each substance could have (Pasnau 2011, 574–96), and about our knowledge of them (Pasnau 2011, 124–34), but there was widespread agreement that there is a close connection between a thing's substantial form(s) and its essence. A thing's substantial form was thought to complement or actualize its matter, thus "completing" its essence, and making the thing a composite substance of a particular kind (Pasnau 2011, 551–2). Substantial forms were invoked to explain a substance's species membership, its diachronic identity conditions, and the possibility that its matter might later constitute a different substance (Pasnau 2011, 554–5).

In the seventeenth century, the doctrine of substantial forms was under attack from many quarters. Some largely forgotten critics of the doctrine in the early decades of the century include Sebastian Basso, William Premble, Joachim Jungius, and Gerard and Arnold Boate (Pasnau 2011, 565–6). Better known enemies of substantial forms include Descartes, Malebranche, and

Hobbes, as well as Boyle and Locke. Descartes contents himself with saying that he did not need to invoke substantial forms in his explanations of natural phenomena, though as he explains in a letter to Regius, "in such matters, saying that one does not wish to make use of these entities is almost the same as saying one will not accept them" (CSMK, 207). Malebranche takes a more direct approach, declaring that substantial forms exist "only in the imagination," and diagnosing the belief in them as a result of the mistake of projecting our sensations on to physical objects (Malebranche 1980a, 74). Hobbes sees the doctrine of substantial forms as positively dangerous, and wishes that "men may no longer suffer themselves to be abused, by them, that by this doctrine of *Separated Essences*, built on the Vain Philosophy of Aristotle, would fright them from Obeying the Laws of their Countrey" (Hobbes 1991, 465). Boyle makes substantial forms the target of a sustained critique in his *Origin of Forms and Qualities* (Boyle 1991, 53–72). He responds to many of the "plausiblest" arguments in favor of them; his chief argument against them is that he finds the whole doctrine unintelligible (Boyle 1991, 55). When Locke disdains the first opinion about real essence, he is adding his voice to a large chorus of those who repudiate the scholastics' substantial forms.

Several commentators have pointed out that there could be corpuscularian versions of the first opinion, for all Locke has said (Bennett 2001, vol. 2, 94; Conn 2003, 38). Perhaps there could be, but these might have to combine contingent claims about corpuscular structures with one or more *a priori* claims about essences and species. It is a feature of the "first opinion" that bodies are supposed to "become of this or that *Species*" (III.iii.17) by partaking in the essences according to which natural things are supposed to be made, and Locke at least does not think that bodies come to belong to species solely by virtue of having certain corpuscular structures.

§21 *Relative and Total Real Essences*

Locke aligns himself with the second of the two opinions about real essences. Yet as other commentators have noted, he himself uses 'real essence' in two different senses, at least when speaking of corporeal substances (Phemister 1990; Owen 1991; Conn 2003; Kaufman 2007). Sometimes, he uses 'real essence' to refer to a constitution that is supposed to be responsible for a particular subset of a body's observable qualities, namely those qualities the ideas of which are constituents of a nominal essence to which the body answers. This is clearest at III.vi.6:

> By this *real Essence*, I mean, that real constitution of any Thing, which is the foundation of all of those Properties, that are combined in, and are constantly found to co-exist with the *nominal Essence*; that particular constitution, which every Thing has within it self, without any relation to any thing without it. But *Essence*, even in this sense, *relates to a Sort*, and supposes a *Species*: For being that real Constitution, on which the Properties depend, it necessarily supposes a sort of Things, Properties belonging only to *Species*, and not to Individuals; *v.g.* Supposing the nominal Essence of *Gold*, to be Body of such a peculiar Colour and Weight, with Malleability and Fusibility, the real Essence is that Constitution of the parts of Matter, on which these Qualities, and their Union, depend; and is also the foundation of its Solubility in *Aqua Regia*, and other Properties accompanying that complex *Idea*.

Here we have a sense of 'real essence' on which the real essence of a body is, in a certain respect, relative to its nominal essence. In just what sense real essence is relative to nominal essence is a matter that we will take up shortly.[2]

A number of scholars claim that Locke always uses 'real essence' in the sense explicated at III.vi.6 (Ayers 1991, vol. 2, 67–8, 70; Guyer 1994, 133). Some add that he speaks of the 'internal constitution' (or 'real constitution') of a body when he wants to refer not to a nominal-essence-relative aspect or part of its constitution, but to the totality of its constitution (Guyer 1994, 133). On this reading, a body's real essence is a part or aspect of its internal (or real) constitution. Its real essence is involved in producing a subset of its observable qualities, whereas its internal (or real) constitution is involved in producing all of them.

Yet other scholars have shown that Locke sometimes uses 'real essence' to refer to the constitution responsible for *all* of a body's discoverable qualities (Owen 1991, 106–8; Conn 2003, 31; Kaufman 2007, 514–16). They point to the very passage in which he introduces the notion of real essence. At III.iii.15, Locke says that the sort of essence that is not unfitly termed "real essence" is the real, internal constitution of things "whereon their discoverable Qualities depend." He says that their *discoverable* qualities depend upon

---

[2] Notice that III.vi.6 is one of the places where we find Locke speaking of *the* nominal essence of something. How many nominal essences a "Thing" has will depend on, among other things, the sort of thing it is. If the "Thing" is an individual (a "parcel of Matter"), there could be as many nominal essences as there are subsets of its observable qualities. If the "Thing" is a kind, then it makes sense to speak of its nominal essence only if we mean the nominal essence that defines the kind it is. In that case, there can strictly speaking be just one nominal essence for each kind. However, we can speak somewhat loosely of their being different nominal essences of gold, if we mean by this different abstract ideas that speakers associate with the word 'gold.'

this sort of essence, not just that certain of their *discovered* qualities do. He then goes on to observe that this is the sense of 'essence' we employ "when we speak of the *Essence* of particular things, without giving them any Name." For Locke, to speak of a particular without giving it a (general) name is to speak of it without ranking it under a nominal essence. So in this passage he is elucidating a sense of 'essence' that he calls "real essence" and that bodies are meant to possess independently of their being ranked under any general term—that is, independently of their relation to any nominal essence. Further evidence that Locke allows for a sense of 'real essence' meaning the totality of a thing's internal constitution is that he frequently treats "real essence" and "internal constitution" as equivalent expressions (II.xxxi.6, 9; III.vi.43; *Works* IV, 84, 91). It is uncontroversial that he regards a body's internal constitution as involved in the production of all of its observable qualities.

So Locke sometimes uses 'real essence' in a sense that is meant to be nominal-essence-relative, and sometimes in a sense that is meant to be nominal-essence-independent. From this point forward, let us use the phrase 'relative real essence' as shorthand for "real essence in the nominal-essence-relative sense," and 'total real essence' as shorthand for "real essence in the nominal-essence-independent sense."[3] This will make the exegesis less clumsy. Let us also pause for a moment to consider what it *is* about a relative real essence that is supposed to be relative to a nominal essence. For each body, there is the totality of its internal constitution, and this is involved in the production of all of its observable qualities. For every possible subset of a body's observable qualities, a nominal essence might be constructed, and for each possible nominal essence there is some part or aspect of the body's total internal constitution that is involved in the production of the observable qualities represented by that nominal essence. However, at any given time each body has *all* of the aspects or parts of its internal constitution that are involved in producing all of the possible subsets of the observable qualities it has then. So when we speak of relative real essences, we must not think that it is a body's *possession* of these real essences that is relative to

---

[3] Some commentators have phrased this distinction as one between the real essences of sorted particulars and the real essences of unsorted particulars (Owen 1991; Conn 2003). I fear that this is potentially misleading because it encourages the impression that we are talking about the real essences of different things. It encourages one to think that "sorted" particulars do not have the real essences that belong to "unsorted" particulars, and that "unsorted" particulars do not have the real essences that "sorted" particulars do.

a nominal essence. Framing an abstract idea and pairing it with a name does not generate a new real essence in any body. The introduction of a nominal essence merely supplies the criterion for distinguishing one existing relative real essence from another. I will consider an objection to this claim below, but first need to explore another distinction.

There is a systematic ambiguity in talk of a body's "internal constitution." One can use this phrase to refer to the body itself (a substance), considered from a certain point of view. On the most plausible way of spelling this out, an internal constitution would not be the inside parts of a body, but rather the whole of a body considered at a certain level of microphysical detail. One can also use the phrase 'internal constitution' to speak of one of a body's complex features (a mode). That is, one can use it to refer to the body's feature of having parts of certain descriptions arranged in certain ways. Again, this is most plausibly understood not as the body's feature of having interior parts of certain descriptions arranged in certain ways, but rather its feature of having all of its parts satisfy descriptions and stand in relations that are specified at a certain level of microphysical detail. To what ontological category—substance or mode—are the real essences of substances supposed to belong? It is not obvious. Locke says that a real essence is "the very being of any thing, whereby it is, what it is" (III.iii.15). To call a real essence "the very being of any thing" suggests that perhaps it is the thing itself (a substance). Yet to say that a real essence is that whereby the thing "is, what it is" suggests that it may be a feature that makes the thing what it is (a mode). We should be alive to the possibility that Locke speaks of real essences—both relative real essences and total real essences—in different ways at different times. It is easy, and generally harmless, to slide between talk of structures *qua* things and talk of structures *qua* features. However, there are contexts in which it does matter which sense one has in mind.

It matters whether the real essences of corporeal substances are things or features when we come to speak of *shared* real essences. If an internal constitution is a substance—a body considered from a certain point of view—then it makes no sense to speak of it as something that might be shared by another body. However, if an internal constitution is a complex feature involving the arrangement of a thing's parts, then it does make sense to speak of the possibility that other bodies share it.[4] So far as I know, Locke does not consider

---

⁴ Of course, since Locke is committed to the thesis that everything that exists is a particular, he must say that the sharing of features is not a matter of an abstract entity being wholly present at two different places, but of two things being similar in certain respects.

the question of shared total real essences. For two bodies to share a total real essence would be for them to be atom-for-atom copies of one another, or something approaching that. Though Locke does not broach the question, this has not kept scholars from trying to answer it on his behalf. Pauline Phemister, who calls total real essences "individual" real essences, argues that he leaves open the possibility of shared individual real essences, and that his atomism may commit him to this possibility (Phemister 1990, 48–50). On the other hand, Kenneth Winkler says of the real essences described at III.iii.15 that each is "an absolutely private possession, no less unique and unrepeatable than the individual possessing it" (Winkler, forthcoming). I suggest that Phemister is silently thinking of real essences as features, and that Winkler is thinking of them as things.[5] If that is right, there is a sense in which they might both be right (though as I have said, whether Locke is speaking of constitutions *as things* at III.iii.15 seems to me uncertain). Of much greater moment than the possibility of shared total real essences is the possibility of shared relative real essences. Locke's attitude toward this is something that we will consider in detail in §24. Here it will suffice to make the point that if shared relative real essences are even to be a possibility, then these too must be modes rather than substances, features rather than things.

Another context in which it matters whether we conceive of real essences as features or as things concerns the relation between relative real essences and total real essences. If total and relative real essences are things, there are likely to be cases in which the relative real essence of a body *is* its total real essence. On the other hand, if either sort of real essence is a feature, then that sort of identification will be unlikely or impossible. To see this, let us start with Winkler's apparent supposition that the real essences described at III.iii.15 are things. For the moment, let us also suppose that the relative real essences of bodies are things. In that case, relative real essences will be physical parts of total real essences, and the different relative real essences of a body may be different-sized parts of it. Suppose that B is a body that is yellow, malleable, soluble in *Aqua Regia*, ring-shaped, dense, and fusible. If Franny associates the abstract idea "yellow, ring-shaped thing" with some general term, then her idea is a nominal essence to which B answers, and

[5] That Winkler is thinking of total real essences as things is further suggested by this remark about real essence in the sense described at III.iii.15: "It might even be viewed *as* the thing itself, but it is the thing in what might be called its active aspect: the thing considered as a generator of everything that makes it what it is" (Winkler, forthcoming).

one that specifies a relative real essence of B. That real essence will consist in the parts of B that are causally responsible for B's being yellow and ring-shaped. It is arguable that these will be parts limited to B's outer surface. (At least, they will be if B is made out of the sort of material that could hold its shape even if it had a hollow core.) So on this scenario, the real essence specified by Franny's idea is a proper part of B's total real essence. Along comes Pearl, and she associates a general term with the abstract idea "yellow, malleable thing that is soluble in *Aqua Regia*." This too is an idea to which B answers, and it specifies a different relative real essence of B. However, in this case it seems much less likely that the real essence specified will be just a proper part of B. We cannot localize the parts of a body that are causally responsible for its being malleable and soluble in *Aqua Regia* as we can localize the parts of it that are responsible for its being yellow and ring-shaped. Pearl's abstract idea may well define a relative real essence of B that is *identical* to B's total real essence.

What happens if we suppose that relative real essences are features rather than things? In that case, there can be no question of any of B's relative real essences being identical to its total real essence. For we are supposing that B's total real essence is B itself, and those relative real essences are features of B.

Now suppose that instead we follow Phemister, and take the total real essence of a body to be a complex feature of it. In that case, if relative real essences are things, then some of the relative real essences of B (perhaps including the one specified by Pearl's idea) will be identical to B, but none will be identical to the total real essence of B. What if relative real essences are features? On this supposition, it seems unlikely that any of B's relative real essences will be identical to its total real essence, but it is hard to be sure. The relative real essence specified by Franny's idea will be the conjunction of those features of B's microstructure responsible for B's color and shape, whereas the total real essence of B will be a complex feature of it having to do with the arrangement of all of its parts. Since we are sure that there could be a number of yellow, ring-shaped things with different chemical or physical properties, we can be sure that the relative real essence specified by Franny's idea is not the same feature as B's total real essence. Taking both relative and total real essences to be features, a relative real essence of B will be identical to the total real essence of B just in case there is some collection of observable properties such that B possesses all of those properties and only an atom-for-atom copy of B *could* possess all of those properties.

It seems highly unlikely that there could be such a collection of observable properties; to be certain that there could not, one would have to know a good deal of physics and chemistry.

Earlier I suggested that we do not bring any new relative real essences into being when we fashion abstract ideas and associate general terms with them. A new nominal essence gives us a way of specifying and referring to a relative real essence whose existence or non-existence is independent of our linguistic and conceptual activity. Now we can see that, if we take relative real essences to be features, there is room for another view of the matter. One might say that for a body to have a relative real essence is for it to have a certain extrinsic feature. One might say that for a body to have a relative real essence is for it to (i) have microphysical features that give rise to certain observable features, and (ii) thereby conform to an abstract idea that somebody associates with a general term. This is to conceive of a relative real essence as something that a body has partly because of its relation to a nominal essence to which it answers. However, there is reason to think that this is not Locke's view. Recall III.vi.6, where he spells out the notion of real essence that we are calling relative real essence. There he says that the real essence of a thing is that constitution "which every Thing has within it self, without any relation to any thing without it." This seems to mean that a relative real essence is an intrinsic feature of the thing whose essence it is. This might be puzzling, since we have also seen that this is the section in which Locke explains that "*Essence*, even in this sense, *relates to a Sort*, and supposes a *Species*." We saw earlier that for a real essence to suppose a species is for it necessarily to stand in some relation to a nominal essence. How can he say both that a body's real essence necessarily stands in some relation to a nominal essence, *and* that it is something that a body has without relation to anything else? He can do this because his view is that a body's relative real essences *exist* independently of its relations to anything else, though picking one out and distinguishing it from the others is something that we do only by considering the body in relation to a nominal essence.

§22 *Workmanship of the Understanding*

Toward the end of a long chapter about the names of substances, Locke draws the conclusion that "[f]rom what has been said, 'tis evident, that *Men make sorts of Things*" (III.vi.35). This is not an observation about the production of artifacts. He does not mean that men make things that belong to sorts. He means that there *are* sorts or species only because of our conceptual and linguistic activity. This claim comes in the course of a wide-ranging discussion about the semantics of general terms, the distinction between essence and accident, the epistemic constraints we encounter in classifying natural and artificial things, and the resulting imperfections in the nominal essences we put together. In the course of this discussion, Locke advances a number of theses about sorts or species, and these are not always clearly distinguished from one another. Several of them take the form of a claim that something or other is made by the mind, or is the "Workmanship of the Understanding." He makes such claims about specific essences (III.vi.25), nominal essences (III.vi.26–28), the boundaries of species (III.vi.30, 37) and the sorting of things under names (III.vi.37). Elsewhere, he adds abstract ideas (III.iii.14; IV.xii.3) and the essences of sorts (III.iii.12) to the list of things that are the workmanship of the understanding. To unravel all of this—to see how these claims are related, and what are his arguments for each—is to do some sorting ourselves.

Earlier in that same chapter, after reminding us of the distinction between real and nominal essences (III.vi.6), Locke considers "by which of those Essences it is, that *Substances are determined into* Sorts, or *Species*" (III.vi.7). His answer is that we determine substances into sorts by nominal essences. The justification he offers is that we determine things into sorts by ranking them under general names, and nominal essences are the only things we signify by general names. There are two points to take note of here. One is that when Locke says that it is the nominal essence alone that a general term "signifies," he does not mean to deny that general terms refer to things in the world. On his view, ideas in the mind of a speaker are all that his words signify primarily and immediately (III.ii.2); still, the names of substances are "not put barely for our *Ideas*, but [are] made use of ultimately to represent Things" (III.xi.24).

The second thing to notice about III.vi.7 is that Locke is not there offering an argument to show that there cannot be sorts or species independent of our sorting and classifying. What we find there is just an argument to show that when *we* rank things into sorts and species, we do so by means of the nominal essences that we make. Let us call this the modest workmanship thesis. It is modest insofar as it concerns only the sorting that we do, and not whether nature makes species. In III.vi, it often seems to be the modest workmanship thesis that Locke is chiefly interested in securing. It is "the *Species of Things to us*" that he says "*are nothing but the ranking them under distinct Names*" (III.vi.8).[6] It is "our *ranking*, and distinguishing natural *Substances into Species*" that is done by nominal essences (III.vi.11), "our *distinguishing Substances into Species*" that is not founded on real essences (III.vi.20). It is "*the boundaries of the Species, whereby Men sort them*" that are made by men (III.vi.37).

Locke thinks that we sort substances by their nominal essences, and these nominal essences are "*made by the Mind*" (III.vi.26). A nominal essence is just an abstract idea associated with a general term. Nominal essences are the workmanship of the understanding because we make the abstract ideas, and we are the ones who associate them with general terms. At this point in the proceedings, Locke does not need to offer new support for these last two claims. He has already argued that words are voluntary signs, and that we cannot make them the signs of things we do not know (III.ii.2). He has already argued that none of our ideas is innate (I.iv), and that we make all of the complex ideas we have out of simple ones received by sensation and reflection (II.ii.1; II.xii.1). He has already given an account of the operation by which we make abstract ideas (II.xi.9; III.iii.6–9).

There are other times when Locke makes a bolder claim. These are times when he says not just that the categories that *we* use to sort things are devised by us, but that sorts themselves, or the essences of sorts, are the workmanship of the understanding. Let us call this the bold workmanship thesis. At III.vi.30, he says that it is evident that men make the sorts of things, though he immediately makes it clear that he is prepared to fall back on the modest thesis if need be:

[T]hese Boundaries of *Species*, are as Men, and not as Nature makes them, if at least there are in Nature any such prefixed Bounds. 'Tis true, that many particular Substances are so made by Nature, that they have agreement and likeness one with another, and so afford a Foundation of being ranked into sorts. But the sorting of Things by us, or the making of determinate *Species*, being in order to naming and comprehending them under general terms, I cannot see how it can be properly said, that Nature sets the Boundaries of the *Species* of Things: Or if it be so, our Boundaries of *Species*, are not exactly conformable to those in Nature.

Locke puts forward the bolder claim again III.vi.35, where he says that "[f]rom what has been said, 'tis evident, that *Men make sorts of Things*." Yet

---

[6] Here and in the rest of this paragraph, the italicization is mine, and is added for emphasis.

further on we find him finessing the issue again. At III.vi.39, he speaks of "how much general Names are necessary, if not to the Being, yet at least to the completing of a *Species*, and making it pass for such."

The position set forth in these passages is a bit slippery, but there is no need to say that it involves any waffling on Locke's part. He says (i) that we make species, (ii) that he cannot imagine how nature could make species, and (iii) that even if nature did make species, there is no reason to think that the categories that we use to classify things map neatly on to the divisions between species as nature makes them. It is because of the fact expressed by (ii) that he holds (i). That is, because he is unable to see how nature could set the boundaries of species, he concludes that setting those boundaries is something that we do. The fact that (ii) is his reason for holding (i) explains his tentativeness about (i). For to be unable to see how nature could set the boundaries of species is not the same as seeing that nature *cannot* set the boundaries between species. Finally, it is because his commitment to (i) is somewhat provisional that he offers claim (iii). If it should turn out that he has overreached with his bold workmanship thesis, he wants to be able to fall back upon the modest workmanship thesis.

When Locke argues for his workmanship theses, he repeatedly contrasts his position with the view that real essences make species (III.vi.9–10, 24, 33). To the extent that the doctrine of substantial forms is his target here, we can see his modest workmanship thesis and his bold workmanship thesis as directed at different scholastic positions. All of the scholastics held that substantial forms determine the species to which substances belong, but some— including Scotus, Ockham, and Francis of Marchia—were pessimistic about our ability to know these forms or essences (Pasnau 2011, 124–9, 635). Boyle notes that the "more candid of the Peripatetics generally do" acknowledge that "the true knowledge of forms is too difficult and abstruse to be attained by them" (Boyle 1991, 54). Some of these skeptical Aristotelians went on to raise the natural worry that the classificatory schemes we actually use might not be correct (Pasnau 2011, 635 n1). Locke's bold workmanship thesis runs counter to the doctrine of substantial forms itself, so it can be seen as directed against all of the scholastics. His modest workmanship thesis can be seen as directed against just those scholastics who are optimistic about our ability to know the essences or forms of things, and so optimistic about our classificatory scheme getting it right.

Locke offers at least three arguments in support of the modest workmanship thesis. The first seems decisive by itself: we cannot sort substances by their real essences because "we know them not" (III.vi.9). A second points to the fact that ordinary folk, who are ignorant of real essences and substantial forms, often know more about sorts than do "those who have in this one part of the World, learned the Language of the Schools" (III.vi.24). Locke may be thinking of what farmers know about the different sorts of livestock, what cheese-mongers know about the different sorts of cheese, what builders know about different sorts of wood. His point is that our divisions of things into kinds are typically the product of practical expertise rather than theoretical expertise:

So that they have not been Philosophers, or Logicians, or such who have troubled themselves about *Forms* and *Essences*, that have made the general Names, that are in use amongst the several Nations of Men: But those, more or less comprehensive terms, have, for the most part, in all Languages, received their Birth and Signification, from ignorant and illiterate People, who sorted and denominated Things, by those sensible Qualities they found in them..." (III.vi.25).

Locke's third argument for the modest workmanship thesis is that the variability in people's views about the boundaries between species shows that our ideas of them are not copied from nature. He puts this somewhat misleadingly when he says that the variability shows that nominal essences "*are made by the Mind*, and not by Nature" (III.vi.26). Locke holds that *all* complex ideas are made by the mind. What he seems to be trying to say is that when we frame ideas of species, we lack an external standard that would ensure that we all draw the lines in the same places.

If Locke is to give us a reason for embracing his bold workmanship thesis, then he has got to explain what is the difficulty with supposing that nature makes species. He does not do this as directly as one might wish. In III.iii and III.vi, he makes a number of observations that speak to the issue; but they are scattered, and often appear side by side with claims offered in support of the weaker, fall-back position. However, it is possible to reconstruct a chain of reasoning from these materials. Locke's skepticism about the idea that nature makes species grows out of his reflection on what it means for there to be a sort or a species.

Locke says that for general terms to stand for sorts is for them to stand for ideas "wherein several particular Substances do, or might agree" (III.vi.1). He explains that he has chosen those words with care:

I say, do or might agree: for though there be but one Sun existing in the World, yet the *Idea* of it being abstracted, so that more Substances (if there were several) might each agree to it; it is as much a Sort, as if there were as many Suns, as there are Stars.

Thus "sun" is a sort or species, even if there is only one individual belonging to that sort. On the other hand, there could well be a million suns.[7] Not only can different sorts have different numbers of individuals belonging to them, but the membership of a sort can grow or shrink.[8]

If a sort can persist despite changes in its membership, then we must distinguish a sort from the collection of individuals who belong to it. Locke makes this point in giving his account of the meanings of general terms:

> The next thing therefore to be considered, is, *What kind of signification it is, that general Words have.* For as it is evident, that they do not signify barely one particular thing; for then they would not be general Terms, but proper Names: so on the other side, 'tis as evident, they do not signify a plurality; for Man and Men would then signify the same; and the distinction of numbers (as Grammarians call them) would be superfluous and useless. That then which general Words signify, is a sort of Things ... (III.iii.12)

Locke's view seems to be that 'Man' is a singular general term standing for a sort to which all men belong, and that 'Men' is a plural term standing for a collection of individuals. Perhaps the idea is that 'Men' serves as something like a proper name for the particular collection of men who exist at the moment the word is deployed. In that case, the referent of 'Men' changes as the population changes, though 'Man' continues to stand for the sort to which all of these different men belong.[9]

If we must distinguish a sort from the individuals that belong to it, then nature does not make a sort of things merely by making some individuals. This will be true however much the individuals resemble one another, true even if they were to share total real essences. For nature to make a sort, it has

---

[7] Locke might go so far as to say that the sort "sun" could exist even if there were *no* suns. He does say such things about sorts of mixed modes. If we frame the idea of adultery and associate a name with it before anybody has committed that act, then a species will be constituted "before any one individual of that Species ever existed" (III.v.5). On the other hand, Locke does think that our ideas of substances are focused on actually existing things in a way that ideas of mixed modes are not (§4), so it is possible that he would say a sort *of substances* exists only when there is at least one substance of that sort.

[8] Indeed, we may be tempted to say that it is a necessary feature of sorts that their memberships can grow and shrink, but that is too strong. There are sorts of mixed modes, and these will include mathematical sorts, whose memberships could not be other than they are. There may also be sorts of substances that must be unique. God may be a substance of that sort.

[9] Another possibility is that 'Men' stands for the collection of all of the men (or all of the people) there ever are. In either case, it is hard to see how Locke's semantic theory is going to accommodate the fact that 'Man' and 'Men' have different significations. To do that it would seem that they must stand for different ideas; yet if 'Men' does not stand for the abstract idea for which 'Man' stands, how is it that 'Men' manages to signify the plurality that it does? Presumably it cannot be that the speaker has in mind the idea of each and every particular man.

to do something besides producing a number of individuals that are similar in various respects. Indeed, it need not do that at all, since there can be a sort to which only one individual belongs, and perhaps even a sort to which nothing belongs. What nature must do if it is to make a sort is to somehow specify the requirements for membership in the sort. It must discriminate between the things that belong to the sort and those that do not, and do this not only with regard to existing things but also with regard to merely possible things. Locke does not see how nature could do that.

It is not only individual substances and modes that have essences. Locke often speaks of sorts or species as having essences.[10] His candidates for this role are the abstract ideas that we associate with general terms: "the *Essences of* the *sorts, or* (if the Latin word pleases better) *Species* of Things, are nothing else but these abstract *Ideas*" (III.iii.12). For there to be a species of thing is for us to frame an abstract idea to which something answers, and then to associate a general term with it:

The measure and boundary of each Sort, or *Species*, whereby it is constituted that particular Sort, and distinguished from others, is that we call its *Essence*, which *is* nothing but that *abstract* Idea *to which the Name is annexed*: So that every thing contained in that *Idea*, is essential to that Sort. (III.vi.2)

An abstract idea can supply the "measure and boundary" of a sort because some things answer to the idea and some do not. Since the real essence of a thing is what makes it the thing it is, and since an abstract idea associated with a general term is a nominal essence, it is not going too far to say that nominal essences are Locke's candidates for being the real essences of sorts.[11]

If we accept Locke's candidate for the essence of a sort, then we have accepted his bold thesis that sorts are the workmanship of the understanding. For his candidate is an abstract idea associated with a general term, and he has already argued that we make abstract ideas and associate them with general terms. One who would like to resist Locke's bold workmanship thesis must be prepared to offer an account of how sorts are constituted independently of human activity. Locke holds that no account that has real

---

[10] See II.xxxii.7; III.iii.12, 15, 17; III.v.1, 2, 9; III.vi.2, 4–5, 24, 27, 37, 40; III.viii.1.

[11] Here I agree with Winkler, though he worries that it is slightly misleading to say that nominal essences are the real essences of sorts, "because Locke works so strenuously to distinguish between the nominal essence of a species and the real essences of the individuals belonging to it" (Winkler, forthcoming).

essences or substantial forms playing that role can succeed. We have already seen his argument that nature does not make sorts merely by making individuals with similar constitutions. He thinks that the view that substantial forms makes for the species of things labors under a special difficulty. On the corpuscularian conception of real essences, we at least have some grasp of what real essences are supposed to be. Of substantial forms, he says, we have "scarce so much as any obscure, or confused Conception in general" (III.vi.10). As he complains in an earlier chapter, "when I am told, that something besides the Figure, Size, and Posture of the solid Parts of that Body, is its Essence, something called *substantial form*, of that, I confess, I have no *Idea* at all, but only of the sound *Form*." If we do not understand what is meant by 'substantial form,' it does little good to suggest that substantial forms are the essences of sorts.

Another possible approach might be to identify the essence of a sort not with a substantial form but with some sort of abstract object, something that is distinct from, but wholly present in, each of its various realizations. In that case, one could explain the difference between the (abstract) sort and the (concrete) things that belong to it. One could also say how the essence of the sort supplies the measure and boundary of the sort: an individual belongs to the sort whose essence is the abstract feature just in case the individual realizes that feature. Locke rejects this possibility too:

[I]t is plain, by what has been said, That *General and Universal*, belong not to the real existence of Things; but *are the Inventions and Creatures of the Understanding*, made by it for its own use, *and concern only Signs*, whether Words, or *Ideas* ... And *Ideas* are general, when they are set up, as the Representatives of many particular Things: but universality belongs not to things themselves, which are all of them particular in their Existence, even those Words, and *Ideas*, which in their signification, are general. When therefore we quit Particulars, the Generals that rest, are only Creatures of our own making ... (III.iii.11)

Locke repudiates abstract objects, and can think of nothing else but nominal essences that might serve to supply the measure and boundaries of sorts.

I have already acknowledged that Locke offers little support for his claim that only particulars exist (§2). In the passage from III.iii.11 quoted above, he suggests that this claim follows from "what has been said." Yet when we look at what has been said earlier in the chapter, there is little to persuade anyone who might be inclined toward realism about universals.

The chapter begins with Locke simply supposing that only particulars exist (III.iii.1). There follows his account of how abstract ideas and general terms are made. If the chapter did contain an argument against universals, we should expect to find it in III.iii.9, a section bearing the heading "*General Natures are nothing but abstract* Ideas." Yet the most we find there is Locke's suggestion that one who thinks that "general Natures or Notions" are something other than abstract and partial ideas "will, I fear, be at a loss where to find them." The rest of the section is occupied with giving further support for his account of abstraction as the formation of a partial conception of some larger complex idea.

§23 *Anti-Essentialism*

We have already seen that the notion of essence plays a major role in Locke's metaphysics. He distinguishes between real and nominal essences, and speaks of real essences in more than one sense. He invokes real essences to explain the conjunctions of observable qualities that we find in corporeal substances. Though he volunteers nothing about what might serve as the real essences of incorporeal substances, he seems equally committed to the idea that they too have essences that explain their salient features. Locke invokes nominal essences to explain the attributes of geometrical figures, and of complex properties and events of various sorts, and also to explain the existence of sorts themselves. Though he countenances much talk of essences, and even of the essential features of different kinds of substances and modes, Locke clearly and emphatically rejects essentialism. An essential feature is one that characterizes a thing necessarily, one that it could not have existed without and one that it could not survive the loss of. Essentialism is the view that the distinction between a thing's essential and accidental features is itself a real feature of the world, independent of how we happen to conceive of, or refer to, the thing. Locke holds instead that we can distinguish between a thing's essential and accidental features only so long as we are considering it in relation to some abstract idea that determines the boundaries of a kind. If we do this, and if the thing has the features represented by the idea, then the thing is properly said to belong to the kind, and the features may be termed essential features. However, the features are essential only to the thing's membership in the kind, and not to the thing itself. The notion of essence, on Locke's view, has "a reference, not so much to the being of particular Things, as to their general Denominations" (III.vi.8). He expresses this by saying that nothing is essential to individuals, but only to species.[12]

Locke offers us a deflationary account of the distinction between a thing's essential features and its accidental ones. On his account, this is merely the distinction between the features that are, and those that are not, included in some abstract idea in relation to which the thing is considered. There are many abstract ideas in relation to which any thing might be considered, and accordingly many possible divisions of each thing's qualities into the essential and the accidental. "[I]n truth," Locke says, "*every distinct abstract* Idea*, is a distinct* Essence*:* and the names that stand for such distinct *Ideas*, are the names of Things essentially different" (III.iii.14). If essentialism were true, then for each thing—or at least each thing that has an essence—there would be just one nominal essence that correctly drew the boundary between its essential and accidental features. Locke denies that any of the nominal essences to which any thing conforms is privileged in this manner. This is what makes his account of the distinction between essence and accident a deflationary one.

Starting at III.vi.4, Locke argues against essentialism by trying to show that his deflationary account of the distinction between essence and accident is the only account of that distinction that is intelligible. He seeks to show this by inviting us to perform certain feats of reflection. First, he asks us to see what happens when we consider a thing independently of its relations to any nominal essence. The result, he says, is that we find ourselves without any basis upon which to say that certain of the thing's features are essential and others not:

That *Essence*, in the ordinary use of the word, relates to *Sorts*, and that it is considered in particular Beings, no farther than as they are ranked into *Sorts*, appears from hence: That take but away the abstract *Ideas*, by which we sort Individuals, and rank them under common Names, and then the thought of any thing *essential* to any of them, instantly vanishes: we have no notion of the one, without the other: which plainly shews their relation.

Then Locke invites us to reflect on what happens when we think of a thing as having certain of its features essentially. If one does this, he says, one finds that there has come into one's mind the complex idea associated

---

[12] See Locke's index to the *Essay*, under the heading "ESSENTIAL, what" (p. 727), and also the marginal heading to III.vi.4–6.

with a general term, and furthermore that "'tis in reference to that, that this or that Quality is said to be *essential*." Finally, he says that if we consider a single thing in two different ways—first independently of its relation to any abstract idea, and then in relation to some particular abstract idea to which it conforms—we find we are able to toggle back and forth between the intuition that a certain one of its features is not essential to it, and the intuition that this same feature is essential to it. Consider Locke in isolation, and reason does not seem to be an essential property of him. Consider him as a man, and it does. Considered by itself, it does not seem essential to the white thing upon which he writes that it has words on it. Call it a treatise, and that does seem an essential feature of it.

At III.vi.5, Locke observes that his account does allow us to speak of features as essential to kinds. Yet this account also entails that which features are essential to a kind will be relative to the abstract idea one uses to define the kind. This means that when people associate different ideas with the same general term, they will in a certain sense quite properly come to different judgments about whether a feature is essential. He illustrates the point with the case of a disagreement over whether solidity belongs to the essence of body:

> Thus if the *Idea* of *Body*, with some People, be bare Extension, or Space, then Solidity is not *essential* to Body: If others make the *Idea*, to which they give the name *Body*, to be Solidity and Extension, then Solidity is essential to *Body*.

Locke thinks that our ordinary notion of body includes not just the idea of extension, but also that of solidity. At II.xiii.11–14, he offers several arguments for that conclusion. Yet here he makes the point that if one does use 'body' to stand just for the idea of an extended something, then in one's own idiolect it will be right to say that solidity is not essential to body. What looks like a disagreement between Locke and Descartes about the essential features of a kind is really just a verbal disagreement. Later on, Locke suggests that this verbal disagreement is also what underlies the dispute about whether a vacuum is possible: "He that with *Des-Cartes*, shall frame in his Mind an *Idea* of what he calls *Body*, to be nothing but Extension, may easily demonstrate, that there is no *Vacuum, i.e.* no Space void of Body" (IV.vii.12). Locke thinks that Descartes is wrong to deny the possibility of a vacuum (II.xiii.21–22), but that ultimately his error is that of altering the signification of words already in common use.

Locke's next move is to consider in what sense we might describe any-thing as lacking an essential feature. He notes that it makes no sense at all to say that any individual lacks any feature that is essential to *it*. If there is any sense to be made of an individual lacking an essential feature, this can only be a matter of its lacking some feature essential to membership in one or another sort. This is just lacking a feature included in the abstract idea that defines some sort. Locke imagines a parcel of matter that has all of the other qualities of iron except "Obedience to the Load-stone" (III.vi.5). Is the dif-ference between it and a piece of iron an "*essential*" difference? The question is unintelligible if we are merely considering the two items in relation to one another. It becomes intelligible only if we consider them in relation to some abstract idea, such as the one that we associate with 'iron':

For I would ask any one, What is sufficient to make an *essential* difference in Nature, between any two particular Beings, without any regard had to some abstract *Idea*, which is looked upon as the Essence and Standard of a *Species*? All such Patterns and Standards, being quite laid aside, particular Beings, considered barely in themselves, will be found to have all their Qualities equally *essential*; and every thing, in each Individual, will be *essential* to it, or, which is more true, nothing at all. (III.vi.5)

Christopher Conn says that this passage commits Locke to "accidentalism," the doctrine that every feature of each thing is accidental to it (Conn 2003, 28).[13] If every feature of each thing is accidental to it, then there is no feature of any thing that it could not exist without.

Another passage that might seem to commit Locke to accidentalism is this, from III.vi.4:

[A] 'Tis necessary for me to be as I am; GOD and Nature has made me so: [B] But there is nothing I have, is essential to me. [C] An Accident, or Disease, may very much alter my Colour, or Shape; a Fever, or Fall, may take away my Reason, or Memory, or both; and an Apoplexy leave neither Sense, nor Understanding, no nor Life.

In [A], Locke concedes that his features are necessary in one sense. He has been caused to have the features that he does have. In [C], he denies that his features are necessary in another sense. But in what sense? On one

---

[13] Following Benardete, Conn distinguishes this position from "relativistic anti-essentialism," accord-ing to which the distinction between essential and accidental features is always relative to a sort or description (Benardete 1989, 149). Conn takes relativistic anti-essentialism, and not accidentalism, to be Locke's "official position" (Conn 2003, 30).

reading, he is denying that any of his features is permanent. Just as God and nature have determined him to have each of the features that he does have, so God and nature could erase any of the features he has. Yet if that is all that Locke is saying, then [C] does not lend the kind of support for [B] that it evidently is meant to. An essentialist can happily concede that we are mutable and impermanent. An alternative is to see [C] as illustrating the point that none of Locke's features is such that he could not exist without it. This is accidentalism, and does entail that none of Locke's features is essential to him.

Jonathan Bennett also sees Locke as committed to accidentalism. Despite confessing some sympathy for accidentalism himself, Bennett exposes the view's more worrisome implications. He asks of an individual heron whether it could become a lizard, and whether it could have been a lizard from the beginning. He claims that Locke should answer yes to both questions (Bennett 2001, vol. 2, 92–3). Accidentalism implies that Locke could have existed without being extended, and even that the Eiffel Tower could have existed without being extended. If we grant that things have negative features as well as positive ones, then the view also implies that each thing that is not a grain of sand and not a plate of scrambled eggs could lose those features:

If Locke agrees that it is absolutely impossible that I—this very thing—should become a plate of eggs, or should have been one from the outset, then he is allowing a *de re* essence after all. It is negative, boringly trivial, absurd even to mention, but it looks like a breach in the wall: it stops Locke from saying that no properties of a thing are essential to it *de re*, which should start us discussing which properties are and which are not essential to this or that thing. (Bennett 2001, vol. 2, 93)

The upshot of Bennett's reasoning would seem to be that if Locke is to reject essentialism, he must hold the line and grant that he could have been, or could become, a plate of scrambled eggs.

Bennett does raise another possibility. His own solution to these problems is to opt for something like David Lewis's counterpart theory. On this view, no individual in the actual world exists in any other possible world, and counterfactual statements about actual individuals are to be evaluated in terms of those individuals' "counterparts" at other possible worlds. Whether the denizen of any other possible world is sufficiently like Locke to be treated as a counterpart of him depends upon the context, and on our interests; but in no case will a plate of scrambled eggs be a decent candidate. Bennett suggests that Locke's rejection of individual essences might reflect a view such as this. This is really to back off the suggestion that Locke is an accidentalist, and instead to see him as a kind of super-essentialist. On this view, nothing could have any feature that it does not have in the actual world, though we can develop a semantics that allows us to accommodate counterfactual talk.

Accidentalism is an enormously implausible doctrine, and to imagine that Locke has anything like Lewisian counterpart theory in mind seems quite a stretch. Fortunately, there is an alternative to both of these readings, and one for which there is also textual support. Locke's view is, first, that we can consider things without considering them as belonging to sorts; and second, that it is wrong to say of things so considered either that any of their features are essential to them, or that any their features are accidental to them. He thinks that we cannot even make good sense of the distinction between essence and accident unless we are considering things in relation to abstract ideas that set the boundaries of sorts:

> For though it may be reasonable to ask, Whether obeying the Magnet, be *essential* to *Iron*? yet, I think, it is very improper and insignificant to ask, Whether it be *essential* to the particular parcel of Matter I cut my Pen with, without considering it under the name *Iron*, or as being of a certain *Species*? (III.vi.5)

Bennett notes this passage, and says that he hopes that it does not represent Locke's considered position, since it is plainly false that 'It is essential to x to be F' is unintelligible. Yet Locke's claim is not that 'It is essential to x to be F' is unintelligible, full stop. His claim is that 'It is essential to x to be F' is unintelligible unless we consider our candidates for x in relation to some abstract idea or other. He thinks that if we do not consider our candidates for x in relation to some abstract idea or other, we find ourselves at a loss about what could elevate some of their features and not others to the status of being essential. To put the point somewhat anachronistically, his view is that we cannot see what might serve as the truthmaker for an instance of 'It is essential to x to be F' without bringing into view some abstract idea to which x answers. Setting aside abstract ideas, the only candidates for the role are the states of affairs that serve as truthmakers for instances of 'x is F' and 'God and nature have caused x to be F.' By themselves, these are not up to the task.

One might resist the suggestion that Locke can reject essentialism without embracing accidentalism. By definition, a thing's essential features just are the ones that it could not survive the loss of, or that it could not have existed without. If one denies that things have any essential features, has one not committed oneself to saying that each thing could survive the loss of any of its features? The answer is that one has not. To say that a feature is accidental is to say something about the persistence conditions that govern the thing whose feature it is. To deny that a thing's features are essential independent of our linguistic and conceptual activity does not commit one to any claim about the thing's persistence conditions. By the same token, to say that some of a thing's features are accidental commits one to certain counterfactual claims about the thing, claims about the features it could have existed without. Yet to deny that a thing's features are essential or accidental independent of our linguistic and conceptual activity does not commit one to any counterfactual claims about the thing.

Locke confesses to encountering a certain difficulty in formulating and defending his brand of anti-essentialism:

I desire, it may be considered, how *difficult* it is, *to lead another by Words into the Thoughts of Things, stripp'd of those specifical differences* we give them: Which Things, if I name not, I say nothing; and if I do name them, I thereby rank them into some sort or other, and suggest to the Mind the usual abstract *Idea* of that *Species*; and so cross my purpose. (III.vi.43)

In order to present his anti-essentialist case, Locke needs to invite us to consider things independent of their relations to the nominal essences by means of which we sort them into kinds. A natural way of doing this is by way of some example, but this presents him with the task of telling his readers which thing they are to imagine independent of its relations to nominal essences. If he does this by means of a description, that is sure to involve a general term, and so his invitation will already be presenting the thing as answering to a nominal essence. Some proper names also include general terms (Statue of Liberty, Kangamangus Highway), and so raise the same problem. Even the use of ordinary proper names typically implies something about the kinds to which their referents belong. For most proper names are almost always reserved for people (or at least animals), and many are gender-specific.

Locke tries several approaches to getting around the difficulty. Sometimes he formulates his anti-essentialist thesis in very general terms, presenting it as a view about the relation between "Individuals" or "Things" and their features. He takes "*Being, Thing*, and such universal terms" to be maximally general, so general that they "stand for any of our *Ideas* whatsoever" (III. iii.9). If *everything* is a being, a thing, an individual, then none of these terms is half of an idea/term pair that draws a boundary between sorts. This means that in using these terms one does not classify the item to which one refers.

A second approach that Locke tries is using an indexical to refer to the thing that he is inviting us to consider independent of its relations to nominal essences. He does not offer us an account of how indexicals work, but he seems to presume that they are not general terms that stand for abstract ideas that set the boundaries between kinds. Recall III.vi.4, where he says that "there is nothing I have, is essential to me," and then goes on to describe how various causes could deprive him of his shape, his sense, understanding, memory and life. The observation about the losses to which he might be subject supports his denial that anything is essential to him only if the point of the observation is that he could persist through those losses. Yet given his own account of what it is for something to be an organism and a person, no organism or person could persist through those losses. So Locke must at least be thinking that 'I' picks out what it does without tacitly ranking its referent as an organism or a person. If we are to generalize from this—if the example is really to show that there is *nothing* that Locke has that is essential to him—then he must be thinking that 'I' picks out what it does without tacitly ranking its referent as any sort of thing.

It may seem that accidentalism has reared its head again. For if 'I' refers to something that could persist through those losses of shape, understanding, memory, and so on, does this not mean that it refers to something that has each of those features accidentally? It does not mean that if 'I' refers to what it does without implying that this thing falls under any particular kind concept that might be used to track it through that loss. To think that 'I' functions in this way might involve thinking that its reference is, in a certain sense, vague or indeterminate. Locke's suggestion that "I" could survive the losses of shape, understanding, and memory may mean just that, for each potential loss, there is some concept or other that could be used to track something that counts as a referent of 'I' through that loss. He may hold that there will be some such concept for any given feature a thing might lose, even though he does not think that there is any one particular kind to which the use of 'I' by itself implies that the speaker belongs—or at least none that could be used to track the speaker through the loss.[14]

A third tactic that Locke uses to refer to things without tacitly ranking them under sorts is to speak of them as particular parcels of matter. We saw this at III.vi.5, where he says that it is improper and insignificant to ask whether it is essential to "the particular parcel of Matter I cut my Pen with" that it obey the magnet. We see it again at III.vi.6, where he says that "there is no individual parcel of Matter, to which any of these Qualities are so annexed, as to be *essential* to it, or inseparable from it."[15] In these passages, he is picking out an individual thing using a very general description, but not a maximally general one. Locke will presumably say that the meaning of 'parcel of matter' is given by an associated abstract idea. That idea will be one in relation to which the feature of being drawn by a magnet (for instance) counts as an accidental feature, since magnets do not attract all parcels of matter. Yet what Locke wants to deny is that it makes sense to speak of obeying the magnet as accidental to some particular parcel of matter unless we are considering that parcel in relation to some nominal essence. Suppose that one insists that it does make sense to speak of that feature as essential or accidental to that particular parcel, and that which it is depends upon whether the parcel could survive whatever changes would make it such that magnets no longer attracted it. Whether it could survive those changes depends on what those changes are (an empirical matter), and on what criteria of identity are supplied by the abstract idea "parcel of matter." Locke has a plausible reply to this. He can say that there is no fact of the matter about whether a particular parcel of matter can survive those changes, because there is no sharp criterion of identity associated with 'parcel of matter.' In that respect, 'parcel of matter' is like 'heap,' 'lump,' and 'chunk.' The idea "parcel of matter" has more content than the idea "individual" does, but not enough to tell us when we do and do not have the same parcel of matter as an earlier one.[16]

[14] How plausible is it that the use of 'I' does not imply that the speaker belongs to any particular kind? It is certainly right to say that 'I' is not itself a general term, not the name of a kind. It is also right that the user of 'I' need not be a person, as Locke understands personhood (see II.xxvii.9, a passage that we will examine closely in §48.) The user of 'I' need not be self-conscious, need not even be conscious, and need not exist for more than a moment. Perhaps the use of 'I' implies that the speaker is a speaker, but the concept of a speaker is not one that has associated with it a criterion of identity that would allow us to track a thing through changes. We track speakers by tracking people that speak, or human animals that speak, or answering machines that speak.

[15] Locke also speaks of parcels of matter at III.vi.35, 50 and at IV.vi.5.

[16] To say this is to deny that the idea associated with 'parcel of matter' is a "sortal concept" in the sense in which P. F. Strawson uses that phrase (Strawson 1959, 168). See §44.

Locke claims that sorts are the workmanship of the understanding, and also that we are responsible for demarcating the boundaries between the essential and the accidental features of things. These are both claims that we are responsible for something that one might have taken to be an aspect of the natural order. In both cases, Locke says that we do what we do by making nominal essences and ranking individuals under them. This naturally raises the question of whether the relationship between Locke's bold workmanship thesis and his anti-essentialism is closer still. Does either one entail the other? Though the two are closely related parts of Locke's metaphysical system, I think that the answer is "no."

First consider whether the bold workmanship thesis entails anti-essentialism. The question is whether one can accept that we make sorts—and accept this for the reasons that Locke does—while embracing essentialism. To embrace essentialism is to hold that for each individual that has some essential features there is a mind-independent fact of the matter about which of its features are essential to it and which accidental. If essentialism is true, then it is possible that there should be a number of different individuals for whom the same set of features is essential. Indeed, we would expect that to be the case. Do those individuals therefore belong to a sort prior to our ranking them under any nominal essence? One who accepts the bold workmanship thesis will say that they do not. If a number of individuals share a number of features, then each of these shared features is one respect in which the individuals are similar to one another. If each of those individuals possesses the same set of features essentially, then this is just one more respect in which the individuals are similar to one another. They are similar not just in regard to some of their occurrent features, but also in regard to some of their modal features. Yet for nature to make a sort it has to do something besides producing a number of individuals that are similar to one another in however many ways. It has to somehow specify what are the requirements for membership in the sort, and to do this not only in regard to existing things but also in regard to merely possible things. There seems to be conceptual space for someone who embraces both the bold workmanship thesis and essentialism.

Next consider whether a commitment to Lockean anti-essentialism entails a commitment to the bold workmanship thesis. We can see this as the question of whether we can accept that nature makes sorts, and yet hold that the distinction between essence and accident is nominal-essence-relative. Suppose that it is a natural fact that a certain number of individuals are conspecifics. Suppose that Hal is one of these individuals, and that he is conspecific to the other individuals we call chimpanzees. Finally, suppose that there were some series of medical interventions that could be performed upon Hal, the end result of which would be a creature genotypically and phenotypically indistinguishable from a living human being. One might take these interventions to be ones that turn a chimpanzee into a human being. Or one might hold that anything that begins life as a chimpanzee can only be a chimpanzee, even if medical interventions make it a very unusual chimpanzee. Either way, the question facing us is whether Hal could persist through this series of medical interventions. The view that nature sets the boundaries between kinds—that it is a natural fact that Hal starts out life conspecific to certain other creatures—does not seem to settle the question. It seems open to a Lockean anti-essentialist to say that whether Hal could persist through the envisaged changes depends upon the abstract idea in relation to which we consider him. If we consider him in relation to the idea "chimpanzee," we may say that he could not, for we may think that the interventions turn a chimpanzee into a human being. If we consider Hal in relation to the idea "organism," we may say that he could survive the interventions, so long as they do not too seriously interrupt the metabolic processes that constitute his life. It would seem that a Lockean anti-essentialist can allow that nature makes kinds.

§24 Natural Kinds

Locke thinks that kinds are the workmanship of the understanding, and that it is we who draw the lines between things' essential and accidental features. Yet he also concedes that nature does not distribute qualities over individuals randomly, or without pattern. Nature makes things that are similar in various respects, and we key on these similarities as we put together the abstract ideas that we use to sort individuals and to mark off certain of their features as essential. Locke makes this point just after giving his account of abstraction:

I would not here be thought to forget, much less to deny, that Nature in the Production of Things, makes several of them alike: there is nothing more obvious, especially in the Races of Animals, and all Things propagated by Seed. But yet, I think, we may say, the *sorting* of them under Names, *is the Workmanship of the Understanding, taking occasion from the similitude* it observes amongst them...(III.iii.13)

The division of labor seems to be this: nature makes many things that are similar to one another, but it is we who decide which similarities make things of the same species, which differences form the boundaries between sorts.

That nature produces many individuals that are similar to one another in various respects is, of course, perfectly obvious. The most casual survey of any part of our world reveals animals that resemble one another in shape and coloration, plants that have similar leaves and flowers, chunks of matter that behave similarly when heated or hammered. These are easily observable similarities, but Locke thinks that it is also likely that some bodies resemble one another in regard to their unobservable features:

Nature makes many particular Things, which do agree one with another, in many sensible Qualities, and probably too, in their internal frame and Constitution: but 'tis not this real Essence that distinguishes them into *Species*; 'tis *Men*, who, taking occasion from the Qualities they find united in them, and wherein, they observe often several individuals to agree, *range them into Sorts, in order to their naming* ... (III.vi.36).

To say that nature probably produces bodies with internal constitutions that are similar to one another is not necessarily to say that these microphysical similarities correspond to, and underwrite, observable similarities. It is not necessarily to say that bodies sharing many observable qualities are more likely to have similar internal constitutions. Yet it is hard to see what reason Locke could have for thinking that bodies resemble one another in their internal frame and constitution unless he infers this from their observable similarities. If that is how he arrives at the view, then it would seem to be a species of causal inference: (i) inner constitutions determine observable features, and (ii) some bodies share a number of observable features, so (iii) those bodies probably share underlying structural features that explain their shared observable features. This chain of reasoning does yield the view that bodies sharing observable features are more likely to share unobservable ones. Indeed, it yields the view that the bodies answering a sufficiently rich nominal essence are likely to share a relative real essence.

We must not rush to the conclusion that Locke believes that some bodies probably share relative real essences. The remark at III.vi.36 is not definitive, and if he does endorse shared relative real essences this raises serious questions. Does a belief in shared relative real essences amount to a belief in natural kinds? Would not such a view be directly at odds with Locke's bold workmanship thesis? Would it not conflict with his anti-essentialism? Before we tackle these questions, let us see what other evidence there is concerning Locke's views about the prospects for shared relative real essences.

Heretofore, we have spoken of real essences in relation to individual substances. The total real essence of an individual substance just is that individual itself, considered at a certain level of microphysical detail. The relative real essence of an individual substance is that part or aspect of its total real essence that is responsible for its having the observable features represented in some nominal essence. Locke also sometimes speaks of the real essences of *kinds* of substances, such as gold and man. Thus:

[1] For let it never be so true, that all *Gold*, *i.e.* all that has the real Essence of *Gold*, is fixed, What serves this for, whilst we know not in this sense, what is or is not *Gold*? (III.vi.50)

[2] For when a Man says *Gold is Malleable*, he means and would insinuate something more than this, that *what I call Gold is malleable*, (though truly it amounts to no more) but would have this understood, *viz.* that *Gold*, i.e. *what has the real Essence of Gold is malleable* ... (III.x.17)

[3] For to what purpose else is it, to enquire whether this or that thing have the real Essence of the Species *Man*, if we did not suppose that there were such a specifick Essence known? (III.x.21)

We have seen that Locke's own candidates for the essences of kinds are abstract ideas associated with general terms. Yet when he speaks in these passages of the real essence of gold, or of man, it is clear that he is not talking about the abstract ideas we associate with 'gold' or 'man.' In each of these passages, the context makes it plain that the real essence to which he is referring is supposed to be unknown to us. He is speaking of internal structural features that are supposed to be common to the members of a kind and responsible for at least some of their observable qualities. Despite this, such passages as these three do not show that Locke believes in shared relative real essences. For in each of these passages, he is discussing a view to which he is not himself committed.

Passage [1] comes from a section in which Locke is making a point about the view that the name of each species stands for the real essence of that species. His point is that even if this were true, this fact would be of little use to us, since we could not say which individuals had the real essence of any given species. Now whatever he thinks about the possibility that there is a real essence for each species, Locke clearly does not think that the names of substances stand for such things. So he is, in this passage, making an observation about what is implied by a package of views that he himself does not hold. In that context, one cannot take a reference to "the real Essence of *Gold*" to show that he believes that there is such a thing. Similar points apply to passages [2] and [3]. Passage [2] comes as Locke is listing various ways in which words are abused. Fifth on his list is the mistake of using words "*in the place of Things, which they do or can by no means signify*" (III.x.17). The view that the general name of a sort of substances stands for the real essence of that sort is offered as an instance of this folly. He refers to "*the real Essence of Gold*" in the course of explaining what '*Gold is Malleable*' means on this mistaken view about the names of substances. Such a reference in such a context does not show that he thinks that there is a real essence of gold. Passage [3] comes later in the same chapter, and in a discussion about the same abuse of language. Locke is claiming that this abuse involves the false supposition that we know real essences of kinds. What would be the point in supposing that the names of substances referred to real essences of kinds, he asks, if one did not take oneself to know which things had those essences? One would have to admit that one never knew when to use those names. This is another spin on the point made in [1], and again shows us nothing about whether Locke thinks that the members of kinds are likely to share relative real essences.

Though not all of Locke's references to the real essences of kinds commit him to there being such things, there are passages in which he does betray the assumption that the individuals falling under a nominal essence will possess the same internal constitution:

[4] Some, who have examined this Species more accurately, could, I believe, enumerate ten times as many Properties in *Gold*, all of them as inseparable from its internal Constitution, as its Colour, or Weight...(II.xxxi.10)

[5] And had we such a Knowledge of that Constitution of *Man*, from which his Faculties of Moving, Sensation, and Reasoning, and other Powers flow; and on which his so regular shape depends, as 'tis possible Angels have, and 'tis certain his Maker has, we should have a quite other *Idea* of his *Essence*, than what now is contained in our Definition of that *Species*...(III.vi.3)

[6] But whilst our complex *Ideas* of the sorts of Substances, are so remote from that internal real Constitution, on which their sensible Qualities depend...(IV.vi.10, ll.22–24)

[7] This being the abstract *Idea*, and consequently the Essence of our Species *Man*, we can make but very few general certain Propositions concerning *Man*, standing for such an *Idea*. Because not knowing the real Constitution on which Sensation, power of Motion, and Reasoning, with that peculiar Shape, depend, and whereby they are untied together in the same Subject...(IV.vi.15)[17]

In each of these passages, Locke speaks as though there is a constitution shared by the members of a kind. He is not discussing a view that he rejects, so we cannot set aside these passages on that account. If we are reluctant to see him as supposing shared relative real essences, we might wish to see his references to the internal constitutions of substances as references to the internal constitutions of *individual* substances. However, in each of these passages Locke makes it clear that he is talking about constitutions had by kinds of substances. In [4], it is the properties of the species "gold" that are said to be inseparable from its internal constitution. In [5], the phrase 'that Species' is an anaphoric reference back to '*Man*,' and so it is the species "*Man*" whose powers are being said to flow from its constitution. In [6], it is the sorts of substances whose sensible qualities are said to depend upon their real, internal constitutions. Passage [7] comes after Locke has asked us to suppose that the nominal essence of man is "a Body of the ordinary shape, with Sense, voluntary Motion, and Reason join'd to it" (IV.vi.15). He is making the point that something like this must be the essence of our species "*Man*," because we are ignorant of the constitution on which those qualities depend. Again, he implies that there is one constitution underlying that collection of qualities when they are found together.

Further evidence of what Locke thinks about the prospects for shared relative real essences can be found in the correspondence with Stillingfleet. In his *Discourse in Vindication of the Doctrine of the Trinity*, Stillingfleet says that when we see a number of individuals with the same powers and properties, we must conclude that there is something that makes them of one kind. If the difference between kinds is to be real, he reasons, that something must be a real essence. The difference between kinds cannot depend on the complex ideas that men put together, for "let them mistake in the *Complication of their Ideas*, either in leaving out, or putting in what doth not belong to them, and let their Ideas be what they please; the *Real Essence* of a Man, and a Horse, and a Tree, are just what they were" (Stillingfleet 1697, 259). In his

---

[17] For other examples, see II.xxiii.37, 317, l. 18 and IV.vi.10, 584, ll.6–8.

reply, Locke suggests that Stillingfleet is making the mistake of supposing both that things are distinguished by real essences and that they are distinguished by nominal essences (Locke 1697, 205–6). Articulating the second half of this charge, he says that Stillingfleet's phrase 'the *Real Essence* of a Man' refers to what it does because of the complex idea that Stillingfleet associates with 'Man.' He adds:

So that taking *Man*, as your Lordship does here, to stand for a kind or sort of Individuals, all which agree in that common, complex Idea, which that specifick Name stands for, it is certain that the real Essence of all the Individuals, comprehended under the specifick name *Man*, in your use of it, would be just the same, let others leave out or put into their complex idea of *Man* what they please; because the real Essence on which that unalter'd complex Idea, *i.e.* those Properties depend, must necessarily be concluded to be the same.

Locke easily concedes that the real essence of the individuals that answer to the abstract idea that Stillingfleet associates with 'Man' will not be affected by other speakers associating different ideas with that term. Yet in making this concession, Locke himself seems to suppose that there will be a single real essence shared by the individuals answering to the idea that Stillingfleet associates with 'Man.'

Locke goes on to suggest that if he and Stillingfleet were to associate different abstract ideas with 'Man,' encompassing somewhat different sets of individuals, Stillingfleet would not insist that 'the real Essence of Man' had the same meaning for both of them. Yet, he says, Stillingfleet has implied as much. Locke presses the point, inviting Stillingfleet to suppose that five different men associate five different ideas with 'Man.' One of these ideas is that of a rational animal, another that of a rational animal of such a shape, another that of an animal of a certain size and shape, and so on. It is plain, he says, that "Man, as standing for all of these distinct, complex Ideas, cannot be supposed to have the same internal Constitution, *i.e.* the same *real Essence*" (Locke 1697, 209). Locke's point is that as we vary the nominal essence associated with a term, we vary the boundaries of the kind picked out by that term, and so probably the real essence of that kind too. Yet here again he seems to assume that there will be a real essence for each kind defined by a nominal essence. This is to assume that, for each of those kinds, the members of that kind will share a relative real essence.

In his *Discourse*, Stillingfleet says that the real essences that make things belong to the kinds they do are "*unchangeable.*" He justifies this with the observation that they depend not on the ideas of men, but on the will of God (Stillingfleet 1697, 259). In reply, Locke first supposes Stillingfleet to be saying that the real essences of individuals are unchangeable. This claim he rejects outright: only God's real essence is unchangeable. The real essences of other things can be changed by God, much as the internal mechanism of a watch can be changed by its maker (Locke 1697, 211). Locke next considers the possibility that it is the real essences of kinds that Stillingfleet means to call unchangeable:

What then is it that is *unchangeable*? The internal Constitution or real Essence of a Species: Which, in plain English, is no more but this, whilst the same specifick Name, *v.g.* of *Man, Horse* or *Tree*, is annexed to or made the Sign of the same abstract, complex Idea, under which I rank several Individuals, it is impossible but the real Constitution on which that unalter'd, complex Idea, or nominal Essence depends, must be the same, *i.e.* in other Words, where we find all the same Properties, we have Reason to conclude there is the same real, internal Constitution, from which those Properties flow. (Locke 1697, 211–12)

The sense in which the real essences of kinds are unchangeable, Locke suggests, is just this: if we hold fixed the nominal essence that defines a kind, then we hold fixed the real essence of that kind. At first he puts this in very strong terms, saying that if we hold fixed the nominal essence that defines a kind, then it is impossible that the real essence of that kind should vary. A moment later, he tones down the claim somewhat, saying that if we hold fixed the nominal essence that defines a kind, then we have reason to conclude that there is the same real essence.

The passage just quoted is a slippery one. It is unclear whether Locke is saying (i) that the real essence of each kind is stable over time, or (ii) that the individuals belonging to each kind do not vary in respect of their relative real essences. Suppose we say that a constitution "supports" a thing's membership in a kind if it gives rise to the conjunction of features definitive of the kind. Each member of a kind must have its membership supported by some inner constitution or other. To say that a kind has a real essence is to say that there is some one real essence supporting the membership of its various members. On reading (i) of the passage above, Locke is presuming that each kind has a real essence, and denying that the real essence of any kind changes. That is, he is denying that the members of any kind have their membership in that kind supported first by one real essence, and then by another. At first he makes the strong claim that such change is impossible. Then he makes the more temperate claim that it is unlikely. On reading (ii), Locke is denying that some of the members of a kind have their membership supported by one internal constitution, and some by another. This is equivalent to saying that each kind has a real essence. At first he makes the strong claim that this is necessary or certain. Then he makes the more careful claim that it is likely.

It may be that there is no evidence decisive between readings (i) and (ii). The beginning of the passage, with its claim that the real essence of a species is unchangeable, suggests reading (i). The end of the passage, with its endorsement of the inference from shared observable features to shared real essences, suggests reading (ii). Either way, this passage shows Locke favoring the view that the members of a kind do share a relative real essence. On reading (i), he is assuming that they do. On reading (ii), he is saying that we have reason to conclude that they do. One commentator has suggested that in this passage Locke is allowing that the members of a kind share a relative real essence, but that he is doing so only for the sake of argument (Jones 2007, 677, n 41). Were this so, we should expect his acceptance to permit the furtherance of some argument from Stillingfleet that he means to challenge at a later point. The exchange does not have that structure. Stillingfleet has said that real essences are unchangeable. Locke has considered one interpretation of that claim on which he rejects it, and now is describing another on which he accepts it. After this, he briefly considers Stillingfleet's suggestion that real essences are unchangeable because God has made them. God has made the real constitutions of things, Locke allows, but he says that "their being ranked into sorts, under such and such Names, does depend, and wholly depend upon the *Ideas* of Men" (Locke 1697, 212–13). After this, Locke drops the issue altogether, and moves on to consider what Stillingfleet has said on the subject of personhood.

We have seen considerable evidence that Locke thinks that the corporeal substances that fall under a nominal essence—bodies with some cluster of observable features in common—are likely also to be similar in regard to their internal constitutions. Once or twice he says that this is a reasonable inference. On other occasions, he seems to presume that there is some internal structure common to men, or to bits of gold. However, we must not exaggerate what it means to presume such a thing. The real essences that are candidates for being shared are not total real essences, but nominal-essence-relative real essences. These are microphysical features of things.[18] The respects in which the microstructure of one thing might be similar to that of another might be quite specific, but they also might be very general. To say that two individuals with one or two observable features in common share a real essence might be only to say that they share some very general structural features, features that might be realized in them very differently. Thus two things might be malleable and fixed, and both of these features might be the result of there being particular cohesive forces governing their very small parts, and yet there might be different mechanisms responsible for those cohesive forces in the two individuals. It would stand to reason that individuals with more observable features in common will be likelier to share more specific microstructural features. Yet even in these cases, one can speak of shared internal constitutions while allowing for different degrees of microphysical similarity. One may hold that the kinds "gold" and "man" both have real essences, and yet think that two lumps of gold will be much more alike at the microstructural level than two men need be.

Locke would also not have us exaggerate the degree to which our nominal essences manage, by indirect means, to sort things according to similarities in their internal constitutions. He observes that it is a mistake to suppose that nature gives "exactly the same real internal Constitution to each individual, which we rank under one general name" (III.x.20). That there should be microphysical differences between the individuals belonging to a kind is no surprise. This will be the case so long as the members of a kind are not atom-for-atom copies of one another. Yet Locke also wants to make the point that our sorting of things by their observable features does not always group them according to the degrees of similarity and difference in their internal constitutions:

[A]ny one who observes their different Qualities can hardly doubt, that many of the Individuals, called by the same name, are, in their internal Constitution, as different one from another, as several of those which are ranked under different specifick Names. (III.x.20)

---

[18] They cannot be parts if they are to be shared, and even talk of shared features is metaphorical. For Locke, to speak of shared real essences is ultimately to speak of similarities between the microphysical features of one thing and those of another.

One can imagine at least two kinds of reasons why taxonomies based upon obvious observable similarities might not group together things whose internal constitutions are most alike. It might sometimes happen that a small and relatively insignificant difference in internal constitution makes for a dramatic observable difference, such as one in color. In such cases, we might classify two individuals as belonging to different types, when in fact they have very similar chemical properties, or very similar physiologies. Alternatively, it might sometimes happen that two very different internal constitutions give rise to individuals with some number of superficial features in common. In these cases, we might classify individuals as being of the same kind though they differ greatly with respect to less obvious features.

If Locke thinks that individuals answering to the same nominal essence are likely to have an internal constitution or real essence in common, does this mean that he thinks that there probably are natural kinds? The answer to this depends upon what it means to say that there are natural kinds. If one takes this to mean that nature makes kinds—that nature draws the boundaries between sorts—then the answer is "no." Locke's view is that for there to be kinds, something has got to determine what are the requirements for membership in each kind. He thinks that the only plausible candidates for this role are the abstract ideas that we frame in our minds and associate with general terms. Nature could make individuals ever so much alike, and it would still be up to us to say which similarities and differences make things belong to the same or to different kinds. This would be true even if we know all about the real essences of bodies. That knowledge would just give us more similarities and differences to take into account.

There are, however, other ways of understanding the claim that there are natural kinds. On some of these, Locke's view that the individuals that we rank together probably have similar internal constitutions may well amount to the view that there probably are natural kinds. Richard Boyd and Hilary Kornblith suggest that we think of natural kinds as "homeostatic property clusters" (Boyd 1988; Kornblith 1993). By a "homeostatic property cluster" they mean a group of features that tends to be stably co-instantiated as a result of a single sort of underlying cause. A biological species such as the American Kestrel counts as a natural kind because the size, shape, coloration, and behavior of its members are features that co-occur with regularity, and do so because of the presence of certain underlying genetic traits. Water counts as a natural kind because its transparency, its boiling point, its freezing point, and the fact that it expands when it freezes are all conse-quences of its chemical structure. If that is what it is for there to be a natural kind, then Locke's view that the observable features represented by nominal essences probably result from internal constitutions that are similar can be understood as the view that there probably are natural kinds.

Another account of natural kinds is offered by Joseph LaPorte. He sug-gests that we conceive of natural kinds as kinds that have a certain kind of explanatory value (LaPorte 2004, 18–23). The knowledge that an indi-vidual belongs to a natural kind explains why it has many of the features it does. Natural kinds are ones that we can usefully invoke to predict and control the members of those kinds. In particular, the knowledge that two individuals belong to the same natural kind justifies the expectation that they will share qualities beyond those that led us to rank them together in the first place. The kind "polar bear" is natural in this sense, and the kinds "green thing" and "thing named on a Tuesday" are not. As we shall see in the next section, Locke thinks that we can improve nominal essences by adding "Properties" to them. In doing this, we raise the chances that our nominal essences group together things that are likely to have still more "Properties" in common. To improve nominal essences by adding "Properties" is thus to make it the case that our nominal essences pick out kinds that are more natural in LaPorte's sense.[19]

Locke's view that the individuals we rank together as men are likely to share an internal constitution or real essence is compatible with his bold workmanship thesis. He holds that the boundaries between kinds are drawn by us, even if our nominal essences succeed in classifying together things that are likely to share microstructural similarities and so to constitute nat-ural kinds (on some understandings of what that means). Is his view of natural kinds also compatible with his anti-essentialism? It is, and to appre-ciate why it is we must remember that essentialism is a doctrine about the relationship between individual things and their features. It is the view that each individual that has an essence has certain of its features necessarily, and

---

[19] On LaPorte's account, the naturalness of natural kinds is a matter of degree, and there may be different measures of naturalness depending upon one's explanatory goals. Thus some of the categories produced by cladistic taxonomists will count as more natural if one wants categories that reflect the line of descent; the traditional evolutionary taxonomists' categories will count as more natural if one wants homogeneous taxa that reflect niche occupation and other ecological factors (LaPorte 2004, 20–1). For some purposes, only the basic categories of physics and chemistry—and not any biological taxa—will count as natural (LaPorte 2004, 24).

others contingently. A thing's essential features are those it could not have existed without, those whose loss it could not survive. Locke holds that we rank certain individuals together as polar bears because we have noticed similarities among them, fashioned an abstract idea to which they answer, and associated a term ('polar bear') with that idea. Suppose we allow that these individuals share a certain internal constitution, and because of this have a number of other anatomical and physiological features in common (including, perhaps, some unknown to us). This still does not imply that any of them has some of its features necessarily and others contingently, independently of our linguistic conventions.

Suppose that Phoebe is one of the individuals answering to the idea that a speaker associates with 'polar bear.' This is what it is for Phoebe to belong to the kind "polar bear." If we consider Phoebe in relation to that abstract idea, we can distinguish certain of her features as essential and others as accidental. Her essential features are those represented in the abstract idea. Locke presumes that these will be observable features, but one can just as well imagine that with the growth of scientific knowledge a speaker might come to include in his idea "polar bear" the representation of some of the unobservable, genetic features common to polar bears. In that case, these too will be essential to Phoebe, but still only insofar as she is considered in relation to that nominal essence. Other of Phoebe's features not included in the idea "polar bear" may be possessed by all polar bears because they result from the internal constitution common to polar bears. These Locke will count as "Properties," but they have this status only in relation to the abstract idea that sets the standards for what are to count as the other polar bears. If Phoebe loses a feature represented in that idea, she ceases to count as a polar bear. This does not necessarily mean that she ceases to exist.

§25 Perfecting Nominal Essences

Locke says that we make the nominal essences of substances "with some liberty" (III.vi.27). How much liberty, and what kind? These are important questions, because there is at least the appearance of a tension in his account. One the one hand, there are considerations seeming to push him toward the view that any nominal essence that one might associate with a general term is as good as any other. Locke's semantic theory tells us that when two people associate different abstract ideas with a term such as 'gold,' they are not really disagreeing about the features belonging to an independently constituted kind. They are simply talking about different kinds. The meaning of a general term is determined for each speaker by the abstract idea that she associates with that term, and every nominal essence defines a kind whose members are just whatever individuals answer to that idea. People construct different nominal essences even when confronted with the same samples and even when they are attempting to use those samples as standards. Locke explains why:

Because these simple *Ideas* that co-exist, and are united in the same Subject, being very numerous, and having all an equal right to go into the complex specifick *Idea*, which the specifick Name is to stand for, Men, though they propose to themselves the very same Subject to consider, yet frame very different *Ideas* about it…(III.ix.13).

Here we have Locke's tic of saying "idea" when he means "quality." Correcting for that, he is saying that people attempting to frame a nominal essence find themselves confronted with an enormous number of co-existing qualities, any of which might be included in a nominal essence, and all of which have an equal claim to being there.[20] If each quality possessed by a sample has an equal claim to inclusion in a nominal essence modeled upon the sample, what could make one such nominal essence better than another?

Yet Locke does imply that some nominal essences are better than others. He says that some people make nominal essences more accurately, others less so (III.vi.31). He distinguishes between the nominal essences that men commonly associate with the names of substances, and those that are, or might be, produced by careful researchers (III.vi.30; III.ix.8, 15). Ordinary nominal essences do well enough for ordinary purposes, he says, but they are apt to disappoint when we are engaged in natural philosophy. Locke suggests that it would be a good thing if "Men, versed in physical Enquiries" were to "set down those simple *Ideas*, wherein they observe the Individuals of each sort constantly to agree" (III.xi.25). He implies that if there were dictionaries of kind terms produced by knowledgeable experts, we ought to defer to them. Alas, he holds out little hope that such a project will come to fruition, because it would require too much work from too many hands.

---

[20] He repeats the claim at III.ix.17.

There is an uninteresting sense in which we have a great deal of liberty in making nominal essences. There is a sense in which we may include the ideas of any qualities we like in any nominal essence. This is uninteresting because Locke thinks that we make ideas in order to be able to use them, and nominal essences made willy-nilly are unlikely to prove useful. We make abstract ideas of substances so that we might think and talk about classes of things within our experience. We want to do this because we want to be able to understand, explain, predict, and control these things. A substance idea is unlikely to be of any use in such endeavors if nothing in the world corresponds to it, and this points to an obvious sense in which our goals in making substance ideas constrain the substance ideas we make. If one is making abstract ideas of substances, it is better to make ones that are real rather than fantastical, better to make ones that are true rather than false.

As we saw in §4, Locke takes ideas to be real when they have "a Foundation in Nature" and "a Conformity with the real Being, and Existence of Things, or with their Archetypes" (II.xxx.1). What it is for an idea to have such a foundation, and to what it must conform to be real, depend upon its maker's intentions. Different sorts of ideas are intended for different ends. As for ideas of substances, Locke says this:

> Our *complex* Ideas *of Substances*, being made all of them in reference to Things existing without us, and intended to be Representations of Substances, as they really are, are no farther *real*, than as they are such Combinations of simple *Ideas*, as are really united, and co-exist in Things without us. (II.xxx.5)

Ideas of substances are intended to model really existing substances. Locke's examples of fantastical ideas of substances include the idea of a centaur, the idea of a yellow, malleable, fusible, and fixed body that is lighter than water, and the idea of "an uniform, unorganized Body, consisting as to Sense all of similar parts, with Perception and voluntary Motion joined to it" (II.xxx.5). They also include ideas of substances that "contain in them any Inconsistency or Contradiction of their Parts" (II.xxx.5).

Locke holds that fantastical ideas of substances are those representing conjunctions of features that are not actually found together. On the most permissive reading of this, a substance idea is real so long as there is, in the history of the universe, at least one thing answering to it. If there ever was, or will be, one centaur, then the idea of a centaur is real after all. However, Locke seems to intend a stronger requirement for the reality of substance ideas. He thinks that we make ideas of substances in order to represent things with which we actually have commerce. This leads him to suggest that for a substance idea to be real, its maker must have modeled it upon something in his experience. Speaking of such ideas as that of a centaur, he says:

Whether such Substances, as these, can possibly exist, or no, 'tis probable we do not know: But be that as it will, these *Ideas* of Substances, being made conformable to no Pattern existing, that we know; and consisting of such Collections of *Ideas*, as no Substance ever shewed us united together, they ought to pass with us for barely imaginary ... (II.xxx.5)

If ideas are real only when they have actually been modeled upon something within our ken, then Locke will need to allow for the possibility of indirect modeling—modeling one's idea upon a substance via another person, or a series of people—or else he will end up with the result that my idea of an elephant is fantastical until I have seen an elephant myself. Locke does, when discussing ideas of mixed modes, speak of one person's taking another's idea as the archetype for his own (III.vi.45). Presumably my idea of a centaur does not become real just because it accurately copies yours. However, it does seem open to Locke to say that a substance idea is real if it is accurately modeled upon another person's idea, and that person's idea is modeled upon a substance that answers to it.

When Locke calls ideas true or false, he takes himself to be complying with our ordinary way of speaking. However, he insists that the "truth" and "falsity" of ideas is in reality a matter of the truth and falsity of judgments that the mind makes (II.xxxii.19). These judgments all have to do with some relation between an idea and something extraneous to it (II.xxxii.4). This extraneous something can be either a thing to which the idea is supposed to conform, or an idea in the mind of another person (II.xxxii.5). There are different judgments that one can make about the relation between an idea and the thing upon which it is modeled, and so there are different ways in which an idea can fail to conform to that thing. A substance idea may be called false if it combines features that are not combined in nature (II.xxxii.22), if it is taken to be adequate when it is not (II.xxxii.23), or if it is taken to represent the real essence of any body when it does not (II.xxxii.24). When ideas of substances are judged by their conformity to the ideas of other people, there would seem to be two possibilities. The first is that for one's substance idea to be true, it need only be an accurate copy of the other person's idea. The second is that for it to be true, it must accurately copy another person's idea *and* that other person's idea must conform to a real object. Locke does not explicitly distinguish these, but it seems likely that the second reading is what he has in mind.

Real substance ideas are better than fantastical ones, true better than false. The next thing to consider is whether Locke thinks that some real and true nominal essences are better than others. I believe that it can be shown that he does. To see what he thinks are the considerations that ought to lead us to make, and make use of, certain nominal essences rather than others, it is useful to begin by considering what he says about the factors that actually *do* lead us to make the nominal essences we make. Locke allows that it would be possible to model a nominal essence upon a single individual. He imagines Adam finding a glittering substance "quite different from any he had seen before," and using it to model the idea of "a distinct Species" he terms "*Zahab*" (III.vi.47). However, he does not think that this is how we typically go about making nominal essences. He says repeatedly that we are prompted to make complex ideas of substance when we notice that a certain number of sensible qualities (or "simple *Ideas*," as he calls them) "go constantly together" (II.xxiii.1). We model ideas of substances on collections of qualities that "have been observed or supposed constantly to exist together" (II.xxxi.6), that are "existing together constantly in Things" (II.xxxii.18), that are "constantly and inseparably united in Nature" (III.vi.30).

Broadly speaking, there would seem to be two different ways of interpreting Locke's talk of certain sensible qualities going together constantly. He could be referring to situations in which when many things instantiate some one set of sensible qualities (or, to speak more carefully, when many things are similar to one another in a number of different respects). Call this the Many Copies interpretation. Alternately, he could be referring to situations in which a thing endures while undergoing little or no change in regard to some of its sensible qualities. Call this the Stable Thing interpretation. On the Many Copies interpretation, a substance idea that represents qualities that go together constantly will be an idea to which many things answer. On the Stable Thing interpretation, a substance idea that represents qualities that go together constantly may have but one thing answering to it. If it is the Many Copies interpretation that captures Locke's meaning, then he must be understood to be talking only about what often prompts us to make a substance idea, and not about what does so in every case. For he does think that we have the abstract idea "sun," though there may be but one thing answering to it (III.vi.1). If, on the other hand, it is the Stable Thing interpretation that captures Locke's meaning, then he may be offering us an account of the genesis of substance ideas that is meant to be exceptionless.

Which interpretation best captures Locke's meaning? It is hard to say. At II.xxiii.1, it would seem to be the Stable Thing interpretation. For immediately after he speaks of our noticing that "a certain number of these simple *Ideas* go constantly together," Locke goes on to say that we presume these "simple *Ideas*" to belong to one thing. Yet elsewhere in the *Essay* he makes it perfectly clear that the reason we frame abstract ideas and associate general terms with them is so that we might refer to large numbers of things without having to name each one individually (III.iii.4). So it stands to reason that it would be the fact that we see a number of individuals as similar in certain respects that would lead us to model nominal essences upon them. Perhaps neither the Many Copies interpretation nor the Stable Thing interpretation captures all of what Locke means when he speaks of our noticing that certain sensible qualities go together constantly. He may think that either sort of constancy among sensible qualities—their homeostasis, or their regular recurrence—can prompt us to make a substance idea. Whether Locke's talk of ideas going together constantly concerns the homeostasis of individual things, similarities between individuals, or both, it is clear why he speaks of sensible qualities as *going together*. We experience sensible qualities not as evenly or randomly distributed, but as occurring in clusters. An individual substance itself may be conceived of as a cluster of qualities or tropes occurring at the same place and time. Other sorts of clustering are involved in the distribution of qualities or tropes across individuals. First, the distribution of any one sort of quality across individuals is not uniform, but patchy and uneven. The world that we experience is not a multi-colored test pattern with dots of color spread about randomly; instead, we find a big blue thing here, a medium-sized yellow thing there, and so on. Similar remarks apply to shapes, sounds, odors, flavors, and so on. Second, the sensible qualities within our ken are not distributed independently of one another. Perhaps we can imagine a world in which the distribution of colors is independent of the distribution of odors, in which the distribution of odors is independent of the distribution of flavors, etc., but that is not our world.

It is less clear what Locke means when he speaks of certain sensible qualities as going together *constantly*. Suppose that Q_1, Q_2, Q_3, and Q_4 are qualities that go together constantly. Does this mean that each of Q_1, Q_2, Q_3, and Q_4 occurs only with all the others? This cannot be right, because it would imply that if gold is yellow then nothing but gold is yellow. Does it mean that Q_1, Q_2, and Q_3 are never found together without Q_4 being there too? This too seems untenable, for it precludes the nesting of kinds that seems an obvious feature of the world. Surely Locke wants to allow for a situation in which Q_1, Q_2, and Q_3 are definitive of the kind "metal," and Q_4 is possessed only by gold. Perhaps the best thing to say is that his talk of qualities going together "constantly" needs to be interpreted at a discount. He is talking about the regular co-occurrence of clusters of sensible qualities, but not about a regularity that is exceptionless or even easily characterized. To say more than that would take us further than Locke goes.

Now let us return to the question of what might make some nominal essences better than others. If Locke thinks that we are prompted to make substance ideas when we notice sensible qualities going together constantly, then he thinks that we are prompted to make substance ideas to which many things answer (the Many Copies interpretation), or substance ideas of long-lasting things that do not change much (the Stable Thing interpretation), or some combination of these. Does he think that we do this because nominal essences of unchanging things are better than those of changing things? Does he think that nominal essences to which more things answer are better than those to which few do? Neither of these claims seems plausible just as it is. If some abstract ideas are better than others, we should be prepared to say what they are better *for*. A nominal essence to which more stable things answer, or to which a greater number of things answer, may be more useful in that a speaker may have more occasion to use it. An idea that one has more occasion to use may be one whose deployment has a greater effect on the furtherance of one's projects. Presumably it is the recognition of these facts that leads Locke to emphasize our tendency to make substance ideas that correspond to sensible qualities that go together constantly. However, when the object of an idea plays an important role in one's projects then that idea may be indispensible though its objects be short-lived, changeable or few in number.

The next thing to consider is whether Locke thinks that nominal essences that represent larger clusters of qualities are better than those that represent smaller ones. Is a nominal essence that is richer and more specific more likely to prove useful, more likely to further our projects? Locke does think that nominal essences that are the products of closer, more careful examinations of things can be superior to those resulting from casual observations. That is why he says that he would have dictionaries of kind terms written by men "versed in physical Enquiries" (III.xi.25), and not simply by competent speakers of the language. However, we should be reluctant to saddle him with the view that nominal essences made by careful researchers will be superior just because they represent larger clusters of features. For a nominal essence to represent a smaller cluster of features just is for it to be more generic, and it will not do simply to say that specific ideas are simply better than generic ones. In many contexts, the idea "tiger" will be more useful than the idea "Indochinese tiger." It may be more important to know that there is no tiger lurking outside than it is to know just that there is no Indochinese tiger there.

What makes the nominal essences that are put together by careful researchers better than those put together by ordinary speakers? Locke's answer is, I think, that the nominal essences put together by careful researchers are more likely to group together individuals with similar internal constitutions. Often it happens that objects sharing a few salient features will, because they have very different internal constitutions, differ in regard to other important, but less obvious, features. Not all red berries are safe to eat, and not all shiny, yellow metal has the same conductive properties. Careful researchers will be more likely to discover when nominal essences are too inclusive to be of much use in furthering our projects. They will be more likely to frame nominal essences that distinguish the edible red berries from the inedible ones, and the gold from the fool's gold.

I have said that Locke thinks that careful researchers are likelier to produce nominal essences that group together things with similar internal constitutions. As a first step toward supporting this claim, I would draw attention to the following passage, which offers us a clue about what Locke thinks about why we include certain features in a nominal essence and exclude others:

Whosoever first light on a parcel of that sort of Substance, we denote by the word *Gold*, could not rationally take the Bulk and Figure he observed in that lump, to depend on its real Essence, or internal Constitution. Therefore those never went into his *Idea* of that Species of Body; but its particular Colour, perhaps, and Weight, were the first he abstracted from it, to make the complex *Idea* of that Species. (II.xxxi.9)

Here Locke seems to say that when we model a nominal essence upon an individual, we aim to include in the nominal essence only the ideas of features that depend upon the individual's real essence. Immediately we face the question of whether the real essence he is talking about is a relative real essence or a total real essence. If it is a relative real essence, then presumably it would have to be the real essence relative to the nominal essence "gold." Yet it cannot be that, since Locke is talking about the first person ever to see a sample of gold and to use it to model a nominal essence upon. So it would seem that Locke must be referring to the total real essence of the parcel. The trouble is that the size and shape of a parcel of gold *do* seem to depend on its total real essence. That total real essence just is the parcel itself, considered at a certain level of microphysical detail. Fix all of the details about the primary qualities of the insensibly small parts of the parcel, and their relations to one another, and you have fixed the size and shape of the whole parcel.

If the "real Essence" to which Locke refers in II.xxxi.9 is neither a nominal-essence-relative real essence nor the total real essence of the parcel, then what else could it be? It could be that in this passage Locke has slipped, and that he is presuming that parcels of the stuff we call "gold" belong to a sort that is constituted prior to, and independently of, our ranking them together. He might be saying that when we model a nominal essence upon an individual, we try to include just those features that depend upon the real essence that independently constitutes the species to which it belongs. This would be quite a slip, for in that case Locke would be presuming exactly the view against which so much of his fire is directed.

I think that Locke has expressed himself inartfully, but that he is not presuming the very position that he spends so much time attacking. The way to see what he *is* trying to say is to reverse-engineer his example. He is imagining the first person to be confronted with a parcel of gold. He says that reason would lead this person to include the parcel's color and density in that nominal essence, and to exclude its size and shape from it. Now what is it that would prompt someone to make just this discrimination between the parcel's features? I suggest that it is the judgment that similarities in the size and shape of naturally occurring lumps of metal are not likely to be indicative of any deeper microstructural features common to them, whereas similarities in color and density may well indicate deeper microstructural commonalities. The person in the situation that Locke describes considers whether adding the size and shape of the parcel before him to the nominal essence that he is making will increase or decrease the likelihood that his final product will collect individuals that have similar internal constitutions. He answers that it will decrease that likelihood, and so he leaves the parcel's size and shape out of the nominal essence.[21]

If this is the logic behind Locke's example, then the person in his example is not to be conceived as making the discrimination that he does solely on the basis of his experience with that one parcel of gold. He may have encountered just one parcel of *gold*, but he knows that naturally occurring lumps of metal with many observable features in common come in all manner of shapes and sizes. That is a fact about naturally occurring lumps of metal, or about non-living things found underground, but it is not something that can be said about individuals generally. It is does not hold for biological organisms. The living things that we are apt to rank together on account of similarities in coloration, behavior, nutrition, gestation, etc. are also likely to be similar in size and shape. A person who wanted to sort living things according to their degree of microphysical similarity would make a good start by sorting them according to size and shape. So the person in Locke's example is deploying some of his knowledge about the clustering of observable features in the world.

Locke thinks that natural philosophers too aim at producing nominal essences that will gather together individuals that are likely to have similar internal constitutions. We can see this from what he says about some of the frustrations encountered by chemists. At III.vi.8, he observes that things classified as being of the same kind sometimes "have yet Qualities depending on their real Constitutions, as far different one from another, as from others, from which they are accounted to differ *specifically*." He explains:

Chymists especially are often, by sad Experience, convinced of it, when they, sometimes in vain, seek for the same Qualities in one parcel of Sulphur, Antinomy, or Vitriol, which they have found in others. For though they are Bodies of the same *Species*, having the same nominal *Essence*, under the same Name; yet do they often, upon severe ways of examination, betray Qualities so different one from another, as to frustrate the Expectation and Labour of very wary Chymists.

---

[21] We can express this in terms of the relation between the parcel's observable features and its real essence, but it is not pretty. We can say that when Locke tells us that the size and shape of the lump do not "depend on its real Essence," he means that they are not determined by the relative real essence that is relative to whatever nominal essence is likeliest to collect things with internal constitutions like that of the parcel.

The chemists hope that the things they have grouped together under the nominal essence "sulphur" will, when subjected to further tests, prove to have other features in common. Sometimes they are disappointed in this. Notice Locke's commitment to the view that the things they pick out with the term 'sulphur' really *are* all parcels of sulphur, however much they may differ in their chemical properties. To be parcels of sulphur, they need only answer to the idea that we associate with that term. Here in III.vi.8 we again find Locke invoking the distinction between those of a parcel's features that depend upon its real essence and those that do not. As with the passage at II.xxxi.9, he expresses himself less well than he might. His point is that we do not look for parcels of sulphur to be the same size or shape, because those are not features we expect to be linked with similarities in internal constitution. Yet chemists *do* look for parcels of sulphur to have in common features that they take to be linked with similarities in internal constitution. This shows that they intend and hope that the nominal essence "sulphur" will group together things that have similar internal constitutions.

Locke thinks that ordinary speakers and natural philosophers alike aspire to make nominal essences that group together things with similar internal constitutions. They seek to do this by including features linked to similarities in internal constitutions, and excluding ones not so linked. This process begins with ordinary speakers fashioning nominal essences that distinguish things by a few "*leading sensible Qualities*" (III.xi.20). These leading sensible qualities usually include color and a few other qualities; in the case of living things, they typically include shape and size (III.vi.29; III.ix.15; III.xi.19). The resulting nominal essences serve us well enough for ordinary purposes, but their limitations become evident when we engage in "*Philosophical Enquiries and Debates*" (III.ix.15).

When we are confronted with the limitations of ordinary nominal essences, Locke says that we ought to work toward more perfect ones, either by engaging in natural philosophy ourselves, or else by deferring to those who do. After reminding us that our nominal essences are supposed to represent not only ideas but "Things," he says:

And therefore in Substances, we are not always to rest in the ordinary complex *Idea*, commonly received as the signification of that Word, but must go a little farther, and enquire into the Nature and Properties of the Things themselves, and thereby perfect, as much as we can, our *Ideas* of their distinct Species; or else learn them from such as are used to that sort of Things, and are experienced in them. For since 'tis intended their Names should stand for such Collections of simple *Ideas*, as do really exist in Things themselves, as well as for the complex *Idea* in other Men's Minds, which in their ordinary acceptation they stand for: therefore *to define their Names right, natural History is to be enquired into*; and their Properties are, with care and examination, to be found out. (III.xi.24)

Locke goes on to explain that it is not enough to have learned the common, but imperfect, idea that is associated with a kind term. If we search after "Knowledge, and philosophical Verity," we need to acquaint ourselves with the "History" of the items upon which we model our nominal essences. In the light of what we learn, we must "rectify and settle our complex *Idea*, belonging to each specifick Name," and then tell one another what ideas we have come to associate with those names.

The best way to make nominal essences that group together things with similar internal constitutions would be to make nominal essences based upon close examination of the internal constitutions of things. Judging that impossible, Locke advises us to study some of the things that fall under an ordinary nominal essence, and to subject them to further tests so that we might discover their "Properties." In this context, the term 'properties' is used in its technical sense. It refers to features that are common to examined samples of some sort, but features not already included in the nominal essence of that sort. Locke imagines Adam trying to discover the "Properties" of "*Zahab*" (III.vi.47). After using an initial sample to put together the idea of "a Body hard, shining, yellow, and very heavy," Adam subjects such bodies to further tests. He knocks them, beats them with flints, bends them and discovers their fusibility.

Locke thinks that for at least some kinds defined by nominal essences, there are apt to be a great many "Properties." He suggests that there are likely to be "infinite other Properties" of gold (II.xxxi.10), or at least so many that nobody will know all of them (III.ix.17). He also thinks that the discovery of the "Properties" of sorts of bodies may require materials and skills that go well beyond Adam's knocking and bending:

He that shall but observe, what a great variety of alterations any one of the baser Metals is apt to receive, from the different applications only of Fire; and how much a greater number of Changes any of them will receive in the Hands of a Chymist, by the application of other Bodies, will not think it strange, that I count the Properties of any sort of Bodies not easy to be collected, and completely known by the ways of enquiry, which our Faculties are capable of. They being therefore at least so many, that no Man can know the precise and definite number, they are differently discovered by different Men, according to their various skill, attention, and ways of handling...(III.ix.13)

The fact that Locke thinks that there are likely to be a great many "Properties" for a kind defined by a nominal essence is itself further evidence that he thinks that at least some of our nominal essences already group together individuals whose internal constitutions are probably similar in significant respects. One would not expect experimental tests on a random collection of bodies to show that they all dissolved in the same acids, reacted in the same way to flames, or exhibited the same changes under extremes of temperature. The difficulty of discovering the "Properties" of the kinds defined by our nominal essences is partly due to the fact that these "Properties" are apt to be relational qualities. This means that their discovery requires the discovery, collection, control, and manipulation of things other than the samples under study. Another obstacle to our discovery of "Properties" is that it rarely if ever happens that we can examine all of the individuals that answer to any of our nominal essences. If we are seeking to learn more of the "Properties" of gold, we can at most test a relatively small percentage of the world's gold to see how it reacts to some newly isolated acid, or how it behaves when subjected to some new set of experiments. This means that we can at most have a well-grounded belief—and not what Locke calls knowledge—that any feature is a "Property" in relation to a nominal essence.

Now we must consider how learning about at least some of the "Properties" of a kind might lead to the perfection or rectification of a nominal essence. Suppose that we examine several individuals that answer to a nominal essence, and discover that they have in common some further, unobvious feature. We then hypothesize that this further feature will be found in all of the other individuals belonging to the kind, and that it results from the relative real essence that is responsible for the kind's leading sensible qualities. We can, at that point, decide to add the idea of the supposed "property" to the nominal essence that defines the kind. This is the outcome that Locke anticipates, for he several times raises the concern that different investigators will discover different "Properties," and that all of these "Properties" have an equal claim to being included in the nominal essence (II.xxxi.8; III.vi.47; III.ix.13, 17). The solution to that problem is to be as explicit as possible about what one takes to be the contents of a nominal essence at the outset, and then to add to it the ideas of *all* of the "Properties" discovered by trusted researchers. If the newly added features really are "Properties" of the bodies that answer to the original nominal essence, then the resulting nominal essence will more completely capture "such Collections of simple *Ideas*, as do really exist in Things themselves" (III.xi.24). This nominal essence is also likely to be superior in another important respect. Its adoption reduces the chances that we are using the associated kind term to refer to individuals that are only superficially similar to one another. By increasing the chances that we are grouping together individuals with similar internal constitutions, it also increases the chances that these individuals will have still more "Properties" in common.

Though we speak of "perfecting" a nominal essence by adding to it, we must not think of this as though it involved a single nominal essence persisting through some metamorphosis. To change the contents of the idea one associates with a term is to associate a different idea with that term. To associate a different abstract idea with a sortal term is to use that term to pick out a different sort. This may or may not change the extension of the term. Suppose that, like Adam, one initially associates with 'gold' the idea of a hard, shining, yellow, and very heavy body. If one examines a number of such things and discovers that they all dissolve in *aqua regia*, one may decide to begin to use 'gold' differently, to stand for the idea of a hard, shining, yellow, and very heavy body that is soluble in *aqua regia*. In doing this, one has decided to use 'gold' to stand for a different sort. It is at least possible that some things belonging to the sort for which 'gold' first stood will not belong to the sort for which it comes to stand. However, it is also possible that all of the actual hard, shining, yellow bodies that are very heavy are also soluble in *aqua regia*. In that case, one will have changed the meaning of 'gold' without having changed its extension.

When Locke speaks of nominal essences as being more or less perfect, he occasionally does so in a way that suggests that this is a matter of their more or less accurately representing independently constituted sorts. He does this in the course of explaining one of the reasons we might call a substance idea false:

When in its complex *Idea*, [the Mind] has united a certain number of simple *Ideas*, that do really exist together in some sorts of Creatures, but has also left out others, as much inseparable, *it judges this to be a perfect complete Idea, of a sort of things which really it is not; v.g.* having joined the *Ideas* of substance, yellow, malleable, most heavy, and fusible, it takes that complex *Idea* to be the complete *Idea* of Gold, when yet its peculiar fixedness and solubility in *Aqua Regia* are as inseparable from those other *Ideas*, or Qualities of that Body, as they are one from another. (II.xxxii.23)

Here Locke considers a scenario on which the term 'gold' is first associated with the idea of a yellow, malleable, dense, fusible substance, and then later associated with the idea of a yellow, malleable, dense, fusible, fixed substance that is soluble in *aqua regia*. One could take him to be saying that the idea initially associated with 'gold' was an imperfect or incomplete idea of a sort, and that the one later associated with 'gold' is a less imperfect or less incomplete idea of that same sort. This would be squarely at odds with Locke's bold workmanship thesis and his account of the semantics of kind terms. He is committed to the view that a kind is brought into being by the association of an abstract idea with a name. He is committed to the view that to associate a different abstract idea with a substance name is to use the name to stand for a different kind.

The principle of charity requires that we look for another reading of II.xxxii.23, and there is one available. Even with his other commitments, it is open to Locke to say that when a collection of features regularly co-occurs, a sortal concept that captures more of them is better than a sortal concept that captures fewer of them. In the scenario that he describes, the idea first associated with 'gold' is an idea of a sort. It is also an imperfect and incomplete idea, not because it imperfectly and incompletely represents the sort that it does represent, but because it does imperfectly and incompletely what we want ideas of substances to do. It imperfectly and incompletely captures the clustering of sensible qualities in the real world. This is also a reason to think that it imperfectly segregates individuals according to whether they are likely to share similar internal constitutions. It is, on Locke's view, inevitable that our ideas of substances will fall short of perfection and completeness. He suggests that all who have studied bodies in earnest will allow that "this, call'd *Gold*, has infinite other Properties, not contained in that complex *Idea*" (II.xxxi.10). These unknown "Properties" are features possessed by all of the individuals that answer to the nominal essence that we currently associate with 'gold.' Locke's reason for thinking that there are apt to be a great many of them is that the serious empirical study of nature is young, and our resources limited, and yet researchers have already discovered many "Properties" common to the individuals that answer to the layperson's idea of gold (II.xxxi.10).

Until we have discovered all of those "Properties," and added them to the nominal essence "gold," our idea of gold is inadequate in Locke's technical sense (II.xxxi.8, 13). For an idea to be inadequate is for it to fail to perfectly represent its archetype (II.xxxi.1). Thus we can see that Locke takes the archetype of our idea of gold to be a regularly co-occurring cluster of qualities, the cluster that includes the relatively small number of qualities already represented in our idea "gold." Yet though our idea of gold is likely to remain inadequate in this sense, this is not a reason to despair. We still can, and ought to, work to associate with 'gold' an idea that is *less* inadequate. We can also try to remain mindful of the inadequacy of all of our substance ideas, and so avoid judgments that render them "false."

It must be admitted that the business of perfecting nominal essences is complicated in ways that Locke does not even begin to discuss. For example, how reasonable it is to add the idea of a feature to a nominal essence will depend in part on how many individuals answering to the nominal essence are tested and found to have the feature. It may also depend upon where those individuals are found. If all of the gold we have tested proves to be soluble in *aqua regia*, and yet we have tested only the gold from a particular hillside, it may be too much to conclude that all gold is soluble in *aqua regia*. On the other hand, it is also too demanding to require that *all* of the individuals tested must have a feature before it can be appropriate to add the idea of that feature to the nominal essence to which those individuals conform. Suppose that researchers find that 90 percent of the samples of yellow, shiny heavy metal that they examine are soluble in *aqua regia*, but that the other 10 percent are not. It could be that the appropriate move is to add solubility in *aqua regia* to the nominal essence "gold," and to bestow some new name on the samples excluded by this addition. If further investigation reveals that the same 90 percent of those samples also have still other features in common, and that these features are not possessed by the other 10 percent, then we have an even stronger case for splitting up the old kind in this way. For these results suggest that the original nominal essence lumped together things that did not all have the same degree of similarity in their internal constitutions. Still, even if Locke does not delve so far as we might like into the question of how we ought to go about perfecting nominal essences, it is at least important to recognize that his semantic theory, his conventionalism about kinds, and his empiricism do not preclude him from saying that some nominal essences are better than others, that the better ones are those likelier to group together individuals with similar internal constitutions, and that there are things that we can do to fashion better nominal essences.

5

Substratum

§26. Locke holds that the idea of each substance includes as parts not only ideas of the features of that substance, but also an idea that he calls "the idea of substance in general." He disparages this idea as confused and obscure. §27. Locke offers two accounts of how we make an idea of substance. On one, we do it by abstraction; on the other, we do it by reasoning that features must be supported by something. These are best understood as accounts of how we make two different ideas: the general idea of something belonging to the category "substance," and the idea of substratum or "substance in general." §28. Locke's remarks about substratum have been seen as endorsements of several different theories about the relation between the features of a thing and that which supports them. None of these readings is entirely adequate. In fact, Locke does very little theorizing about substratum. A closer look at his complaints about our idea of substance shows why. §29. Locke calls the idea of substance obscure at least partly because he takes its constituents or their order to be "undetermined." By this he means that we do not consistently associate a single idea with the term 'substance.' §30. Locke also complains that the idea of substance is confused, by which he means that it is part of an idea/term pairing that leads us to neglect distinctions that we ought to be making. He suggests that we might do this because the idea has too little content, or because it presents its object as something unclassifiable. §31. Locke also complains that our idea of substance is vague, and that it portrays only the relational features of its object. On his view, we are all muddled in our thinking about substratum. Though he tries to describe in general terms how our idea of substance is defective, he does not regard himself as able to sort out the resulting muddle.

§26 *The Idea of Substance*

We began our examination of Locke's metaphysics with a look at the basic categories of his ontology: substance and mode. Because these are the basic categories, there is a sense in which the rest of his metaphysical theorizing is a matter of fleshing them out and exploring the relations between them. We gave close attention to what he says about the nature and status of the modes that most concern him, the qualities of bodies. Then we began to explore some important strands in his thinking about the relations between substances and modes, focusing in particular on what he says about the modes that serve as the essences of substances. We will investigate further aspects of his thinking about the relations between substances and modes when we turn to what he says about the relation between mental features and material substance, about the individuation of substances, and about the possibility of thinking matter. Before proceeding to that, let us devote some attention to Locke's most general observations about the relation between qualities and substances.

Nothing has done more to damage Locke's reputation as a metaphysician than his remarks about the idea of substance. This is so despite the fact that there is no general agreement about the import of these remarks. Some of the damage is due to the fact that Locke confesses to finding it necessary to invoke and to employ an idea that he also disparages as confused and unclear. He offers his readers little comfort when he suggests that we are all in this position. Also taking its toll is the worry that Locke's empiricist theory of ideas cannot account for our possession of this supposedly indispensible but still problematic idea. Perhaps most damaging is the suspicion that in his remarks about the idea of substance Locke commits himself to a metaphysic of bare particulars. On that picture of reality, ordinary physical objects resolve into two different kinds of ontological parts: qualities, and a substratum in which they inhere. Each man, horse, statue, or stone is supposed to consist of a collection of qualities or quality-instances that is somehow anchored in or supported by an intrinsically featureless but self-subsisting item.

In this chapter I seek to limit the damage. I aim to do so primarily by showing how modest Locke's theorizing about substance is, how arrested and inconsequential and unambitious it is. He gives a theory of substance very little to do, and this is because he is conscious of having very little to offer in the way of a theory of substance. When we examine carefully what he has to say about the idea of substance—about why we need it, about its contents, and how we make it—we find a philosopher who is pulled in different directions, and ultimately at a loss. We find a philosopher who is in a muddle, but one who *knows* that he is in a muddle. Locke does not articulate and defend a theory of substance. If he several times takes a step or two in the direction of one, he does not go further. He flounders, as indeed he thinks we all do when it comes to this set of issues. He is unprepared to anatomize his own false starts and missteps in any detail, but he does own up to the fact that his thinking about the relation between modes and substance is profoundly inadequate.

We will begin by taking a closer look at what Locke says about the idea of substance and how we make it. His remarks on this score have spawned a number of interpretations, and we will weigh the merits of the most important of these. We will also pay careful attention to Locke's complaints about the idea of substance. He says that it is obscure and confused, that it is vague, and that it is not a positive idea. These complaints have often been noted, but rarely has it been asked just what he means by them. To uncover this requires a detour through his epistemology, but this proves worthwhile. We come to see that Locke's complaints have to do with the poverty of our idea of substance, and with our unsteady use of the term 'substance.' We also come to see that in making these complaints he implicates himself along with the rest of us, making it plain that he sees himself in no position to offer a substantial theory of substance.

Locke tells us that each idea of a substance is a complex idea whose components include ideas of some of the qualities possessed by that substance. Each idea of a substance also includes another idea, one that he frequently calls the idea of substance. That this latter idea is the "idea of substance" we encountered in §3—the general idea of an ontologically independent thing—is but one of several possibilities to consider. Locke says that we get the idea of lead by joining the idea of substance with the ideas of such qualities as a particular color, a degree of weight, and so forth (II.xii.6). He says that we get the idea of a man by joining the idea of substance with the idea of a certain figure, and the ideas of the powers of motion, thought, and reasoning (II.xii.6).

As we noted in §1, Locke couches much of his metaphysical talk in terms of ideas, and it can be difficult to tell when he is just making a claim about our ideas, and when he is saying something about the character or structure of the real things our ideas represent. This is certainly true when it comes to his discussions about our ideas of qualities and substance. Locke holds that the idea of a substance cannot just be the idea of a number of qualities, but his reason for holding this seems to be his conviction that a substance cannot just *be* a number of qualities. His reason for thinking that a substance cannot just be a number of qualities is that qualities are not self-subsisting. Qualities require something to support them, something in which to inhere or subsist. The idea of substance that is a component of each idea of a substance is the idea of that which supports qualities, that in which the substance's qualities inhere or subsist.

Locke repeatedly characterizes qualities as needing to subsist in, or to be supported by, something else. We get a good deal of this in the opening sections of II.xxiii, "*Of our Complex* Ideas *of Substances*." There he is especially concerned with sensible qualities, and particularly with the qualities responsible for producing what he calls simple ideas. Simple ideas, for Locke, are ideas that present "*one uniform Appearance*" (II.ii.1). They include ideas of colors, flavors, odors and sounds (II.iii.1), and ideas of such features as solidity (II.iii.2), motion, and extension (II.v). At II.xxiii.1, Locke says that the mind is furnished with a great number of these simple ideas, and that we cannot imagine "how these simple *Ideas* can subsist by themselves." There he speaks of "simple *Ideas*," but he seems to be making a claim about qualities. He seems to be saying that we cannot conceive how the qualities that cause our simple ideas can subsist by themselves; instead we "accustom our selves, to suppose some *Substratum*, wherein they do subsist." In the next section, Locke speaks of "those Qualities, we find existing, which we imagine cannot subsist, *sine re substante*, without something to support them" (II.xxiii.2). Two sections later, he notes that our idea of a horse or a stone is "but the Complication, or Collection of those several simple *Ideas* of sensible Qualities, which we use to find united in the thing called *Horse* or *Stone*." "[B]ecause we cannot conceive, how they should subsist alone, nor one in another," we take sensible qualities to be "existing in, and supported by some common subject; *which Support we denote by the name Substance*" (II.xxiii.4). Locke's denial that we can conceive how a collection of sensible qualities could exist "one in another" seems to rule out one of them serving as the support for the others, as well as the members of the collection somehow mutually supporting one another.

Though it is often sensible qualities that Locke characterizes as needing support—as being unable to subsist by themselves—the characterization is one that he applies to modes generally. At II.xxiii.5, he applies it to mental events, denying that the "Operations" or "Actions" of the mind can subsist by themselves. There are also a number of places in the first letter to Stillingfleet where Locke says that actions, or modes generally, are incapable of subsisting by themselves and so require the support of something. He quotes and endorses the passage from II.xxiii.4 cited above, but then makes its point in somewhat broader terms. He says the mind "cannot conceive how [modes or accidents] should subsist of themselves" (*Works* IV, 13). Several pages later, he says:

[A]ll the ideas of all the sensible qualities of a cherry come into my mind by sensation; the ideas of perceiving, thinking, reasoning, knowing, &c. come into my mind by reflection: the ideas of these qualities and actions, or powers, are perceived by the mind to be themselves inconsistent with existence; or as your lordship well expresses it, 'we find that we can have no true conception of any modes or accidents, but we must conceive a substratum or subject, wherein they are;' *i.e.* that they cannot exist or subsist of themselves. Hence the mind perceives their necessary connexion with inherence or being supported. (*Works* IV, 21)

Here we have not only mental actions, but "any modes or accidents," said to be incapable of subsisting by themselves. Locke makes the point about mental events and properties once more when he says that the idea of the "action or mode" of thinking is "inconsistent with the idea of self-subsistence, and therefore has a necessary connexion with a support or subject of inhesion" (*Works* IV, 33).

Locke usually uses the terms 'substance' (I.iv.18; II.xxiii.2,4) and 'substratum' (I.iv.18; II.xxiii.1, 37; IV.vi.7) when referring to what is supposed to support modes or qualities. The *idea* of what is supposed to support modes or qualities he calls not only "the *Idea* of substance" (I.iv.18; II.xii.6), but also the "*Notion of pure Substance in general*" (II.xxiii.2) and the "idea of substance in general" (II.xxiii.3). The 'in general' in '*Idea* of Substance in general' could be understood either as modifying 'idea' or as modifying 'substance.' If it modifies 'substance,' then it would seem that 'idea of substance in general' refers to the idea of a special sort of substance. If it modifies 'idea,' then 'idea of substance in general' may refer to the general idea associated with 'substance.' Several commentators alter Locke's typography in order to disambiguate in favor of the reading on which 'in general' modifies 'substance.' Thus Woolhouse refers to Locke's "idea of Substance in General" (1971, 67ff), the capitalization suggesting that Locke's 'Substance in general' is a name. Alexander and Newman achieve the same result by inserting hyphens; they speak of Locke's "idea of substance-in-general" (Alexander 1985, 210; Newman 2000, 291). However, the other reading is a more natural way of understanding Locke's slightly odd locution. This becomes obvious if one substitutes anything else for 'substance.' Suppose that a friend were to speak of his "idea of dog in general." It would be far and away more plausible to construe him as talking about the general idea he associates with 'dog' rather than about "dog" in some special or restrictive sense, dog-in-general. It is also worth noting that Locke uses the phrase 'substance in general' only in contexts where 'in general' could be modifying something other than 'substance.' He never speaks of substance in general being this way or that, but always of the *idea*, *notion*, or *nature* of substance in general being this way or that.

Locke has many disparaging things to say about the idea of substance. At II.xii.6, he calls it "the supposed, or confused *Idea* of Substance," sending a rather mixed message. To call the idea of substance "supposed" suggests that we are mistaking something else for the idea of substance, and even raises the possibility that we may not have an idea of substance. Compare this with a storyteller's reference to "the supposed prince." This would seem to imply that something that is not a prince is being mistaken for a prince. Depending on the context, it might even invite us to doubt whether there is a prince. On the other hand, Locke's calling the idea of substance "confused" suggests that we do at least have the idea, but that it is defective. To call an idea confused and then to deny that we have it is like saying that a truck is red but that it does not exist.

The *Essay*'s earliest discussion of the idea of substance also goes some way toward suggesting that we do not have that idea. At I.iv.18, in the midst of his critique of innatism, and just after denying that we have an innate idea of God, Locke says this:

I confess, there is another *Idea*, which would be of general use for Mankind to have, as it is of general talk as if they had it; and that is the *Idea of Substance*, which we neither have, nor can have, by *Sensation* or *Reflection*. If Nature took care to provide us any *Ideas*, we might well expect it should be such, as by our own Faculties we cannot procure to our selves: But we see on the contrary, that since by those ways, whereby other *Ideas* are brought into our Minds, this is not, We have no such *clear Idea* at all, and therefore signify nothing by the word *Substance*, but only an uncertain supposition of we know not what; (*i.e.* of something whereof we have no particular distinct positive) *Idea*, which we take to be the *substratum*, or support, of those *Ideas* we do know.

The denial that we have a *clear* idea of substance, that we have a *distinct, positive* idea of substance, is not quite the denial that we have the idea of substance. Yet if Locke stops short of denying that we have the idea of substance here, he does not do so as clearly as he might have. He says that the idea of substance is not brought into our minds by those ways that other ideas are brought into our minds (i.e., sensation and reflection). His marginal heading also makes the reader understand that the "Idea *of Substance* [is] *not innate*." This would seem to rule out the idea of substance entering our minds by the most obvious alternative to the ways that other ideas are brought into our minds. A reader could be forgiven for thinking that Locke means to deny that the idea of substance has entered our minds at all. In the first three editions, that suggestion was even stronger, for Locke did not add the qualifying phrase 'particular distinct positive' until the fourth edition. Before then, I.iv.18 told readers that we signify nothing by the word 'substance' but the uncertain supposition of "something whereof we have no *Idea*." A similar passage survives at II.xxxi.13. There Locke says that "a Man has no *Idea* of Substance in general."

That man has no idea of substance in general is not Locke's considered position. In the *Essay* and afterwards, he makes various claims about this idea—about its contents, its genesis, and its role as a constituent in other ideas—and these claims make sense only if he thinks that we do have this idea. In the *Essay*, Locke says that the idea that we associate with the general term 'substance' is that of the unknown support of qualities (II.xxiii.2), and that this idea is an important constituent of every idea that we have of a kind of substance (II.xii.6; III.vi.21). In the correspondence with Stillingfleet, he defends himself against Stillingfleet's characterization of him as one of the "Gentlemen of this new way of thinking [who] have almost discarded *Substance* out of the reasonable part of the World" (Stillingfleet 1697, 234). Unsure of what it means to discard substance out of the reasonable part of the world, Locke first responds to the charge that he has denied the existence of substance. Once he takes himself to have shown that the "being...of substance [is] safe and secure," he then considers whether "the idea of it be not so too" (*Works* IV, 18). He says that it is, that the idea of substance is "a complex idea, made up of the general idea of something, or being, with the relation of a support to accidents" (*Works* IV, 19), and that we make this idea by abstraction (*Works* IV, 21, 16).

Though Locke allows that we have an idea of substance, he also regards it as deeply inadequate. That is the moral of his digression about the idea of substance in II.xiii, a chapter about our ideas of space, place, figure, and extension. At II.xiii.17, he considers the question of whether empty space is substance or accident. To this, he says: "I shall readily answer, I know not: nor shall be ashamed to own my Ignorance, till they that ask, shew me a clear distinct *Idea* of *Substance*." He presses the point further in the next section by posing a dilemma: Is the same idea of substance being invoked when we say that the concept of substance applies "to the infinite incomprehensible GOD, to finite Spirit, and to Body"? If the answer is "yes," he suggests, one commits oneself to "a very harsh Doctrine," the doctrine that "God, Spirits, and Body...differ not any otherwise than in a bare different modification of that *Substance*; as a Tree and a Pebble, being in the same sense Body, and agreeing in the common nature of Body, differ only in a bare modification of that common matter." If the answer is "no," then 'substance' is ambiguous in a way likely to breed confusion, and one is saddled with the task of explaining its different meanings.

At II.xiii.19 Locke says, "They who first ran into the Notion of *Accidents*, as a sort of real Beings, that needed something to inhere in, were forced to find out the word *Substance*, to support them."[1] He compares their situation to that of an Indian philosopher who explains that the earth is supported by an elephant standing upon a tortoise. He again flirts with the denial that we have the idea of substance, saying that "we have no *Idea* of what it is, but only a confused obscure one of what it does." In the section that follows, he suggests that the explanation that substance is that which supports accidents has an unhelpful circularity about it. It is like saying that a pillar is a thing supported by a basis, and a basis a thing that supports a pillar. It is like saying that a book consists of paper and letters, "and that Letters were things inhering in Paper, and Paper a thing that held forth Letters" (II.xiii.20).

Locke reprises the story of the Indian philosopher at II.xxiii.2, this time adding that the Indian was asked what holds the tortoise up, and that he could answer only "something, he knew not what." In its first appearance, the moral of the story was that "*European* Philosophers" who can say of substance only that it supports accidents are no better off than the Indian philosopher (II.xiii.19). There it was not clear whether Locke meant to include himself among those European philosophers. Here, by contrast, he clearly indicts not only himself but his readers. *We* are the ones who "talk

---

[1] Note the use/mention confusion here: he is ostensibly talking about the *word* 'substance,' but he gives it a task that no word could perform—that of supporting attributes.

like Children" when we can say of substance little more than that it is something. *We* are the ones who use the "general name Substance" to stand for nothing but "the supposed, but unknown support of those Qualities, we find existing, which we imagine cannot subsist, *sine re substante*, without something to support them."

§27 *Making the Idea of Substance*

In his *Discourse in Vindication of the Doctrine of the Trinity*, Stillingfleet portrays Locke as holding that all ideas come from sensation and reflection, but also as denying that the idea of substance comes from either of these sources. That is the basis for his characterization of Locke as one of the "Gentlemen of this new way of thinking [who] have almost discarded *Substance* out of the reasonable part of the World" (Stillingfleet 1697, 234). Stillingfleet offers what he takes to be an alternative: he says that the idea of substance is one of those "*general Ideas*, which the mind doth form, not by *meer comparing those Ideas it has got from Sense or Reflection*; but by forming distinct general Notions, of things from particular *Ideas*" (Stillingfleet 1697, 235).

Locke responds by correcting Stillingfleet: his view is not that all ideas come from sensation and reflection, but that all *simple* ideas come from those sources (*Works* IV, 11). Stillingfleet's suggestion about how we get the idea of substance is not an alternative to his view; it *is* his view. Locke calls Stillingfleet's attention to the *Essay*'s two main discussions of abstraction. He quotes some of III.iii.6, and cites II.xi.9 as another place where he expresses himself "to the same purpose" (*Works* IV, 12).[2] Then, after some remarks about the idea of substance and about abstraction in brutes, he says:

I beg leave to remind your lordship, that I say in more places than one, and particularly those above quoted, where ex professo I treat of abstraction and general ideas, that they are all made by abstracting; and therefore could not be understood to mean, that that of substance was made any other way ...(*Works* IV, 16)

In the *Discourse*, Stillingfleet had cited II.xxiii.1 as showing that Locke thinks that the general idea of substance is not made by abstraction but is instead "*a Complication of many simple Ideas together*" (1697, 236). As Locke explains,

---

[2] *Works* IV (p. 12) has Locke citing I.xi.9, as does the original printed edition of the first letter to Stillingfleet. However, Book I of the *Essay* has only four chapters, and Locke surely means to be pointing to his discussion of abstraction at II.xi.9.

this is mistaking a remark about the ideas of particular substances for one about the idea of substance in general. Quoting the relevant portions of II.xxiii.1, he observes that it contains no words "that deny the general idea of substance to be made by abstraction," because he was "speaking in that place of the ideas of distinct substances, such as man, horse, gold, &c." (*Works* IV, 17).

In the *Essay*, Locke does say that we can arrive at a general idea of substance by abstraction. At III.iii.9, he explains that one can form the general idea of man or horse by beginning with the ideas of particular men (Peter, Paul), or of a particular horse (Bucephalus), and then "leaving out something, that is peculiar to each Individual." Leaving out more ideas yields the general idea "animal." By leaving out still more, one arrives at ideas of still greater generality:

> Leave out of the *Idea* of *Animal*, Sense and spontaneous Motion, and the remaining complex *Idea*, made up of the remaining simple ones of Body, Life, and Nourishment, becomes a more general one, under the more comprehensive term, *Vivens*. And not to dwell longer upon this particular, so evident in it self, by the same way the Mind proceeds to *Body*, *Substance*, and at last to *Being*, *Thing*, and such universal terms, which stand for any of our *Ideas* whatsoever.

Locke's characterization of "body," "life," and "nourishment" as simple ideas is initially puzzling. This is one of several places in which he speaks of "simple ideas" in a loose way, meaning *simpler* ideas.[3] What he is saying is that the ideas "body," "life," and "nourishment" are less complex than the idea "animal," and that they are constituents of it. By "*Vivens*" Locke seems to mean "living thing." The idea "*Body*" is more general than that, because there can be inanimate bodies. "*Substance*" is more general still, because there can be immaterial substances. "*Being*" or "*Thing*" is the most general idea, because beings include not only substances but also modes.

In the correspondence with Stillingfleet, Locke offers a different description of how we make the idea of substance. He begins by saying that he and Stillingfleet agree that "the substratum to modes or accidents, which is our idea of substance in general, is founded in this, 'that we cannot conceive how modes or accidents can subsist by themselves'" (*Works* IV, 19). A couple

---

[3] He warns us of this locution at II.xxiii.7, telling us that "for brevity's sake" he sometimes calls ideas of "active Powers, and passive Capacities" simple, though they are in fact complex. This loose sense of 'simple ideas' is to be distinguished from two other stricter senses of the phrase, one that implies homogeneity and one that implies the stronger condition of partlessness (Stuart 2010).

of pages later, he expands upon this by way of examples. He says that simple ideas of the sensible qualities of a cherry enter the mind by sensation, while simple ideas of such mental features as perceiving and thinking enter it by reflection. The mind perceives that these features are "by themselves inconsistent with existence," and so is led to judge that there must be something that supports them, something in which they inhere:

Hence the mind perceives their necessary connection with inherence and being supported; which being a relative idea superadded to the red colour in a cherry, or to thinking in a man, the mind frames the correlative idea of a support. For I never denied, that the mind could frame to itself ideas of relation, but have showed quite the contrary in my chapters about relation. But because a relation cannot be founded in nothing, or be the relation of nothing, and the thing here related as a supporter or support is not represented to the mind by any clear and distinct idea; therefore the obscure, indistinct, vague idea of something, is all that is left to be the positive idea, which has the relation of a support or substratum to modes or accidents; and that general indetermined idea of something, is, by the abstraction of the mind, derived also from the simple ideas of sensation and reflection: and thus the mind, from the positive, simple ideas got by sensation or reflection, comes to the general relative idea of substance; which, without the positive simple ideas, it would never have. (*Works* IV, 21–22)

In this passage, Locke says that we perceive that modes or accidents must inhere in, or be supported by, something else. He presumes that this perception involves the idea of a two-place relation of inherence or support. The mode that is supported is one relatum, and the mind concludes that there must be another. In addition to the thing supported and the relation of support, there must be a supporter. Locke says that we do not have any clear or distinct idea of this supporter. He also says that the only positive idea that can serve as our idea of it is the general, indetermined idea of something. The upshot seems to be that the idea of substance in general is a complex idea whose constituents include (i) the indetermined idea of something, and (ii) the idea of the relation of support.

We have seen Locke offer two descriptions of processes that are supposed to yield a general idea of substance. What is supposed to be the relation between their products, and between the processes themselves? There are at least three possibilities to consider. One is that Locke is offering conflicting stories about how we arrive at the same idea. In that case he is deeply confused. The principle of charity would seem to require that we settle upon this explanation only as a last resort. A second possibility is that Locke is offering different descriptions of processes that are supposed to yield the same idea, but that these are meant to be two parts of a single story. Though Locke may conceive of the process described at III.iii.9 and the one described in the first letter as producing the same idea, it does not seem that he could be intending these as different descriptions of the same process. The input to the process described at III.iii.9 is the fully-saturated idea of a particular substance, whereas the process described in the first letter begins with the idea of a mode or accident. So if Locke is giving us two descriptions of processes that give rise to the same idea, it must be that he thinks that two different processes yield the same idea. Perhaps the process described in the first letter is meant to be the story about how we make the complex idea of substance in the first place, and the process described at III.iii.9 is the story of how we can arrive at that idea by abstracting from the larger complex idea of a particular substance. There is some analogy in the case of simple ideas, where Locke gives one description of how we originally acquire them, but also gives an account of abstraction on which they can be reached by removing the other parts of a complex idea that we have put together.[4]

The trouble with this second interpretation lies in the claim that the idea produced by the process described at III.iii.9 is the same as that produced by the process described in Locke's first letter. The idea produced by the process described in the *Essay* is the general idea of the category substance. The one produced by the process described in the first letter is the idea of something that supports modes or accidents. If the idea of substratum *were* the idea of the ontological category of substance, then it would not seem as though the idea of substratum should be any more mysterious or problematic than the ideas "animal," "*vivens*," and "body." It should be, like these ideas, a general idea to which many unmysterious, commonplace things answer. It is tempting to say that this is what Locke should have said about the idea of substratum. He should have said that the thing that "supports" the features of Caesar just is Caesar himself (Lowe 2005, 70). Yet this does not seem to be Locke's position.[5] If it were his position, then he should not say that the idea of substance in general is obscure or confused. He should

---

[4] Locke holds that we passively receive only simple ideas, and that we make all of the complex ideas we have. See II.ii.1; II.xii.1; and *Works* IV, 11. For discussion of dissenting interpretations, see Stuart 2008.

[5] According to Robert Pasnau, it is Locke's position (Pasnau 2011, 159–167).

not call it a "supposed" idea. He should not say that we lack positive ideas of substrata. He should not say that we have only a confused and obscure idea of what substance does. If Caesar and Caesar's horse were substrata, then the items answering to our idea of substance in general would be familiar things, not somethings we knew not what.

A third possibility is that the two processes that Locke describes are supposed to yield different ideas. At III.iii.9, Locke describes an ascent through ever more general categories to which an individual man or horse belongs: animal, living thing, body, substance, being. This suggests that the idea of substance that we arrive at by abstraction stands to the idea of being as the idea of animal stands to that of a living thing. An animal is a living thing that has certain other features (those that distinguish animals from plants), so the implication is that a substance is a being that has some other feature or features. The obvious candidate for the distinguishing feature of substances is ontological independence. This would mean that the idea of substance that we reach by the process described at III.iii.9 is the idea of substance that we identified in §3, the idea of an ontologically independent thing. This of course is an idea to which many commonplace things answer. By contrast, the process that Locke describes in the first letter to Stillingfleet seems to yield not a general idea to which many commonplace things answer, but rather a general theoretical idea. It seems to yield the idea of something that is not directly observable, but that we are supposed to have solid reasons to believe in. In that respect, it is like our idea of the force of gravity, or our idea of an electron.

If the two processes described at III.iii.9 and in the first letter are meant to produce different ideas, that solves one puzzle. Other problems remain. To see what these are, let us proceed on the assumption that Locke's complaints about our confused and obscure idea of substance are complaints about the idea of substratum—the idea of something that supports modes or accidents—and not complaints about the idea of the ontological category to which men and horses belong. Locke holds that both these ideas are constituents of every complex idea of a particular substance. At III.iii.9, he implies that we can reach the idea of the ontological category of substance by abstraction upon the idea of any particular substance. At II.xii.6 and III.vi.21, he says that the idea of substratum is also a constituent of each idea of a particular substance or sort of substance. Locke is led to both these conclusions because he holds that the idea of a kind is a complex idea whose constituents are ideas of the sensible qualities or introspectible features that define the kind. This leads him to think that the full-dress idea of any particular substance—the idea that represents all of the sensible qualities or introspectible features that we notice in it—will contain the constituent ideas of all of the kinds to which that substance belongs. The idea of a particular lump of gold will contain whatever simple ideas go into the general idea of gold; the idea of a particular tiger will contain whatever simple ideas go into the general idea we associate with 'tiger.' For the same reason, Locke presumes that the full-dress idea of each particular substance will contain the constituents of the general idea of the category substance.

One problem with the Lockean view just described is that parallel reasoning leads to the conclusion that the idea of any particular mode or accident must contain the general idea of the ontological category mode. This is a problem because the ideas of many modes are supposed to be simple ideas. A second and perhaps deeper worry is that Locke's theory of ideas may not have the resources to explain how our idea of a particular substance could come to contain the idea of an ontologically independent thing as a constituent. The trouble is that he thinks of the idea of a kind as the idea of a cluster of sensible or introspectible features that define the kind, and there does not seem to be any cluster of sensible or introspectible features possessed by all and only ontologically independent things. This is a serious and general problem with his theory, as there are many kinds that cannot plausibly be understood as defined by any cluster of observable features. They include philosophers, mousetraps, musical instruments, and dollars (Stuart 2008). Locke will confront the same problem if he tries to explain how our ideas of particular substances come to include the idea of substratum. He seems to think that the idea of substratum has as constituents the idea of something, and the idea of the relation of inherence or support. He may want to say that the general idea of something is a simple idea that can be acquired through any experience.[6] The other constituent of the idea of substratum—the idea

---

[6] At II.vii.7, Locke suggests that the idea of existence is, like the idea of unity, a simple idea "suggested to the Understanding, by every Object without, and every *Idea* within." He may think that the ideas of existence, of being and of something are the same idea, or at least that they are to be given the same treatment. To say that an idea is suggested by every object of perception is not yet to say how we first acquire it, but at II.xiii.25 and II.xvi.1 Locke does say that the idea of unity accompanies every other idea that enters the mind. Perhaps he would have us think the same of the idea of being or something. As Ayers (1991, vol. 2, 303n77) points out, Draft A includes a deflationary account of "Entity Being Something Existing," an account that does not appear in the *Essay*. In the draft, Locke denies that any of those terms stands for a maximally general idea, and says instead that they are simply terms that can be applied to anything (Locke 1990, 19).

of inherence—must be a complex idea, since all ideas of relation are complex ideas (II.xii.3,7; II.xxix.1; II.xxxi.14). If this is supposed to be a collection of simple ideas of sensible or introspectible features that define that relation, it is hard to see what those simple ideas could be (Stuart 2008).

Another worry concerns the relation between the general ideas of substance produced by the two processes that we have been considering. It would seem that there must be a close connection between them, since the idea of the ontological category substance is the general idea of an ontologically independent thing, and the idea of substratum is the idea of that on which ontologically dependent things depend. Yet these are different ideas, so perhaps the idea of substratum is the idea of a component belonging to each thing that answers to the idea of the category substance. In that case, perhaps Locke should reckon the idea of substratum among the constituents of the idea of the ontological category. Yet if he were to do that, it would seem that whatever defects the idea of substratum possessed would also infect the idea of the category substance. So it may be that the idea of the ontological category substance is as vexed as the idea of substratum after all.

§28 A Variety of Readings

Locke's remarks about the idea of substance in general or substratum have given rise to a number of different interpretations. The one with perhaps the longest pedigree is an interpretation to which we have already alluded. This is the reading on which Locke commits himself to an ontology of bare particulars (Gibson 1917, 96; O'Connor 1952, 79–83; Bennett 1987; Jolley 1999, 74–8, Bennett 2001, vol. 2, 108–23). Locke certainly does not use the phrase 'bare particular,' or anything like it. Nor does he explicitly claim that the substance or substratum that supports a thing's qualities is devoid of any intrinsic qualities or accidents. Yet there is a case for saying that both his positive and his negative remarks about substance or substratum point in that direction. His arguments for the necessity of supposing a substratum, and also his disparaging comments about our idea of substratum, encourage the thought that a substratum is a bare particular.

Locke maintains that qualities and other modes are ontologically dependent. He thinks that we cannot conceive of them as existing without the presence of something that supports them. He seems to presume that whatever serves as the support of qualities is something self-subsisting. To suppose otherwise is to invite the possibility of a potentially endless series of entities dependent upon one another. Since Locke seems to think that the ontological dependency of modes is perfectly general, there would be an obvious difficulty if he were conceiving of the self-subsisting support of qualities as something that had features of its own. For in that case, the metaphysical problem solved by positing a substratum would simply re-appear at a deeper level. If the substratum that is invoked as the support of a thing's features has features of its own, then there will be the need to invoke a second substratum to account for the support of the features of that first substratum. Again we are threatened with an endless series of entities supporting one another. Locke would seem to avoid this difficulty if he conceives of substratum as something that has only the features it "supports."

Locke says that we do not acquire our idea of substance or substratum through sensation or reflection. He thinks of it as an idea with minimal content. It is an "uncertain supposition of we know not what" (I.iv.18). At one point, he claims that we have no idea of what substratum is, but "only a confused obscure one of what it does" (II.xiii.19). Later he says that we have only an "obscure and relative *Idea* of Substance in general" (II.xxiii.3). We can explain why he says all of these things on the supposition that substrata are bare particulars. Locke holds that the ideas we acquire through sensation and reflection are all simple ideas of the features of things. The idea of a bare particular could not be acquired in this way, because a bare particular is not a feature of anything. The idea of a bare particular must be an idea with minimal content because it is the features of things that supply the content to our ideas of them. One will think that a bare particular must in a certain sense be unknowable if one thinks that really knowing something involves grasping some of its intrinsic features. All there is to know about a bare particular is what it does, and what it does is just to stand in a certain relation to the features of a thing.

There are a few Lockean texts that do not fit comfortably with the suggestion that he conceives of substratum as a bare particular. At II.xxiii.1, he says, in reference to a cluster of co-occurring qualities, that "not imagining how these simple *Ideas* can subsist by themselves, we accustom our selves, to suppose some *Substratum*, wherein they do subsist, and from which they do result, which therefore we call *Substance*." The trouble for the bare particular reading is the characterization of sensible qualities as *resulting* from the supposed substratum. If to "result" from a substratum means to have that substratum as an efficient cause, then it would not seem that Locke could be thinking of the substratum as a bare particular. A bare particular seems ill-suited to be the efficient cause of anything. For the bare particular reading to accommodate this passage, it needs to read the talk of "resulting" non-causally. Some scholars point to the fact that one may think of a bare particular as responsible for the unity of the various qualities that inhere in it. Locke may mean that it is not the qualities themselves but their unity that "results" from an underlying bare particular (Jolley 1999, 74; Bennett 2001, vol. 2, 123). There may be an even more straightforward non-causal reading of the claim that a thing's sensible qualities result from its substratum. The ontological dependence of qualities entails that they would not exist were it not for the item or items upon which they depend. The defender of bare particulars may say that a thing's qualities "result" from the bare particular in which they inhere because they would not exist without it.

Another passage that seems to pose a problem for the bare particular interpretation is this one, which comes just a few sections later:

> Whatever therefore be the secret and abstract Nature of *Substance* in general, all *the* Ideas *we have of particular distinct sorts of Substances*, are nothing but several Combinations of simple *Ideas*, co-existing in such, though unknown, Cause of their Union, as makes the whole subsist of itself. (II.xxiii.6)

Here we do have Locke invoking substance as the cause of the union of a thing's sensible qualities. It is the suggestion that substance may have a "secret and abstract Nature" that poses a difficulty. A bare particular does not seem to be the sort of thing that could have a nature of its own. Yet perhaps this passage too can be accommodated by the bare particular interpretation.

In his first letter to Stillingfleet, Locke cites this passage from II.xxiii.6 as showing that he did not deny that the general idea of substance is made by abstraction (*Works* IV, 17). This suggests that for there to be an "abstract Nature" of substance may just be for us to have an abstract idea we associate with 'substance.' Locke's use of the phrase 'abstract nature' later in the correspondence lends further credibility to this. In the second letter, he speaks of the abstract nature of man, and of the even more abstract nature of animal. He suggests that these are notions or ideas (*Works* IV, 171). In the third letter, he speaks of "that specific abstract nature, which Peter and James, for their supposed conformity to it, are ranked under" (*Works* IV, 433). In all of these cases, an abstract nature seems to be just a nominal essence. This leaves the problem of how the "abstract Nature" or nominal essence of substance can be "secret." The answer may be supplied by the *Oxford English Dictionary*, which tells us of a use of 'secret' now obsolete, but current in the seventeenth century, to mean "abstruse" or "recondite." Something is abstruse if it is remote from apprehension, recondite if it is little known or obscure. Given the disparaging things that Locke has to say about the idea of substance or substratum, it is easy to see why he would call the nominal essence of substance "secret" in that sense.

Those who have resisted the suggestion that Locke endorses a metaphysic of bare particulars have typically done so not on the grounds that his texts cannot support that reading, but on grounds of charity. Philosophers are nearly unanimous in rejecting the notion of a bare particular as empty or confused. It seems an empty claim to say that there is an *x* but that *x* does not have any features of its own. It seems a contradiction to say that *x* supports a number of qualities and does not have any features of its own. If the defender of bare particulars says that "supporting" qualities is not having qualities, then he owes us an account of what it is to support qualities. Even were such an account forthcoming, supporting qualities would seem to be a feature of sorts, and one would think that in order to support qualities a thing would have to have some other features qualifying it for that role.[7]

A number of commentators reluctant to see Locke saddled with bare particulars have suggested that instead we see his talk of the idea of substance or substratum as linked with his account of real essences or internal constitutions (Mandelbaum 1964; Yolton 1970; Bolton 1976; Ayers 1977). They point out that both substratum and real essence are supposed to be unknown and possibly unknowable by us, and that Locke characterizes sensible qualities as depending on both. They suggest that he invokes talk of substratum as a sort of "surrogate" (Mandelbaum 1964, 39) or "'dummy' concept" (Ayers 1977, 85) standing for the unobserved and unknown structural underpinnings of material or immaterial substances. On this reading, the substratum underlying a thing's qualities is not a featureless platform that is unknowable in principle because of its featurelessness. It is a structure or a structural

---

[7] It seems unlikely that a satisfactory account of the relation of "support" can be forthcoming. The defender of bare particulars makes the mistake of treating what are abstractions—the idea of a quality, the idea of a thing that has qualities—as though they represent parts. Having made this mistake, he appropriates language that can be used to speak sensibly about relations between parts ("supports," "inheres in"), but does so without giving it any clear new meaning.

feature that is unknown and perhaps unknowable in practice because of the limitations of our sense organs and of our microscopes.

As many scholars have pointed out, this attempt to coalesce Locke's handling of substratum with his treatment of real essence or internal constitution faces serious difficulties. There is no direct textual evidence linking substratum and real essence in this way; his discussions of them are kept quite separate (Bennett 1987, 202; McCann 1994, 82). Indeed, a rare passage in which real essence and the idea of substance in general make an appearance together—II.xxxi.13— just seems to reinforce the notion that Locke conceives of them as different topics (Bennett 1987, 204–5; Jolley 1999, 72–3). This is further confirmed by material in the correspondence with Stillingfleet (Alexander 1985, 218–21). When Stillingfleet points to ancient authors who sometimes use 'substance' as equivalent to 'essence,' Locke says that he does not use 'substance' that way. He uses it to mean the substratum of accidents (*Works* IV, 23).[8] Though Locke does portray us as ignorant of both substance and real essence, there are significant differences in his attitudes toward these two ideas. He takes the idea of substratum to be implied by ordinary ways of talking and thinking; but the concept of real essence he treats as a theoretical posit (Bennett 1987, 204). He treats the idea of substratum as an embarrassment; but his remarks about our ignorance of real essences seem the expressions of epistemic modesty (Bennett 2001, vol. 2, 117). Finally, there is the fact that Locke seems to invoke substratum and real essence to answer different questions (Lowe 1995, 76–7; Jolley 1999, 73). In the substratum passages, his topic is the instantiation of qualities by bodies and minds (Alexander 1985, 217–18; Bennett 2001, vol. 2, 109–10). When he comes to speak of real essences, he is concerned with the causal explanation of the observable features of bodies.

Another interpretation that avoids saddling Locke with bare particulars is offered by Peter Alexander (1985, 221–35). He suggests that the idea of substance in general is the idea of the stuff out of which things are composed. One strength of this reading is that it makes the relations between an individual substance, its qualities, and substratum relatively intelligible. The relationship between qualities and the substratum in which they inhere is the relationship between the shape of a ring and the material of which it is composed. The

---

[8] Later Stillingfleet invokes Boyle as someone who allows that 'nature' can be used to mean the essence of a thing. Stillingfleet draws the conclusion that as "the Real Essence of a thing is a Substance," so "Nature and Substance are of the like Importance" (Stillingfleet 1698, 102–3). Locke responds that Boyle does not even mention substance in the work cited by Stillingfleet. He goes on to suggest that Stillingfleet's use of 'substance' to mean "nature" is a confusing innovation (*Works* IV, 364–5).

relationship between an individual substance and its substratum is that of a thing to the stuff out of which it is composed. Gold and silver are stuffs out of which rings are made, but Alexander's suggestion is that Locke's idea of substance in general is the idea of stuff in an even more general sense: it is the idea of matter. Alexander does not want to say that Locke conceives of matter as featureless, because that would lead to "all of the difficulties of the scholastic *materia prima*" (Alexander 1985, 224). Yet he is also reluctant to allow that Lockean matter can have any qualities of its own, presumably because he sees Locke as invoking substance as the support of all of the qualities of bodies. His solution is to say that Locke conceives of matter as essentially solid, but that he does not conceive of solidity as a quality (Alexander 1985, 224).

Locke invokes the notion of substratum not only in connection with material things, but also in connection with spirits. After telling us that our ideas of "*Horse*" and "*Stone*" include the idea of a support that we denominate "substance," he says:

The same happens concerning the Operations of the Mind, *viz.* Thinking, Reasoning, Fearing, *etc.* which we concluding not to subsist of themselves, nor apprehending how they can belong to Body, or be produced by it, we are apt to think these the Actions of some other *Substance*, which we call *Spirit*…*We have as clear a Notion of the Substance of Spirit, as we have of Body*; the one being supposed to be (without knowing what it is) the *Substratum* to those simple *Ideas* we have from without; and the other supposed (with a like ignorance of what it is) to be the *Substratum* to those Operations, which we experiment in our selves within. (II.xxiii.5)

Alexander takes Locke to be a substance dualist, and so portrays him as holding that there are two kinds of substance in general. In addition to matter, which serves as the support for the qualities of bodies, there is a spiritual stuff that serves as the support for immaterial minds. He suggests that in the *Essay* Locke treats thinking as standing to immaterial substance in general as solidity does to material substance in general (Alexander 1985, 226). In the correspondence with Stillingfleet, he claims, Locke is less confident about what characterizes immaterial substance in general (Alexander 1985, 227).

Alexander's reading faces insuperable objections. The evidence that Locke took solidity to be a quality is overwhelming (McCann 2007, 178–9). Solidity appears on several of his lists of primary qualities (II.viii.9; II.viii.22; II.x.6). Even if we set this aside, there are problems. On Alexander's reading, Locke explains the exemplification of qualities in terms of their support by underlying stuff. Yet he does not explain why a thing's solidity does not also need to be supported by underlying stuff. Another difficulty is that Alexander's reading cannot accommodate Locke's claim that the general idea of substance is the same whether we are conceiving of substances as solid or as unsolid:

[T]he general idea of substance being the same every where, the modification of thinking, or the power of thinking joined to it, makes it a spirit, without consider- ing what other modifications it has, as whether it has the modification of solidity or no. (*Works* IV, 33)

Alexander tries to evade this difficulty by insisting that at this point in the correspondence with Stillingfleet Locke is speaking as though he holds a view that Stillingfleet suspects him of holding, but one that he does not in fact hold—namely the view that we are wholly material (Alexander 1985, 228). Alexander's reading of this passage is not plausible (McCann 2007, 182). Stillingfleet does not accuse Locke of being a materialist, and there is nothing in the text to suggest that he is doing anything but articulating a view that he actually holds. Locke is saying that when we combine the general idea of substance with that of thinking we have made the idea of a spirit, and that this fact is not altered by our further adding the idea of solidity to it. He goes on at some length trying to show that it is not a misuse of language to call something a spirit without insisting upon its immateriality (*Works* IV, 33–6). He notes that one finds references to material spirits or souls in the Old and New Testaments, as well as in the writings of Cicero and Virgil. He is also quick point out that he does insist that God at least is an immaterial spirit.

Though Alexander's reading will not work, this does not mean that we must immediately abandon the suggestion that Locke's notion of substance in general is the idea of the stuff out of which individual substances are com- posed. One possibility is that he holds that the idea of substance in general is the idea of stuff that has no features of its own. Call this the Featureless Stuff reading. On this reading, stuff composes individual substances that have many features, but these are features that are "supported" by the stuff, not ones that are exemplified by it. This is not a very promising line of thought. It seems vulnerable to many of the objections that imperil the doctrine of bare particulars. How could there be stuff that has no features? How could arrangements of featureless stuff give rise to things with features?

Another possibility is that Locke thinks that the idea of substance in general is the idea of the stuff that composes individual substances, and that the nature of this stuff is unknown to us. Call this the Mysterious Stuff reading. Michael Ayers defends something like this reading (Ayers 1991, vol. 2, 40). If Locke holds that the nature of the stuff that composes individual substances is thoroughly mysterious, we should expect him to be agnostic about whether there are one or more basic kinds of stuff. Perhaps a single kind of stuff composes bodies and minds, or perhaps bodies and minds are composed of different stuffs. The second possibility can be reconciled with Locke's remark about our *idea* of substance being the same in both cases so long as he denies that we have any idea of the differences between material stuff and spiritual stuff. The main difficulty with the Mysterious Stuff reading is one that it shares with Alexander's reading: it implies that Locke's candidate for the role of that which supports features is something that has features of its own. To exempt these features from needing support seems unacceptably arbitrary; yet to postulate a support for them seems to threaten the possibility of an infinite regress.

Yet another possible view is that (i) the idea of substance in general is an idea of stuff so general that material stuff and immaterial stuff both answer to it, and (ii) when we speak of any stuff as having features, this is to be understood in terms of the exemplification of those features by *quantities* of that stuff. Call this the Quantity of Stuff reading. Quantities of stuff are things of a sort, things that stand in a particularly intimate relation to other things that they compose. Quantities of stuff have many, but not all, of the very features that are had by the things they compose. If a man is 6 feet tall, then the quantity of stuff that composes him is 6 feet tall. If he weighs 150 pounds, then so does the quantity of stuff that composes him. However, the man and the quantity of stuff that composes him do not have all of the same features. They do not have the same modal features, for instance. The stuff that composes the man will be able to survive changes that would spell the end of the man. The stuff that composes a man may also lack certain features that the man has because of the nature or condition of some of his proper parts. The man may have ginger colored hair and a limp, but it does not seem right to say that the stuff that composes him has these features.[9] The account of matter or stuff contained in the Quantities of Stuff reading seems more attractive than those

---

[9] One might explain this by saying that although quantities of stuff have smaller quantities as parts, and although these smaller quantities may compose things that are parts of the individual thing that the entire quantity composes, quantities of matter do not have anything but quantities of matter as parts. They do not have hair or legs as parts, and so cannot have ginger colored hair or limps. This explanation commits one to saying that quantities of matter cannot have atoms as parts, though it allows one to say that quantities of matter can have as parts small quantities that compose atoms.

contained in the Featureless Stuff reading or the Mysterious Stuff reading. It is more attractive because it makes the stuff that composes substances relatively unmysterious. Yet for this very reason, the Quantities of Stuff reading fares poorly as an interpretation of Locke's account of substratum. He clearly regards that idea of substratum as mysterious and problematic.

There are texts that suggest that Locke conceives of substratum as matter or stuff. The most noteworthy of these are passages in his early drafts of the *Essay*. In the opening section of Draft A, in a passage that strongly foreshadows II.xxiii.1, we find this:

The senses by frequent conversation with certain objects finde that a certaine number of those simple Ideas goe constan⟨t⟩ly together & soe are all Ideas of substances as man, horse sun water Iron, upon the heareing of which words every one who understands the language presently frames in his imagination the severall simple Ideas which are the immediate objects of his sense, which because he cannot apprehend how they should subsist alone he supposes they rest & are united in some fit & common subject which being as it were the support of those sensible qualitys he cals substance or mater, though it be certain that he hath noe other idea of that matter but what he hath barely of those sensible qualitys supposed to be inhærent in it. (*Drafts*, 1–2).

A very similar passage appears in section 19 of Draft B (*Drafts*, 130). The phrase "substance or matter," which appears in both, suggests an equivalency. It suggests that Locke is thinking of "substance" as the stuff out of which material objects are composed. In both passages, substance or matter is given the role of supporting the qualities that belong to such things as men and horses, and in both Locke says that we have no idea of substance or matter beyond those we have of the sensible qualities that are supposed to inhere in it. This requires either the Featureless Stuff reading or the Mysterious Stuff reading rather than the Quantity of Stuff reading.

Locke is a substance dualist, holding that God and angels, at least, are immaterial thinking substances. In Drafts A and B, he seems to presume that the "substance or matter" that composes ordinary physical objects does not also compose thinking substances. For he contrasts this substance or matter with another kind of substance that he calls spirit. This is implicit in Draft A, where he mentions "by the by" that "the Idea of matter is as remote from our understandings & apprehensions as that of spirit" (*Drafts*, 2). It is explicit in Draft B, where he compares our knowledge of the "matter or substan‹c›e" that composes horses and stones with that of "some other substance which we call spirit":

The one being supposd to be without knowing what it is, the substratum to those simple Ideas we have from without, & the other supposd, (with a like ignorance of what it is) to be the substratum to those actions or workings which we experiment in our selves within. (*Drafts*, 130)

If the "substance or matter" that supports the qualities of animals and rocks is a stuff that composes them, then Locke's view would seem to be that a different kind of stuff composes human minds. This would be compatible with his later view that our idea of substance is the same in both cases only if he thinks that we have no idea of what distinguishes the two kinds of substances. That may in fact be what he thinks. In the passage above from Draft A, he says that we have no idea of material substance beyond our ideas of the qualities that are supposed to inhere in it. In Draft B, he says that the ideas of matter and spirit are equally "remote from our understandings & apprehensions" (*Drafts*, 130). He portrays us as "not haveing any notion of the essence" of either.

If matter and spirit are two different stuffs composing bodies and minds respectively, then they are not featureless stuffs. There must be something that distinguishes them, making the one fit for composing things like rocks and human bodies and the other fit for composing human minds. This would seem to speak in favor of a dualist version of the Mysterious Stuff reading—a Mysterious *Stuffs* reading—and against the Featureless Stuff reading. However, Locke does seem to face a serious problem here. There is a tension between his confidence that he is dealing with two kinds of substance, and his insistence upon the mysteriousness of these stuffs. If we know nothing about the nature of the stuff that composes bodies and minds, how do we know that it is not the same "substance or matter" doing both? In Draft C, the references to "substance or matter" disappear, and are replaced with language very close to what we find in the *Essay*.[10] This could be an indication that Locke ceases to think of the substance that supports qualities as stuff at all. However, it could also be that he continues to think of substance as stuff, and moves toward the view that there might be one stuff

[10] In Draft C, the passage that most closely corresponds to the "substance or matter" passages of Drafts A and B is II.xxvii.1, which is not significantly different from the *Essay*'s II.xxiii.1. Indeed, much of Draft C's II.xxvii appears with little change in the *Essay*'s II.xxiii. See Mattern 1981.

supporting the features of bodies and minds. He might have perceived the tension between his dualism about stuffs and his profession of ignorance about their nature, and this might have pushed him from a Mysterious Stuffs view and toward a more neutral Mysterious Stuff view.

Locke also sometimes employs a locution that may encourage us to see him as holding that the idea of substance in general is the idea of the stuff out of which individual substances are composed. These are the times when he speaks of the substance *of* something or other: "the *Substance* of Spirit" (II.xxiii.5), "the Substance of Body" (II.xxiii.16), "the substance...of that thinking thing" (II.xxiii.23), "the substance...of that solid thing" (II.xxiii.23), "the substance of my body and soul" (*Works* IV, 345).[11] The "substance of" locution is easily explained if the idea of substance in general is the idea of the stuff out of which individual substances are composed. For it is natural to speak of individual things ("that solid thing," "that thinking thing") as composed of stuff, and of kinds of things ("Spirit," "Body") as composed of kinds of stuff. The "substance of" locution is somewhat less easily accommodated by the other readings that we have considered.[12]

There is one more reading that we must consider. Edwin McCann presents Locke as holding what he calls a "no theory" theory of substance (McCann 1994, 2001, 2007). McCann identifies a number of phenomena that theories of substance have traditionally been called upon to explain. These include the nature of predication, the independent existence of certain things, the

---

[11] See also II.xxiii.30 and *Works* IV, 306.

[12] The substance of a particular body or mind might be the bare particular that supports its features, but talk of the substance of spirit, or of the substance of body, is harder to make sense of on the bare particular reading. It seems to commit Locke to the view that there is one bare particular supporting all of the features of spirits, one supporting all of the features of bodies. The idea that Locke might embrace monism about material substance is not beyond the pale, but that he believes in a single group mind seems spectacularly improbable. One could try to read "the substance of" locution as a reference to real essence. Locke certainly thinks that individual bodies have real essences, and perhaps he would allow that individual minds do as well. Here again it is harder to make sense of his talk of the substance of body, or of the substance of mind. Though it is harder, it may not be impossible. Locke accords "extended solid thing" something like the status of the nominal essence of body (III.vi.21), which at least raises the possibility that there might be a real essence responsible for the features included in that nominal essence. Locke conceives of the real essences of bodies as atomic or corpuscular structures of some sort. Since atoms and corpuscles *are* bodies, one cannot hope to explain the nominal essence of body in terms of their arrangement. However, there is one passage in which he hints at the possibility of a deeper factor that might explain extension and solidity, if not thinghood. He describes secondary qualities as depending upon primary qualities, "or if not upon them, upon something yet more remote from our Comprehension" (IV.iii.11). One could take this to mean that even if secondary qualities depend upon primary qualities, these might depend on some deeper factor. If Locke did think that some unknown factor might explain such primary qualities as extension and solidity, he could also allow an analogous unknown factor to explain thinking in spirits. Perhaps these unknown factors could be "the Substance of Body" and "the Substance of Spirit."

co-location of certain sensible qualities, the individuation of objects, the unity or integrity of certain objects, and the number of basic kinds of things or stuffs (McCann 2001, 88–90). According to McCann, Locke thinks that our idea of substance in general is so confused and obscure that it cannot explain any of these things. He also suggests that it is a part of Locke's "no theory" theory that there is no need to explain any of them (McCann 2001, 91).

McCann's reading seems to me largely correct, though he goes too far if he means that Locke abrogates all theorizing about substance. Locke does hold that the existence of such ontologically dependent things as qualities stands in need of explanation, and that substance is what fills this role. McCann says that to claim that *something* must support the qualities and powers of a body is "not to explain, or even begin to explain, anything" (McCann 2007, 191).

It is true that Locke does not explain the existence of modes, but he is at least describing an explanatory or causal role that must be filled. To do this is at least to begin to theorize. Consider analogous situations in the sciences. A look at the fossil record leads us to conclude that something must explain the sudden disappearance of the dinosaurs. The observation of a tiny wobble in the rotation of a distant star leads us to conclude that something or other must account for the wobble. Even before we are in a position to offer hypotheses about what killed the dinosaurs, or what caused the wobble, it is some contribution to have identified an explanatory hole that must be filled by something or other. We have also seen that there are places where Locke seems to be engaging in very tentative, under-developed, almost abortive theorizing about what it is that supports modes. There are places where he seems to be thinking of the supporter as a featureless thing, or as a stuff whose intrinsic features are unknown and perhaps unknowable.

McCann's "no theory" reading highlights Locke's complaints about the obscurity and confusedness of the idea of substance. These complaints are data that any reading must accommodate, but they present us with something of a puzzle when we consider them in relation to his remarks about the transparency of the mind. Locke holds that knowledge is the perception of the agreement and disagreement of ideas. Our capacity for knowledge depends upon our ability to perceive the ideas in our minds. Locke takes a very measured view about the knowledge we are capable of: we do not have all the ideas we might have (IV.iii.23–25), and often have difficulty discerning relations between the ideas we do have (IV.iii.28). Yet he makes strong claims about our ability to perceive the ideas we do have. Ideas are as we perceive them to be:

For a Man cannot conceive himself capable of a greater Certainty, than to know that any *Idea* in his Mind is such, as he perceives it to be...(IV.ii.1)

Perhaps even more importantly, we perceive ideas to be as they are:

[T]here can be no *Idea* in the Mind, which it does not presently, by an intuitive Knowledge, perceive to be what it is, and to be different from any other. (IV.iii.8)[13]

What is not clear is how to reconcile these claims with Locke's confession that certain of our ideas remain confused and obscure despite our best efforts. One would think that for an idea to be confused and obscure would be for us to find it difficult to make out its contents, difficult to distinguish it from other ideas. Yet Locke seems to hold that we can always do this for any of our ideas. To resolve this we must take a closer look at what he says about what it is for ideas to be confused and obscure. If we can come to a better understanding of that, we may come to better understand his complaints about the idea of substance in general.

§29 *Obscurity*

Locke devotes a whole chapter—II.xxix—to explaining the distinctions between clear and obscure ideas, and between distinct and confused ones. He says that what is required for an idea to be clear depends on whether it is simple or complex. Simple ideas are clear so long as "they are such as the Objects themselves, from whence they were taken, did or might, in a well-ordered Sensation or Perception, present them" (II.xxix.2). Two sections later, he says that an idea is clear if the mind has "such a full and evident perception, as it does receive from an outward Object operating duly on a well-disposed Organ" (II.xxix.4). In this second passage, he is ostensibly defining what it is for any idea to be clear, but it is evident that the ideas he has in mind are simple ideas of sensation. One suspects that it is also ideas of sensation that he has in mind in the first passage, though perhaps 'Perception' could be taken to encompass acts of reflection as well. In any case, Locke could presumably explain the clarity of simple ideas of reflection in something like the way he explains the clarity of simple ideas

---

[13] See also II.xxix.5, quoted in §30.

of sensation, though he would likely not want to commit himself to saying that reflection involves physical organs. In both of the above passages, the upshot seems to be that a simple idea is clear if it is as would be produced by a well-functioning mechanism.

This raises the question of what it means for a sense organ, or a mechanism of idea-acquisition generally, to be well-disposed. Locke does not say. If he were to explain the well-disposedness of sense organs in terms of their tendency to produce accurate representations, this would raise the threat of circularity. For in that case, he would be saying that clear simple ideas are ones produced by good mechanisms, and that good mechanisms are ones that produce accurate representations. Trouble would be averted only if he had an account of accuracy on which there are accurate and inaccurate simple ideas (distinguishing the good mechanisms from the poor ones), and on which accuracy does not presuppose clarity. The prospects for that line of thought do not look good. A better option would be for Locke to say that organs of sensation (and mechanisms of reflection) are "well-disposed" if and only if they function in the manner that is typical of our species.[14] This avoids the threat of circularity. It also allows one to say that a human being's visual organs can be perfectly well-disposed despite being less acute than an eagle's.[15] This way of unpacking what it is for a sense organ to be well-disposed has an interesting consequence that will prove to be of some importance later. It allows us to make sense of the claim that a particular person's simple idea of X is obscure; but it does not allow us to make sense of the claim that everybody's (i.e., every human being's) simple idea of X is, and always has been, obscure. Thus we might say of an old woman blind since childhood that her idea of yellow is obscure if it has dulled over time,

[14] There might be some reason to define well-functioning organs in terms of their conformity with a norm specified in reference to a smaller, privileged subset of one's conspecifics, such as young adults. This would allow us to say that the gradual deterioration of organ function could begin (as it seems to) before one reaches the median age for one's species. However, the cost of this is having to say that children are defective to the extent that their organs do not function like those of adults. Perhaps a better option would be to relativize the notion of proper function not only to species but to age.

[15] One might object that it should be possible to make inter-species comparisons with respect to the clarity of simple ideas, and that on the view that I am suggesting this is not possible since the notion of clarity is species-relative. Yet I suspect we do not really want to say that the eagle has clearer *simple* ideas of sight than we do, or that the golden retriever has clearer *simple* olfactory ideas than we do. What makes the eagle's vision and the retriever's sense of smell superior to ours is that they can make discriminations where we cannot. In Lockean terms, this is a matter of them having more and different simple ideas produced in them than we do in the same situations. On occasions where I have no simple ideas of olfaction, or perhaps only the one of an ammoniac odor, my dog Trout may—and apparently does—have produced in him a fascinating array of sensory ideas.

and is not as it would be were her organs of sight to function normally again. However, we cannot say that everybody's idea of yellow is, and always has been, obscure. For it does not make sense to claim that everybody's organs of sight are, and have always been, atypical of the species.[16]

For a complex idea to be clear, Locke says, it is necessary both that its constituent ideas be clear, and that their "Number and Order" be "determinate and certain" (II.xxix.2). This seems to mean that the complex idea must have a determinate number and order of constituent ideas, and that one must be certain about what they are. There are problems about how to understand the first of these requirements. To begin with, it would seem that we understand talk of the number of a thing's constituents only if we have some idea of how to count them. How might one go about counting the constituents of a complex idea? Is this a matter of attending to the phenomenologically available features of an introspectible particular? Or is it a task of conceptual analysis, akin to the formulating of a definition? This will depend partly on what sorts of things Locke's ideas *are*, which is of course a much-disputed question. Yet even if we know what ideas are for Locke, there may still be a problem about how to count their constituents. Many of Locke's claims about ideas seem to be driven by analogies with visual images or with language. He speaks of complex ideas as having more or fewer constituents depending on how abstract the ideas are. The thought seems to be that just as a more detailed drawing might contain more lines or colors, and as a more specific description might contain more terms, so a more specific idea will have more constituent simple ideas. Yet notice how little this tells us about what it means for an idea to have a determinate number of constituents. For it is not obvious how to count the lines or colors in a picture. Counting words is straightforward, but perhaps the number of words is not really the best measure of the specificity of a description.

It is also not obvious what it means for the constituents of a complex idea to have an order. Presumably here too Locke is leaning on analogies with visual images or with language. He may be thinking about the order of lines and colors on the surface of a canvas. Just as different distributions of the same

---

[16] Perhaps there are scenarios on which we would say that every *living* person's idea of yellow is obscure. If a disease caused everybody's visual systems to change in a way that the idea of yellow was no longer produced in anybody, then perhaps everybody's idea of yellow would begin to "fade." Their "faded" ideas of yellow would count as obscure so long as what is typical of a species is understood to be fixed not just by how most representatives of *Homo sapiens* are now, but by how most representatives of *Homo sapiens* are over some suitably broad span of evolutionary history.

colors across the surface of a canvas could make for paintings with different representational contents, so different arrangements of the same simple ideas might make for different complex ideas. Or he may be thinking of the order of ideas as analogous to the order of words in a description. We can imagine Locke's wanting to say that the complex ideas "uncle" and "nephew" have the same constituents (e.g., "male," "person," "parent of," "sibling of") in different orders (corresponding to the difference between "male person who is the sibling of a person who is a parent of one" and "male person whose parent is one's sibling"), while the complex ideas "uncle" and "aunt" have different constituents but the same order (since "aunt" would have an order corresponding to "female person whose parent is one's sibling").

Even if we understood what it means for complex ideas to have a certain number of constituents, and for these constituents to have an order, there would seem to be a problem with Locke's claim that complex ideas are clear only if the number and order of their constituents is determinate. The trouble is that it is not clear how the number and order of an idea's constituents could *fail* to be determinate. Locke thinks that the content of a complex idea is a function of its constituents and their order. To say that it is indeterminate how many constituents a complex idea has, or that the order of its constituents is indeterminate, is to say that it is indeterminate what the idea's content is. This is saying of a complex idea that it is indeterminate *which* idea it is, which is incoherent. If we are told that a person associates with a term an idea whose constituents are indeterminate, or whose constituents have an indeterminate order, we should insist that the situation has been mis-described. The situation should be re-described as one in which the person fails to associate any single complex idea with the term. It might be suggested that although idea *tokens* cannot have indeterminate contents, idea *types* can do so by having tokens that vary in their composition. However, this faces the same objection. Ideas are individuated by their contents, and the contents of a complex idea are determined by its constituents and their order. Any two token ideas that differed in their constituents, or in the order of their constituents, would be tokens belonging to different idea types.

The way out of our difficulty lies in understanding the peculiar meaning that Locke generally attaches to the claim that an idea is determinate or determined. One might characterize ideas as "determined" or "determinate" and mean by this that they are detailed rather than abstract. Thus one might say that the idea of a dozen is more determinate than the idea of a multitude;

that the idea "red scarf" is more determinate than the idea "colored scarf." Though this is a natural way to understand talk of determinate and indeterminate ideas, there are no clear cases of Locke using these terms in that way. There are a few passages in which he speaks of a "determined idea" or a "determinate idea" and may mean nothing more than "a certain idea," or "a particular idea." If so, then these are the exceptions rather than the rule.

When Locke speaks of ideas as determined, determinate, undetermined, or indeterminate, he is almost always using these terms in his own rather idiosyncratic way. He explains his use of these terms in two places. One of these is a page-long discussion specifically addressing the terminology of "determinate *or* determined" ideas, a discussion added to the "Epistle to the Reader" in the *Essay*'s fourth edition. There Locke says that "Clear and distinct Ideas, *are terms, which though familiar and frequent in Men's Mouths, I have reason to think every one, who uses, does not perfectly understand*" ("Epistle," p. 12). He give this as his reason for preferring talk of "determinate *or* determined" ideas instead, though he does not explain why he expects this language to be better understood. Perhaps his thought is that these terms, being less frequent in men's mouths, have the ring of technical terms, making it more likely that readers will attend to the meanings that he explicitly associates with them.[17] Locke offers a single explanation of what it is for an idea to be "determinate *or* determin'd," showing that he regards the terms as equivalent. An idea may fitly be called "determinate *or* determin'd," he says, when it is objectively in the mind and "*annex'd, and without variation* determined *to a name or articulate sound.*"[18] Thus for an idea to be "determined" or "determinate," as Locke uses these terms, is for the idea to be consistently associated with one word.

[17] Locke explains that he has "*therefore in most places chose to put* determinate *or* determined, *instead of* clear and distinct, *as more likely to direct Men's thoughts to my meaning in this matter*" ("Epistle," p. 13). He is exaggerating when he says that in *most* places he has opted for talk of determinate or determined ideas. Even in the fourth edition, there is much more talk of clear ideas, distinct ideas, and so forth, than of determined or determinate ideas. However, there are a number of places in the fourth edition where he replaces talk of clear and distinct ideas or notions with talk of determinate ideas (see, for example, II.xiii.14, 18; II.xxi.26; II.xxviii.4; III.x.3). The timing of these changes, and of the addition of this passage to the Epistle, suggests that they were prompted by Locke's long and frustrating exchanges with Stillingfleet about what does and does not follow from ideas being clear and distinct.

[18] One might see "Epistle," p. 13, ll.11–13 as suggesting that simple ideas are "determinate" and complex ideas are "determined." Yet at III.xi.9 we find Locke giving an account of what it takes for complex ideas to be "determinate" that is essentially the same as the earlier account of what it takes for them to be "determined." In the "Epistle," Locke goes on to try to "explain ....a little more particularly" what "determinate" simple ideas and "determined" complex ideas are, but not all of what he says is very helpful. For example, we are not much the better for learning that a determinate simple idea is a "*simple appearance, which the Mind has in its view, or perceives in it self, when that Idea is said to be in it*" ("Epistle," p. 13).

Locke repeats essentially the same explanation later, in his discussion of the abuse of words. He says that when people fail to take the pains to settle "determined" ideas in their minds, they use "such unsteady and confused Notions as they have…as if their very sound necessarily carried with it constantly the same meaning" (III.x.4). This is a "loose" use of words that serves well enough for common life, but that is not sufficient for philosophical enquiries, which require "precise determinate *Ideas*" (III.x.22). In the next chapter, he explains that a complex idea is determinate if there is a "precise Collection of simple *Ideas* settled in the Mind, with that Sound annexed to it, as the sign of that precise determined Collection, and no other" (III.xi.9).

There are in fact several different virtues that ought to be distinguished: (i) a person consistently associating one idea with one term; (ii) a linguistic community generally associating one idea with one term; and (iii) a person consistently associating one idea with one term in conformity with her linguistic community. Notice that (ii) could not occur unless most members of the relevant linguistic community instanced (i), and that (iii) could not occur unless a person instanced (i) and her community instanced (ii). Locke does not explicitly distinguish between (i), (ii), and (iii). He sometimes speaks of an idea's being determined or undetermined and seems to intend this as a general observation. In these cases, he can be understood to be asserting or denying that (ii) holds with respect to some idea or term. However, when he speaks of a person as having an idea that is determined or undetermined, it is often (iii)—and not just (i)—that he has in mind. Instancing (i) is necessary for having a clear idea: in the "Epistle," he says that a person who fails to annex the same idea to the same term "*in vain pretends to* clear or distinct Ideas*" (p. 13). However, intra-personal consistency by itself does not suffice to make one's ideas determined in the sense that Locke has in mind. For he holds that the indeterminacy of ideas is the cause of endless verbal disputes, and is optimistic that these disputes will vanish if disputants have ideas that are determined. Locke makes this point in the "Epistle,"[19] and again at III.xi.7:

And here I desire it may be considered, and carefully examined, whether the greatest part of the Disputes in the World, are not meerly Verbal, and about the Signification of Words; and whether if the terms they are made in, were defined, and reduced in

---

[19] "[*W*]*here Men have got such* determined *Ideas of all, that they reason, enquire, or argue about, they will find a great part of their Doubts and Disputes at an end*" ("Epistle," p. 13).

their Signification (as they must be, where they signify any thing) to determined Collections of the simple *Ideas* they do or should stand for, those Disputes would not end of themselves, and immediately vanish.

If having determined ideas were merely a matter of maintaining consistent associations between ideas and terms intra-personally, then determined ideas would not be a cure for verbal disputes between persons.

When Locke complains about an idea being "undetermined," "indetermined," or "indeterminate," he is complaining about there not being a consistent association between one idea and one term. This is why, in the "Epistle," he says that to have an "indetermined" idea is just to misuse language in a certain way:

The greatest part of the Questions and Controversies that perplex Mankind depending [sic] on the doubtful and uncertain use of Words, or (which is the same) indetermined Ideas, which they are made to stand for. ("Epistle," p. 13)

A case in which there fails to be a single idea associated with a single term could conceivably fit either of two profiles: (i) several ideas are associated with one term, or (ii) one idea is associated with several terms. If one were to use the phrase "an undetermined idea" in describing one of these scenarios, the type (ii) scenario would seem to be a more plausible candidate. There, at least, one is dealing with *an* idea. Yet Locke speaks of there being an undetermined idea when he has in mind a type (i) scenario. He does this when he says that men are likely to disagree about whether an "odly-shaped *Fœtus*" is "a *Man*, or no," and this because the idea of our own species is "undetermined" (III.vi.27). He does it when he says that men have "*uncertain, and undetermined*" ideas insofar as they associate a different idea with "church" or with "idolatry" each time they use one of these words (II.xxix.9).

In reference to this last example, Locke offers a somewhat convoluted diagnosis of what goes wrong when one has an undetermined idea. He says, "a mutable *Idea* (if we will allow it to be one *Idea*) cannot belong to one Name, rather than another; and so loses the distinction, that distinct Names are designed for" (II.xxix.9). Here he speaks as though different mental contents are all the same idea so long as they are—in a person at different times, or in a number of people within a linguistic community—associated with the same word. This is misleading, and his parenthetical remark is the acknowledgment that it does not *really* make sense to speak of a mutable idea. Ideas are individuated by their contents. What is mutable is *which* idea is associated with "the church" (or "idolatry," or whatever). The problem that Locke is trying to draw the reader's attention to is that "the church" has more than one meaning in the hands of some men. Here, as elsewhere, he says that the *idea* of φ is undetermined, but his real complaint is that several different ideas are associated with the *word* 'φ'. Locke may also say that the idea of φ is undetermined if we sometimes use 'φ' without associating any idea with that term. He would better get his point across were he to say that it is the signification of the word 'φ' that is undetermined. In fact, Locke does sometimes describe type (i) cases that way. For instance, he says that the names of mixed modes frequently have a "very loose and undetermined, and consequently obscure and confused signification" (III.ix.9). He explains that this is the source of endless controversies among intelligent men about "*Honour, Faith, Grace, Religion, Church*, etc."[20]

We have been considering what Locke means in calling an idea determined or undetermined, determinate or indeterminate. However, what he says is required for a complex idea to be clear is that the *number* and *order* of its constituents be determinate.[21] If we try to understand this by analogy with what he thinks is involved in an idea's being determinate, it would seem that the number and order of an idea is determinate so long as one term is consistently associated with token ideas having the same number of constituents in the same order. Notice that in that case, a complex idea whose constituents have an indeterminate number or order of constituents *is* an undetermined idea. For token ideas with different numbers of constituents, or with the same constituents in different orders, will have different contents. It is a bit odd that in specifying what is needed for a complex idea to be clear Locke focuses on the determinateness of the *number* and *order* of the idea's constituents. Surely what he really cares about is that ideas with the same *content* are associated with the same terms—that is, that the idea itself is determined or determinate. What fixes the content of a complex idea is not just what number of constituents it has in a particular order, but *which* constituents it has in a particular order. The complex ideas "aunt" and "uncle" may have the same number of constituents in the same order, but surely Locke would regard it as a source of obscurity were one to vacillate between associating one and then the other of these ideas with the word 'aunt.'

---

[20] For other examples of Locke speaking of indeterminacy of meaning rather than of an idea, see III.ix.20; III.x.6; III.xi.9; IV.iii.30.

[21] He speaks this way not only at II.xxix.2, but at II.xxix.10 and 12.

Though it is a bit odd that Locke focuses on the need for clear ideas to have constituents of a determinate number and order—rather than on the stronger requirement that the complex ideas be determinate—he does suggest the stronger requirement elsewhere. Where a man does not keep a term "*steadily annex'd*" to a "determined *Idea*," he says in the "Epistle," "*he in vain pretends to* clear or distinct Ideas" (p. 13). It may also be possible to dispel the oddness of Locke's formulation at II.xxix.2 by supposing that when he says that the number of a complex idea's constituents must be determinate for the idea to be clear, he is using "number" to refer to the constituents rather than to their cardinality. We use "number" this way when we say such things as that "some of their number departed." If Locke were doing that at II.xxix.2, he would be saying that a complex idea is clear only if there is a consistent association between its constituents-ordered-in-a-certain-way and some term. This is to say that a complex idea is clear only if there is a consistent association between *it* and some term—which is to say that a complex idea is clear only if it is determined.

Locke says that for a complex idea to be clear, the number and order of its constituents must be determinate and *certain*. If this last requirement adds anything, it would seem to be that for an idea of φ to be clear, one must be certain exactly which mental contents are associated with the term 'φ'. Locke's transparency doctrine threatens to render this requirement superfluous if the certainty required for clarity is intra-personal. The certainty requirement has real bite if the certainty required for clarity involves certainty about which ideas others associate with a given term.

§30 *Confusedness*

Let us now turn to Locke's account of the distinct/confused distinction. He initially says that a distinct idea is one "wherein the Mind perceives a difference from all other," and that a confused idea is one that is "not sufficiently distinguishable from another, from which it ought to be different" (II.xxix.4). Almost immediately, he raises the objection that the transparency of the mental renders it impossible for ideas to be confused in that sense: "For let any *Idea* be as it will, it can be no other but such as the Mind perceives it to be; and that very perception, sufficiently distinguishes it from all other *Ideas*, which cannot be other, i.e. different, without being perceived to be so" (II.xxix.5). This prompts Locke to offer a more elaborate account of confused ideas. It begins this way:

Now every *Idea* a Man has, being visibly what it is, and distinct from all other *Ideas* but it self, that which makes it *confused* is, when it is such, that it may as well be called by another Name, as that which it is expressed by, the difference which keeps the Things (to be ranked under those two different Names) distinct, and makes some of them belong rather to the one, and some of them to the other of those Names, being left out; and so the distinction, which was intended to be kept up by those different Names, is quite lost. (II.xxix.6).

Here Locke is giving us an account of confusedness according to which it is not an intrinsic feature of an idea, but a feature having to do with the idea's relations to other ideas and terms, and to the distinctions those terms are intended to capture. He is saying that a confused idea is one that is part of an idea/term pairing that promotes confusion by leading to the neglect of distinctions that should be made. I am going to suggest that this is Locke's understanding of what it is for an idea to be confused, even though he does in this passage seem to offer a more specific analysis of confusedness. On that more specific analysis, a person's idea is confused because it is overly general. What looks like a more specific analysis of confusedness is really intended as an example of one sort of confusedness. For Locke immediately goes on to say that the case in which someone associates a term with an overly general idea is but the first of three "*Defaults which* usually *occasion*" the confusion of ideas (II.xxix.7).

This first "default" that occasions confused ideas happens when a complex idea is made up of "*too small a number of simple Ideas*, and such only as are common to other Things, whereby the differences, that make it deserve a different Name, are left out" (II.xxix.7). Locke gives the example of a person who associates the idea "a Beast with Spots" with the term 'Leopard' (II.xxix.7). The idea is too meagre to capture the respects in which leopards differ from lynxes, panthers, and other spotted beasts. So the person who pairs 'Leopard' with this idea counts lynxes, panthers, and other spotted beasts as leopards. It is not that there is anything inherently confused or confusing about the idea of a spotted beast. Nor is Locke pointing to the confusion that results simply because a person associates one idea ("spotted beast") with more than one term ("leopard" and "spotted beast"). That situation occurs every time someone knows a synonym, or speaks two languages. The trouble comes from the fact that here a person lacks ideas that are sufficiently detailed and rich to permit her to make distinctions that she ought to be making. Which distinctions she ought to be making will presumably depend upon what her interests are, and many of these will be dictated by what is necessary for self-preservation and the achievement of pleasure. One also fails to make distinctions that others in one's linguistic community are making with the very terms one is using. If the members of one's linguistic community use 'leopard,' 'panther,' and 'lynx' as *we* do, then one is apt to be confused if one simply associates 'leopard' with the idea "spotted beast."

Looking forward, we see that the third of Locke's three defects occasioning confused ideas is when any idea is "*uncertain, and undetermined*" (II. xxix.9). The passage in which Locke says this is one that we considered earlier, one in which he chides men for changing the ideas they associate with "idolatry" or "church" almost as often as they use the terms. Locke is saying that an idea's being undetermined in this sense suffices for its being confused as well as obscure.

Locke identifies another common cause of confused ideas, and it is "when though the particulars that make up any *Idea*, are in number enough; yet they are so *jumbled together*, that it is not easily discernable, whether it more belongs to the Name that is given it, than to any other" (II.xxix.8). He suggests that we think of this sort of confusion by analogy with anamorphic images, a kind of visual parlor trick popular in England and Holland in the early modern period. Anamorphic images result from one or another kind of systematic spatial distortion. Viewed directly from a "normal" perspective, they present an unintelligible swirl of lines or color. However, when viewed from a particular and unusual perspective, or (in other cases) as reflected in a cylindrical or conical mirror set in the center of the original, they become easily recognizable representations of familiar objects. A famous example of anamorphosis in a serious work of art is to be found in Hans Holbein's *The Ambassadors* (1533), an impressively realistic portrait of two members of the court of Henry VIII in their finery, surrounded by elaborate tapestries, books, and scientific and musical instruments. At the bottom of the painting is a large colored elliptical smear. Only if the painting is viewed from high on the right side at a low angle does the smear resolve into a realistic image of a human skull.

One thing that Locke says about anamorphic images is that the confusedness of such an image is not a matter of its asymmetry. A realistic picture of a cloudy sky will show "as little order of Colours, or Figures" (II.xxix.8). He also notes that "another Draught made, barely in imitation of this [anamorphic image], could not be called confused." Just so, a painstakingly accurate copy of a Jackson Pollock painting would, in a certain sense, be quite the opposite of a confused image. Both of these points illustrate the more general fact that the confusedness of an image is not an intrinsic feature of it. What makes us regard the anamorphic image as confused is "applying to it some Name, to which it does no more discernibly belong, than to some other" (II.xxix.8). With images, the opportunity for confusion arises only when words are used to say what the image represents. Locke wants to say something like that of ideas:

No one of these mental Draughts, however the parts are put together, can be called confused, (for they are plainly discernable as they are,) till it be ranked under some ordinary Name, to which it cannot be discerned to belong, any more than it does to some other Name, of an allowed different signification. (II.xxix.8).

Locke's view seems to be that an image or an idea confuses when words are used to indicate that it represents something that it does not obviously seem to represent. One might object that a person viewing *The Ambassadors* from an ordinary perspective would find the elliptical smear at the bottom of the painting confusing even before the word 'skull' was mentioned in connection with it. Locke should reply that because of the context in which the smear appears—that is, in an otherwise impressively realistic painting—the viewer is encouraged to see that smear as an object of some recognizable kind. Trying to classify a thing is trying to see it as falling under an idea that one already associates with a name. "Applying" a name to a thing need not involve uttering the name. The unwitting viewer finds the elliptical smear confusing because he tries and fails to classify it as of some familiar sort of thing. Contrast this with the case of a knowledgeable art lover contemplating one of Jackson Pollock's later works. The art lover will not find Pollock's image confusing, because he will not try to classify it as being of any sort of object.

Locke begins II.xxix.8 by observing that because some ideas are jumbled, we cannot tell what names to associate with them. He ends the section by saying that ideas become confused only after we rank them under names. If the jumbledness or unjumbledness of an idea is supposed to make its ranking under names more or less problematic, then it must be a feature that an idea has prior to being ranked under a name. In that case, jumbledness must be different from confusedness, though it causes or contributes to confusedness.

What does it mean for an idea to be jumbled? Since Locke does not explain what it means for an idea's constituents to have an order, it is not surprising that he fails to explain what it is for them to be disordered. It again seems likely that he has in mind some analogy with pictures or language. The difference between jumbled and unjumbled visual images is fairly obvious. Some patterns of line and color immediately strike us as resembling familiar objects, and others do not. This is largely a matter of whether or not we detect spatial isomorphisms between images and familiar things. Images are jumbled or unjumbled prior to our ranking them under names, and their being jumbled or unjumbled makes it more or less difficult to rank them under names—that is, to identify their objects as belonging to familiar types. A late Jackson Pollock painting will strike any viewer as jumbled. Whether or not it is also confused depends on whether the viewer is thinking of it as representational, and hence whether the viewer tries and fails to rank under the name of some familiar kind. A linguistic analogue would be a certain kind of nonsense verse—one with mostly familiar words ordered so as to make no literal sense.

If Locke is not to contradict himself, it must be possible for ideas to be jumbled and yet at the same time "plainly discernable as they are" (II. xxix.8). Recall that on his transparency doctrine, we can always perceive the ideas that are in our minds, but we are not always able to perceive the relations that hold among them. One way to explain jumbledness while trying to respect the transparency doctrine would be to say that jumbled complex ideas are ideas the order of whose constituents we have difficulty apprehending. There are two problems with this. One is that it is not clear that Locke can allow that we can perceive which complex ideas we have without perceiving the order of their constituents. Another problem is that the suggested account of jumbledness does not fit well with the analogy he draws between jumbled ideas and anamorphic images. The jumbledness of the smear at the bottom of *The Ambassadors* is not a consequence of our failure to grasp the relations that hold among its constituents. Rather, we succeed at apprehending those relations, and see that they are not isomorphic with the spatial relations that hold between the constituents of any familiar object.

Locke's analogy between jumbled ideas and anamorphic images suggests that a jumbled idea is simply a complex idea whose parts are so arranged that what it represents is not easily recognizable or classifiable. To recognize or classify something is to see it as answering a nominal essence. This suggests that for an idea to be jumbled is for it to present its object as something that does not obviously seem to answer to a nominal essence. Of course, anything that can be presented by an idea will answer to the maximally general nominal essence "thing." Perhaps Locke will say that an idea is jumbled if its object does not seem to answer to a more specific nominal essence. Jumbledness so conceived might be a matter of degree.

In the correspondence with Stillingfleet, Locke charges the Bishop with having misunderstood his account of confused ideas (*Works* IV, 379–80). Not wanting to repeat himself, he refers Stillingfleet to II.xxix.4–6. However, Locke does go on to flesh out the account a bit more. Stillingfleet had suggested that Locke's transparency doctrine commits him to the view that an idea must be clear and distinct if we are to have certainty about its object (Stillingfleet 1698, 110). Locke says that on his account an idea can be sufficiently distinct in one's mind, and yet be confused. In such a case, he says, "the confusion [is] made by a careless application of distinct names to ideas, that are not sufficiently distinct." He offers the example of a person who has different ideas of the liquor in a sheep's heart (red, opaque, warm) and of that in a lobster's heart (aqueous, pellucid, cold), and yet uses 'blood' to refer to both. Locke clearly thinks of this as a case in which someone fails to use language to mark a distinction that he should be making. If it is also to be a case of someone using a non-standard idea/ term pairing, then perhaps it is non-standard in relation to the specialized linguistic community of natural philosophers. It is less clear how it is supposed to be an example of the careless application of distinct names to ideas that are not sufficiently distinct. In the example, we seem to have one name ('blood') and two sufficiently distinct ideas. Perhaps all he means by the "careless application of distinct names to ideas, that are not sufficiently distinct" is the application of one or more names to ideas that are not sufficiently distinguished linguistically. In that case, the example does fit the description.

Locke goes on to tell Stillingfleet that there are two sorts of cases in which we may have certainty about the truth of a proposition even when some of the ideas corresponding to terms in the proposition are not clear and distinct.[22] The first are cases of undetermined ideas, cases in which a term "comes to stand sometimes for one idea, sometimes for another" (*Works* IV, 380). The second sort of case is one in which someone supposes a "name to stand for something more than really is in the idea in our minds, which we make it a sign of" (*Works* IV, 380). He gives the example of a man who has forgotten the taste of a pineapple, but who remembers the other observable features of that fruit. This man associates an idea with 'pineapple,' but the idea that he associates with 'pineapple' contains less information than does that in the mind of one who "newly eat of that fruit, and has the idea of the taste of it also fresh in his mind" (*Works* IV, 380).

§31 *Problems with the Idea of Substance*

Locke complains that the idea of substance is not clear,[23] that it is not distinct,[24] that it is confused,[25] and that it is obscure.[26] These are two complaints really, since he contrasts obscure ideas with clear ones, and confused ideas with distinct ones. He also complains that our idea of substance is not a positive idea,[27] and that it is undetermined[28] and vague.[29] We are now in a position to begin to see what these complaints come to.

What Locke means when he complains that the idea of substance is obscure depends on whether he takes it to be a simple idea or a complex one. He does at one point refer to the idea of substance as simple, but the context is not one that encourages us to take that characterization seriously. In the first letter to Stillingfleet, he says:

The obscurity I find in my own mind, when I examine what positive, general, simple idea of substance I have, is such as I profess, and further than that I cannot go; but what, and how clear it is in the understanding of a seraphim, or of an elevated mind, that I cannot determine. (*Works* IV, 28)

Locke has just admitted to "the dimness" of his "conceptions." There is fairly obvious irony in his suggestion that Stillingfleet might have a clearer

---

[22] In the exchange with Stillingfleet, Locke does not mention ideas being confused because they are jumbled.

[23] I.iv.18; II.xiii.17; II.xxiii.3,4, etc.

[24] II.xiii.17; II.xxiii.2,4; *Works* IV, 21, 27, etc.

[25] II.xii.6; II.xiii.19; II.xxiii.3; *Works* IV, 27, 29, etc.

[26] II.xiii.19; II.xxiii.3; *Works* IV, 21–2, 25, 27–9, etc.

[27] I.iv.18; II.xxiii.15; IV.iii.23.

[28] *Works* IV, 29.

[29] *Works* IV, 21, 27.

understanding of substance on account of his having an "elevated" mind more like an angel's. There is also reason to think that his description of the idea of substance here is somewhat facetious. His idea of substance may be general, but he makes it clear on several occasions that he does not think that any of us has a *positive* idea of substance.[30] Since Locke holds that all simple ideas originate in sensation or reflection, he could not consistently maintain that it is a simple idea while denying that it comes from either of those sources (as he does at I.iv.18). Thus it is not surprising to find him telling Stillingfleet quite directly that it is a complex idea (*Works* IV, 19).

If the idea of substance is complex and obscure, then either one or more of its constituent simple ideas is obscure, or else it is undetermined or uncertain. There is at least one reason for thinking that the obscurity of the idea of substance cannot be a matter of its having an obscure simple idea as a constituent. Locke's view is that the clarity of a simple idea is a matter of its being produced by a well-disposed organ. He does not explain what it is for an organ to be well-disposed, but earlier I suggested that he should say that a well-disposed organ is one that functions in a manner typical for one's species. If that is the way that he is thinking about "well-disposed" organs, then he cannot make sense of the claim that a simple idea is obscure for all, or even most, people. Yet Locke does think that the idea of substance is obscure for all of us, and presumably for the same reason, whatever that is.[31]

If Locke thinks that the idea of substance is complex and obscure, but not that it is obscure on account of having obscure simple constituents, then he must think that it is undetermined or uncertain. In fact, he does complain of its being undetermined. At II.xiii.18, having just raised and then set aside the question whether empty space is substance or accident, he says:

It helps not our Ignorance, to feign a Knowledge, where we have none, by making a noise with Sounds, without clear and distinct Significations. Names made at pleasure, neither alter the nature of things, nor make us understand them, but as they are signs of, and stand for determined *Ideas*.

---

[30] See note 27 above.

[31] As we have already glimpsed, Locke does sometimes say that others beside himself might have clear and distinct ideas of substance, but this is mere rhetoric. To Stillingfleet, he says:[Y]our lordship must enjoy the privilege of the sight and clear ideas you have: nor can you be denied them, because I have not the like; the dimness of my conceptions must not pretend to hinder the clearness of your lordship's, any more than the want of them in a blind man can debar your lordship of the clear and distinct ideas of colours (*Works* IV, 28). Clearly he is having a bit of fun at the Bishop's expense.

Locke goes on to pose a dilemma about whether we are invoking the same idea of substance when we apply "these two Syllables, *Substance*" to God, finite spirit, and body. He thinks that there are serious problems with both "yes" and "no" answers, and does not himself try to resolve the dilemma. What matters for us at the moment is that he is using the case of substance to illustrate what goes wrong when we use words that do not stand for "determined *Ideas*."

That is not the only place that Locke complains about "substance" being an undetermined idea. In the first letter to Stillingfleet, after explaining how we arrive at the idea of substance, he says:

> And thus I come by a certainty of the existence of that something which is a support of those sensible modes, though I have but a very confused, loose, and undetermined idea of it, signified by the name substance.[32]

For Locke, the complaint that the idea of substance is undetermined could conceivably mean either that (i) the term 'substance' is associated with more than one idea, or that (ii) more than one term is associated with a single idea, "substance." Both (i) and (ii) could come in intra-personal and inter-personal versions. Internal evidence suggests that at II.xiii.18 and in this passage it is (i) that Locke has in mind. At II.xiii.18 that is quite clear, since the whole point is to raise the question of whether we are using 'substance' in different senses in different contexts. Here in the letter to Stillingfleet, there is the fact that he mentions just one "name"—'substance'—as he tells us that the idea is undetermined.

That Locke has (i) in mind when he complains of the idea of substance being undetermined is also what we should expect given the depth of his pessimism about philosophical accounts of substance. That is because (i) presents a much thornier problem than (ii) does. On the intra-personal version, the worst that (ii) seems likely to yield is fairly harmless redundancy, as when non-philosophers talk of "morals and ethics" or "soul and spirit." Even on the inter-personal version—when several parties use different terms but have the same idea in mind—this seems likely to give rise to temporary confusion rather than intractable disputes. It seems likely to generate the sort of confusion that arises when one person does not—and others do—know an idiom, a technical term, or an out-of-the-way word such as 'defenestration.'

---

[32] This passage appears at *Works* IV, 29, but with an error: the *Works* has "the same substance" whereas the passage should read "the name Substance," as it does in Locke 1697, 58.

Eventually the parties will turn to talk of examples, and will discover that their terms or phrases have the same extension, that theirs is merely a problem of translation. By contrast, (i) can make for deeper muddles. In an intra-personal case of (i), one's reasoning about substance is likely to be permeated by the fallacy of ambiguity. In the inter-personal case, disputes arising from the fact that 'substance' is used in different senses may masquerade as disputes about the features possessed by candidates for the title of substance. The worst is when intra-personal and inter-personal versions of (i) combine, when people who are themselves unknowingly veering between different senses of 'substance' in their reasonings go on to argue with one another about substances or substance-hood. This is just the sort of predicament that Locke seems to think that we are in, for he confesses that his *own* idea of substance is undetermined, and yet he thinks that his problem is a general one.

Locke's view that he, and we, associate more than one idea with the term 'substance' could account for both his verdict that the idea of substance is obscure, and his verdict that it is confused. For as we have seen, he holds that an idea's being "*uncertain, and undetermined*" is one of the common defects that leads us to call them "Confused" (II.xxix.9). When we unwittingly use a term first in one sense, and then in another, we get muddled, we confuse other people, and we fail to mark distinctions that we should be making. Yet Locke also leaves open the possibility that the idea of substance is confused for other reasons—because it is too meager to enable us to make distinctions that we ought to be making, or because it presents its object as jumbled and so as not readily classifiable. Indeed, the fact that Locke thinks that we are unsteady in the idea we associate with 'substance' opens up the possibility that various of the ideas we associate with 'substance' have these different defects.

So far we have considered what Locke means when he calls the idea of substance undetermined, obscure, and confused. He also complains that it is vague, and that we have no positive idea of substance. Locke offers no account of vagueness, and does not seem to have any technical notion in mind. Perhaps he is thinking that an idea is vague if it is unclear what exactly belongs to the extension of the associated term. If he thinks that we unwittingly waver between using 'substance' in different senses, it is easy to see why he might think the idea of substance is vague in that sense.

To understand Locke's complaint that we lack a positive idea of substance, we must appreciate that he contrasts positive ideas with relative ideas.

We see this in the *Essay* when he speaks of seemingly positive ideas that conceal tacit relations (II.xxv.3; II.xxvi.4). We see it in the correspondence with Stillingfleet when he speaks of ideas as simple or complex, positive or relative, general or particular. A positive idea is one that presents, or seems to present, intrinsic features of its object. Locke thinks that the idea of substratum is not a positive idea because he thinks that it is simply the idea of something that stands in the relation of support to modes or accidents.

Let us try to sum up Locke's complaints about the idea of substratum. (i) Individually and collectively we associate different ideas with 'substance' and unwittingly slide between them. (ii) This fact, and perhaps also certain features of one or more of the idea/'substance' pairs, leads us to neglect distinctions that we ought to be making. The features of idea/'substance' pairs that might lead us to neglect distinctions that we ought to be making may include (but are not necessarily limited to) (iii) one or more of the ideas containing too little detail, and (iv) one or more of them presenting its object as something that is not readily classifiable. (v) The extension of 'substance' is vague, perhaps because of (i), (iii), and (iv). (vi) One or more of the ideas we associate with 'substance' is a wholly relational idea, and does not represent intrinsic features of its object. At the end of §28, we raised the question of how Locke can allow the idea of substance to be confused and obscure while also holding to his transparency doctrine. We can now see that the answer lies in understanding what he is complaining of when he complains that the idea of substance is confused and obscure. He is not saying that we are unable to make out, at any particular moment, the contents of an idea of substance that is in our mind. Problems (i)–(vi) are ones to which we may be liable even if Locke's transparency doctrine is true.

Looking back over the ground that we have covered, we can see that Locke's own texts lend credence to his worry that he is juggling several different notions of substance and not always managing to keep them separate. When he speaks of "the idea of substance in general," he often has in mind not the general idea of the category substance, but the idea of a supporter of qualities. Whether he always keeps these ideas distinct, and what he thinks of the relation between them, is unclear. He offers two descriptions of how we arrive at the idea of substance, but does not tell us whether these are meant to be descriptions of the same process or whether these processes are supposed to yield the same idea. At times he seems to presume that our idea of substance is the idea of a thing, at other times he seems to be thinking of it as the idea of a stuff. At times he suggests that the idea of substance represents something altogether feature-less; at other times, he suggests that bodies and minds are composed of different sorts of substance. Despite all of this, it is unlikely that Locke thinks that the only problem with our idea of substance is that 'substance' is ambiguous. To know that a term is ambiguous one must already have some idea about what are the different meanings associated with the term, and to do this is already to be on one's way toward solving the problem. Locke is less optimistic than he should be if he thought that he was in this position.

To the extent that Locke explains what goes wrong when an idea is unde-termined, obscure, confused, relative, or vague, we can see him as offering the beginnings of a diagnosis of where we go wrong in our thinking about substratum. Yet it is also perfectly clear that Locke does not think that he is in a position to set us straight about where we go wrong, and how to avoid it in the future. Locke is in the unenviable position of being a philosopher who realizes that he is in a muddle, and has some inkling of the sort of mud-dle that he is in, without his being able to see his way through it entirely. He writes like a man who is beginning to see that he has painted himself into a corner. He may see that his thoughts about substance lead him to troubling or even paradoxical conclusions about the relations between properties and property-bearers. He may also have reason to suspect that the trouble lies in the unsettled meaning he gives 'substance.' He may see that he has trouble producing a helpful definition of 'substance,' and that he has trouble answer-ing questions about the extension of 'substance.' Nevertheless, he cannot put his finger on just how and where he, and we, have gone wrong.

Our closer look at Locke's complaints about the idea of substance shows that he does not take himself to be offering solutions to any of the long-standing puzzles that philosophical theories of substance have traditionally been called upon to solve. His modest reflections about the ideas of sub-stance and substratum do not amount to a theory about what are the onto-logically independent things upon which modes depend. They do not tell us how many basic kinds of stuff there are, or what their natures are. They do not answer questions about the ontological categories to which God and space belong, or resolve puzzles about the individuation of bodies, or spirits, or people. Some of these traditional problems Locke simply leaves unsolved, mindful as always of his limitations and ours. Others he does have more to say about, outside the context of a theory of substance. It is to these we turn next, beginning with his theory of identity and individuation.

6

Mind and Matter

§32. Locke is a substance dualist. He holds that God and angels are immaterial substances, and that it is likely that our minds are immaterial substances too. §33. In the course of arguing for the existence of God, Locke considers and rejects a number of materialist scenarios, including one on which a single atom thinks, another on which every particle of matter thinks, and a third on which a compound material thing thinks because of the arrangement or motion of its parts. §34. Though Locke is no materialist, he holds that we cannot rule out the possibility that God can give powers of thought to material substances. He offers no account of how God might do this, though he rules out the possibility that He might do it just by creating a body with certain mechanical features. Locke is not committed to the view that a body's powers of thought would have to be grounded in any of its more basic features. §35. In fact, he holds that God clearly does give bodies some powers that we cannot understand as grounded in their more basic features. These include the powers that bodies have to produce sensory ideas in us, and their gravitational powers. §36. Locke invokes the arbitrary will of God to explain the cohesion of matter, the communication of motion through impulse, and the laws of motion. This voluntarism is compatible with the view that mechanical interactions are relatively intelligible, and it does not commit him to occasionalism. §37. Mechanism is best understood as involving a commitment to the view that all natural phenomena can be explained in terms of the mechanical affections of bodies, and also to the view that bodies act upon one another only through contact. Locke's views about thinking matter and gravitation show that he is not committed to mechanism.

§32 Immaterial Substances

Substance dualism is the view that there are fundamentally two different kinds of things or stuff: material things or stuff, and non-material things or stuff. Locke offers what he takes to be absolutely decisive arguments for God's existence and for God's immateriality. This is enough to make him a substance dualist. If we are to have any reluctance about affixing that label to him, it is only because he may be seen as leaving open the possibility that there are *more* than two basic kinds of substances. We saw earlier (§26) that he raises and does not answer the question of whether God, finite spirits, and body agree "in the same common nature of *Substance*" (II.xiii.18). One way to understand this is to see him as allowing for the possibility that God, finite spirits, and bodies represent three different basic kinds of substances. One might call this position substance trialism rather than substance dualism. Yet even if we read Locke this way, it is not clear that there is anything wrong with calling him a substance dualist. For even if God, finite spirits, and bodies are substances of fundamentally different kinds, there is a contrast to be drawn between the kinds to which God and finite spirits belong, and that to which bodies belong. Though God's special nature may make Him a substance of a different sort, or in a different sense, than any finite thing, Locke's God is wholly immaterial and has this in common with finite spirits as they are ordinarily conceived. Thus the sort of trialism that Locke considers would also seem to be a form of dualism. It contrasts with the trialism that some have ascribed to Descartes, on which a third kind of substance combines the natures of material substance and immaterial substance (Cottingham 1985).

Locke conceives of God as eternal, omnipotent, and omniscient. If we can show that there is something with these features, he says, we have shown that God exists, even if we are (mistakenly) conceiving of this thing as material (IV.x.13). We make our idea of God in much the same way as we make complex ideas of finite spirits. We combine simple ideas that we acquire by reflection, including the ideas of existence, duration, knowledge, power, pleasure, happiness, and so on (II.xxiii.33). At least some of these ideas represent features that we conceive of as coming in various degrees (II.xxiii.34). Of these, the ones that we include in our idea of God we join with the idea of infinity (II.xxiii.35). Thus we conceive of God as having infinite knowledge, infinite power, and so on. This idea of infinity is all that distinguishes our idea of God from our ideas of other spirits (II.xxiii.36). Yet we must not be overly bold and suppose that we have anything like an adequate conception of God (II.xxiii.35). We do not know God's essence, and He may be simple and uncompounded even if our idea of Him is not.

Locke believes that it is likely that there are angels; and that if there are, they are partly or wholly composed of immaterial substances. He thinks that we cannot know whether angels exist (I.iv.9; IV.iii.27), but that divine revelation supplies us with one reason for thinking that they do (IV.iii.27). Another derives from the sort of analogical reasoning that justifies our belief in material beings too small or distant for us to perceive. We see subtle gradations between beings in the visible world, and so "have reason to be perswaded, that by such gentle steps Things ascend upwards in degrees of Perfection" (IV.xvi.12). Locke allows that angels may be able to "assume to themselves Bodies of different Bulk, Figure, and Conformation of Parts" (II.xxiii.13). Whether this would involve an angel's being partly composed of something material, or its merely standing in some special relation to something material, he does not say. He suggests that angels may be able to assume organs of perception that give them ideas of the corpuscular structures of things. He presumes that they have greater knowledge than we do, however they come by it (II.xxiii.36). He also presumes that they have greater happiness than we do, and more perfect ways of communicating their thoughts.

Locke also thinks it is likely that our minds are immaterial substances. In the *Essay*, he says that "the more probable Opinion" is that our consciousness is "annexed to, and the Affection of one individual immaterial Substance" (II.xxvii.25). Later he tells Stillingfleet that arguments in the *Essay* "prove it in the highest degree probable, that the thinking substance in us is immaterial" (*Works* IV, 33). He repeats the claim a few pages later (*Works* IV, 37).

Locke holds that there are certain features common to material and immaterial substances. The ideas of existence, duration, and mobility are, he says, common to bodies and spirits (II.xxiii.18). We might be reluctant to saddle him with the view that existence and duration are properly counted as affections at all, but in fact he does unhesitatingly call them that (II.x.6; II.xv.4). Number is another affection that Locke says is possessed by both material and immaterial substances (II.x.6). The idea of number "applies it self to Men, Angels, Actions, Thoughts, every thing that either doth exist, or can be imagined" (II.xvi.1). Earlier (§11) I suggested that this means just that each thing is one thing, and so is possessed of number.

When he first addresses the relation of spirits to space, Locke is circumspect, saying that we cannot know "what Spirits have to do with Space, or how they communicate in it" (II.xv.11). Yet even there he insists that human intelligence cannot conceive of "any real Being, with a perfect Negation of all manner of Expansion." When the issue comes up again, he is more forthright in ascribing mobility to spirits. He argues that they must move, because they can operate only where they are, and they clearly operate in different places at different times (II.xxiii.19–21). Locke unflinchingly maintains that God is literally present at every location in space. We cannot so much as imagine "any Expansion where he is not" (II.xv.2). To say otherwise is to limit God in a way that is contrary to His nature. We easily admit that God fills eternity, and Locke says that we will have a difficult time finding a reason to deny that he also fills "Immensity" (II.xv.3). It is infinite extent, and not immateriality, that prevents God from being able to move (II.xxiii.21).

As for the features that are peculiar to immaterial substances, Locke's most helpful remarks about these come in II.xxiii, where he argues that our knowledge of immaterial substances is roughly on a par with our knowledge of material ones.[1] We know that bodies are composed of cohering solid parts, and that they possess the power to communicate motion though impact, though we understand neither cohesion nor impulse. Likewise, we know that immaterial spirits are thinking things with powers to initiate actions, though we understand neither the basis of thought nor how spirits move bodies. Sensation provides us with ideas of many particular qualities in bodies: color, shape, size, and so forth. Similarly, reflection provides us with ideas of "the several modes of Thinking, viz. Believing, Doubting, Intending, Fearing, Hoping," and of "Willing, and Moving the Body consequent to it" (II.xxiii.30).

Early in the Essay, Locke gives a quick survey of several modes of thinking—sensation, recollection, contemplation, attention, intention, and dreaming—and then promises that he will have "occasion hereafter to treat more at large of Reasoning, Judging, Volition, and Knowledge, which are some of the most considerable Operations of the mind" (II.xix.2). He keeps his promise. He gives his account of volition in II.xxi ("Of Power"), and we shall give this close attention later on. His account of the nature,

---

[1] Locke sometimes speaks of our knowledge of bodies and of spirits, rather than of material and immaterial substances. This might be thought consequential because spirits for him are not necessarily immaterial (Works IV, 32). However, he makes it abundantly clear in II.xxiii that his topic is our knowledge of bodies and of *immaterial* spirits (see II.xxiii.16, 22, 26, 31).

extent, and improvement of knowledge occupies much of Book IV, and he devotes a chapter apiece to reason and judgment (IV.xvii and IV.xiv, respectively). Locke says that knowledge is the perception of the agreement or disagreement between ideas (IV.i.2). In what he calls intuitive knowledge, the agreement or disagreement of ideas is immediate and perspicacious (IV.ii.1). In demonstrative knowledge, it is perceived only with the aid of intermediate ideas (IV.ii.2). Reasoning is the operation by which we discover and order these intermediate ideas (IV.xvii.2). Sensitive knowledge is what Locke calls the awareness that we have of the existence of things outside us (IV.ii.14), an assurance that he says extends only to bodies while we are perceiving them (IV.xi.9, 11). In general, knowledge is scanty; often the best that we can manage is probable judgment. Judgment involves not the perception of agreement or disagreement between ideas, but rather the presumption of such agreement or disagreement.[2] Locke's accounts of knowledge, reason, and judgment belong more to epistemology than to metaphysics, and a detailed examination of them lies outside the purview of the present work.

When Locke describes immaterial spirits as thinking things, he means that they possess the capacity for thought. He is suspicious of the Cartesian claim that the soul is always actually thinking (II.i.9–19). The soul's property of thinking is comparable to a body's power of moving, he says, it being no more "necessary for the *Soul always to think*, than for the Body always to move" (II.i.10). Locke also distinguishes between a broad sense of 'thinking' on which even the passive reception of ideas counts, and a narrower and more proper sense on which thinking requires activity and attention on our part (II.ix.1). This raises the question of whether it is the capacity to think in the broader sense that is supposed to be basic to spirits, or whether it is the capacity to think in the narrower and stricter sense. A change that Locke makes in the *Essay*'s fourth edition suggests the former.

The chapter "Of Power" ends with a list of the "very few primary, and original" ideas on which the rest of our ideas are supposed to depend. In the first edition, the list includes extension, solidity, and mobility, said to be received by our sense from body; thinking and the power of moving, said to be received by reflection upon our minds; and existence, duration, and

---

[2] For a fuller treatment of Locke's account of judgment, see Owen 2007.

number, said to "belong" both to body and mind (II.xxi.47 [1st]). In the fourth edition, Locke substitutes '*Perceptivity*, or the Power of perception, or thinking' for '*Thinking*' (II.xxi.73 [4th]). He explains that he has coined the term 'perceptivity' so as to avoid the potential for misunderstanding that comes with the use of an equivocal term such as 'thinking.'[3] Here Locke makes it clear that the "thinking" that is the primary and original idea associated with spirit is the power of perception. At II.ix.1, he equates perception with thinking in the broad sense—that is, with the capacity for awareness in general, rather than the narrower capacity for focused mental activity. So it is thinking in the broad sense that Locke means to identify as a primary idea or property of spirit.

§33 A Case for Dualism

Because Locke conceives of God as an immaterial substance, his argument for the existence of God amounts to an argument for substance dualism. Theism is generally taken to entail substance dualism, but in Locke's case the connection between the case for theism and the case for dualism is particularly close. He argues for the existence of God by arguing that nothing but God's existence could account for the existence of finite thinking things; in the course of this argument, he commits himself to principles that rule out a materialist metaphysics. Locke argues for what is often called property dualism, and uses that to argue for the existence of God and for substance dualism. Property dualism is the view that mental features and physical features form two closed sets, none of the members of either being ultimately explicable in terms of, or reducible to, members of the other. Property dualism by itself does not necessarily entail substance dualism. It is possible for the property dualist to hold that there is just one kind of substance, and that this one kind of substance has both mental and physical features. In fact, though he is a property dualist, Locke allows that there may be material substances that have both mental and physical features. However, he argues that material substances could come to possess mental features only through the agency of an immaterial God. Thus for him property dualism does entail substance dualism.

---

[3] The OED does cite II.xxi.73 as the first appearance of 'perceptivity.'

Locke's argument for the existence of God is so obviously fallacious that its interest for us lies almost entirely in its component parts and what they tell us about Locke's philosophy of mind and matter. His first pass over the argument occupies IV.x.2–7. His case for theism begins where Descartes's does, with a claim about the certainty that each of us has that he exists. It is, Locke says, "beyond Question, that *Man has a clear Perception of his own Being*" (IV.x.2). He also regards it as intuitively certain that something cannot come from nothing. From this, he fallaciously infers the existence of something eternal:

If therefore we know there is some real Being, and that Non-entity cannot produce any real Being, it is an evident demonstration, that from Eternity there has been something; Since what was not from Eternity, had a Beginning; and what had a Beginning, must be produced by something else. (IV.x.3)

If it is granted that something cannot come from nothing, and if one makes the natural supposition that one is not eternal, this licenses the conclusion that at some time there must exist something that caused one to exist. Locke's glaring mistake is to draw the much stronger conclusion that there must be something eternal that caused one to exist. He neglects the possibility that each of us is a non-eternal thing that is caused to exist by a non-eternal thing, which was in turn caused to exist by a non-eternal thing, and so on. He also neglects the possibility that there might be several eternal things, and that different eternal things may be ultimately responsible for the existence of different non-eternal things. He moves directly to the conclusion that there is one eternal thing that is the ultimate cause of the existence of every non-eternal thing. Locke then reasons that whatever is the ultimate cause of the existence of all of the non-eternal things must also be the cause of their having the powers they do. He may be thinking that if created things have powers, they must have gotten them from their causes, or else something would have come from nothing. He concludes that the ultimate cause of the existence of all of the non-eternal things is a single, eternal and most powerful thing.

From this point, Locke goes on to argue that the eternal cause of all non-eternal things must be a thinking thing. He contends, as Descartes does, that each of us is certain not only of his own existence, but of the fact that he is a thinking thing. He reasons that either the eternal cause is a thinking thing, or else he and other non-eternal thinking things have an unthinking thing as their ultimate cause. He then claims that it is absolutely impossible for an unthinking thing to be the ultimate cause of a thinking thing:

It being as impossible, that Things wholly void of Knowledge, and operating blindly, and without any Perception, should produce a knowing Being, as it is impossible that a Triangle should make it self three Angles bigger than two right ones. For it is as repugnant to the *Idea* of senseless Matter, that it should put into it self Sense, Perception, and Knowledge, as it is repugnant to the *Idea* of a Triangle, that it should put into it self greater Angles than two right ones. (IV.x.5)

Locke concludes that the eternal thing that is the ultimate cause of non-eternal thinking things must itself be a thinking thing. He quickly and silently moves from this to the conclusion that this eternal thing must be a "*most knowing Being*" (IV.x.6). Perhaps, if pressed, he would again justify this by invoking the principle that something cannot come from nothing. He may suppose that any knowledge, or capacity for acquiring knowledge, that is possessed by non-eternal things must ultimately derive from their ultimate cause. This might be thought to entail that the ultimate cause has whatever knowledge can be possessed by non-eternal thinking things. Having argued for the existence of an eternal, most powerful, and most knowing being that is the ultimate cause of all non-eternal things, Locke takes himself to have shown that God exists.

Locke has enormous confidence in his argument for the existence of God. He suggests that anyone who attends to it carefully will find its cogency irresistible (IV.x.7). Nonetheless, given the importance of its conclusion, he deems it worthwhile to revisit and to enlarge upon certain parts of his exposition. In the course of this, he says more about why it is that unthinking matter could never, by itself, give rise to a thinking thing. He begins at IV.x.10, with the claim that an eternal parcel of matter would be "in it self, able to produce nothing." He illustrates this in reference to motion. An eternal parcel of matter could not, he says, produce motion in itself. He then goes on to say that even if an eternal parcel of unthinking matter had motion always, it could not by itself give rise to a thinking thing:

I appeal to every one's own Thoughts, whether he cannot as easily conceive Matter produced by *nothing*, as Thought to be produced by pure Matter, when before there was no such thing as Thought, or an intelligent Being existing....[Y]ou may as rationally expect to produce Sense, Thought, and Knowledge, by putting together in a certain Figure and Motion, gross Particles of Matter as by those that are the very minutest, that do any where exist. They knock, impell, and resist one another, just as the greater do, and that is all they can do.

Locke suspects that we may be tempted to imagine that if matter is divided into sufficiently small parts, it may become "spiritualized" and acquire powers of thought. He thinks that this is a mistake. Tiny bits of matter can interact only in the ways that larger chunks can, and it is inconceivable that mechanical interactions should give rise to thought. From our perspective, there are several failures of imagination here: the assumption that there is no difference between microphysics and macrophysics, the assumption that bodies interact only by knocking against one another, and the inability to conceive that interactions between material parts might give rise to thought.

Locke has argued that an eternal parcel of unthinking matter cannot give rise to thought. This still leaves the possibility that an eternal parcel of *thinking* matter does. He regards this too as inconceivable, and offers a reason for thinking so. If we suppose an eternal parcel of thinking matter, he says, "then Sense, Perception, and Knowledge, must be a property eternally inseparable from Matter and every Particle of it" (IV.x.10). Locke is saying that if we admit the possibility of an eternal material thinking thing, we are forced to an absurd form of panpsychism. He then goes on to offer an argument for this:

Not to add, that though our general or specifick conception of Matter makes us speak of it as one thing, yet really [A] all Matter is not one individual thing, [B] neither is there any such thing existing as one material Being or [C] one single Body that we know or can conceive. And therefore [D] if Matter were the eternal first cogitative Being, there would not be one eternal infinite cogitative Being, but an infinite number of eternal finite cogitative Beings, independent of one another, of limited force, and distinct thoughts, which could never produce that order, harmony, and beauty which is to be found in Nature.[4]

This is a curious argument, and a somewhat obscure one. In [A], he denies that the totality of matter is one individual thing. In [C]—and possibly in [B] as well[5]—he denies that we can know or conceive of one single material being. It is not obvious what these claims amount to, or what reasons Locke has for making them.

---

[4] I have inserted the letters in brackets for ease of reference.

[5] Whether in [B] and [C] he is ruling out two possibilities or only one depends on whether we take '…that we know or can conceive' to modify [C] alone or [B] as well. On the second option, [B] and [C] are equivalent, the only difference being the substitution of 'Body' for 'material Being.' Locke is denying that there is one body that we can know or conceive. On the first option, [B] says that there is one material being and [C] that there is one conceivable or knowable material being. This would make the denial of [B] even stronger than the denial of [C].

Let us begin by considering how we might understand Locke's denial, in [B] that there is such a thing as one material being. Here are three interpretations of the claim:

(6.1)   It is not the case that there are any material things.

(6.2)   It is never the case that a number of particles jointly compose a material thing.

(6.3)   It is never the case that any body we pick out is *just* one thing.

Reading (6.1) is a non-starter. Locke surely does not mean to be saying that there is not even one material thing in existence.

On reading (6.2), Locke is saying that there are no complex bodies. The only material things are atoms or particles. What we ordinarily take for complex bodies are in fact just collections of atoms or particles. Any mental features belonging to material things are mental features of particles. Taken by itself, the claim that there is not "any such thing existing as one material Being" does not sound like an expression of (6.2). However, coming on the heels of [A] we can read [B] that way. In [A], he tells us that the totality of matter is not a compound material thing, and [B] might be seen as making the more general point that nothing is a compound material thing. The trouble with (6.2) is that it conflicts with much that Locke says, and it is not at all clear how to construct an argument for it out of Lockean materials. We saw in §3 that substances comprise one of the fundamental categories of Locke's ontology, and that he conceives of these as distinct particular things. Many of the items that he calls substances are compound material things. These include men, animals, and artifacts.

It may be suggested that Locke often allows himself to speak as though there are such complex material things, but that when he is doing ground-floor metaphysics he regards this as loose talk about what are really collections of particles. The problem is that this requires us to say that he buried his deepest thoughts about the identity and individuation of material bodies in the middle of his argument for God's immateriality, and left them *out* of his chapter-long exploration of identity and individuation. In II.xxvii ("*Of Identity and Diversity*"), Locke enunciates principles about the identity of simple material things, but also ones about the identity of such compound material things as masses and persons. There is no suggestion that any of this is provisional or loose talk.

I conclude that reading (6.3) offers the most plausible way to understand Locke's denial that there is "any such thing existing as one material
Being." In [A] he is telling us that the totality of the world's matter is not
just one thing, and in [B] and [C] he is making the point that this is one
instance of a more general truth. Locke is in fact independently committed to the view that each of the compound material bodies that we see,
talk about, and navigate around is both an individual unified thing and
a collection of particles. He is, as we shall see (§§45–46), committed to
the view that almost all identity judgments are relative to sortal concepts.
Each of the bodies that surrounds us falls under indefinitely many sortal
concepts, and in the case of most these include the concept of a collection
of atoms or particles. We can also see that Lockean principles take us from
(6.3) to [D]. Reading [B] as (6.3), we have the claim that any compound
material thing is not just one thing, but a collection of particles. Those
particles will also be the ultimate parts of the thing. Locke presumes that
the features of any complex thing must be explicable in terms of its ultimate parts and their features. He has just argued that thought cannot
arise from the arrangement of *unthinking* particles. He concludes that if
an eternal parcel of matter thinks, it must do so because it is composed of
thinking particles.

One reason that Locke regards the possibility of thinking particles as patently absurd is that he takes it to involve each particle having sense, perception, and knowledge. He neglects the possibility that bits of matter might
have some kind of proto-mental features falling short of conscious experience like ours, features that somehow combine to make for sense, perception,
and knowledge in the compound thing they jointly compose. This does not
seem a possibility to him because he holds that all mental activity is a matter of having ideas, and that one cannot have ideas without being aware that
one has them.[6] To have any mental activity is to have conscious awareness,
which is what he calls having "perception." Locke may reason that anything
with any mental features must receive ideas somehow, and so must have
something like sense or reflection. He may also reason that anything with
conscious experience must have knowledge, at least about the contents of

---

[6] Locke allows two senses in which it is possible to have ideas in mind, an episodic sense and a dispositional sense (Stuart 2010). It is the former that is primary for Locke, and in this sense having an idea
entails awareness of the idea. He also speaks of having ideas laid up in memory. To do this is to have had
an idea episodically before, and to have the ability to make oneself have it episodically again.

those ideas. Locke concludes that if there were an eternal, material thinking being, there must be an infinite number of such beings. Presumably this is supposed to follow because of the infinite divisibility of matter (§9).

We have just seen Locke argue that if we admit an eternal, material thinking thing, this commits us to the view that every particle of matter thinks, which makes for a *reductio*. He does not take this result for granted in the rest of the chapter. Instead, he engages in a sort of tactical retreat for rhetorical purposes. At IV.x.14–17, he continues to examine the possibility of an eternal, material thinking thing, and he surveys three possibilities: (i) that every constituent particle of the eternal parcel thinks; (ii) that one constituent particle of the eternal parcel thinks; and (iii) that no constituent particle of the eternal parcel thinks. He argues that none of these will do, and so again draws the conclusion that the eternal thinking thing is immaterial.

At IV.x.14, Locke remarks that those who would claim that the eternal, thinking being is material "will scarce say" that every particle of matter thinks. This time he not only presumes that panpsychism is absurd, but suggests that it has untoward theological consequences. To suppose that every particle of matter thinks is, he says, to suppose that there is an "infinity of Gods." It is unclear how seriously Locke means this. Earlier, he had claimed that if every particle of matter thinks, these will be "independent one of another, of limited force, and distinct thoughts" (IV.x.10). Such things would seem to be less than gods. In the intervening passages, Locke has offered no reason for taking thinking particles to be more godlike. Perhaps at IV.x.14 he is speaking loosely, and calling the particles "Gods" just because they, like God as traditionally conceived, are eternal thinking things.

Locke then considers the possibility that there is only one eternal, thinking material thing, and that this thing is a single atom. He says that either this atom would be the one eternal thing that causes everything else, or the rest of matter would also be eternal. If a thinking atom is the lone eternal thing, and the cause of everything non-eternal, then "we have the creation of Matter by a powerful Thought, which is what the Materialists stick at" (IV.x.15). Locke reasons that since thought is what distinguishes the eternal atom from the non-eternal ones, it must be the eternal atom's thought that accounts for the creation of everything else.[7] He thinks that a materialist

---

[7] Here Locke seems to neglect the possibility that it is the eternal atom's eternality that allows it to create the non-eternal atoms. One might say that it is simply the fact that it is around to do the creating that gives it pre-eminence among the other atoms.

will find this unacceptable. He does not explain why, but perhaps he supposes that the materialist wants to explain thought in terms of basic features
common to all matter. Locke imagines the materialist retreating to the view
that the eternal atom creates non-eternal atoms not by thinking, but in some
manner above our conception. To this he replies: "it must still be Creation;
and these Men must give up their great Maxim, *Ex nihilo nil fit*" (IV.x.15).
Locke seems to be saying that anyone who takes a single atom to be the
ultimate cause of everything else runs afoul of the principle that something
cannot come from nothing. He does not explain how the hypothesis of a
lone eternal atom violates that principle. Perhaps it is because a single atom
does not have all of the perfections included in the rest of creation. This
means that those perfections cannot all have come from the atom. Some of
them must have come from nothing.

The defender of the single-thinking-atom hypothesis may try to get
around the problem by supposing all matter to be eternal. If matter was
not created, then it was not created *ex nihilo*. Locke dismisses this possibility
quickly. He thinks that on this scenario we cannot explain why one eternal
particle should have thought, and the others not. He says:

> Every particle of Matter, as Matter, is capable of all the same Figures and Motions
> of any other; and I challenge any one in his Thoughts, to add any Thing else to one
> above another (IV.x.15).

Locke seems to be presuming that all of the features of bodies supervene
upon their shapes and motions. If all particles are capable of the same shapes
and motions, then there cannot be any reason why one of them should have
the power to think while the others do not. In elaborating this point, Locke
seems to fumble matters somewhat. He says that on the scenario being
considered we cannot explain how one particle should be "in Knowledge
and Power infinitely above all the rest" (IV.x.15). Yet on the scenario under
consideration, there is no reason to say that the one thinking particle is distinguished from the others by anything but the fact that it thinks. Since the
other particles are eternal, the one thinking particle need not be invoked as
their cause. This means that there is no reason to suppose that it contains all
of the powers or perfections that they do, no reason to suppose that it is all
knowing or most powerful. Perhaps Locke will say that any thinking thing
must be, in knowledge and power, infinitely above every non-thinking
thing. He has not argued for that.

The last of the materialist scenarios that Locke considers is one on which the eternal, thinking thing is *"some certain System of Matter* duly put together" (IV.x.16). He expects us to find this less strange than the scenarios involving thinking particles, but he argues that it is no less absurd. His initial argument is very similar to one that we encountered at IV.x.10. There he declared it inconceivable that mechanical interactions should give rise to thought. Here he denies that thought can possibly result from the arrangement of material parts:

For to suppose the eternal thinking Being, to be nothing else but a composition of Particles of Matter, each whereof is incogitative, is to ascribe all the Wisdom and Knowledge of that eternal Being, only to the *juxta*-position of parts; than which, nothing can be more absurd. For unthinking Particles of Matter, however put together, can have nothing thereby added to them, but a new relation of Position, which 'tis impossible should give thought and knowledge to them. (IV.x.16).

When he says that it is absurd to suppose that thought and knowledge could be "ascribed" to the juxtaposition of parts, Locke seems to be deny-ing that mental features can supervene upon, or just be a matter of, the arrangement of material parts. The term 'juxtaposition' was newly coined in Locke's day. Like 'arrangement,' it can refer either to the static condi-tion of being arranged in space, or to the action of arranging things in space. Locke denies that thought and knowledge can be a matter of the juxtaposition of parts in either sense, as he makes clear in the section that follows.

If the eternal thinking thing is a *"corporeal System,"* Locke says, then either that system has no moving parts or its thinking consists in its having certain moving parts. He rules out the first possibility very quickly:

If it be perfectly at rest, it is but one lump, and so can have no priviledges above one Atom. (IV.x.17)

This argument is condensed, and requires a bit of unpacking. Its basic struc-ture is as follows:

(6.4)   An atom cannot think.

(6.5)   A compound material thing with no moving parts is in all relevant respects like an atom.

(6.6)   Therefore, a compound material thing with no moving parts can-not think.

Premise (6.4) is at this stage in the proceedings being assumed. Locke has already considered scenarios on which atoms or particles are supposed to think, and has found them wanting. To see what grounds he has for asserting premise (6.5), we must remind ourselves of his views about atoms and infinite divisibility.

We have seen (§9) that Locke commits himself to the infinite divisibility of matter, though he acknowledges that this embroils him in difficulties that he cannot solve (and that he does not describe). We have also seen that what makes a portion of matter count as an atom for him is its having an unchangeable outer boundary. An atom cannot be dented, smashed, or broken. If a body's chemical and physical features are the consequence of its having the outer boundary that it does, then the chemical and physical features of Lockean atoms are stable. Yet atoms are not partless. Premise (6.5) says that there is no relevant difference between an atom and a macroscopic body whose parts do not move in relation to one another. In both cases, Locke will say, there is a material thing with infinitely many parts, and in both cases the parts on their outer surface are Frozen. The only difference between the atom and the larger body is size, and Locke has already suggested that this alone cannot be the difference between a thinking body and an unthinking one (IV.x.10). We have set aside the possibility that thought is a possession of matter qua matter. It must therefore be the particular arrangement of the parts of a "*corporeal System*" that makes it a thinking thing. Yet for any arrangement of parts that might be possessed by such a system, there could in principle be an atom with smaller parts arranged in the same way. Since premise (6.4) tells us that atoms cannot think, we may conclude that thinking is not the result of any static arrangement of material parts.

If it is not the static arrangement of the parts of a thinking material system that accounts for its thought, then it must be the motion of its parts that does so. Locke then offers a new argument against this possibility. At IV.x.10, he had insisted that collisions between material parts could not possibly give rise to thought. Here he argues for the narrower contention that the motions of unthinking parts could not possibly give rise to certain kinds of mental features or abilities that we take ourselves (and God) to possess:

If it be the motion of its parts, on which its Thinking depends, [A] all the Thoughts there must be unavoidably accidental, and limited; since [B] all the Particles that by Motion cause Thought, being each of them in it self without any Thought, cannot regulate its own Motions, [C] much less be regulated by the Thought of the whole;

[D] since that Thought is not the cause of Motion, (for then it must be anteced-
ent to it, and so without it) but the consequence of it, whereby [E] Freedom,
Power, Choice, and all rational and wise thinking or acting will be quite taken away.
(IV.x.17)

Locke's conclusion here is not that the motion of unthinking particles could
not give rise to thought, but that any thought to which the motion of
unthinking particles did give rise must be accidental, limited, and narrow.[8]
To have thoughts of that sort could not be to exercise freedom, power, or
choice. It could not be rational thought, wise thinking, or wise acting.

Let us try to re-state the argument a bit more clearly. Locke argues that
on the thinking-corporeal-system scenario, (A) thoughts must be accidental
and limited because (B) the moving particles that cause them cannot regulate their own motions, much less (C) have their motions regulated by the
thinking of the corporeal system they jointly compose. The particles cannot
(C) have their motions regulated by the thinking of the corporeal system
they jointly compose because (D) their motions cause that thinking and so
must be antecedent to it. He concludes that on this scenario (E) free choice
and rational thought are impossible. Locke's use of 'much less…' suggests
that what is *really* required if the thoughts of a corporeal system are not to
be (A) accidental and limited is (C) for the motions of at least some of its
constituent particles to be regulated by the system or mind itself. It suggests
that the absence of this kind of regulation is enough to make (E) free choice
and rational thought impossible. Why does he think that a corporeal thinker
must exercise control over the motions of some of its constituent particles
if it is to have free choice and rational thought? He thinks this because he
is supposing that those motions are what determine the corporeal thinker's
thoughts. The point is that a free chooser and rational thinker must be able
to direct the course of his own thoughts to some degree. He must be able to
do what he wants to do, and to think about what he wants to think about.
Locke's claim is that even if certain motions of a system's material parts
gave rise to thought, undirected motions could only give rise to undirected
thoughts. In particular, motions not directed by the thinker could not give

---

[8] In characterizing the form of Locke's argument thus, I part company with Jonathan Bennett. He
sees Locke as arguing that there is a feature that *all* thought must have, and that nothing that is ultimately
caused only by unthinking particles could have (Bennett 2005, 169–70). He suggests that the feature is
teleology (Bennett 2005, 170–1).

rise to thoughts directed by the thinker, and these are required for free agency and rational thought.

Locke argues that (C) a thinking corporeal system cannot regulate the motions of its constituent particles because (D) its thinking is the consequence of those motions. He seems to be thinking that the motions of the particles cannot be both the causes and the effects of the corporeal system's thoughts. Causes must be antecedent to their effects, and so they cannot also be caused by them. Locke has surely moved too quickly here. It is possible for a machine's state at one time to affect the states of some of its parts at a later time. Its total state at the later time will be, in some sense, a consequence of the states of all of its parts at that later time. Thus the states of some of the parts at the later time will be both caused by the machine's total state, and causing it. Yet there is no paradox: we are talking about the machine's total states at different times, and different senses of 'cause' are at work. By the same token, the motions of the particles that compose a system of matter may be what they are partly because of the system's earlier thoughts, even if the system's thoughts at any given time supervene on the state of its constituent particles at that time. Indeed, this must be the case if the system is to learn, or to plan for the future. Learning and planning involve making changes in one's own total package of mental states. If the mental supervenes on the physical, this means making changes in one's own total package of physical states going forward. It need not involve effects preceding their causes.

In the argument at IV.x.17, Locke makes the point that (B) the moving particles that comprise a corporeal thinking system cannot regulate their own motions. Why does he do this? Does he think that if those particles *did* direct their own motions, this would enable the system to be a free chooser and a rational thinker? In that case, he might be trying to undermine the claim that the system could be a free chooser and a rational thinker by ruling out one way in which its constituent particles might be thought to come by the required sort of regulation. The trouble is that it does not seem that particles directing their own motions would make for the required sort of regulation.

Suppose that there were a million minds and a million atoms, that each of the minds exerted some control over one of the atoms, and that the atoms jointly composed an organism of some sort. The fact that each of the atoms is controlled by a mind does not by itself give us any reason to think that the organism can choose freely or think rationally. The organism may have no mind at all. It may be like a mob, or an army, which does not really have thoughts of its own. If the organism retains its integrity for any period of time, and if its motions are anything but random, then we must assume either that the minds are very limited in the degree to which they can control the atoms' motions (like a mob being forced through narrow streets), or that their efforts are somehow coordinated (like an army carrying out a planned assault). Now on the corporeal-thinking-system scenario that Locke considers, the system *is* supposed to have a mind, its thoughts are supposed to arise from the motions of the atoms, and the thoughts that direct the atoms are supposed to belong to the atoms. So let us add these suppositions to our story. In this case, the organism's thoughts will supervene upon the total package of the atoms' motions. Still, the fact that each atom's motions are directed by its own thoughts does not make it more likely that the organism is able to choose freely or to think rationally. For the organism to do those things, its thoughts must influence the atoms' motions (and so the organism's future mental states) in ways that allow the organism to do what it wants to do, to think about what it wants to think about, to respond to reasons, to plan ahead. Perhaps the organism's thoughts could do this by influencing the atoms' minds. In that case, the organism's regulation of atomic motions may be compatible with the atoms' regulation of their own motions. Still, this does not mean that the organism is freer and more rational because its constituent atoms think. What matters is that it can affect its own future states in certain ways, and an army of unthinking atoms may be as responsive as an army of thinking atoms. An army of robots may be as efficient and as easy to control as an army of people.

If the atoms in a corporeal system were guided by their own thoughts, this would not increase the likelihood that the system was capable of free choice, rational thought, or wise action. It is uncharitable to suppose that Locke thinks otherwise. We do better to read his remark (B) about atoms not regulating their own motions as a rhetorical flourish. He is making the point that the atoms' motions are not regulated by *any* thoughts, though what he needs to establish is just the narrower conclusion that their motions are not regulated by the thoughts of the corporeal system.

In his second pass over the question of whether the eternal, thinking thing could be material, Locke rules out in turn the possibility that every atom thinks, that some one atom thinks, and that a corporeal system thinks.

Thus he bolsters his conclusion that the eternal thinking thing is immaterial, and so his case for dualism.

Locke ends the chapter with a coda in which he defends the traditional view that God created matter. This is in response to those who would say that God cannot have created matter because creation *ex nihilo* is inconceivable. At least initially, Locke seems willing to grant that we cannot conceive of how God could create matter out of nothing.[9] He does not see this as giving us reason to conclude that creation *ex nihilo* is impossible. His defense of the possibility of creation *ex nihilo* takes the form of a condensed dialogue:

Matter must be allowed eternal: Why? Because you cannot conceive how it can be made out of nothing; why do you not also think your self eternal? You will answer, perhaps, Because about twenty or forty Years since, you began to be. But if I ask you what that *You* is, which began then to be, you can scarce tell me. The Matter whereof you are made, began not then to be: for if it did, then it is not eternal: But it began to be put together in such a fashion and frame, as makes up your Body; but yet that frame of Particles, is not You, it makes not that thinking Thing You are ...therefore when did that thinking Thing begin to be? If it did never begin to be, then have you always been a thinking Thing from Eternity; the absurdity whereof I need not confute....If therefore you can allow a thinking Thing, to be made out of nothing, (as all Things that are not eternal must be,) why also can you not allow it possible, for a material Being to be made out of nothing [?] (IV.x.18)

Here Locke imagines his opponent wanting to say both that matter is eternal and that he came into being 20 or 40 years ago. Locke asks how he came into being when he did, and the opponent offers a couple of unsatisfactory responses. First he suggests that he came into being when the matter that composes him was made. This will not do because that matter is supposed to be eternal. Next he suggests that he came into being when a quantity of eternal matter was organized in a certain way. This will not do because, as Locke has already argued, the mere arrangement of matter cannot give rise to a thinking being.[10] So the opponent must say that he

---

[9] A bit further on in the same section, Locke suggests that after all "we might be able to aim at some dim and seeming conception how Matter might at first be made, and begin to exist by the power of that eternal first being" (IV.x.18). For enlightening discussion of this remark, see Bennett and Remnant 1978 and Bennett 2001, vol. 2, 127–30. In §40 below, I respond to an argument that Locke's suggestion about the creation of matter shows that he is a four dimensionalist.

[10] Locke seems to go too far when he says that all things that are not eternal must be created *ex nihilo*. Even if we grant that rearranging matter will not bring a thinking thing into existence, might it not bring an organism into existence? Or an artifact?

is a thinking thing, and that he was created *ex nihilo*. Having said this, he is no longer in a position to deny the possibility that God creates things *ex nihilo*.

In the passage quoted above, Locke seems to have moved silently from the conclusion that substance dualism is true—the conclusion that there is at least one immaterial substance—to the assumption that each of us is partly or wholly composed of an immaterial substance. This is less obvious than one might think. As Locke generally uses the term, a thinking substance counts as a "spirit" whether or not it is immaterial. Moreover, as we are about to see, he thinks that we cannot rule out the possibility that human thinkers are material substances. Yet here the structure of his argument shows that he is thinking of human spirits as immaterial. The argument depends on extracting the concession that God creates spirits *ex nihilo*. It cannot depend on the assumption that matter is created, since that is the very point at issue. Now if matter is eternal and human spirits were material, then it would not be obvious that the creation of spirits involved creation *ex nihilo*. So Locke's assumption that the creation of a spirit involves creation *ex nihilo* shows that at IV.x.18 he is thinking of spirits as immaterial.[11]

§34 *Thinking Matter*

Locke insists in the strongest terms that it is impossible that any arrangement of unthinking matter should of itself give rise to a thinking thing. That unthinking matter should produce a thinking thing is, he says, as impossible as that nothingness should produce matter (IV.x.10). For it is impossible that the mere juxaposition of material parts should give thought and knowledge to them (IV.x.16). Despite these strong claims, Locke does not think that it is impossible that matter should think. He does not claim that thinking matter is possible, but he does insist that we are not in a position

---

[11] The only way to resist this conclusion is to say that the creation of a material spirit would involve creation *ex nihilo* because it would involve the creation of the *feature* of thought from nothing. There is presumably some sense in which the creation of any feature involves bringing into being something when before there was nothing. When one bends a formerly straight pipe cleaner, one brings into being an instance of crookedness rather than re-locating an already-existing instance of crookedness. Yet this would seem to make creation *ex nihilo* utterly commonplace. It seems quite unlikely that this is Locke's understanding of 'creation *ex nihilo*.'

to rule out its possibility. He makes this point to illustrate how limited is our ability to perceive the agreement or disagreement even between ideas that we have:

We have the *Ideas* of *Matter* and *Thinking*, but possibly shall never be able to know, whether any mere material Being thinks, or no; it being impossible for us, by the contemplation of our own *Ideas*, without revelation, to discover, whether Omnipotency has not given to some Systems of Matter fitly disposed, a power to perceive and think, or else joined and fixed to Matter so disposed, a thinking immaterial Substance: It being, in respect of our Notions, not much more remote from our Comprehension to conceive, that GOD can, if he pleases, superadd to Matter a Faculty of Thinking, than that he should superadd to it another Substance, with a Faculty of Thinking; since we know not wherein Thinking consists, nor to what sort of Substances the Almighty has been pleased to give that Power, which cannot be in any created Being, but merely by the good pleasure and Bounty of the Creator. (IV.iii.6)

Locke is here defending not the possibility that matter might think, but rather the "epistemic" possibility that matter might think. He is arguing that we cannot rule out the possibility that matter might think. The argument turns on what we can and cannot say about what might be done by an omnipotent being. An omnipotent being can bring about whatever is not logically impossible—that is, any scenario whose description does not involve a contradiction. We cannot always tell when a scenario is logically impossible, and so we cannot always tell whether a scenario might be brought about by an omnipotent being. Locke thinks that we cannot tell whether God's giving the power of thought to a system of unthinking matter is logically impossible. He can see no contradiction in it, though he cannot be sure that it does not contain some hidden contradiction.

One of the main factors that leads Locke to think that we must remain open-minded about the possibility of God giving thought to matter is that we do not know "that wherein Thinking consists." It is true that we do not understand how material substances might be made to think, but we also do not understand how it is that immaterial substances think, or how God would go about uniting an immaterial substance with a human body. We should not dismiss the possibility that God makes it the case that bodies have pleasures and pains when they or certain of their parts are moved in certain ways, because no matter what we must say that He has given to the motions of bodies effects whose production is mysterious:

> Body as far as we can conceive being able only to strike and affect body; and Motion, according to the utmost reach of our *Ideas*, being able to produce nothing but Motion, so that when we allow it to produce pleasure or pain, or the *Idea* of a Colour, or Sound, we are fain to quit our Reason, go beyond our *Ideas*, and attribute it wholly to the good Pleasure of our Maker. For since we must allow he has annexed Effects to Motion, which we can no way conceive Motion able to produce, what reason have we to conclude, that he could not order them as well to be produced in a Subject we cannot conceive capable of them, as well as in a Subject we cannot conceive the Motion of Matter can any way operate upon? (IV.iii.6)

The bodies around us have the capacity to trigger sensations of colors and sounds in us, and we have no clue how they do it. If our minds are immaterial substances, then God has given these bodies the power to act on unsolid things. We cannot understand how He could do this any better than we can understand how He might give bodies powers of sense and thought.

When Locke speaks of the possibility of God giving thought to a material system, he speaks of the possibility of God "superadding" a power of thinking. The word is somewhat unfamiliar, but we should not leap to the conclusion that it is a technical term. The *Oxford English Dictionary* records its use as a transitive verb as early as 1641, and defines it this way:

> To add over and above; to add to what has been added; to put as a further addition. Often a mere strengthening of *add*: To add besides; 'to join any thing extrinsick' (Johnson).

There is considerable difficulty about what Locke has in mind when he speaks of the possibility of God superadding thought to matter. Yet this does not mean that we should look for a Lockean account of superaddition in general, as though he thinks of superadding a feature as a special way of adding a feature. Indeed, his other uses of 'superadd' and its cognates give us reason to think that he uses the term in its ordinary sense. In his first letter to Stillingfleet, Locke speaks of superadding the idea of inherence to the red color of a cherry (*Works* IV, 21). In his third letter, he offers an example in which he describes God as first creating a solid extended substance without superadding anything else to it, then as superadding motion to some parts of it, and then as superadding the properties of a rose, a peach, or an elephant to various parts of it (*Works* IV, 460). What this shows is that Locke uses 'superadd' and its cognates in a sense broad enough to encompass different kinds of interventions that add a feature to something. To superadd one idea to another is to perform the mental operation he usually calls "compounding." To superadd motion to matter is to move parts of it somehow or other. To superadd the features of an elephant is to manipulate material parts so that they come to be in a certain fairly stable arrangement. If no juxtaposition of material parts could give rise to thought, then to superadd thought to matter must be a different sort of intervention altogether.

What kind of intervention is Locke thinking of when he refers to the possibility of God superadding thought to matter? Michael Ayers has suggested that he is thinking of God's carefully selecting the initial distribution of matter and motion in the universe to ensure that certain very specific arrangements are achieved, ones that make for thinking corporeal substances (Ayers 1981, 234; 1991, vol. 2, 170). The obvious difficulty with this line of interpretation is that it seems at odds with the principles to which Locke gives expression in the course of arguing for the immateriality of the eternal thinking being. It seems at odds with his claim that it is impossible that unthinking matter should give rise to a thinking thing, and his claim that it is impossible that the mere juxtaposition of a body's parts should give it thought and knowledge. Ayers responds to this difficulty by urging that the tension dissipates once Locke's claims are properly taken in context. According to Ayers, Locke's claim that it is impossible for the juxtaposition of material parts to make for thought or knowledge is to be understood as the claim that it is impossible for *random or unguided* juxtapositions of material parts to make for thought or knowledge (Ayers 1981, 245; 1991, vol. 2, 178). His claim that it is impossible for unguided, unthinking matter to give rise to a thinking thing is to be understood in terms of his conviction that no perfection or excellency—not even a mechanical modification of matter—can arise without an appropriately powerful external cause (Ayers 1981, 241; 1991, vol. 2, 175).

As best I understand him, Ayers takes Locke's position to be that (i) thought is not essential to matter, that (ii) some arrangements of matter may suffice to make a thinking thing, and yet that (iii) it is impossible that matter should acquire the perfection of thought anywise but by the direction of a thinking being. About (i) there is no dispute. It is reconciling (ii) and (iii) that is the problem. Articulating (iii), Ayers says:

If matter supposed necessarily in motion would not itself *necessarily* produce a certain perfection, then it could not do so by itself *accidentally*. Indeed, an excellency or perfection of matter is superior to the "properties" of matter, and to random or undirected accidents (i.e., to what happens to matter "accidentally" in something like the modern sense) precisely in that it could not possibly have arisen by bare chance. (Ayers 1981, 241)

The view that Ayers is ascribing to Locke is not just that it is spectacularly unlikely that unguided matter should come to form a thinking thing, but that it is absolutely impossible that it should do so. So the picture is that there may be some configuration of particles that is possible, and that if realized would constitute a thinking thing; but that it is absolutely impossible that unguided particles should come to be in such a configuration, even if we presume that the particles are in motion and that they might interact for an eternity. This picture seems to me incoherent. If we are willing to grant any possible distribution of matter and motion, and if we impose no constraint on time, then any configuration that it is possible for matter to be in is one that could, in principle, be arrived at without the guidance of an agent. To say otherwise is to draw a line that is utterly arbitrary. We should resist ascribing such an arbitrary and incoherent view to Locke unless his text permits no other interpretation. In fact, a straightforward reading of his text does not lead us to ascribe (ii) to him. That any arrangement of matter suffices to make a thinking thing seems plainly ruled out by IV.x.10 and IV.x.16.

Lisa Downing has described two different scenarios that Locke might have in mind when he speaks of God superadding thought to matter (Downing 2007). Common to both is the notion that the distinction between real and nominal essences may apply not only to particular material things (individual men, horses, etc.) and to kinds of material things (gold, steel, etc.), but to matter itself.[12] Downing suggests that Locke may regard "solid, extended stuff" as being the nominal essence of matter, and that he may take matter to have an underlying real essence that accounts for its solidity and extension.[13]

---

[12] Downing prefers to speak of an underlying "real constitution" of material substances. She suggests that we regiment Locke's terminology in a way that he does not, reserving 'real essence' for what I have called "relative real essence," and using 'real constitution' for what I have called "total real essence" (Downing 2007, 370–1).

[13] Ayers (1991) pursues a similar line of interpretation (see 1991, vol. 2, 42, 52, 181–2). I focus on Downing's later formulation because it is more fully developed.

In that case, she says, there are two ways that he might be thinking about the superaddition of thought to matter (Downing 2007, 372–3). On one scenario, the real constitutions of unthinking material substances would be of one type, and those of thinking material substances of another. The former real constitutions may be wholly describable in terms of mechanical features—size, shape, solidity, and motion or rest—but the latter possess some "non-mechanical" features. These non-mechanical features account for the capacity for thought. God superadds thought to matter just by making some material substances whose total real essences are of the second type.

On Downing's second scenario, all material things have real constitutions with non-mechanical features. When those features are "configured" in a certain way, this gives rise to thought. God superadds thought to matter just by configuring portions of it in ways that make for thinking things. As we have seen, Locke denies that the arrangement of material parts, and their consequent juxtaposition, can give rise to thought. This means that on Downing's second scenario the configuring that God does to make matter think is not a spatial reorientation of material parts, but some other sort of re-distribution of the non-mechanical features of matter. Downing does not (and need not) speculate about what this might be.[14]

Nothing in Locke's philosophy prevents us from applying the distinction between real and nominal essences to matter itself, but nothing demands that we do so either. Locke clearly takes "solid extended thing" to be the abstract idea that most of us associate with 'body' (II.xiii.11). This is enough to make "solid extended thing" count as a nominal essence, an abstract idea that defines a kind. Yet this does not necessarily mean that there is a cor-responding real essence to account for the co-instantiation of the features included in that nominal essence. Locke may well think that there are some ultimate or basic features of matter, and that matter is a basic kind of sub-stance. If the most basic features of a basic kind are included in the nominal essence that defines it, then there cannot be a real essence underlying them.

---

[14] Downing says that her second scenario requires that "some particular co-instantiations of primary qualities will work to produce thought and others will not" (Downing 2007, 373). Yet as she makes clear in a footnote, she is not talking about co-instantiations of extension, shape, solidity, etc. She is using 'primary qualities' to refer to the non-mechanical features of real constitutions. I would resist this ter-minological move, on the grounds that it is a departure from Locke's usage. On the reading that I have defended above (§8), primary qualities are of necessity features that *we* associate with 'body.' This means that there cannot be unknown primary qualities.

There cannot be any constellation of more basic features to account for the co-instantiation of features that are already basic.

Locke does not commit himself on the question of whether solidity, extension, and the other primary qualities are the most basic features of bodies. That he is open to the possibility that there are more basic features is suggested by his characterization of the secondary qualities of bodies as "depending all...upon the primary Qualities of their minute and insensible parts; or if not upon them, upon something yet more remote from our Comprehension" (IV.iii.11). Still, as I remarked earlier (§9), extension would seem to be a strong candidate for being an ultimate feature of bodies. It is hard to imagine any other feature accounting for the fact that bodies are extended rather than unextended. Locke does occasionally suggest that the extension of bodies is a consequence of cohesion, but there he seems to mean that the particular dimensions of bodies are to be explained in terms of the mutual cohesion of their parts. Since those parts are themselves extended things, this is not a case of him treating extension *per se* as something that stands in need of explanation. Solidity is another good candidate for an ultimate feature of bodies. Locke conceives of solidity as repletion, an intrinsic feature that entails imperviousness to mutual co-location (§10). That two bodies cannot be at the same place at the same time is something that he treats as obvious, rather than as a mystery to be explained.

Another way to understand the suggestion that God may superadd thought to matter is to see it as the suggestion that God may be able to give thought to certain material systems without manipulating or arranging any of their other, more basic features. One could read him this way without supposing that he means to offer, or to rely upon, any particular theory about how God accomplishes the feat. Or else one could take him to be committed to some particular story about how God does what He does. One might see Locke's superaddition claim as grounded in his conception of a substratum as a sort of platform upon which any feature might in principle be placed. Leibniz seems to read Locke this way (Leibniz 1981, 379). Or one might see his claim about God superadding thought to matter as the suggestion that God may decree that a certain Humean regularity holds. On this reading, he is suggesting that God may will that whenever matter attains certain configuration, it thinks (McCann 1994, 74–5).

The suggestion that God might add thought to bodies without altering or re-distributing their more basic features has been the target of criticism.

Leibniz complains that it involves a mistaken conception of the relation between the features of things and their natures or essences:

[I]t must be borne in mind above all that the modifications which can occur to a single subject naturally and without miracles must arise from limitations and variations of a real genus, i.e. of a constant and absolute inherent nature. For that is how philosophers distinguish the modes of an absolute being from that being itself; just as we know that size, shape and motion are obviously limitations and variations of corporeal nature (for it is plain how a limited extension yields shapes, and that changes occurring in it are nothing but motion). Whenever we find some quality in a subject, we ought to believe that if we understood the nature of both the subject and the quality we would conceive how the quality could arise from it. So within the order of nature (miracles apart) it is not at God's arbitrary discretion to attach this or that quality haphazardly to substances. He will never give them any which are not natural to them, that is, which cannot arise from their nature as explicable modifications. (Leibniz 1981, 66)

Leibniz makes at least three related claims here:

(6.7)   The modifications of a substance must arise from limitations or variations of its nature.

(6.8)   If we understood both the nature of a substance and the nature of a feature it has, we would be able to conceive how the feature could arise from that nature.

(6.9)   Within the order of nature (i.e., miracles aside), it is not at God's arbitrary discretion to attach features to substances.

With (6.7), Leibniz says that each of the modifications of a substance must be related to its nature in the way that size, shape, and motion are related to extension. To be some size and shape just is to be extended in a certain way; it is for one's extension to be limited to certain dimensions. To be moving is to stand in certain changing spatial relations to various other things. Claim (6.8) is an epistemological corollary to (6.7). The relation between a general feature and a way of instancing that feature is an intelligible one; so if each modification is a limitation or variation of a nature, the relation between the two should be intelligible to one who grasps both. Claim (6.9) invokes a distinction between the natural order and the miraculous. Leibniz is willing to allow that God might bestow features on things arbitrarily—that is to say, despite their being no intelligible connection between the features and the things—but he says that in such cases God is performing a miracle.

Within the order of nature, the features of bodies must arise from basic features shared by all bodies. Leibniz thinks that by neglecting (6.7)–(6.9), Locke effectively re-introduces the "occult qualities" or "bare faculties" of the scholastics (Leibniz 1981, 65, 379).

A possible Lockean move in response to (6.9) might be to say that God can superadd thought to matter, but then to allow that if He does so it involves a miracle. To this one could imagine Leibniz insisting that miracles must be rare, whereas Locke seems to allow that *all* human thought may be the result of divine superaddition. In fact, it does not look as though Locke will allow that the superaddition of thought to matter is miraculous. For he says that an event counts as a miracle with respect to some spectator only if it is "in his opinion contrary to the established course of nature" (*Works* IX, 256). If all human thought were the consequence of divine superaddition, it would be hard to say that thinking matter was contrary to the established course of nature. Yet this also shows how Locke can respond to a complaint that is sometimes made, the charge that the superaddition of thought to matter would amount to a standing miracle. The correct Lockean reply to this is to say that "standing miracle" is an oxymoron.

Those who see Locke as offering, or relying upon, a specific account of how God gives thought to matter may also object to that more specific account. Leibniz, who sees something like the bare particular conception of substratum as lying behind Locke's proposal about thinking matter, complains that he is treating the features of bodies as like "little subsistent beings which can fly in and out like pigeons with a dovecote" (Leibniz 1981, 379). He says that Locke is unwittingly turning the powers of substances into substances themselves. Another concern may be raised by those who see Locke as proposing that God simply decrees that thinking is to happen whenever certain configurations of matter are realized. They may worry that the proposal amounts to a form of occasionalism. They may worry that, on the scenario described, a body's coming to be in a certain configuration will be merely an occasion for God to cause a certain mental event. It will not avail to resist this by pointing out that Locke's God would be acting by general decree rather than intervening on a case-by-case basis. For the occasionalists too say that God acts by a general will (Malebranche 1980b, 157).[15]

---

[15] According to Malebranche, God's acting by a general will is not a matter of his willing at the time of creation and resting thereafter. Instead, he says, "God wills unceasingly though without variation, without succession, without necessity" (Malebranche 1980b, 157).

We have considered several interpretations of Locke's suggestion that God may superadd thought to matter. We considered, and set aside, a reading on which he is proposing that thought may be the natural consequence of matter achieving configurations that matter can achieve only by divine direction. We considered a reading on which he is proposing that God may give matter, or certain bodies, non-mechanical features that give rise to thought. We also considered a reading on which he is proposing that God may give powers of thought to certain material systems without these being grounded in any of the more basic features of bodies. I am now going to propose an additional reading, one that I will call the "no theory" interpretation of Locke's superaddition claim. As the name suggests, this reading is analogous to McCann's "no theory" interpretation of Locke's remarks about substance. McCann says that Locke abstains from offering any metaphysical theory about substance, and I largely agree. I say that Locke also does not offer or presuppose any particular story about how God might accomplish the feat of superadding thought to matter. We can presume that he would reject any story that conflicted with his own express claims, but otherwise he is to be seen as agnostic about the metaphysics of thinking matter. He offers metaphysical theories about a great many things, but that is not one of them.

The strongest argument for the "no theory" interpretation is that Locke says almost nothing about how God might superadd thought to matter. He does not even attempt to show that God *can* superadd thought to matter, never mind attempt to explain how God would accomplish the feat. Locke simply reports that he sees no contradiction in the claim that God might somehow or other give thought to certain parcels of matter. He concludes that we are in no position to dismiss that possibility. Locke does say enough to rule out the possibility that God can add thought to matter merely by moving or arranging material parts. Beyond this, he does not exclude any scenarios, but also does not endorse any. He does not deny that God might give certain bodies basic non-mechanical features that give rise to thought, or that God might configure non-mechanical features of matter so that certain bodies might think. Yet he also does not deny that God might give thought to certain bodies directly, without adding to or manipulating any of their more basic features. Leibniz assures us that God will never give bodies features that do not arise from their natures as explicable modifications of them. Locke is more cautious, and less inclined to issue pronouncements about what God will or will not do.

Downing portrays Locke as holding a view about bodies and their features that is much like Leibniz's. She portrays him as holding that "the qualities and behavior of a body follow from its real constitution (some particular configuration of its intrinsic and irreducible qualities), together with the real constitutions of other bodies and the spatial relations among bodies" (Downing 2007, 368). As evidence for this, she points to a passage in which Locke reflects on what it would be like if we had knowledge of the real essences of bodies. He says that if we knew the real essences of bodies, then our knowledge of their properties would be like our knowledge of the properties of geometrical figures:

Had we such *Ideas* of Substances, as to know what real Constitutions produce those sensible Qualities we find in them, and how those Qualities flowed from thence, we could, by the specifick *Ideas* of their real Essences in our own Minds, more certainly find out their Properties, and discover what Qualities they had, or had not, than we can now by our Senses: and to know the Properties of *Gold*, it would be no more necessary, that *Gold* should exist, and that we should make Experiments upon it, than it is necessary for the knowing the Properties of a Triangle, that a Triangle should exist in any Matter, the *Idea* in our Minds would serve for the one, as well as the other. (IV.vi.11)

Exactly what analogy Locke is drawing here is contested. Some take him to be saying that if we knew the real constitutions of bodies then we could have *a priori* knowledge of their observable features (Yolton 1970; Woolhouse 1971; Wilson 1979). Yet this does not fit with Locke's claim that many of the observable features of bodies depend on background conditions and on interactions with other bodies, a claim that he makes emphatically in the very section in which this passage appears. Downing takes Locke to be saying that a body's features and its behavior are fixed by its own real constitution and those of the bodies with which it interacts. This is better, but neglects the role played by the laws of motion and impact, which Locke ascribes to "the arbitrary Will and good Pleasure of the Wise Architect" (IV.iii.29).[16] Downing's reading may also have trouble accounting for the strength of Locke's skepticism about a science of bodies, because her reading implies that knowledge of the real constitutions of bodies should suffice for knowledge of all of their features. Locke despairs about our ever having

---

[16] In Stuart 1996, I argue that the point of Locke's geometrical analogy is that if we had knowledge of real essences and of how qualities flow from them, then we should be able to offer explanations that take the form of deductive arguments from premises about which we are certain.

exhaustive knowledge of the features of bodies—declaring it "lost labour" to seek after a science of bodies—though he does not say that real constitutions are unobservable in principle.

A closer look at IV.vi.11 suggests that it does not commit Locke to anything so strong as the principle that Downing ascribes to him. She takes him to be saying that every feature of each individual body is fixed by its total real essence together with the total real essences of the other bodies in its environment.[17] Yet there is good reason to think that his concern in IV.vi.11 is with relative real essences of bodies, and with "Properties" in the narrow, Aristotelian sense. He is saying that if we knew the relative real essence common to the members of a nominal-essence-defined kind, then we could say what other features must be shared by those members. When Locke compares knowledge of bodies to knowledge of a triangle, he is not thinking of the knowledge we might have in virtue of possessing the fully-detailed idea of some particular triangular-shaped physical object. He is thinking of the knowledge that we *do* have in virtue of possessing the general idea "triangle." For he makes the point that we would equally well know "the Properties of a Triangle" even if there were no particular triangles in existence. If the analogy is to be on all fours, the idea of a body that he is talking about should also be a general idea. It will be that if he is talking about the knowledge we would possess if we had ideas of the *relative* real essences of bodies. These are general ideas of the structures that give rise to the observable features represented in the nominal essences we make. If we had ideas of relative real essences, and of the relevant laws of nature, we should know what features must be possessed by anything answering to one of these nominal essences. That this is Locke's point is suggested by his observation that our possessing ideas of real constitutions would give us knowledge of the "Properties" of "*Gold.*" He seems to be saying not that we would know all of the features possessed by some particular parcel, but rather that we would know all of the features common to the members of some kind of body.

This reading of IV.vi.11 gains further support when we look at other passages in which Locke speaks of what it would be like if we had ideas of

---

[17] I have taken the liberty of translating from Downing's terminology to my own. Where I speak of total real essences, she speaks of "real constitutions." Where I speak of relative real essences, she speaks of "real essences" (Downing 2007, 370–1). I think that we agree that Locke does not consistently use any pair of terms to demarcate the two concepts.

the real essences of bodies. At II.xxxi.6 (a passage also cited by Downing), he says that if the nominal essence of a corporeal substance were its real essence, then "the Properties we discover in that Body, would depend on that complex *Idea*, and be deducible from it; as all Properties of a Triangle depend upon, and as far as they are discoverable, are deducible from the complex *Idea* of three Lines, including a Space." Here the geometrical idea is again the general idea "triangle," not the idea of some particular triangular object. Again this suggests that the corresponding idea of body will be the general idea of a real essence. Locke illustrates his point about our knowledge of bodies by observing that malleability, which we look upon as a "Property" of iron, is not included in the nominal essence of iron, and is not deducible from it. He implies that if we had the idea of iron's *real* essence, we could deduce that all bits of iron must be malleable. That is just what we should be able to do if we had the idea of the relative real essence of iron and understood the laws of nature. Later in II.xxxi.6, Locke refers to a particular bit of gold, the parcel of matter on his finger. Yet when he speaks of its real essence he speaks of the "real Essence, whereby it is *Gold*." This is the relative real essence of gold, not the total real essence of that parcel. When he goes on to remark that a certain color, density, and "fitness to have its Colour changed by the touch of Quicksilver" are "Properties" that depend on this essence, he is selecting these features because they are ones that this bit of gold has in common with every other bit of gold.[18]

Locke invokes the example of gold again at III.xi.22, saying that knowledge of the constitution of "this shining, heavy, ductil Thing (from whence all these its Properties flow)" would give us a more perfect understanding of "the signification of the word *Gold*." If knowledge of this constitution would give us a more perfect understanding of the meaning of a general term, it would again seem that the constitution he has in mind is a relative real essence. If it were knowledge of the thing's total real essence that we had, we should not know which of the features flowing from the thing belonged to the signification of the word 'gold,' and which did not.

What all three of these passages tell us is not that all of a body's features are fixed by its total real essence and those of the bodies in its environment.

---

[18] Since Locke here seems to include the color of gold among its "Properties," and since he always presumes that the color of gold belongs to its nominal essence, he is evidently using "Properties" in the wider of the two narrow, Aristotelian senses, the one that includes both the features essential to a kind and those non-essential features possessed by every member of the kind.

They tell us is that if we knew the real essence responsible for the cluster of observable features included in a nominal essence, then we would also be able to say what other features (if any) must be common to the individuals answering to that nominal essence. To say this does not commit one to any very general account of the relations between the qualities of things and their underlying natures. Moreover, even if we suppose that "solid extended substance" is the nominal essence of matter, and that matter has an unknown real essence, these passages do not tell us that thought must flow from that real essence. For thought is surely not a property of matter in the Aristotelian sense of 'property.' It is not one of those features that must be possessed by everything that answers to the nominal essence of matter.

I have suggested that Locke has no theory about how God might add thought to matter. Downing, on the other hand, portrays him as holding that the superaddition of thought to matter must involve the creation or manipulation of a real essence or constitution that has non-mechanical features. In support of her reading, she points to two passages from the correspondence with Stillingfleet. The first comes as Locke is making the point that it is incomprehensible to us how God could bestow the power of thought upon any substance, whether material or immaterial. He compares the incomprehensibility of thinking matter to the incomprehensibility of gravitation:

If it be asked, why they limit the omnipotency of God, in reference to the one rather than the other of these substances; all that can be said to it is, that they cannot conceive how the solid substance should ever be able to move itself. And as little, say I, are they able to conceive how a created unsolid substance should move itself; but there may be something in an immaterial substance, that you do not know. I grant it; and in a material one too: for example, gravitation of matter towards matter, and in the several proportions observable, inevitably shows, that there is something in matter that we do not understand, unless we can conceive self-motion in matter; or an inexplicable and inconceivable attraction in matter, at immense and almost incomprehensible distances: it must therefore be confessed, that there is something in solid, as well as unsolid substances, that we do not understand. (*Works* IV, 464–5)

Downing takes Locke to be saying that the hypothesis of thinking matter leads not to the view that God could bestow thought on mere solid, extended stuff, but to the view that there is something in material substances that we do not know. This, she says, "strongly suggests that there must be something internal to the thinking thing that would, in principle, explain its ability to think" (Downing 2007, 374).

In glossing the passage as she does, Downing may over-reach. Locke does say that there is something in solid substances that we do not understand. However, there is nothing in what he says to suggest that this something is an underlying non-mechanical feature that explains gravitation. On what seems to me the most natural reading of the passage, he is saying that the something in matter that we do not understand *is* gravitation. It is this "attraction in matter" that he calls "inexplicable and inconceivable." Gravitation is inexplicable and inconceivable because we do not understand how God can give bodies the power to attract other bodies across immense distances. We can only conceive of bodies as being able to act upon one another by impulse (II.viii.11). Locke makes his point about gravitation in the service of a broader claim: there are some features that God is able to give to bodies though we cannot understand how He gives them to bodies. Gravitation is one thing in matter that we do not understand, he says, and thought may be another.

A second passage that Downing mentions in support of her reading is one in which Locke responds to the charge that there is a tension between (i) his admission that God might give thought to matter and (ii) his denial (II.xi.10–11) that brutes are capable of abstraction. He says:

This seems to suppose, that I place thinking within the natural power of matter. If that be your meaning, my lord, I neither say, nor suppose, that all matter has naturally in it a faculty of thinking, but the direct contrary. But if you mean that certain parcels of matter, ordered by the divine Power, as seems fit to him, may be made capable of receiving from his omnipotency the faculty of thinking; that indeed I say, and that being granted, the answer to your question is easy, since if Omnipotency can give thought to any solid substance, it is not hard to conceive, that God may give that faculty in an higher or lower degree, as it pleases him, who knows what disposition of the subject is suited to such a particular way or degree of thinking. (*Works* IV, 468)

Downing suggests that if Locke were open to the possibility that God can give to bodies powers not rooted in their natures, then he should not speak of God needing to make parcels of matter "capable of receiving" powers. There are other passages that could be used to make the same point. At IV.iii.6, when he first raises the possibility of thinking matter, Locke describes this as the possibility that God might add thought to "fitly disposed" systems of matter. When he repeats the suggestion later in the section, he says that God may add thought to "certain Systems of created sensless matter, put together as he thinks fit." He uses similar language in the correspondence with Stillingfleet (*Works* IV, 466). Downing's challenge is this: if God can add to bodies features that are not rooted in their basic natures, then what could possibly make some material things fitter than others for receiving the features He gives them?

When Locke introduces the possibility of thinking matter, he does so by saying that we may be unable to discover which of two possibilities obtains: (i) that God has given thought to certain "fitly disposed" systems of matter, and (ii) that God has "joined and fixed *to Matter so disposed*, a thinking immaterial Substance" (IV.iii.6, italics mine). This shows him presuming that even if the substance dualist account of us is correct—so that thinking is in no way a product of our physical features—it is still only creatures with fitly disposed bodies to whom God gives the power of thought. Locke assumes that God has some reason to enjoin a certain correspondence between the mental and the physical, even if the mental is not grounded in the physical. What might Locke think those reasons are? We can only speculate. So far as his argument goes, we cannot rule out the possibility of God superadding the power of thought to a solid block of marble. Nonetheless, Locke does think that God creates thinking people and sensing organs, and that He does not create thinking, sensing blocks of marble. To explain why God does that, one would need to explain why He creates at all, and why He creates organisms and people in particular. So far as I am aware, Locke does not express an opinion about this. Let us not do so either. Let us simply suppose that God has some reasons for creating organisms and people. Why does He give powers of thought to them, and not to blocks of marble?

An obvious, but reasonable, suggestion is that many of the mental states of organisms and people help them to do what they need to do if they are to survive and flourish. The mental states of people and other organisms allow them to obtain food and other necessities, to avoid predators and other dangers, to form social relationships, to plan and realize their projects, and perhaps to worship their God. So if God has reasons to create organisms and persons, and if their survival and flourishing depend upon their abilities to eat, find shelter, avoid predators, form social relationships, carry out projects, and perhaps praise their God, then God has reasons to give those beings thoughts. He does not have similar reason to endow blocks of marble with the power of thought. God not only has reasons to give organisms and persons the power of thought, he has reasons to give them particular sorts of mental states. He has reasons to give them sensory states that accurately represent nearby opportunities and threats, and volitional states that permit them to respond to those opportunities and those threats effectively.

§35 Arbitrary Determinations

Locke maintains that there is no apparent contradiction in the proposition that God gives the power of thought to certain systems of matter. He concludes that we should remain open to that possibility, though we do not understand how God could accomplish the feat. One of the ways that he argues for this stance is to point to other cases in which we must say that God has given to bodies powers that we cannot conceive of as grounded in the nature of matter. He points to the powers that bodies have to produce ideas in us, and to those that bodies have to attract one another. In both of these cases, he says, we find ourselves unable to explain why bodies have these powers, except to say that God has determined that they will have them. What is particularly interesting is that Locke goes beyond saying that we do not understand how God bestows the powers. He says that the powers that bodies have to produce ideas in us are arbitrary determinations, and that powers of gravitation cannot be explained in terms of the natural operations of matter. This shows that he does not accept Leibniz's view about what relations must obtain between the natures or essences of substances and their other features. He does not agree that the features of bodies must be limitations and variations of corporeal nature. He thinks that God not only can but does give to bodies some features more arbitrarily than that. Whether or not Leibniz was right about the metaphysics of matter, he was right about the interpretation of Locke on this issue.

We saw earlier (§12) that secondary qualities immediately perceivable are powers that bodies have to trigger simple sensory ideas in us. Locke thinks that bodies have such powers, even if they only have them when they are exercising them (§15). In a chapter on what it means for ideas to be true, he says something about how bodies come by these powers:

Our simple *Ideas*, being barely such Perceptions, as God has fitted us to receive, and given Power to external Objects to produce in us by established Laws, and Ways, suitable to his Wisdom and Goodness, though incomprehensible to us, their Truth consists in nothing else, but in such Appearances, as are produced in us, and must be suitable to those Powers, he has placed in external Objects, or else they could not be produced in us...(II.xxxii.14)

It is not surprising to hear Locke say that God gives bodies powers to trigger sensory ideas in us, since he thinks that God is ultimately responsible for giving every contingent thing all of its features. His suggestion that bodies produce ideas in accordance with divinely established laws is perhaps of greater interest. It is one of just a few places in which Locke speaks of laws of nature in what is now the familiar sense of that phrase.[19] He offers no account of what a law of nature is, but in this case he seems to be thinking of a divinely instituted correspondence between the physical features of external objects and the simple ideas they produce in us. He implies that different pairings of external stimuli and ideas are conceivable, and that God has established one that is better than some of the other ones possible. For unless other pairings were possible, and unless some of these were worse than the actual pairing, God's establishing this pairing could hardly reflect His goodness and wisdom. Locke tells us that there is something about the powers that bodies have to produce simple ideas in us that is incomprehensible. It is not exactly clear what he is calling incomprehensible. It may be how God gives bodies those powers, or it may be the laws that govern the distribution of those powers, or it may be both.

When he comes to survey the extent of human knowledge, Locke again discusses the powers that bodies have to produce ideas in us. He takes it for granted that bodies do have these powers, and leverages this into an argument for the possibility of thinking matter:

Body as far as we can conceive being able only to strike and affect body; and Motion, according to the utmost reach of our *Ideas*, being able to produce nothing but Motion, so that when we allow it to produce pleasure or pain, or the *Idea* of a Colour, or Sound, we are fain to quit our Reason, go beyond our *Ideas*, and attribute it wholly to the good Pleasure of our Maker. For since we must allow he has annexed Effects to Motion, which we can no way conceive Motion able to produce, what reason have we to conclude, that he could not order them as well to be produced in a Subject we cannot conceive capable of them, as well as in a Subject we cannot conceive the motion of Matter can any way operate upon? (IV.iii.6)

The argument is that God gives bodies one sort of power that we cannot conceive as arising from their more basic features, so we should allow that He might just as well give them other powers we cannot conceive as arising

---

[19] Another is IV.iii.29, a passage that we will consider below (§36). Usually Locke reserves the phrase 'law of nature' for talk about moral laws (eg, I.iii.2; II.xxviii.11; Locke 1954).

from their more basic features. At present, our interest lies not in Locke's defense of thinking matter, but in what he says about the etiology of the powers that bodies have to produce ideas in us. Here Locke says that God has "annexed Effects to Motion, which we can no way conceive Motion able to produce" (IV.iii.6). He might mean that God annexes effects to the motions of insensibly small corpuscles on a body's surface, but it is not clear what grounds he would have for thinking that colored surfaces are always composed of particles in motion. More likely, he means that God annexes effects to the motions of the light corpuscles that reflect off the surfaces of colored bodies (and to the motions of the corpuscles that bring odors and sounds to our noses and ears).

In the passage just quoted, Locke says both that it is inconceivable to us that the motions of bodies should produce ideas in us, and that the motions of bodies *do* produce ideas in us. So the sort of inconceivability that he has in mind is not an inconceivability that entails impossibility. It is incomprehensibility. The production of ideas in us by the motions of external bodies is incomprehensible to us for two reasons, according to Locke. First, it is a case of a body affecting something other than another body. At this point in the proceedings, Locke is assuming for the sake of argument that ideas belong to immaterial substances. He is, in effect, trying to show us how that assumption might unravel. A second reason why the production of sensory ideas in us is incomprehensible is that it is a case of a motion causing something other than another motion.[20] Locke assumes that the having of ideas is not reducible to, or explicable in terms of, the motion of parts in the subject of those ideas, whether that subject is material or immaterial.[21]

When we allow that motions cause ideas in us, Locke says, we quit our reason and go beyond our ideas. Reason is the faculty by which we discover the intermediate ideas that we must have for demonstrative knowledge. Locke says that we quit our reason, and go beyond our ideas, because

[20] Perhaps he should put the point more carefully, and say that it seems to be a case in which the motion causes a feature that cannot be reduced to, or explained in terms of, the arrangement or motion of a thing's parts. For Locke hypothesizes that heat is molecular motion, and yet presumably wants to allow that it is comprehensible that the application of heat should change certain of a thing's chemical features. This is comprehensible because we can understand how changes in certain of a body's chemical features might reduce to, or be explicable in terms of, changes in the motions or the arrangement of its parts.

[21] Locke holds that immaterial substances have spatial locations and that they can move, but he is evidently dubious about the prospects of explaining their states or features in terms of the motions of their parts.

he thinks that we do not have ideas that would allow us to perceive an agreement between the ideas of moving bodies and such ideas as those of pleasure or color. The only way that we can understand such a connection is to see it as forged by a God who wills that certain motions should cause certain experiences.

Later in IV.iii, Locke explains that our inability to grasp why bodies have powers to produce ideas is not just the result of our ignorance of the primary qualities of their insensibly small parts. "[T]here is yet another and more incurable part of Ignorance," he says, "…and that is, that there is no discoverable connection between any *secondary Quality, and those primary Qualities* that it depends on" (IV.iii.12). Even if we knew the primary qualities of the insensibly small parts of bodies, we should not understand why arrangements of microscopic parts produce particular sensory ideas in us. We should not understand this because of the lack of a certain kind of connection between cause and effect in these cases. What is the connection that is wanting? It is a "visible necessary" connection assuring us that two features—in this case, a configuration of primary qualities and the power to produce a certain idea—will co-occur (IV.iii.10). Locke's examples suggest that the desired connection is a conceptual one, like that involved when we see that "Figure necessarily supposes Extension," and that "receiving or communicating Motion by impulse, supposes Solidity" (IV.iii.14). Yet he also seems to allow that the extent to which a cause/effect pair displays the required sort of connection might be a matter of degree. He says that when a body with one configuration of primary qualities strikes another, and so brings about a change in the second body's primary qualities, there seems to us to be "some *connexion*" between cause and effect (IV.iii.13). Locke presumably does not mean that the connection between cause and effect is a wholly conceptual one, for that would require him to say that the laws of impact were conceptual truths. I defer until §36 the question of how he can allow that there being "visible necessary" connections between cause and effect might be a matter of degree, and also that of why he thinks we see "some *connexion*" in cases of mechanical interaction.

At IV.iii.28, Locke repeats his claim that we are unable to grasp why bodies have powers to produce ideas, and that this is because of "a want of *a discoverable Connection* between those *Ideas* which we have." He says that it is obvious that the sizes, shapes, and motions of bodies around us cause our sensations of colors and sounds, our pleasures and pains. Yet, he says, there is "no conceivable connexion between any impulse of any sort of Body, and any perception of a Colour, or Smell, which we find in our Minds." Indeed, we understand neither how any body can produce an idea, nor how any thought can produce a bodily motion. We observe that there are constant and regular connections or correspondences between certain kinds of physical events and certain kinds of mental ones; but because these are not discoverable "in the *Ideas* themselves," we can only attribute them to "the arbitrary Determination of that All-wise Agent, who has made them to be, and to operate as they do, in a way wholly above our weak Understandings to conceive."

There are other features of bodies that Locke thinks must be ascribed to the hand of God because they cannot be explained in terms of more basic features of matter. These include powers that bodies have to move themselves, and one another, in certain ways. Locke does not discuss gravitation in the *Essay*, but in *Some Thoughts Concerning Education* (1693) he offers it as an example of something that can only be explained on the supposition that there is an immaterial, superior being:

[I]t is evident, that by mere matter and motion, none of the great phænomena of nature can be resolved: to instance but in that common one of gravity, which I think impossible to be explained by any natural operation of matter, or any other law of motion, but the positive will of a superior Being so ordering it. (*Works* IX, 184)

Downing tries to accommodate this passage by locating the emphasis on the impoverishment of our idea of matter. She reads Locke as saying that we cannot explain gravity with *our* idea of matter, and so we must invoke God to explain it. She sees this as leaving open the possibility that "what [God] did was to create material stuff whose nature transcends our ideas" (Downing 2007, 376 n40). Yet Locke does not say that *we* cannot explain gravitation in terms of *our* idea. He says that it is impossible to explain gravitation in terms of any natural operation of matter.[22] He also implies that there is a distinction between the natural operations of matter and such features as gravitation. The obvious way to cash this out is as a distinction between those features that are (at least in part) consequences of a thing's nature, and those that are not. On Downing's reading, there are no features of body that are not (at least in part) consequences of its nature.

---

[22] Downing's reading has an easier time with Locke's remarks about gravitation at *Works* IV, 467–8, where he insists that God can "put into bodies powers and ways of operation above what can be derived from our idea of body, or can be explained by what we know of matter."

Though Downing concedes that the sentence quoted above is somewhat awkward for her interpretation, she argues that the sentence that follows it vindicates her reading. After telling us that gravity is evidence of God's involvement in the world, Locke makes a suggestion about the cause of Noah's flood:

And therefore since the deluge cannot be well explained, without admitting something out of the ordinary course of nature, I propose it to be considered, whether God's altering the centre of gravity in the earth for a time, (a thing as intelligible as gravity itself, which perhaps a little variation of causes, unknown to us, would produce), will not more easily account for Noah's flood, than any hypothesis yet made use of, to solve it. (*Works* IX, 184)

Downing sees this as supporting her interpretation because "it implies that gravity has some underlying cause, which might be altered in some fashion so as to shift the Earth's center of gravity" (Downing 2007, 376 n40). She seems to be thinking that the "little variation of causes" to which Locke refers might involve the re-configuration of non-mechanical features of the Earth's matter. However, Locke's language is vague and there are other equally good ways of accommodating what he says. He might just as well be thinking that solidity and extension are the whole essence of matter, that bodies attract one another because God wills that they do, and that the flood was caused by His moving about masses inside the Earth so as to alter its center of gravity.[23]

The topic of gravity also comes up in Locke's exchange with Stillingfleet. There Locke invokes the case of gravity in opposition to those who would say that "God can give no power to any parts of matter, but what men can account for from the essence of matter in general" (*Works* IV, 461). He says:

For it is visible, that all the planets have revolutions about certain remote centres, which I would have any one explain, or make conceivable by the bare essence or natural powers depending on the essence of matter in general, without something added to that essence, which we cannot conceive: for the moving of matter in a crooked line, or the attraction of matter by matter, is all that can be said in the case; either of which it is above our reach to derive from the essence of matter, or body in general; though one of these must unavoidably be allowed to be superadded in this instance to the essence of matter in general. (*Works* IV, 461)

[23] I made this suggestion in Stuart 1998, 356 n21.

To explain the movements of the planets, we must either suppose that matter has an inclination to move in crooked lines, or that is has the power to attract matter. We can conceive of neither of those features as included in, or grounded in, the essence of matter. So we must conclude that one or the other of them is superadded to that essence by God.

There are two ways that one might understand Locke's talk of God adding something to the essence of matter to give bodies powers of gravitation. One might take him to be suggesting that God expands the features included in the essence of matter, or one might take him to be suggesting that God adds features to things that possess the essence of matter. On the second reading, he need not be taken to be suggesting that powers of gravitation, or features that give rise to them, belong to the essence of matter. The first reading fits better with Downing's suggestion that Locke's God adds powers of gravitation to matter by giving matter certain non-mechanical features and configuring them in a certain way. One problem with this reading is that it does not really make sense to speak of adding essential features to a kind of stuff. Any stuff with a different set of essential features is a different stuff. To add to the essence of matter would be to make something other than matter, though of course one might help oneself to the word 'matter' to name the new stuff. Another problem with this reading is that Locke makes it clear that the features that he conceives of God as adding to matter are non-essential features of matter. Just a paragraph earlier, he says that "[t]he idea of matter is an extended solid substance," and that "wherever there is such a substance, there is matter, and the essence of matter, whatever other qualities, not contained in that essence, it shall please God to superadd to it" (*Works* IV, 460). Locke goes on to explicitly position himself against those who charge that adding thought to matter "changes the essential properties of matter." Against them, he maintains that "whatever excellency, not contained in its essence, be superadded to matter, it does not destroy the essence of matter, if it leaves it an extended solid substance; wherever that is, there is the essence of matter" (*Works* IV, 460–1).

§36 *Voluntarism*

Locke thinks that bodies might have powers to think, and that they do have powers to produce sensory ideas and to attract other bodies. In each of these cases, he invokes divine choice or activity of some kind to explain how it is that bodies might, or do, have the features in question. He also describes certain other aspects of matter as being the products of arbitrary decisions on God's part. He draws a contrast between our understanding of these and our grasp of geometrical truths:

In some of our *Ideas* there are certain Relations, Habitudes, and Connexions, so visibly included in the Nature of the *Ideas* themselves, that we cannot conceive them separable from them, by any Power whatsoever. And in these only, we are capable of certain and universal Knowledge. Thus the *Idea* of a right-lined Triangle necessarily carries with it an equality of its Angles to two right ones. Nor can we conceive this Relation, this connexion of these two *Ideas*, to be possibly mutable, or to depend on any arbitrary Power, which of choice made it thus, or could make it otherwise. But the coherence and continuity of the parts of Matter; the production of Sensation in us of Colours and Sounds, *etc.* by impulse and motion; nay, the original Rules and Communication of Motion being such, wherein we can discover no natural connexion with any *Ideas* we have, we cannot but ascribe them to the arbitrary Will and good Pleasure of the Wise Architect. (IV.iii.29)

One of the features here ascribed to God's will is the cohesion of bodies. Locke is dissatisfied with the prevailing natural philosophical explanations of cohesion, as he explains at II.xxiii.23–27. He points out that those who would account for cohesion in terms of the ambient pressure of air or æther are left with the problem of explaining the cohesion of the air or the æther (II.xxiii.23, 27). He adds that an experiment involving two polished pieces of marble shows that such pressure is not enough to explain cohesion in any case (II.xxiii.24).[24] At IV.iii.29 Locke also ascribes the "original Rules and Communication of Motion" to God's will. He is trying to explain both why the laws of impact (the "Rules…of Motion") are what they are, and how the "Communication of Motion" from one body to another is effected. Regarding the latter, he says that our only conception of it involves "the passing of Motion out of one Body into another," and he regards this as being "as obscure and unconceivable, as how our Minds move or stop our Bodies by Thought" (II.xxiii.28). The difficulty is that it would not seem that a mode can literally be detached from one body and transferred to another as a physical part might be.

---

[24] In the correspondence with Stillingfleet, Locke again remarks on the mysteriousness of cohesion: "If God cannot join things together by connexions inconceivable to us, we must deny even the consistency and being of matter itself; since every particle of it having some bulk, has its parts connected by ways inconceivable to us" (*Works* IV, 465–6).

In the passage above, Locke draws a contrast between the truths of geometry and those having to do with how bodies cohere, what laws govern their
motions, and how they communicate motion when they strike one another.
Immediately afterwards, he goes on to observe that the resurrection of the
dead and the future of the Earth are things that are acknowledged by everyone to depend "wholly on the Determination of a free Agent" (IV.iii.29).
Locke characterizes the truths of geometry as ones that we grasp by apprehending necessary connections between ideas. These are truths that we cannot conceive of as depending upon anyone's arbitrary choice. By contrast,
he offers the resurrection of the dead and the fate of the Earth as examples
of factors that everyone thinks of that way. The main point of the passage is
that the facts about cohesion, the laws of motion, and the communication
of motion belong with the second lot, and not the first. We cannot grasp the
facts about the cohesion and the motions of bodies by apprehending necessary connections between ideas; we must reckon them the consequences of
arbitrary divine decisions.

In what sense are God's decisions about cohesion, the laws of motion and
the production of ideas arbitrary? It is not that they are random, or to no
purpose. Locke says that when God gives bodies powers to produce ideas
in us, he does so "by established Laws, and Ways, suitable to his Wisdom
and Goodness, though incomprehensible to us" (II.xxxii.14). For help in
understanding what he does mean in calling these divine choices arbitrary,
we do well to consider the other connections that he calls arbitrary. These
are the signification of words (III.ii.8), and the composition of ideas of
mixed modes (III.iv.17).[25] Locke points out that each of us can make any
word stand for whatever idea we like, and none can force another to associate any particular idea with any particular word or sound (III.ii.8). We
are constrained to associate particular words with particular ideas only if
we have the goal of communicating in a common language already in use.
The arbitrariness of language is also illustrated by facts perhaps too obvious
for Locke to mention: the fact that different groups speak different languages, and that languages change over time.[26] As for ideas of mixed modes,

<hr/>

[25] Locke also talks about the arbitrariness of the signification of sounds III.iv.11. The sounds he is
thinking of are spoken words, so this is just a special case of the arbitrariness of words.

[26] A curiosity he does mention is that authors write in their own idiolects even when they share a
common language. Locke says that the uncertainty in the signification of words "is so evident in the
Greek Authors, that he, that shall peruse their Writings, will find, in almost every one of them, a distinct
Language, though the same Words" (III.ix.22).

I suggested earlier (§4) that Locke thinks their arbitrariness is a matter of there being many more kinds of fleeting features and events than we have any reason to think or talk about. Which ones we should make ideas of depends on our interests and our circumstances.

If we abstract a general account of arbitrariness from the sort of arbitrariness that we see in language and in concept formation, we get something like this: a state of affairs is arbitrary if (i) it is one of several logically possible arrangements; (ii) it depends upon the choice of an agent or agents; (iii) when the agents choose that it should obtain, there is no such thing as getting it right or wrong, except insofar as the choice does or does not serve their interests; and (iv) the agents responsible could in principle replace it with a different state of affairs. To a certain kind of theist, this kind of arbitrariness can also be seen as applying to the nature and strength of cohesive and gravitational forces. It can be seen as applying to the fact that certain kinds of events at the surfaces of our organs of sense trigger certain ideas in us, and to the laws that govern the communication of motion through impact.[27]

Locke is not the only theist who embraces voluntarism about the laws that govern the behavior of bodies. Descartes holds that God is the primary cause of motion, and that His immutability accounts for laws of nature that are "the secondary and particular causes of the various motions we see in particular bodies" (CSM, 1:240). These laws determine that objects at rest or in motion remain that way until they are acted upon by other things, and that all motion is in itself rectilinear (CSM, 1:240–2). They also determine what happens when bodies collide with one another (CSM, 1:240–4). Boyle too defends a voluntarist account of the laws of motion. Several times he puts forward the idea that God did more than just create matter and give motion to it. He established laws about how that motion would be communicated in the ordinary course of nature, and He intervened in extraordinary ways at the early stages, to ensure that living things came to be:

I plead only for such a philosophy as reaches but to things purely corporeal, and, distinguishing between the first *original of things* and the subsequent *course of nature*, teaches concerning the *former*, not only that God gave motion to matter, but that

---

[27] In contrast, triangles having internal angles equal to two right ones is a state of affairs that meets none of conditions (i)–(iv). Locke will say that our making certain ideas of substances, and associating terms with them, fails condition (iii) because such ideas are reckoned defective if nothing in the world answers to them (see §4).

in the beginning he so guided the various motions of the parts of it as to contrive them into the world he designed they should compose (furnished with the *seminal* principles and structures or models of living creatures), and established those *rules of motion*, and that order amongst things corporeal, which we are wont to call the *laws of nature*. (Boyle 1991, 139).[28]

In "Some Physico-Theological Considerations about the Possibility of the Resurrection," Boyle goes so far as to suggest that God can change the laws of motion whenever He likes: "the most free and powerful Author of those laws of nature, according to which all the phenomena of qualities are regulated, may (as he thinks fit) introduce, establish or change them in any assigned portion of matter" (Boyle 1991, 207).

Locke's voluntarism about the laws of motion gives rise to a puzzle. For though he says that we must ascribe the "Rules…of Motion" to the arbitrary will of God, he also draws a contrast between the relative intelligibility of mechanical interactions, and the unintelligibility of the relation between primary qualities and powers to produce particular sensory ideas in us. Regarding mechanical interactions, he says:

That the size, figure, and motion of one Body should cause a change in the size, figure, and motion of another Body, is not beyond our Conception; the separation of the Parts of one Body, upon the intrusion of another; and the change from rest to motion, upon impulse; these, and the like, seem to us to have some *connexion* one with another. (IV.iii.13).

And yet, he continues, "we can by no means conceive how any *size, figure, or motion* of any Particles, can possibly produce in us the *Idea* of any *Colour, Taste,* or *Sound* whatsoever; there is no conceivable *connexion* betwixt the one and the other" (IV.iii.13). The puzzle is this: if the rules of motion are arbitrary, and if the connections between primary qualities and secondary qualities are also arbitrary, why are the former more intelligible than the latter? If they all depend upon God's arbitrary decisions, why are they not all equally mysterious?

The solution to the puzzle is to recognize that Locke does see there as being some connection between the idea of a collision and the sorts of changes that can result from it. It is not that the specific laws of motion are conceptual truths, but rather that our idea of body imposes a constraint on what can happen in consequence of a collision. Our idea of body includes

[28] See also Boyle 1991, 19, 69.

the idea of solidity. It is an upshot of this that no conceivable scenario could count as one in which bodies come to be co-located. If one body strikes another, the result cannot be that the first passes through the second. Instead, we must see its motion as being halted, re-directed, or transferred somehow. This is why Locke thinks that we can grasp some connection between the intrusion of a body and the separation of another body's parts, between impulse and a consequent change from rest to motion. It is the specific manner in which the motions of colliding bodies are halted, re-directed, or transferred that is arbitrary, and decided by God. Now compare this to the case of bodies striking our sensory organs. These too are cases of collisions, yet neither our idea of body nor our idea of motion entails anything about any mental effects of these collisions. They give us no reason to think that these collisions must give rise to any ideas in the owner of the sense organs. Locke explains the fact that they do, and the facts about which particular stimuli give rise to which particular sensory ideas, as consequences of God's arbitrary will.

One might perhaps worry that Locke's voluntarism amounts to occasionalism. The voluntarist makes God responsible not only for creating matter of a certain sort, and imparting motion to portions of it, but also for deciding what matter will do with those motions. God decides whether moving bodies will continue to move when they are uninhibited; and if He decides that they will move, then He decides how they will move. God also decides what will happen when moving bodies collide with other bodies. If God makes all of these decisions, and if His omnipotence means that bodies cannot fail to behave as He wills, one might worry that there is nothing left for finite causes to do. This sort of thinking has prompted occasionalist readings of Descartes and Boyle, at least so far as body-to-body causation is concerned.[29]

Yet whether voluntarism leads to occasionalism depends on what the voluntarist says about the causal contributions of God and of created substances. The voluntarist might hold that God can establish the laws that govern moving bodies without moving the bodies Himself. One sort of theory about this, recently dubbed "mere conservationism" (Freddoso 1991), has it

---

[29] Occasionalist readings of both Descartes and Boyle date back to the seventeenth century (Della Rocca 1999, 70 n1; Anstey 2000, 166). Daniel Garber is one recent scholar who defends an occasionalist reading of Descartes on body-to-body causation (Garber 1993). J. E. McGuire's reading of Boyle has been described by some as an occasionalist reading (McCann 1985, appendix; Anstey 2000, 160), though McGuire denies that Boyle accepted occasionalism (McGuire 1972, 532).

that God gives bodies genuine active and passive powers when He creates them, and from that point on He merely conserves them. Sometimes it is added that this conservation is equivalent to continual creation. Another option for the voluntarist is to say that God's establishing the laws of motion involves more intervention from Him than mere conservation. An approach called "concurrentism" has it that God and finite things can both be genuine causes of the same events. A defender of concurrentism might say that God establishes the laws of motion by consistently making the contributions He does toward moving bodies about.[30]

The majority of recent scholarly opinion speaks against reading Descartes and Boyle as occasionalists, even about body-to-body causation, and in favor of reading them as concurrentists of some sort.[31] There is no *more* reason to read Locke an occasionalist. He characterizes finite things as causes in the very section we have been discussing:

> The Things that, as far as our Observation reaches, we constantly find to proceed regularly, we may conclude, do act by a Law set them; but yet by a Law, that we know not: whereby, though Causes work steadily, and Effects constantly flow from them, yet their *Connexions* and *Dependancies* being not discoverable in our *Ideas*, we can have but an experimental Knowledge of them. (IV.iii.29)

Even after God has "set" finite things to act in accord with laws, those things—or events that feature them as constituents—are causes. Those causes work, and effects flow from them. The possibility that 'Causes' here refers to divine acts of will can be discounted, since Locke goes on to say that we have experimental knowledge of them. Unfortunately, he does not offer any general account of what God does to set things to act in accord with laws, or how this divine activity is to be understood as consistent with the view that there are genuine finite causes.

If we take seriously Locke's commitment to the view that there are no relations (§5), then there is at least one model that we can rule out. This would be a model on which God fixes the laws of motion—and perhaps gives bodies powers to produce ideas as well—by bestowing upon bodies relational features that are not grounded in their intrinsic features.[32] For

---

[30] For characterizations of mere conservationism and concurrentism, and discussions of some of their scholastic adherents, see Freddoso 1991 and Freddoso 1994.

[31] On Descartes, see Nadler 1994; Della Rocca 1999; Pessin 2003; Schmaltz 2008; Platt 2011a, 2011b. On Boyle, see McCann 1985 (appendix); Shanahan 1988; Jacobs 1994; Anstey 2000.

[32] This is a point that I came to appreciate only after reading Ott 2009, 178.

presumably there cannot be relational features if there are no relations; and if there are no relational features, then it cannot be strictly true that God bestows relational features upon bodies. Locke would be able to countenance talk of God giving things relational features, but only so long as he held that such claims were ultimately reducible to claims about His creating bodies with certain intrinsic features, or to claims about His manipulating bodies somehow. This means that if Locke were to turn to a conservationist account of what God does when He sets bodies to laws, he would be compelled to say that God fixes the laws of motion by fixing the intrinsic features of bodies. However, he might just as well opt for some form of concurrentism, as Descartes and Boyle seem to do. In that case, he could say that God establishes the laws of nature partly by creating bodies with their intrinsic features, and partly by His manner of acting in the world. He could say that the solidity of bodies is partly responsible for their behavior (since it places some constraint on the motions that are possible for them), and yet that divine activity is also needed to make them gravitate, cohere, and move as they do.

§37 Mechanism

Locke's suggestion that God might add powers of thought to bodies—and his claims that their powers to attract one another, to cohere, and to move one another are also to be chalked up to His arbitrary will—have provoked a great deal of discussion among commentators. Much of it has centered on the question of what all of this reveals about Locke's commitment to mechanism.[33] Here the waters are muddied some by disagreement over what is, or ought to be, meant by 'mechanism' in this context. I suppose that it is pointless to quarrel much over a word. Still, the term 'mechanism' does have an obvious lexical relation to 'machine,' and as the name for a project in seventeenth-century natural philosophy, it is clearly related to the idea that natural things are like machines. The sorts of machines to which seventeenth-century adherents of the new science compared natural things were clocks, machines whose overt behavior can be explained in terms of the pushes, pulls, and collisions of their internal parts.[34] Our understanding of what mechanism is ought to do

---

[33] See, for example, Wilson 1979, Ayers 1981, 1991; McCann 1985, 1994; Downing 1998; Stuart 1998; Rozemond and Yaffe 2004; Ott 2009.

[34] See, for example, CSM 1:108, 288, 2:58; and Boyle 1991, 71, 148, 160.

justice to this.[35] It ought to capture the methodological commitments of the seventeenth-century natural philosophers who were most drawn to compare natural things and processes to the workings of clocks—those who saw explanations cast in terms of the sizes, shapes, pushes, and pulls of smaller parts as models of clarity and intelligibility. If one's definition of 'mechanism' yields the result that Descartes and Boyle were not mechanists, this is an indication that one has run off the rails.[36] Indeed, I would have us look to Descartes and Boyle to see what a commitment to mechanism involves.

In the *Principles of Philosophy*, the most finished statement of his physics, Descartes lays out three fundamental laws of nature for bodies. The first is that each thing always continues in the same state until it is acted upon by some external cause (CSM, 1:240). The states he has uppermost in mind are those of motion and rest, but the point is perfectly general: "if a particular piece of matter is square, we can be sure without more ado that it will remain square for ever, unless something coming from outside changes its shape" (CSM, 1:241). The point is perfectly general because Descartes holds that all physical differences between bodies ultimately depend on differences in motion (CSM, 1:232). Descartes's second law says that "all motion is in itself rectilinear," and his third describes what happens when moving bodies collide (CSM, 1:241–2).[37] Of paramount importance is Descartes's observation that his third law covers *all* changes that result from physical causes (CSM, 1:242). According to Descartes, any time one body causes a change in another, it does so in consequence of contact or collision.

Boyle endorses something like Descartes's first law,[38] but he does not articulate specific laws of mechanics. He calls shape, size, motion, and texture the "primary"

---

[35] Thus Micheal Ayers's definition of "pure mechanism" as the view that "the laws of physics can be explained, in principle if not by us, by being deduced from the attributes possessed essentially by all bodies *qua* bodies" (Ayers 1981, 210) seems to me to stumble out of the gate. Ayers does better when he says that 'mechanism' "can provisionally and roughly be defined as the view that the perceptible functioning of machinery supplies an overt illustration of the intelligible principles which covertly govern nature as a whole" (Ayers 1991, vol. 2, 135). Walter Ott's definition of "course of nature mechanism" as the view that "physical objects behave as they do in virtue of their properties and natures" (Ott 2009, 36) also strikes me as too untethered from the analogy between natural things and machines. Only somewhat better is his characterization of "ontological mechanism" as the view that "the only properties of bodies are size, shape, and motion or rest, plus or minus derivative properties like situation, position, and so on" (Ott 2009, 36).

[36] The first definition mentioned in the previous footnote has this defect.

[37] A collision can alter a body's state of motion or rest because the first two laws apply to all of the bodies involved in the collision. So, for example, one body's tendency to remain in motion and moving in a straight line might work against another body's tendency to remain at rest. Something has to give.

[38] Once accidents are introduced into matter, he says, "[w]e need not seek for a new substantial principle to preserve them there, since, by the general law or common course of nature, the matter qualified by them must continue in the state such accidents have put it into, till by some agent or other it can be forcibly put out of it and so divested of those accidents" (Boyle 1991, 62).

or "mechanical" affections of bodies. He holds that every body must have some determinate size and shape (Boyle 1991, 51), and that aggregate bodies must have textures in virtue of the sizes and shapes of their constituent parts (Boyle 1991, 30, 51). Like Descartes, Boyle sees motion as having a special preeminence among the affections of matter. God is the first cause, he says, but *"local motion seems to be indeed the principal among second causes, and the grand agent of all that happens in nature"* (Boyle 1991, 19).[39] All change in bodies requires some motion of the bodies or their parts (Boyle 1991, 141), and "if an angel himself should work a real change in the nature of a body, it is scarce conceivable to us men how he could do it without the assistance of local motion" (Boyle 1991, 146). God creates and preserves "this great *automaton*, the world (as in a watch or clock)," and even directs the motions of bodies in the early stages, but the naturalist's task is to explain corporeal phenomena in terms of the mechanical affections alone:

[W]hen the skillful artist has once made and set it a-going, the phenomena it exhibits are to be accounted for by the *number, bigness, proportion, shape, motion* (or *endeavour*), *rest, coptation*, and other mechanical affections, of the spring, wheels, pillars, and other parts it is made up of; and those effects of such a watch that cannot this way be explicated must, for aught I know, be confessed not to be sufficiently understood. (Boyle 1991, 71)

Though here Boyle stops short of asserting that all natural phenomena have mechanistic causes, that is clearly the leading idea of his research project. He is not always so cautious. At one point he says that "whatever is done among things inanimate...is really done but by particular bodies, acting upon one another by *local motion*" (Boyle 1991, 191).

Though Boyle does not come right out and say that the motions of one body can work changes on another body only by virtue of contact or collision, that is his working assumption. This is evident from the fact that he sees the question of how an incorporeal substance might move a body "which it may pass through without resistance" to be "hardly explicable" and above reason (Boyle 1991, 224). We also see it in his commitment to explaining away the appearance of action at a distance. Descartes explains gravity as being the result of downward-spiraling funnels of celestial matter (CSM, 1:269). Boyle is doubtful that anybody has yet offered a satisfactory explanation of it:

[T]hough the effects of gravity indeed be very obvious, yet the cause and nature of it are as obscure as those of almost any phenomenon it can be brought to explicate....And indeed, the investigation of the true nature and adequate cause of

---

[39] See also Boyle 1991, 44 and 109.

gravity is a task of that difficulty that, in spite of aught I have hitherto seen or read, I must yet retain great doubts whether they have been clearly and solidly made out by any man. (Boyle 1991, 156)

Nevertheless, when Boyle does mention possible causes of a body's gravitational descent, he mentions "the pressure of some subtle matter incumbent on it" and "magnetical steams of the earth" (Boyle 1991, 161). These "magnetical steams" he conceives of as corpuscular. In *Experiments and Notes about the Mechanical Production of Magnetism*, he invokes them to explain changes in the magnetic features of iron when it is heated. He judges it "probable that the great commotion of the parts, made by the vehement heat of the fire, disposed the Iron, whilst it was yet soft, and had its pores more lax...to receive much quicker impressions from the Magnetical *effluvia* of the earth" (Boyle 1676, 14).

I have suggested that our understanding of seventeeth-century mechanism should be firmly rooted in the suggestion that the corporeal realm is a sort of vast machine, and in the scientific methodologies of those who take that suggestion most seriously. If we approach the issue this way, we should say that a commitment to mechanism involves a commitment to the view that all of the workings of nature can be explained in terms of the shapes, sizes, and motions of bodies. It also involves the supposition that bodies can act on one another only by communicating motion through contact action. If a commitment to mechanism involves at least this much, then Locke is not committed to mechanism. He thinks that it is epistemically possible that God adds powers of thought to bodies, and he thinks this despite categorically ruling out the possibility that bodies might think in virtue of the sizes, shapes, and motions of their smaller parts. This violates the first requirement for a commitment to mechanism. Locke also thinks that it is impossible to explain gravitation in terms of the natural operations of matter and the laws of motion. He holds that we can explain it only as a consequence of God's positive will. This violates the second requirement for a commitment to mechanism. This does not mean that Locke is committed to saying that the worldview of mechanism is false. It is just that he cannot see how it could be true, and he is not committed to its being true.

7

Identity

§38. Early in his chapter on identity, Locke endorses principles of individuation that go some way toward specifying the relations between things, places, and times. He also offers some account of the diachronic identity conditions that govern atoms, masses of matter, and organisms. §39. These principles do not answer every question about identity. One question they do not answer is how a compound material thing is related to the mass that composes it at any given instant. Locke has variously interpreted as a four dimensionalist, as a relativist about identity, and as countenancing distinct, coincident entities. §40. Locke's tentative endorsement of Newton's account of how matter might be made does not show that he is a four dimensionalist. §41. Neither does the fact that he sometimes refers to the substances that constitute persons as parts of those persons. §42. Locke's explanations of why identity proves so puzzling can be accommodated by both the coincident objects reading and the relative identity reading. His principles about things, places, and times also fail to decide between these two readings. §43. However, Locke's argument against the possibility of co-located bodies spells trouble for the coincident objects reading. §44. The relative identity reading can accommodate Locke's claim that each thing has only one beginning. §45. Locke's remarks about an oak and a horse lend some support to the relative identity reading. §46. Locke's rejection of essentialism speaks against the coincident objects reading. If his anti-essentialism does not by itself commit him to relativism about identity, it does when combined with another view that he seems to hold—the view that nominal essences supply diachronic identity conditions. §47. Locke's anti-essentialism makes nearly all judgments about the persistence of things nominal-essence-relative. The exceptions are judgments that a body or an immaterial substance has been annihilated.

§38 *Principles of Individuation*

Locke added the chapter "*Of Identity and Diversity*," which became II.xxvii, to the *Essay's* second edition in response to William Molyneux's suggestion that he "Insist more particularly and at Large on…the Principium Individuationis" (*Corresp.*, 4, #1609, 650). The problem of the *principium individuationis* was an inheritance from scholasticism. Medieval philosophers and later scholastics who were moderate or "Aristotelian" realists about universals held that if two individuals belonged to the same species, they did so in virtue of possessing the same general or substantial form. This left the problem of accounting for an individual's distinctness from others of the same species.[1] Scholastic candidates for the principle of individuation included matter, "designated" matter, an individual "haecceitas" or "thisness," existence, and the entity itself.[2] Surprisingly, Locke opts for one of these traditional answers. At II.xxvii.3, he announces that "tis easy to discover what is so much enquired after, the *principium individuationis*; and that, 'tis plain, is Existence it self."

Locke's candidate for a principle of individuation is, at first sight, distinctly unpromising. To say that existence is the principle of individuation looks like an unilluminating tautology. Locke seems to be telling us just that each thing exists where and when it exists. Yet if we consider what he says before and after he says that existence is the principle of individuation, we will discover that his claim is not the vacuity it seems to be. Immediately after offering existence as the *principium individuationis*, Locke notes that existence "determines a Being of any sort to a particular time and place, incommunicable to two Beings of the same kind" (II.xxvii.3). Existence, for him, is spatiotemporal existence. Locke repudiates abstract objects (III.iii.1); he holds that finite spirits occupy places and move about (II.xxiii.19–21; II.xxvii.2); and he thinks that God is "every where" (II.xxvii.2; II.xv.2). So when Locke says that existence is the principle of individuation, he is saying that existence in space and time is the principle of individuation.

---

[1] Evidence that Locke shares this conception of the *principium individuationis* can be found in the exchange with Stillingfleet. Stillingfleet addresses the question of what is the ground of the distinction of several individuals, Peter, James, and John. He glosses this as a question about "the distinction between several individuals in the same common nature," and Locke treats this as equivalent to a question about "the *principium individuations*" (*Works* IV, 438–9).

[2] For an overview, see Thiel 1998.

A second clue to understanding Locke's claim that existence is the *principium individuationis* lies in his observation that this fact is easy to discover "[f]rom what has been said." This comes at the beginning of II.xxvii.3, so "what has been said" must refer to something to be found in II.xxvii.1–2. Locke begins II.xxvii by offering some remarks about how we form the idea of identity, and by endorsing four principles about things, places, and times. The account of how we form the idea of identity is fraught with difficulties, but we can set these aside as lying out of our way.[3] It is Locke's principles about things, places, and times that hold out the greater promise of showing how he arrives at the view that existence is the *principium individuationis*. The four principles that he endorses in II.xxvii.1 are these:

(7.1)   Nothing can be at more than one place at a time

(7.2)   No two things of the same kind can be at the same place at the same time

(7.3)   One thing cannot have two beginnings

(7.4)   Two things cannot have one beginning

There are questions about how to interpret each of these.

It seems fairly obvious that in endorsing (7.1), Locke does not mean to deny that a thing can occupy two different places by having parts that occupy two different places. He will allow that there is a sense in which my body occupies both the place that is occupied by my left hand and the place that is occupied by my right hand. What Locke means to rule out is something like the possibility that my favorite coffee mug might be both in the cupboard and in the dishwasher below the cupboard. It also seems best to find a way of understanding (7.1) on which it does not preclude the possibility of scattered objects.[4] We can do this by allowing for the possibility of scattered regions—regions whose parts are not contiguous—and interpreting (7.1) as the claim that for each thing there is only one region that contains all and only its parts.

---

[3] Locke holds that all ideas of relations are complex ideas formed by acts of comparing (II.xi.4). He says that we form the ideas of identity and diversity by "considering any thing as existing at any determin'd time and place" and then comparing it "with it self existing at another time" (II.xxvii.1). However, he says much less than we might like about what acts of comparing involve, and about the constituents of complex ideas of relations. If the idea of identity is complex, then what are the simple ideas that are its parts? Do these include the idea—or parts of the idea—of the particular thing whose existence at one time is compared with its existence at another? In that case, how can the idea of identity be as general as it seems it must be? For more on the problems with Locke's account of how we make ideas of relations, see Stuart 2008.

[4] Michael Jacovides argues that we should understand Locke as holding that fluids are scattered objects (Jacovides 2008).

In order to understand (7.2), we need to know what it means for two things to be of the same kind. One possibility is that the answer is supplied in II.xxvii.2, where Locke explains that there are but three sorts of substances: God, finite "Intelligences" or spirits, and bodies. If these are the kinds referred to in (7.2), then (7.2) tells us that it is not possible for two spirits to be co-located, or for two bodies to be co-located, though it may be possible for a spirit and a body to be co-located. In §42, I will argue that this is in fact the correct reading of (7.2). Other commentators have suggested that the notion of "kind" at play there is more fine grained, with bodies including things of more than one kind. So it has been suggested that Locke takes organisms and the masses of matter that compose them to belong to different kinds. In that case, (7.2) would permit the co-location of an organism with a mass, while precluding the co-location of two organisms or two masses.

If a *principium individuationis* is meant to tell us what it is that distinguishes two contemporaneous individuals of the same species, then Locke's commitment to (7.2) explains his conclusion that existence is the *principium individuationis*. Since two contemporaneous individuals of the same species will be things of the same kind, principle (7.2) tells us that at any one time the two must be at different places. Spatial location will distinguish them. Since Locke holds that to exist is necessarily to exist at a place, he will put this by saying that existence distinguishes any two contemporaneous individuals of the same species.

In Locke's hands, the claim that existence is the *principium individuationis* is not tautologous, but neither does it amount to an overall account of identity. It leaves unanswered many questions about the individuation of things at a moment and about their persistence over time. This is not a problem with Locke's claim. Rather, it points to the narrow compass of the *principium individuationis* as he and his predecessors understood it. It is a principle addressed to one very specific question about individuation, and there are many other questions about identity and individuation that Locke wants to answer. His four principles about things, places, and times take us some way toward answering some of these, but they still do not answer all of them. In fact, the total package of principles (7.1)–(7.4) leaves us with a serious problem about identity at a time, and principles (7.3) and (7.4) presuppose an account of identity over time rather than offering us one. Let us take these points in turn.

Principle (7.3) implies that if x and y begin to exist at different times and places, then x and y are different things. Now consider the relation between a statue and the piece of marble that constitutes it. If the statue is a human creation, it will likely have begun to exist long after the piece of marble did, and perhaps in a different place as well. Thus Locke seems committed to saying that the piece of marble and the statue are two things. Yet if they are two things, they would seem to be two bodies that, for a time, occupy the same place. This would seem to be a violation of (7.2), which forbids the co-location of things of the same kind. This is clearest if the kinds referred to in (7.2) are the three kinds of substances mentioned in II.xxvii.2, for statues and pieces of marble both seem to count as bodies. One may try to circumvent the problem by saying that the kinds referred to in (7.2) are not those mentioned in II.xxvii.2. In that case, one owes an account of what those kinds are, and of where the distinction between them is to be found in Locke. It is of course uncontroversial that there is *some sense* in which statues and blocks of marble are different kinds of things. Yet if one reads (7.2) as permitting the co-location of x and y whenever x answers a nominal essence that y does not (or *vice versa*), then one so weakens (7.2)'s proscription of co-location that (7.2) no longer rules out much of anything.

A moment ago, I said that principles (7.3) and (7.4) presuppose an account of identity over time rather than offering us one. Consider the scenario on which we invoke (7.3) and (7.4) to settle some questions about the individuation of things. If we discern that x and y have different beginnings, we might use (7.3) to deduce that x is not the same thing as y. If we discern that x and y have the same beginning, we might use (7.4) to deduce that x is the same thing as y. The difficulty comes when we consider what is involved in discerning the beginnings of things. A beginning is a time and place of first existence. To know that some time and place, $<t, p>$, constitutes the beginning of x, we must know that x exists at $<t, p>$, and that x does not exist earlier than t. If t is the present moment, then we can know that x does not exist earlier than t only by knowing that no earlier thing is the same thing as x. If t is earlier than the present time, then we can know that x exists at $<t,p>$ only if we are able to judge when a thing is the same thing as an earlier one. So to know that a time and place constitutes the beginning of a thing, we must already be in a position to make diachronic identity judgments about that thing.

A reasonable suggestion, at this point, is that Locke is presuming that spatiotemporal continuity is what links each thing to its beginning. If that is so, he might think that we can settle the question of whether x is the same thing as y by asking whether the earliest thing with which x is spatiotemporally continuous is also the earliest thing with which y is spatiotemporally continuous. There are two problems with this suggestion. One is that it cannot accommodate what Locke says about personal identity. Though he surely does think that spatiotemporal continuity is required for diachronic identity in most cases, he leaves open the possibility that a person may be able to exist at different times despite profound spatiotemporal discontinuity. We will consider his account of personal identity in the next chapter. A second problem with the suggestion is that the notion of spatiotemporal continuity is too vague to adjudicate questions of diachronic identity.

One might see the requirement of spatiotemporal continuity as demanding greater or lesser degrees of overlap between the regions occupied by a continuous object at successive times.[5] On the most demanding conception, spatiotemporal continuity obtains only when the extent of non-overlap between regions occupied by an object at successive moments can be made as small as you like by selecting moments that are close enough together. On this version, however, continuity fails when a thing is subject to the sudden acquisition or loss of a material part that alters its borders ever so slightly. Thus continuity fails to obtain when a plank is added to a ship, or when an oak tree loses a leaf in the wind. Less demanding concepts of spatiotemporal continuity will require some degree of overlap between the regions of space occupied at successive moments, but will also allow for the sudden attachment or loss of parts if they are small enough. To give an account of diachronic identity, it is not enough to say that diachronic identity is a matter of spatiotemporal continuity. One must also say something about the sort of continuity that is required. This might involve saying a good deal about the organization of the particular kind of thing one is dealing with, and of the changes in composition that might be compatible with—or even necessary for—its persistence. For it seems likely that different degrees of spatiotemporal continuity may be required for the persistence of different sorts of things, even that different degrees of spatiotemporal continuity may be required for the persistence of the different parts of one thing.

---

[5] See Hirsch 1982, 15–21 for a fuller treatment of this.

I have said that principle (7.3) seems to commit Locke to saying that a statue and the stone out of which it is made are two things, while principle (7.2) seems to commit him to saying that they are one thing. Another way to raise essentially the same problem is to note that Locke offers different criteria of persistence for atoms, masses of matter, organisms, and persons. These differences seem to entail that a mass of matter will be distinct from the organism that it constitutes, and that an organism will be distinct from any person it constitutes. Since it seems possible that masses, organisms, and people are wholly material, this seems to violate Locke's proscription on the co-location of things of the same kind.

Before we consider how Locke resolves the problem of material constitution, let us take a look at what he says about the identities of some basic kinds of material things. After telling us that existence is the *principium individuationis*, and that existence determines each being to a time and place that it does not share with others of the same kind, Locke observes that this is "easier to conceive in simple Substances or Modes," but that it is "not more difficult in compounded ones, if care be taken to what it is applied" (II.xxvii.3). He then proceeds to tell us something about the identity conditions that govern atoms, masses, plants, and animals. The structure of the opening lines in II.xxvii.3 suggests that what Locke has to say about each of these cases is supposed to be an application of his insight that existence is the *principium individuationis*. However, his remarks about the identities of atoms, masses, plants, and animals actually take us farther than a mere application of that principle could do. Locke's *principium individuationis* seems to answer a question about synchronic identity, but he is also interested in what it takes for atoms, masses, plants, and animals to persist over time.

Locke asks us to suppose that an atom is a "continued body under one immutable Superficies, existing in a determined time and place" (II.xxvii.3). He then offers these remarks about atomic identity:

'[T]is evident, that, considered in any instant of its Existence, it is, in that instant, the same with it self. For being, at that instant, what it is, and nothing else, it is the same, and so must continue, as long as its Existence is continued (II.xxvii.3).

This is pure tautology. Any atom is what it is, and must continue to exist so long as its existence is continued. However, there is a better account of atomic identity buried in here. One thing that Locke manages to make clear with his tautology is that the identity of atoms is a simple, straightforward affair. His supposition about what an atom is explains why this is. An atom, for Locke, is a body whose outer boundaries are immutable. This does not mean that an atom is partless, but it does mean that an atom cannot acquire parts or lose parts. This means that atoms cannot undergo the sorts of changes that give rise to philosophical puzzles about identity. Atoms, as Locke conceives them, can satisfy the most straightforward and demanding criterion for spatiotemporal continuity. Which region of space an atom occupies can change only as a result of the atom's moving about as a whole, and not by its growth or diminution.

Atoms sometimes cohere together to form masses. Locke conceives of these masses as being, like atoms, incapable of acquiring or losing parts, and thus as obeying the strictest sort of spatiotemporal continuity. He stipulates that 'mass of matter' be understood in such a way that mereological essentialism is true of masses. A mass survives any rearrangement of its component atoms, but not the separation or addition of any atoms. If one component atom ceases to be contiguous with a mass, or one new atom becomes contiguous with a mass, that mass goes out of existence and a new mass comes into being. A Lockean mass is therefore not an ordinary physical object, something capable of undergoing a limited and orderly change in its composition. An ordinary physical object will, over the course of its career, be composed of many masses of matter, but masses themselves do not undergo compositional change. Neither is a Lockean mass a "quantity of matter" in one technical sense of that phrase, that is, a portion of stuff that continues to exist so long as its component portions do, no matter how they are scattered about. If Locke countenances scattered objects, each will be composed of more than one mass at a time.

The persistence conditions for organisms are quite different from those for masses. For in the case of living creatures, "the variation of great parcels of Matter alters not the Identity" (II.xxvii.3). Locke explains that an oak tree differs from a mass of matter in that the one is "only the Cohesion of Particles of Matter any how united," while the other consists of parts organized for self-maintenance (II.xxvii.4). The capacity to receive and distribute nourishment, and in turn to grow and maintain organs (including those responsible for receiving and distributing nourishment), is what constitutes vegetable life. According to Locke, the same oak persists as long as these metabolic processes are uninterrupted. "[I]t continues to be the same Plant," he says, "as long as it partakes of the same Life, though that Life be communicated to new Particles of Matter vitally united to the living Plant, in a like continued Organization, conformable to that sort of Plants" (II. xxvii.4). Some degree of spatiotemporal continuity is presumably required for the persistence of a plant, but this must be consistent with plants acquiring and losing parts in a certain orderly way.

Locke offers an account of the persistence conditions for animals that is much like his account of the persistence conditions for plants. He also suggests that a similar account might apply to artifacts. A living animal body is, Locke says, something like a machine:

> For Example, what is a Watch? 'Tis plain 'tis nothing but a fit Organization, or Construction of Parts, to a certain end, which, when a sufficient force is added to it, it is capable to attain. If we would suppose this Machine one continued Body, all whose organized Parts were repair'd, increas'd or diminish'd, by a constant Addition or Separation of insensible Parts, with one Common Life, we should have something very much like the Body of an Animal...(II.xxvii.5)

A living animal body is like a machine in that it is composed of parts, its parts are organized in a particular way so that it can perform certain functions, and it can survive the acquisition and loss of parts so long as it has some parts or other organized in that way to perform those functions. A living plant body is machine-like in the same way. What distinguishes the living animal from both is that "in an Animal the fitness of the Organization, and the Motion wherein Life consists, begin together, the Motion coming from within" (II.xxvii.5).

It is clear that Locke thinks that plants and animals can survive the acquisition and loss of parts so long as the parts they have are swept up into one continuing life. Less clear is how seriously he is committed to giving a similar account of artifact identity. In order to get us to appreciate that living animal bodies are machine-like, Locke asks us to imagine (i) that a watch is one body; (ii) that it survives the replacement of some of its insensibly small parts; and (iii) that its parts participate in one common life. This feat of imagination is supposed to show us that animals are machine-like, but one might equally well take it to show that machines are animal-like. We do ordinarily suppose that a watch is one persisting thing (though some philosophers resist this). We also ordinarily suppose that a watch can survive the replacement of some of its parts (though these are not insensibly small). What about the supposition that the parts of a watch have "one Common Life"? Locke could be asking us to imagine that a watch is alive; or he could be speaking figuratively (we do sometimes speak of the life of an artifact, as we speak of the life of an idea or a movement). Either way, we might understand him to be encouraging us to think of a watch as something that persists through the replacement of parts so long as it has some parts or other that allow it to perform the function of keeping time.

§39 *The Problem of Constitution*

Locke needs to explain the relation between an organism or an artifact and the mass of matter that constitutes it at any given moment. There are a number of strategies that one might employ to do this. One solution to the problem of overpopulated places is to deny the existence of some of the things whose existence we ordinarily take for granted. Call this the nihilist approach. The nihilist might deny that organisms exist, or even that masses of matter exist. The nihilist might say, for example, that what we loosely speak of as organisms are successive organism-shaped masses of matter, or that they are collections of atoms participating in a certain complex activity.

A second approach uses four dimensionalism to solve the problem of constitution. The four dimensionalist says that material things have temporal extent as well as spatial extent. A commonsense view of objects supposes that all of a thing exists at each moment of its existence. The four dimensionalist says that at any given moment only a temporal part of each thing exists. Each thing is the sum of its temporal parts, just as each instantaneous temporal part is the sum of its spatial parts. Common sense allows for the possibility that two three-dimensional objects may have a part in common—as when two apartments share a wall between them. The four dimensionalist says that two four-dimensional things may have temporal parts in common. An organism and the mass of matter that briefly constitutes it can thus be explained as different four-dimensional things that share a temporal part. If a mass constitutes an organism from t_1 to t_2, then the temporal part of the mass that occupies t_1 to t_2 will be identical with the temporal part of the organism that occupies that span. However, the mass and the organism will be two different things so long as they do not have all of their temporal parts in common.

A third way of solving the problem of constitution is to allow that there can be more than one material thing at a place at a time. We may call this the coincident objects approach. On this approach, it is said that distinct material things may be co-located so long as they belong to different kinds. So one might say that a mass of matter is distinct from the organism that it momentarily constitutes, and that their co-location is unproblematic because organisms and masses are different kinds of things. One who allows for this kind of co-location will see it everywhere, with organisms, artifacts, rivers, and planets being composed of—but not identical to—collections of atoms or quantities of material stuff.

A fourth approach to the problem of constitution derives from the thesis that identity is relative. This thesis says that judgments of identity are relative to sortal concepts that supply criteria of identity. Thus a single relation of absolute identity is replaced by a vast number of identity relations, one for each sortal concept. On this view, it does not make sense to ask how many things there are in a region. Instead we should ask how many Fs there are— how many atoms, or masses of matter, or organisms. Rather than positing two or more distinct things at a place, the relativist will say that any place may be occupied by something that falls under two or more sortal concepts. The judgment that "x is the same as y" is also incomplete at best, shorthand for a judgment of the form "x is the same F as y." The relativist about identity then goes on to say that x can be the same F as y without being the same G as y, even if x and y are both Fs and Gs. The thing in front of us may be a mass of matter, and an organism, and it may be the same organism as an earlier thing without being the same mass of matter as that thing.

Locke has been variously interpreted as advocating the coincident objects approach (Chappell 1989, 1990; Bolton 1994), the four-dimensionalist approach (Conn 1999, 2003) and the relative identity approach (Langtry 1975; Mackie 1976). If it has not been seriously proposed that he favors the nihilist approach, it has been suggested that this would be "the only way to develop his position with complete logical rigor" (Van Inwagen 1990, 144). I will argue that it is the relative identity reading that makes the best overall sense of Locke's remarks about identity and individuation. The nihilist reading we can set aside almost immediately: it has no defenders, and there is no evidence in Locke's writings that he means to deny the existence of animals, houses, or other compound material things. The four-dimensionalist reading does have at least one able defender. Christopher Conn has argued that

Locke is a four dimensionalist. In the next two sections I consider two of his arguments for that conclusion.[6] In the rest of the chapter, I confine myself to arguments that seek to decide between the relative identity reading and the coincident objects reading. We return to the topic of four dimensionalism in the next chapter, where I offer an argument that Locke's account of personal identity requires that persons be three-dimensional things that endure through time (§54).

§40 *Matter and Temporal Parts*

Christopher Conn argues that Locke is committed to a four-dimensionalist account of physical objects by his endorsement of Newton's suggestion about how God might make matter. At IV.x.18, in the second and later editions of the *Essay*, Locke alludes to a possible explanation of the creation of matter:

> Nay possibly, if we would emancipate our selves from vulgar Notions, and raise our Thoughts, as far as they would reach, to a closer contemplation of things, we might be able to aim at some dim and seeming conception how Matter might at first be made, and begin to exist by the power of that eternal first being: But to give beginning and being to a Spirit, would be found a more inconceivable effect of omnipotent Power.

Locke says no more about what the dim and seeming conception might involve. However, in a footnote published twenty-five years after Locke's death, Pierre Coste relates that he asked Isaac Newton about the passage, and was told "that it was he himself who had devised this way of explaining

---

[6] Conn at one point describes himself as having a third argument for Lockean four dimensionalism, but this evaporates on closer inspection. Early in his book, Conn says that he will offer an argument for four dimensionalism deriving from Locke's treatment of space and time (Conn 2003, 24). However, this proves to be merely an argument that Locke recognizes some similarities between space and time (Conn 2003, 157–9). Conn says that this gives Locke a "strong—if subliminal—motive for taking objects to have both spatial and temporal extent" (Conn 2003, 159). I do not see how it does anything to decide between three-dimensionalist and four-dimensionalist accounts of ordinary physical objects. Conn also points to a passage in *Draft B* where Locke alludes to temporal and spatial parts (Locke 1990, 250). Yet Locke does not there suggest that any one thing has both. Indeed, he suggests that "Duration" has the former, and "Space" has the latter. Finally, Conn claims that Locke possesses the concept of spacetime (Conn 2003, 159–60), which one might see as some kind of evidence that he is a four dimensionalist. The claim is based on Locke's observation that "Expansion and Duration do mutually imbrace, and comprehend each other; every part of Space, being in every part of Duration; and every part of Duration, in every part of Expansion" (II.xv.12). However, Locke's observation may mean only (i) that every place exists for an eternity, and (ii) that for each time it is, it is that time everywhere. To say these things is not to say that space and time are combined in a single manifold.

the creation of matter, the thought of it having come to him one day when he happened to touch on this question in company with Mr. Locke and an English lord" (Bennett and Remnant 1978, 5). Coste goes on to explain that Newton's suggestion was that God might create a material thing by conferring impenetrability upon a region of space. He says that Newton suggested that the mobility of matter might be accounted for by God's communicating this impenetrability to other similar portions of space.

One might challenge the suggestion that Locke *endorses* the Newtonian theory to which he alludes, but I will let that pass. Let us suppose that Locke tentatively endorses the theory that bodies are, or might be, adjectival on regions of space. Conn claims that on this theory, bodies are identified with regions of space. He says that, "If God creates an atom by conferring the property of impenetrability upon an atom-sized and atom-shaped region of space, then it follows that an atom *is* a region of space" (Conn 2003, 165). Conn then argues that the identification of bodies with regions of space entails four dimensionalism about material objects. He invites us to consider an atom, a, that persists from t_1 to t_n, occupying region r_1 at t_1, r_2 at t_2, and so on. He claims that on the Newtonian theory, r_1 is a body at t_1, and r_2 is a body at t_2, and so on. He calls the first of these bodies a_1, the second a_2, and so on. Conn reasons that a cannot be an enduring three-dimensional body:

If a body is simply a divinely modified region of space, then different divinely modified regions of space must be *different* bodies. In other words, a_1 and a_3 must be numerically distinct bodies, since $a_1 = r_1$, since $a_3 = r_3$ and since $r_1 \neq r_3$. This, in turn, entails that a_1, a_2, and a_3 cannot possibly be identical with a. Hence, a must be a temporally extended object, and a_1, a_2, and a_3 must all be *parts* of a. (Conn 2003, 169)

According to Conn, Newton's theory makes no room for the possibility of three-dimensional bodies that both persist and move. Since Locke clearly holds that bodies do both, Conn concludes that he is committed to four dimensionalism.

From the claim that bodies are regions of space, and that different regions of space might constitute the same body at different times, Conn infers that bodies must be four-dimensional things. In doing so, he neglects several other possible accounts of the relation between bodies and regions. We have seen that if one treats masses as basic substances, and allows that an organism might be constituted by different masses at different times, there are a number of things one might say about the relation between masses and organisms. Likewise, if one treats regions of space as basic, and allows that a mass might be constituted by different regions at different times, there are a number of things one might say about the relation between masses and regions. To say that masses are four-dimensional things whose parts are four-dimensional regions of spacetime is one possibility. Another is to say that masses and regions are distinct but co-located things. On that approach, one might say that constitution is a ubiquitous relation not to be confused with identity, and that a mass may be constituted by different regions at different times just as an organism may be constituted by different masses at different times. Another approach would be to say that judgments of identity are relative. One might say that they are relative to time, and that a_1 is identical to r_1 in relation to t_1, that a_2 is identical to r_2 in relation to t_2, and so on. Or one might say that judgments of identity are sortal-relative, and that a_2 is the same mass as a_1, but not the same region as a_1, though a_2 is both a mass and a region. There is, of course, much that might be said for and against each of these accounts. What matters for present purposes is just that even if Locke does endorse Newton's suggestion about how matter might be made, this does not show that he is committed to four dimensionalism about physical objects.

§41 *Persons and their Parts*

Conn has also argued that Locke's remarks about persons and substances prove him to be a four dimensionalist. He draws our attention to the fact that Locke sometimes describes the successively existing substances that constitute a person at different times as being parts of that person. He argues that the only way to make sense of this is to suppose that Locke is conceiving of people as four-dimensional objects. The strongest textual evidence that Conn offers along these lines is II.xxvii.25, where Locke says:

But the same continued consciousness, in which several Substances may have been united, and again separated from it, which, whilst they continued in a vital union with that, wherein this consciousness then resided, made a part of that same *self.*

And:

Any Substance vitally united to the present thinking Being, is a part of that very *same self* which now is: Any thing united to it by a consciousness of former Actions makes also a part of the *same self*, which is the same both then and now.[7]

---

[7] Conn also cites passages from II.xxvii.13, 16, 17 and 23, discussing them at Conn 2003, 128–30.

Conn invites us to suppose that over a period of time the mental life of a person named Fred is upheld by a succession of ten mental substances, substance s_1 at time t_1, s_2 at t_2, and so on (Conn 2003, 131). He asks how Fred is related to these substances. Is Fred's mind wholly composed of each of them in succession, or is it partly composed of each and wholly composed of the aggregate of them? According to Conn, the second passage quoted above decides in favor of the second alternative, because "according to this passage, s_1, s_2, and s_3 are distinct parts of him '*both then and now*'" (Conn 2003, 131). He concludes that "on Locke's view, in the event that a person's mental life is the product of successively existing thinking substances, then this person's cognitive nature would be the temporally extended aggregate of these substances" (Conn 2003, 132).

One potential problem with Conn's argument is that even if we were to accept that Fred is an aggregate of s_1, s_2, s_3 etc., this only leads us directly to four dimensionalism if we are assuming that s_1, s_2, s_3 and so on are four-dimensional objects. If s_1, s_2, s_3 and so on are three-dimensional objects, then they are not the sorts of things that could be aggregated to make a four-dimensional object. However, if we are assuming that s_1, s_2, s_3 and so on are four-dimensional objects, then we are assuming that Locke is a four dimensionalist. A second problem with Conn's argument is that his gloss on the last sentence of II.xxvii.25 gets it wrong. As he describes it, Locke tells us that s_1, s_2, and s_3 are parts of Fred '*both then and now*.' Looking back at the passage however, we see that what Locke says is "the same both then and now" is the *self*, not some substance's being a part of that self. What Locke says entails that Fred is Fred at t_1 and at t_{10}, not that s_1 is a part of Fred at t_1 and at t_{10}.

If Conn's argument is reframed to avoid the appearance that it begs the question, we get something like this:

Locke tells us that a thing once united to a present self by consciousness is a part of that self. He thinks that this is so even if the thing is a different substance than that which constitutes the present self. The best way to account for this is to suppose that Locke regards both the thing and the self as four dimensional objects, with the former being a temporal part of the latter.

To undermine this argument, one must show that there is another, equally good way of reading Locke. One must show that it is possible to accommodate talk of s_1, s_2, and s_3 being parts of Fred without supposing that they are four-dimensional things that are temporal parts of Fred. I think that this can be done. There is a manner of speaking of parts on which we say that x is a part of y if x is a sometime constituent of y. Consider the Green Monster, the high left field wall at Boston's Fenway Park. Originally covered in painted tin, it now has a surface of hard, green plastic. Suppose that from time to time repairs are made to the wall, and that when sections of the plastic covering are removed they are divided into small squares and sold to fans as mementos. One would not be surprised to find the Red Sox organization advertising that you could own a part of the Green Monster, or to find a purchaser of one of these mementos describing it to his friends as a part of the Green Monster.

One might reply on Conn's behalf by pointing to a disanalogy between the case of Fred and the case of the Green Monster. What are being called parts of the Green Monster are items that were once proper parts of the Green Monster, but what is being called a part of Fred is (according to the three dimensionalist) an item that once constituted the whole of Fred. If the Red Sox were to replace the entire left field wall during an off-season, and if they were able to remove the retired wall section as one piece, surely we would not call that piece a part of the Green Monster?[8] This might be offered as evidence that we call a sometime constituent of a thing a part of it only when the sometime constituent was at some time a *proper* part of it. I think that what it shows instead is just that ordinary language does not supply us with any natural way of talking about the items that previously constituted, but no longer constitute, all of some currently existing thing. This is not surprising, since outside of philosophy there is seldom any call to refer to such things. Locke is having to stretch ordinary language to talk about the relation between such things as s_1, s_2, s_3, etc. and a persisting self. He does this in a slightly awkward way using 'part' to mean a sometime constituent. He does it less awkwardly when he suggests that two thinking substances might successively "make but one Person" (II.xxvii.13).

---

[8] How would we refer to the retired left field wall if it were to be put on display somewhere? We might call it the Green Monster of 1990–2011 (or something like that), but there would be no implication that it was a temporally extended thing, and people would undoubtedly continue to speak of the Green Monster as a feature of Fenway Park that had been there since at least 1947 (the moniker 'Green Monster' is a recent one, and before 1947 the wall was covered in advertisements). The concepts of some material objects operate like the concepts of political offices. Just as 'the President' refers to whatever person serves as the chief executive, so 'the Green Monster' refers to whatever tall green structure serves as the left field wall in Fenway Park.

If s_1, s_2, s_3 are "parts" of Fred because they are sometime constituents of him, then one might say that their claim to parthood depends on the fact that s_1 was an improper part of Fred at t_1, and s_2 an improper part of Fred at t_2, and so on. Conn claims that this cannot be how Locke thinks of the relations between s_1, s_2, s_3, etc. and Fred:

> In the first place, he does not have the concept of an improper part. But even if he did, the clear implication of these passages [from II.xxvii.25] is that these substances are parts of him at t_{10}, and this is clearly incompatible with s_1's being an *improper* part of him at t_1, to say nothing of s_{10}'s being an improper part of him at t_{10}. (Conn 2003, 131)

To say that Locke does not have the idea of an improper part, but that he does have the idea that ordinary physical objects are four-dimensional things, strikes me as tendentious. Surely he could have the thought that 90 per cent of a material object is a large part of it. What is to prevent him from having the further thought that 100 per cent of a material object is an even larger part of it? In ordinary talk, we contrast talk of parts with talk of wholes. To speak of the whole of a material object as a part of it is a departure from ordinary language, but then so is speaking of a material object as something with temporal parts. Conn claims that it is incompatible to say both that s_1 is a part of Fred at t_{10} and that s_1 is an improper part of him at t_1. However, there is the appearance of incompatibility here only if we fail to distinguish two senses in which something might be called a part of an enduring material object. In a somewhat relaxed sense, we can call any sometime constituent of an object a part of it. In a stricter sense, we count only the current constituents of an object as parts of it. The small squares of green plastic purchased by Red Sox fans are parts of the Green Monster on one manner of speaking, but on the other they are no longer parts of the Green Monster.

§42 *The Difficulty About this Relation*

At several points in II.xxvii, Locke offers summary explanations of why identity has proved so puzzling to philosophers, and what must be done to make it less so. Unfortunately, his summary explanations are themselves puzzlingly indeterminate. At II.xxvii.1, he says, "That which has made the Difficulty about this Relation, has been the little care and attention used in having precise Notions of the things to which it is attributed." He makes a similar remark near the end of the chapter:

[T]he difficulty or obscurity, that has been about this Matter, rather rises from the Names ill used, than from any obscurity in things themselves. For whatever makes the specifick *Idea*, to which the name is applied, if that *Idea* be steadily kept to, the distinction of any thing into the same, and divers will easily be conceived, and there can arise no doubt about it. (II.xxvii.28)

Locke's advice seems clear enough: when we ask a question about the identity or persistence of some thing, we should be clear to ourselves and others about the idea we have in mind. If we are using a general term to pick out a thing whose identity or persistence we are asking about, we should be clear about which idea we associate with that general term. Locke evidently holds that the answers to our questions about identity and persistence will differ depending on the ideas that we have in mind as we ask these questions. What is not so clear is exactly why he believes this to be so.

Two possibilities suggest themselves—one compatible with the coincident objects approach to the problem of constitution, and the other with the relative identity approach. One possibility is that Locke thinks that we must take care about which idea we have in mind as we pose questions or make judgments about identity because different ideas pick out different things. If one simply points in the direction of an occupied region of space, asking whether this thing is the same as was here yesterday, it may be unclear whether one is asking about the identity of the golden retriever that one is ostending, or about the identity of the mass of matter that is co-located with the golden retriever. It is important to be clear about this, because the answer to one's question may differ depending on the object to which one is referring: golden retrievers and masses of matter have different identity conditions. Another possibility is that Locke thinks that we must take care about which idea we have in mind because there are indefinitely many identity relations, and which one we intend to be raising a question about depends on which general idea that we have in mind. If one points to the thing asleep on the living room floor and asks whether it is the same as was sleeping there yesterday morning, one may intend to be asking whether this thing and that stand in the relation "same golden retriever" to one another, or one may intend to be asking whether this thing and that stand in the relation "same mass of matter" to one another. It is important to be clear about which of these questions one means to be asking, because the answers to them may differ.

The chapter contains one other general pronouncement about how to avoid confusion about identity. At II.xxvii.7, shortly before launching into his account of personal identity, Locke says:

'Tis not therefore Unity of Substance that comprehends all sorts of *Identity*, or will determine it in every Case: But to conceive, and judge of it aright, we must consider what *Idea* the Word it is applied to stands for: It being one thing to be the same *Substance*, another the same *Man*, and a third the same *Person*, if *Person*, *Man*, and *Substance*, are three Names standing for three different *Ideas*; for such as is the *Idea* belonging to that Name, such must be the *Identity*: Which if it had been a little more carefully attended to, would possibly have prevented a great deal of that Confusion, which often occurs about this Matter, with no small seeming Difficulties.

Here the talk of "sorts of identity" fits well with the relative identity reading, and it is tempting to see "such as is the *Idea*...such must be the *Identity*" as reaching for the point that "same man as" and "same person as" are different relations rather than one relation ("same as") between different things. However, this cannot be regarded as conclusive. Locke's talk of sorts of identity might be an incautious way of speaking about identity between different sorts of things, and he may hold that it is one thing to be the same man and something else to be the same person because men and persons are different things.

To decide between the coincident objects reading and the relative identity reading, one might look to the general principles that Locke endorses at the beginning of the chapter. They are, again:

(7.1)   Nothing can be at more than one place at a time
(7.2)   No two things of the same kind can be at the same place at the same time
(7.3)   One thing cannot have two beginnings
(7.4)   Two things cannot have one beginning

Vere Chappell has argued that Locke's endorsement of (7.3) shows that he regards organisms as distinct from the masses of matter with which they are co-located (Chappell 1989, 73–5 and 1990, 22). The argument is as follows. Given Locke's account of the identity conditions for masses of matter, any tree that has grown from a seedling will have come into existence much earlier than the mass of matter that now constitutes it. Such a tree thus has a different beginning of existence than does the mass of matter now constituting it. If one thing cannot have two beginnings, it follows that the tree and the mass are two things. Nevertheless, they are two things at the same place at the same time. Chappell anticipates the objection that the co-location of the tree and the mass would seem to violate (7.2). He responds by denying that the "kinds" spoken of in (7.2) are the three kinds of substances mentioned in II.xxvii.2 (God, finite intelligences, and bodies). According to Chappell, Locke regards atoms, masses, and organisms as being things of different kinds, in the sense of 'kind' that is invoked in (7.2).

One problem with Chappell's argument is that it depends on an interpretation of (7.3) that Joshua Hoffman has shown to be unlikely (Hoffman 1980). Taken in isolation, it would be natural to suppose that the upshot of (7.3) is that nothing can begin to exist at two different times. (This could, in turn, be construed either as the truism that nothing can *first* exist at two different times, or as the repudiation of intermittent existence.) This seems to be the way that Chappell reads (7.3). The problem with this reading is that Locke evidently regards (7.3) and (7.4) as following from (7.1) and (7.2). His endorsement of (7.3) and (7.4) comes after his statement of (7.1) and (7.2), and is prefaced with the phrase "from whence it follows." Moreover, immediately after endorsing (7.3) and (7.4), he justifies these principles on the grounds that it is impossible "for two things of the same kind, to be or exist in the same instant, in the very same place; or one and the same thing in different places" (II.xxvii.1). This is, of course, just a re-statement of (7.1) and (7.2). If (7.3) is to follow from (7.1) and (7.2), then surely (7.3) must be supposed to follow from (7.1), the principle that it is impossible for one thing to be at more than one place at a time. However, if (7.3) is to follow from (7.1), then (7.3) must be understood as precluding one thing's having two "beginnings" in some sense that would involve that thing being at two different places at the same time. Hence, if Locke is to be saved from an obvious *non sequitur*, (7.3) should be understood as saying is that it is impossible for one thing to simultaneously begin to exist at two different places. So understood, (7.3) does not entail that no thing could begin to exist at two different times. This means that it does not entail the claim needed to get the result that the tree and the mass are distinct.

There is also a problem with Chappell's response to the objection that the co-location of trees and masses would violate (7.2). Chappell's response is to say that the reference to kinds in (7.2) is not a reference to the three kinds of substances mentioned in II.xxvii.2. He says that in (7.2) Locke is using 'kind' in such a way that an organism and a mass of matter belong to different kinds. The problem is that Locke clearly does commit himself to a version of (7.2) on which all bodies do belong to the same kind. At II.xxvii.2, shortly after telling us that God, finite intelligences, and bodies are the only three sorts of substances that we have ideas of, he says:

For though these three sorts of Substances, as we term them, do not exclude one another out of the same place; yet we cannot conceive but that they must necessarily each of them exclude any of the same kind out of the same place...

Here there can be no doubt that Locke is saying that there are three kinds of substances—God, finite spirits, and bodies—and that a substance belonging to one of these kinds may be co-located with one belonging to another, but not with one of the same kind. Thus a substance that is a body can be co-located with God, or with a substance that is a finite spirit, but not with another substance that is a body. The only way to reconcile the co-location of organisms and masses with this passage is to deny that organisms or masses are substances.

The evidence certainly speaks in favor of Locke's taking masses and organisms to be substances. At II.xxvii.3, he introduces a distinction between simple and compound modes and substances. He then seems to offer atoms as examples of simple substances, and masses as examples of compound substances. William Uzgalis reads the passage that way, but then goes on to say that Locke regards organisms as compound modes rather than compound substances (Uzgalis 1990, 287). Yet this is contradicted by the many passages in which men, sheep, horses and birds figure as prototypical substances for Locke.[9]

---

[9] II.xii.6, p. 165; II.xxiii.3–6, pp. 296–8; II.xxiii.14, p. 305; II.xxiv.1, p. 317; *Works* IV, pp. 17, 460. It is true that these passages occur outside the identity chapter. One might argue that Locke uses 'substance' differently in the identity chapter (see Alston and Bennett 1988). One might then say that Locke takes organisms to be substances in one sense of that term, but not in the sense employed within II.xxvii. However, the thesis that 'substance' means something different in the identity chapter than it does outside it is something to be established only on the basis of our failure to make sense of the identity chapter otherwise; it is not something to be presumed from the outset.

§43 *Against Co-location*

At II.xxvii.2, shortly after the passage last quoted, Locke argues that if the possibility of co-located bodies were to be admitted, our conceptions of identity and diversity would unravel:

[C]ould two Bodies be in the same place at the same time; then those two parcels of Matter must be one and the same, take them great or little; nay, all Bodies must be one and the same. For by the same reason that two particles of Matter may be in one place, all Bodies may be in one place: Which, when it can be supposed, takes away the distinction of Identity and Diversity, of one and more, and renders it ridiculous.

The argument in this passage is elliptical and unclear, but it does show Locke thinking along lines that are difficult to reconcile with the coincident objects reading. He presumably does not mean to rule out the sort of co-location that obtains between a body and the larger whole of which it is a part, or the partial co-location that obtains between two bodies that share a part. What Locke seems to mean is that if we were to allow that two bodies of exactly the same dimensions could be completely co-located, then we would lose our grip on the individuation of bodies. He seems to think that it must always be possible to distinguish bodies by their spatial locations. The trouble for the coincident objects reading is that it is hard to imagine Locke having grounds for this that do not militate against the co-location of masses and organisms as well as against the co-location of two or more masses. Let us explore this more deeply.

What grounds does Locke have for denying that two bodies can be at the same place at the same time? To answer this question, we must settle something about the structure of the passage quoted above. In that passage, Locke is telling us something about the relations between these three claims:

1. Two bodies may be at the same place at the same time
2. All bodies may be at the same place at the same time
3. There is no distinction between the identity and diversity of bodies

It is clear that Locke thinks that if we accept (1) then we are committed to (3), and that he offers this as a reason for rejecting (1). Less clear is whether he thinks that the argument from (1) to (3) necessarily goes through (2). One way to read the passage above is to take Locke to be suggesting that there is an argument that takes us from (1) to (3), and that requires (2) as an intermediary step. In that case, his rejection of co-location is grounded on a single, two-step *reductio* of (1), so let us call this the two-step interpretation. A second interpretation takes Locke to be suggesting two different *reductio* arguments, one that takes us from (1) to (2), and another that takes us from (1) to (3). Call this the double *reductio* interpretation.[10]

On the two-step interpretation, the first step will be an argument that takes us from (1) to (2), and the second one that takes us from (2) to (3). Locke's argument from (1) to (2) would seem to be just that that if we accept the co-location of two bodies, then we can have no principled reason for resisting the co-location of more bodies. What does he mean when he speaks of the possibility of all bodies being in the same place? He seems to mean that if it were possible for two parcels of matter of the same dimensions to wholly occupy the same region at the same time, then it would be possible for the whole of the world's matter to be divided up into parcels of just those dimensions, and for all of them to be at that place at that time. The challenge, on the two-step interpretation, is to find an argument that takes us from (2) to (3), and that makes (2) a load-bearing premise in the overall argument from (1) to (3).[11] I suggest the following. If it is possible for all bodies to be at the same place at the same time, then two worlds might differ just in that the first contains a single body at some place and the second contains a large number of co-located bodies at that place. If we imagine that in the second world the co-located bodies always traveled around together, we find ourselves unable to say what makes for the difference between the two worlds. Is there one body where the ancient, black rotary phone sits on my desk, or are there many co-located and co-traveling bodies there? What does the difference between the scenarios come to? To confess that we cannot answer the question is tantamount to confessing that there is no distinction between the identity and diversity of bodies.[12]

---

[10] A third possibility is that Locke rests his rejection of co-location on a single argument from (1) to (3), but one in which (2) serves as a superfluous premise, a sort of red herring. In that case, Locke's argument against co-location is in effect just the second of the two *reductio* arguments that I describe below in connection with the double *reductio* interpretation.

[11] Several commentators have suggested arguments that Locke might have in mind at II.xxvii.2, ll. 15–20, but none meets the demands of the two-step reading. Martha Bolton suggests an argument that would show that (2) is incoherent, but that is not an argument that (2) entails (3) (Bolton 1994, 109). Conn and Bennett both suggest arguments that get us to (3) (Conn 2003, 66–8), but these are arguments that would just as easily take us from (1) to (3) without the need for (2) as an intermediate step.

[12] This idea for how step two might go was suggested to me by Samuel Levey.

On the double *reductio* interpretation, Locke is again seen as arguing that (1) implies (2), and again his argument seems to be just that if one allows for the co-location of two bodies then there is no principled way to resist the possibility of further co-locations. The difference is that now he is taken to be offering (2) as an absurdity, a consequence that shows that it is wrong to accept (1). This raises the question of whether (2) is any greater an absurdity than (1). Why should someone who is untroubled by the possible co-location of two bodies balk at the possible co-location of all of them? The second step on the two-step reading gives us one possible reply. Let me suggest another.

Locke might begin with a point about the possible size of the physical universe. Suppose that all the world's matter is composed of atoms of uniform dimension. In that case, if all bodies could be co-located, then all of the world's matter could be contained within a space the size of a single atom. Notice that the claim is not just that an atom-sized universe is possible, but that all of the matter that actually exists in our universe could fit within a space the size of one atom, and that it could do so without being compressed in any ordinary sense. That is a result that might seem more obviously absurd than the mere co-location of two bodies. Locke could also build on this. If it were possible for the entire physical universe to fit within a very small space, then we face the question of why the actual universe is not like that. What prevents the universe's collapse by co-location? If the question is unanswerable, we have another respect in which (2) seems an absurdity.[13]

On both the two-step interpretation and the double *reductio* interpretation, Locke argues from (1) to (2). In both cases, his argument seems to be just that if one allows the co-location of two bodies, then one has no grounds on which to deny the possibility that all bodies might be co-located. This speaks against the coincident objects reading. For on that reading, Locke holds that there are good reasons for thinking that some material objects may be co-located, and that others cannot be. If he thinks that co-location is possible in some cases and not others, then why should he think that (1) opens the flood-gates to (2)?

---

[13] It does not look as though the defender of co-location can say that it is the solidity or impenetrability of bodies that prevents the universe's collapse by co-location. For what is the sense in which bodies are solid or impenetrable if it is not impossible for them all to be at the same place at the same time? Yet if the defender of co-location gives up the idea that matter is impenetrable, then he faces the task of explaining the difference between body and space.

On the double *reductio* reading of II.xxvii.2., ll.15–20, the second *reductio* will be an argument that takes us from (1) to (3), without necessarily going through (2). It will be an argument to the effect that if one allows that two bodies might be at the same place at the same time, then one cannot say what features distinguish those bodies. Again, to account for the fact that Locke does not bother spelling the argument out, it should be a quick and easy one. I think that it is possible to construct such an argument on his behalf. Locke might think that co-located bodies will be bodies with exactly the same dimensions, that bodies with exactly the same dimensions will be bodies with the same atomic structure, and that bodies with the same atomic structure must have the same intrinsic features. In that case, he will think that bodies that are co-located could be distinguished only by their extrinsic features. If bodies are to be distinguished by their extrinsic features alone, it seems reasonable to say that they must be distinguished by spatial features. Co-located bodies could not be distinguished by those, and so we are left with the result that they cannot be distinguished at all.

If the argument that I have just sketched is Locke's second *reductio* of (1), this too speaks against the coincident objects reading. For if the problem with co-location is that co-located bodies must have all the same intrinsic features, this would seem to apply not only to bodies of the same kind (e.g. two masses), but to ones of different kinds (e.g. a mass and an organism). A defender of the coincident objects approach may reply that bodies belonging to different kinds or ontic levels will not have all of their intrinsic features in common, because they will have different modal features that distinguish them. Thus an organism will have the feature of being able to survive the loss of one of its constituent atoms, whereas the mass that constitutes it will not have that feature. The problem with this reply is that it saddles Locke with the problem of explaining how objects that have the same atomic constitutions can have different modal properties. In general, it seems that differences in the modal properties of things must be explicable in terms of differences in their non-modal properties. We are not content to admit it as a brute fact that a lump of sugar has the possibility of dissolving in water, and that a lump of bronze does not. Instead, we seek to explain these modal differences in terms of non-modal differences between the physical properties of sugar and bronze. The coincident objects approach seems to require differences in modal properties that are not grounded in differences in non-modal properties.

§44 *Women and Masses*

William Uzgalis has argued that the relative identity solution to the problem of constitution runs afoul of (7.3), Locke's principle telling us that no one thing can have two beginnings:

Consider a woman and the mass of particles which composes her at different times. Each of the masses of particles which compose her at various times will have a different beginning in time from each other and from the woman they compose. But *ex hypothesi* the woman and the mass of particles are simply one individual. It follows that one individual will have many different beginnings in time and place. But nothing could be further from what Locke says about identity than the [*sic*] one individual has many beginnings in time and at many places. (Uzgalis 1990, 293)

In §42, we noted an argument of Joshua Hoffman's about the import of (7.3). Locke presents (7.3) as following from (7.1) or (7.2). Of these possibilities, it seems much likelier that (7.3) is meant to follow from (7.1). In that case, we must take (7.3) to be ruling out not the possibility that one thing begins to exist at two different times, but the possibility that one thing simultaneously begins to exist at two different places. If that is the correct understanding of (7.3), then the scenario described by Uzgalis does not begin to show that there is a conflict between the relative identity reading and (7.3). For even on his description of what the relative identity reading entails, it does not involve a commitment to anything having two simultaneous beginnings.

This reply to Uzgalis may be good as far as it goes, but it is not fully satisfying. It fails to satisfy because even if (7.3) is telling us just that nothing can simultaneously begin to exist at two different places, one might think that Locke should also deny that anything can begin to exist at two different times.[14] If he does hold that nothing can first exist at two different times, would this conflict with what the relative identity reading would have him say about women and masses? I will argue that it does not. Before I do that, it will help to introduce a few technical terms having to do with the words and concepts that we use to categorize things.

Locke introduces the word 'sortal' to the English language, deriving it from 'sort' as we do 'general' from 'genus' (III.iii.15). As he uses the word,

---

[14] In §54 I show that such a principle would need to be spelled out with some care if it is to be compatible with Locke's account of personal identity.

a sortal term (or "*Sortal* Name") is any general term, any term that stands for an abstract idea. These days, many philosophers follow P. F. Strawson in using 'sortal' in a narrower sense, as standing for a term that supplies criteria of identity sufficient for counting (Strawson 1959, 168; Griffin 1977, 34; Lowe 2009, 13). I will use 'sortal' in this more restrictive sense unless otherwise specified. In order to supply criteria for counting Ss, a term must not only supply criteria that distinguish Ss from non-Ss, but also ones that individuate Ss over time, so that we do not count the same S twice.[15] Ideas or concepts associated with sortal terms we may call sortal ideas or sortal concepts. Sortals can be nested in the sense that the things falling under one sortal may comprise a subset of the things falling under another sortal. This is sometimes put by saying that some sortals are "restrictions" of others. Somewhat intuitively, a term 'F' restricts another term 'G' (and the concept of an F restricts the concept of a G) if and only if an F is a G that is P, where P is some predicate. Thus, for example, 'graduate student' restricts 'student' (and the concept of a graduate student restricts the concept of a student) because a graduate student is a student enrolled in a graduate program.[16] A sortal term that is not a restriction of any more general sortal term may be called an "ultimate" sortal.

The term 'book' is a sortal, because we can easily make sense of the request to count the books in a room, and of the question whether the book in one's hand is the same book as one held earlier. To say that 'book' is a sortal is not to say that there can be no difficulties about how to count books. It is easy enough to count them in the most cases, but it may be less clear what to do when one literary work occupies several volumes, when novels by several authors are bound together, or when a collection of writings are first bound together and later broken up and bound separately. A term can supply some criteria of identity without providing criteria so thorough as to settle every question that might arise. Still, there does seem to be an important difference between a sortal term such as 'book' and a non-sortal such as 'thing.'

---

[15] The sense of 'criteria' employed here is intended to be metaphysical rather than epistemological. If 'F' is a sortal term, the criterion of identity associated with 'F' is one that tells us not what counts as good evidence that x and y are the same F, but what it is for x and y to be the same F.

[16] In order to preclude terms or concepts from restricting themselves, we may require that P be a predicate that need not apply to all G's. Our example satisfies this requirement, because not all students are enrolled in graduate programs.

If we are instructed to count the things in a room, we might begin by counting the table, the chairs, the lamps, the pictures on the wall. Yet soon we run into trouble. Do we count the table legs? The left halves of the pictures? Do we count momentary table stages as well as tables? Is there a thing composed of the back of one chair and the left half of a picture? Many of us find ourselves at a loss about how to answer such questions. There are philosophers who do defend answers to them, but even their success would not necessarily show that 'thing' is a sortal. For 'thing' to be a sortal, it would have to be the case that the answers to the above questions are delivered by criteria that are grasped implicitly by understanding the meaning of, or mastering the use of, the ordinary word 'thing.' If that were the case, then we would expect to be able to answer those questions as easily, and with as much consensus, as we do questions about which items are books. The unsettled state of the debate about the metaphysics of physical objects suggests that this is not the case.

Some point out that we sometimes use 'thing' and 'object' to mean something like "bounded, coherent material object" (Geach 1968, 145; Xu 1997), and that we sometimes do count such things. If a child's six wooden blocks sit alone on a table, it does seem very natural to say that there are just six things on the table. If a car drives across a plain, it seems likely that even an observer who had never before encountered a transporting vehicle would conceptualize it as a single moving thing (Hirsch 1976, 361). Yet problems arise about how to cash out the notions of boundedness and coherence. Is a desk lamp that is plugged into an outlet a bounded thing? What about a light fixture on the ceiling? A steam radiator that is connected to other radiators by pipes? To be sure, problems also arise about how to count books, but the counting and tracking of bounded, coherent material objects seems to involve more vagueness, and less easily remedied vagueness, than does the counting of books. So if we do sometimes use the concept of a bounded, coherent material object to count and to track "things" or "objects," it may be best to say that in such cases 'thing' and 'object' function as quasi-sortals rather than as genuine sortals.

Terms that take the grammatical form of count nouns, but that do not supply criteria for counting, are sometimes called "dummy sortals." A dummy sortal can stand in proxy for one or more genuine sortals. Even if we cannot track "things" or "objects" *per se*, we can understand someone who says: "Those things on the table were there yesterday." We can understand this remark because we see, or presume that we could come to see, that there are sortals that do apply to the things on the table and that might be used to ground diachronic identity judgments about them. Dummy sortals can function as labor-saving devices. It would have been more cumbersome to say that the six books, three pencils, one fountain pen, one stapler, and seventeen loose sheets of paper that are on the table were there yesterday.

We are now in a position to explain why Uzgalis's argument against the relative identity reading fails even if Locke were to deny that anything can begin to exist at two different times. Suppose that Rebecca was conceived in 1975, and that at some particular time, t, on some particular day, she is composed of a mass of atoms that came to cohere together at t minus three minutes. The relativist about identity can say that this is a case of something existing at t that is (in the predicative sense of 'is') both a woman and a mass. He can say that there is at t a woman who began to exist in 1975, and that there is at t a mass that began to exist at t minus three minutes. However, he ought not to say that there is at t something that began to exist in 1975 and that also began to exist at t minus three minutes. If he did say that, the 'something' in his claim would be functioning as a dummy sortal, one that must be presumed to be standing in for some proper sortal that supplies criteria of identity that connect a clump of cells in Rebecca's mother's uterus in 1975 to the thing that is both a woman and a mass at some place at t. To do this, the sortal will have to be one that both 'woman' and 'mass' restrict. There is no such sortal. Moreover, even if one were to contrive a sortal, 'S,' that both 'woman' and 'mass' restrict, the relativist should say that there is an S that began to be a female human being in 1975, and that began to be a particular mass at t minus three minutes, but not that the S (or anything else) began to exist at both those times.

Here a critic may respond by pointing out that when the relativist says that there is something existing at t that is both a woman and a mass, he too would seem to be using 'something' as a stand-in for some sortal that both 'woman' and 'mass' restrict. If there is no such sortal, how are we to make sense of the relativist's claim? The relativist can respond by pointing out that the function of a sortal is to supply criteria that distinguish an object from its environment. That task is much simpler when the scope is limited to a single moment, which is the case when the relativist says that something existing at t is both a woman and a mass. One can distinguish a thing from its environment at a moment without having recourse to the principles of individuation associated with proper sortals. If t is the present and Rebecca is nearby, the relativist who wants to distinguish a thing that is both a woman and a mass may achieve this partly by pointing. Pointing may not do the whole job, since pointing at Rebecca is inevitably pointing at her body parts. Yet if one points and says, "*This* is both a woman and a mass of particles," then anyone who understands 'woman' will understand that the item being ostended is not merely Rebecca's nose. If one cannot point at Rebecca, one can distinguish the thing that is both a woman and a mass by means of a description that involves a non-sortal term and reference to a location. One might say, for instance: "The material object that is at place p is both a woman and a mass of particles."

§45 *The Oak and the Horse*

Let us now consider Locke's remarks about a particular case of constitution, the constitution of an organism by a mass of matter, to see what help it offers in deciding between the relative identity reading and the coincident objects reading. At II.xxvii.3, he explains the relation between organisms and masses as follows:

> An Oak, growing from a Plant to a great Tree, and then lopp'd, is still the same Oak: And a Colt grown up to a Horse, sometimes fat, sometimes lean, is all the while the same Horse: though, in both these Cases, there may be a manifest change of the parts: So that truly they are not either of them the same Masses of Matter, though they be truly one of them the same Oak, and the other the same Horse.

The situation is that at t_1 there is a seedling and a colt, while at t_2 there is an oak tree and a grown horse. On the coincident objects reading, this entails the existence of at least six distinct entities. They are (i) an oak that persists from t_1 to t_2; (ii) a mass that is distinct from, but co-located with, the oak at t_1; (iii) another mass that is distinct from, but co-located with, the oak at t_2; (iv) a horse that persists from t_1 to t_2; (v) a mass that is distinct from, but co-located with the horse at t_1; and (vi) another mass that is distinct from, but co-located with, the horse at t_2. On the relative identity reading, his remarks will imply that there is something at t_2 that is the same oak as something at t_1, but not the same mass of matter as it. They also imply that there is, at t_2, something that is the same horse as something at t_1, but not the same mass of matter as it.

A careful reading of this passage shows that it speaks in favor of the relative identity reading. What is crucial is Locke's claim that "they are not either of them the same Masses of Matter, though they be truly one of them the same Oak, and the other the same Horse." We may begin by asking what 'they' refers to in this claim. His use of the word 'either' implies that whatever "they" are, there are two of "them." Of these two things, he says that one is the same oak as the young plant, the other the same horse as the colt. Clearly, "they" are the oak tree at t_2 and the grown horse at t_2. Now, consider Locke's denial that "they" are the same masses of matter. The grammar makes it clear that he is not stating the obvious fact that the matter composing the tree at t_2 is different from the matter composing the horse at t_2: he denies that "they" are the same "Masses," not that they are the same mass. What he means in denying that "they" are the same masses is that the mass composing the tree at t_2 is different from the mass that composed the tree at t_1, while the mass composing the horse at t_2 is different from the mass that composed the horse at t_1.

The problem for the coincident objects reading is that in denying that "they" are "either of them the same Masses of Matter," Locke suggests that "they" are *different* masses of matter. On the coincident objects approach, this does not make sense. Nothing can be both an oak and a mass of matter, so no oak can be either the same mass of matter as anything, or a different mass of matter than anything. The advocate of the coincident objects reading must say that Locke has denied that "they" are the same masses of matter when he meant to deny that "they" are masses of matter at all. By contrast, Locke's remark that "they are not either of them the same Masses of Matter" is just what we should expect him to say if his solution to the problem of constitution is to relativize identity. On this reading, "they" are two things existing at t_2, and he is discussing the relations between these things and two things that existed at t_1. He is saying that one of "them" stands in the relation "same oak as" to one of the things at t_1, without standing in the relation "same mass as" to that thing. He is saying that the other of "them" stands in the relation "same horse as" to one of the things at t_1, without standing in the relation of "same mass as" to it.

Though the passage we have been discussing lends support to the relative identity reading, it is immediately followed by perhaps the most straightforward bit of evidence for the coincident objects reading. Just after the sentence that we have been scrutinizing, Locke says, "The reason whereof is, that in these two cases of a Mass of Matter, and a living Body, *Identity* is not applied to the same thing" (II.xxvii.3). If he means that a living body and the mass that momentarily constitutes it are distinct things, then he would seem to be countenancing the co-location of distinct material objects. However, that is not the only way to understand his remark. We might begin to see this if we ask what it means to apply identity to a thing. Elsewhere in the identity chapter, he speaks of identity as being "attributed" or "applied" to ideas (II.xxvii.1, l.11), to things (II.xxvii.1, ll.27–30), and to names (II.xxvii.7, ll.25–26). What can all of this mean?

It seems fair to suppose that to "attribute" or "apply" identity is to make a judgment about the identity of something. However, the cases in which Locke speaks of "applying" identity to ideas or names do not seem to be cases where he is concerned with judgments about the identities of concepts or linguistic items. His concern in all of these passages is to highlight the importance of attending to exactly what we judge when we judge that things are the same or different. When he speaks of the need for "precise Notions of the things to which [the relation of identity] is attributed" (II.xxvii.1), and of the need to consider "what *Idea* the Word it is applied to stands for" (II.xxvii.7), he seems to be urging us to take care about precisely what we are judging. Ironically, these warnings are themselves formulated rather carelessly. Locke drifts haphazardly between talk of ideas, words, and things, perhaps lulled by his views about the tight connections between the ideas in our minds, the meanings of our words, and the referents of our thought and talk. When he says that "*Identity* is not applied to the same thing" in these "two cases of a Mass of Matter, and a living Body," this may mean no more than that these are different identity judgments.

§46 *Essence and Identity*

Another reason for reading Locke as a relativist about identity is that relativism about identity fits comfortably with his rejection of essentialism, whereas the view that organisms and masses are distinct, co-incident entities does not. In §23, we saw that Locke maintains that the distinction between essence and accident is nominal-essence-relative. He holds that any attempt to distinguish between the essential and the accidental features of a thing can be made only in relation to one of the abstract ideas to which the thing answers. Each such idea is a nominal essence that defines a kind. The features included in the nominal essence are those necessary for a thing's membership in the kind. A thing that has all of those features belongs to the kind, and may be said to have those features essentially in relation to that nominal essence. Its other features may be called accidental in relation to that nominal essence. Yet each thing answers to many nominal essences, and different nominal essences draw the line between essence and accident in different places. Locke holds that we cannot conceive of anything to privilege one such division above the others.

The coincident objects reading sits uneasily with Locke's views about essence and accident. If an organism and the mass that constitutes it are distinct but co-located entities, then they will have many of the same features. Some of the features they share will be features that the organism has essentially, and that the mass has only accidentally. The existence of an organism of a certain kind depends on its maintaining a certain shape, and on its having internal parts arranged in a certain way. A mass may have the same shape, and the same arrangement of internal parts, but could exist without those features. If the organism and the mass are composed of the same atoms at the same time, then the fact that the one has certain features essentially and that the other has them only accidentally is at least part of what accounts for the distinctness of these two things. The question is whether we can make sense of this without supposing essentialism. If an organism and the mass that constitutes it really are distinct from one another, then their distinctness must be a fact that is independent of our conceptual activities. It would be absurd to say that the organism and the mass are distinct from one another but that one or both of them come into being just because we judge something, or because we conceptualize something in a certain way. We cannot create new material objects merely by judging or thinking. If the distinctness of the mass and the organism is independent of our conceptual activities, and if part of what accounts for their distinctness is the organism's having certain features essentially that the mass has contingently, then the distinction between essence and accident must obtain independently of our conceptual activities. Thus the coincident objects approach to the problem of constitution seems to presuppose the essentialism that Locke rejects.

In contrast, Locke's account of the distinction between essence and accident fits comfortably with the thesis that judgments about diachronic identity are nominal-essence-relative. Indeed, if his account of essence and accident does not commit him to the relativity of identity, it strongly pushes him in that direction. We can begin to appreciate this by looking at what his account of essence and accident implies about things perishing.

Locke's account of the distinction between essence and accident entails that some facts about the persistence conditions of things are nominal-essence-relative. It entails that whether or not a thing can survive the loss of a feature generally depends upon the nominal essence in relation to which the thing is considered. A thing possesses a feature essentially if it could not exist without that feature, and possesses it accidentally otherwise. The loss of an essential feature means the end of the thing whose feature it is. To lose an accidental feature, on the other hand, may be to persist through a change. Locke holds that the only sense in which things possess some of their features essentially and others accidentally is in relation to one or another nominal essence. Each thing answers to more than one nominal essence. This raises the possibility that the loss of a feature may count as the end of a thing on one nominal essence, but as a survivable change on another. Suppose that a thing answers to nominal essences "F" and "G," and that it possesses a feature that is included in the idea "G" but not in the idea "F." If it loses that feature, we are faced with the question of whether to say that it has gone out of existence or that it may have persisted through a change. Locke must say that which it is depends on the abstract idea in relation to which we consider the thing.[17] After the loss of the feature, there may still be a thing that is the same F as the earlier thing; but this later thing is not a G, and hence is not the same G as the earlier thing. It may seem that this already entails a commitment to the relativity of identity, but that is too quick.

The considerations adduced so far show only that Locke should allow that there are true statements of the form:

R1: x is the same F as y, but not the same G as y, though x is a G

However, we have characterized the view that identity is relative as the view that there are true statements of the form:

R2: x is the same F as y, but not the same G as y, though x and y are both Gs

---

[17] In §47 below I show the need to qualify this point. Locke's account of essence and accident entails that whether a thing perishes or not is nominal-essence-relative in every case except those where a body or an immaterial thinking substance is annihilated.

Whether instances of **R1** would establish that identity is relative in any interesting sense is somewhat contentious.[18] In any case, it is the stronger **R2** formulation of the relative identity thesis that Locke will need later if he is to allow for the possibility that x and y may be the same organism and different persons.

There is another reason we should be reluctant to say that Locke's account of essence and accident commits him to the relativity of identity. That account implies something about the relativity of perishing, but to show this is not yet to show that it implies the relativity of identity over time. It will be suggested that if facts about whether something perishes are nominal-essence-relative, then so must be facts about whether something persists, since something persists just in case it does not perish. Even so, this does not take us all the way to the conclusion that Locke is a relativist about identity.[19] The claim that identity over time is nominal-essence-relative is not just the claim that whether a thing persists is nominal-essence-relative; it is the claim that which later thing is to be identified with a given earlier thing is nominal-essence-relative. To show that Locke is committed to this claim, one must say something about what he thinks it takes for x to be the same F as y.

For x to be the same F as y, x must be an F and y must be an F. Locke holds that for something to be an F is for it to answer to the nominal essence, "F." This leaves us with the question of what more, beyond x and y answering to the nominal essence "F," he takes to be required for x to be the same F as y. An obvious possibility to consider is that he thinks that the additional requirement is spatiotemporal continuity under the sortal concept "F." Perhaps he thinks that x is the same F as y if and only if there is a continuous

---

[18] Harry Deutsch formulates the relative identity thesis as the view that it may be true that x and y are the same F though x and y are different Gs (Deutsch 2007). He says that this schema is only trivially satisfied when y is not a G at all, and describes what I call **R2** as the "nontrivial core claim" of the relativist about identity. On the other hand, David Wiggins, a critic of relative identity, deems it worth his while to argue against the view that there are instances of **R1** in which y is not a G (Wiggins 2001, 29–30). He considers the case of Sir John Doe, the Lord Mayor of London, who is the same human being as an earlier boy, but not the same boy as that earlier boy (because the Lord Mayor is not a boy at all). Wiggins contends that if we are careful about tenses, we will see that this is not a case that lends support even to the weaker formulation of the relative identity thesis.

[19] Another objection is that the suggestion neglects the possibility that nothing does persist. We have shown only that if a thing answers to the nominal essence "F," and does not lose any of the features included in "F," then it *may* persist. However, the view that nothing persists is a strange and implausible one, and I think that we can safely dismiss the possibility that Locke held it.

spatiotemporal path linking x and y, with something answering to "F" at each location on that path.

Earlier we considered, and dismissed, the suggestion that Locke holds that x is the same thing as y just in case x and y are spatiotemporally continuous. We dismissed that suggestion for two reasons: because he does not hold that personal identity requires spatiotemporal continuity, and because the requirement of spatiotemporal continuity is too vague. The present proposal overcomes one of these objections, but still falls to the other. To say that diachronic identity is a matter of spatiotemporal continuity under a sortal does address the concern about vagueness. The requirement of continuously satisfying a sortal places real restrictions on the sorts and speeds of compositional change to which a thing can be subject. Even so, this reading cannot be right, because Locke does not hold that spatiotemporal continuity of any sort is required for a person to be the same person as an earlier person. The proposal may point us in the right direction though, because it invites us to think about the relationship between seeing something as answering to a nominal essence and seeing it as being governed by certain identity conditions.

Let us say that a feature is "instantly observable" if one can see whether something has that feature simply by observing the thing at an instant. The size, shape, and motion of a body are instantly observable. Photographs and other sorts of static images can directly represent only the instantly observable features of things. If we were to conceive of nominal essences as static images of some sort, then we would have to say that they too can represent only instantly observable features. This does not seem to be how Locke thinks of nominal essences.

Locke suggests that the nominal essences of gold and lead include dispositional features such as malleability, fusibility, and solubility in *aqua regia*. These are not instantly observable features. One can see that something is soluble by watching it dissolve, but dissolution takes time. Dispositional features are forward-looking, they are features that tell us something about what their bearers might do. There is reason to think that Lockean nominal essences represent backward-looking features as well. Something answers to the nominal essence "organism" just in case it has been participating in a life, and something answers to the nominal essence "work of art" only if it has been created or altered by someone with artistic intentions. If nominal essences can impose forward-looking and backward-looking constraints on the things that answer to them, might they not also include forward-looking and backward-looking constraints on which past and future things can be identified with the things that presently answer to them? If that were so, then what it takes for x to be the same F as y would be determined by the nominal essence "F."

Locke does not say, in so many words, that the persistence conditions that govern things of a kind are built into the nominal essence that defines the kind. However, that does seem to be his view. At III.iii.9, he tells us that the abstract ideas "man" and "horse" include the idea "animal." This means that a thing answers to the idea "man" or the idea "horse" only if it answers to the idea "animal." At II.xxvii.8, he says this about the idea "animal":

An Animal is a living organized Body; and consequently, the same Animal, as we have observed, is the same continued Life communicated to different Particles of Matter, as they happen successively to be united to that organiz'd living Body.

From the fact that an animal is a living organized body, Locke says, it *follows* that a later animal is the same animal only if it participates in the same continued life. Locke thinks that to see something as answering to the idea of a living organized body is to see it as having certain diachronic identity conditions. Putting these two passages together, we get the result that seeing something as answering to the idea "horse" means seeing it as governed by certain diachronic identity conditions. To count something as a horse commits one to seeing a later horse as being the same horse only if that later horse participates in the same continued life.

The interesting result of all this is that if the persistence conditions for things of a kind are determined by the nominal essence that defines the kind, then whether there are any true statements of the **R2** type will depend on the particular nominal essences we happen to have. Locke's view about the particular nominal essences we have does seem to lead to the result that there are some true statements of the **R2** type. It will be an upshot of our decision to rank something under the nominal essence "mass" that we count a later mass as being the same mass as the present one if and only it is composed of the same atoms and these have remained contiguous (however they might have been jumbled about). It will be an upshot of our decision to rank something under the nominal essence "organism" that we count a later organism as being the same organism so long as it participates in the same life. There will be occasions on which we can rank two things at different times under both of these nominal essences, and some of these will be occasions when the later thing participates in the same life as the earlier one, but is composed of different atoms. This will be a case in which an x is the same organism as an earlier y, but not the same mass as that y, though both x and y are both masses and organisms.

Let us summarize the ground that we have covered in this section. Our topic has been the relationship between Locke's anti-essentialism and his solution to the problem of constitution. First we saw reason to think that the coincident objects approach to the problem of constitution requires a sort of essentialism that Locke rejects. Then we considered whether his account of the distinction between essence and accident commits him to the view that identity judgments are nominal-essence-relative. We saw that the account does entail that there are true statements of the form **R1**, but that it is not clear that this suffices to make Locke a relativist about identity. In any case, we are interested in whether he is a relativist of a more robust sort, one involving the view that there are true statements of the form **R2**. To show that he is a relativist of the more robust sort, we must also show that he takes the question of whether an individual at one time is to be identified with an individual at another time to be nominal-essence-relative. One might hold such a view because one holds that the persistence conditions for things of a kind are determined by the nominal essence that defines that kind. I have offered evidence that Locke does hold that view.

§47 *Annihilation*

Locke's account of essence and accident entails that whether a thing persists through a change, or perishes because of it, may depend upon the nominal essence in relation to which we consider the thing. This raises the worry that he may be unable to explain the palpable difference between something's ceasing to be an F and its ceasing to exist altogether. Locke can explain that difference, but we must tread carefully.

If the world loses a student because someone graduates, this is no cause for sorrow; if it loses one because someone is hit by a bus, that is another matter. Both cases might be thought to involve something ceasing to answer to a certain idea or nominal essence. In the first case, something ceases to answer to the idea "student"; in the second, something ceases to answer to the idea "human being." David Wiggins suggests that we should distinguish between those concepts that "present-tensedly apply to an individual x at every moment through-out x's existence … and those that do not" (Wiggins 2001, 30). He calls the former "substance concepts" and the latter "phased sortal concepts." If one says that "human being" is a substance concept and "student" a phased sortal concept, then one can say that nothing really goes out of existence when a student graduates, but that something does really go out of existence when a student dies.

Wiggins's account of the difference between ceasing to be a student and ceasing to be a human being is not available to Locke. He can say only that whether a thing continues to answer to the nominal essence "human being" is something that we care about much more than we do whether it continues to answer to the nominal essence "student." To distinguish between substance concepts and phased sortal concepts would be to say that there *is* something that privileges some nominal essences over others. It would be to say that some nominal essences delineate the features that are necessary for the existence of an individual, and not just those necessary for an individual's membership in a kind. Locke's anti-essentialism does not allow him to say this. Or rather, it allows him to say this only about two nominal essences, and only in reference to "individuals" in an anemic sense. To understand these caveats, we must consider what account Locke can give of annihilation.

Locke wants to allow for the possibility of annihilation. At II.xiii.21 [*bis*], he contends that those who argue against the possibility of empty space must "deny a power in God to annihilate any part of Matter."[20] He does

---

[20] The argument is as follows. God can surely put an end to all motion in matter. If He does this, and if He annihilates any part of matter, then the region formerly occupied by that part will be empty, for it will have been vacated and no other matter will have moved into it. Therefore, if there cannot be empty space, then it must be that God cannot annihilate any part of matter.

this in the course of arguing for the possibility of empty space, so we are encouraged to think that he would say (and expects his readers to say) that God can annihilate parts of matter. Though he wants to allow for the possibility of annihilation, Locke also makes the point that our idea of it does not represent what this divine activity would consist in so much as what its effects would be:

[M]any words, which seem to express some Action, signify nothing of the Action, or Modus Operandi at all, but barely the effect, with some circumstances of the Subject wrought on, or Cause operating; v.g. Creation, Annihilation, contain in them no Idea of the Action or Manner, whereby they are produced, but barely of the Cause, and the thing done. (II.xxii.11)

A Lockean account of annihilation will be an account of the cause of annihilation, and of the circumstances of the subjects of annihilation. Locke does not give us such an account, but let us consider what account might be available to him.

It seems safe to assume that Locke would say that only God can annihilate things, and this because he thinks that God's omnipotence ensures that only He can undo His act of creation. As for the circumstances of the subjects of annihilation, there are at least two ways that Locke could explain the difference between something's merely ceasing to be an F and its being annihilated. He could point out that cases in which something merely ceases to be an F are cases in which at least some of the parts of the F survive. These include cases in which something ceases to be an F because its parts are re-arranged or re-located, but also cases in which something ceases to be an F just because time passes. Cases of annihilation, by contrast, may be understood as cases in which all of a thing's parts cease to be when it ceases to be. Another way Locke might distinguish cases in which something merely ceases to be an F from cases of annihilation is by pointing out that the former are cases that can be described as something's persisting through a change. Cases of annihilation are cases in which there ceases to be an F and this cannot be re-described as a case of anything's persisting through a change.

Let us pursue a bit further the second way of characterizing annihilation. If the situation of something ceasing to be an F is describable as one of something persisting through a change, the description must employ a kind term that 'F' restricts, to characterize what it is that ceases to be an F. We say that it is a human being who ceases to be a student (and 'student' restricts 'human being' because a student is a human being who studies). We say that it is a dog who ceases to be a pup (and 'pup' restricts 'dog' because a pup is a dog that is immature). A case of something ceasing to be an F, if it is a case that cannot be re-described as a case of something persisting through a change, will be one in which there is no term other than 'F' that might be used to characterize what it is that ceases to be an F. It will be a case in which something ceases to be an F and 'F' is an ultimate sortal, at least in the Lockean sense of 'sortal.' We have already seen Locke's candidates for these. His three most general categories of substances are God, finite intelligences, and bodies. We can set aside the case of God, since God is not a candidate for ceasing to exist. This leaves us with the view that if something is annihilated, this must be either a case in which something ceases to be a finite intelligence, or one in which something ceases to be a body. If a "finite intelligence" is a finite *immaterial* thinking substance, this is what we should expect. For to say that "body" and "finite immaterial thinking substance" are the ultimate (Lockean) sortals for Locke is to say that he is a substance dualist.

We can now see that Locke's anti-essentialism does allow him to make a distinction between "substance concepts" and "phased sortal concepts," but the substance concepts are limited to "body" and "finite immaterial thinking substance." Does this mean that he is, after all, committed to saying that some of the features that individuals have are necessary for their persistence, and not just for their membership in a kind? One could say that, but the sense of 'individual' in play is not robust. Anything answering to the nominal essence "body" must be extended and solid, and the loss of either of these features spells its annihilation. However, in Locke's hands 'body'—unlike 'mass'—is merely a Lockean sortal, and not a Strawsonian one. The idea "body" does not supply criteria that tell us what it takes for x to be the same body as y. To say that each body has the feature of solidity essentially is not to say something about an individual that is distinct from other individuals, an individual whose movements might in principle be tracked. In order to refer to a distinct individual body we must employ some other nominal essence that restricts "body."

The assumption that God can annihilate His creatures, together with Locke's account of the distinction between essence and accident, leads to the view that every judgment that something perishes is either (i) the judgment that a body or an immaterial substance has been annihilated, or (ii) a nominal-essence-relative judgment concerning a scenario that could be re-described as a case of something's persisting through a change.[21]

[21] Locke *could* treat even the "annihilation" of bodies and immaterial thinking substances as a case of (ii). Suppose that he holds that space exists necessarily, and that he endorses the Newtonian account of the origin of matter. In that case, even what one might call the annihilation of a material object will be re-describable as a region of space losing certain features without any other region of space acquiring those or similar features. We can go further. Locke holds that if there are finite immaterial thinking substances, these have spatial locations and move about as bodies do. This raises the possibility that he might account for the creation of spirits as Newton proposed to account for the creation of bodies. For a spirit to exist would be for some region of space to have some feature or features distinctive of spirits. For a spirit to move about would be for different regions to acquire and lose that feature. In that case, neither the annihilation of spirits or of bodies would amount to anything more than qualitative changes to regions of space. This is a road that Locke could have gone down, but not one that we can say that he did go down. He does consider a metaphysic like this one, however. In his discussion of space, he raises the question of whether space is substance or accident (II.xiii.17). Locke declines to answer until his imaginary interlocutor can show him a clear, distinct idea of substance. He then responds with questions of his own:

"I desire those who lay so much stress on the sound of these two Syllables, *Substance*, to consider, whether applying it, as they do, to the infinite incomprehensible GOD, to finite Spirit, and to Body, it be in the same sense; and whether it stands for the same *Idea*, when each of those three so different Beings are called *Substances*? If so, whether it will not thence follow, That God, Spirits, and Body, agreeing in the same common nature of *Substance*, differ not any otherwise than in a bare different modification of that *Substance*; as a Tree and a Pebble, being in the same sense Body, and agreeing in the common nature of Body, differ only in a bare modification of that common matter; which will be a very harsh Doctrine." (II.xiii.18)

Here Locke entertains the possibility that God, spirits, and bodies are all modifications of one common substance. He does not propose space as a candidate for being that substance, but the possibility seems an obvious one, coming as this does on the heels of his discussion about whether space is a substance. The difference between this view and the one that I described above is that this view makes even God adjectival upon the one substance. Presumably it is this that leads Locke to declare it a harsh doctrine. He might think it harsh because it does not make God sufficiently distinct from His creation, or because it makes God not only omnipresent but extended.

8

Persons

§48. A person, according to Locke, is a rational being who can conceive of himself as a self persisting over time. Consciousness determines the extent of a self at a moment, and also the extent of its past. To extend one's consciousness to a past thought or action is to remember having the thought or performing the action. Locke defends the "simple memory theory," according to which a past thought or action is correctly attributed to a present self just in case the self remembers the earlier episode in a certain first-personal way. §49. There is a longstanding puzzle about how Locke can consistently treat persons as substances and yet deny that the persistence of a substance is either necessary or sufficient for the persistence of a person. The solution involves the recognition that he is a relativist about identity. This leaves us with the challenge of explaining what it means to deny that x is the same substance as y. We can meet this challenge by supposing either that Locke uses 'substance' as a quasi-sortal, or that he uses it as a dummy sortal. §50. The memory continuity theory says that for an event to be in one's past one need not remember it, so long as one is connected by ties of memory in the right way to someone who remembers it. Some have ascribed the memory continuity theory to Locke; others offer it as a friendly amendment to his simple memory theory. Both are mistakes. These readings fail to do justice to Locke's view that what determines the extent of a self at a moment is also what determines its past extent. §51. Locke is best understood as holding that an event does not belong to one's past if one tries and fails to remember it, even if one will remember it minutes later. §52. Locke needs to distinguish genuine memories from mere apparent memories. The best way to do this is to say that genuine memories have certain causal connections to the remembered events. In Locke's case, this is complicated by his desire to accommodate mortalism. §53. In a notorious passage about false memory, (II.xxvii.13) Locke stumbles but does not—as some have alleged—forget his own account of personal identity. §54. Locke's simple memory theory

can be defended against many objections, and in several cases his commitment to the relativity of identity supplies the key to its defense. Yet his theory fails to offer a satisfactory account of survival. The trouble is that his is a backward-looking theory and survival is largely a forward-looking matter.

§48 Introducing Persons

Locke sees there as being an important distinction between human beings and persons. This may be a bit surprising, but more surprising still is the account that he gives of the nature of persons. Many commentators have sought to interpret that account in ways that minimize its strangeness. Where Locke's words seem to lead away from the familiar, his interpreters stretch to find readings that domesticate his account of personhood.[1] In doing so, they risk missing some of the points that he is keenest to make. Locke thinks that the concept "person" behaves in ways that are radically unlike most of the sortal concepts that we employ. In particular, he thinks that the criteria for diachronic identity that we associate with 'person'—or, at least, the ones we *ought* to associate with 'person'—differ from those we associate with 'mass' and 'man' in fundamental ways. Locke thinks that a mass or a man is the same mass or man as an earlier one only if there is some degree of spatiotemporal continuity between them. He also thinks that the span of the existence of a mass or a man must gradually increase with the passage of time, until the mass or man ceases to exist altogether and forever. By contrast, Locke thinks that spatiotemporal continuity is *not* required of persons; and he thinks that the span of the existence of a person can be "gappy." He also thinks that the span of a person's existence can decrease or increase abruptly as time passes. His account of persons is at once weirder, more interesting, and less easily refuted than it is frequently taken to be, though ultimately it fails to do all that he needs it to do.

Locke introduces the topic of personal identity at II.xxvii.9, and it remains his exclusive concern for the rest of the chapter. In his opening salvo, he does a number of things: he describes the conditions that something must meet in order to count as a person, he makes some observations about the relation between consciousness and selfhood, and he gives us a first look at his account of the diachronic identity conditions for persons. All of this is

---

[1] A refreshing exception is Strawson 2011.

important, and the section is worth considering in some detail. It begins with Locke giving us an account of what the word 'person' means:

[W]e must consider what *Person* stands for; which, I think, is a thinking intelligent Being, that has reason and reflection, and can consider it self as it self, the same thinking thing in different times and places...

To count as a person, Locke holds, a subject must: (i) have reason, (ii) have reflection, (iii) have the ability to consider itself as itself, and (iv) have the ability to think of itself as the same thinking thing in different times and places.

To have reason is to possess a mental faculty that Locke thinks is responsible for much of our knowledge and also much of our superiority to "Beasts" (IV. xvii.1). To understand what reason does, we must recall that on his account knowledge is perception of the agreement or disagreement of ideas (IV.i.2). Sometimes we can perceive this agreement or disagreement immediately; these are cases of what he calls "*intuitive Knowledge*" (IV.ii.1). Other times, we can perceive the agreement or disagreement of ideas only by interposing a chain of ideas intermediate between them; these are cases of what he calls "*demonstrative Knowledge*" (IV.ii.5). The difficulty of acquiring demonstrative knowledge is that of finding the appropriate intermediate ideas, and arranging them in the proper order so that each is immediately or "intuitively" apprehended to agree or disagree with its neighbors.[2] Reason is the faculty by which we are supposed to discover these intermediate ideas and "what connexion there is in each link of the Chain, whereby the Extremes are held together" (IV.xvii.2).

To have reflection, the second requirement for personhood, is to be able to perceive the operations of one's own mind. Reflection is, along with sensation, one of the two original sources of the simple ideas we possess. It furnishes the understanding with "another set of *Ideas*, which could not be had from things without" (II.i.4). Ideas of reflection include the ideas of such mental activities as thinking, believing, and willing, but also those of "Passions arising sometimes from them, such as is the satisfaction or uneasiness arising from any thought" (II.i.4).

Locke's third criterion for personhood is the ability of a subject to consider itself as itself. This is the capacity for a kind of self-consciousness that

---

[2] Besides the much-discussed problem of what Locke's ideas *are*, there is a difficulty about how to understand this talk of ideas as having a spatial or quasi-spatial ordering. I will not attempt to solve these problems here.

goes beyond the awareness of oneself that is involved just in virtue of reflection. Locke uses 'self' and 'person' interchangeably.[3] The upshot is that on Locke's view in order to *be* a person one must be able to employ the *idea* "person," and to apply it to oneself. Some creatures fall short of personhood because despite having an experiential awareness of their own mental activities, they cannot think of themselves as selves. A tiger chasing its prey might meet requirement (ii) for personhood, but not requirement (iii). Its desire to catch and eat a certain deer may be reflectively available to it as a component of its experience—it may *feel* the desire, or the hunger—but it cannot think "I am the subject of a desire to catch and eat that deer."

Though I have distinguished (iii) and (iv), it might be more accurate to say that for Locke these constitute a single requirement for personhood, since (iv) incorporates (iii). Requirement (iv) is that one be able to consider oneself as oneself—the same thinking thing—at different times and places. This requirement for personhood is epistemic in nature. Locke is saying that in order to count as a person, one must be able to conceive of oneself in a certain way, or have certain knowledge about oneself. Less clear is exactly how one must conceive of oneself, or what one must know about oneself, to qualify as a person. Perhaps he means only that one must be able to conceive of oneself as the sort of thing that could exist at different times and places. To do this would be to recognize oneself as enjoying a different mode of existence than actions and thoughts—"things whose Existence is in succession," and that cannot exist at different times and places because they perish as soon as they begin (II.xxvii.2). However, requirement (iv) can also be given a stronger reading. It may be taken as requiring that one believe or know something about one's own particular history. Locke may mean that something counts as a person only if it knows something about its existence at earlier times and at other places.

After listing these requirements for personhood, Locke goes on to say something about how we meet them. He says that we do this "only by that consciousness, which is inseparable from thinking, and as it seems to me

---

[3] At II.xxvii.26 he announces that "*Person*, as I take it, is the name for this *self*." Earlier in the chapter, we find him switching between 'self' and 'person' merely for stylistic variation. Thus the section heading for section 16 is "*Consciousness makes the same Person*"; that for section 17 is "*Self depends on Consciousness*"; and that for sections 23–25 is "*Consciousness alone makes self*." He also uses the phrase "personal self" as equivalent to both "person" and "self" (II.xxvii.10, 11). At II.xxvii.17, he defines 'self,' saying that a self is a "conscious thinking thing,...which is sensible, or conscious of Pleasure and Pain, capable of Happiness or Misery, and so is concern'd for it *self*, as far as that consciousness extends." That this is equivalent to personhood will emerge in what follows.

essential to it: It being impossible for any one to perceive, without perceiving, that he does perceive."[4] In the remainder of II.xxvii.9, Locke makes a number of observations about role of consciousness in the constitution of the self:

Thus it is always as to our present Sensations and Perceptions: And by this every one is to himself, that which he calls *self*: It not being considered in this case, whether the same *self* be continued in the same, or divers Substances. For since consciousness always accompanies thinking, and 'tis that, that makes every one to be, what he calls *self*; and thereby distinguishes himself from all other thinking things, in this alone consists *personal Identity*, *i.e.* the sameness of a rational Being: And as far as this consciousness can be extended backwards to any past Action or Thought, so far reaches the Identity of that *Person*; it is the same *self* now it was then; and 'tis by the same *self* with this present one that now reflects on it, that that Action was done. (II.xxvii.9)

Here Locke makes at least three important claims about consciousness and selfhood. First, it is consciousness of one's present sensations and perceptions that makes one the self that one is. Second, what makes for selfhood in the present is also what makes for the persistence of a self over time. Third, a present self is to be identified with a past self if the present one's consciousness extends backwards in time to the past one's thoughts or actions. We shall have a closer look at each of these claims in what follows. It is the third claim that has gotten the lion's share of the attention from commentators, but it is a mistake to neglect the other two. If we are to understand what Locke says about the identities of persons over time, and *why* he says what he does about that, we must understand his views about selfhood in the present and its relation to selfhood over time.

What Locke does say about selfhood over time he casts in terms of the reaches of consciousness and personal identity. Personal identity, he says, extends as far back as consciousness does:

'[T]is plain consciousness, as far as ever it can be extended, should it be to Ages past, unites Existences, and Actions, very remote in time, into the same Person, as well as it does the Existence and Actions of the immediately preceding moment: So that whatever has the consciousness of present and past Actions, is the same Person to whom they both belong. (II.xxvii.16)

---

[4] There is some ambiguity about what it is that we are supposed to do "only by that consciousness, which is inseparable from thinking." Locke could mean that it is by consciousness that we meet requirement (iv); or he could mean that it is by consciousness that we meet all four of the requirements for personhood. The latter strikes me as the more plausible reading. It is also suggested by his punctuation (with the semi-colon separating 'places' and 'which'), though it must be admitted that in keeping with the standards of his day Locke's use of punctuation is somewhat haphazard.

Locke illustrates this by saying that if he possessed a consciousness of Noah's flood, he could no more doubt that he had viewed the great deluge than he can doubt that he saw the Thames overflow last winter. "I [am]," he says, "as much concern'd, and as justly accountable for any Action was done a thousand Years since, appropriated to me now by this self-consciousness, as I am, for what I did the last moment" (II.xxvii.16).[5] Locke holds not only that personal identity reaches back as far as consciousness does, but also that it reaches no farther. "[P]ersonal Identity [reaches] no farther than consciousness reaches" (II.xxvii.14), he says, and "it is impossible to make personal Identity to consist in any thing but consciousness; or reach any farther than that does" (II.xxvii.21).[6]

Locke is as concerned to tell us what personal identity does *not* consist in, as he is to tell us what it does consist in. One of the central themes of II.xxvii is that personal identity is not the same thing as identity of substance. He allows that the two may coincide, but he insists that they do not do so as a matter of necessity. He notes that the material substance that composes one's body can undergo a sudden change in composition—the loss of a limb—without this affecting personal identity (II.xxvii.11). He then argues that even if we presume persons to be wholly constituted by immaterial substances, personal identity and substantial identity can come apart. If the consciousness of past actions were transferred from one immaterial substance to another, he says, personal identity could be preserved despite the change in substances (II.xxvii.13). On the other hand, the persistence of a thinking substance is no guarantee of the persistence of the person it once constituted. One's soul might be the same as was in Nestor at the siege of Troy, but if one lacks consciousness of Nestor's actions, then one is no more the same person as Nestor than one would be just because one's body contained some material particles that had once belonged to Nestor's (II.xxvii.14). Locke says that we can also imagine a single immaterial thinking substance alternately constituting two different persons. He notes that men sometimes part with their consciousness of past actions, and later recover it. "Make these intervals of Memory and Forgetfulness to take their turns

---

[5] For more evidence that Locke holds that personal identity reaches as far back as consciousness does, see II.xxvii.10, p.336, ll.14–15 and ll.21–24; II.xxvii.17, p.341, ll.28–32.

[6] For more evidence that Locke holds that a person's thoughts and actions include only those to which his consciousness extends, see II.xxvii.14, p.339, ll.28–32; II.xxvii.17, p.341, ll.28–32; II.xxvii.23, p.344, ll.13–14; II.xxvii.24, p.345, ll.20–24; II.xxvii.26, p.346, ll.28–29.

regularly by Day and Night," he says, "and you have two Persons with the same immaterial Spirit" (II.xxvii.23).

If we are to understand Locke's account of personal identity, we must know what he means when he speaks of consciousness reaching back to an earlier thought or action. Making this more of a challenge is the fact that he seems to use the term 'consciousness' in quite different ways. When he speaks of "the consciousness of past Actions" (II.xxvii.13), he seems to be thinking of consciousness as a state or event, a mental happening. However, when he entertains the possibility that a detached body part might come to have "its own peculiar consciousness" (II.xxvii.18), and when he reflects on the implications of "two distinct incommunicable consciousnesses acting the same Body" (II.xxvii.23), he seems to be treating *a* consciousness as something more thing-like. The waters are further muddied by the fact that Locke speaks of consciousness being extended not only to past thoughts and actions, but to present ones; and not only to thoughts and actions, but to particles and body parts. Finally, there is his curious and fluid use of the phrase "the same consciousness," which at several points he uses in formulating his views about personal identity.[7] Sometimes when Locke speaks of "the same consciousness," he seems to be talking about a mental state that is like an earlier one. Thus he speaks of a being's ability to repeat the idea of a past action "with the same consciousness it had of it at first" (II.xxvii.10). At other times, he seems to use 'the same consciousness' to refer to a locus of consciousness, as when he speaks of "the same consciousness going along with the Soul" that inhabits a certain body (II.xxvii.15).

One thing that does seem sufficiently clear is that for Locke extending one's consciousness to a past thought or action involves memory. For he speaks of consciousness being "interrupted" by forgetfulness (II.xxvii.10), and of one who forgets his past actions as parting with his consciousness of them (II.xxvii.23). He also seems to equate consciousness of a past action with memory of it, as when he says that "to remember is to perceive any thing with memory, or with a consciousness, that it was known or perceived before" (I.iv.20); and again, when he speaks of a spirit being "stripp'd of all its memory or consciousness of past Actions" (II.xxvii.25). Such passages

---

[7] At II.xxvii.10, he says that a person will be "the same *self* as far as the same consciousness can extend to Actions past or to come." At II.xxvii.13, he says that "the same consciousness being preserv'd, whether in the same or different Substances, the personal Identity is preserv'd."

suggest that his talk of extending consciousness to past thoughts and actions may simply be an exotic way of talking about remembering those episodes in a certain first-personal way. If this reading is correct, then he seems to be saying that a past thought or action is correctly attributed to a present self just in case the present self remembers having had the thought or having performed the action. Let us call this the "simple memory theory."[8] We can think of it as consisting of a necessity claim and a sufficiency claim. Let S be any person existing at time t_2, and A be a mental or physical action that was performed at some earlier time t_1. The necessity claim says that it is a necessary condition of S's having performed A that S can remember having performed A. The sufficiency claim says that if S can remember having performed A, then S did perform A.

Many of Locke's readers have taken him to be forwarding the simple memory theory, and many of these have argued that the theory is badly mistaken. Some objections to the theory—such as Joseph Butler's "circularity" objection, and Thomas Reid's "brave officer" objection—have become as well-known as the theory itself, and continue to figure prominently in the literature on personal identity. There is also a long line of commentators who have come to Locke's defense. Some of these argue that he does not advocate the simple memory theory after all. Others concede that he does, but suggest that the theory can be modified so as to circumvent the standard objections to it. Often they suggest that these refinements are in keeping with Locke's broader aims, and that they would be welcomed by him. I will argue that he does mean to endorse the simple memory theory, and that he would not welcome the attempts to rescue him from it. However, I will also show that while the simple memory theory seems to yield strange results about the relations of persons to their pasts, Locke's commitment to the relativity of identity does much to mitigate the strangeness. He holds that the concept "person" is but one of the many nominal essences under which each of us falls, a concept having especially to do with our liabilities as moral agents. The episodes in one's personal history are those for which one might be duly punished or rewarded. Yet as a relativist about identity, Locke holds that the actions belonging to one's personal history may not be all of those performed by the human being one is.

[8] In this terminological matter, I follow Yaffe 2007.

§49 *Persons and Substances*

Before we delve more deeply into Locke's account of personal identity, let us consider a problem about his view of the relation between persons and substances. On Locke's ontology, people seem to count as substances, and yet he denies that the persistence of a person requires the persistence of a substance. This is puzzling: if a person *is* a substance of a certain kind, then how can the persistence of a person not involve the persistence of a certain kind of substance? This is not just a difficulty about people. The same problem arises in relation to other complex things, including plants, animals, and perhaps artifacts. Each tree or horse would seem to count as a substance for Locke, and yet he says that the persistence of an organism is a matter of "Identity of Life, and not of Substance" (II.xxvii.12). He holds that plants and animals persist through the acquisition and loss of material parts so long as those parts are swept up in one ongoing life, and he implies that identity of substance is something else.

Some commentators have claimed that Locke holds that a person is not a substance but a mode (Uzgalis 1990; LoLordo 2010). Even if this were right, it would solve the puzzle only if he also held that organisms (and perhaps artifacts) were also modes rather than substances. Yet 'man' is Locke's term for a human organism, and he offers the idea of a man as an example of an idea of a substance (II.xii.6). A possible response to this is to say that Locke uses the term 'substance' differently inside II.xxvii than he does outside that chapter. Some commentators claim that outside the identity chapter a "substance" is any thing-like item (as opposed to a property or a relation), but that inside this chapter only *simple* thing-like items qualify as substances (Alston and Bennett 1988; Uzgalis 1990). Men and other organisms are substances in the broad sense; but being complex things they are not substances in the stricter sense that is supposedly in play in II.xxvii. The obvious problem with this reading is that it seems terribly *ad hoc*. Locke nowhere suggests that he uses 'substance' differently inside II.xxvii than he does outside it, and nowhere inside that chapter does he say that simples are the only substances.

If we read Locke as a relativist about identity, this offers us a better solution to the puzzle about people and substances. The relativist can say that x is the same person or organism as y, but not the same substance as y, though x and y are both substances. For the relativist about identity, sameness of personhood and sameness of substance can come apart, even if people are substances. This is promising, but more will have to be done if we are to show that the relative identity reading solves the puzzle about people and substances. For we must be able to explain how Locke can meaningfully and consistently say both (i) that people are substances, and (ii) that being the same person does not entail being the same substance.

Claim (i) can be parsed in more than one way. The absolutist about identity may want to understand it as the claim that for every x that is a person, there is a y that is a substance and $x = y$. The relativist should say that the 'is' in 'Each person is a substance' is that of predication rather than that of (absolute) identity. In Lockean terms, to say that each person is a substance is to say that anything answering to the abstract idea "person" also answers to the abstract idea "substance." To make sense of this, we need to understand what it means for something to answer to the idea "substance." In §27, we saw reason to think that Locke calls at least two different ideas "the idea of substance." One of these is the general idea of an ontologically independent thing, and the other is the vexed idea of substratum. It is the first of these that is the obvious candidate for being an abstract idea to which all people answer.

It is understanding claim (ii) that poses the bigger challenge for the relative identity reading. The relativist about identity holds that x can be the same F as y without being the same G as y, even if x and y are both Gs. This formula presumes that we possess some criteria of identity for Fs and for Gs, and that these are different criteria. To make sense of claim (ii), on the relative identity reading, we must see Locke as holding that there are criteria of identity for persons and for substances, and as holding that these are different criteria. There is no doubt that he offers an account of the criteria of identity for persons, and we have begun to investigate what that account is. Less clear is whether he has an account of the criteria of identity for substances. We can approach this by asking: when Locke says such things as (ii), is he using 'substance' as a sortal, a quasi-sortal, or a dummy sortal?

If Locke's conception of a substance is that of an ontologically independent thing, then 'substance' is not a sortal in his hands. We may be able to sort the ontologically independent things from the ontologically dependent ones, but how are we to track and count the ontologically independent things? If every ontologically independent thing is a substance, then 'substance' has much the same status as 'red thing.' We can sort red things from the non-red things, but counting red things presents us with much the same challenge as counting things.

Perhaps Locke uses 'substance' as a quasi-sortal? It cannot be that he reserves 'substance' for bounded, coherent material objects, since he countenances immaterial substances as well as material ones. However, it may be that he reserves the term for extended, ontologically independent things whose persistence involves some degree of spatiotemporal continuity. As we have seen, Locke holds that immaterial substances, like material ones, have spatial locations (II.xxvii.2) and move about (II.xxiii.19). Perhaps he also thinks that some kind of spatiotemporal continuity is required for substances to persist. If immaterial substances are partless, they would seem to be candidates for the strictest sort of spatiotemporal continuity. On the other hand, Locke may want to allow for the possibility of complex, scattered material substances. He seems to count water as a substance (II.xxiii.3), and Michael Jacovides has argued that he takes fluids to be scattered objects (Jacovides 2008). Locke could allow for the possibility of scattered objects if he held that the spatiotemporal continuity required for their persistence is the sort that obtains so long as all of their simple parts enjoy the strictest sort of spatiotemporal continuity. Putting the two cases together, we get the possibility that Locke's notion of a substance is that of an extended, ontologically independent thing that persists only if its simple (improper or proper) parts enjoy the strictest sort of spatiotemporal continuity. This might be enough to make 'substance' a quasi-sortal in his hands. It would give him some account of the criteria of identity associated with 'substance,' and of how these differ from the criteria associated with 'person.' It would not commit him to any very specific principles of individuation for substances, but it would explain why sameness of person does not entail sameness of substance. For on this reading, sameness of substance requires some degree of spatiotemporal continuity, and sameness of person does not.

Another possibility is that Locke uses 'substance' as a dummy sortal. In that case, 'substance' would function for him much as 'red thing' does for us. Any ontologically independent thing will qualify as a substance, and diachronic identity judgments about substances rely upon criteria of identity supplied by other, unvoiced sortals. If we are to make sense of such judgments, we need to be able to say something about the truth conditions that govern them. Consider this affirmation:

A: x is the same substance as y

If 'substance' is a dummy sortal, then we may say that **A** is true just in case there is some sortal, 'S,' such that each S is ontologically independent and x

is the same S as y. If we read Locke as a relativist about identity, we will need to make sense of **A** as it appears in the following relativistic claim:

B: x is the same substance as y, but x is not the same person as y

If one supposes that the substance in question is a material one, one might take **A** as it appears in **B** to be true because one thinks that x is the same mass as y, or because one thinks that x is the same organism as y. If we suppose that the substance is immaterial, it is less clear what might be the sortal for which 'substance' stands in proxy. Since Locke takes immaterial substances to occupy places and to move about, one possibility would be a sortal concept modeled on his notions of atom and mass. This would be the idea of a kind of immaterial substance whose diachronic identity is a matter of perfect spatiotemporal continuity. We might call such a substance an "immaterial mass."

If we say that 'substance' is a dummy sortal in Locke's hands, then we must also be able to offer some account of the truth conditions for the following denial:

C: x is not the same substance as y

There would seem to be two possibilities. The first is to say:

C is true just in case there is no sortal, 'S', such that each S is ontologically independent and x is the same S as y

The second is to say:

C is true just in case there is some sortal, 'S', such that each S is ontologically independent and x is not the same S as y

On the relative identity reading of Locke, we need to consider **C** as it appears in the following relativistic claim:

D: x is the same person as y, but x is not the same substance as y

If everything that is a person is a substance, then the first reading is a non-starter. For if we plug the first reading into **D**, we turn **D** into a contradiction. So we must go with the second reading. On this reading, **D** is equivalent to:

E: x is the same person as y, but there is at least one sortal 'S' such that an S is ontologically independent and x is not the same S as y

Locke will hold that **E** is true if x has autobiographical memories of y's actions and x is not the same mass as y (or not the same organism as y, or not the same immaterial mass as y, etc.).

A possible worry is that **D** seems an awkward way to express **E**. This may lead one to doubt whether Locke could mean anything like **E** when he says something like **D**. Consider a parallel case. Suppose that a relativist about identity wants to solve the ship of Theseus problem by endorsing the following:

H: x is the same ship as y, but x is not the same collection of planks as y

We would not expect the relativist to express himself by saying:

J: x is the same ship as y, but x is not the same thing as y

We would not expect him to do this because there is a natural reading of **J** on which it is a contradiction. By the same token, one might not expect the relativist who holds **E** to assert **D**, because there is a natural reading of **D** on which it is a contradiction.

Is this a decisive knock against reading Locke as a relativist about identity who uses 'substance' as a dummy sortal? I do not think so. One thing to notice is that **D** and **J** are not simply awkward *as* expressions of **E** and **H**, respectively. They are simply awkward. In the ship of Theseus case, the relativist has no reason to employ the potentially misleading dummy sortal formulation **J**, and will instead opt for the clearer formulation with a proper sortal, **H**. Locke, however, may well have reason to employ the dummy sortal in the context of talking about persons, even at the cost of some awkwardness. He wants to remain agnostic about thinking matter, and this means adopting a non-committal stance about what is the sortal for which 'substance' stands in proxy in **D**. He does not know whether that which thinks within us is material or immaterial, and he does not go so far as to explicitly formulate sortal concepts for immaterial things. We should thus not be surprised if he resorts to using a dummy sortal in **B** and **D**. This makes him rather like the person who is unsure about what specific sorts of things are on the table (machines? works of art?), and yet who can say that they are (or are not) the same things as were there yesterday.

Those who allege that Locke uses 'substance' differently inside and outside of II.xxvii are in effect saying that 'substance' functions as a dummy sortal outside of II.xxvii, but as a proper sortal inside it. It is an advantage of the relative identity reading that it does not portray Locke as guilty of this particular inconsistency. However, it is not much of an advantage if we cannot explain what diachronic identity judgments about substances come to on the relative identity reading. I have suggested two possibilities: that Locke consistently uses 'substance' as a quasi-sortal, and that he consistently uses it as a dummy sortal. I have not tried to decide between them, because I see no clear way to do that. We are talking about the presumptions that lie behind certain of Locke's identity statements, and not about positions that he self-consciously forwards.

§50 The Necessity Claim

Let us now take a closer look at Locke's account of personal identity. As we have seen, he holds that a person's past reaches as far back as that person's consciousness extends, and no farther (§48). We saw evidence that what he means by one's consciousness reaching back to past experiences is one's having a certain kind of first-personal memory of them. On the most straightforward reading of him, Locke is endorsing what we called the simple memory theory. This theory identifies a person with an earlier person if, and only if, she remembers in a certain autobiographical way one of the earlier person's thoughts or actions. A common objection to the simple memory theory is that its requirement that one must remember an experience for it to belong to one's past is too demanding. The problem is that it does not seem to allow for the possibility of a person's forgetting any of her earlier thoughts and actions. Yet it seems that we can and do sometimes forget having thought and done things.

Reid's "brave officer" objection can be seen as developing this worry. He bids us to consider the following:

> Suppose a brave officer to have been flogged when a boy at school, for robbing an orchard, to have taken a standard from the enemy in his first campaign, and to have been made a general in advanced life: Suppose also, which must be admitted to be possible, that when he took the standard, he was conscious of his having been flogged at school, and that when made a general he was conscious of his taking the standard, but had absolutely lost the consciousness of his flogging. (Reid 1983, 217–18)

Reid says that Locke's account of personal identity implies both that the general is, and that he is not, the person who was flogged. It implies that he is the person who was flogged because identity is transitive, and the memory account entails both that the general is the same person as the brave officer, and that the brave officer is the same person as the boy who was flogged. It implies that the general is not the person who was flogged, because he cannot remember the flogging.

One might avoid the objection, and still explain personal identity in terms of memory, by conceding that the kind of memory continuity displayed in Reid's example does after all suffice for personal identity. Thus one might give up the idea that the general must remember the flogging for it to be in his past, and instead say that it is enough that the general's memory links him in the appropriate way to an earlier person who remembers receiving the flogging. One might say that the relation in which S must stand to an action, A, for A to be in S's past is not that of remembering having performed A, but the ancestral of that relation. So S must either remember having performed A, or remember having performed an action that was performed by a person who remembers having performed A, or remember having performed an action that was performed by a person who remembers having performed an action that was performed by a person who remembers having performed A, etc. Let us call this the "memory continuity theory." Many who would like to rescue Locke from the objection that the necessity claim is overly demanding have ascribed to him the memory continuity theory (or something close to it), or else have proposed the memory continuity theory (or something close to it) as a friendly amendment of his position. As we weigh the resources of these interpretive options, it will be good to consider a representative of each approach.

Don Garrett ascribes something very much like the memory continuity theory to Locke, and he clearly regards it as a plus that on his reading Locke avoids the brave officer objection (Garrett 2003, 109). It is not the memory continuity theory *exactly* that Garrett ascribes to Locke, for he reads Locke as holding that the extension of one's consciousness to a past action does not necessarily involve standing to that action in the relation that is the ancestral of remembering the performance of it. On his reading, for one's consciousness to extend back to a past action is just for one to appropriate that action to oneself. Typically one does this by remembering the performance of the action, but one might sometimes do it on the basis of third-person evidence. Whether our consciousness is extended back by memory or by third-person evidence, to appropriate a past action is to appropriate all of the actions of the past self who performed that action.

The textual evidence against Garrett's reading is strong. At II.xxvii.20, Locke explicitly considers the objection that his account of personal identity allows for the possibility that we might lose portions of our pasts by losing our memories of them:

> But yet possibly it will still be objected, suppose I wholly lose the memory of some parts of my Life, beyond a possibility of retrieving them, so that perhaps I shall never be conscious of them again; yet am I not the same Person, that did those Actions, had those Thoughts, that I was once conscious of, though I have now forgot them?

Here Locke speaks of losing the memory of past parts of his life, and he treats this loss of memory as entailing a loss of the consciousness of those parts. This is not what he should say if Garrett were right about what he means by his talk of consciousness extending back to past actions. If that talk meant what Garrett says it does, then Locke's memory loss need not entail the loss of consciousness of the forgotten parts of his life, since he might still have good third-person evidence about the forgotten parts. Indeed, on Garrett's reading Locke's memory loss would not even raise the threat of a loss of consciousness of those parts unless the missing parts were those immediately preceding the time at which the memories were lost. Consciousness of the forgotten parts would be guaranteed so long as Locke's present consciousness extended back to an earlier self whose consciousness extended back still further to the forgotten parts.

Garrett could say that the passage quoted above does not count against his reading because in that passage Locke is not speaking for himself, but rather speaking on behalf of an imagined objector. However, Locke's own reply to the objection is equally bad for Garrett's reading. Instead of assuring us that actions in the forgotten span may yet belong to the past of the person who forgot them, he offers an error theory for the intuition that they do belong to that person's past. He says:

> To which I answer, that we must here take notice what the Word *I* is applied to, which in this case is the Man only. And the same Man being presumed to be the same Person, *I* is easily here supposed to stand also for the same Person. But if it be possible for the same Man to have distinct incommunicable consciousness at different times, it is past doubt the same Man would at different times make different Persons...(II.xxvii.20)

If Garrett's reading were correct, Locke should not be conceding that forgotten actions no longer belong to the person's past. Yet he seems to do just that. He allows that if I suffer a complete and irreversible loss of the memories of some part of my life, I may still say that I performed the actions during that forgotten span; but if I do so, he says, the 'I' refers to "the Man only," and not the person. Locke's point is that those who neglect the distinction between a man and a person will be apt to miss this, and that this is what gives the objection its apparent traction.

Another passage that is trouble for Garrett is II.xxvii.23, where Locke again brings up the subject of memory loss:

> For granting that the thinking Substance in Man must be necessarily suppos'd immaterial, 'tis evident, that immaterial thinking thing may sometimes part with its past consciousness, and be restored to it again, as appears in the forgetfulness Men often have of their past Actions, and the Mind many times recovers the memory of a past consciousness, which it had lost for twenty Years together.

Here again we see Locke presuming that to forget a past action entails parting with one's consciousness of it, which on Garrett's reading he should not do. If Garrett's reading were right, Locke should think that consciousness of a past action might always be secured by third-person evidence; and he should think that consciousness of a past action would be ensured so long as one was linked to that action by a chain of selves appropriating earlier selves' actions.

The textual support that Garrett offers for ascribing his version of the memory continuity theory to Locke is inconclusive. He draws our attention to the fact that when Locke wants to discuss situations in which there is identity of a thinking substance (or a man) without personal identity, he chooses cases in which "there are two different persons precisely because *no* perception or action of the one person can properly be appropriated by *any* conscious memory of the other person" (Garrett 2003, 110). Garrett cites II.xxvii.14, where Locke considers an immaterial being "wholly stripp'd of all the consciousness of its past Existence"; and II.xxvii.23, where he entertains the possibility of "two distinct incommunicable consciousnesses acting the same Body, the one constantly by Day, the other by Night." It is true that we should expect Locke to select examples like these if he thought that appropriating any of a past self's actions entailed appropriating all of them. However, given the point that Locke is making in these passages, he also needs examples like these if he embraces the simple memory theory. Consider the first passage. If Locke accepts the simple memory theory, then the case of an immaterial being stripped of all but *one* of its memories of past actions would not constitute a case in which there was sameness of substance without sameness of person. If he is to make his point, he needs the immaterial being to be stripped of all consciousness of its past existence. Now consider the second passage. Suppose that the consciousnesses acting the body were *not* entirely distinct. Suppose Day Man could remember doing some of what Night Man did. In that case, the simple memory theory tells us that Day Man would be the same person as the one who performed those nighttime actions. So here too, even if Locke endorses the simple memory theory, the example had to be as it was to make his point about the possibility of sameness of substance without sameness of person.

The other passage that Garrett points to in support of his reading is II.xxvii.14, where Locke says that if a person "once find[s] himself conscious of any of the Actions of *Nestor*, he then finds himself the same Person with *Nestor*." Garrett says that to find oneself to be the same person as Nestor is "much more then finding merely one single and discrete *act* of Nestor's also to be an act of one's own." (Garrett 2003, 109). He takes Locke to be telling us that one who appropriates any of Nestor's actions thereby appropriates all of the actions that Nestor appropriates. Is he saying that? Not necessarily. A person's finding himself to be the same person with Nestor may be just finding that the relation "...is the same person as..." holds between his present self and the self performing the earlier action. That need not mean his appropriating all of Nestor's actions. To this Garrett could respond that because of the transitivity of identity, finding oneself to be the same person as the self that performed one of Nestor's actions *is* to find oneself the author of all Nestor's actions. For if we say that the present self is the same person as the self who performed the remembered action, and if the self who performed the remembered action is the same person as the self who performed all of the rest of Nestor's actions, it must follow that the present self performed all of the rest of Nestor's actions. We can see this as the lesson of the brave officer objection.

Kenneth Winkler also draws that lesson from the brave officer objection, though he takes Locke's talk of consciousness reaching backwards to be talk about memory, and does not deny that Locke endorses the simple memory theory. Indeed, Winkler emphasizes the degree to which the self is, for Locke, subjectively constituted (Winkler 1991, 205). He notes Locke's tendency to adopt the first-person perspective when discussing personal identity, and also his interest in the appropriation of thoughts and deeds as constitutive of the self. Quite rightly, he sees both of these strands as coming out dramatically in the passage from II.xxvii.20 that we considered a moment ago. Winkler characterizes Locke's view as one on which "my self is constituted by what I take to be included in it" (Winkler 1991, 205). Nevertheless, he insists that there is a severe limit on the authority of the self, namely that imposed by the transitivity of identity. Reid is right to say that the general and the schoolboy are the same person, he says, but this only delimits and does not undermine the view that the self is subjectively constituted. Locke does need to modify his account; he needs to move from the simple memory theory to the memory continuity theory. This does not mean that the self does not constitute itself, but that "constitution is not a feat of the moment: what the self includes at any moment depends on the past" (Winkler 1991, 208). Winkler concludes that although Locke does not endorse the memory continuity theory, it can naturally be joined with his view about the constitution of the self.

Winkler is right to portray Locke as holding that one's history consists of the thoughts and actions that one appropriates to oneself, and he is right to interpret the talk of consciousness reaching backwards as being about remembering. The passages that prove so much trouble for Garrett suffice to show that. Yet he is wrong to suppose that the move from the simple memory theory to the memory continuity theory would be a natural development of, or a friendly amendment to, Locke's view. To see why this is so, we must consider why Locke thinks that a person's consciousness must extend back to an action for it to be his. For the answer to that question, we must return to his claims about selfhood in the present and its relation to selfhood in the past.

Locke—like Descartes, and unlike Leibniz—holds that one's present thoughts and actions consist of just those thoughts and actions that one is currently aware of oneself as having or doing. Let us take thoughts first. Locke thinks that mental items exist only in minds. He makes the point about ideas, saying that they are "nothing, but actual Perceptions in the Mind, which cease to be any thing, when there is no perception of them" (II.x.2). Locke also holds that for something to be in a mind is for that mind to be aware of it. He makes this point with respect to propositional knowledge when, in the course of arguing against innatism, he denies that we can have knowledge of truths without perceiving that we do. It is, he suggests, "near a Contradiction, to say, that there are Truths imprinted on the Soul, which it perceives or understands not; imprinting, if it signify any thing, being nothing else, but the making certain Truths to be perceived" (I.ii.5). Two chapters later, he makes the same point about ideas: "Whatever *Idea* was never perceived by the mind, was never in the mind" (I.iv.20). Ideas not only must be perceived to be; they also cannot be other than they are perceived to be. "[L]et any *Idea* be as it will," Locke says, "it can be no other but such as the Mind perceives it to be" (II.xxix.5).

Just as Locke holds that thoughts are my thoughts only if I am aware of myself having them, so he thinks that actions are my actions only if I am aware of myself performing them. Indeed, given his views about the nature of actions, this follows from his notion of the ownership of thoughts. Locke countenances both mental and physical actions. Mental actions presumably include such activities as adding a series of numbers, or dredging up the name of an old acquaintance. Locke thinks that we are necessarily aware of our present mental actions for just the same reason as we are necessarily aware of all of the mental items that constitute our present selves. As for physical actions, he holds that they too have a mental component. Locke is a volitionist, and holds that every action has, as an essential constituent, an act of will. A bodily motion is not an action of mine unless it is triggered by an act of my will. The act of will and the motion together constitute the action. Since acts of will are necessarily self luminous in the way that all mental acts are for Locke, it follows that a present action cannot be one's own without one's being aware of performing it.

One can lose one's watch or one's wallet. One can own an object that one cannot locate. However, Locke thinks that with present thoughts and actions it is different. One owns a present thought or action only by virtue of its being something to which one has access through consciousness of it. It is only by virtue of one's consciousness of them that such items are constituents of oneself. Locke thinks this not only about present thoughts and actions, but also about past ones. At II.xxvii.9, he tells us that it is because consciousness accompanies thinking, and makes one to be the self that one is, that consciousness also makes for personal identity or "the sameness of a rational Being." In the next section, he repeats the point:

For it is by the consciousness [an intelligent being] has of its present Thoughts and Actions, that it is *self* to it *self* now, and so will be the same *self* as far as the same consciousness can extend to Actions past or to come ... (II.xxvii.10)

Toward the end of the chapter, he makes the point yet again, this time even more forcefully:

This personality extends it *self* beyond present Existence to what is past, only by consciousness, whereby it becomes concerned and accountable, owns and imputes to it *self* past Actions, just upon the same ground, and for the same reason, that it does the present. (II.xxvii.26)

Locke holds that the scope of one's past is subjectively constituted, and for precisely the same reason as one's present self is subjectively constituted. Just as it is consciousness of a present thought or action that makes it one's own, so it is the reach of consciousness to a past thought or action that makes it one's own. Thus Locke's view that I must be able to remember an action for it to be mine is grounded in his more general account of the ownership of mental items. The memory continuity theory would not be a friendly amendment to his view, because it would require him to abandon that account of the ownership of mental items.

§51 *Remembering and Forgetting*

Locke holds that my consciousness must reach to a past thought or action for the thought or action to be mine, and he takes this reaching to involve the memory of having that thought or of performing that action. What is less clear is just what kind of access I must have to a past thought or action for it to be mine. A present thought or action is mine only if I am currently aware of it as mine. Yet Locke does not mean to say that my consciousness reaches to a past thought or action just in case I am currently thinking about it and appropriating it. If we are to understand what he thinks is required for one to appropriate a past thought or action, we must distinguish several senses in which he speaks of someone's forgetting, or failing to remember, something.

At II.xxvii.10, Locke describes a kind of forgetting that he says is ubiquitous. He is considering the question of whether there is just one substance that does one's thinking over the course of one's existence, and he says that what makes it possible to doubt this is a certain kind of forgetfulness to which we are subject:

But that which seems to make the difficulty is this, that this consciousness, being interrupted always by forgetfulness, there being no moment of our Lives wherein we have the whole train of all our past Actions before our Eyes in one view:

But even the best Memories losing the sight of one part whilst they are viewing another; and we sometimes, and that the greatest part of our Lives, not reflecting on our past selves, being intent on our present Thoughts, and in sound sleep, having no Thoughts at all, or at least none with that consciousness, which remarks our waking Thoughts.

The "forgetfulness" that Locke describes here is simply a consequence of the fact that the scope of our attention is finite. Let us call this sort of forgetfulness "inattention." On this understanding of forgetfulness, I forget an event in my past whenever I am not actively thinking about it.

To call inattention "forgetfulness" at all is a stretch, and Locke quite rightly does not see it as posing any threat to one's appropriation of past events. If we label anything that is not the object of our current attention "forgotten," then the corresponding notion of remembering is that of an occurrent state, rather than a dispositional one. Yet Locke uses dispositional language when formulating his criterion for linking a present self to a past action. He says that personal identity reaches back as far as consciousness *can* be extended (II.xxvii.9,16), as far as one *can* repeat the idea of that past action (II.xxvii.10). This is in keeping with our ordinary way of thinking and talking about memory. I remember my third grade teacher, Mrs Wantland, even though I rarely think of her, and even when I am not thinking about her. Locke also says that a part of the history of the substance that constitutes me is not part of my personal history if "I cannot upon recollection join [it] with that present consciousness, whereby I am now my *self*" (II.xxvii.24). That phrase 'upon recollection' seems to refer to an attempt at remembering. Locke seems to be saying that a past action belongs to my personal history only if I can recall it upon making the attempt to do so.

Locke describes other sorts of forgetting as he canvasses the defects to which human memory is subject. He characterizes memory as "the Store-house of our *Ideas*," and explains that we need such a faculty because our narrow minds are incapable of having many ideas in view at the same time (II.x.2). Ideas in memory are "dormant Pictures" that are sometimes recalled by efforts of will, and other times "rouzed and tumbled out of their dark Cells, into open Day-light, by some turbulent and tempestuous Passion" (II.x.7). One defect to which our memories are subject is the inability to retrieve ideas quickly enough for their retrieval to be of use. In these cases, the ideas are there in the storehouse, but we cannot locate them in time. This is what is going on when we forget a person's name, or the title of a book, though we are sure that it will come to us later. Locke says that this defect constitutes a kind of mental dullness, and in extreme cases it makes for "*Stupidity*" (II.x.8). Let us call this kind of forgetting "mental dullness" or "dullness of mind." A second sort of defect is the loss of ideas that were once stored in memory. Locke thinks that ideas fade over time, and that if little notice is taken of them, and they are not repeated or resurrected from time to time, they can wear out until "at last there remains nothing to be seen" (II.x.5). Let us call this sort of forgetting "memory loss."

It is tempting to suppose that Locke takes the difference between dullness of mind and memory loss to be the crucially important one. It is tempting to suppose that he wants to allow that I might have difficulty remembering the performance of actions that do belong to my past, and that it is only when such memories have vanished altogether from the storehouse of my mind that he will say that the actions no longer belong to my personal history. Yet this reading has its difficulties. One is that it seems to place more weight on the storehouse metaphor than it can bear. For Locke does not really think that particular token ideas enter the mind and then remain there after we are no longer attending to them. At II.x.2, he says:

But our *Ideas* being nothing, but actual Perceptions in the Mind, which cease to be any thing, when there is no perception of them, this *laying up* of our *Ideas* in the Repository of the Memory, signifies no more but this, that the Mind has a Power, in many cases, to revive Perceptions, which it has once had, with this additional Perception annexed to them, that it has had them before. And in this Sense it is, that our *Ideas* are said to be in our Memories, when indeed, they are actually no where, but only there is an ability in the Mind, when it will, to revive them again...

We are considering the suggestion that I can be said to remember the performance of an earlier action so long as my ideas of that performance are somewhere in the storehouse of my mind (even if I have trouble finding them). Yet here Locke tells us that to say that an idea is not in someone's mental storehouse is just to say that she does not have the ability to revive it again with the additional perception that she has encountered it before. On Locke's view, reviving an idea again with the additional perception that one has encountered it before just *is* remembering what the idea represents. So the claim that an idea is not in someone's mental storehouse just means that she cannot remember what it represents. There is the whiff of circularity here.

Locke's empiricism may seem to offer us a way to spell out the difference between memory loss and dullness of mind. He holds that once ideas have entered by sensation or reflection, they become available to the mind in a way that they were not before. Let "Y_{21}" be the idea of a certain shade of yellow, and suppose that it first enters Pat's mind by way of sensation on the occasion of Pat's seeing a flower in her garden. Locke's view is that the particular token of "Y_{21}" that is involved in Pat's visual experience of the flower ceases to exist when Pat closes her eyes or turns her head, or at least when she ceases to think about the flower. Yet having once seen that shade of yellow, Pat may later come to have another token of "Y_{21}" before her mind, and she may do this without her having again seen something of that shade of yellow. To say that an idea is stored in one's memory does not mean that there is a token of it existing somewhere, but it does mean that one can come to have another token of that type without a fresh experience of what it represents.

We are trying to explain the difference between mental dullness and memory loss, hoping to account for the difference between (i) struggling to remember a performance that is in one's past and (ii) failing to remember a performance that is (therefore) not in one's past. We are considering the suggestion that an idea type is in the storehouse of one's mind so long as one could at some later time have another token of that type without the necessity of its being delivered anew through sensation or reflection. The problem is that this suggestion really only applies to simple ideas, and not to complex ones. On Locke's view, no complex ideas are delivered through experience. So every complex idea that could be made from the simple ideas in the storehouse of one's mind is an idea that one could, in principle, have come to without the necessity of its being delivered anew through experience. This means that on the proposed reading the inability to summon up any such idea, if it has formerly been in the mind, will always count as dullness of mind and never as memory loss. Yet it seems likely that nearly all our memories of the things we have done will involve complex ideas whose constituents are simple ideas that remain in the storehouse of our memories. So on the proposed reading, we never really lose memories of any of our past performances. This is a problem because Locke clearly does want to say that this sort of memory loss is commonplace. We will do better to find a reading on which retaining a complex idea in the storehouse of memory involves more than just having the materials out of which it might be fashioned.

There is another problem with the present reading, and it is that Locke allows for a kind of forgetting that is temporary and remediable, but that threatens one's connection with the past. He does this in the course of arguing that consciousness, rather than identity of substance, is what unites remote existences into the same person. At II.xxvii.23, he says:

For granting that the thinking Substance in Man must be necessarily suppos'd immaterial, 'tis evident, that immaterial thinking thing may sometimes part with its past consciousness, and be restored to it again, as appears in the forgetfulness Men often have of their past Actions, and the Mind many times recovers the memory of a past consciousness, which it had lost for twenty Years together.

Locke says that one sometimes forgets an episode from one's past, only to remember it again decades later. One might expect him to go on to say that in such cases the idea of the forgotten episode lay buried deeply in the storehouse of a person's mind, and that its being there sufficed to make the forgotten episode a part of his past. Instead, what he says in the very next line is this: "Make these intervals of Memory and Forgetfulness to take their turns regularly by Day and Night, and you have two Persons with the same immaterial Spirit." So here we have a kind of forgetting that is temporary, but that is enough to make for a distinction between persons. Locke's view seems to be that for the twenty years that he forgets the performance of an action, the man who forgets is not the same person as the one whose action it was. Only when he remembers doing it does the action again become his. What makes this particularly interesting is that Locke is talking about a kind of forgetting that he regards as happening in the real world, and not just in philosophical thought experiments.

At this point, there are two options. If we retain the notion that the difference between mental dullness and memory loss is the difference between an event's being in one's past or not, then we must see Locke as making a distinction between remediable memory loss and irremediable memory loss. We could then see him as holding that the person who takes several minutes to recall the name of an acquaintance suffers from mental dullness, but that one who forgets a college prank for twenty years, and then spontaneously remembers it, has suffered from remediable memory loss. The challenge on this reading is to explain the difference between mental dullness and remediable memory loss. An obvious thing to say is that in cases of remediable memory loss what is forgotten is forgotten for much longer. The trouble is that the difference between short-term forgetting and long-term forgetting is a matter of degree, whereas the question of whether an event belongs to one's past seems to be of the all-or-none variety.

There is, I think, a better option. We can give up the idea that Locke takes the difference between mental dullness and memory loss to be the difference between an event's being in one's past or not. We can see him as holding that the difference between dullness of mind and memory loss is merely a matter of degree; and we can see him as holding that whenever one tries, and fails, to remember a past performance this entails that the performance does not belong to one's personal history. This means that if it takes me a minute to remember yesterday's lunch, then during that minute I am not the person who ate the leftover curry. After that minute, I may again be the person who ate the leftover curry. This is strange, but most of the strangeness is the upshot of the simple memory theory, and not the application of it to cases of short-term forgetting. It would be stranger still to stipulate some arbitrary time at which mental dullness becomes remediable memory loss—to say, for instance, that one may forget an episode in one's past for three and a half hours, but that forgetting it a minute longer entails that the episode is no longer in one's past. The simple memory theory does yield surprising results about which episodes belong to a person's past, but it is at least based upon a coherent principle—the principle that a mental episode or a body part belongs to a person in virtue of his first-personal consciousness of it.

A potentially serious problem for Locke is that it does not seem that he can consistently describe any person as having forgotten anything that he thought or did. For on his account, if a person is unable to remember having an earlier thought, or acting in some way, then that thought or that action does not belong to his past. The trouble is that of course Locke does say that we all forget much of what we have thought and done. The solution to this problem again lies in his relativism about identity. Locke can allow talk of forgetting actions and losing memories so long as what is doing the forgetting or the losing is being tracked under a nominal essence other than "person." Suppose that there is an x that is both a man and a person, and that at time t_2 x cannot remember performing an action, A, that y performed at t_1. Locke can say that x is not the same person as y, but that x is the same man as y. He can say that A does not belong to x's personal history—to x's history when that is tracked under the nominal essence "person"—while allowing that A does belong to x's past when x is tracked under the nominal essence "man" (or under some other nominal essence, such as "mind," "spirit," or "thinking substance"). In fact, that is the way that Locke does speak about forgetting. It is not a person, but an "immaterial Being" (II.xxvii.14), an "immaterial thinking thing" (II.xxvii.23), a "Spirit" or a "Mind" (II.xxvii.25) that might lose consciousness of its past existence. Most telling is a passage we considered earlier, in which Locke considers the objection that I might lose the memory of parts of my life, and yet still be the person that "did those Actions, had those Thoughts, that I was once conscious of, though I have now forgot them" (II.xxvii.20). Locke replies that the objector must take notice of what "the Word *I* is applied to, which in this case is the Man only." The objector's mistake is to presume that the same man is the same person.

§52 *The Sufficiency Claim*

The simple memory theory says not only that you must remember an earlier performance for it to be yours, but also that if you do remember an earlier performance then it is yours. As we have seen, Locke commits himself to this second claim at II.xxvii.16, where he says that if he had the same consciousness of seeing the ark and Noah's flood that he has of seeing the Thames overflowing last winter, then he could not doubt that he viewed the flood any more than that he is the same self he was yesterday. He says that if he appropriates an action that occurred a thousand years ago, he is as "much concern'd" in it, and as "justly accountable" for it, as he would be if he appropriated an action that occurred a moment ago.

The view that to remember having done something suffices for having done it seems to fall to an obvious objection. It seems not to account for the possibility that one might falsely remember doing something that one did not do, even something that was done by somebody else. Such cases of mis-remembering seem not only possible, but commonplace. The objection can be overcome if we insist upon the distinction between genuinely remembering a past thought or deed and merely seeming to remember it. The distinction between apparent memory and genuine memory is one that we must insist upon in any case. The challenge is to explain what more it takes, beyond seeming to remember something, to genuinely remember it.

One may be tempted to say that the genuine memories of one's past actions are just those that represent the things one actually did. Yet if Locke were to say such a thing, he would succumb to Joseph Butler's charge that "Consciousness of personal Identity presupposes, and therefore cannot constitute, personal Identity" (Butler 1736, 302). A more promising approach is to say that a genuine memory is distinguished from a false one by there being the right sort of causal link between the memory and the event remembered. Garrett suggests that there is the basis for such an account in Locke's suggestions that the operations of memory might depend upon the "right Constitution" of our organs (II.xxvii.27), and that memory might involve the storage and revival of images in the brain (II.x.5) (Garrett 2003, 100, 107–8). Though he acknowledges that Locke does not actually develop such an account, Garrett suggests that a Lockean account might take the storage of memories to involve the retention of material traces in the brain, or of immaterial traces in the soul (Garrett 2003, 108, 116).

We need to be very cautious about ascribing to Locke any particular account of how memory works. He does point to the fact that fever and disease can destroy memories, and cites this as a reason for thinking it probable that "the Constitution of the Body does sometimes influence the Memory" (II.x.5). Yet there is reason to think that he does not hold that genuine memories must be grounded in continuously preserved traces in us. For he is committed to the view that personhood can bridge the discontinuity that might be involved between death and resurrection, and he seems to hold that we might go out of existence altogether during this period.

The time between death and resurrection was the subject of an important theological debate stirred by the Protestant rejection of the Catholic doctrine of Purgatory (Burns 1972; Wainwright in Locke 1987; Spellman 1994). Many Protestants, including Calvin and the Cambridge Platonists, held that we continue enjoy a conscious existence during this intermediate period. Others, including Martin Luther and Thomas Hobbes, favored a doctrine called mortalism. One version of the doctrine, called thnetopsychism, held that the soul ceases to exist when the body dies. Another, called psychosomnolence, held that the soul persists but goes into a kind of suspended animation. For the mortalist, resurrection thus involves either bringing back into existence a person who has gone out of existence, or reawakening a sleeping soul. It is quite clear that Locke wants to be able to accommodate thnetopsychism, and at times he seems to go so far as endorsing some sort of mortalism.

Locke holds that we may be wholly material, and that God may have superadded powers of thought to our bodies. In a lengthy exchange with Stillingfleet, he also argues that scripture leaves open the possibility that resurrection involves not the restoration of our earthly bodies, but the restoration of us as persons in different bodies (*Works* IV, 303–334). If we consider these possibilities together—if we suppose that we might be wholly material, that our bodies might be destroyed when we die, and that we might have new bodies at the resurrection—this amounts to the scenario described by thnetopsychism.

Other writings also provide evidence of Locke's desire to accommodate mortalism. In his *Paraphrase and Notes on the Epistles of St. Paul*, and in marginal notes in his copy of the Bible, he offers alternate readings of two passages in *2 Corinthians* (5: 4 and 8) that had been taken by Calvin and others as references to disembodied souls between death and resurrection. Locke seems to prefer a reading on which they are silent about any such intermediate state.[9] Moreover, in his *Reasonableness of Christianity*, Locke says things that seem to imply that we go out of existence when we die, and that we are not restored to life until the resurrection. He quotes several passages from scripture in support of the view that death is our fate because of Adam's fall.[10] He says that in these passages we must understand 'death' in the most straightforward sense, one on which it entails ceasing to be (Locke 1695, 6).[11] Later he repeats the suggestion that "whoever is guilty of any sin should certainly die, and cease to be" before being restored to life by Christ at the resurrection (Locke 1695, 15).

Does Locke's attitude toward mortalism preclude him from saying that genuine memory requires certain causal connections between a memory and the remembered event? Not necessarily. One possibility would be to admit the possibility of direct causal links between events at non-adjacent

[9] See Locke 1987, vol. 1, pp.284–5, 466–7. Locke confesses that *2 Cor.* 5:4 is "noe very easy passage" (Locke 1987, 284n), and the same could be said of Locke's own glosses on both passages. Yet Wainwright notes that Locke's comment on the second of these passages "gives the impression that he does not understand the passage to refer to an intermediate state" (Locke 1987, 467).

[10] "*By one man sin entred into the world, and death by sin*" (Rom. 5:12), "In Adam all die" (1 Cor. 15:22) (Locke 1695, 4).

[11] Locke argues against those who favor recherché interpretations of the "death" we earn by Adam's fall (Locke 1695, 4–6). He reminds us that the language of scripture is intended for the instruction of the "illiterate bulk of Mankind" (Locke 1695, 2). In marginal notes inscribed in his own copy of the first edition of the *Reasonableness*, he expands upon this, saying that "Scripture speaks not to us so much in the tongue of the learned Sophies of the world as in the plainest and most vulgar dialect that may be" (Locke 1999, 8).

times. If action at a temporal distance were possible, then genuine memories might be preserved by casual links between an ante-mortem person's last soul or brain events and a resurrected person's first soul or brain events. A less strange possibility would be a causal chain that goes outside the person and his constituent parts for a time, perhaps through the mind of God. We might think of this as analogous to transferring one's CD collection on to a hard-drive for a while, and then burning it back on to CDs. Memories might be grounded in soul or brain events while we are alive; there might be causal relations between the last such events in our lifetime and some aspect of the divine mind; and then at the resurrection there might be further causal connections between the divine mind and soul or brain events in resurrected persons. This would seem to raise a theological problem about God's being acted upon by events outside Himself, but that is a problem that any theist—or any theist who believes in the power of prayer—must deal with in any case.

§53 *A Fatal Error?*

Locke does not explain the difference between apparent memories and genuine ones, but he does recognize the need to make the distinction. He does so clearly at II.xxvii.13, a passage that is frustratingly obscure in other respects. This difficult section is worth considering in some detail, not least because there is a natural reading of it on which Locke stumbles badly there. The section consists of nine sentences, which I distinguish below by means of numerals in brackets. The first two and the last two together raise and answer the question that is the main business of II.xxvii.13; sentences 3–7 constitute something of a digression, and that is where the trouble is. Let us deal with the main business first, and then move on to the more worrisome digression.

At II.xxvii.12, Locke poses a two-part question: "whether if the same Substance, which thinks, be changed, it can be the same Person, or remaining the same, it can be different Persons." In that section, he also begins to answer the first part of the question. He says that if one takes thinking things to be *material*, then one will surely grant that personhood can be preserved across different thinking substances. He thinks that it is obvious that we persist as persons despite changes in the material substances that compose our bodies. Now the main business of II.xxvii.13 is to answer the same question on the supposition that thinking things are *immaterial*:

[1] But next, as to the first part of the Question, Whether if the same thinking Substance (supposing immaterial Substances only to think) be changed, it can be the same Person. [2] I answer, that cannot be resolv'd, but by those, who know what kind of Substances they are, that do think; and whether the consciousness of past Actions can be transferr'd from one thinking Substance to another.

There is a bit of confusion here, for after making the supposition that thinking things are immaterial, Locke still goes on to say that the answer to our question depends on what sort of substance thinks. What is clear enough is Locke's suggestion that whether one person can persist through a change in immaterial substances depends on whether consciousness of past actions can be transferred from one thinking substance to another.

At the end of the section, Locke picks up that thread, and tells us what follows if memories can be transferred:

[8] But yet to return to the Question before us, it must be allowed, That if the same consciousness (which, as has been shewn, is quite a different thing from the same numerical Figure or Motion in Body), can be transferr'd from one thinking Substance to another, it will be possible, that two thinking Substances may make but one Person. [9] For the same consciousness being preserv'd, whether in the same or different Substances, the personal Identity is preserv'd.

The basic idea is plain enough: if consciousness of a past action, A, is transferred from immaterial thinking substance S1 to immaterial thinking substance S2, then S2 meets the criterion for being the person who performed A, and this despite the change in thinking substances.

What is less clear is what Locke means when he speaks of consciousness of a past action as being transferred from one immaterial substance to another. Garrett reads Locke as holding that such a transfer occurs whenever "one thinking substance represents its *self* (i.e., the *self* that it now helps to constitute) as having had a perception that was, in point of fact, previously represented by *another* thinking substance as being perceived by its *self* (i.e., the *self* that that other substance then helped to constitute)" (Garrett 2003, 116). On this reading, transfers of consciousness might be person-preserving, or they might not. They are person-preserving just in case the substance's representation of itself as having had the earlier perception is a genuine memory, that is, an apparent memory that stands in the right causal relationship to the original perception.

I think that Garrett's reading is mistaken. It is one thing to have an apparent memory that corresponds to the experience of another substance; it is another for a stored memory to be *transferred* from one substance to another. Garrett would have us say that Caesar's consciousness of a past action has been "transferred" to me any time that I happen to have an apparent memory of some experience once had by Caesar, no matter why I happen to have it. So if I receive a head injury, and as a consequence come to have an apparent memory of crossing the Rubicon in 49 BC, Caesar's memory has been "transferred" to me though my only link to him comes by way of history books I read long before the injury. I think that Locke's word choice suggests a different picture. For the consciousness of a past action to be transferred is for stored memories to be relocated. It is of course difficult to say what it takes for a stored memory to be relocated, and what difference there is between this and the production of a new memory with similar content. My own intuition is that brain transplants relocate stored memories, but that Star Trek transporters produce new memories with similar contents. Others will have different intuitions. It would be challenge enough to try to draw upon such intuitions to develop a satisfying account of the difference between relocating stored memories and producing new ones with similar contents. It would be more challenging still to develop such an account on the supposition that immaterial substances are the media for memory storage.

If one sees a difference between relocating stored memories and producing new ones with similar contents, one is then likely to think of the relocation of stored memories as a process that preserves the genuineness of genuine memories. Just as the relocation of a genuine Picasso does not make it less genuine, so we should not expect a genuine memory to become less genuine because it is relocated. That Locke is thinking of the transfer of consciousness from one substance to another as a process that preserves the genuineness of the donor memories is clinched by the conclusion he draws in sentence [8]. There he says that if it is possible to transfer the consciousness of a past action from one immaterial substance to another, then it is possible for two thinking substances to make one person. That it is possible for two thinking substances to make one person is a conclusion that he can reach only if he has established that it is possible for one substance to have a genuine, autobiographical memory of an experience had by a different substance. On Garrett's reading, the claim that consciousness of a past action can be transferred from one thinking substance to another does not entail that it is possible for one substance to have a genuine, autobiographical memory of an experience had by another. For on his reading the supposition that consciousness can be transferred will be established even if what is possible is just the production of false memories that happen to correspond to real actions from the past.

Now let us turn to the somewhat convoluted digression in II.xxvii.13, where Locke considers the problem of false memories. Having raised the question of whether it is possible for consciousness of past actions to be transferred from one immaterial substance to another, he makes the point that this is very different from asking whether the actions themselves could be transferred:

[3] I grant, were the same Consciousness the same individual Action, it could not: But it being but a present representation of a past Action, why it may not be possible, that that may be represented to the Mind to have been, which never really was, will remain to be shewn.

Actions cannot be transferred from one substance to another. Locke may think this because he thinks that events are individuated by the substances that figure in them as constituents. Or because he holds that actions perish the moment they begin (II.xxvii.2). We might expect him to go on to say that representations of past actions are different, and that their relocation is less obviously impossible. Yet that is not what he does. What he does is to suggest that some representations of ourselves as performing past actions may be false. This is obviously true, but why does he make this claim here, and what has it got to do with transfers of consciousness?

One possibility is that Locke is thinking that transfers of consciousness might give rise to false memories. This might seem to be a problem for my reading of what he means by transfers of consciousness. How could transfers of consciousness give rise to false memories if the transfer of consciousness from one substance to another is a process that preserves the genuineness of genuine memories? To answer this, we must consider the scenarios on which we might call an autobiographical, first-person memory a false memory. One is when the imagination of a past experience is mistaken by its bearer for a memory. Perhaps this is how we should account for the chapter in Salvador Dalí's autobiography about his intra-uterine experiences (Dalí 1942). Another scenario involves the genuine memory of a past experience that comes with mistaken beliefs about its contents. One might genuinely recall the experience of seeing a great flood, and mistake this for a memory of Noah's flood.[12] Even a defender of the simple memory theory will allow that transfers of genuine memories can give rise to false memories of this second sort. They are especially likely to do so if the transfers are done piecemeal. For if the transplanted memory is isolated—if it is a single memory of an event that occurred hundreds of years ago, for instance—then it will be impossible to locate the remembered event in the narrative of the rest of one's life, and yet one will be apt to try to make room for it somehow. This might well involve arriving at false beliefs about when or where the remembered experience took place.

It may also be that Locke raises the issue of false memories in [3] because he sees both memory transfers and false memories as possibilities that arise only because the connection between a substance's performance and a substance's representation of that performance later is a contingent connection. He has just made the point that there is a necessary connection between a thinking substance and the actions it performs. If there is not a necessary connection between an action and the representation of it, this opens up the logical space for memory transfers and false memories alike. Something like this is suggested by the obscure sentence that comes next:

[4] And therefore how far the consciousness of past Actions is annexed to any individual Agent, so that another cannot possibly have it, will be hard for us to determine, till we know what kind of Action it is, that cannot be done without a reflex Act of Perception accompanying it, and how perform'd by thinking Substances, who cannot think without being conscious of it.

Here Locke seems to be trying to imagine a kind of action whose character would inseparably bind consciousness of it to the agent. He seems to be thinking that if there were actions of that sort, then either the transfers of memories of them, or false memories of them, would be impossible. However, there is much that is puzzling here. Not least is why he thinks

---

[12] Probably most ordinary cases of false autobiographical memories involve aspects of both scenarios. We fill the blanks in our genuine memories with acts of imagination. Or we take genuine memories of looking at photograph albums, change them slightly in imagination, and mistake them for first-person memories of the scenes depicted in the photographs.

that there being a sort of action that "cannot be done without a reflex Act of Perception accompanying it" would have the implications he seems to envision. What reason is there to think that the memory of a self-luminous action would be untransferable, or that one could not have false memories of having performed a self-luminous act?[13]

In the two sentences that come next, Locke worries about a substance representing itself as doing something it never did, and then suggests that God will not allow this to happen:

[5] But that which we call the *same consciousness*, not being the same individual Act, why one intellectual Substance may not have represented to it, as done by it self, what it never did, and was perhaps done by some other Agent, why I say such a representation may not possibly be without reality of Matter of Fact, as well as several representations in Dreams are, which yet, whilst dreaming, we take for true, will be difficult to conclude from the Nature of things. [6] And that it is never so, will by us, till we have clearer views of the Nature of thinking Substances, be best resolv'd into the Goodness of God, who as far as the Happiness or Misery of any of his sensible Creatures is concerned in it, will not by a fatal Error of theirs transfer from one to another, that consciousness, which draws Reward or Punishment with it.

This is deeply puzzling. In sentence [5], Locke raises a worry about someone who represents himself as having done something that he did not do. In sentence [6], he seems to attempt to allay that worry by assuring us that God will not transfer memories that leave their recipients open to punishment for things they did not do. Yet on Locke's view, it is only genuine memories that make people deserving of reward or punishment for what they remember doing, and here he seems to be talking about a false memory. Is he assuring us that God will not transfer a genuine memory to a new owner because it would be unjust for that new owner to become liable for the remembered action? In that case, it would seem that he must be supposing that the new owner is not really the person who performed the action, despite his remembering doing so. So it would seem as though Locke first

---

[13] More puzzles: (1) If agents are persons, then the simple memory theory would seem to imply that there *are* necessary connections between agents and consciousness of the actions they perform. Can 'Agent' here mean "thinking substance"? (2) Locke seems to imply that he does not know whether there might be a kind of action that requires self-awareness on the part of the actor. Yet his volitionism and his commitment to the transparency of the mental seem to entail that every action necessarily involves awareness of it. (3) If there were an action that required self-awareness on the part of the actor, what is the difficulty of it being performed by an agent whose thoughts are all conscious ones?

forgets which problem he is trying to solve, and then forgets what his own account of personal identity is.

We can begin to untangle this by getting clear about what scenario Locke is envisioning in [5]. This turns on what he means when he describes the intellectual substance as representing something as done by "it self." One possibility to consider is that Locke is envisioning a scenario on which a substance, S1, represents S1 as having performed an action, A, that S1 did not perform, and that some other substance might have performed. That scenario need not be a case of false memory, and it need not be a scenario that God has reason to prevent. For it might simply be a case in which there is sameness of person despite a change in substance. If mortalism is true, then God will ensure that such a scenario *does* occur. So this cannot be the scenario that Locke is concerned about. What concerns him is the possibility of a thinking substance representing the *self* that it is as having done something that it did not do. As we saw in §48, Locke uses 'self' and 'person' interchangeably. In [5], Locke is raising a concern about the possibility of a person's having a false memory.

In [5], Locke is telling us that it is difficult to see why it is not possible for a person to have a false memory. In [6], he offers the goodness of God as a reason for thinking "that it is never so." There is no way of reading this on which Locke is not making a mistake. People *do* sometimes represent to themselves that they have done things that they did not do. Any attempt to reassure us that this never happens is misguided. So the question is not whether Locke makes a mistake here, but what mistake he makes. There are at least two possibilities worthy of serious consideration. One is that in [5] Locke fails to describe the problem that he is really interested in, the one that he means to solve. He is not really concerned about the possibility of false memories in general, but only about the possibility that transfers of consciousness from one thinking substance to another might result in people having false memories, and that this might lead to people being unjustly punished or unjustly rewarded. On this reading, the first half of [6] is meant to be the assurance that this never happens, not that false memories never happen. A second possibility is that in [5] and [6] Locke makes the mistake of shifting his attention between two problems that interest him, and fails to see that they need to be handled separately. One problem that interests him is the problem of false memories, and the other is a worry about transfers of memory leading to unmerited punishments or unmerited rewards. Failing to distinguish the problems sufficiently, he fails to see that he only has a solution to offer to the second.

These two accounts of how Locke stumbles in [5] and [6] open up different ways of reading the passage as a whole. Let us start with the first reading, on which he is really just trying to address the problem of the false memories to which transfers of consciousness might give rise. These false memories might conceivably be of two kinds: those that result from the relocation of stored false memories, and those that result from the relocation of genuine memories that come to be paired with false beliefs about their contents. It is rather hard to imagine a case of the second sort that would invite unmerited punishment. This would have to be a case in which a genuine memory of an innocent action is mistaken for the memory of a guilty one. Yet there is also a problem with the suggestion that Locke is concerned about the relocation of false memories. He assures us that God will not transfer "that consciousness, which draws Reward or Punishment with it." Since he holds that we are accountable only for the actions that we genuinely remember performing, this seems to be the assurance that God will not transfer *genuine* memories. One possibility is that the reward and punishment to which Locke alludes there is not divine reward and punishment, but human reward and punishment. On one way of understanding this, he is thinking that false memories might lead to false confessions or to false boasts, which might lead society to punish the innocent or to reward the undeserving.[14] Garrett objects that "the prevention of such criminal punishments as these seems no more central to God's concerns than does the prevention of unjust punishments based on the dishonest testimony of others—something that Locke does not describe God as taking any special care to prevent" (Garrett 2003, 115). His objection succeeds if we read Locke as assuring us that God will protect us against false memories; but it fails if we read him as assuring us that God will not cause us to have false memories that leave us vulnerable to unmerited punishments. For God presumably does take special care to see that *He* does not cause anyone to suffer unmerited treatment at the hands of others.[15]

---

[14] Garrett ascribes this reading to Paul Helm (Garrett 2003, 115).

[15] Garrett suggests another way of seeing Locke's allusion to reward and punishment as an allusion to *human* reward and punishment. He reads Locke as assuring us that God will not transfer false memories that would lead us to punish ourselves with internal disgrace, or to reward ourselves with internal credit, for what we have not done (Garrett 2003, 117). Garrett's suggestion can easily be combined with the previous one. If we take Locke to be assuring us that God will not produce false memories that would invite unmerited reward or punishment of human origin, we may see him as assuring us that God will not cause us to suffer unjust treatment at the hands of others *or* ourselves.

Now consider the second reading, on which Locke runs together what are really two different concerns, one about false memories and one about transfers of consciousness giving rise to unmerited reward or punishment. On this reading, his slide from thinking about false memories to thinking about the implications of transfers of consciousness is the mirror image of the slide he made back in [3]. Earlier I suggested reasons why he might associate the two issues. The present hypothesis is that he associates them so closely that he blurs them together: he shifts his attention from the problem of false memories to the troubles that might be caused by relocating memories, and he does this without fully appreciating that these are different problems. His muddle is responsible for his thinking that he can offer some assurance that false memories do not occur. He cannot do that, because false memories are a fact of life. Locke does, however, have grounds for assuring us that God will not transfer consciousness of past actions if this is likely to result in unmerited reward or punishment.

On this second reading, we need not see Locke as concerned only with the production of false memories that would make their recipients vulnerable to undeserved human rewards and punishments. When he assures us that God's goodness will keep Him from transferring "that consciousness, which draws Reward or Punishment with it," Locke might mean to assure us more generally that God will not transfer consciousness of past actions when this would invite undeserved reward or punishment. The relocation of genuine memories might do that if it were done in a piecemeal fashion, and not only because the recipients might develop false beliefs about what they remember.

Suppose that Benet is a vicious criminal, and Beth a virtuous, law-abiding citizen. Suppose that God were to take Benet's memory of one of his crimes, and transfer just this one memory to Beth. Given the simple memory theory, it would become true that Beth was the person who committed the crime. Her consciousness of having committed the crime would draw divine punishment in the sense that it would *invite* that punishment: she would be the guilty party. But would she *merit* divine punishment? Locke need not say that. Beth finds herself with this horrible memory, but she cannot weave it into the narrative of her own life. She remembers plunging the dagger into innocent flesh, but cannot remember the sequence of decisions that led her to do it, cannot remember the childhood traumas or the bad choices that set Benet on his violent path, cannot reconcile the act itself with her own values or her conception of herself. It might even be that the crime happened centuries before Beth's birth, in a far away place, and that she finds herself unable to make any sense of how the memory *could* be a real one, convincing though it is in its presentation. Does she deserve to be punished for the crime? At II.xxvii.26, Locke says that for a self to be punished for an action to which it cannot extend its present consciousness is "all one, as to be made happy or miserable in its first being, without any demerit at all." It would be wrong to punish such a person, he thinks, because he would be incapable of fully understanding his responsibility for that action. Much the same could be said about Beth, despite the fact that she can extend her consciousness back to the crime. Locke must say that she owns the crime, but he can also say that her predicament is one that a just God would not put her in.

I cannot find any clear and decisive evidence favoring one of our readings of [5] and [6] over the other, but the second reading strikes me as more plausible. I find it suggestive that Locke drifts between the same issues of false memories and memory transfers in [3]; and somewhat improbable that he is thinking only of human reward and punishment at the end of [6]. It might be said that considerations of charity speak in favor of the first reading, since on that reading he is less confused. On the other hand, there is independent reason to think that Locke was confused as he was writing this section. It is hard to avoid that conclusion as one struggles to extract a coherent train of thought from sentence [4]. Also confusing, and perhaps confused, is his observation in [6] that because of His concern for His creatures, God will not "by a fatal error of theirs transfer from one to another, that consciousness." What could it mean for God to effect a transfer of consciousness *by* an error of His creatures? Even if we could make sense of Him effecting a transfer of consciousness *by* an error of His creatures, would this not preclude the error's being the product of that transfer? I know of no commentator who has even tried to make good sense of this.[16] Locke is

---

[16] The digression on false memories and transfers of consciousness also ends on note of mystery, if not confusion:

[7] How far this may be an Argument against those who would place Thinking in a System of fleeting animal Spirits, I leave to be considered.

It is unclear (i) what 'this' refers to, (ii) which view about the nature of thought Locke sees as possibly being threatened, and (iii) what the threatening argument might be. Is he suggesting that the possibility of false memories poses a special problem for materialism? Or that the possibility of transfers of consciousness poses a special problem for some particular version of materialism? Could he be suggesting that the fact that we must invoke God's goodness to stave off worries about certain cases of undeserved punishment somehow counts against materialism or some version of it? None of these suggestions seems very plausible.

not at his best in II.xxvii.13. He expresses himself poorly, and at moments his train of thought is confused. However, at least we do not need to see him as committing the "fatal error" of presuming a different account of personal identity than the one he is supposed to be defending.

§54 *Assessing the Simple Memory Theory*

Though many sympathetic commentators have tried to save him from it, Locke does hold the simple memory theory. If we think of him as trying to offer an analysis of personal identity that aims at preserving our ordinary notions about our extent over time, this comes as a disappointment. His account of the extent of persons is quite a departure from our ordinary way of thinking about our histories. Ordinarily we presume that our temporal extent can only increase, until such a time as we go out of existence altogether. On Locke's account, the temporal extent of a person can decrease simply by his forgetting some of what he once thought or did. Ordinarily we presume that our temporal extent can increase only by the addition of segments at the later end, through the accumulation of thoughts and actions in the present. On Locke's account, a person's temporal extent can increase by the addition of thoughts and actions that occurred in the past. Ordinarily we presume that our existence is, and must be, continuous. On Locke's account, the temporal extent of persons can be very gappy. The individuation of us as persons is thus, for Locke, a very different matter from the individuation of us as human beings.

Locke's simple memory theory of personhood may begin to seem less a disappointment if one appreciates that it is not intended to capture all of our ordinary ways of thinking about ourselves and our pasts. Locke's commitment to the relativity of identity means that questions about the individuation and persistence of a thing are always relative to some sortal concept or nominal essence. The abstract idea "person" is not the only nominal essence under which we can consider ourselves when we are looking back to past thoughts and deeds. At II.xxvii.20, a passage we considered in §§50–51, Locke allows that we can sensibly say "I did that, though I do not recall doing it." It is just that when one says this one is thinking oneself as a man that is the same man as an earlier man, rather than as a person that is the same person as an earlier person. Locke's concept of "person" is narrow, and tailored to reflect a particular set of concerns having to do with reward, punishment, accountability for the past, and concern for the future. That is what he means when he says that 'person' is "a Forensick Term appropriating Actions and their Merit" (II.xxvii.26). The question of whether I am the same person as performed an earlier action is, first and foremost, a question about whether I might justly be held accountable for it. It is not the only way of raising the question of whether or not an action is, in some sense or other, in my past.

The way to take the measure of any philosophical theory is to see how it stands up against objections. This can show us more than just whether the theory stands or falls. It can give us a fuller picture of what the theory says, what its resources are, what it can and cannot explain. I have already mentioned the most famous objection to Locke's simple memory theory, Reid's brave officer objection. Reid sees it as a fatal flaw of Locke's theory that it makes the old general a different person than the naughty schoolboy. Locke's reply to this should be: *that's not an objection, that's the theory*! Reid asks us to suppose that one person robbed the orchard, stole the enemy's standard and was made a general in later years, and also that the general cannot remember robbing the orchard. Locke should say that given his understanding of what 'person' means, that supposition is incoherent.

Reid's objection shows that Locke must reject the transitivity of identity when it comes to persons. His simple memory theory says that the general is the same person as the brave officer, that the brave officer is the same person as the naughty schoolboy, but that the old general is not the same person as the naughty schoolboy. This seems a disastrous result, until we bear in mind Locke's relativism about identity. When logicians treat it as fundamental that identity is a transitive relation, they are speaking about the relation of absolute identity. Locke dispenses with that relation altogether, and in its place he countenances indefinitely many sortal-relative identity relations—such relations as " …is the same person as…," " …is the same man as…," and " …is the same father as …." To avoid contradiction on his simple memory theory, he needs to deny that " …is the same person as…" is a transitive relation. So in that respect, he views the relation " …is the same person as…" as like the relation " …is the friend of…," and as unlike the relation " …is taller than …."

Some might object that the very idea that a thing's existence might be discontinuous is incoherent. If something goes out of existence, how could *that very thing* come back into existence again? Whatever force the objection has derives from a certain explanatory challenge. Suppose that a thing, S, exists for a time and then ceases to exist. At some later time, there is a thing, S★, that for one reason or another seems a candidate for being S redux. The challenge is to explain what makes it the case that S★ *is* S, rather than S★'s being something that is qualitatively similar to, but numerically distinct from, S. Locke thinks that he can meet that challenge. He does this, of course, by offering the general explanation that what makes a mental state, an experience, an action, or a body part *mine* is that I can extend my consciousness to it; and by supposing that I extend my consciousness to a past experience by remembering it in a certain autobiographical way.

It is worth highlighting just how peculiar are the results that Locke's account delivers. It is not just that people can go out of existence for a time and then come back into existence. His view entails not only that there might be periods between Kate's beginning and Kate's end during which she does not exist; but also that whether a particular span of time is one of those periods or not is itself something that can change over time. On Locke's theory, it might be that at t_2 the span between t_1 and t_2 is a period during which Kate existed, while at some later time, t_3, it is not the case that she existed during that period. Not only is Kate's existence gappy, but where the gaps are is something that might change continuously.[17] One might think that whether or not Kate existed between t_1 and t_2 is a fact that is determined entirely by what goes on between t_1 and t_2. One might argue that a continuous series of exhaustive inventories of the world conducted during the period from t_1 and t_2 should be able to settle once and for all whether Kate existed then. Locke's reply should be that each inventory of the world conducted at a moment between t_1 and t_2 will tell you what exists at that moment, but it will not tell you how those things are related to the things that exist at other moments. It will not tell you whether the thing that is called "Kate" on one inventory is the same as the thing called "Kate" on another, nor whether either is the same thing as any particular Kate who exists after t_2. To decide these questions, one needs a theory of identity, which is of course what Locke is offering us.

Locke's simple memory theory entails that which events belong to Kate's past is something that may change over time, and not simply by the accumulation of more events to her recent history. This can be parlayed into

---

[17] Strawson illustrates this point nicely with diagrams (Strawson 2011, 84–6).

an argument that Locke does not hold a four-dimensionalist account of persons. The four dimensionalist says that a person is a temporally extended thing, a thing that has temporal parts. He also says that things with different temporal parts are different things, even if they have many parts in common. That is how the four dimensionalist solves the puzzle about the relation between masses and organisms, statues and lumps of clay. The organism and the mass that we say briefly constitutes it are really to be thought of as distinct temporally extended things, the latter being a small temporal part of the former. The four dimensionalist translates our ordinary talk about the events in Kate's past or future into talk about Kate's temporal parts. If he concedes the reality of the distinction between past and future, he might accommodate talk about Kate's growing past by saying that this is a matter of her temporal parts acquiring and losing certain features (pastness, futurity). But the four dimensionalist cannot make sense of there being changes in regard to which events are temporal parts of Kate. Temporally extended things are not items that can undergo changes in their composition over time, because they are not things that endure through time. Kate *is* a particular collection of temporal parts, and any other collection of temporal parts is something other than Kate, even if is it something that shares many of her parts.

One might worry that Locke is in no position to allow for discontinuously existing persons. For, it might be said, discontinuously existing persons would conflict with Locke's principle that one thing cannot have two beginnings of existence (7.3). The reply to this is to remind ourselves that what Locke's principle means is that a thing cannot simultaneously come into existence at two different places (§42). That principle does not preclude a thing's going out of existence and then coming back into existence later. Earlier we entertained the possibility that Locke might be willing to endorse another "no two beginnings" principle, one that said that for each thing there can only be one time that is the earliest time at which it exists (§44). Such a principle would have to be formulated with care if it were to be compatible with his account of personal identity. Locke's simple memory theory implies that there is a sense in which one person might have two beginnings. For it might be that at t_1 Kate's earliest memory is her third birthday party; but that she later forgets the party, so that at t_2 her earliest memory is one of cowering in her bedroom during a tornado warning some months after the party. In that case, there would be, at different times, different times that were the earliest time at which there existed a person who was the same person as Kate. Locke could, however, accommodate a "no two beginnings" principle that was relativized to time. He could say that for each time t, and for each person, p, who exists at t, there is but one time, $t^\star$, that is at t the earliest time that p exists.

It might be argued that it is a problem for the simple memory theory that one might be able to extend one's consciousness back to one thought or action of an earlier person, p, without being able to extend one's conscious-ness back to another one of p's thoughts or actions. In this case, the simple memory theory seems to yield the absurd result that one both is, and is not, the same person as p. Here we need to consider two cases: the case in which the two thoughts or actions are simultaneous, and the case in which they are non-simultaneous. The case in which they are non-simultaneous just is the brave officer objection again. Suppose that at t_1 person p_1 performs action a_1, that at t_2 person p_2 performs action a_2, and that at t_3 there is a person p_3. If t_1 and t_2 are different times, then Locke can allow that p_3 is the same person as p_2, that p_2 is the same person as p_1, and that p_3 is not the same person as p_1. He can do this because he is a relativist about identity, can deny that "...is the same person as..." is a transitive relation, and so can deny that the inference that p_3 is the same person as p_1 goes through. However, let us change the example slightly and suppose that at t_2 p_2 performs two actions simultane-ously: $a_{1.1}$ and $a_{1.2}$, and that p_3 has an autobiographical memory of perform-ing one of them but not the other. Then we do get the unacceptable result that at t_3 p_3 both is the same person as p_2 and is not the same person as p_2.

I think that Locke can solve the problem by resisting the suggestion that we perform distinct actions simultaneously, or at least by insisting that there is more than one legitimate way to think about the relation between our simultaneous doings. Suppose that at t a person, p_1, is both whistling and thinking about what to make for dinner, and that later p_2 remembers having the thoughts about dinner but does not remember the whistling. It seems to me that Locke can say that although it may be natural to charac-terize the whistling and the thinking as distinct actions, one could just as well characterize them as parts of a single, complex action that is imper-fectly remembered. Nearly all of one's actions are complex and have other actions as parts. To ride a bicycle is to voluntarily exert oneself in a large number of different ways simultaneously (pedaling, shifting one's weight in subtle ways, turning the handlebars, scanning the road ahead, etc.). We

can characterize the bicycle rider as doing one complex thing, or as doing
many simpler things simultaneously, and there is no real difference between
these. So Locke can say that p_2 has a partial or incomplete memory of a
complex action that is what he was doing at t. There will of course be many
cases where he will have to say that our autobiographical memories are
very incomplete or sketchy, because we remember only a small portion of
what we were doing at an earlier time. However, that is something that we
must say anyway. I remember biking to campus today, but do not remember
each individual pedal stroke. I remember last night's conversation about a
colleague's divorce, but do not remember every word I contributed to that
conversation.

Another problem for Locke's account is that it seems possible that one
might extend one's consciousness back to two actions that were performed
by different people. Suppose that at t_1 person $p_{1.1}$ performs action $a_{1.1}$ and that
at the same time a different person, $p_{1.2}$, performs another action, $a_{1.2}$. Later, at
t_2, a person, p_2, remembers performing both $a_{1.1}$ and $a_{1.2}$. The simple memory
theory entails that p_2 is the same person as $p_{1.1}$, and also that p_2 is the same
person as $p_{1.2}$. Is this a problem? If it is a problem, it is not because Locke's
theory entails that $p_{1.1}$ is the same person as $p_{1.2}$, yielding a contradiction. The
non-transitivity of the "...is the same person as..." relation blocks that result.
However, it does look as though Locke's theory yields a strange result. It
seems to yield the result that there might be two actions that were performed
by different persons when they happened, though at a later time there is one
person who performed both of them. A case like that just described—in
which a person remembers distinct but simultaneous performances—might
seem especially troublesome, since it could be described as a case in which
one person was at two different places at the same time. It is perhaps going
too far to describe this case as one in which two persons have been fused
into one; but if p_2 shared a great many genuine, autobiographical memories
with $p_{1.1}$ and $p_{1.2}$, that description might seem apt. We can also imagine cases
in which a person's memories are divided among a number of different later
persons. The contemporary literature on neo-Lockean theories of personal
identity is, of course, replete with discussions of cases such as these.[18] Our
question is whether Locke's own account entails that such cases are possible,
and if so what that means for his account.

---

[18] Parfit 1984 is the *locus classicus*, though not the first work to raise those issues.

Locke's simple memory theory will entail that fusion and fission cases are possible only if it is possible for genuine, stored memories to be transferred either (i) from one wholly material thinking organism to another, or (ii) from one immaterial thinking substance to another. One can imagine cases of (i) involving partial brain transplants, or rational creatures who undergo amoeba-like divisions on which their memories are split between their descendants. Locke does not consider any version of (i). He is clearly agnostic about whether type (ii) transfers are possible. At the very least, he seems to be in a position to say that it is not clear that—and perhaps cannot be shown that—his theory of personal identity entails that a person might remember the performances of two different persons, or that persons might fuse or divide in these ways. However, even if his theory does imply that the fusion and fission of persons is possible, I think that this is not something that need concern him much.

If we are wholly material, then Locke's account will entail strange results if brain parts are transplanted, or if organismic division is possible. One reason why he should be untroubled by this is that on some of these scenarios (the ones involving amoeba-like persons) the same results are delivered by the major materialist rival to Locke's view, the view on which biological continuity is the criterion for personal identity. Another is that his account generates these strange results because we are asking about the identities of persons on strange scenarios. Partial brain transplants are the stuff of science fiction, and rational creatures who could divide like amoebas would be very odd beings. Though initially we may balk at the idea of one person being responsible for the actions of two, it is not as though we have, or ought to have, strong pre-theoretical intuitions about how responsibility for past actions is distributed in these very unusual cases.

If our minds are immaterial thinking things, then Locke's account allows for the fusion or fission of persons only if memories stored in one mind are transferred to another. Presumably this is something that would have to be done by God. As we have seen (§53), Locke presumes that God will not transfer the consciousness of a past action where this might produce a false memory that could lead to someone's being unjustly punished or rewarded. I suggested that it is also possible to read II.xxvii.13 as offering the more general assurance that God will not transfer consciousness of past actions whenever this would lead to someone who is unable to fully understand his guilt or desert, as might happen if God were to transfer genuine memories piecemeal. Locke is probably not worried about bizarre scenarios on which one person's memories are divided among several people, or several persons' memories are transferred to one person. He presumes that God would not do such things because the results would be people who are profoundly and irremediably confused about who they are, where they belong, and what they value.[19]

Another worry is that the simple memory theory might allow for the possibility that two or more persons could remember performing the same action. Here we are imagining not that one person's memories might be divided among several later persons, but that a single memory or set of memories might be transferred to two different people. If this is possible, the theory seems to lead to the result that two people might both be appropriately punished for a crime that was committed by one person. Whether it is possible to transfer stored memories from one person to a number of persons may depend on facts about how memories are stored, and on how genuine memories are distinguished from new memories with similar contents. What these facts might be if memories are stored in immaterial souls is anyone's guess. So again it is far from clear that the threatened scenario is even possible. If it is possible, the medium of memory storage may place a limit on the number of persons to whom one person's genuine memories might be transferred. If stored memories are brain states, for example, then the duplication of memory in the two cerebral hemispheres might allow for transfers to two different people, but perhaps no more.

In any case, if it is possible in principle for a genuine stored memory to be transferred to several persons, there would again seem to be reasons for thinking that God would not effect such transfers. This is particularly clear in the case of autobiographical memories of the commission of crimes. If two people both have genuine memories of the commission of a crime that was committed by one person, then there are two persons who are deserving of punishment, whereas there might have been only one. To engineer such a situation would be akin to police entrapment. We would be

[19] Of course, there *are* people who are seriously confused about such things, including people with dissociative identity disorder. Why does God allow there to be such people? Is there a difference between His allowing there to be such people and His intervening to produce them? These are real problems, but no more pressing for Locke than for any other theist.

disappointed by police who enticed law-abiding citizens into violating the law, and we would be disappointed by a God who took positive steps to increase the number of those who deserve punishment.

One of the most insightful criticisms of Locke's simple memory theory is J. L. Mackie's complaint that it is not really a theory of personal identity at all, but a theory about the ownership of actions. Mackie puts it this way:

Since a man at t_2 commonly remembers only some of his experiences and actions at t_1, whereas what constituted a person at t_1 was all the experiences and actions that were then co-conscious, Locke's view fails to equate a person identified at t_2 with any *person* identifiable at t_1. It is only a theory of how some items which belonged to a person identifiable at t_1 are appropriated by a person who can be identified as such only at t_2. It is therefore hardly a theory of personal identity at all, but might be better described as a theory of action appropriation. (Mackie 1976, 183)

Here Mackie takes for granted a Lockean conception of the self as subjectively constituted. He presumes that a person at a time just is the totality of her experiences and actions then. He bases his complaint on the fact that a person remembers only some of what he was experiencing or doing at any earlier time. One can imagine Locke replying that his simple memory theory entails that each person *does* have perfect recall. Anything a person cannot remember doing is something that person did not do. Yet Mackie's concern cannot be dismissed so quickly. Think of the total package of your present experiences and actions. For each of us, it is almost certain that there is no future person who will remember all of these. On the most optimistic scenario, only some of what one currently sees, smells, thinks, and does will be recorded in an autobiographical episodic memory two hours from now, two days from now, two weeks from now. So on the simple memory theory, one's consciousness rarely if ever reaches back to every facet of a subjectively constituted self.

I think that Mackie has run together what are really two different criticisms of Locke's account, and that one is more compelling than the other. The first criticism is that Locke's simple memory theory fails to give us criteria for identifying a whole person at one time with a whole person at another, and this because memory is imperfect. The second is that Locke's simple memory theory amounts to a theory of action appropriation rather than one of personal identity. Let us take the first criticism first. Mackie makes the point that a person's consciousness typically extends back to only some of what an earlier person was doing and thinking at a given time. We have already considered this, when we worried that Locke's theory might deliver the result that p_2 both is the same person as an earlier p_1 and is not the same person as p_1. I suggested a reply on Locke's behalf. He might say that what is typically the case when one has an autobiographical memory of the experiences of an earlier person is that one has an imperfect recall of the total package of that earlier person's momentary (or short-lived) experience. There may be many gaps in the times to which one's consciousness reaches back; but when it does reach back, we might think of it as apprehending a whole person sketchily rather than some parts of a person perfectly. In the same way, the person with blurry vision sees whole persons, though she is unable to make out all of their features. Even if it is consciousness that makes for personal identity, it is overly demanding to say that consciousness reaches back to a whole person at an earlier time only if it perfectly represents every facet of that person's experience at that time.

Mackie's second criticism is that Locke has offered us a theory of action appropriation, rather than a theory of personal identity. This is astute. Locke's account of the "…is the same person as…" relation does have to do particularly with the assignment of responsibility for actions. We might say that it answers some of the questions that we want a theory of personal identity to answer, but not all of them. We do want to be able to track people over time so that we can determine who is a fit subject for reward or punishment. Yet we also want to be able to track people over time so that we can count them, so that we can give them appropriate medical treatments, so that we can predict their behavior, so that we can meet our obligations to them, and so on. As a theory of the diachronic identity of people, Locke's simple memory theory has serious limitations. If we understand sameness of personhood as Locke would have us do, the judgment that x is the same person as an earlier y does tell us that x is in some sense responsible for what y does; but it does not tell us that x has y's medical history, that x is likely to have y's batting average next season, or that our promises to y obligate us to x.

At this point, it is tempting to imagine a reply from Locke that invokes the relativity of identity again. He could concede that the concept of personhood that he has been concerned to articulate is one tailored spe-cifically to questions about which actions are one's own. He could say that he is particularly interested in explaining how someone who is standing before God in judgment could understand himself to be liable for actions performed earlier by someone who might have had a different body, some-one who might have died and gone out of existence long before. Yet Locke could also remind us that the idea of personhood that he is articulating is but one of the many sortal concepts under which each of us falls, and that some others supply different criteria of diachronic identity. Which sortal concept is germane will depend upon the questions that we are asking. When making medical decisions or baseball predictions, it may be best to track individuals under the nominal essence "organism" or "man." How it is best to track those to whom you have obligations may depend upon sub-stantive facts about moral or legal obligation. For example, if our promises put us under moral obligations even to those who can no longer remember our promises, then we should track promisees under some other sortal than "person" as Locke understands it.

The above reply is good as far as it goes, but it underestimates the limitedness of Locke's account of personhood. His account is limited not only because it is built to answer questions about the ownership of actions, but also because it is built to answer backward-looking ques-tions rather than forward-looking ones. Consider this forward-looking question about the ownership of actions: "Which future actions will be mine?" One traditional way of answering this question is to say that my future actions include whatever actions are initiated by acts of will that are performed by my soul. Those who defend an animalist conception of ourselves have a different, but equally straightforward, way of answering the question: my future actions include all those performed by a future organism participating in the same life as me. Locke's account, on the other hand, has the resources to answer the forward-looking question only by turning it into a backward-looking one. Let t_1 be the present, and t_2 some time in the future. Locke can say that if there is a person at t_2 who has autobiographical memories of my present thoughts or actions, and if that person also has autobiographical memories of some thoughts and actions, $a_{1.1}, a_{1.2} \ldots a_{1.n}$, that happen between t_1 and t_2, then that person will be the same person as me and $a_{1.1}, a_{1.2} \ldots a_{1.n}$ will be his actions. One might take this to be tantamount to the claim that $a_{1.1}, a_{1.2} \ldots a_{1.n}$ will be my actions. The simple memory theory answers the question about the ownership of future actions only by going still further into the future and looking back.

Locke's backward-looking theory of personal identity is unable to do all that he needs it to do, and all that we want a theory of personal identity to do. He needs an account of personal identity on which the prospect of reward or punishment on judgment day can motivate me to behave well now. He needs an account on which I can now understand that the person who will be rewarded or punished will be *me*, even though I shall die before judgment day, and even if my death means me going out of existence entirely. The fact that this future person will remember doing things that I remember doing may help to justify that reward or that punishment to that future person, but how does it suffice to motive me to behave well now? The trouble is that Locke's theory fails to give us an adequate account of the sort of survival that we care about deeply.

Survival is essentially a forward-looking matter, and Locke's simple memory theory gives a poor account of it. I want to persist, but I do not necessarily want any future person to remember my present experience (which is just that of writing in my study as I have done ever so many times). Still less do I want any future person to remember every aspect of my present experience, every patch of color in my visual field, the sounds of each passing car, the sweat on my palms this humid day, the tightness in my back around my left shoulder blade, the mental labor of crafting this sentence. Worse still is the thought of that future person—me!—being burdened with such vivid memories of millions of such moments. Whenever it is the case that my experience is unremarkable (as it is now), it is unlikely that there will be, two or three days hence, any person with an autobiographical memory of my present experience. On Locke's theory, this means that it is unlikely that there will be a person two or three days hence who is the same person as me. So whenever my experience is unremarkable, it is unlikely that my self will survive for two or three days. This Lockean account of survival does not accommodate our ordinary beliefs about our prospects, and it does not capture our hopes for ourselves. I want a future person to have autobiographical memories of some of the experiences that I have had, and perhaps also of some of those that I will have between now and that future person's present. However, my desire to persist as a self is independent of my desire that there be such a person, and prior to it. I want there to be a future person who has some of my autobiographical memories *because* I want to survive and *because* I do not want to lose all of my memories!

9

Agency: The First Edition

§55. Locke is a volitionist. In the first edition of the Essay, he slides between two accounts of volition: one on which willing to φ is occurrently wanting to φ, and another on which it is something more like trying to φ. §56. Locke holds that the objects of volition are narrowly circumscribed: we can will only episodes of thinking and the motions of our own bodies. §57. He holds that actions and forbearances are voluntary when they are consequent to one's volition. Locke's unfortunate tendency to think of willing as wanting leads him to suggest that a falling man wills not to fall, and that a complacent paralytic forbears walking. §58. On Locke's view, an agent is free with regard to an action if and only if both of the following are true: if the agent wills to perform the action he does perform it, and if he wills not to perform it he does not. An unwitting prisoner's stay in a locked room may be voluntary but unfree. It has been argued that this last example does not serve its purpose, but this analysis fails to take account of Locke's view about the narrow scope of volition. §59. There are good reasons for a volitionist to favor a deflationary account of negative actions, but Locke puts forward a robust account on which forbearances involve volitions directed at not doings. §60. Locke's view that forbearing involves willing to not do something threatens to yield the result that nobody ever forbears doing anything. This is so even if we construe the view somewhat charitably as telling us that in cases of forbearing one's act of will is the INUS condition of one's not doing something. §61. Locke denies that our wills are free, that we are free in regard to willing, and that we are free in regard to our preferences. He thinks that a person cannot forbear willing one way or the other on a course of action once he considers it. He may think that because he thinks that the scope of volition is limited to actions that would begin in the next instant. §62. In the first edition, Locke largely takes for granted an account of motivation that is hedonistic and egoistic: each person always wills to do that which seems to her likeliest to bring her the most pleasure. When he says that the appearance of

greater good "determines" the will, Locke is using 'determines' in a teleologi-
cal sense rather than a causal one. Whether the behavior of agents is causally
determined he does not say.

§55 *Volition as Preference*

Locke's chapter on power (II.xxi) is first and foremost a discussion of
human agency. At the heart of it are accounts of volition, freedom, and
motivation. The chapter also contains discussions of the idea of cause, the
pitfalls of faculty psychology, and the cause of sin, as well as some won-
derful examples and thought experiments. Despite all of this interesting
material, this chapter has received much less attention from commentators
than Locke's discussions of substance, secondary qualities, and personal
identity have. This may be partly due to the complicated state of the text.
Locke revised II.xxi more heavily than any other chapter in the *Essay*. The
biggest changes come between the first and second editions, but there are
also significant later changes, especially between the fourth and fifth editions. Some of the revisions to II.xxi are cases of Locke changing his mind;
others merely his attempts to communicate better. It can be difficult to
tell of a particular change whether it is of the first sort or the second. He
sometimes retains material from the first edition that appears to be motivated by philosophical positions that he has since abandoned. It is also not
always clear that the later additions are consistent with what was retained
from the first edition. Finally, there is important material outside the *Essay*
that bears on Locke's views about agency. These include his correspondence with William Molyneux, and his correspondence with Phillipus van
Limborch.

Work on Locke's philosophy of action has typically given the most attention to the fifth edition of the *Essay* (1706), the last to be prepared at least
partly under Locke's supervision. Scholars have looked back to earlier editions only fleetingly (if at all) for points of contrast. Yet though the fifth
edition does give us Locke's final statement on the issue of agency, I doubt
that we can achieve the best understanding of his views by beginning there.
I think that the best course is to carefully examine his treatment of agency
in the first edition before moving on to the revisions and emendations
he introduced later. The advantages of this approach are considerable. We
learn how much of Locke's final philosophy of action was there from the

beginning. With a better understanding of the original account, we are in a better position to adjudicate claims that doctrines added to later editions conflict with material retained from the first. We are also better placed to spot material in the later editions that is premised upon or motivated by views he has in fact abandoned. In this chapter, I will consider the first edition accounts of volition, freedom, and motivation as though they were finished products, which is of course how Locke viewed them for a time. In the next, I discuss his dissatisfaction with the first edition account, the major changes he introduces in the second edition, and the still further changes he made after his exchange with van Limborch.

Locke is a volitionist, and if we are to understand and assess his account of agency, we must come to grips with his conception of volition. Talk of volition was a commonplace in seventeenth-century theories of agency, appearing center stage in philosophies as different as those of Thomas Hobbes and Ralph Cudworth. Theories of volition have come in for a good deal of criticism since the mid-twentieth century, though they now seem to be enjoying something of a resurgence.

To say that Locke is a volitionist is not yet to say very much. Volitionists agree that there is a species of mental state or event that has content, that is forward-looking, and that plays an important role in explaining human action. Volitionists agree in calling a bodily movement voluntary only if it accords with a volition of the person whose body moves. Yet they do not all agree about the nature of volitions, the relation of volition to bodily movement, and the relation of volition to action. Some treat volition as a species of desire or intention, while others regard it as *sui generis*. Some count volitions as actions, others as components of actions. Of those who count volitions as actions, some hold that all actions are volitions, and others deny this. Some volitionists say that volitions have a distinctive phenomenological character, and others make no such claim. Some invoke volitions to explain the difference between action and mere bodily movement, while others allow for the possibility of non-voluntary or involuntary action. Some conceive of the contents of volitions as activities that take time to complete; others insist that we can frame volitions only about what to do in the next instant. It would be anachronistic to presume that Locke stakes out positions on all of these issues. Still, we should do what we can to flesh out his conception of volition by looking at his explicit pronouncements about volitions, and also at what is implied by his reasoning about volition.

Locke introduces the notion of volition at II.xxi.5 [1st]:

This at least I think evident, That we find in our selves a Power to begin or forbear, continue or end several, Thoughts of our Minds, and Motions of our Bodies, barely by the choice or preference of our Minds. This Power the Mind has to prefer the Consideration of any *Idea*, to the not considering it; or to prefer the Motion of any part of the Body, to its Rest, is that, I think, we call the *Will*; and the actual preferring one to another, is that we call *Volition*, or *Willing*.

For Locke, 'Will' names a capacity that a person has, while 'volition' and (equivalently) 'willing' refer to an exercise of that capacity. A Will is a power; a volition or willing is an episode in a person's mental life. Locke repeats the point at II.xxi.15 [1st], saying that a volition is an "actual choosing or preferring forbearance to the doing, or doing to the forbearance, of any particular Action in our power, that we think on," while the Will is the "Faculty to do this."[1] To have a volition is to be preferring or choosing the doing of an action or the forbearance of one. He regards volitions themselves as actions. He speaks of "those Actions of Understanding and Volition" at II.xxi.6 [1st], and of "the Actions of Choosing and Perceiving" at II.xxi.17 [1st]. At II.xxi.23 [1st] he explicitly relies on the supposition "That Willing, or Choosing [is] an Action." Every action falls under one of two headings: thinking and motion (II.xxi.4,8 [1st]). We may safely assume that Locke conceives of volitions as episodes of thinking rather than as motions.[2]

In his characterizations of volition, Locke speaks of "choosing or preferring" (II.xxi.15 [1st]), and of the "Ability, to preferr or choose" (II.xxi.17 [1st]), seeming to imply an equivalency between choosing and preferring. Neither 'choosing' nor 'preferring' seems particularly apt for capturing the mental exertion or impetus suggested by 'willing.' Of the two terms, 'choosing' seems a better candidate than 'preferring': when I choose, it seems, I *do* something, whereas it is not so clear that my preferring one thing to another need involve me doing anything at all. Yet oddly, Locke more often characterizes willing as preferring. He also explicates 'preferring' in a way that is not very suggestive of activity. At II.xxi.28 [1st], he says:

---

[1] See also II.xxi.17 [1st]

[2] Though volitions are surely episodes of thinking for Locke, there is at least the appearance of a problem in that he contrasts volition and thinking at II.vi.2 [1st], calling these the two "great and principal Actions of the Mind." The solution is that he is using 'thinking' in two senses: one that applies to all mental doings, and another that applies only to those mental doings that are exercises of the Understanding. Volitions are mental doings, but they are exercises of the Will rather than the Understanding. In II.xxi [1st], Locke uses 'perceiving' to refer to those mental doings that are exercises of the Understanding (see II.xxi.5, 17 [1st]).

[W]e must remember, that *Volition* or *Willing* ...*is* nothing but the *preferring* the doing of any thing, to the not doing of it; Action to Rest, & *contra*. Well, but what is this *Preferring*? It *is* nothing but the *being pleased more with the one, than the other.*

Gideon Yaffe invokes this passage in support of his claim that in the first edition Locke equates having a volition with having a positive attitude toward a course of conduct:

[I]n the first edition, Locke took volitions to be no more than preferences: anytime an agent has a positive attitude toward a course of conduct, she is having a volition in favor of that course of conduct. Under this account of volition, volitions aren't exertions, they aren't efforts to produce conduct...[V]oluntariness never requires, on this view, causation by volition. (Yaffe 2000, 100–1)

Yaffe observes that there are occasions when one prefers to do something, and yet one makes no effort to do it and does not think that one will do it. He claims that "such desiderative states would count as volitions according to the first edition account of volition" (Yaffe 2000, 98). He says that this account of volition is much less sophisticated than the one that Locke offers in later editions. One might even say that on Yaffe's reading, Locke is not offering an account of *volition* at all in the first edition. Volition is usually conceived of as a sort of trigger—something that explains how an agent goes from merely having reasons or feelings that favor a course of action to actually performing the action. On Yaffe's reading of the first edition account, to be the subject of a volition is just to have one more feeling.

Locke says a good deal in the first edition that does not fit with Yaffe's reading, especially if having a positive attitude toward a course of conduct is supposed to be a matter of being positively *disposed* toward it. He characterizes volitions not only as preferences, but as willings, choices, and actions. These terms suggest that he thinks of volition as involving more than merely favoring an action; they suggest an exercise of agency, the actualizing of a disposition rather than mere possession of one. He also portrays volitions as causing actions. He says that by willing we can move parts of our bodies (II.xxi.4 [1st]); that by the choice or preference of our minds, we begin motions (II.xxi.5,7 [1st]); that "by choice, or preference of the existence of any Action" the free man can "make it to exist" (II.xxi.21 [1st]). The causal role that Locke assigns to acts of will does not seem to be one that could be filled by the dispositional state of liking or favoring. The cause of a movement or an action must be a datable episode rather than a disposition.

We might develop a friendly amendment of Yaffe's reading by considering II.xxi.28 [1st] in the light of Alvin Goldman's view of agency. Goldman articulates a theory of action that he hesitates to call volitionist, but that has certain strong affinities with volitionism. He draws a distinction between standing wants and occurrent wants (Goldman 1970, 86–91).[3] A standing want is a desire that is dispositional in character, whereas an occurrent want can be identified with a datable mental episode (frequently, but not necessarily, a conscious one). If, while drawing up my grocery list, I desire cheese in a way that involves my focusing my attention on the prospect of cheese, this desire is an occurrent want of mine. On the other hand, when I later do my shopping and the cheese entirely slips my mind (I have not paid sufficient attention to my list), I may still be the subject of a standing want for the cheese, but I am no longer occurrently wanting it. The distinction is supposed to be parallel to a distinction between dispositional and occurrent belief. Before reading this sentence you likely had a belief about the date your mother was born, but it is unlikely that you happened to be actively thinking about that date. Ten minutes ago your belief about your mother's birthday was a dispositional state. Now, if you are actively thinking that she was born on June 3rd (or whenever), you are having an occurrent belief with that content.

Goldman says that what it is for a piece of behavior to be a voluntary action is for it to be caused by an occurrent want. He cites Locke's first edition account as an antecedent (Goldman 1976, 68). We have seen that Locke equates willing an action with being more pleased at the prospect of performing it than at the prospect of not doing so. Considerations of charity might lead us to take this as the view that willing to ψ is occurrently wanting to ψ more than not to ψ. The "occurrent desire" reading of Locke (as we might call it) accommodates his idea that having a volition is being pleased with an action. It also accommodates his view that volitions cause actions. Moreover, it does better than Yaffe's reading because it treats volitions as discrete episodes of mental activity—the sort of thing that could conceivably serve to trigger bodily motions.

However, the notion that willing an action is occurrently wanting to perform it does not fit with all that Locke says about volition, even as we confine ourselves to the first edition. It does not fit well with his view that

---

[3] Though the distinction is associated with Goldman's theory, he credits it to William Alston (Goldman 1970, 86n).

volitions are themselves actions. Not all volitionists consider volitions to be actions, but the view has considerable plausibility. The unwitting paraplegic who wakes up in the hospital and tries to move his legs seems to be engaging in a certain kind of mental activity, a mental exertion that in an able-bodied person precedes muscular contraction. Moreover, this mental activity seems to go beyond wanting to move his legs. Another paraplegic— one who *knows* that he will never move his legs again—may experience the strongest desire to move his legs, without engaging in the mental exertion of willing to move them (since he knows that it would be futile). Even if volition is conceived of as occurrent (rather than dispositional) wanting, the idea that willing an action is wanting it does not fit well with the view that willing is an action. One who is the subject of an occurrent desire need not be engaged in any kind of activity in virtue of being so. Though one who is pleased with a prospective action is "doing" something in a denatured sense (he is undergoing a certain experience), feeling pleasure at the prospect of an action is not an expression of one's agency. It is instead a passion in the original sense of that term, a passive quality or attribute. We can make decisions about what actions to perform, but we *discover* what desires we have. We cannot decide what to want, except indirectly, by deciding upon a course of action likely to promote or suppress certain desires in us.

The idea that willing to do something is occurrently wanting to do it also fits poorly with Locke's own explanation of why he characterizes volition in terms of preference. This comes at II.xxi.33 [1st]:

I have rather made use of the Word *Preference* than *Choice*, to express the act of Volition, because choice is of a more doubtful signification, and bordering more upon Desire, and so is referred to things remote; whereas Volition, or the Act of Willing, signifies nothing properly, but the actual producing of something that is voluntary.

Yaffe claims that on Locke's first edition account a merely "desiderative state" qualifies as a volition. Here, by contrast, Locke says that he favors 'preference' over 'choice' in order to *avoid* a meaning that is too close to "desire." He seems not to be thinking of volition as merely a matter of wanting something to occur. Yet it must be conceded that his explanation is puzzling on two counts. First, it seems to get things backwards: 'prefer' seems closer in meaning to 'desire' than 'choose' does. If I merely desire a glass of wine but make no effort to get one, it seems more accurate to say that I prefer a glass of wine than that I choose one. Second, there is the question of what Locke means when he says that the reference of 'choice' includes "things remote," while that of 'volition' is nothing but the actual production of something voluntary. I will address the first of these puzzles now, and take up the second in the next section.

Locke's linguistic intuitions about 'preference' and 'choice' may be explained by taking into account some drift in the meanings of these terms. Even now, the first sense of 'prefer' given in the *Oxford English Dictionary* is "to put forward or advance, in status, rank, or fortune; to promote." ("To favor or esteem more" is the third meaning.) One of the sub-entries for this first meaning—now obsolete, but with citations spanning from 1574 to 1647—is "to forward, advance, promote (a result); to assist in bringing about." Thus an author writing in the mid-seventeenth century says that "A little shaking prefers the growth of the tree." To prefer an action in this sense would be not merely to have a positive attitude toward it, but to put it forward as to be done, to help make it happen. The *OED* also cites seventeenth-century sources in which 'preference' is used, in a manner now rare, to mean "preferment, promotion" or "advancement." Many contemporary volitionists characterize volition as an episode of trying to do something.[4] It seems fair to say that on one use of 'prefer' common in the seventeenth century, preferring an action is a matter of trying to do something. At the same time, the *OED*'s third entry for 'choose' tells us that "the notion of a choice between alternatives is often left quite in the background, and the sense is little more than an emphatic equivalent of, To will, to wish." The next entry includes a now obsolete use of 'choose' dating from the fifteenth century to the nineteenth, meaning "to exercise one's own pleasure, [to] do as one likes." So perhaps Locke's linguistic intuitions would not have to have been defective for him to think that 'choice' suggested desire more than 'preference' did.

In the first edition of the *Essay*, Locke consistently characterizes volition as the preferring of an action to its forbearance (or *vice versa*). Despite the appearance of a single, consistently held account, there are two strands in his thinking about volition and they are at odds with one another. The difference is papered over by the fact that there is a sense of 'preferring' to cover each of his two ways of thinking about volition. On the one hand, he

---

[4] These include Prichard (1949), O'Shaughnessy (1973), Hornsby (1980), Ginet (1990). For a volitionist who explicitly repudiates the notion that willing is trying, see Odegard 1988.

sometimes thinks of willing to ψ as a matter of being occurrently pleased by the prospect of ψ-ing. On this way of thinking about volition, having a volition to ψ is occurrently wanting to ψ more than not to ψ. There is, of course, a sense of 'prefer' on which preferring an alternative is wanting it more. On the other hand, Locke also thinks of willing as itself a kind of activity—as something that one *does* rather than something that one discovers about oneself. When he is thinking of volition in this way, he thinks of preferring an action as different from merely desiring it. Preferring an action in this sense is a matter of promoting it, helping to realize it, trying to do it.

Both ways of thinking about volition appear throughout the first edition version of II.xxi, with sometimes one and sometimes the other in the ascendant. It is unfortunate that Locke tends to think of willing as a matter of being pleased with a prospective action. The other strand in his thinking about volition is better, and the two are incompatible. Later in the chapter I will offer an hypothesis about why he finds it natural and attractive to conceive of volition as being pleased with an action (§62).

§56 The Objects of Volition

The second puzzling aspect of Locke's remark at II.xxi.33 [1st] has to do with the contrast that he draws between volition properly understood and choice in a sense that is supposed to border upon desire. Locke says that 'choice' in the sense bordering on desire is "referred to things remote," whereas 'volition' signifies nothing but the production of something voluntary. I suggest that he is drawing a contrast having to do with the objects of desire on the one hand, and of volition on the other. He means that the object or target of a desire may be something further removed from the agent than the object or target of a volition can be.

The content of a desire may be specified by reference to an object ("Chris wants that autographed copy of *The Ambassadors*"), a state of affairs ("Chris wants the Dolphins to win the Super Bowl"), or a proposition in the subjunctive mood ("Chris wishes that we would visit him in Tennessee next Christmas"). Perhaps one of these ways of characterizing the content of desire is more fundamental than the others. No matter. For our purpose, we need only observe that desires may have as their objects things or states of affairs that are spatially and temporally distant from the agents whose desires they are. (That copy of *The Ambassadors* may be on another continent, and Christmas and the Super Bowl may be weeks or months away.) Can the same be said of the objects of volition?

Locke holds that the objects of volition are performances and non-performances of actions. Recall that he equates having a volition with willing, and willing with choosing (presumably in a sense *not* bordering on desire) and preferring. *What* he repeatedly and consistently characterizes us as willing, choosing, and preferring are actions and forbearances. This is worth emphasizing, as it has gone unappreciated and it has significant implications. At II.xxi.7 [1st], Locke defines volition as the exercise of the mind's power to "prefer any particular one of those Actions to its forbearance, or *Vice versa*." At II.xxi.15 [1st], he says that "*Volition* ... is nothing but the actual choosing or preferring forbearance to the doing, or doing to the forbearance, of any particular Action in our power." At II.xxi.23 [1st]—and again at II.xxi.27 [1st]—he portrays agents as willing the "existence, or not existence" [*sic*] of actions. At II.xxi.28 [1st], he says that "*Volition* or *Willing* ... is nothing but the *preferring* the doing of any thing, to the not doing of it; Action to Rest, & *contra*." Finally, at II.xxi.46 [1st], he says that our idea of Will contains the idea of "a Power to prefer the doing, to the not doing any particular Action (& *vice versâ*)." As we saw earlier, Locke also holds that volitions are themselves actions. Volitions are thus actions directed at the doings and not-doings of other actions.

Ignoring Locke's claims that volitions are actions, and that what we will are actions, Lowe ascribes to him a Millian conception of action (Lowe 1986, 1995). In *A System of Logic*, Mill writes:

> Now what is an action? Not one thing, but a series of two things; the state of mind called a volition, followed by an effect. The volition or intention to produce the effect, is one thing; the effect produced in consequence of the intention, is another thing; the two together constitute the action. (Mill 1973, 55)

On Mill's account, neither a volition nor the change in body or mind that it produces is an action. Instead, each is part of an action that they together constitute. Lowe portrays Locke as holding that an ordinary case of voluntary action—that of an agent φ-ing—consists in the agent having a volition to φ, and this causing what Lowe calls a "φ-result." As an example of the distinction between an action (the φing) and its "result," he offers the distinction between the raising of an arm and that arm rising. The arm rising is an event that begins at the shoulder, as it were. The rising of a person's arm is a sort of thing that could happen even if the person did not raise her arm—if the relevant muscles were electrically stimulated by a probe inserted into the shoulder, or if her arm were lifted by some other person or blown by a strange gust of wind. The raising of an arm consists of a subject's having a volition to raise his arm, and this causing the arm's rise. Locke could accept this distinction between raising and rising. What does not fit well with the text of II.xxi is the view that our willings cause not actions but "results." Lowe cites a passage from IV.x.19 [1st]:

My right Hand writes, whilst my left Hand is still: What causes rest in one, and motion in the other? Nothing but my Will, a Thought of my Mind; my Thought only changing, the right Hand rests and the left Hand moves.

Lowe notes that "Locke is *not* in fact saying that my thought or volition causes *my action of writing*, but rather that it causes *the motion of my hand* which occurs when I write voluntarily" (Lowe 1986, 151). However, since 'motion' is the term that Locke uses to refer to a large class of actions—all those actions that are not episodes of thinking—this hardly shows that he conceives of volitions as bringing about "results" rather than actions.

Locke says that all the actions we can conceive of are either episodes of thinking or of moving (II.xxi.4,8 [1st]). Coupled with the view that actions are the objects of volition, this yields the thesis that what we will are episodes of thinking, motions of our bodies, and forbearances of these.[5] Locke is giving expression to part of this when he says that "all the Actions of our Body" consist in the motion of "several parts of our Bodies," by which means we "move our selves, and other contiguous Bodies" (II.vii.3 [1st]). Since our own thoughts and bodily motions cannot be remote from us spatially, it follows that the objects of volition cannot be spatially remote, as objects of desire can be. The picture this leads to is one on which the contents of our volitions are more circumscribed than our ordinary ways of talking suggest. Sometimes we speak of agents as acting voluntarily when they turn on lights, throw touchdown passes, or hit targets with arrows. Yet on Locke's view, what an agent *wills* is that certain thought processes occur in his mind or that his body moves in certain ways. The agent's contribution toward the turning on of a light is his moving his body in a certain way, and likewise his contribution toward throwing a touchdown pass or hitting a target with an arrow. Locke will of

---

[5] One philosopher who *has* appreciated this is W. F. R. Hardie (see Hardie 1971, 196).

course acknowledge the obvious fact that certain motions of our bodies are likely to have certain effects some distance from us. He will allow that we frequently act with the intention that our bodily motions will have effects on "contiguous Bodies" and on more remote things. However, these external effects are produced by the world's contribution as well as our own. Though we may desire, intend, or expect such remote effects, we do not *will* them. Our volitional activity is directed solely at realizing *our* share of what goes into causing a light to go on, a football to land in the receiver's hands, or an arrow to hit its target.

Carl Ginet has defended an account of volition with certain affinities to Locke's. Ginet maintains that willing is a simple mental act not to be confused with intending, wanting, or deciding (Ginet 1990, 11, 32). He says that in the case of a physical action, what one wills is to exert a part of one's body with a certain force in a certain direction (Ginet 1990, 33). He rejects the Lockean notion that we will *motions* of our body parts, doing so on the grounds that we sometimes will exertions in order to resist motion.

Ginet holds that the contents of volition are narrowly circumscribed not only spatially, but temporally. On his view, volitions are unlike desires, intentions, and decisions in that they concern only what is done at the present instant. "Volitions do not plan ahead," he says, "not even very slightly" (Ginet 1990, 33). He sees the contents of volition as being in constant flux:

Volition is a fluid mental activity whose content is continually changing...I can all at one time decide to swim another length of the pool, but I cannot all at one time *will* the whole sequence of bodily exertions involved in swimming another length, any more than I can *perform* the sequence of exertions all at one time. Indeed, I cannot all at one instant will the whole sequence of exertions involved in just taking one more complete stroke with my right arm. (Ginet 1990, 32–3)

On this view, we are unselfconsciously modulating the contents of our volitions as we make our way through the world. The content of volition is like an active counterpart to the continuous, frequently repetitive, shifting contents of perception. Might Locke too think of the contents of volition as temporally circumscribed? Might this be another sense in which our desires may be "referred to things remote," but our volitions cannot be? Later I will suggest that he does think this way, and that this explains his view that we cannot forbear willing on a question once we have taken it up (§61).

§57 *Voluntary Action*

What 'volition' signifies, according to II.xxi.33 [1st], is "the actual producing of something that is voluntary." At II.xxi.7 [1st], Locke says this about what it means for an action or its forbearance to be voluntary:

The power the Mind has at any time to prefer any particular one of those Actions to its forbearance, or *Vice versa*, is that Faculty which, as I have said, we call the *Will*; the actual exercise of that Power we call *Volition*; and the forbearance or performance of that Action, consequent to such a preference of the Mind, is call'd *Voluntary*.

The phrase 'consequent to' can bear several meanings. A thing may be said to be "consequent to" another when it merely follows the other, when it follows the other as an effect or result, or when it follows the other as a logical consequence. Presumably it is only the first two meanings that are relevant here. Still, this yields three possible readings of his criterion for voluntariness: an action or forbearance's voluntariness is either a matter of its conforming with a prior volition, of its being caused by a prior volition, or both. We have already seen that Locke employs causal language to describe the relation between successful volitions and their objects. He says that by willing we *produce* voluntary motions, *begin* motions, *make* actions exist, *cause* motion in our hands. However, this does not show that an action's being voluntary is a matter of it being caused by a prior volition. Even if physical actions are bodily motions caused by volitions, it could be conformity with volition rather than causation by volition that gives them their status as voluntary. Indeed, conformity with a precedent volition could be the criterion for voluntariness even if it is the fact that our actions are caused by our volitions that usually explains their conforming with our volitions. Later I will suggest that this seems to offer Locke a way out of a difficulty that he encounters in his account of forbearing (§60).

Since Locke holds that actions and forbearances are voluntary when they are "consequent to" volitions, and that volitions are themselves actions, he cannot use voluntariness to delineate the class of actions. Locke does not offer a general criterion for an event's counting as an action, but he does say something important about what it takes for the movement of a body to count as one. At II.xxi.4 [1st], he implies that the movement of a body counts as an action only if it involves the beginning of motion rather than the transfer of motion:

A Body at rest affords us of no *Idea* of any active Power to move; and when it is set in motion its self, that Motion is rather a Passion, than an Action in it: For when the Ball obeys the stroke of a Billiard-stick, it is not any action of the Ball, but bare passion.

Locke regards it as evident that when I move parts of my body through the exercise of my will, I am beginning motions rather than merely transferring them. In fact, he says, our experience of volition is our only source of the idea of *beginning* motion (II.xxi.4 [1st]). Bodies can transfer motion, but it is spirits or souls that have "the power of *exciting of Motion by Thought*" (II. xxiii.28 [1st]). He says that we would do well to consider whether "active power be not the proper attribute of Spirits, and passive power of Matter" (II.xxiii.28 [1st]).

Locke uses three thought experiments to flesh out his accounts of voluntariness and freedom: the falling man, the complacent paralytic, and the locked room. We will consider the first two here, and the third in the next section.

At II.xxi.9[1st], Locke is making the point that inanimate objects such as tennis balls cannot be free because they cannot have volitions. He adds this:

Likewise a Man falling into the Water, (a Bridge breaking under him,) has not herein liberty, is not a free Agent. For though he has Volition, though he preferrs his not falling to falling; yet the forbearance of that Motion not being in his Power, the stop or Cessation of that Motion follows not upon his Volition; and therefore therein he is not free.

What is supposed to be the point of similarity between the tennis ball and the falling man? The answer seems to be this: neither the tennis ball nor the falling man is free in respect of its motion, because in both cases the motions are not voluntary. The tennis ball moves in the absence of a volition to move on its trajectory, because it moves in the absence of volition altogether. The falling man moves in the absence of a volition to hurtle toward the ground, because he lacks that particular volition. Now a somewhat harder question: Does Locke attribute some particular volition to the falling man? His observation that the man "has Volition" could just mean that he has a general capacity to will, in distinction from the tennis ball. However, in light of Locke's characterization of willing as preferring, it seems natural to read the next clause—"he preferrs his not falling to falling"—as ascribing to the man a volition not to fall. This is problematic. Locke conceives of volitions as directed at actions and forbearances. Yet the man's falling is not an action: it is something that happens to him, and not an exercise of his agency. If the man wills his not falling, then it would seem that he must be willing to forbear from falling. Yet he cannot refrain from doing what is not an action in the first place.

If Locke means that the falling man is willing himself not to fall, this may also be in tension with a principle about willing that he endorses. He defines volition as the choosing or preference of actions "in our power" (II.xxi.15 [1st]). He describes volition as "regarding only what is in our power" (II.xxi.28 [1st]). For a being "to *Will*," he says, is for it "to preferr the being, or not being of any thing in its power, which it has once considered as such" (II.xxi.23 [1st]). In these passages, Locke gives oblique expression to a principle that might best be put by saying that we cannot will to do what we firmly believe to be impossible under the circumstances. Perhaps I can will to jump a foot higher than I have ever jumped before. I may doubt that I will be able to jump that high, but I am not sure that I cannot. However, I am sure that I cannot jump over a house, and because of this I cannot will to do it. I might will to jump my highest near the house, but that is not the same thing as willing to jump over the house. Only somebody who is delusional—somebody who does not appreciate the impossibility of what he proposes to do—could pull off willing to jump over a house. Thus it would seem that the falling man could will not to fall only if he thought it possible that he could do something to stop his fall. It seems unlikely that Locke is supposing that the falling man thinks he can levitate. Perhaps Locke sees the thrashings of a falling man as vain attempts to stop his fall, attempts that show that he does not quite grasp that he cannot help himself in that way.[6]

It might seem that we can make sense of Locke's remarks about the falling man by supposing that he is thinking of willing as occurrently wanting to do something. For if having a volition is just having an occurrent desire, then the man's having a volition not to fall is a matter of his

[6] Thanks to Don Garrett for this suggestion.

occurrently wanting not to fall. Surely a person can want not to fall? However, this merely papers over the difficulty. If there is such a (negative) state of affairs as the man's not falling, then presumably it is one that the falling man can want to obtain. Yet even when Locke is thinking of willing as occurrent desire, the objects of volition are supposed to be actions. To will is to prefer the performance of an action to the forbearance of it (or *vice versa*). Locke's unfortunate tendency to think of willing as being pleased makes it easy for him to drift into the mistake of characterizing agents as willing states of affairs that are not actions. This is understandable, for one can certainly be pleased at the prospect of states of affairs that are not actions.

At II.xxi.11 [1st], Locke says that, "[T]he sitting still even of a Paralitick, whilst he preferrs it to removal, is truly voluntary." He does not say just how immobile the paralytic is supposed to be, but it seems fair to assume that we are to imagine him as being quite unable to move and as being fully aware of this. In that case, there is a problem with the notion that the paralytic has a volition to sit still, which is implied by Locke's claim that his sitting is voluntary. For it does not seem that the paralytic who is aware of his paralysis should be able to willingly forbear moving. Willing the forbearance of an action, where one believes the action to be impossible anyway, is problematic in much the same way as willing an action that one believes to be impossible under the circumstances. I cannot willingly forbear jumping over the house any more than I can will to jump over the house. As in the falling man case, Locke's handling of the example is probably the result of his first thinking of willing an action as being pleased with it, and then drifting into the mistake of supposing that one can will any state of affairs that one can be pleased with.

§58 *Freedom and Forbearance*

Philosophical discussions about human freedom often involve the supposition that our freedom or unfreedom is a pervasive metaphysical condition, an all-or-nothing affair. Either the sort of freedom we value is a wholesale illusion and none of us has ever really had it, or else it is enjoyed by all adults of sound mind. This is not how Locke thinks about freedom. To be free is, on his view, to be free with respect to a kind of action under some set of circumstances at a certain time. One can be free with respect to a kind of action at one time, but unfree with regard to that same kind of action a moment later, if the circumstances have changed. One can simultaneously enjoy freedom with regard to one sort of action, and unfreedom with regard to another. In fact, given Locke's account of freedom, it is inevitable that each of us is always free with regard to some kinds of actions, and unfree with regard to others.

Our introduction to Locke's first edition conception of freedom comes at II.xxi.8 [1st]:

All the Actions that we have any *Idea* of reducing themselves, as has been said, to these two, *viz.* Thinking and Motion, so far as a Man has a power to think, or not to think; to move, or not to move, according to the preference of his own choice, so far is a Man *Free*. Where-ever any performance or forbearance are not equally in a Man's power; where-ever doing or not doing, will not equally follow upon the preference of his Mind, there he is not *Free*, though perhaps the Action may be voluntary.

Locke holds that being free with respect to a certain kind of action is a matter of being able both to perform and to forbear from performing an act of that kind under the prevailing circumstances. 'Forbearing' is Locke's term for voluntary not-doing. His view is that one acts freely only when one could have forborne acting in that way; one forbears freely only when one could have done what one forbears doing. The second of these claims simply follows from the analysis of what it is to forbear: we do not say that a person can refrain from doing what he could not have done anyway. The first claim is more controversial.

Locke's first edition conception of freedom can be characterized this way:

An agent, A, is free with respect to a kind of action, φ, if and only if: (1) If A were to will to φ, A would φ, *and* (2) If A were to will not to φ, then A would forbear φ-ing.

Locke usually speaks of *agents* as being free or not. We can also speak of *acts* as free or not, but if we are being careful we will keep in mind that agents and acts cannot be free in the same sense. Acts cannot will, act, and forbear. When we call an action or a forbearance free what we mean is just that the agent performing that action or forbearance is free in regard to that performance.

Locke sometimes speaks of "liberty" rather than "freedom." His term for unfreedom is 'necessity.' He says that "Where-ever Thought is wholly wanting, or the power to act or forbear, there *Necessity* takes place" (II.xxi.13 [1st]). Necessity thus "takes place" throughout the inanimate realm. Necessity so understood is different from both causal necessity and logical necessity. A truly random sequence of events produced by indeterministic causes and involving inanimate objects would exhibit necessity in Locke's sense, though it may involve occurrences that were neither causally nor logically necessary.

We are now in a position to appreciate more of what Locke was trying to show with his examples of the falling man and the complacent paralytic. The falling man case is supposed to bolster the intuition that doing as one wills is necessary for freedom. The falling man is unfree because his falling is not voluntary. The case of the complacent paralytic is supposed to show that doing as one wills is not sufficient for freedom. The paralyzed person is unfree because, in a certain sense, he cannot do otherwise than he does. He is content to stay where he is, but he would stay where he is even if he were not content to do so.

Locke's example of the complacent paralytic illustrates his thesis that "*Voluntary…is not opposed to Necessary; but to Involuntary*" (II.xxi.11 [1st]). At II.xxi.10 [1st], he uses another example to the same end:

[S]uppose a Man be carried, whilst fast asleep, into a Room, where is a Person he longs to see and speak with; and be there locked fast in, beyond his Power to get out: he awakes, and is glad to find himself in so desirable Company, which he stays willingly in, *i.e.* preferrs his stay to going away; I ask, Is not this stay voluntary? I think, no Body will doubt it…

Like the case of the complacent paralytic, the case of the man in the locked room is supposed to be one in which an agent acts voluntarily, but under "necessity" in Locke's sense.

Lowe argues that the example of the man in the locked room does not actually support Locke's thesis (Lowe 1986, 155–7). He suggests the following as an interpretation of what would be involved in an action being done voluntarily but under "necessity" in Locke's sense:

(9.1)   A φ'd *both under necessity and voluntarily* if and only if A φ'd voluntarily and if A had had a volition not to φ, he would not have succeeded in not-φ-ing voluntarily (Lowe 1986, 154).

What the man does voluntarily is to stay in the room. But *staying* is not an ordinary, straightforward, "positive" action. It is what is sometimes called a "negative" action: to stay in the room voluntarily is to voluntarily *not* do something. What is it, precisely, that the man is voluntarily not doing when he stays in the room? A natural suggestion is that he is voluntarily not leaving the room. Lowe rejects this on the grounds that a person cannot refrain or forbear from doing what he could not do under the circumstances. Since the man cannot leave the room, Lowe says, he cannot forbear leaving it. This leads to the suggestion that what he is voluntarily not doing is *trying* to leave the room. He could have tried to leave the room—walking to the door and pushing against it—and he voluntarily refrains from doing that.

Lowe substitutes "refrain from trying to leave the room" in place of "φ" in (9.1). This yields the result that the man's voluntary stay in the locked room was "necessary" in the relevant sense only if the following is true:

(9.2)   If the man had had a volition not to refrain from trying to leave the room, he would not have succeeded in not refraining from trying to leave the room voluntarily.

In this case, "φ" is a so-called negative action. To understand what would be required for the man's stay to be necessary, we must understand what would be involved in his willing to not perform this negative action. Willing to not perform this negative action would seem to be willing the performance of a "double negative" action—willing to refrain from refraining from trying to leave. Lowe has two things to say about this. First, he says that refraining from refraining from trying to leave the room does not entail trying to leave the room. He does not say what it does entail.[7] Second, he says that even if

---

[7] The suggestion that an agent might forbear from forbearing is a bit mind boggling. Lowe denies that forbearing from forbearing φ-ing would entail φ-ing, but his argument does not convince. He observes, "It is not the case that I *omitted* to fly to the moon last night: but it doesn't follow that I *did* fly there last night. So omitting to omit to φ is not the same as φ-ing" (Lowe 1986, 156). He concludes, "Forbearing to forbear to attempt to leave the room is not, then, the same as attempting to leave the room—it's 'less' than that." However, there is an important difference between omitting and forbearing. Forbearing, unlike omitting, necessarily involves intending or willing not to do something. Therefore, if it makes any sense to speak of forbearing from forbearing φ-ing, this must involve intending or willing not to intentionally or willingly not φ. Whether this will entail φ-ing will depend on the particular account of negative action we presume. (On the account of negative action that I endorse in the next section—which is Robert Moore's account, not Locke's—forbearing from forbearing from φ-ing *does* entail φ-ing. For it involves an agent not refraining from φ-ing, and doing so as a result of his decision not to refrain from φ-ing. One can decide not to refrain from φ-ing only by deciding to φ.) In any case, Locke will say that it does not make sense to speak of forbearing to forbear φ-ing, since (as we shall see below) he regards as absurd the suggestion that an agent can will to will. Fortunately, we can avoid the whole question of what is involved in forbearing from forbearing φ-ing. It arises only because of Lowe's peculiar formulation of the issue. I give an account of the complacent prisoner's volition that does not have the prisoner forbearing from forbearing.

did entail trying to leave the room, that is something the man can do even if the room is locked. It is not the case that if he had had a volition to try leaving the room, he would have failed at that. Therefore, Lowe concludes, the man's negative action is not necessary in Locke's sense (Lowe 1986, 157).

We can begin a reply on Locke's behalf by reminding ourselves of his view of the contents of volition. Lowe notes that the man cannot forbear leaving the room, since he cannot leave the room. However, if our earlier account of Locke's view of the content of volition is correct, then he will say that leaving the room is not something the man could *will* to do even if the door were unlocked and the man knew it was. Leaving a room with a closed door is an event that—like turning on a light or throwing a touchdown pass—depends partly on the agent's contribution, and partly on the world's cooperation. When a man leaves a room by opening an unlocked door and stepping outside, what he *wills* is the series of bodily motions that would—if the world were to cooperate—constitute his rising, approaching the door, turning the handle, opening the door, and walking outside.

Earlier we left open the question of whether Locke would allow that a man can will a series of bodily motions at one go, or whether instead he would say that willing such a series requires a series of willings. Suppose that Locke does think that a man can, at one go, will a series of motions that will take some time to complete. Let 'φ' stand for the series of motions that would—if the world were to cooperate—constitute the man's rising, approaching the door, turning the handle, opening the door, and walking outside. Because the door is locked, φ-ing is something that the man cannot do. He can perform some of the motions that are early constituents of φ; but upon turning the handle and pulling, he would find that he cannot perform all of the constituents of φ. He cannot, for instance, keep his hand firmly gripped around the handle while simultaneously pulling his arm back in the way that would constitute his opening the door if only the door were not locked. The man cannot φ, but because he was *asleep* when he was put in the room, he does not know that he cannot φ. Since he does not know that he cannot φ, there is nothing to prevent him from being able to will to φ. Since he can will to φ, there is nothing to prevent him from being able to will not to φ. Locke should say that when the unwitting prisoner wills to stay in the room, what he wills is not to φ. He wills not to perform the series of bodily motions that would, if the world were to cooperate, constitute his getting up and leaving the room.

Matters are just slightly more complicated if we suppose that Locke would deny that a man can, at one go, will to φ. Suppose that he holds that we can will only those bodily motions that occupy the vanishingly small immediate present. Let us then say that φ—the series of bodily motions that would constitute the man's leaving the room if the door were unlocked—consists of bodily motions $\varphi_1, \varphi_2, \varphi_3 \ldots \varphi_n$. Locke will deny that a man can will to φ, but he will allow that a man can will to φ_1, and that he can do so with the intention of subsequently voluntarily φ_2-ing, φ_3-ing....φ_n-ing. In that case, Locke should say that the unwitting prisoner who stays in the room voluntarily wills not to φ_1, and also intends not to $\varphi_2, \varphi_3 \ldots \varphi_n$.

Is the unwitting prisoner's stay an example of a voluntary but unfree action, as Locke suggests? Harkening back to our earlier characterization of Locke's account of freedom, we can see that the prisoner's stay is not free. If we allow that a man can will a series of motions that would take some time to complete, then we should say that it is not the case that if the unwitting prisoner were to will to φ, he would φ. The state of the door would prevent the prisoner from performing the bodily motions that constitute the later stages of φ-ing. If we insist that a man can will only his actions in the next instant, then we should say that the unwitting prisoner is unfree because it is not the case that if he were to will to φ_1 with the intention of subsequently voluntarily $\varphi_2, \varphi_3 \ldots \varphi_n$, then he would perform φ_1 and would subsequently perform $\varphi_2, \varphi_3 \ldots \varphi_n$. Again, that is because he cannot perform the later members of that series of actions. So if there is a problem with Locke's example of the unwitting prisoner, it lies not with the contention that the prisoner's stay is unfree, but with the contention that it is voluntary. Locke says that no one will doubt that it is voluntary. Yet real questions can be raised about what is involved in voluntarily *forbearing* to do something. We shall return to the man in the locked room after a detour on the topic of forbearing.

§59 *Volition and Negative Action*

Lowe offers a more direct argument against Locke's thesis that our acts can be voluntary but "necessary." This argument invites us to delve more deeply into Locke's volitionism, and his handling of so-called negative actions in particular. Lowe asks us to consider a particular instance in which an agent, A, raises his arm voluntarily. He says that for it also to be the case that A's arm raising is "necessary" in Locke's sense, the following must be true:

(9.3) Even if A had willed not to raise his arm, A would still have raised his arm (Lowe 1995, 130).

Lowe then argues that (9.3) could rarely, if ever, be true (Lowe 1995, 130–1). It could easily be that even if A had willed not to raise his arm, his arm would still have *risen*. However, it does not seem that A could *raise* his arm even while willing not to raise it. For *raising* one's arm is an action that necessarily involves one's arm rising consequent to one's willing it to rise. This means that (9.3) could be true only if A had simultaneously willed not to raise his arm and willed to raise his arm, and that is of doubtful coherence.

Lowe presumes that if A wills to not raise his arm, A achieves the object of his volition so long as it is not the case both that A wills to raise his arm and that this results in his arm rising. Since A's willing not to raise his arm seems necessarily to preclude A's willing to raise his arm, A's volition to not raise his arm seems guaranteed to achieve its end whether or not A's arm goes up. This looks a bit too easy. Consider the case in which an agent's arm does rise despite his willing not to raise it. Suppose that it is wartime and that an evil neurosurgeon implants a device allowing him to control a certain draftee's body. The commanding officer of the draftee's platoon asks for volunteers for a very dangerous mission. Wanting as little danger as possible in his life, the draftee wills not to raise his arm. The surgeon, for reasons of his own, causes the draftee's arm to rise anyway. The officer commends the draftee on his patriotism, takes his protestations to be an attempt at self-effacing humor, and hurries him off on the dangerous mission. By Lowe's reasoning, we should say that the draftee has achieved the object of his volition to not raise his arm, since it was not the draftee but the surgeon who raised the draftee's arm. The draftee tried to not raise his arm, and he did what he set out to do, since *he* did not raise his arm. Yet we feel considerable unease in saying this.

Voluntarily staying in a room and voluntarily not raising one's arm are both so-called negative actions. The unease we feel in saying that the draftee's volition achieved its object raises the question of what counts as success or failure in the case of negative action. One way to approach this is to consider negative actions in relation to ordinary "positive" actions on the one hand, and to mere not-doings on the other. By a mere not-doing, I mean something that is not done, where this does not involve any contemplation on the part of the agent. In all likelihood, walking on the moon, standing outdoors in your underwear, and reciting poetry in Japanese are some of the many things that you are now merely not-doing (or at any rate, they are things that you were merely not doing a moment ago, since you may now be contemplating these actions just by virtue of reading this page). By comparing so-called negative action with ordinary, positive action on the hand, and mere not-doing on the other, we can raise the question of whether a negative action is, properly speaking, an action. For the volitionist, this is not mere wordplay. An action is necessarily something that an agent might try to do, and for a volitionist this means that an action is something that might be the target of a volition. To ask whether a negative action is really an action is to ask whether *not* doing something can be the target of a volition.

We do not think of mere not-doings as actions of any sort. Suppose that the thought of reciting Japanese poetry outdoors in your underwear had never occurred to you before. We do not think of your *not* reciting Japanese poetry outdoors in your underwear yesterday at 2:30 in the afternoon as one of your actions then. All that is required for that particular not-doing to be correctly ascribed to you is that it not be the case that you were performing certain positive actions at 2:30 yesterday afternoon. Observing that negative actions are a species of not-doing, the volitionist might consider giving negative actions a similar deflationary treatment. On the resulting account, we are at best speaking loosely when we say that A wills to not raise his hand. The state of affairs thus inaptly characterized does not involve an agent having a voli-tion whose target is the not raising of his hand; rather, it involves its not being the case that A raises his hand, and then some further condition or conditions being met. Some further condition must be allowed in order to distinguish the kind of *mindful* not-doing sometimes called negative action from mere not-doing. However, the volitionist need not account for the mindfulness of so-called negative actions by supposing that they involve volitions to not do.

What further condition or conditions must be met for A's not φ-ing to amount to the negative action that we might call *refraining* from φ-ing? Various accounts of refraining have been offered that make no use of volitions to not-do, and the volitionist who takes a deflationary view of negative action can take his pick.[8] One that seems promising is Robert Moore's. Moore says that

---

[8] See Brand 1971, Moore 1979, Green 1980, Milanich 1983. Yaffe proposes another account of refraining. He says that on Locke's view an agent refrains from φ-ing if and only if (i) the agent considers φ-ing, (ii) the agent ψ-s voluntarily, and (iii) ψ-ing is incompatible with φ-ing (Yaffe 2001, 378). However, this fails to capture the ordinary notion of refraining. Suppose that S is unaware that ψ-ing is incompatible with φ-ing. In that case, S might voluntarily start ψ-ing while also planning to φ at the first opportunity. S would satisfy Yaffe's requirements, yet we should not say that S has refrained from φ-ing. Plugging this hole seems likely to yield an account like Brand's, on which an agent refrains from φ-ing if and only if he performs another act, ψ, *in order that* he not perform φ (Brand 1971, 49). Moore criticizes Brand's account on the grounds that it does not actually require that A's ψ-ing prevents his φ-ing, and that it misclassifies cases of avoiding as cases of refraining (Moore 1979, 407).

A refrains from φ-ing if and only if (i) A does not φ, and (ii) A has decided not to φ, and (iii) it is because of this decision that A does not φ, and (iv) this decision does not deprive A of the opportunity to φ (Moore 1979, 420). The first condition requires what would, by itself, constitute mere not-φ-ing: namely, at some time, *t*, its not being the case that A φ-s. Refraining is then distinguished from mere not-doing by conditions (ii) and (iii), which require that at some time (presumably earlier than *t*) A decided against φ-ing at *t*, with this decision accounting for the fact that it is not the case that A φ-s at t.[9] Condition (iv) is added to exclude certain cases in which we hesitate to say that an agent has refrained from φ-ing despite the fact that his decision not to φ causes him not to φ (Moore 1979, 417–19). These include cases in which the agent decides against φ-ing at *t*, consequently fails to make the necessary preparations for φ-ing at *t*, and then changes his mind so that at *t* he would φ if he could. The upshot is that a volitionist can give an account of mindful not-φ-ing that does not involve a volition to not-φ.[10]

Whether or not one is a volitionist, there are good reasons to favor a deflationary account of negative action. In "Negative 'Actions'," Gilbert Ryle—no friend of volitionism—catalogues some of the reasons for denying that so-called negative actions are actions (Ryle 1979). He notes that most actions can be done well or poorly, but that this does not seem to be true of so-called negative actions, such as forgiving or keeping a secret (Ryle 1979, 107). The performance of actions often requires certain materials or implements, but the "performance" of so-called negative actions never does. Most significantly, there is a kind of hierarchical structure to action that is absent in negative action. Ryle uses the nomenclature of *supra*-actions and *infra*-actions: one resigns (*supra*) by writing (*infra*) a letter; one writes (*supra*) a letter by moving (*infra*) one's hand in certain ways while holding a pen over paper (Ryle 1979, 107–8).[11] There does not seem to be anything like

---

[9] It might be objected that deciding not to φ entails willing not to φ. In that case, the volitionist who follows Moore will be treating not-doings as possible objects of volition after all. However, the volitionist may have independent grounds for distinguishing deciding and willing. For example, he might insist that one can make decisions about future action long in advance, but that one can will only what one does in the immediate present.

[10] Though mindful not-φ-ing itself need not involve volition, the volitionist need not deny that one can be willing some other action as one refrains from φ-ing.

[11] Many writers prefer the terminology of basic and non-basic actions, or basic and non-basic descriptions of actions. There are controversies about how to properly draw the distinction, and about how it relates to the individuation of actions (see Davidson 1963, Danto 1965, Brand 1968, Goldman 1970, Hardie 1971, Hornsby 1980, Smith 1988, Ginet 1990). I will enter into these no farther than is necessary to understand and assess Locke's account.

this in the case of so-called negative actions. Ryle says: "Where the preacher had (*infra*) to voice vowels and consonants if he was (*supra*) to deliver his sermon, there is no corresponding *infra*-x-ing without which the climber could not have *paused*" (Ryle 1979, 108). This is related to a more general point about negation: statements about not-doings are non-committal in a way that statements about doings typically are not. If you know only that a person is not smoking, you know very little about him. The full story of an action must involve the specification of a vast number of details about the circumstances and mechanism of its performance, but the full story of a so-called negative action need specify no more than what the agent did not do.

There are also particular reasons for a volitionist to favor a deflationary account of negative action. Volition is usually conceived of as a type of mental episode that triggers occurrences in the body or mind. Not-φ-ing would seem a non-occurrence rather than an occurrence. It is hard to see how a non-occurrence could be triggered by anything. (We could say that a not-φ-ing is triggered by a volition when the volition triggers an action incompatible with φ-ing, but that is just a version of deflationism—the view that our willings bring about not-doings indirectly, by bringing about other doings.) Another reason for the volitionist to deny that not-doings are the targets of volitions is that otherwise there would sometimes seem to be one volition too many. Suppose that S considers φ-ing at a time, t, but in the end refrains from φ-ing at t and ψ-s then instead. If S's ψ-ing at t is voluntary, the volitionist must say that it is proceeded by a volition to ψ. It seems gratuitous to insist that in order to fully account for S's state at t we must invoke not only the successful volition to ψ, but also the distinct and equally successful volition to not-φ.

While the volitionist has reason to adopt a deflationary account of negative action, this is not what Locke does. Instead, he treats not-doings as possible objects of volition. In his discussions of freedom, he speaks of agents having the power to prefer the forbearance of an action (II.xxi.5, 7–8, 15 [1st]), the "not considering" an idea (II.xxi.5 [1st]), the resting of a finger (II.xxi.21 [1st]), the "non-existence" of an action (II.xxi.21 [1st]), and the "not doing" of something (II.xxi.28 [1st]). If he were using 'prefer' in its modern sense, none of this would entail that not-doings are the targets of volitions. But as we have seen, he equates preferring an action with willing it, and willing it with having a volition to do it. He also speaks of the "*not*

Existence" of an action as dependent on "*our Volition of it*" (II.xxi.27 [1st]). Finally, the idea that not-doing can be the target of a volition is suggested by his characterization of us as able to "produce" the forbearance of an action (II.xxi.8 [1st]), and to "produce" silence, and rest (II.xxi.21 [1st]).

We have seen what the volitionist who favors a deflationary account of action might say about what it is to succeed at not-φ-ing. The volitionist who regards not-doings as possible targets of volition will see things differently. He favors a robust conception of negative action, rather than a deflationary one. From his perspective, the claim that negative actions are *actions* means more than just that we can be held accountable for them, or that they can be intended, or that they can be the results of our decisions. From the perspective of a volitionist who favors a robust conception of negative action, a negative action is more akin to positive action than to mere not-doing, and so we should expect him to model his conception of negative action on his conception of positive action.

On Locke's view, the performance of a positive physical action involves an agent having a volition to move his body in a certain way, and his thereby causing his body to move in that way. Thus for Locke:

> (9.4)   A raises his arm if and only if: (i) A wills to raise his arm, *and* (ii) A's willing is followed by an upward motion of his arm, *and* (iii) his willing is the cause of that motion.

A question might be raised about what it is for A to will to raise his arm, as (9.4)(i) requires. Since the satisfaction of all three conditions is being offered as what it is for A to raise his arm, one might worry that A's willing to raise his arm will involve (among other things) his willing what is required for the satisfaction of (9.4)(i), and hence that it will involve his willing to will to raise his arm. It might seem that a regress looms.

Volition does involve a kind of self-reference, but not one that launches a regress. When A wills to raise his arm, he is not willing *to* will anything; he is not willing that he perform another mental act. When A wills to raise his arm, he wills that his arm rise. However, he is willing not *just* that his arm rise, for his will would not be satisfied by an evil neurosurgeon's subsequently causing his arm to rise. What A wills when he wills to raise his arm is that his arm rise as a result of the very act of will that he is at that moment engaged in. The content of his volition thus includes a reference to the volition of which it is the content.[12] Locke does not explicitly draw attention to the self-referential character of volition's content. However, as we have seen, he does frequently speak of agents as preferring or willing not motions or periods of rest, but actions and forbearances. We have also seen that for a motion of one's body to qualify as an action, on his view, it must be initiated by the agent's own willing (rather than having been transferred from another body). Forbearing too is not mere not-doing, but voluntary not-doing. Therefore, when Locke characterizes us as willing actions and forbearances, he is implicitly committing himself to something very like the picture I have just suggested. What the agent wills when he wills an action is not just that a certain motion occur in his body, but that there occur in his body a certain motion with the right causal history—he wills that there occur a motion initiated by his willing. By the same token, Locke is committed to saying that what the agent wills when he wills a forbearance is not just that his body does not move in a certain way, but also that its not moving has a certain causal history—that its not moving be a consequence of his willing it not to move.

It therefore seems fair to see Locke as committed to the following:

(9.5)   A raises his arm if and only if: (i) A wills that his arm rise as a consequence of his so willing, *and* (ii) A's willing is followed by his arm's rising, *and* (iii) his willing is the cause of his arm's rising.

Now we are in a position to offer a qualified defense of Locke against Lowe's critique. We are supposing that A voluntarily raises his arm. Lowe says that the following would have to be true for A's voluntary arm raising to be "necessary" in Locke's sense:

(9.3)   Even if A had willed not to raise his arm, A would still have raised his arm (Lowe 1995, 130).

He then goes on to argue that the truth of (9.3) would require A's willing both to raise and not to raise his arm at the same time, a scenario of doubtful coherence. However, in deriving (9.3), Lowe presumes that the failure

---

[12] This is a point that Ginet makes: "The intentional object of my volition is not just my body's exertion but my voluntary control of its exertion. I will that my willing—this very willing of whose content we speak—cause the exertion. The content refers to the volition of which it is the content and says that this volition should cause the body to exert in a certain way" (Ginet 1990, 35). He notes that Harman makes a similar observation about intention (Harman 1976), and that Searle makes this point about what he calls "intention in action" (Searle 1983).

of A's willing to not raise his arm entails A's raising his arm. From the point of view of a volitionist who believes that not-doings can be the targets of volitions, that is not a valid presumption.

Since Locke is a volitionist who favors a robust conception of negative action, we should expect him to hold an account of negative action that runs parallel to his account of positive action. We should expect him to say this about what would be involved in A's voluntarily not raising his arm:

> (9.6)   A succeeds in voluntarily not raising his arm if and only if: (i) A wills that his arm not rise as a consequence of his so willing, *and* (ii) A's willing is followed by his arm's not rising, *and* (iii) his willing is the cause of his arm's not rising.

A volitionist holds that in the case of an ordinary, "positive" action, there is a mental exertion of the agent directed toward the realization of some state of his body or mind. If that state is not realized as a consequence of his exertion, then his exertion is for naught and is deemed a failure. For the volitionist who favors a robust conception of negative action, an agent's voluntarily *not* doing something also involves a mental exertion on his part directed toward the realization of a state of his mind or body (albeit a negative state). If that state is not realized as a consequence of his exertion, the volitionist who favors a robust conception of negative action will say that the exertion was for naught, that it was a failure. Thus we should expect Locke to hold that the non-satisfaction of condition (9.6)(ii) alone is enough to ensure that A does not succeed in voluntarily not raising his arm. He should say that the rising of the draftee's arm consequent to his willing to not raise it renders that willing a failure even if the rising is brought about by the machinations of an evil neurosurgeon. Thus Locke should deny that volitions to not-do are automatically guaranteed to succeed, and he eludes Lowe's criticism.

§60 *A Problem for Locke's Account*

In order to understand Locke's philosophy of action, we have tried to see things from the perspective of a volitionist who thinks that not-doings can be the targets of volitions. From this point of view, the successful performance of a negative action seems to require the realization of the targeted negative state of affairs. Because of this, Locke eludes Lowe's criticism. This is not to say that all is well with Locke's account of freedom. I have already mentioned some general considerations favoring a deflationary account of negative action, and have suggested that the volitionist has special reason to embrace such an account. There is also a deeper problem for the volitionist who takes a robust view of negative action—one that threatens to undermine Locke's verdict about the unwitting prisoner, his view that we sometimes forbear actions, and ultimately his view that we sometimes act freely. To see this, we must first generalize the account of voluntary not-doing that we have ascribed to Locke.

To produce a general account of forbearing modeled on (9.5), we need a way of capturing the distinction marked by our talk of arm raisings *versus* arm risings. If an arm *raising* occurs, somebody has acted; if an arm *rising* occurs, this might or might not be a case of somebody acting. (The Millian will say that an arm rising is *part* of an action if it is caused by a volition to raise the arm that rises. Locke will say that an arm rising *is* an action if it is caused by such a volition.) That difference is captured by the distinction between the transitive and intransitive uses of certain verbs, such as 'to move.' I can move [transitive] my hand, and when I do so my hand moves [intransitive]. The transitive use entails agency, whereas the intransitive use leaves it an open question whether an action has occurred. Jennifer Hornsby introduces subscripts to distinguish the two uses: if the agent moves [transitive] his arm, he moves$_T$ it; if the arm moves [intransitive], it moves$_I$ (Hornsby 1980). Nominalizations exhibit the same ambiguity: it is one thing to speak of an agent's movement$_T$ of his arm, and another to speak of his arm's movement$_I$. Locke thinks of all physical actions as bodily motions initiated by volitions (as opposed to bodily motions initiated by the transfer of motion from other bodies). This means that for him all physical actions are movements$_I$. Where ψ is a movement$_I$, let us say that a ψ-movement$_I$ is the sort of movement$_I$ of his body that an agent brings about when he ψ-s. With this in mind, if we model a general account of forbearing on (9.5), we get:

(9.7)   If ψ is a bodily motion, A forbears ψ-ing if and only if: (i) A wills to not ψ in consequence of his so willing, (ii) A's willing is followed by the absence of a ψ-movement$_I$ of his body, and (iii) A's willing is the cause of that absence of a ψ-movement$_I$ of his body.[13]

[13] One might doubt whether negative states of affairs can be causal relata, as (9.7)(iii) requires. This is essentially the doubt raised earlier about whether we can make sense of episodes of volition "triggering" non-occurrences. If negative states of affairs cannot be causal relata, then it is a mistake to model a causal requirement for voluntary not-doing on a casual requirement for voluntary doing. As suggested earlier, this is a reason for favoring a deflationary account of negative actions.

Earlier we left hanging the question whether Locke was justified in supposing that the man's stay in the locked room was voluntary. I suggested that he
conceives of the man's willing to stay in the room as his willing to forbear
φ-ing, where 'φ' stands for the series of motions that would, if the door were
unlocked, constitute his standing up, opening the door, and walking out of
the room. Because the door is locked, the man is not free with respect to
φ-ing. It is not the case that if he willed to φ, he would φ. Does the man
in the locked room forbear φ-ing on the above account? Locke's description of the case ensures that (9.7)(i) and (9.7)(ii) will be satisfied when we
substitute 'φ' for 'ψ.' The matter comes down to whether the man's willing
to not-φ is the cause of there being no φ-movement$_1$ of his body. Since the
locked door ensures the non-occurrence of a φ-movement$_1$ of his body
however he wills, it does not seem right to say that his willing is the cause
of that non-occurrence. The non-occurrence of a φ-movement$_1$ in this case
is at best overdetermined. Thus it seems that the man in the locked room
fails as an example of necessary but voluntary action not (as Lowe had suggested) because the man's voluntary action fails to qualify as necessary, but
because what he does fails to qualify as a negative action.

It is not just that the above account of forbearing a physical action gives
us the wrong answer about the case of the man in the locked room. It
threatens to give us the wrong answer even if we are thinking about a man
who decides to remain in an *unlocked* room. The difficulty lies with condition (9.7)(iii) and its requirement of a causal connection between the agent's
volition and his not-doing. What sort of causal connection does (9.7)(iii)
require? If it requires that the agent's volition be a necessary condition of his
not-doing, it would in all likelihood never be satisfied, and we would have
an account of forbearing on which nobody ever forbears doing anything.
For even if the door to the room that a man occupies is unlocked, it will
almost always be true that it *could* have been locked. This will be enough to
ensure that the man's willing to refrain from opening the door is not a *necessary* condition of his body's not moving in just those the ways that would
be required to open an unlocked door. Because there are so many ways for
any event *not* to happen, it is hard to imagine a case in which an agent's
volition to not ψ would be a necessary condition of the non-occurrence of
a ψ-movement$_1$ of his body.

In response, we might observe that events singled out as causes are rarely
necessary conditions of the events they are supposed to cause. Indeed, as J.

L. Mackie has shown, typically the events that we pick out as causes are neither necessary nor sufficient for the events they are taken to cause (Mackie
1965). Mackie asks us to consider a scenario in which a short-circuit causes
a house fire. The short circuit by itself, independent of other conditions,
does not suffice for the house fire. Nor, presumably, is the occurrence of that
particular short circuit necessary for the occurrence of a fire at that time
and place. Mackie says that the short circuit is, though itself *insufficient* for
the house fire, a *necessary* (i.e., non-redundant) part of a state of affairs that
was itself *unnecessary* but *sufficient* for occurrence of the fire (Mackie 1965,
245). Though the short circuit is neither necessary nor sufficient for the
occurrence of a fire at that place and time, it is part of a prior condition that
actually sufficed to cause the fire, and a feature absent which that fire would
not have occurred. Mackie expresses this by saying that the short circuit is
an INUS condition of the house fire.

Shall we then read (9.7)(iii) as requiring that A's volition be an INUS
condition of the absence of a ψ-movement$_1$ in A's body? In that case, we
still get the result that the man in the locked room fails to count as forbearing the motions that would, if the world were to cooperate, constitute his
leaving the room. For his willing not to perform these actions is a *redundant*
part of the state of affairs that belongs to the causal sequence that results in
his body's not moving in the relevant ways. The state of the door is another
part of that state of affairs, and would have ensured the same result even if
the man had not willed as he did.

The bigger problem for Locke is that even if (9.7)(iii) requires only that
A's volition be an INUS condition of the absence of a ψ-movement$_1$ in his
body, we still get the result that there can be few if any cases of forbearing. Suppose that A stays voluntarily in an unlocked room. Is his volition
to forbear moving in the ways that would constitute his opening the door
and leaving—let us once again call it his volition to forbear φ-ing—an
INUS condition of his body's not moving$_1$ in those ways? The volitionist
will maintain that A's volition belongs to the actual causal sequence that
explains the absence of a φ-movement$_1$ of his body. However, for it to be
an INUS condition of the absence of a φ-movement$_1$ of his body, it has to
be a *necessary* part of the condition that actually suffices for the absence of
that movement$_1$. The way we test whether the volition is a necessary part
of that condition is to ask whether the result would still have occurred
absent the volition. But since there is no reason to think that A's *failure* to

will to forbear φ-ing would result in a φ-movement, of his body, his volition to forbear φ-ing seems not to be an INUS condition of the absence of a φ-movement, of his body. So it seems that (9.7)(iii) will rarely if ever be satisfied, and few if any cases of not-doing will qualify as forbearings. Since Locke holds that an agent acts freely only when he could have forborne, it follows that he can recognize few if any cases of free action if the above account of forbearing is his.

Is there a reading of Locke that avoids this result? Perhaps in framing his account of voluntary not-doing, we have modeled it too closely upon his conception of positive physical action. There may be a sort of halfway position between the deflationary view of negative action and the robust view of negative action. Locke does think of positive physical action as involving volitions directed at actions, and he does think of the volitions as *causing* the actions when the volitions are successful. He also does think of forbearing as involving volitions directed at not-doings. Yet perhaps he does not think of volitions to not-do as having to *cause* not-doings in order to be successful. Recall that at II.xxi.7 [1st] he says an action or forbearance is voluntary if it is consequent to a preference of the mind for it. We saw that this is open to three possible readings. The voluntariness of an action or forbearance could be a matter of its conforming with a prior volition, of its being caused by a prior volition, or both. Suppose that the first interpretation is what Locke has in mind. In that case, he will still hold that positive physical actions are bodily motions caused by volitions. Even if a bodily motion does not need to be caused by a volition to qualify as voluntary, it does need to be caused by a volition to qualify as a physical action. Yet Locke could say that an agent succeeds in voluntarily not-doing something so long as he wills not to do it and does not do it, no matter what is the cause of that not-doing. Thus he might adopt the following account of voluntarily forbearing bodily motion:

(9.8)   If ψ is a bodily motion, A forbears ψ-ing if and only if: (i) A wills to not ψ, *and* (ii) A's willing is followed by the absence of a ψ-movement, of his body.

If we applied this to the case of the man in the locked room, Locke would get the result that he wants. When the man wills to stay in the room he wills to forbear those motions that would, if the world were to cooperate, constitute his opening the door and exiting. Subsequently, his body does not engage in those motions. So on the account in (9.8), he voluntarily forbears those motions. At the same time, if he had willed to perform those motions the locked door would have kept him from performing some of them. So he is not free with respect to those motions. Having dropped the causal requirements, (9.6)(iii) and (9.7)(iii), Locke would also get the desired result in the case in which the man willingly stays in an unlocked room. Cases of voluntarily forbearing bodily motions would be easy to come by.

The trouble with this account of voluntary not-doing is that if a volition is supposed to be a mental episode directed at bringing about a targeted state of the mind or body, it is hard to understand why one would invoke volitions to explain forbearance once the causal requirement for forbearance is dropped. Why say that forbearing involves volition if successful forbearing need not involve the volition's *doing* anything? If volitions are conceived as episodes of trying to bring about some state of the body or mind, it does not seem that a volition could be said to succeed except by causally contributing to the realization of the targeted state. The reading of Locke as endorsing a halfway position on negative action fares much better if we suppose that he is thinking of volition as occurrent desire. For a desire to be satisfied, all that is required is that the desired state is realized. It does not matter whether it is realized as a result of its being desired. As we shall see, in the second edition of the *Essay* Locke abandons the idea that willing is wanting (§63). At that point, the suggestion that he endorses a halfway position on negative action no longer seems viable.

§61 *Freedom of the Will*

Locke believes that the sort of freedom that he has already demarcated—the sort an agent possesses with respect to a type of action when his performing or forbearing an act of that type depends upon his choice or preference—is all the freedom we have, all the freedom we need, and all the freedom we ought to want. "For," he asks, "how can we think any one freer than to have the power to do what he will?" He continues:

And so far as any one can (by preferring any Action to its not being; or Rest to any Action) produce that Action or Rest, so far can he do, what he will: For such a preferring of Action to its absence, is the willing of it: and we can scarce tell how to imagine any *Being* freer, than to be able to do what he will: So that in respect of Actions, within the reach of such a power in him, a Man seems as free, as 'tis possible for Freedom to make him. (II.xxi.21 [1st])

Yet Locke says that the motive of shifting off "all thoughts of guilt"—the motive of evading responsibility for some of our actions—leads some to say that "a Man is not free at all, if he be not as free to will, as he is to act, what he wills" (II.xxi.22 [1st]). He considers three questions under the rubric of "freedom of the will." The common thread running throughout his discussion of them is that the desiderata conceived under this heading involve one or another sort of confusion.

Locke first considers the question "*Whether Man's Will be free, or no*" (II. xxi.14 [1st]). Taking the question very much at face value, he rejects it as incoherent. Freedom, as he conceives it, is a trait possessed by agents, not the faculties of agents. To speak of the will as free or not is to make a category mistake. As Locke puts it, "it is as insignificant to ask, whether Man's Will be free, as to ask, whether his Sleep be Swift, or his Vertue square" (II.xxi.14 [1st]). To ask whether the will has freedom is to ask whether one power or ability has another power ability; in reality both are attributes that can be possessed only by substances that are agents (II.xxi.16 [1st]). Locke warns against the homunculization of mental faculties, and indeed against the homunculization of faculties generally. He suggests that it is the mistake of treating powers as though they are little agents that lies behind the widespread acceptance of pseudo-explanations in natural philosophy: digestion is "explained" as being carried out by the digestive faculty, and bodies as being moved by the motive faculty (II.xxi.20 [1st]).

Locke's second and third questions about freedom of the will both concern whether agents can be free in regard to performing acts of will. What prompts him to consider these questions is the suggestion that "a Man is not free at all, if he be not as free to will, as he is to act, what he wills" (II.xxi.22 [1st]). His second question is "*Whether a Man be free to will*" (II. xxi.22 [1st]). Locke's somewhat rambling argument for a "no" answer occupies II.xxi.23–24 [1st], and even spills over into II.xxi.25 [1st], but the core of it is as follows:

[*A*] *Man in respect of willing any Action in his power once proposed to his Thoughts, cannot be free.* The reason whereof is very manifest: for it being unavoidable that the Action depending on his Will, should exist, or not exist; and its existence, or not existence, following perfectly the determination, and preference of his Will, he cannot avoid willing the existence, or not existence, of that Action; it is absolutely necessary that he *will* the one, or the other, *i.e. prefer* the one to the other: since one of them must necessarily follow; and that which does follow, follows by the choice and determination of his Mind; that is, by his *willing* it: for if he did not *will* it, it would not be. So that in respect of the act of willing, a Man is not free ...(II.xxi.23 [1st])

Vere Chappell offers a reconstruction of this argument that I shall paraphrase as follows (Chappell 1994a, 105–6):

Each contemplated action must either exist or not exist. If it exists, this is because the agent wills it to exist. If it does not exist, then this is because the agent wills it not to exist. Either way, the agent wills. So an agent must will with regard to each contemplated action.

Chappell says that the argument is valid, but not sound. It falters on the false premise that if a contemplated action does not exist, this is because the agent has willed it not to exist. On Chappell's reading, Locke fails to appreciate that an action can fail to exist for reasons other than an agent's willing it not to exist.

If Chappell's reconstruction is correct, then Locke neglects the possibility that an action once contemplated might fail to occur because an agent is prevented by external circumstances or by another agent from performing it. Locke does seem to be neglecting that possibility when he declares that the "existence, or not existence" of an action follows "perfectly the determination, and preference" of an agent's will (II.xxi.23 [1st]). On Chappell's reading, Locke also neglects the possibility that an action might fail to exist because an agent puts off deciding whether or not to perform it. In this, Chappell sides with Leibniz's spokesman in the *New Essays*, who says this about II.xxi.23:

I should have thought that we can and very frequently do suspend choice, particularly when other thoughts break into our deliberations. So that, although the action about which we are deliberating must exist or not exist, it does not follow that we must necessarily *decide* on its existence or non-existence; for its non-existence may come about for want of a decision. This is how the Areopagites in effect acquitted a man whose case they had found too difficult to decide: they adjourned it to a date in the distant future, giving themselves a hundred years to think about it. (Leibniz 1981, 181)

As Chappell points out, the error that he and Leibniz accuse Locke of making is particularly unpardonable in light of the fact that most of II.xxi.23 [1st] is retained in the *Essay*'s later editions, which also contain Locke's own discussion of the importance of our ability to suspend decisions between alternate courses of action.

I think that there is a more charitable, and also a more plausible, reading of Locke's argument that we are not free to will. It will help to get clearer about precisely what question is being addressed. Locke is asking whether an agent who is considering whether or not to perform an action can be free with respect to willing. Suppose that A is deciding whether or not to ψ—that is, whether to ψ or to forbear ψ-ing. Both ψ-ing and forbearing ψ-ing would involve A's willing. Thus if A decides to do one or the other, A can be said to will on the question of whether to ψ. To will on the question of whether to ψ is, on Locke's view, to perform an action of a certain sort. Locke is asking whether *that* action is one in regard to which A can be free. Already this suggests another reading of his observation that the action of the man who has deliberated follows "perfectly the determination, and preference of his Will" (II.xxi.23 [1st]). If we take that remark to be about actions generally, then Locke is advancing the absurd view that we always do as we will—that nothing can prevent an agent from accomplishing what he wills to do. Yet if we take the remark in context, as concerning *the action of willing on the issue of whether or not to perform some particular action*, it makes much better sense. For it is plausible to say of *that* action that it must follow perfectly the determination and preference of the agent. External circumstances and other agents may keep me from ψ-ing, but they cannot keep me from willing to ψ, or from willing not to ψ.[14]

For Locke, the answer to the question of whether we can be free in regard to willing on the question of whether to ψ depends on what we get when we plug 'will on the question of whether to ψ' for 'φ' in his account of freedom. What we get when we make that substitution is:

(9.9)   An agent, A, is free with respect to willing on the question of whether to ψ if and only if: (i) If A were to will to will on the question of whether to ψ, A would will on the question of whether to ψ, *and* (ii) If A were to will not to will on the question of whether to ψ, then A would forbear willing on the question of whether to ψ.

---

[14] Thinking back to our earlier discussion of the impossibility of willing to do what one is absolutely convinced one cannot do under the circumstances, one might object that external circumstances or other agents could keep me from willing to ψ by so convincing me of the impossibility of successfully ψ-ing that I am rendered incapable of willing to ψ. In that case, however, it is not the external circumstances alone that are doing the work. It is in large part my own rationality and knowledge that keeps me from willing to ψ. For external circumstances or other agents to be fully responsible for preventing me from willing to ψ, they would also have to somehow be responsible for my rationality and good sense.

The question of whether a person can be free with regard to willing on whether to ψ is the question whether (9.9)(i) and (9.9)(ii) can both be satisfied. Locke in fact thinks that neither condition can be satisfied, but what he argues first and foremost is that (9.9)(ii) cannot be satisfied. He denies that we can forbear willing on a question once we have taken it up.

Shortly after the passage already quoted from II.xxi.23 [1st], Locke says:

> Nor is any Being, as far as I can comprehend Beings above me, capable of such a freedom of Will, that it can forbear to *Will*, {*i.e.* to preferr the being, or not being of} any thing in its power, which it has once considered as such.[15]

He repeats the point at II.xxi.24 [1st]. Of the "Actions in our power," he says:

> [T]hey being once proposed, the Mind has not a power to act, or not to act, wherein consists Liberty: It has not a power to forbear *willing*, it cannot avoid some determination concerning them, let the Consideration be as short, the Thought as quick as it will, it either leaves the Man in the state he was before thinking, or changes it: whereby it is manifest it prefers one to the other, and thereby either the continuation, or change becomes unavoidably voluntary.

On Locke's view, A cannot forbear willing on the question of whether to ψ once A considers whether or not to ψ. Thus he holds that (9.9)(ii) cannot be satisfied, and so that A cannot be free with regard to willing on the question of whether to ψ.

Why does Locke think that an agent cannot forbear willing on a choice once he is considering it? He does not say. Yet we can offer a plausible argument on his behalf, one that relies on a conception of volition that he should find congenial, and one that I suspect reflects what he actually had in mind. The basic idea this: if one decides not to will on whether to ψ, this is in effect to will not to ψ. As a sort of loosening-up exercise, consider Leibniz's remark about the Areopagites.[16] Leibniz offers the story as an example of agents forbearing to will on a question, but the example plays right into Locke's hands. Do we really want to say that the Areopagites did not decide the man's case? Even Leibniz concedes that "in effect" they acquitted him. At least sometimes, deciding not to decide whether to do something is deciding not to do it. Deciding to postpone for a hundred

---

[15] Locke's text does not include the curvy brackets. I have inserted them to indicate which portion of the sentence I take to be an aside giving us an explication of what it means "to *Will*."

[16] The Areopagus was an ancient Athenian judicial council.

years the decision about whether to punish a man *is* deciding not to punish him. I suggest that Locke goes further, holding that *every* case in which an agent postpones a decision about whether to ψ is a case in which the agent wills not to ψ.

One could argue for that position as follows. To postpone the decision of whether to ψ is to will not to ψ now, while also resolving to consider again at some future time the question of whether to ψ. If postponing the decision of whether to ψ entails willing not to ψ now, then it does not involve forbearing to will on the question of whether to ψ. It will naturally be objected that we need to distinguish between forbearing to will on the question of whether to ψ now, and forbearing to will on the question of whether to ψ sometime. It may be that postponing the decision about whether to ψ sometime involves willing not to ψ now, but this is consistent with forbearing to will on whether or not to ψ sometime. Thus whether to ψ sometime would at least seem to be a question in regard to which it is possible to forbear willing. Against this objection, Locke's position can be defended by denying that it is possible to will on the question of whether to ψ sometime except by willing to ψ *now*. Locke's view that it is impossible to forbear willing with regard to an action under consideration makes good sense if he holds the independently plausible view that all volitions are volitions to do (or not to do) something *now*.

Earlier we briefly considered Carl Ginet's view of volition. According to Ginet, the contents of volition are narrowly circumscribed not only spatially, but temporally. He takes all volitions involved in physical action to be directed toward exertions of one's body in the immediate present. On his view, the act of walking across a room involves a continuous series of willings to exert the muscles in one's lower body in what are for most of us thoroughly familiar ways. Ginet's account is one incarnation of a view that ought to have considerable appeal to most volitionists. This is the view that all volitions are volitions to do something *now*. Ginet says that volitions do not plan ahead even slightly. Another version of the thesis might allow for volitions that do plan ahead. One might grant that the objects of volition can extend beyond the immediate present, so long as they include the immediate present and extend forward without temporal discontinuities. Thus one might hold that one can now, all at one go, will to perform an action that will take some time to complete, while insisting that what one wills is necessarily to begin performing that action now.[17]

To one thinking of willing as wanting, the thesis that all willing is willing to begin doing something now will have little appeal. It seems perfectly possible to have a current desire to eat chocolate cake at tomorrow's birthday party. Yet if one is thinking of willing an action as promoting it, helping to realize it, *trying to do it*, then there is good reason to say that all willing is willing to begin doing something now. For although one can now decide, plan, or intend to do something later, one cannot now try to do something later. One can now try to do something that one hopes or intends will have certain later effects; but that is not the same as now trying to *do* something later. One cannot now exert oneself to bring about some considerably later event, except by now exerting oneself to bring about a contemporaneous event that one expects will have the desired later effect. This is still to will to begin doing something now.

If Locke does suppose that all willing is willing to begin doing something now, then he has good reason to deny that one can forbear willing on a question once it has been taken up. To take up a question is to reflect on whether to ψ or not to ψ. One can now decide to ψ later, but one cannot now *will* to ψ later. If one decides to ψ later, one wills not to ψ now, while planning to ψ later. In that case, one wills on the only question about ψ-ing that one *could* will on now—namely, whether to ψ now. If one postpones deciding whether to ψ or not to ψ, one decides not to ψ now, and resolves to consider ψ-ing again some time in the future. Again, one wills on the only question about ψ-ing that one could possibly will on now. Since one cannot forbear an action that one could not have performed, one cannot forbear willing on the question of whether to ψ except by forbearing to will on the question of whether to ψ now. Yet one cannot forbear willing on the question of whether to ψ now by deciding to postpone the decision of whether to ψ. Hence one cannot forbear willing on the question of whether to ψ. If Locke holds that all volitions are volitions to begin doing something now, this justifies his denial that we can forbear willing on whether or not to perform an action once we have taken the matter under

---

[17] A consideration favoring Ginet's version is that it does not saddle us with questions about what finite number of volitions one performed in a finite period of time. As W. F. R. Hardie observes, "We have no conventions which would enable us to count our volitions and to say how many there were between breakfast and lunch" (Hardie 1971, 194). Hardie adds, "This is not, of course, a decisive objection to 'volitions': the question how many actions we performed in the same period is similarly unanswerable."

consideration. That in turn justifies his view that willing on the matter of whether to perform an action is not itself an action in regard to which we can be free.

Locke has another reason for thinking that neither (9.9)(i) nor (9.9)(ii) can be satisfied, and so that one cannot freely will on whether to ψ. Both (9.9)(i) and (9.9)(ii) require that agents will to will something, and Locke thinks that this is incoherent. This is also his reason for giving a "no" answer to the third question he considers under the heading of freedom of the will: "*Whether a Man be at liberty to will which of the two he pleases, Motion or Rest*" (II.xxi.25 [1st]). This question, Locke says, "carries the absurdity of it so manifestly in it self, that one might thereby sufficiently be convinced, that Liberty concerns not the Will in any case." He justifies that verdict as follows:

For to ask, whether a man be at liberty to will either Motion, or Rest; Speaking, or Silence; which he pleases, is to ask, whether a Man can will, what he wills; or be pleased with what he is pleased with. A Question which, I think, needs no answer.

A puzzling aspect of this passage is Locke's handling of the idea that willing an action is being pleased with it. He suggests that (i) willing to will is equivalent to (ii) being pleased with what one is pleased with. Yet there is a problem about the syntax of (ii), and about what the threatened absurdity is supposed to be. In (i) we have an act of will with another act of will as its object. This is something that a volitionist might have reason to challenge, if volition is conceived as trying or exerting to perform an action. On the other hand, there are two possible readings of (ii), and neither seems to involve an absurdity. On one reading, the claim that one is pleased with what one is pleased with is simply redundant. If am pleased with the book I have just purchased, then that is what I am pleased with and I am pleased with it. There is nothing absurd about that, and this does not involve one episode of being pleased with something taking another as its object. To preserve the syntactical parallel, we could take (ii) to mean (iii) being pleased *that* one is pleased with what one is pleased with. In that case, one episode of being pleased with something does take another as its object, but there still seems no threat of absurdity. For it seems I might not only take pleasure in the book I have just purchased, but also experience a pleasing sense of superiority at being the sort of person who gets pleasure from buying a book rather than drugs, video games, or lottery tickets.

Whatever Locke thinks about being pleased with what one is pleased with, he evidently thinks that the prospect of willing what one wills is absurd. This is well motivated if he is thinking of volition as a kind of mental exertion directed at bringing about some state of one's body or mind. We understand the claim that an agent *wants* to try raising his arm, or *intends* to try raising his arm, and these are clearly distinct from the claim that he tries to raise his arm. Yet it does not seem that we can make sense of the claim that an agent *tries* to try raising his arm. The sort of mental act that we might be inclined to describe as trying to try to raise one's arm is just the act of trying to raise one's arm, undertaken with an air of tentativeness or an expectation of failure. Nor does it make sense to speak of mentally exerting oneself to mentally exert oneself to raise one's arm. One could perhaps mentally exert oneself to do something in order to increase the likelihood that one would then mentally exert oneself to raise one's arm. In that case, the second mental exertion is not the target of the first mental exertion, but a hoped-for consequence of the target of the first mental exertion.[18] This is especially clear if we suppose that all volitions are volitions to begin doing something *now*, since in the case just described the second mental exertion need not begin immediately after the first.

If it is impossible to forbear willing, then an agent cannot be free in regard to willing. By the same token, if willing to will is impossible, then an agent cannot be free in regard to willing. Locke concludes that free willing cannot be a requirement for an agent's being free. Yet at II.xxi.23 [1st], in the midst of his argument that one cannot forbear willing, he raises another difficulty for those who think that a man is not free unless his acts of will are free. He says:

So that to make a Man free in this sense, there must be another antecedent *Will*, to determine the Acts of this *Will*, and another to determine that, and so *in infinitum*: for where-ever one stops, the Actions of the last Will cannot be free ...

---

[18] Suppose that a call has been issued for volunteers to go on a dangerous mission. One could mentally exert oneself to undertake certain reflections, in hopes of increasing the likelihood that one will have the courage to mentally exert oneself to raise one's hand to volunteer. One might exert oneself to reflect on the importance of the mission's success, or on the unpleasantness of going through life thinking of oneself as a coward. Yet if one undertook the process of reflection and ultimately did not volunteer for the mission, it would be wrong to say that one had not done as one willed when one willed to undertake the process of reflection. One might not have done as one wished, in that one did have a (relatively weak) desire to volunteer, and this went unsatisfied. One might also have other desires that went unsatisfied, such as the second-order desire that one's desire to volunteer overwhelm one's fear. But the mental exertion to engage in a certain thought process was not fruitless.

He returns mid-sentence to the point about the impossibility of forbearing to will. Yet in this brief interlude he raises a worry that he can take to be relevant only if, *per impossibile*, acts of will could be free. The worry is that if a man's being free required that his acts of will be free, this would precipitate an infinite regress. The argument appears again at II.xxi.25 [1st]. There, as we have just seen, Locke claims that the question of whether one can will what one wills is absurd and "needs no answer." Having said this, however, he goes on to say that those who can "make a Question" of whether a Man can will what he wills "must suppose one Will to determine the Acts of another, and another to determine that; and so on *in infinitum*, an absurdity before taken notice of."

In both passages, Locke suggests that the infinite series that his opponent finds himself saddled with is a series of wills—a series of mental faculties. He seems to be offering the following *reductio*. Suppose that one is a volitionist who holds:

> (9.10)   A acts freely only if A's action is produced by the free exercise of a will.

In that case, one must say that A freely raises his hand only if the rising of A's hand is produced by the free exercise of a will. The exercise of that will—call that episode "w1"—is itself an action. Principle (9.10) tells us that it is a *free* action only if it is produced by the free exercise of a will. Call the will whose exercise results in the free exercise of w1 "w2." Principle (9.10) tells us that the exercise of w2 will be free only if it is produced by the free exercise of a will, "w3." And so on. Yet it is absurd to suppose an endless series of wills exercising freely. Hence, we should reject (9.10). As Chappell points out, the problem with this argument is that (9.10) commits the volitionist to a multiplicity of wills only if a will cannot determine itself to will (Chappell 1994a, 111–12). For if w2 and w3 are the same will as w1, then (9.10) does not generate an endless series of wills. Moreover, those of Locke's contemporaries who accepted (9.10) and who might be presumed to be the targets of his argument did hold that the will determines itself to will (Chappell 1994a, 112).

It is striking the extent to which Locke's half-sentence *reductios* at II.xxi.23 [1st] and II.xxi.25 [1st] depend upon just the sort homunculizing of mental faculties that he complains of elsewhere in the chapter. If one were to recast the argument in such a way as to make it clear that it is *agents*, not wills (which are powers of agents) that perform acts of will, it should be quite obvious that the philosopher who thinks that freedom requires free willing is not committed to an endless series of distinct mental faculties. At the same time, recasting the argument in this way yields a stronger challenge to the view that agents are free only when they will freely.

The problem with the requirement that acts of will be free is not that it threatens to generate an endless series of mental *faculties*, but that it threatens to generate an endless series of mental *acts*. Consider a volitionist who holds the following:

> (9.11)   A acts freely only when A's action issues from an act of will that is itself free.

Our volitionist will say that A freely raises his arm only if A's arm rises as a consequence of A's volition to raise his arm, and only if that volition—call it "v_1"—is itself a free act. Since (9.11) is a doctrine about what it is for any act to be free, and since it presupposes that volitions are acts, the volitionist committed to (9.11) must say that for v_1 to be a free act, it too must issue from a volition that is itself a free act. Call the volition from which v_1 issues "v_2." Notice that whereas v_1 is a volition to raise an arm, v_2 is a volition to will to raise an arm. It should be obvious that our volitionist must say that v_2 is a free act only if it issues from another volition, v_3, and so on *ad infinitum*. Furthermore, our volitonist must say that is a necessary condition of A's arm raising being free that v_1 is free; that it is a necessary condition of v_1 being free that v_2 is free; and so on *ad infinitum*. Thus our volitionist can say that A's arm-raising is free only if there is an infinite series of volitions ending at A's volition to raise his arm and stretching backwards. It is absurd to suppose that each time an agent freely raises his arm he produces an infinite succession of volitions, and so it seems the volitionist must reject (9.11).

This argument is Lockean in spirit if not in fact. Like the argument that Locke actually offers, its conclusion is that the view that agents act freely only when their acts are produced by free acts of will leads to an infinite regress. Unlike the argument that Locke actually offers, this one does not violate his proscription against homunculizing the will, and it does pose a problem even for those who hold that the will can determine itself. It would be too much to say that this argument refutes the view that free physical actions must be produced by free acts of will. What it does show is that it is untenable to hold that *all* free acts must be the products of free acts of will. One who wants to defend the view that a free physical action must be produced by a free act of will cannot give the same account of what it is for a physical act to be free and what it is for an act of will to be free. One cannot say that every act must be produced by a free act of will in order to be a free act.

§62 *Motivation and Preference*

In a chapter entitled "Of Modes of Pleasure and Pain," Locke says this about good and evil:

> Things then are good or evil, only in reference to Pleasure or Pain; That we call *Good*, which is apt to cause or increase Pleasure, or diminish Pain in us; or else to procure, or preserve us the possession of any other Good, or absence of any Evil. (II.xx.2 [1st]).

Here we have a hedonistic theory of goodness: for something to be good is for it to cause pleasure or to lessen pain. This is a view that Locke presumes, not one for which he argues (despite the second word in the quoted sentence, which suggests otherwise).

Locke also holds a hedonistic account of human motivation. For he not only identifies goodness with pleasure, but says that each person always wills to do that which seems to him likeliest to produce more good. Initially he puts this by saying that "*the greater Good is that alone which determines the Will*" (II.xxi.29 [1st]). Though he repeats this formulation (II.xxi.35, 36 [1st]), it is misleading. For as he makes abundantly clear, his view is not that the greater good *per se* determines the will, but that the *appearance* of greater good does. At II.xxi.33 [1st], he says that "the preference of the Mind [is] always determined by the appearance of Good, greater Good." At II.xxi.37 [1st], he says:

> [T]hat which has the *Preference*, and makes us will the doing or omitting any Action in our Power, is the *greater Good*, appearing to result from that choice in all its Consequences, as far as at present they are represented to our view.

This passage spills over into the succeeding section, where he says that "*that which determines the choice* of the Will…*is still Good, the greater Good*: But it is also only Good *that appears*." Finally, at II.xxi.39 [1st] (which due to a misprint in the first edition is labeled as a second "II.xxi.36"), he says that men "always prefer the greater apparent Good."

So what explains why A wills to ψ rather than to forbear ψ-ing? In the first edition, Locke holds that the correct answer is always this: it appeared to A at the time that ψ-ing was better than not ψ-ing. The sense of 'appeared' here is cognitive rather than perceptual. A wills to ψ because A judges or believes that at that time ψ-ing is better than not ψ-ing. The view that Locke is endorsing is both hedonistic and intellectualist. It is hedonistic because the good is identified with pleasure, and pleasure is said to be the ultimate object of all human action. It is intellectualist because it says that whenever a man wills to do the wrong thing—whenever he wills to ψ and not doing so would actually be better—this is because of an error in calculation on his part, not a deficiency of virtue or willpower.

Locke's theory of motivation is also egoistic. For what he means is that each man wills to ψ when ψ-ing appears to him more apt to increase *his* pleasure than not ψ-ing does.[19] As A. P. Brogan observes, "The egoistic or selfish theory is taken so much for granted by Locke that one must search his sentences to find a clear statement of it" (Brogan 1959, 80). Perhaps the only such general statement in the *Essay*'s first edition is this one, which at least could not be clearer:

For since I lay it for a certain ground, that every intelligent Being really seeks Happiness, and would enjoy all the pleasures he could, and suffer no pain; 'tis impossible any one should willingly put into his own draught any bitter Ingredient, or leave out anything in his Power, that could add to its sweetness, but only by a wrong Judgment. (II.xxi.40 [1st])[20]

Locke's commitment to psychological egoism also occasionally burbles up to the surface when it is not the main topic. Consider, for example, his

---

[19] Of course, we are rarely if ever faced with the isolated choice about whether or not to perform a single action—whether to ψ or to forbear ψ-ing. To perform one action at a time is to rule out performing indefinitely many other possible actions then. For the prospect of ψ-ing to seem more apt to produce pleasure in one than the prospect of not ψ-ing, the prospect of ψ-ing has got to seem more apt to produce pleasure in one than the prospect of doing the other things one considers doing if one does not ψ then.

[20] Locke's general commitment to egoism is also evident in this passage from "Of Ethics in General," a manuscript which according to von Leyden dates from Locke's stay in Holland in the 1680s (Locke 1954, 69), and which was printed in King's *Life*:

"And an understanding free agent naturally follows that which causes pleasure to it and flies that which causes pain; *i.e.* naturally seeks happiness and shuns misery. That, then, which causes to any one pleasure, that is good to him; and that which causes him pain, is bad to him...[N]othing can be good or bad to any one but as it tends to their happiness or misery, as it serves to produce in them pleasure or pain: for good and bad, being relative terms, do not denote any thing in the nature of the thing, but only the relation it bears to another, in its aptness and tendency to produce in it pleasure or pain..."(King 1830, 122–3) justification for thinking that we cannot make mistakes about present good or evil:

> For the Pain or Pleasure being just so great, and no greater, than it is felt, the present Good or Evil is really so much as it appears. And therefore were every Action of ours concluded within it self, and drew no Consequences after it, we should undoubtedly always will nothing but Good; always infallibly prefer the best. (II.xxi.37 [1st])[21]

Locke thinks that each individual is an unchallengeable authority on what he currently finds pleasant and unpleasant. He infers from this that if actions did not have later consequences, we would infallibly choose the good. Only to one who accepts an egoistic form of hedonism does that look like a legitimate inference.

Locke's commitment to egoism is also evident in his reply to the objection that the diversity of intentional human behavior renders it improbable that everyone always pursues pleasure. He says:

> Were all the Concerns of Man terminated in this Life; why one pursued Study and Knowledge, and another Hawking and Hunting; why one chose Luxury and Debauchery, and another Sobriety and Riches, would not be, because every one of these did not pursue his own Happiness; but because their Happiness lay in different things … (II.xxi.34 [1st])

Each man pursues *his own* happiness, Locke holds, but different things make different men happy.

Locke does at one point try to argue for his view that the will is determined by the greater apparent good. He says that it follows from what he has established about the nature of volition:

> [T]he Will, or Preference, is determined by something without it self: Let us see then what it is determined by. If willing be but the being better pleased, as has been shewn, it is easie to know what 'tis determines the Will, what 'tis pleases best: every one knows 'tis Happiness, or that which makes any part of Happiness, or contributes to it; and that is it we call *Good*. (II.xxi.29 [1st])

---

[21] Chappell claims that this passage tempers Locke's intellectualism. When the will is determined by thoughts of the future, bad choices are always the result of cognitive errors on the part of the agent. Yet, Chappell says: "The situation is different for choices prompted solely by present pleasure and pain. Here the agent's will may be determined directly by what he is feeling, so that no judgment or prediction or hope or intellectual activity of any other kind need be involved" (Chappell 1994b, 202). I see no grounds for ascribing to Locke the idea that present pleasures and pains ever determine the will. As I suggest below, the sense of 'determine' that he has in mind throughout II.xxi in the first edition is teleological. What "determines" the will in this sense must necessarily be a prospective action—something in the future. Thus I see his first edition account as thoroughly intellectualist.

Here Locke is again thinking of willing an action as being more pleased with it. Since willing to ψ is being more pleased at the prospect of ψ-ing, he reasons, no agent wills to ψ when he finds the prospect of not ψ-ing more pleasing. Cases one might have been apt to describe that way are not to be taken at face value. If A does something unpleasant out of a sense of duty, it must be that he finds the prospect of failing to do his duty even more unpleasant. Locke also assumes that if A finds the prospect of ψ-ing more pleasing than the prospect of not ψ-ing, this entails, or is equivalent to, A judging that ψ-ing will yield more pleasure *for A* than not ψ-ing would. Again, apparent counterexamples must be explained away. What about the parent who labors at a dreary job so that her children will have a better life? Locke must say that she has judged that her life of drudgery is likelier to contain more pleasure *for her* than a life in which she lives with the knowledge that she failed to do all she could to improve the lives of her children.

Here we have an argument that is supposed to take us from his theory of volition to an egoistic, hedonistic account of human motivation. The trouble is that the argument seems unlikely to convince anyone who does not already accept egoistic hedonism. In fact, absent some independent support for egoistic hedonism, it could be viewed as a *reductio* of the idea that willing an action is being better pleased with it. For it is antecedently quite plausible that the motive of duty can lead an agent to sacrifice his own pleasure; or that a parent can value her children's happiness more than her own. Perhaps these are intuitions that can be dislodged, but Locke has done nothing to dislodge them. Despite the claim to have previously "shewn" that willing is being better pleased with an action, Locke has done little to motivate the conception of volition that here serves as the starting point. We find ourselves asking why Locke finds it natural and appealing to think of volition in this way.

Locke invites the reader to deduce an egoistic, hedonistic theory of motivation from his conception of volition as occurrent wanting. It seems more plausible that in *his* case the explanation really runs in the other direction. It is Locke's commitment to egoistic hedonism that explains why he finds that conception of volition attractive in the first place. For one who assumes egoistic hedonism will hold that the actions that A *wills* necessarily coincide with the ones that A judges to be most likely to produce pleasure in A. By the same token, one who assumes egoistic hedonism will say that the actions that seem to A likeliest to cause A pleasure are of necessity the ones whose prospect will be most pleasing to A. To one who believes that the actions that A wills necessarily coincide with those whose prospect is most pleasing to A, it will be very tempting to simply *identify* A's willing an action with his being pleased at the prospect of it.

Locke identifies the good with pleasure, and says that each person always chooses to do that which seems to him at the time likeliest to bring him the most pleasure. He also holds that the actions that best serve an agent's interest are those that are the best morally. However, this does not mean that he would have us act like desperados in a Hobbesian state of nature. For an all-powerful God demands certain behavior of us, rewards with the bliss of heaven those who comply, and punishes with eternal torment those who do not. This bliss and that torment more than outweigh whatever short-term gains or losses accrue from disobeying God's laws during the course of our natural lives:

To him, I say, who hath a prospect of the different State of perfect Happiness, or Misery that attends all Men after this Life, depending on their Behaviour here, the measures of Good and Evil, that govern his choice, are mightily changed. For since nothing of Pleasure and Pain in this Life, can bear any proportion to endless Happiness, or exquisite Misery of an immortal Soul hereafter, Actions in his Power will have their preference, not according to the transient Pleasure, or Pain that accompanies, or follows them here; but as they serve to secure that perfect durable Happiness hereafter. (II.xxi.38 [1st])

Unfortunately, we do not always keep in mind the prospects of a life hereafter, and so are prone to making mistakes about what serves both our own long-term interests, and the interests of morality.

Locke thinks that we are susceptible to several different sorts of error when thinking about what actions will bring us the most pleasure. One is a kind of temporal foreshortening: present pains and pleasures loom larger than those in the distance, and we tend to weigh them disproportionately (II.xxi.41 [1st]). Another is that due to the "*weak and narrow Constitutions of our Minds,*" present pleasure and pain absorb our attention, making it difficult to think of anything else (II.xxi.42 [1st]). We are usually able to enjoy only one pleasure at a time, and lose sight of all pleasure when experiencing pain. "A little bitter mingled in our Cup, leaves no relish of the sweet," he says. We are also prone to making mistakes about the consequences of our actions, and the effects these will have on our future pleasures and pains

(II.xxi.43 [1st]). We frequently make these errors as the result of culpable ignorance and inadvertency: we fail to learn all we could about the likely consequences of our actions, and we overlook what we do know about them (II.xxi.44 [1st]). We are more prone to the latter sort of mistake when our "feeble passionate Nature" is in the grips of some current pleasure. Fortunately, "To check this Precipitancy, our Understanding and Reason was given us, if we will make a right use of it, to search, and see, and then judge thereupon" (II.xxi.44 [1st]).

Locke frames his account of motivation by asking what it is that *determines* the will. There are different senses in which we might speak of an agent as being determined to will as he does. To the modern reader, the claim that A is determined to will as he does is most naturally construed as a claim about the efficient cause of A's willing as he does. It is likely to be taken as the claim that if A wills to ψ, there was a prior state of the world that, together with the laws of nature, entails that A wills to ψ then. Locke's answer to the question of what determines the will suggests that this is not how he is understanding the question. What determines the will, on his view, is the appearance of greater good. By this he means that an agent wills to do that which appears likeliest to maximize his pleasure. What is doing the "determining" here is an anticipated feature of *prospective* actions—actions that have yet to occur when the will is determined. The determination of the will that Locke has in mind is thus a pull rather than a push. He is using 'determines' in a teleological sense, rather than a causal one. For an agent's will to be determined in this sense is for the contents of his volitions to be co-variant with the apparent goodness of available courses of action.[22]

This is not to deny that Locke believes that agents are causally determined to will as they do. Nor is it to say that he does believe that agents are causally determined to will as they do. The question of whether the behavior of agents is governed by deterministic causal laws is one that he does not take up. Whether his teleological determinism commits him to causal determinism depends on the contested question of how the teleological explanation of an action relates to the causal explanation of it. That too is a question that he does not take up. He does not even explicitly distinguish

---

[22] Yaffe makes this observation, saying that agents who track the good with their representations have their volitions "determined" by the good in a sense that must be non-causal since "no event or state can cause an event that precedes it in time" (Yaffe 2000, 35). Surprisingly, he then goes on to claim that in the first edition "Locke is insistent that our choices are causally determined by what appears to us to be good" (Yaffe 2000, 36).

the pull of teleological determination from the push of causal determination, and he sometimes moves from one to the other in a way that suggests no great sensitivity to the difference between them. At II.xxi.30 [1st]—a passage quoted below—he discusses the "determination" of volitions by features of prospective actions, but in the same sentence speaks of the will as "determining" something. When he speaks of the will as determining, he seems to have in mind an act of will determining an action or forbearance. That "determination" is causal: the act of will precedes and causes an action or forbearance.

Locke endorses a sort of compatibilism, but given the sort of "determination" that he is chiefly concerned with, it is not the same doctrine that usually goes by that name today. He says:

But though the preference of the Mind be always determined by the appearance of Good, greater Good; yet the Person who has the Power, in which alone consists liberty to act, or not to act according to such preference, is nevertheless free, such determination abridges not that Power. He that has his Chains knocked off, and the Prison-doors set open to him, is perfectly at liberty, because he may either go or stay, as he best likes; though his preference be determined to stay by the darkness of the Night, or the illness of the Weather, or want of other Lodging. (II.xxi.33 [1st])

Locke means that an agent can be free despite the fact that his actions are always aimed at doing what seems to him likeliest to bring him the most pleasure. An agent can be free despite the fact that he acts for reasons, with his choices "determined" by what seems to advance his goals. He does not mean that an agent can be free despite the fact that his choosing is governed by deterministic causal laws. That being said, his account of freedom certainly seems to be compatibilist in that sense too. For on his view, an agent is free if he acts as he wills, and if he would have refrained from doing so had he willed to refrain. An agent whose acts are causally determined can satisfy those requirements.

In the following rather tortuous passage, Locke argues that the fact that we always choose what seems to us the best is no threat to the sort of freedom we value:

A perfect Indifferency in the Will, or Power of Preferring, not determinable by the Good or Evil, that is thought to attend its Choice, would be so far from being an advantage and excellency of any intellectual Nature, that it would be as great an imperfection, as the want of Indifferency to act, or not to act, till determined by the Will, would be an imperfection on the other side. A Man is at liberty to lift up his Hand to his Head, or to let it rest quiet: He is perfectly indifferent to either; and it would be an imperfection in him, if he wanted that Power, if he were deprived of that Indifferency. But it would be as great an imperfection, if he had the same Indifferency, whether he would prefer the lifting up his Hand, or its remaining in rest, when it would save his Head or Eyes from a blow he sees coming…(II.xxi.30 [1st])

Here we are being invited to consider a person whose choices about whether or not to perform an action are completely independent of which of these options appears better or worse to him. The "Indifferency of the Will" possessed by such a creature is not what we want. Locke compares this "Indifferency of the Will" with the "Indifferency to act" that characterizes a person before he wills. The latter indifferency he calls a "Power." It is the power to do either of two things: to perform an action, or to forbear from performing it. When we lack this (as the paralyzed person does with respect to walking and the man in the locked room does with respect to leaving), we lack something of value that detracts from our freedom. Locke's point is that *having* "Indifferency of the Will" would be as much an imperfection as *lacking* an "Indifferency to act" is. One whose choices about what to try to do were independent of what seemed to him better or worse might have every reason to raise his hand—to ward off a blow, for instance—and yet find himself willing not to. Such a creature would not be more free than we are. The actions of such a creature would not tend to be those that promoted its interests.

As Locke points out, there is a category of actual creatures whose actions do not promote their interests, and we do not envy them:

Would any one be a Changeling, because he is less determined, by wise Considerations, than a wise Man? Is it worth the Name of Freedom to be at liberty to play the Fool, and draw Shame and Misery upon a Man's self? If want of restraint to chuse, or to do the worse, be Liberty, true Liberty, mad Men and Fools are the only Free-men: (II.xxi.32 [1st])

Locke also argues that a view on which freedom required the ability to will the apparently worse option would face grave theological difficulties. Speaking of God and the angels, he says that "we shall have reason to judge they are more steadily *determined in their choice of Good* than we: and yet

we have no reason to think they are less happy, or less free, than we are"
(II.xxi.31 [1st]). Presumably he means not that "Superior Beings" choose to
do what seems to them the best more often than we do (since we *always* do
that), but that they succeed in choosing the best more steadily than we do. It
is a certainty that when God chooses, He chooses both what seems to Him
the best and what *is* the best. Yet we do not want to say that He is therefore
unfree.

10

Agency: The Revised Account

§63. In the second and later editions of the Essay, Locke drops the suggestion that willing is wanting, and offers a single account of willing as commanding or ordering a performance. He also places greater emphasis on his insight that the objects of volition are more narrowly circumscribed than the objects of desire. He retains his robust account of negative action as involving volitions directed at not doings. §64. Between the first and second editions of the Essay, Locke undergoes a major shift in his thinking about motivation. He comes to hold that we are motivated not by the prospect of future good, but by present uneasiness. He continues to take for granted hedonism and psychological egoism. §65. In the second edition of the Essay, Locke hints that it was his catching a "scarce observable slip" in the first edition that precipitated his change of heart about motivation. Catching that slip involved him getting clearer about desire and volition having different scopes. This led him to reject the conception of willing as wanting, which in turn deprived him of his reason for thinking that one always wills that which promises to bring one the most pleasure. §66. In the second and later editions of the Essay, Locke says that we can suspend the prosecution of our desires. He intends this as a commonplace observation, not an esoteric theoretical claim. It has been suggested that he means to revise his account of freedom, to qualify his new account of motivation, and to contradict his earlier claim that we cannot forbear willing on an action once it is proposed. There are reasons to resist all of these suggestions. §67. Some read Locke's remarks about suspension as evidence that he is a libertarian incompatibilist, but in fact it is unclear what he thinks of determinism. Some passages in Locke's correspondence do suggest a lean toward incompatibilism, but these are inconclusive. §68. In the second and later editions of the Essay, Locke says that the ability to suspend the prosecution of our desires is the source of all liberty, and yet he continues to offer his original account of freedom. The best explanation is that he takes the ability to suspend the prosecution of our desires to be a prerequisite for fully fledged agency. §69. Locke's 1701

correspondence with van Limborch shows that he continues to hold that volition always follows a judgment about what it is best to do. §70. In the fifth edition, Locke adds several passages that (again) seem to indicate that he changed mind about whether it is possible to forbear willing on a proposed course of action. Evidence from the correspondence with van Limborch shows conclusively that he did not.

§63 Rethinking Volition

On September 20, 1692, Locke wrote to William Molyneux about his plans for a second edition of the *Essay* (*Corresp.*, 4, #1538, 523). He asked Molyneux to indicate any "superfluous" passages that might be left out of the new edition. He also asked Molyneux to call his attention to anything he took to be mistaken in the first edition account. Molyneux did not propose any cuts, but he did offer a few suggestions, including these:

The Next place I take Notice off [*sic*] as requiring some Farther Explication is Your Discourse about Mans Liberty and Necessity. this Thread seems so wonderfully fine spun in your Book, that at last the Great Question of Liberty and Necessity seems to Vanish. and herein you seem to make all Sins to proceed from our Understandings, or to be against Conscience; and not at all from the Depravity of our Wills. Now it seems harsh to say, that a Man shall be Damn'd, because he understands no better than he does. (*Corresp.*, 4, #1579)

Locke's response is gracious. "I do not wonder to find you think my discourse about liberty a little too fine spun," he says, "I had so much that thought of it myself, that I said the same thing of it to some of my friends before it was printed."[1] Spurred by Molyneux's criticism, Locke revised II.xxi heavily for the second edition, lengthening it considerably, but also changing his mind about some important matters.

---

[1] Yaffe misunderstands Molyneux's complaint—and Locke's concession—that Locke's first edition account of agency was "too fine spun." He says that "Molyneux's challenge suggests…that Locke needs to say something more nuanced about a large class of actions and agents than he said in the first edition" (Yaffe 2000, 42). He takes the point of the metaphor to be that "a fabric made from thread spun too finely lacks richness of texture." Really, the point is just the opposite. Used figuratively, the expression 'fine-spun' means "Elaborated to flimsiness, excessively subtle or refined" (*Oxford English Dictionary*). The complaint is not that Locke needs to make more, or more nuanced, distinctions, but that his account is already too nuanced. However, it cannot be said that the account he offered in later editions was any less fine-spun.

The first edition of the *Essay* contains two conceptions of volition, and Locke shows no sign there of appreciating that they are different and incompatible. Each can be put by saying that willing is a matter of "preferring" an action, but that is because 'preferring' can have different senses. On the one hand, Locke thinks of having a volition as a matter of being pleased with a prospective action. I have suggested that he is led to think of volition in this way because he presumes an egoistic form of hedonism. He presumes that the action that appears to an agent most likely to maximize his pleasure is always the one that pleases him more, and always the one that he wills to perform. From this it is a short slide to saying that an agent's willing an action just *is* his being more pleased with it. On the other hand, Locke also says that willing is itself a kind of action. In seventeenth-century usage, to "prefer" something could mean to promote it or to assist in bringing it about. Locke thinks of willing as a mental activity that makes a thought or bodily motion happen. He distinguishes volition from desire, saying that desires are "referred to things remote; whereas Volition, or the Act of Willing, signifies nothing properly, but the actual producing of something that is voluntary" (II.xxi.33 [1st]). I have argued that this should be understood as the claim that desires can have spatially and temporally remote things as their objects, whereas the objects of volition are limited to one's actions (voluntary thoughts and bodily motions) in the next instant.

Locke's conception of volition as the state of being pleased with an action does not fit with his views that volition is a kind of action and that it is different from desire. Being pleased with an event that has yet to occur seems at least to involve wanting it to occur, if it is not simply to be identified with that. Being pleased with something is a passive state, not an expression of one's agency. It is not something that one *does* in the same way that walking or adding are things that one does. One typically *discovers* that one is pleased with this or that, whereas one does not typically discover that one is doing something like walking or adding.[2] Of Locke's two ways of thinking about volition in the first edition, the more attractive is his conception of willing as a mental activity directed at the production of thoughts or bodily motions. Volition is fruitfully thought of as a certain sort of trying.

---

[2] The drunk who finds himself walking up his front steps is probably not literally making a discovery, but rather giving more attention to facts to which he was giving very little attention before. Perhaps a person who awakens from sleep-walking could literally discover that he was walking. However, one might challenge the claim that his walking in his sleep was a fully fledged action of his, an expression of his agency.

In the second edition (1694) and afterwards, Locke offers a single account of volition. This account contains at least one novel element, but it is basically a version of the more attractive strand from the first edition. The novel element is that volition is now said to be a matter of commanding or ordering a performance. The first edition claim that we find within ourselves the power to begin or forbear actions "barely by the choice or preference of our Minds" (II.xxi.5 [1st]) becomes the claim that we find the power to do these things "barely by a thought or preference of the mind ordering, or as it were commanding the doing or not doing such or such a particular action" (II. xxi.5 [2nd]). Locke no longer says that willing an action is a matter of being pleased with it. Where in the first edition he had said that preferring an action is "nothing but the *being pleased*" with it (II.xxi.28 [1st]), he now says that "Volition or Willing is an act of the Mind directing its thought to the production of any Action, and thereby exerting its power to produce it" (II.xxi.28 [2nd]). He now positively repudiates the idea that willing is desiring:

> I have above endeavored to express the Act of *Volition*, by *chusing*, *preferring*, and the like Terms, that signifie *Desire* as well as *Volition*, for want of other words to mark that Act of the mind, whose proper Name is *Willing* or *Volition*; yet it being a very simple Act, whosoever desires to understand what it is, will better find it by reflecting on his own mind, and observing what it does, when it *wills*, than by any variety of articulate sounds whatsoever. This caution of being careful not to be misled by Expressions, that do not enough keep up the difference between the *Will*, and several Acts of the Mind, that are quite distinct from it, I think the more necessary: Because I find the Will often confounded with several of the Affections, especially *Desire*; and one put for the other, and that by Men, who would not willingly be thought not to have had very distinct notions of things, and not to have writ very clearly about them. (II.xxi.30 [2nd])

One cannot help but think that Locke means to include his former self among the men who thought of themselves as clear thinkers and writers and yet confounded willing and desiring.

Has Locke entirely rid himself of the idea that willing is being pleased with an action? In the second and later editions, he continues to characterize willing as a matter of "preferring" an action, though he expresses some misgivings about this:

> I must here warn my Reader that *Ordering*, *Directing*, *Chusing*, *Preferring*, &c. which I have made use of, will not distinctly enough express *Volition*, unless he will reflect on what he himself does, when he *wills*. For Example *Preferring* which seems perhaps

best to express the Act of *Volition*, does it not precisely: For though a man would preferr flying to walking, yet who can say he ever *wills* it? Volition, 'tis plain, is an Act of the mind knowingly exerting that Dominion it takes it self to have over any part of the man by imploying it in, or witholding it from any particular Action. (II.xxi.15 [2nd])

It is clear that Locke feels that none of the ways that he can think of to describe volition quite captures its nature. Yet this passage is vexing. He says that 'preferring' does not quite capture the idea of willing, and when he goes on to justify this remark he seems to be thinking of 'preferring' in the sense of "wanting more." For he observes that we can prefer flying to walking, and yet that we do not will to fly. Surely the uncontroversial sense in which one can prefer flying to walking is that one can want to fly more than one wants to walk. So it would seem that he is saying that willing an action is not *exactly* wanting it more, though this description conveys the idea better than any other. There is, however, another reading of the passage. When he says that one can prefer to fly without willing to fly, we can understand this in light of a point that he makes later: 'preferring' is not equivalent to 'willing' because 'preferring' can be used to "signifie *Desire* as well as *Volition*" (II. xxi.30 [2nd]). That is to say, 'preferring' does not precisely express the act of volition because it is ambiguous in a way that 'willing' is not. If this is what he means, then he need not be understood as holding that 'preferring' in the sense of "wanting more" gets anywhere close to the meaning of 'willing.'

In the second edition, Locke advances more explicitly a view that was present in the first edition, but that was considerably less prominent there. This is the view that the objects of volition are more narrowly circumscribed than are the objects of desire. One can desire distant things or events, but one can will only one's own actions:

For he, that shall turn his thoughts inwards upon what passes in his mind when he *wills*, shall see, that the *will* or power of *Volition* is conversant about nothing, but our own Actions; terminates there; and reaches no farther...Whereby the *Will* is perfectly distinguished from *Desire*...(II.xxi.30 [2nd])
For we producing nothing by our *willing* it but some action in our power, 'tis there the *will* terminates, and reaches no farther. (II.xxi.40 [2nd])

In all of the *Essay*'s editions he says that the only actions we can conceive of are episodes of thinking and bodily motions. So the view that he is espousing more prominently in the second edition is that an agent may desire distant things, but he can will only his own voluntary thoughts and bodily motions.

After the first of the passages just quoted, Locke goes on to explain that will and desire may be at odds. He offers a nice example:

A Man, whom I cannot deny, may oblige me to use persuasions to another, which at the same time I am speaking I may wish may not prevail upon him. In this case 'tis plain the *Will* and *Desire* run counter: I will the Action, that tends one way, whilst my desire tends another, and that the direct contrary. (II.xxi.30 [2nd])

The example illustrates several points. One is that an agent can will to perform an action that he does not want to perform. This is our first indication that Locke's thoughts about motivation have undergone a major shift. For on the first edition view, the action one wills to do always coincides with the action (of those available) that one most wants to do. We will consider Locke's change of heart about motivation shortly (§64). The example also illustrates the related point that the objects of volition and desire can be contrary in a sense. The object of the volition is persuasive speech, while the object of desire is that the hearer not be moved by that speech. Finally, Locke's example illustrates the point he has just made about volition and desire having different sorts of objects. What he wills in the example is to perform certain vocalizations, certain motions of his throat and mouth. The object of his desire, on the other hand, is a particular reaction on the part of the man to whom he is talking. The object of his *volition* is necessarily an action of his, but the object of his *desire* can be something more remote.

Locke also makes this last point in correspondence with Phillipus van Limborch. Van Limborch was a Dutch minister and theology professor belonging to a liberal nonconformist sect known as the Remonstrants or Arminians. Jacobus Arminius (1560–1609) was a Dutch theologian who rejected the Calvinistic doctrine of predestination. The Remonstrants were so called because in the year following Arminius's death, a number of Dutch ministers signed a document called the Remonstrance and stating their anti-predestinarian views. The Remonstrants suffered political persecution in the years immediately following the Remonstrance, but achieved legal toleration by 1630. Van Limborch and Locke formed a warm friendship during Locke's stay in Holland in the 1680s. Van Limborch did not read English, but read the *Essay* in Pierre Coste's French translation (1700) and then in Ezekiel Burridge's Latin translation (1701), both renderings of the fourth edition. His correspondence with Locke is conducted in Latin. Van Limborch was particularly interested in Locke's handling of the free will problem. He attempts an exposition of what he takes to be some of Locke's central claims, and compares them with accounts of liberty in Remonstrant writings (*Corresp.*, 7: #2881, 270-8). Responding to the first of van Limborch's letters about freedom, Locke offers this correction:

> But when you say that 'whatever a man wills is considered by him to be agreeable' I fear that you are confusing Will with Desire, as I see is done by most of those who treat this subject, not without great damage to truth or at least to perspicuity. I grant that Desire is directed to the agreeable, but Will is directed only to our actions and terminates there...For Longing [*Cupido*] is a passion moved by an absent good; Volition on the other hand is an act of the will or of the soul exercising command over the operative powers of man. (*Corresp.*, 7: #2925, 327)

Three months later, Locke makes the point again, observing that "Will terminates solely in our actions and cannot be further extended to anything else or directed to a remote and absent good" (*Corresp.*, 7: #2979, 403). Van Limborch eventually concedes that will and desire are distinct, and that he had spoken carelessly (*Corresp.*, 7: #3010, 449).

Events can be "remote and absent" not only by involving objects that are at a distance from one's body, but by belonging to the non-immediate past or future. Furthermore, it seems that temporally remote events are no more possible objects of volition than spatially remote events are. I may now desire to eat tomorrow's breakfast, but I cannot now *will* to eat tomorrow's breakfast. If Locke means to include one's future doings among the "remote and absent goods" that one can now desire but that one cannot now will, then his view is that an agent can will only his own mental actions and bodily motions in the next instant.[3] This is significant because in the previous chapter I offered a reading of Locke's argument against freedom of the will that involved just this view of the objects of volition. In the second and fifth editions, Locke revises the passage containing his argument against freedom of the will (II.xxi.23–24), but the argument remains essentially unchanged. We will consider the revisions later.

---

[3] Is Locke's more explicit endorsement of the view that volition and desire have different objects further evidence that he has completely abandoned the idea that willing is occurrent wanting? Desires can have remote and absent goods as objects and volitions cannot; but this is consistent with volitions being occurrent desires of a particular, narrowly-defined sort (i.e., occurrent desires about actions to be performed in the next instant).

If Locke has completely abandoned the idea that willing is being pleased with an action, this leaves him with a more consistent and attractive account of volition. However, the fact that he no longer equates willing an action and being pleased with it makes his mishandling of the falling man example and the complacent paralytic example more mysterious to one who reads only a later edition of the *Essay*. As we saw in the previous chapter, Locke seems to fall into the mistake of supposing that a man who would rather not fall *wills* not to fall, and that a paralyzed person who is happy to remain where he is *wills* to remain where he is, because he equates willing and being pleased with an action (§57). Though his thinking about volition changes in the later editions, his first edition comments about the falling man and the complacent paralytic remain.

In the previous chapter, we examined Locke's first edition account of what it is to forbear doing something (§59). I argued that he favors a "robust" conception of such negative actions as staying in a room and keeping still. Rather than thinking of these as actions only in a deflationary sense, he thinks of them much as he thinks of ordinary, positive actions. He thinks that when one voluntarily refrains from doing something, this involves one's having a volition directed at the non-performance of an action. He presumes that just as an attempt at physical action is successful only if the desired bodily motion$_1$ occurs, so an attempt at not-doing something with one's body is successful only if the relevant bodily motion$_1$ does not occur.

Locke's account of what it is to forbear doing something is essentially unchanged in the later editions. Nearly all of the first edition passages in which he speaks of acts of volition or will directed at not-doings are retained in the later editions.[4] One new passage makes it even clearer that he thinks of negative action as involving volitions not do to things. After giving his updated characterization of what volition is, he says:

To avoid multiplying of words, I would crave leave here, under the word *Action* to comprehend the forbearance too of any Action proposed, *sitting still*, or *holding ones peace*, when *walking* or *speaking* are propos'd, though mere forbearances, requiring as much the determination of the *Will*, and being often as weighty in their consequences, as the contrary Actions, may, on that consideration, well enough pass for Actions too ... (II.xxi.28 [2nd]).

---

[4] I have in mind II.xxi.5, 8, 15, 21, 27. The exception is II.xxi.7, but that is just because material from II.xxi.7 [1st] was re-located to II.xxi.5 [2nd].

One who favors a deflationary account of negative actions can allow that they may be as weighty in their consequences as ordinary, positive actions are. What makes for a robust view of negative action is the claim that forborne actions are as much determined by the will as ordinary, positive actions are.

Though Locke's conception of negative action remains the same, the changes to his conception of volition do foreclose an avenue of interpretation that we had earlier seen as having some appeal. Locke thinks that a bodily motion must be initiated by a volition in order to qualify as an action (II.xxi.4). Supposing his account of forbearance to be closely modeled upon his account of positive action, we should expect him to hold that to forbear a bodily motion the absence of the relevant motion$_1$ in one's body must be caused by one's volition. In the previous chapter we saw reasons for thinking that this condition could rarely if ever be met. This prompted us to consider the possibility that Locke does not model his conception of forbearance *quite* so closely upon his conception of positive action. We considered the possibility that he conceives of forbearance in a way that does involve volitions directed at not-doings, but that does not require the volitions to cause the not-doings. We considered the possibility that Locke holds the following:

(9.8) If ψ is a bodily motion, A forbears ψ-ing if and only if: (i) A wills to not ψ, and (ii) A's willing is followed by the absence of a ψ-movement$_1$ of his body.

If willing were a matter of being pleased with an action, then one can see how one might be drawn to say that an agent successfully forbears ψ-ing when he prefers not to ψ and subsequently there is no ψ-movement$_1$ of his body. For one might say that an episode of occurrent wanting is successful if one gets what one wants, even if one does not get it *because* one wants it. However, if volition is an act by which the mind exerts its power to produce an action (II.xxi.28 [2nd]), then successful not doing must require a causal connection between the volition and a resultant negative state of affairs. If what explains the absence of a movement$_1$ is an exertion of power to produce it, then surely that exertion is a success only when it does produce that absence.

§64 Rethinking Motivation

Between the first and second editions, Locke undergoes a major change of heart about the nature of motivation. In the first edition, he says that it is the appearance of greater good that determines an agent to will as he does.

In the second edition and afterwards, he reports that "upon second thoughts" he is apt to imagine that what determines the will "is not, as is generally supposed, the greater good in view: But some (and for the most part the most pressing) uneasiness a Man is at present under" (II.xxi.31 [2nd]). He wavers on whether to identify uneasiness with desire or to portray them as necessary concomitants:

This, Uneasiness we may call, as it is *Desire*, which is an uneasiness of the mind for want of some absent good. All pain of the body of what sort soever, and disquiet of the mind is uneasiness: And with this is always join'd Desire, equal to the pain or uneasiness felt; and is scarce distinguishable from it. (II.xxi.31 [2nd])

Locke seems to regard the precise relation between uneasiness and desire as being of no great moment. In these two sentences, we are told that uneasiness *is* desire, that it is scarcely distinguishable from desire, and that it is joined with desire.[5] Later he suggests that there are other sorts of uneasiness associated with aversion, fear, anger, envy, and shame (II.xxi.39 [2nd]). This much at least is clear: uneasiness is a state of the agent rather than a feature of prospective actions, and it is an affect or feeling rather than a belief or judgment.

In the second edition, Locke holds that a person can be unmotivated to perform an action despite fully appreciating that he could obtain more pleasure overall by performing it. Not all absent goods stir uneasiness or desire in us, even when we reflect on them and see that we could get them. He suggests that a case may arise in which a poor person fully apprehends that "plenty has its advantages over poverty," and yet because he is content with his poverty "his *will* never is determin'd to any action, that shall bring him out of it" (II.xxi.35 [2nd]). He says that a person can be fully "perswaded of the advantages of virtue," and yet not be moved to behave virtuously until he "*hungers and thirsts after righteousness*" (II.xxi.35 [2nd]).

In the second edition, Locke also holds that agents are sometimes moved by uneasiness to perform actions that they know will not maximize their own pleasure in the long run. These are cases of weakness of the will. He gives the instance of a drunkard whose "habitual thirst after his Cups at the usual time drives him to the Tavern, though he have in his view the loss of

---

[5] Locke's casualness about the relation between uneasiness and desire is also evident in a summary of the second edition account that he sends to Molyneux: "That which in the train of our voluntary actions determines the will to any change of operation, is some present uneasiness, which is, or at least is always accompanyed with that of [*sic*] desire" (*Corresp.*, 4: #1655, 722).

health and plenty, and perhaps the joys of another life; the least of which is no inconsiderable good, but such as, he confesses, is far greater, than the tickling of his pallat with a glass of Wine, or the idle chat of a soaking Club" (II.xxi.35 [2nd]). On the first edition view, we would have to explain away such a case by saying that although in reflective moments the drunkard recognizes the deleterious effects of his behavior, he is nevertheless subject to a persistent series of cognitive errors. When he sets out for the tavern, or lifts his glass of wine, he does at that moment mistakenly believe that it is the action of those available to him that is likeliest to most augment his pleasure. In contrast, on Locke's second edition view he can say that there are agents who are, even as they act, fully aware that their actions are likely to diminish their own pleasure in the long run, and yet who are not sufficiently motivated by this to do something else.

At II.xxi.36 [2nd], Locke proposes to explain "why 'tis uneasiness alone operates on the *will*, and determines it in its choice." The argument is not a model of clarity. He says:

[W]e shall find, that we being capable but of one determination of the will to one action at once, the present uneasiness that we are under, does naturally determine the will in order, to that happiness we all aim at in all our actions: For as much as whilst we are under any uneasiness, we cannot apprehend our selves happy, or in the way to it. Pain and uneasiness being by every one concluded, and felt, to be inconsistent with happiness, spoiling the relish, even of those good things we have; a little pain serving to marr all the pleasure we rejoyced in. And therefore that, which of course determines the choice of our *will* to the next action, will always be the removing of pain, as long as we have any left, as the first and necessary step towards happiness.

To understand this passage, we must look ahead.

Locke says that we constantly desire happiness (II.xxi.39 [2nd]), that we are always pursuing it (II.xxi.43 [2nd]), and that the want of it underlies all of our other desires (II.xxi.41 [2nd]). He has a very demanding conception of what happiness is: "Happiness...in its full extent is the utmost Pleasure we are capable of...And the lowest degree of what can be called happiness is the being eas'd of all pain, and enjoying so much Pleasure, as without which any one cannot be content" (II.xxi.42 [2nd]). Happiness is thus a state that is rarely if ever achieved. One is not in this state unless one is absolutely free from uneasiness; and as he explains at II.xxi.45 [2nd], we are nearly always beset with one sort of uneasiness or another. Some kinds of uneasiness are physical in origin, as when we are cold, or hungry, or tired. Others are "fantastical uneasinesses" that are transmitted culturally, as when we feel the want of honor, power, or riches. The result is that "We are seldom at ease, and free enough from the sollicitation of our natural or adopted desires" (II. xxi.45 [2nd]).

The crux of the argument at II.xxi.36 [2nd] is the claim that the elimination of uneasiness is the first and necessary step toward happiness. Pain and uneasiness are supposed to so "marr" the pleasures we experience, "spoiling the relish" of them, that we cannot be motivated to pursue any absent goods until we have first completely rid ourselves of pain and uneasiness. Since that rarely if ever happens, we are always or nearly always determined to act by the uneasiness we experience. Locke repeats the argument at the end of II.xxi.46 [2nd]:

Because, as has been said, the first step in our endeavours after happiness being to get wholly out of the confines of misery, and to feel no part of it, the *will* can be at leisure for nothing else, till every uneasiness we feel be perfectly removed, which in the multitude of wants, and desires, we are beset with in this imperfect State, we are not like to be ever freed from in this World.

He seems to be conceding that if we only had peace of mind to attend to absent goods, they might suffice to motivate us. It is just that we are "seldom at ease," so they are "jostel'd out, to make way for the removal of those uneasinesses we feel" (II.xxi.45 [2nd]). Clearly the weak point of the argument is the contention that in our pursuit of happiness we must rid ourselves of every pain and uneasiness before we can be motivated to secure absent goods. It is rather like saying that a company must pay off all of its debts before going about the business of earning money. Locke's reason for thinking that we must rid ourselves of uneasiness before we can be attracted to absent goods is that the slightest pain or uneasiness spoils any enjoyment of pleasure. Yet if this were so, we would never experience any pleasure, since as Locke says we are always subject to some discomfort or other. In fact, one can derive considerable pleasure from reading a novel or tickling one's four-year-old daughter even while one's back is hurting.

At II.xxi.37 [2nd], Locke offers another argument for his new view of motivation. At first this argument seems to be wholly *a priori*:

Another reason why 'tis uneasiness alone determines the will may be this. Because that alone is present, and 'tis against the nature of things, that what is absent should operate, where it is not.

He is invoking a version of the principle that there cannot be action at a distance. That is a causal principle in physics, and thus here Locke seems to be suggesting that what determines a person to will as he does must be some state of the person, and not a desideratum that is merely prospective and hence "absent." These *a priori* considerations do not get us far, however. For as Locke realizes, a defender of his first edition view can say that when prospective goods "determine" the will in the sense of being the target of volition, this also involves a state of the agent "determining" her will. When an agent apprehends that one course of action is likely to bring her more pleasure than another, her representation of this fact may explain her willing as she does. Locke allows that, "The *Idea* of [absent good] indeed may be in the mind, and view'd as present there." He responds with the empirical observation that representations of absent goods are by themselves inefficacious: "How many are to be found, that have had lively representations set before their minds of the unspeakable joys of Heaven...and all that while they take not one step, are not one jot moved toward the good things of another life."

At II.xxi.38 [2nd], Locke presses further this point that people do not seem to be sufficiently motivated by the prospect of eternal bliss. If people were moved to will as they do by the prospect of securing absent goods, we should expect the possibility of eternal and infinite bliss to trump the possibility of any lesser pleasure. In that case, we should expect everyone to live a blameless life in obeyance of God's laws. The obvious response is that one may be more confident of enjoying worldly pleasures in the next moment than of enjoying heavenly pleasures someday, and so act to obtain the former. Locke anticipates this. He says that even if we grant that worldly pleasures are "the more probable to be attain'd," we should expect the greater potential payoff of heavenly reward to trump any other absent goods that might tempt us. Locke seems to invite the reader to conclude that his original account cannot explain the fact that people sin.

One might object that if the chances of a potentially infinite payoff are small enough, then prudence and rationality would not necessarily dictate following the course of action with the potentially infinite payoff. A greater problem for Locke's argument is the fact that even if the course of action with the potentially infinite payoff *were* the one that prudence and rationality dictated, people are not always prudent and rational. In the first edition, Locke explains willful flouting of the divine law as the consequence of several types of cognitive error. Chief among these is a kind of short-sightedness: in our practical reasoning, we tend to give present pleasures and pains disproportionately more weight than future pleasures and pains. Related to this is the fact that we have narrow attention spans that tend to get filled up by pleasures and pains, leaving us without the cognitive wherewithal for practical reasoning. The passages in which he ascribes these errors to us are retained in the second and later editions, and show how sin can be accounted for even on the view that the will is moved by the allure of absent goods.[6]

While Locke's second thoughts about motivation do represent an important departure, it is also easy to exaggerate the extent to which his view changes. Indeed, it is remarkable how much of the original account is preserved. The idea that uneasiness determines the will does not so much supplant his first edition account as get inserted into it. Locke continues to endorse an egoistic form of hedonism. As before, he identifies good and evil with pleasure and pain (II.xx.2 [2nd]). In the first edition, his most explicit avowal of egoism comes at II.xxi.40 [1st]. In the second and later editions, this passage is revised and relocated, but the gist of it is the same:

For since I lay it for a certain ground, that every intelligent Being really seeks Happiness, which consists in the enjoyment of pleasure, without any admixture of uneasiness; 'tis impossible any one should willingly put into his own draught any bitter ingredient, or leave out any thing in his power, that he could desire, or would tend to his satisfaction, and the compleating of his Happiness, but only by a wrong Judgment. (II.xxi.62 [2nd])

Locke still maintains that many of our bad choices result from miscalculations about which course of action is likeliest to maximize our pleasure. We make mistakes about the consequences of our actions (II.xxi.66 [2nd]). We undervalue pleasures that we have to wait for (II.xxi.63 [2nd]). We are ignorant of much, and frequently act too precipitately to make use of the knowledge we do have (II.xxi.67 [2nd]).

Whereas before Locke said that an agent is determined to choose the action that appears likeliest to cause the most pleasure in him, he now says that an agent's choice is determined by the uneasiness or desire that is produced in him as he considers various courses of action. He still holds that we are always driven toward pleasure or away from pain. Yet now he

---

[6] These passages are II.xxi.41–2 in the first edition, II.xxi.63–4 in the second.

maintains that prospective pleasure moves us to act by stirring uneasiness or desire in us. He sees this intermediate step as loosening, but not severing, the connection between the pleasure an act promises to yield, and our motivation to perform it. For now he emphasizes that motivation need not be *proportional* to apparent goodness. Though "every little trouble moves us, and sets us on work to get rid of it," not every prospective pleasure stirs uneasiness or desire in us (II.xxi.44 [2nd]). Moderate goods are often enough to render men content, and in this case the prospect of further goods need not stir any desire or uneasiness in them.

§65 *A Mistake of One Word*

In a curious passage found only in the *Essay*'s second edition, Locke offers a glimpse at what led him to reconsider his accounts of volition and motivation:

To conclude this enquiry into humane Liberty, which as it stood before, I my self from the beginning fearing, and a very judicious Friend of mine, since the publication suspecting, to have some mistake in it, though he could not particularly shew it me, I was put upon a stricter review of this Chapter. Wherein lighting upon a very easie, and scarce observable slip I had made, in putting one seemingly indifferent word for another, that discovery open'd to me this present view, which here in this second Edition, I submit to the learned World…(II.xxi.71 [2nd])

Teasingly, Locke leaves the reader in the dark both about the identity of the judicious friend, and the verbal slip in the first edition.

The judicious friend was almost certainly Molyneux, and with him Locke is more forthcoming. Writing to Molyneux in July of 1693, Locke says:

[B]y observing only the mistake of one word (viz. having put things for actions, which was very easy to be done in the place where it is, viz. p. 123. as I remember, for I have not my book by me here in town) I got into a new view of things, which, if I mistake not, will satisfie you, and give you a clearer account of humane freedom than hitherto I have done…[*Corresp.*, 4: #1643, 700]

As others have noted, 'things' does not appear on page 123 of the first edition (which page comprises II.xxi.25–28 [1st] and the first two and a half sentences of II.xxi.29 [1st]). However, 'thing' appears on that page three times, and two of these occurrences were replaced with 'action' in the second edition.

In his next letter, Molyneux shows that he takes Locke to mean that the verbal slip occurred at II.xxi.28 [1st]. "I plainly perceive the Mistake of sec.28 pag.123. where you Put *Thing* for *Action*," he says, "And I doubt not, but in your next Edition, you will fully rectify this Matter" (*Corresp.*, 4:#1652, 716). In the first edition, II.xxi.28 reads:

Secondly, in the next place we must remember, that *Volition* or *Willing*, regarding only what is in our power, *is* nothing but the *preferring* the doing of any thing to the not doing of it; Action to Rest, & *contra*.

However, another possibility is that the slip occurred at II.xxi.25 [1st]:

Since then it is plain, a Man is not at liberty, whether he will *Will*, or no; (for when a thing in his power is proposed to his Thoughts, he cannot forbear Volition, he must determine one way or other;) …

In both of these cases, 'action' was substituted for 'thing' in the second edition.[7] No other occurrence of 'thing' or 'things' in II.xxi was replaced with either 'action' or 'actions' in the second edition, so we can be pretty sure that Locke remembered the page number correctly when he wrote to Molyneux. Since he does not correct Molyneux's description of the slip as occurring at II.xxi.28 [1st], it seems fair to begin with the assumption that it is the passage he had in mind. Indeed, I believe that it is the passage that he had in mind, and will now suggest how his realization that he had put 'thing' for 'action' there might have led him in the direction of his second edition views about volition and motivation.

At II.xxi.28 [1st] Locke is explaining what "*Volition* or *Willing*" is. In the first edition, he says that it is nothing but preferring of the doing of any *thing* to the not doing of it. What he should have said is that it is nothing but preferring of the doing of any *action* to the not doing of it. When he apprehends this as a slip he comes to a greater appreciation that it is *actions*, and actions alone, that are the proper objects of volition. It becomes clearer to him that volition must be distinguished from desire, and that the objects of volition are more narrowly circumscribed than the objects of desire are. We can desire states of affairs that are not actions; we can desire to perform actions that we believe are impossible under the circumstances; we can desire that others perform actions. All that we can *will* is to perform actions

---

[7] What I have said up to this point about Locke's "scarce observable slip" has been said before (*Corresp.*, 4, 700n1; Chappell 1994b, 198n3).

that we take to be within our capacities under the circumstances. As we have seen, Locke's fuller appreciation of this is one of the substantial differences between his first and second edition accounts of volition (§63). In the first edition, while he does frequently say that it is actions and forbearances that are the objects of volitions, he also tends to think of volition as occurrent wanting. In the second edition, and later in the correspondence with van Limborch, he emphatically distinguishes volition and desire, saying that the chief difference between them is that volitions can be directed only at actions that one takes to be within one's power. Desires, on the other hand, can be directed at almost any object or future state.

Now consider the implications of this for Locke's account of motivation. In both editions, he presumes that what is good for an agent is whatever brings him the most pleasure. This is his egoistic hedonism. In the first edition, he also presumes that each person always wants to perform the action that will be the best for him. He then invokes the idea that willing an action is wanting it more, and concludes that each person always wills to do what seems the best (II.xxi.29 [1st]). After catching his slip at II.xxi.28 [1st], he comes to realize more fully that willing and desiring are different operations of the mind with different scopes. No longer thinking of willing as wanting, he is deprived of his argument for the conclusion that each person always wills the action that promises to deliver him the most pleasure. This leads him to consider (or to consider anew) the possibilities that one might see that an action would deliver the most pleasure without being motivated to perform it, or will to perform an action without thinking that it will deliver the most pleasure. He reflects on actual cases that seem to fit this description—the drunkard who acknowledges that his drinking is ruining his life but who continues to drink, the Christian who acknowledges that eternal damnation awaits the sinner but who sins anyway—and comes to the conclusion that it must be something other than apparent goodness that determines the will. We cannot, of course, know whether Locke had just this sequence of thoughts. Yet we can see how he might have "got into a new view of things" by "observing only the mistake of one word."

§66 Suspending Desire

In the second and later editions, Locke calls attention to the fact that we have the capacity to suspend the prosecution of our desires. "[I]n most cases," he says, the mind has "a power to suspend the execution and satisfaction of any of its desires; and so all one after another is at liberty to consider the objects of them; examine them on all sides, and weigh them with others" (II.xxi.47 [2nd]). He claims that there is an important relation between this capacity and the freedom of agents: the power to suspend the prosecution of our desires is "the source of all liberty" (II.xxi.47 [2nd]), the "hinge on which turns the liberty of intellectual Beings" (II.xxi.52 [2nd]).

These remarks raise some difficult questions. One is whether Locke's view that we can suspend the prosecution of our desires is compatible with his denial that we can forbear willing on an action once it is contemplated by us. On the face of it, suspending the prosecution of one's desire to φ might seem to involve—or even to be the same thing as—forbearing to will on whether to φ. To decide whether Locke is contradicting himself, we must explore in greater detail what is involved in the sort of suspension that Locke has in mind. Another issue is whether Locke has changed his mind about what is involved in an agent's being free. Some see his "doctrine of suspension" (as it has been called) as committing him to a libertarian version of incompatibilism. This would represent quite a departure from the first edition account of freedom. Even if he is not endorsing libertarian incompatibilism, his claim that the power of suspension is the source of all liberty might seem to alter or extend his first edition account of freedom.

To say that Locke has a "doctrine of suspension" in the later editions of the *Essay* is to exaggerate the theoretical content and status of what is intended by him as a commonplace observation. That the mind can suspend the prosecution of its desires is, Locke says, "evident in Experience"—it is something that "every one dayly may Experiment in himself" (II.xxi.47 [2nd]). He is calling attention to the plain, obvious fact that even when we have an initial preference about whether or not to perform a certain kind of action, we usually have the ability to put off acting on that preference, and to do so long enough to evaluate whether acting on it would really best serve our long-term interests. We do not always exercise that ability. Frequently we act precipitously, and sometimes we deserve censure for this. There are, on the other hand, times when we do not have the ability to rationally evaluate the long-term consequences of various courses of action. These include cases in which we are gripped by some "extreme disturbance" of mind, such as a severe pain or a violent passion (II.xxi.53 [2nd]). The notion that agents can usually refrain from acting on their desires long enough to weigh matters judiciously was actually present in the first edition, though less prominent and without the language of "suspension." In the first edition, he explains that people sometimes act contrary to their own interests because they choose their actions in haste. "To check this Precipitancy," he says, "our Understanding and Reason was given us, if we will make a right use of it, to search, and see, and then judge thereupon" (II.xxi.44 [1st]).

Locke does not say a great deal about exactly what goes on when one suspends the prosecution of a desire. This is what we should expect, since he is alluding to a fact of ordinary experience rather than promulgating an esoteric theory. It is clear that when he introduces the talk of suspending desire, he is thinking about the common case in which there are a great many "uneasinesses" soliciting an agent's will—that is, a number of competing desires about which of several incompatible actions one ought to perform. "[I]t is natural," he says, "that the greatest, and most pressing should determine the *will* to the next action" (II.xxi.47 [2nd]). For the most part, an agent simply performs the action that he has the strongest desire to perform. Yet we have the ability to suspend the prosecution of that desire in order to "examine, view, and judge, of the good or evil of what we are going to do" (II.xxi.47 [2nd]). In that case, Locke seems to be saying, the will is not determined by the greatest and most pressing uneasiness.

If on some occasion the greatest and most pressing uneasiness does not determine the will, then what does? One possibility is that the will is then determined by another, weaker, desire or uneasiness. One might take this to be implied by Locke's statement that what determines the will is "some (and for the most part the most pressing) uneasiness a Man is at present under" (II.xxi.31 [2nd]). Yet it is hard to make sense of the claim that a weaker desire occasionally overpowers a stronger one. The very fact of its winning the competition would seem to show that it was, at that moment, the stronger of the two desires. Furthermore, when Locke says at II.xxi.47 [2nd] that the most pressing uneasiness determines the will "for the most part, but not always," he is not thinking about the case of a weaker desire winning out against a stronger one. He is thinking about a case in which several competing desires for positive action are put in abeyance as the agent reflects on the likely consequences of those actions.

Another possibility is that the greatest uneasiness determines the will only "for the most part" because sometimes the will is determined by something other than an uneasiness. Yet it seems unlikely that this is what Locke has in mind. He qualifies his claim that the will is determined by the most pressing uneasiness, but he does not qualify his claim that the will is determined by uneasiness.

Still another possibility is that sometimes the will is not determined at all. But what would *that* mean? The will is just the agent's capacity for willing, for producing volitions. The will is "determined" one way or another if an agent has volitions with one or another determinate content. For the will not to be determined would be for the agent not to have volitions with determinate contents. It would be for the agent not to be doing any willing. Could that be what goes on when the agent suspends the prosecution of his greatest and most pressing uneasiness?

There may indeed be a temptation to interpret Locke's talk of suspension as implying the total disengagement of the will's gears, as it were, so that during a period of suspension an agent's will is not determined by anything and the agent does not will. Yet it is good to remember what it is that Locke says we suspend. It is not volition altogether, or even any particular volition, but the "prosecution of this or that desire" (II.xxi.47 [2nd]). It is also significant that Locke thinks of suspension as a voluntary activity, rather than as something that happens to a person unbidden. To suspend the prosecution of one's desire is to do something. This is suggested by his observation that we sometimes have a duty to suspend the prosecution of our desires (II. xxi.52 [2nd]). One's duties pertain only to one's actions. Suspending the prosecution of one's desire would seem to be a negative action, a mindful not doing. Locke thinks of mindful not doing as involving a volition directed at the not doing. Therefore, when an agent suspends the prosecution of his strongest desire for positive action, he must do so by means of a volition to not perform that positive action. The uneasiness prompting him toward the positive action is outweighed by his uneasiness for the non-performance of that (and perhaps any other) positive action.

Let us imagine that an agent is deciding which of three acts to perform (A1, A2, or A3) and that he has a corresponding desire (D1, D2, and D3) to perform each of them. Suppose that D1 is a greater and more pressing uneasiness than either D2 or D3. Usually we would expect our agent to attempt A1, but Locke tells us that he might suspend the attempt to satisfy D1 in order to further reflect on his choice between A1, A2, and A3. Just as Locke holds that refraining from leaving a room involves a volition to not do something, so we should expect him to hold that refraining from attempting any of A1, A2, and A3 involves a volition to not do something.

The involvement of volition here distinguishes the *suspension* of D1 from the mere failure to satisfy D1 (as when, for example, the agent dozes off before he can get around to satisfying D1). Locke thinks that we are always subject to an uneasiness or desire for our own happiness, and that sometimes an agent may become particularly cognizant that there are risks and benefits at stake in the decision about which of several actions to perform. This may lead the agent to refrain from performing any of them while he thinks the matter over more. Putting this in terms of our example, we can say that the agent's awareness of the potential risks and benefits of the various actions that he is considering generates a desire—call it D4—to not perform any of A1, A2, or A3 at present.

While the agent suspends the attempt to satisfy D1, and reflects on the likely consequences of each of A1, A2, and A3, D4 is stronger than D1. Reflection can alter the balance of power between an agent's desires for positive action. "[B]y a due consideration and examining any good proposed," Locke says, "it is in our power, to raise our desires, in a due proportion to the value of that good" (II.xxi.46 [2nd]). This is particularly true when we look past the action considered and toward the longer-range end it serves. An action can be "rendred [*sic*] more or less pleasing" by "the contemplation of the end, and the being more or less perswaded of its tendency to it, or necessary connexion with it" (II.xxi.69 [2nd]). Eventually one of the agent's desires for positive action becomes stronger than D4, reflection ends, and the agent acts.

Locke qualifies his principle that the most pressing uneasiness determines the will. He says that it is only "for the most part" that it does so. We can now see two reasons for the qualification. First, the will is not always determined by the most pressing *of those desires inclining the agent to perform positive actions*. The will of the agent deciding between A1, A2, and A3 need not be determined by the most pressing of D1, D2, and D3. It might instead be determined by a desire to refrain from A1, A2, and A3 in order to reflect on which of these actions is likeliest to promote his happiness. Second, the will need not *ever* be determined by the desire that was most pressing prior to reflection. Once the agent reflects on the long-term consequences of A1, A2, and A3, the relative strengths of D1 and D2 may change. When D4 weakens enough to allow one of the competing desires for positive action to produce a volition, it may be that D2 has become stronger than D1, leading him to perform A2 instead of A1.

Suspending the attempt to satisfy one's strongest desire for positive action might seem to be a case of forbearing to will something. While one's desire is suspended, one does not will to perform the action that would satisfy it, and if the suspension is voluntary then one's not willing to satisfy the desire would seem to be voluntary too. Thus it might seem as though Locke's second edition remarks about suspending desire conflict with his view (retained from the first edition) that we cannot forbear willing. Chappell considers an argument to this effect, one that turns on the claim that "[i]f one is able to suspend all of one's desires then…one can avoid performing some volition" (Chappell 1994a, 115).[8] We have just seen reason to doubt that Locke thinks that we are able to suspend the prosecution of all of our desires at one time. Still, that does not much affect the argument that Chappell considers. He could just as well have said: "If one is able to suspend one of one's desires, then one can avoid performing some volition."

For there to be a conflict between Locke's second edition views about suspending actions and his first edition denial that we can forbear willing, it would have to be the case that our ability to suspend the prosecution of a desire shows that we can sometimes forbear willing one way or the other on a proposed action. Given the account that I have offered of Locke's view of suspension, there is no such conflict. Earlier, I explained why Locke thinks that we cannot forbear willing (§61).[9] If forbearing to will on whether to φ were possible, it would involve postponing φ-ing. To a volitionist who favors a robust treatment of negative action, postponing φ-ing will be taken to involve willing not to φ now. I maintained that Locke also presumes a view that has independent plausibility to a volitionist thinking of willing as trying to bring an action about. This is the view that the will can be directed only at actions that would begin immediately. To one who makes this presumption, there is no matter about φ-ing that the will can weigh in

---

[8]   In the end, Chappell finds the argument inconclusive, being balanced by an equally plausible argument for the opposite conclusion (Chappell 1994a, 117).

[9]   There *is* a harmless sense in which suspending the prosecution of one's desire to φ involves forbearing to will something. Suspending the prosecution of one's desire to φ involves intentionally not generating a particular volition—the volition *to φ now*. This does not show that there is any conflict between Locke's second edition views about suspending actions and his first edition denial that we can forbear willing. When Locke says that we cannot forbear willing, he never means to deny that we can intentionally refrain from willing *particular actions*. He means that we cannot forbear willing *one way or the other* on whether to perform a proposed action. We intentionally refrain from willing *particular* actions (positive or negative) every time we will to do anything. If, after a moment's reflection, one wills to φ, one is refraining from willing to not-φ; by the same token, if after a moment's reflection one wills not to φ, one is refraining from willing to φ.

on besides whether to φ now. From this point of view, forbearing to will on whether to φ will be seen to be impossible. Putting off the decision about whether to φ would not mean forbearing to will on whether to φ. It would mean planning to revisit the question of whether to φ at some point in the future, but also willing not to φ now, where that is the only matter about φ-ing that one *could* will on.

Suspending the prosecution of one's desire to φ is a matter of postponing φ-ing as one weighs the likely consequences of φ-ing against those of several other possible actions. We have just seen that Locke thinks of this as a voluntary activity, one that a person sometimes has a duty to perform. Suspending the prosecution of a desire is thus a negative action, a case of mindfully not doing something one might have done. When one suspends the desire to φ, one wills not to φ now. If I am right about how to understand his denial that we can forbear willing, then for him suspending the desire to φ is as far as can be from forbearing to will about whether to φ. It involves active contemplating whether φ-ing in the near future would serve one's broader interests, but it also involves willing on whether to φ now, which is the only matter relating to φ-ing that one could will on.

Locke says that the power to suspend the prosecution of our desires is the foundation of liberty (II.xxi.51 [2nd]), the source of liberty (II.xxi.47 [2nd]), and the hinge on which liberty turns (II.xxi.52 [2nd]). He says that it is in this capacity that man's liberty lies (II.xxi.47 [2nd]). All of this suggests that in order for a performance to be free, an agent must have been able to suspend the prosecution of the desire that moved him to act as he did. In the first edition, Locke had seemed to hold that an agent, A, is free with respect to an action, φ, if both of the following are true: (i) if A were to will to φ, A would φ, and (ii) if A were to will not to φ, then A would forbear φ-ing. Is he giving us a different account of freedom in the second edition?

One compelling reason for thinking that Locke does not mean to be giving a new account of freedom in the second edition is that he continues to give the old account of freedom. The first edition passages in which he tells us what freedom is—II.xxi.8, 12, 21, 23 [1st]—are retained in the second edition and afterwards with few changes. Thus in the second edition we find Locke saying:

[S]o far as any one can, by the direction or choice of his Mind, preferring the existence of any Action, to the non-existence of that Action, and, *vice versâ*, make it to exist, or not exist, so far he is *free*. (II.xxi.21 [2nd])

What is new here is just the characterization of volition as involving the direction of the mind. (This is of a piece with his tendency, in the second and later editions, to characterize volitions as the mind's orders or commands.)[10] Not only does he retain passages from the first edition; Locke continues to produce very similar ones in new writings until the end of his life. In May of 1701 we find him saying that "liberty…consists solely in the power to act or not to act consequent on, and according to, the determination of the will" (*Corresp.*, 7: #2925, 329). In August of that same year, he writes that "if a man is able to do this if he will to do it, and on the other hand to abstain from doing this when he wills to abstain from doing it: in that case a man is free" (*Corresp.*, 7: #2979, 406). In September of 1702, in the last of his surviving letters to van Limborch, Locke writes that "a man is free in every action, as well of willing as of understanding, if he was able to have abstained from that action of willing or understanding; if not, not" (*Corresp.*, 7: #3192). Finally, in the fifth edition of the *Essay*, published posthumously, he adds new material including the claim that "Liberty 'tis plain consists in a Power to do, or not to do; to do, or forbear doing as we *will*" (II.xxi.56 [5th]).

It is, of course, possible that beginning with the second edition of the *Essay* Locke offers two different accounts of freedom without appreciating that he is doing so: one retained from the first edition, and another that assigns an important role to the capacity to suspend one's desires. We should regard that as a reading of last resort, since it imputes to Locke a higher degree of confusion about his own text than one would like to imagine. It would be more charitable to say, as Chappell does, that he is being careless when he claims that the power to suspend the prosecution of our desires is the foundation and source of liberty. What he really means, Chappell says, is that the power to suspend the prosecution of our desires is the foundation and source of *the proper use* of freedom (Chappell 2000, 247). Locke does say that "the end and use of our Liberty" (II.xxi.48 [2nd]) is to act in accordance with the "last result of a fair Examination" (II.xxi.47 [2nd]), the sort of examination that requires an opportunity for careful thought about consequences. Chappell's interpretation is the one to settle for if we cannot find a reading of the second edition on which

---

[10] In the first edition, this passage reads: "[S]o far as any one can, by choice, or preference of the existence of any Action, to the non-existence of that Action, and, *vice versâ*, make it to exist, or not exist; so far he is *free*."

it contains a single, consistent account of freedom that makes the ability to suspend desire a prerequisite for free action. Yet Chappell's interpretation does require us to dismiss Locke's repeated claims about the role of suspension; surely it would be preferable to find one that can accommodate them.

§67 Suspension and Indeterminism

Peter Schouls offers one reading on which the ability to suspend the prosecution of desires is a prerequisite for free action. He portrays Locke as a libertarian incompatibilist. He says that on Locke's view, "[a] person avoids being incorporated into the mechanism of nature through the complex act that includes suspension of natural desires, examination of these desires and their potential consequences, contemplation of true good, judgment of the suspended desires in terms of the good contemplated, and submission to the outcome of that judgment" (Schouls 1992, 145). To avoid being incorporated into the "mechanism of nature" is presumably to avoid having one's actions be governed by the deterministic causal laws that reign over the rest of the material realm (or at least over the inanimate portions of the material realm). According to Schouls, Locke thinks that what makes agents suspend the prosecution of desire is not uneasiness, but "a determination that has its cause solely in the agents themselves" (149), a "pure self-determination" (161). He thus portrays Locke as an agent causalist, one for whom the process of suspension is an indeterministic breaching of deterministic processes.[11]

One difficulty for Schouls's reading is that Locke regards it as a plain deliverance of experience that we can suspend the prosecution of our desires, and it is surely not a plain deliverance of experience that we can abrogate deterministic causal laws. A more basic problem is that Schouls presents Locke as taking a forthright stand on the issue of determinism. In fact, the evidence for Locke's attitude toward determinism is rather murky. Such evidence as there is suggests that he does not regard himself as having a solution to the traditional problem of freedom and determinism.

[11] Schouls claims that Roderick Chisholm's "Freedom and Action" (1966)—a *locus classicus* of twentieth-century agent-causal libertarianism—is "at many points...a contemporary retelling of Locke's story" (Schouls 1992, 147n1).

One searches in vain for a clear statement from Locke about the idea that every event is fixed by prior events plus the laws of nature. Chappell has suggested that he explicitly endorses determinism in Book IV, when he makes these two back-to-back claims (Chappell 2000, p.248 n2):

[B]are *nothing can no more produce any real Being, than it can be equal to two right Angles* (IV.x.3 [1st])
[W]hat had its Being and Beginning from another, must also have all that which is in, and belongs to its Being from another too (IV.x.4 [1st]) .

Yet it is overreaching to call this an explicit endorsement of determinism. These passages come as Locke is arguing for the existence of an eternal thinking being. In the first one, we have a version of the principle that something cannot come from nothing. Locke seems to be thinking about the coming-into-being of a substance (a "Being") rather than the coming-into-being of an event or a state of affairs, but we might suppose that he would endorse a more expansive version of the principle that applies to events and states of affairs as well as substances. Even so, the principle says that everything must have a cause, but not that all causation is subsumed under deterministic laws. One might see that gap as being filled by the second passage. If it too is construed broadly, it could be taken to mean that if a substance, event, or state has an external cause, then every aspect of that substance, event, or state must have been fixed by its external cause. Yet whether this amounts to causal determinism, or instead leaves the door open for undetermined agents causing their own states, is still unclear. The latter seems possible if Locke thinks that some of the states of agents do not have external causes.

One might expect to find a statement of Locke's attitude toward determinism in his accounts of what determines agents to will as they do. Yet we saw in the previous chapter that when Locke says in the first edition that acts of will are "determined" by the pleasure that various courses of action promise, he is talking about the features of prospective actions that attract us to them, not about the efficient causes of our behavior (§62). Thus when he says in the first edition that our behavior may be free despite being determined, he means that its being goal-directed does not preclude it from being free. He insists that a man deciding whether to go or stay is not the less free because his preference is "determined to stay by the darkness of the Night, or illness of the Weather, or want of other Lodging"

(II.xxi.33 [1st]). In describing the man's preference as determined in this way, he does not mean that bad weather is the efficient cause of the man's preferring to remain indoors. The point is that the man prefers to remain indoors because the bad weather has implications for his goals of remaining warm and dry.

It is somewhat more plausible to imagine that Locke has causal determination in mind when, in the second edition, he says that uneasiness determines the will. For uneasiness is at least a state of the agent, and one that precedes volition. Yet even so, there is good reason to think that he is not giving an account of the efficient causes of acts of will. In the second edition, he raises the question of what determines the will at II.xxi.29 [2nd]. There he says that to ask "*what determines the Will*" is the same as to ask "What moves the mind, in every particular instance, to determine its general power of directing, to this or that particular Motion or Rest." He answers that question as follows:

[T]he motive, for continuing in the same State or Action, is only the present satisfaction in it; The motive to change, is always some uneasiness; nothing setting us upon the change of State, or upon any new Action, but some uneasiness. This is the great motive that works on the Mind to put it upon Action, which for shortness sake we will call *determining of the Will*, which I shall more at large explain.

So in the second edition Locke is using 'determines' in such a way that what determines the will is equated with the agent's *motive* for willing as he does. This suggests that he is still thinking about the agent's goals or reasons for acting, rather than about the event or state of affairs that causally necessitates his acting as he does. He is saying that agents always act as they do in order to relieve themselves of some uneasiness.

Looking outside the *Essay*, we find that there are passages in Locke's correspondence that can be seen as pointing in the direction of incompatibilism, but none that does so conclusively. One important text is the 1693 letter in which he responds to Molyneux's criticisms of the first edition. This letter offers a fascinating glimpse at some of Locke's doubts about his first edition account of liberty, but it also raises many questions. As we saw at the outset of this chapter, Molyneux offers, in the course of a few sentences, three criticisms of the first edition account of liberty. He says that it is too "fine-spun," that as a consequence of its being too fine-spun "the Great Question of Liberty and Necessity seems to Vanish" in it, and that it is too harsh because it makes men damnable for their intellectual shortcomings (*Corresp.*, 4: #1579, 600-1). In his response, Locke first notes that he had not originally intended to weigh in on the free will debate, and then makes what might be a surprising confession:

When the connection of the parts of my subject brought me to the consideration of power, I had no design to meddle with the question of liberty, but barely
pursued my thoughts in the contemplation of that power in man of choosing or
preferring, which we call the will, as far as they would lead me without any the
least bypass to one side or other; or if there was any leaning in my mind, it was
rather to the contrary side to that where I found my self at the end of my pursuit.
But doubting that it bore a little too hard upon man's liberty, I shew'd it to a very
ingenious but professed Arminian, and desired him, after he had consider'd it, to
tell me his objections if he had any, who frankly confessed he could carry it no
farther. (*Corresp.*, 4: #1592, 625)

On one reading of this passage, Locke is telling Molyneux that he followed the argument where it led him, but that he was not convinced by his
own account even as he published it. Another reading of it has him telling
Molyneux only that the arguments took him toward the side he originally
leaned against.

   If Locke did find himself unable to believe the conclusion of one of
his own arguments, which was it? Is it the notion that people sometimes
act freely? Or his account of what freedom consists in? His account of
motivation? Locke's fear that his discourse bore "too hard upon man's
liberty" could be the fear that his account of what is required for an agent
to be free was too demanding. On the other hand, the defining feature of
Arminianism was the rejection of Calvinistic doctrines of predestination,
so one might take the fact that he looked to an Arminian for criticism
as indicating that he was worried that his account was too friendly to
determinism. Perhaps the most likely reading of this passage is that Locke
means to be joining in Molyneux's concern about the harshness of the
first edition's account of motivation. That account could be thought to
bear "too hard on men's liberty" because it denies that men can choose
those actions that do not seem likely to maximize their own pleasure.
One might also expect a critic of predestination to object to that account
for that reason, which would explain Locke's turning to the Arminian for
critical input.

After inviting Molyneux to point out to him his particular missteps in the first edition, Locke says this:

But if you will argue for or against liberty, from consequences, I will not undertake to answer you. For I own freely to you the weakness of my understanding, that though it be unquestionable that there is omnipotence and omniscience in God our maker, and I cannot have a clearer perception of any thing than that I am free, yet I cannot make freedom in man consistent with omnipotence and omniscience in God, though I am as fully perswaded of both as of any truths I most firmly assent to. (*Corresp.*, 4: #1592, 625-6)

It is not obvious what it means to argue "for or against liberty, from consequences." This could mean arguing that we are free or not by pointing to the consequences of our freedom or unfreedom. Yet it seems more likely that arguing "for or against liberty, from consequences" means arguing about whether we are free in light of the apparent fact that each state of affairs is a consequence of some other. The reason that Locke gives for declining to argue "for or against liberty, from consequences" is that he is baffled about how to reconcile human freedom and divine omniscience. The problem would seem to be that if God knows in advance what we will do, then what we will do must already be fixed.

Locke holds that for the performance of an action to be free, it must not only be true that the agent acts voluntarily, but also that he could have forborne that action. The worry about divine omniscience is that if God knows now (or timelessly) that A will voluntarily ϕ tomorrow, then it would seem that A cannot forbear ϕ-ing tomorrow, and so A's ϕ-ing cannot be free. A similar worry can be raised about determinism: if A is determined to will to ϕ tomorrow, then (it could be argued) A cannot forbear ϕ-ing tomorrow, and so A's ϕ-ing cannot be free. There are, of course, strategies for responding to both of these arguments. Since Locke does not go into the matter, we cannot say which he considered or why he found them unconvincing. We can say that much would turn on what he thinks is required for A to have had an unexercised capacity to forbear ϕ-ing. Much depends on the sort of possibility that is at issue in Locke's claim that A has ϕ-d freely only if it was *possible* for A to forbear ϕ-ing. In the previous chapter, I presumed that he means that A is free with respect to ϕ-ing only if the following is true: if A had willed not to ϕ, then A would have forborne ϕ-ing. Yet it is possible that he has in mind a more demanding requirement for free action. He could think that A did not have the power to forbear φ-ing unless it was possible for A to *will* not to φ. He could also think that it was not possible for A to will not to φ if A was *determined* to will to φ. In that case, Locke's account of free action would entail incompatibilism. However, his text does not tell us one way or the other whether this is what he has in mind.

It would be very surprising if Locke were thoroughly convinced of the compatibility of freedom and determinism while so evidently hopeless about the prospect of explaining how freedom and foreknowledge could be compatible. This is a reason for doubting that he is a convinced compatibilist about freedom and determinism. At the same time, this letter to Molyneux does not show us that he is a convinced incompatibilist. He tells Molyneux that he is as persuaded of both human freedom and divine omniscience as he is of anything. If he believes in both, then presumably he does not believe that divine omniscience and human freedom are incompatible, despite his confessed inability to explain how they could be compatible. For all we have been able to show, he could take a similar view of freedom and determinism. He could presume them to be compatible without taking himself to have a satisfactory explanation of their compatibility.

What this letter does show is that in 1693 Locke does not think that he has a satisfactory story to tell about how it could be that we are free. After confessing his inability to reconcile our freedom with God's omniscience, he says:

And therefore I have long since given off the consideration of the question, resolving all into this short conclusion, That if it be possible for God to make a free agent, then man is free, though I see not the way of it. (*Corresp.*, 4: #1592, 626)

Molyneux had complained that the great question of liberty and necessity seemed to vanish in Locke's account.[12] Locke's response seems to be that he had not set out to solve that problem, and that he is not prepared to solve it now.

The letter that we have been considering was written in January of 1693. In July of that year, Locke again writes to Molyneux on the subject of liberty, and reports that he has gotten into "a new view of things, which, if I mistake not, will satifie you, and give a clearer account of humane freedom than

---

[12] One might think that making an age-old philosophical problem "Vanish" would be a good thing, but what Molyneux means—and what Locke takes him to mean—is that in the *Essay* Locke ducked the traditional problem of how we could be free if our actions are necessitated by prior states of affairs.

hitherto I have done" (*Corresp.*, 4: #1643, 700). That is the letter in which says that he was prompted to revise his account after noticing "the mistake of one word." He writes again another month later, telling Molyneux that "upon review of my alterations, concerning what determines the will, in my cool thoughts I am apt to think them to be right, as far as my thoughts can reach in so nice a point" (*Corresp.*, 4: #1655, 722). It is the question of motivation that has occupied his attention, and he is evidently satisfied with his new account. There is no indication that he is beset with doubt as he may have been when the first edition went to press. Yet he has done nothing to address the problem of divine omniscience, or to respond to arguments against liberty "from consequences." He is as open as ever to Molyneux's charge of having ducked the "Great Question of Liberty and Necessity." This is further reason to think that his earlier doubts about the first edition had to do with the issue of motivation, and that he had not set himself the task of showing whether determinism is true and whether it is compatible with human freedom.

Locke's later correspondence contains one more inconclusive remark about the issue of determinism. In a letter to van Limborch in 1701, Locke reminds his friend that "as you know there are some who deny that a man has any dominion over his actions, but [hold] that all things are governed by predetermined and ineluctable fate" (*Corresp.*, 7: #3043, 503). The implication seems to be that Locke does not regard all things as being governed by "predetermined and ineluctable fate." This could mean that he does not believe that every event is determined by prior events or states, or that he does not believe that every event is absolutely or metaphysically necessary. Nothing about the context of this passage requires the first reading rather than the second.

All told, there is little evidence that Locke took himself to have offered a solution to the problem of freedom and determinism, and even less that he saw our capacity to suspend the prosecution of desires as a way of resisting incorporation into the mechanism of nature.

§68 Suspension and Freedom

There would seem to be two ways of reading the second edition so that it offers a single account of freedom on which the ability to suspend the prosecution of desire is a prerequisite for free action. One is to suppose that

Locke means to add the ability to suspend the prosecution of desire to the requirements for free action recognized by the first edition account. In that case, for A's φ-ing to be free it must not only be the case that A could have forborne φ-ing, but also that A could have postponed φ-ing long enough to reflect on whether φ-ing really served A's long-term interests. The trouble with this reading is that it forces us to say that Locke is speaking carelessly on many occasions on which he tells us what freedom is. Whenever he repeats the first edition formula that an agent is free with respect to an action so long as he has "a power to act, or not to act" (II.xxi.23[2nd]), he would be neglecting to mention the further requirement his account now demanded. There are enough of these occasions that it seems more charitable to follow Chappell and to say that Locke does not really mean that the ability to suspend desire is a prerequisite for freedom.

A second possibility is that Locke does not view the demand that one be able to suspend the prosecution of desire as an *additional* requirement on free action because he views it as already somehow built into the account of freedom that he gave in the first edition. To see how this might go, let us consider what is attractive about the idea that freedom requires the ability to suspend, for a time, the attempt to satisfy one's strongest desire for positive action. Suppose that Fred always acts upon his first impulse, never exercising the restraint that would be needed for him to evaluate whether his first impulse serves his long-term interests. Knowing just this, we might be inclined to say that Fred is impetuous rather than that he is unfree. However, if we then learn that Fred not only continually fails to postpone actions long enough to decide whether they are in his long-term interests, but that he is *incapable* of doing so, this might change our estimation. We might then say that his agency is diminished, as a young child's is, and for much the same reason. The grounding of Fred's behavior in reasons that he has for acting may be too tenuous for that behavior to fully qualify as an expression of agency. Every parent of a toddler knows that there are times when a child is best regarded as a force of nature to be managed rather than an agent to be reasoned with. An adult who is *unable* to reflect on the long-term consequences of his actions—whose behaviors are necessarily the product of instinct rather than reflection—might be properly viewed in much the same light.

Suppose that Locke, thinking along these lines, holds that a person is not a real agent, or not really acting, unless he has at least the capacity to suspend

the prosecution of his desires long enough to reflect on the wisdom of trying
to satisfy them. In that case, we would expect Locke to hold that a person
who does not have the ability to suspend the prosecution of his desires is not
even a *candidate* for being free with respect to actions. An account of what it
takes for an agent to be free with respect to an action would just not apply to
such a person. The capacity to suspend desire would be the source or foundation of liberty—the hinge on which liberty turns—because it is a prerequisite for genuine agency. Locke's second edition remarks about suspending
desire would not reflect a change in his view of what is required for an agent
to be free with respect to a type of action; they would serve to make more
explicit his presumption about what is required for agency in the first place.

One of Locke's letters to van Limborch provides some support for this
interpretation. On July 8, 1701, in the course of explaining his own views
about freedom, van Limborch writes that there are three ways that a man
can act. A man can act in accordance with his judgment about what he
ought to do, contrary to that judgment, or by "brute impulse." His description of this third possibility is somewhat clumsy:

[B]efore his understanding, after a careful examination of the reasons, has judged
what ought to be done[, a man] can by brute impulse do, not what is in accordance
with reason, but what carnal desire dictates. (*Corresp.*, 7: #2953, 369–70)

Van Limborch means that a man might act without first examining the reasons that speak for or against his doing what he does. Locke challenges this
claim in his reply, dated August 12, 1701. He takes van Limborch to be suggesting that liberty involves "a power of willing…without previous cogitation" (*Corresp.*, 7: #2979, 410). "Liberty cannot consist in such a power," he
answers, "because, as I have said, liberty presupposes cogitation." He refers
van Limborch to II.xxi.8–9. In his next letter, van Limborch explains that
in speaking of action by "brute impulse" he was referring to precipitate
action, not action without *any* previous cogitation. He agrees that there is
no willing without prior cogitation. One who acted without any "preceding cogitation," he says, "I should conceive not a man" (*Corresp.*, 7: #3010,
454). There Locke lets the matter lie.

In the first of the passages to which Locke refers van Limborch, he says
that "Liberty cannot be, where there is no Thought, no Volition, no Will"
(II.xxi.8). In the second, he says that a tennis ball is not a free agent because
it does not think, does not have volition, and does not prefer motion to rest

or *vice versa* (II.xxi.9). Taking these remarks by themselves, one might take his point to be that only creatures with certain general cognitive capacities are candidates for being free. However, the letter to van Limborch shows that he has in mind a more demanding requirement—that a particular sort of cognitive episode is a necessary component of each case of free action. Locke explains to van Limborch that "every single volition is always preceded by some judgement of the understanding," though the cogitation may be "slight and momentary" (*Corresp.*, 7: #2979, 411, 410). He holds that one does not will to φ unless one has judged that φ-ing is the thing to do now, or at least that it is the thing to try to do now. His claim that liberty presupposes cogitation amounts to the view that one does not act freely unless one's action is the product of a *decision*. One's decisions may be precipitate or ill-advised, but still he holds that there is an important difference between a precipitate decision and an automatic or impulsive response.

Locke takes the claim that liberty presupposes cogitation to entail that a person does not act freely if his behavior is the product of brute impulse. There is a good case to be made for saying that if one is *incapable* of postponing a contemplated action long enough to reflect on its consequences, then one's behavior is the result of brute impulse. It is of course possible to make snap decisions. This involves making a very quick calculation about which of several available actions is best. One can make a snap decision when it is obvious which action is best, or when one has already done some of the calculation up front, in anticipation of likely scenarios. Yet a person who *must* immediately act to satisfy her strongest desire—a person who cannot stop to reflect on the consequences of her actions even when the circumstances are unanticipated and it is not obvious what is in her long-term interests—acts instinctively or compulsively rather than making a series of snap decisions. Such a person is not a fully fledged agent on Locke's account. If this is right, then the ability to suspend the prosecution of desire is necessary not just for free agency as that is understood in the *Essay*'s second edition; it is necessary for agency as that is understood in the *Essay*'s first edition.

§69 *Motivation and Judgment*

Locke's insistence that each volition follows upon a judgment of the understanding might seem to fit poorly with his revamped account of motivation. In the first edition, he had held that the content of an agent's volition is determined by a judgment about which action is likeliest to maximize his pleasure. In the second edition and afterwards, he says that volitions are determined by affective states—feelings of uneasiness. Has he, in the correspondence with van Limborch, reverted to his first edition view? To see that he has not, we must appreciate the role played by the understanding even in his second edition account.

Locke has been described as moving from an internalist account of motivation in the first edition, to an externalist one in the second (Vailati 1990, 215; Magri 2000, 58). An internalist is supposed to think that being motivated to φ is "internal" to the process of judging that one should φ; an externalist, on the other hand, sees the link between judgment and motivation as at best contingent. Locke has also been described as shifting from an intellectualist account of motivation to a non-intellectualist one (Yolton 1970, 144). An intellectualist thinks that agents are moved to perform bad actions only when they mistake them for good ones. A non-intellectualist allows that one might be motivated to perform a bad action without making any sort of cognitive error. Both of these ways of describing the shift in Locke's views about motivation suggest that in the second edition judgment and the understanding play a diminished role. That is mistaken. In the second edition and afterwards, he continues to hold that volitions are triggered by, and their contents determined by, judgments of the understanding.

The second edition relocates, but preserves with only minor changes, the following passage:

A perfect Indifferency in the Mind, or Power of Preferring, not determinable by its last judgment of the Good or Evil, that is thought to attend its Choice, would be so far from being an advantage and excellency of any intellectual Nature, that it would be as great an imperfection, as the want of Indifferency to act, or not to act, till determined by the Will, would be an imperfection on the other side ... Nay were we determined by any thing but the last result of our own Minds, judging of the good or evil of any action, we were not free. (II.xxi.48 [2nd])[13]

Here Locke is arguing that the determination of our actions is no threat to our freedom so long as the actions are being determined by our own judgments about what to do. Here in the second edition, he is still talking of choices as being determined by judgments about good or evil.

---

[13] Compare II.xxi.30 [1st].

It is van Limborch's response to this passage that precipitates the discussion about liberty presupposing cogitation. Writing in March of 1701, van Limborch makes the point that he and other Remonstrant writers do not hold the view being criticized at II.xxi.48—the view that freedom consists in an indifference that obtains even when "that last judgment, in which the act of volition properly consists, has been made" (*Corresp.*, 7: #2881, 276). Instead, he says, he and the other Remonstrants take freedom to consist in an indifference that occurs earlier. In May, Locke replies that he cannot see how an "indifferency" located before the "last judgment of the understanding" would have any bearing on an agent's freedom:

For before the judgement of the understanding [a man] is altogether unable to determine himself, and so it is idle to inquire whether in that state he has liberty to determine himself to one or another alternative. (*Corresp.*, 7: #2925, 328–329)

Van Limborch does not write again on the subject of liberty until July, by which time he has "read, reread, and seriously pondered" what Locke has written about it (*Corresp.*, 7: #2953, 365). When he does weigh in, one of the things that he tries to do is to clarify what is meant by the "last judgement of the understanding." It is, he says, the "judgement by which a man decrees what he ought to do" (*Corresp.*, 7: #2953, 369). Van Limborch is inclined to think that what people call the "practical last judgement of the understanding" is an act not only of the understanding, but also of the will. What he insists upon, however, is that "a judgement which is an act of the understanding alone proceeds no further than 'This ought to be done, this ought to be forborne'" (*Corresp.*, 7: #2953, 369). He says this in order to allow for the possibility that one might *judge* that one ought to perform one action, but *will* the performance of another.

When Locke responds to this letter in August, most of his attention is devoted to undermining the idea that freedom consists in any kind of "Indifferency." Van Limborch had defined the relevant "Indifferency" as an "energy of the spirit by which, when all requisites for acting are present, it can act or not act" (*Corresp.*, 7: #2953, 367). Locke says that if we assume that the last judgment of the understanding is among the requisites for acting, then freedom cannot consist in an indifferency because "when any action has once been proposed to the understanding the Will is not in a state in which it can act or not act" (*Corresp.*, 7: #2979, 407). His point is that the last judgment of the understanding involves, if it does not just amount to, an action's being "proposed to the understanding." Once an action is proposed to the understanding, the agent cannot remain indifferent toward it—he cannot forbear willing on it.

In the course of arguing against van Limborch's conception of freedom, Locke repeatedly makes the point that volitions follow immediately upon acts of judgment that originate in the understanding:

For an action of willing this or that always follows a judgement of the understanding by which a man judges this to be better for here or now. (*Corresp.*, 7: #2979, 410)

[E]very single volition is always preceded by some judgement of the understanding about the thing to be done, and that that judgement that immediately precedes the volition or act of willing is in that case the last judgement of the understanding. (*Corresp.*, 7: #2979, 411)

I am speaking of that judgement which in every volition immediately precedes Volition; which is in reality the last judgement, whether it has been well pondered and recast by mature deliberation, or is extemporaneous and spring from a sudden impulse; and equally determines the will, whether or not it is in accordance with reason. (*Corresp.*, 7: #2979, 411)

These passages leave no doubt that even after his change of heart about motivation Locke thinks of volitions as being immediately preceded by, and determined by, judgments of the understanding.

If there were any doubts on that score, they should be removed by a passage that Locke adds to the end of II.xxi.48 in the fifth edition:

And therefore every Man is put under a Necessity by his Constitution, as an intelligent Being, to be determined in *willing* by his own Thought and Judgement, what is best for him to do: Else he would be under the Determination of some other than himself, which is a want of Liberty. And to deny, that a Man's *Will*, in every Determination, follows his own Judgment, is to say, that a Man *wills* and acts for an End that he would not have at the time that he *wills* and acts for it. For if he prefers it in his present Thoughts before any other, 'tis plain he then thinks better of it, and would have it before any other, unless he can have, and not have it; *will* and not *will* it at the same time; a Contradiction too manifest to be admitted.

What is being rejected here is van Limborch's idea that the last judgment of the understanding might vote for one course of action, with the agent willing another. Locke says that the content of an agent's volition is determined by his judgment about what is the best thing for him to do.

In the second edition and afterwards, Locke holds that the content of an agent's volition is determined by uneasiness the agent experiences. Yet as we have seen, he also continues to say that acts of will are preceded by, and determined by, judgments of the understanding. Is he offering a single, coherent view of action? Chappell suggests one way of reconciling the two claims. He says that by the time of the fifth edition Locke's view is that "desire, when effective, is always prompted by a judgment as to the goodness or badness of the desired object" (Chappell 1994b, 207). On this reading, the last judgment of the understanding stirs uneasiness, which in turn determines the content of the agent's volition. The problem with this reading is that Locke says more than once that every volition follows immediately upon the last judgment of the understanding. As Chappell has it, an episode of uneasiness comes between the judgment and the volition.

A better solution is to suppose that Locke thinks of episodes of uneasiness and acts of judgment as related not as Chappell suggests, but in the reverse order. We can accommodate both of Locke's claims about what determines the will by taking him to hold that uneasiness determines the content of an agent's volition *by* determining the content of an agent's judgment about what to do. At any given moment, each agent is subject to various kinds of uneasiness. An agent is prompted to attempt φ-ing when he judges that by φ-ing he will relieve a greater uneasiness than he would by performing the other actions that he is considering (including, possibly, the negative action of refraining from any positive action). This judgment might be the product of careful reflection, or it might be the result of a snap decision. Either way, uneasiness determines the will, and so does the last judgment of the understanding. Uneasiness determines the will by determining the last judgment of the understanding.

Earlier we saw reason to think that when Locke says that uneasiness determines the will, he means that uneasiness is the agent's motive for acting, not that it is the efficient cause of the agent's behavior. When he says that the last judgment of the understanding determines the will, he might or might not be using 'determines' in a causal sense. Either way, his view is that every time an agent wills to do something, he is willing to do what he has just judged it would be best for him to do in the next instant. The chief difference between Locke's first and second edition accounts of motivation is not that judgment plays a more prominent role in the first than in the second. Rather, it has to do with the factor that leads agents to judge that one course of action or another is the best. In the first edition, Locke holds that agents are moved to attempt the actions they do because they judge them most likely to be productive of future pleasure. In the second edition, he portrays agents as moved to attempt the actions they do because they judge them most likely to ease current uneasiness.

§70 *Forbearance in the Fifth Edition*

In the fifth edition of the *Essay*, Locke added material to II.xxi.23–25 and II.xxi.56 that bears on the question of whether it is possible to forbear willing. These new passages have been said to show that at the end of his life he changed his mind about that issue, which would also mean changing his mind about whether it is possible to will freely. Yet a closer look at the circumstances in which the new passages were composed tells against the idea that he had any such change of heart.

In the first edition of the *Essay*, Locke says at II.xxi.23 that "Willing, or Chusing being an Action, and Freedom consisting in a power of acting, or not acting, *a Man in respect of willing any Action in his power once proposed to his Thoughts, cannot be free*." The passage, and the reasoning behind it, are familiar: a man cannot be free in respect of willing because he cannot forbear willing on any proposal of action on which he might will. This passage is retained in the second, third, and fourth editions, but with '*Volition*' in place of 'Chusing.' In the fifth edition, however, a new clause is added, so that what is denied is only that a man can be free in respect of willing actions proposed to his thoughts "*as presently to be done*." The implication would seem to be that actions may be proposed to a man's thoughts in some other way, and that in such cases a man may after all be free with respect to willing. A similar change is introduced to II.xxi.24 in the fifth edition. Where earlier Locke had said that "*a Man is not at liberty to will, or not to will*," he now adds the caveat "in all Proposals of present Action." Again, this suggests a willingness to countenance freedom with respect to willing in cases involving proposals of action that are not proposals of *present* action.

What comes next is an example that appears in all of the editions. A man is walking, and it is proposed to him that he stop. Locke contends that the man cannot forbear willing on the question of whether to stop. In the fifth edition, he adds this further observation:

[S]o it is in regard of all other Actions in our Power so proposed, which are the far greater Number. For considering the vast Number of voluntary Actions, that succeed one another every Moment that we are awake, in the Course of our Lives, there are but few of them that are thought on or proposed to the *Will*, 'till the time they are to be done: And in all such Actions, as I have shewn, the Mind in respect of *willing* has not a power to act, or not to act, wherein consists Liberty: The Mind in that Case has not a Power to forbear *willing* (II.xxi.24 [5th]).

Locke thinks of the proposal to stop walking as a proposal of present action (perhaps a proposal of negative action), and as a proposal on which the man must will immediately. Again Locke seems to be allowing that people are sometimes faced with proposals of action that are not proposals of present action, and that in such cases one may forbear willing.

The puzzle is why Locke should think that *willing* on a proposal about what to do in the non-immediate future is even an option. Earlier we were able to make the best sense of his repudiation of freedom of the will by supposing that he subscribes to the view that all willing is willing to begin doing something *now*. To be sure, he should grant that one can *entertain* proposals about what to do in the non-immediate future. One can, on Wednesday morning, think about whether to go to the movies on Friday night. One can even, on Wednesday, *decide* to go to the movies on Friday night. But why think that, on Wednesday, one can *will* Friday night's moviegoing? If one cannot will Friday night's moviegoing on Wednesday, then it should be equally impossible to forbear Friday night's moviegoing on Wednesday.

The next section, II.xxi.25, begins this way in the fourth edition:

Since then it is plain, a Man is not at liberty, whether he will *Will*, or no; (for when an action in his power is proposed to his Thoughts, he cannot forbear Volition, he must determine one way or the other;) the next thing to be demanded is...

In the fifth edition, this passage reads:

Since then it is plain, that in most Cases a Man is not at Liberty, whether he will *Will*, or no; the next thing demanded is...

Here again Locke seems to be allowing for the possibility that a man can sometimes be free with regard to willing.

Perhaps the most interesting passage added to II.xxi in the fifth edition comes later, in the midst of Locke's discussion of why people pursue different courses of action and why some choose bad ones. At II.xxi.56, he repeats the familiar line that liberty consists in the ability to do or forbear. He then anticipates the question of whether willing is itself an action that one might be able to do or forbear doing. He answers it this way:

[I]n most Cases a Man is not at Liberty to forbear the Act of Volition; he must exert an Act of his *Will*, whereby the Action proposed, is made to exist, or not to exist. But yet there is a Case wherein a Man is at Liberty in respect of *Willing*, and that is the chusing of a remote Good as an End to be pursued. Here a Man may suspend the Act of his Choice from being determined for or against the thing proposed, till he has examined, whether it be really of a Nature in its self and Consequences to make him happy or no.

Here Locke finally offers an example of a situation in which he takes it to be possible to forbear willing, and so for one to be free with respect to willing. It is the situation of choosing a temporally remote good as a goal. While that much is clear, much else about the passage is not.

Chappell takes this passage to show that in his final years Locke comes to think that the "doctrine of suspension" conflicts with the thesis that we cannot forbear willing, and hence with the thesis that we cannot be free with regard to willing (Chappell 1994a, 118). He sees this passage as one in which Locke repudiates theses he had previously accepted. However, *pace* Chappell, this passage does not include any concession that there is a conflict between the thesis that we can suspend actions and the denial that we can forbear willing. It might have done so had Locke claimed that we can forbear willing in the case of choosing a remote good *because* we can suspend the prosecution of desire in that case. What Locke does claim is just that in the sort of case in which we can forbear willing, doing so involves suspending an action, namely "the Act of [one's] Choice." That is to say, when one forbears from choosing a remote good as an end, one suspends one's choosing of a remote good. That is to be expected. By the same token, when one forbears from raising one's hand one suspends the raising of one's hand. What is unusual about the present case is just the suggestion that what one suspends when one forbears from choosing a remote good as an end is an act of *willing* something.

Why Locke thinks that choosing a remote good as an end is an instance of willing something is one of the puzzles raised by II.xxi.56 [5th]. Another is why he thinks that this is a situation—perhaps *the* situation—in which one can forbear willing. Finally, there is the question of how II.xxi.56 [5th] relates to II.xxi.23–25 [5th]. Does Locke think that choosing a remote good as an end involves willing on a proposal about what to do in the non–immediate future? We should begin our quest for the answers to these questions by looking at the correspondence with van Limborch, for it was that exchange that prompted Locke to add these passages to the fifth edition.

As we saw earlier, van Limborch's claim that "whatever a man wills is considered by him to be agreeable" (*Corresp.*, 7, #2881, 275) inspires Locke to warn him against confusing will with desire (*Corresp.*, 7, #2925, 327). Desire may be directed toward whatever is agreeable, Locke says, whereas the objects of will are limited to our own actions. In reply, van Limborch concedes the distinction between desire and will, but says that the will can have two different sorts of objects: "I think that we will two things, an end and the means that lead to an end" (*Corresp.*, 7, #2953, 366). A few sentences later, he fills out the suggestion that one can will an end. He says:

A prudent man will choose from many desirables, and set before himself as the end of all of his actions, that one which is perfect in all respects and in which are joined all the reasons that make a thing desirable. But that choice is not made without a determination of the will by which a man decrees that he will set before himself this good, which he judges to be preferable to all the rest, as the end of his actions. I have accordingly believed that it can rightly be said that the will of a man is directed to a good, and that that good is always apprehended by him as agreeable.

Van Limborch holds that setting a goal or end before oneself is a kind of activity. It is a cognitive performance of some kind—what he elsewhere calls an "internal action" (*Corresp.*, 7, #2881, 275). He then adds that when an agent wills the performance of the action of setting a goal before himself, it is right to speak of him as willing not only that action, but also the goal he sets before himself.

Locke's initial reaction is to insist again that, strictly speaking, we will nothing but our own actions. He sees this as following from the definition of 'will':

[I]f 'Will' signifies the power that a man has to begin, to stop, or to forbear any action of his mind or body, as I have set forth at greater length in bk. II, ch. xxi, § 5, etc., in which you also appear to acquiesce: if, I say, this is the idea that the word 'Will' signifies, and if we have it present in mind when we speak of Will, nothing can be more certain than that Will terminates solely in our actions and cannot be further extended to anything else or directed to a remote or absent good. (*Corresp.*, 7, #2979, 403)

Locke thinks that if one speaks of us as willing not only our actions but the ends to which our actions are the means, one must be using 'will' in a different sense than that employed in the *Essay*. He encourages van Limborch to explain what idea he associates with the word 'will,' so that "we may agree about the sense of the word, that is, about the thing that we are discussing" (*Corresp.*, 7, #2979, 404).

Locke does not leave the matter there, however. After an excursus about van Limborch's distinction between "complete" and "incomplete" desires and volitions, he returns to the suggestion that a man's setting a good before himself is his willing an end. Locke agrees with van Limborch that the choosing of a good as an end is a voluntary act:

When many goods, not subordinate to, or consistent with, one another, are present to the understanding at the same time, a man, neglecting the others, proposes one to himself as an end, that is, as a thing to be pursued, this he does voluntarily and so far the will is directed to that action of the mind by which he proposes to himself one thing as an end in preference to the rest, and it terminates in that action in the same way as it terminates in computation when he wills to number or in movement of the feet when he wills to walk. I grant that, owing to this voluntary proposing of that good as an end, it is not infrequently said in every-day speech that the will is directed to that end or to that good, whether appropriately, and as befits philosophical precision, you can judge. (*Corresp.*, 7, #2979, 405)

Locke agrees that there is a sort of mental activity involved in selecting one among several possible goods as one's goal. Where van Limborch speaks of the activity of setting a good before oneself, Locke speaks of proposing a good to oneself as an end. It is clear from the context that "proposing" a good here means more than merely considering the possibility of embracing it as a goal. For it is after the man has considered several goods as possible goals, and when he settles upon one of them, that Locke says the man proposes that one to himself as an end. In this passage, Locke also concedes that when one voluntarily proposes a good to oneself, then there is a loose, everyday sense in which one might say that one has willed the goal itself. Yet he makes it quite clear that he regards this as an imprecise way of talking.

Both Locke and van Limborch seem to be thinking of endorsing or embracing a goal as a voluntary mental doing, on a par with calculating a sum in one's head, or directing one's attention to a particular memory. These are activities that need not involve any outward display, but that can be voluntarily undertaken or forborne. What is less clear is what Locke and van

Limborch think that one *does* when one embraces a long-term goal. Perhaps they think of this as bringing about a kind of cognitive restructuring in oneself. It does seem that when one embraces a goal, one changes one's cognitive and behavioral dispositions in certain ways, altering the tracks in which one's mind is apt to run in the future.

An example might help to fill out the suggestion. Suppose that Felix loves old books, antique typewriters, and fountain pens. Until now, he has acquired these things haphazardly: a first edition of Hume's *History of the Tudors* here, an Underwood #3 with glass-covered keys there. He is attracted by the idea of becoming a more systematic collector, but torn about what to collect. Signed first editions of Updike? Pre-WWII Remington portables? Early Mentmore pens with the ball clip? All of these projects appeal to him, but he can afford to pursue only one of them seriously. On the view suggested by Locke and van Limborch, Felix could *will* himself to choose one of them. He could wake up one morning with the thought that he will no longer dither about it, he will embrace one of these projects. He could then embrace one of them in consequence of a volition to do so. When at long last he settles on the project of collecting Mentmore pens, he instantly gives himself reasons to think and act differently than he did before. He may still love old books, but conscious of his limited disposable income he is less apt to spend Saturday afternoons in used book stores. He may still love American typewriters of the 1920s and 1930s, but now he is more likely to scour the internet auction sites for English pens instead. Felix is also disposed to approach certain decisions differently than he did before. A decision that might previously have occupied him for days—such as whether to spend $100 on an autographed but water-damaged copy of *Rabbit, Redux*— could now be dispatched instantly, almost automatically. Another—such as whether he should spend $80 on a Mentmore Auto-Flow button-filler that is just a *slightly* different shade of brown than one he already has—might loom much larger.

In claiming that one can will a remote good, van Limborch meant just that one can perform an act of will that influences one's future doings, an act of will that channels them in the direction of a particular remote good. When he writes to Locke again, it is clear that he was not seriously committed to the idea that we will the goals of our actions as well as the actions themselves. He confesses to having spoken somewhat carelessly, and accepts both Locke's definition of 'will' and the distinction between will and desire

(*Corresp.*, 7, #3010, 449). He says that when he claimed that the will could be directed toward an end, "I meant nothing else than what you yourself say in your letter." Quoting Locke's remark about the man who voluntarily proposes a good to himself as an end, van Limborch adds: "This choice is therefore an action of the will: when a man has made this choice for himself he is directed by his desire to that good which he chose for himself; and by his will governs his actions by which he hopes to obtain the desired good" (*Corresp.*, 7, #3010, 450). He is willing to concede that a man cannot will anything but the beginning, stopping, or forbearing of an action of his mind or body.[14]

In what survives of his next letter, Locke does not pursue the issue further. There is no need to, since van Limborch has capitulated. However, it is significant that this letter contained an enclosure that is now lost. Locke gives us some idea of its contents:

As regards the remaining things about which you seem to be in doubt, lest the reply should extend to too great length and bulk I think that I shall give satisfaction better and more compendiously by inserting here and there in chapter xxi some explications by which I may make my meaning clearer where it is set down perhaps rather negligently or obscurely, so that it may in future be plain to the reader even if, as happens, he is in a hurry, provided that he does not disdain keeping in mind what has been set down. (*Corresp.*, 7, #3043, 504)

In his closing paragraph, Locke again expresses the hope that the "annexed explications" will allow van Limborch to understand his meaning (*Corresp.*, 7, #3043, 505). Evidently he either enclosed sheets from the fourth edition of II.xxi with his interpolations written in the margins, or else sent just the manuscript interpolations with indications of where they should be inserted. It seems quite likely that the missing enclosure included passages that were also intended for the fifth edition of the *Essay*. For one thing, there is precedent. Three months earlier, Locke had sent van Limborch a postscript concerning the sort of "indifferency" that liberty consists in. He told van Limborch that the passage should be added to II.xxi.71, and in the posthumously published fifth edition it was. Even more compelling is the

---

[14] Later in the letter he suggests once again that he agrees with Locke's handling of the issue: "I also welcome with both thumbs what you write in your letter, that a man is directed to an absent good or end; and that when many goods, not subordinate to, or consistent with, one another, are present to the understanding at the same time, a man, neglecting the others, proposes one to himself as an end, that is, as a thing to be pursued: and this he does voluntarily; and therefore his will is directed to that action of the mind by which he proposes to himself one thing as an end in preference to the rest; and it terminates in that action" (*Corresp.*, 7, #3010, 458).

fact that in this letter Locke speaks of the effects his interpolations will have on future readers. Though they were occasioned by his exchange with van Limborch, they were evidently meant to be read by a wider audience.

It seems quite likely that the lost enclosure contained the passages that were added to II.xxi.23–25 and II.xxi.56 in the fifth edition.[15] This is significant because in his letter Locke makes it clear that the material in the enclosure is meant to prevent the misunderstanding of views that he had already advanced, not to change his position on matters of consequence. If the enclosure contained the passages later added to II.xxi.23–25 and II.xxi.56, this is a reason for thinking that Locke did not intend those passages as retractions of any sort.

Locke's clarifications did not answer all of van Limborch's questions. When he replies a month later, van Limborch says that "even regarding those things that you have added by way of explication, I am uncertain whether you hold that that judgment, after whose formation there is no longer in a man liberty of not willing, is purely an action of understanding, and whether you hold that that action of understanding is free or necessary" (*Corresp.*, 7, #3055, 520). Earlier he had suggested that what Locke calls the last judgment of the understanding is actually a hybrid of judging and willing (*Corresp.*, 7, #3010, 460). His own view is that any act that is wholly an act of the understanding—a judgment with no admixture of volition—is necessary rather than free (*Corresp.*, 7, #3010, 457).

Though Locke writes in a few months to recommend blood-letting for his friend's heart palpitations (*Corresp.*, 7, #3130, 606), almost ten months pass before he returns to the topic of liberty. When he does, it is his final letter on the matter. He does not directly answer either of van Limborch's questions despite having in front of him the letter in which they were posed (*Corresp.*, 7, #3192, 680). As he had done once before, he passes over the question about whether the last judgment of

---

[15] Chappell simply says that the material added to II.xxi.56 *was* in the enclosure, as though this were a known fact (Chappell 1994a, 119). One might dispute the idea that the passages added to II.xxi.23–5 and II.xxi.56 were in the enclosure. For Locke says that the enclosure is meant to clarify matters on which van Limborch still has questions, and at that point van Limborch was no longer pressing him on the issues addressed in those passages. Van Limborch did still have questions about Locke's view of the roles played by the understanding and the will, and at II.xxi.48 [5th] Locke inserts a passage about that. Presumably this passage was in the missing enclosure. Yet it consists of just a few sentences. Surely the enclosure must have contained more than that? Besides the addition to II.xxi.71—which Locke had sent van Limborch earlier—the only other significant fifth edition changes to II.xxi *are* the additions to sections 23–5 and 56. What seems likely is that these passages were in the missing enclosure, and that Locke addressed the questions that van Limborch had raised—not just the ones that he was still pressing—because Locke was writing not just for van Limborch but for future readers of the *Essay*.

the understanding is an act of the understanding alone.[16] He also re-casts van Limborch's question about whether that last judgment is free: "[Y]ou appear to doubt whether I hold that a man is free in Willing or in Understanding" (*Corresp.*, 7, #3192, 680). Then he offers some general pronouncements. He says:

To this question I answer thus:

1. Generally, indeed, that in my opinion a man is free in every action, as well of will-ing as of understanding, if he was able to have abstained from that action of willing or understanding; if not, not.

2. More particularly, as regards the will: there are some cases in which a man is unable not to will, and in all those acts of willing a man is not free because he is unable not to act. In the rest, where he was able to will or not to will, he is free. (*Corresp.*, 7, #3192, 680).

Here the first numbered reply is simply a re-statement of his general view about what is required for a man to be free with respect to an action. His second adds that agents are sometimes unfree with regard to their acts of will. Given his position in the *Essay*, that is rather an understatement. Locke then goes on to suggest that the question of whether acts of the understand-ing are free is ambiguous. He thinks that a person is usually free to reflect on the topics or problems he wants, but not free about the judgments he arrives at concerning matters of fact. A person who judges that 52 and 23 equal 75 is free in that he might have forborne this little feat of addition; yet, having undertaken it, he is not free in arriving at the solution he does.

In this, his final letter on the topic, Locke does not deny that men are sometimes free with respect to acts of will. In fact, he seems to be leaving that possibility wide open. On the other hand, he also does not claim that men *are* ever free with respect to acts of will. He does not say that men "will" freely in any cases but the one sort that he has already conceded, and he does not say that men ever will freely in the strict, philosophically pre-cise, sense of 'will.' There may be some temptation to read between the lines, and to see this letter as conceding that there are many situations in which men will freely. However, in that case Locke would be making a much bigger concession here than he does in the fifth edition of the *Essay*. What seems more likely is that he is retreating to non-committal generalizations

---

[16] There seems to be every reason to think that when Locke speaks of the last judgment of the understanding, he means to be referring to an act of judging, period.

as a way of mollifying van Limborch, while at the same time disengaging himself from further debate on the matter.

What light does the correspondence with van Limborch shed on Locke's final thoughts about our ability or inability to forbear willing? One thing that it shows is that it is quite unlikely that anything that van Limborch said convinced Locke that there was a conflict between his view about suspending the prosecution of desires and his view that we cannot forbear willing. Van Limborch does not even make that suggestion. Early in their exchange about agency, he does call attention to a possible conflict between Locke's view about suspension and another of his views (*Corresp.*, 7, #2953, 370). However, the other is not—as Chappell suggests (Chappell 1994a, 119)—the view that we do not will freely. It is Locke's view that freedom does not consist in an indifferency obtaining before the last judgment of the understanding (*Corresp.*, 7, #2953, 370).[17]

Earlier we asked why, at II.xxi.56 [5th], Locke seems to think that choosing a remote good involves willing something, and why he thinks that it presents us with a case—perhaps the *only* case—in which we can forbear willing. What a careful reading of the correspondence with van Limborch suggests is that Locke does *not* seriously think that choosing a remote good is a matter of willing something. Even van Limborch, who was responsible for suggesting to Locke that we can will a remote good, seems not to have meant that exactly. He seems to have meant just that it is possible to will a mental action that increases the likelihood that one will later act to secure some particular remote good. Like van Limborch, Locke does think that embracing a good—or, as he puts it, proposing a good to oneself as an end—is a mental activity that might be willed or forborne. He may be thinking of this as a kind of rearranging of one's cognitive furniture. In the correspondence, Locke grants that in a loose, everyday way of talking, we may speak of ourselves as willing the good that we embrace when we will

---

[17] In an earlier letter, Locke had said that "before the judgement of the understanding [a man] is altogether unable to determine himself, and so it is idle to inquire whether in that state he has liberty to determine himself to one or [an]other alternative" (*Corresp.*, 7, #2925, 329). His point is that an agent does not have the opportunity of exercising his will—of producing a volition—until he arrives at a judgment about what he should do. Though van Limborch does not press the objection, Locke is surely overstating his case here. On his own account of volition, the volition to φ or not to φ must come immediately on the heels of his last judgment about whether to φ. Therefore, if it were idle to inquire whether an agent is free with respect to φ-ing before he has decided whether he should φ, it would be idle to describe an agent as free with respect to an action except in retrospect. Locke has not said enough to justify such a strange and sweeping conclusion.

the embracing of it. Yet he clearly holds that the act of proposing the end to oneself is not, strictly speaking, a willing of that end.

Locke thinks that the act of setting a goal for oneself is an activity that may be somewhat loosely characterized as willing on a proposal about what to do in the non-immediate future. Given that, we can also understand why he says that it supplies us with a case in which one may be said to have the ability to forbear willing. Earlier, we explained his denial that we can forbear willing by attributing to him the view that the objects of volition are thoughts or bodily motions that would begin immediately. If one is thinking about whether to will into existence a particular thought process or bodily motion in the next instant, the closest that one could come to forbearing to will on the matter would be to decide not to do it now, while entertaining the possibility of initiating the same sort of process or motion at some time in the future. That is not forbearing to will, for it involves deciding not to perform the action that had been under consideration. In contrast, consider the situation of someone deciding whether or not to run a marathon four months from now. That is a decision that *could* be put off, at least for a while. (If one puts it off too long, one effectively decides not to run the marathon, since running the marathon requires time for training.) If one is going to speak in a loose, imprecise way of the decision to run a marathon as a matter of willing to run it, then one can also speak in a loose, imprecise way of postponing that decision as forbearing to will on whether to run the marathon. However, just as Locke does not think that one can, strictly speaking, will to run a marathon that is months away, so he should not allow that, strictly speaking, one can forbear willing on whether to run a marathon that is months away.

Locke does not, in the fifth edition of the *Essay*, suggest any argument that might have convinced him that we can exercise our wills on proposals about what to do in the non-immediate future. Nor does he offer any explanation of why choosing a remote good might really involve *willing* it. Of course, it is possible that he came to believe these things in consequence of some argument that he does not share with his readers. That is why we look to the circumstances in which he composed these passages and added them to the *Essay*. Doing this we discover, first, that in all likelihood he wrote them in response to letters from van Limborch; and second, that van Limborch did not change Locke's mind about much of anything. He certainly did not convince Locke that choosing a remote good involves willing it, strictly speaking, and thus that a man can will something other than his own thought or bodily motion in the next instant. What is involved in choosing a remote good is not a point of contention between the two men. They discuss just the sort of case that Locke mentions at II.xxi.56 [5th], and they *agree* that it is only in a loose, everyday sense of 'will' that one can be said to will the goals one adopts.

It was the correspondence with van Limborch that served as the original impetus for the passages in which Locke seems to be allowing that we can sometimes forbear willing. Writing to van Limborch, he could presume that his reader would understand that he was speaking loosely when he allowed that we can forbear willing on proposals concerning the non-immediate future, and in particular when he allowed that we can forbear willing the goals we set for ourselves. He then left instructions for the material to be inserted in II.xxi in the *Essay*'s next edition. What he did not do is take sufficient care to ensure that the inserted material made it clear to a reader of the *Essay* how little Locke was actually conceding. He did not take sufficient care that the new passages would be understood as he knew that van Limborch would understand them, and as he meant for them to be understood. To explain this editorial failure, we might remind ourselves of the excuse that Locke offers van Limborch in the letter that included these interpolations: "If there are in your letter any things that you think I have not answered clearly enough," he says, "please make allowance for uncertain health, which renders me more languid and less fit for writing" (*Corresp.*, 7, #3043, 505).

Bibliography

Aaron, Richard. 1937. *John Locke*, 1st ed., Oxford: Oxford University Press.

Aaron, Richard. 1971. *John Locke*, 3rd ed., Oxford: Oxford University Press.

Acworth, Richard. 1971. "Locke's First Reply to John Norris." *Locke Newsletter* 2, 7–11.

Alexander, Peter. 1974. "Curley on Locke and Boyle." *Philosophical Review* 83, 229–237.

Alexander, Peter. 1985. *Ideas, Qualities and Corpuscles*, Cambridge: Cambridge University Press.

Allaire, Edwin. 1963. "Bare Particulars." *Philosophical Studies* 14, 1–8.

Allaire, Edwin. 1965. "Another Look at Bare Particulars." *Philosophical Studies* 16, 16–21.

Alston, William and Bennett, Jonathan. 1988. "Locke on People and Substances." *Philosophical Review* 97, 25–46.

Anstey, Peter. 2000. *The Philosophy of Robert Boyle*, London: Routledge.

Arbini, Ronald. 1983. "Did Descartes Have a Philosophical Theory of Sense Perception?" *Journal of the History of Philosophy* 22, 317–37.

Ariew, Roger. 1999. *Descartes and the Last Scholastics*. Ithaca: Cornell University Press.

Ariew, Roger and Cottingham, John, and Sorrell, Tom, eds. 1998. *Descartes's Meditations: Background Source Materials*. Cambridge: Cambridge University Press.

Aristotle. 1984. *The Complete Works of Aristotle: The Revised Oxford Translation*, 2 vols. J. Barnes ed. Princeton: Princeton University Press.

Aristotle. 1995. *Selections*. T. Irwin and G. Fine eds. and trans. Indianapolis: Hackett Publishing Company.

Armstrong, D. M. 1997. *A World of States of Affairs*. Cambridge: Cambridge University Press.

Armstrong, D. M., Martin, C. B., and Place, U. T. 1996. *Dispositions: A Debate*. Tim Crane ed., London: Routledge.

Austin, J.L. 1961. *Philosophical Papers*. Oxford: Oxford University Press.

Ayers, Michael. 1974. "Individuals Without Sortals." *Canadian Journal of Philosophy* 4, 113–48.

Ayers, Michael. 1977. "The Ideas of Power and Substance in Locke's Philosophy." *Philosophical Quarterly* 25, 1–27.

Ayers, Michael. 1981. "Mechanism, Superaddition and the Proof of God's Existence in Locke's *Essay.*" *Philosophical Review* 90, 210–51.

Ayers, Michael. 1991. *Locke*, 2 vols. London: Routledge.

Ayers, Michael. 1997. "Is *Physical Object* a Sortal Concept? A Reply to Xu." *Mind & Language* 12, 393–405.

Ayers, Michael. 2011. "Primary and Secondary Qualities in Locke's *Essay.*" In *Primary and Secondary Qualities: The Historical and Ongoing Debate*, L. Nolan, ed. Oxford: Oxford University Press, 136–57.

Barber, Kenneth and Gracia, Jorge (eds). 1994. *Individuation and Identity in Early Modern Philosophy*, Albany: SUNY Press.

Blackburn, Simon. 1990. "Filling in Space." *Analysis* 50, 62–65.

Benardete, José. 1989. *Metaphysics*, Oxford: Oxford University Press.

Bennett, Jonathan. 1971. *Locke, Berkeley, Hume: Central Themes*, Oxford: Clarendon Press.

Bennett, Jonathan. 1984. *A Study of Spinoza's* Ethics, Indianapolis, IN: Hackett Publishing Co.

Bennett, Jonathan. 1987. "Substratum." *History of Philosophy Quarterly* 4, 197–215.

Bennett, Jonathan. 1996. "Ideas and Qualities in Locke's Essay." *History of Philosophy Quarterly* 13, 73–88.

Bennett, Jonathan. 2001. *Learning From Six Philosophers*, 2 vols. Oxford: Oxford University Press.

Bennett, Jonathan. 2005. "God and Matter in Locke: An Exposition of *Essay* 4.10." In *Early Modern Philosophy: Mind Matter and Metaphysics*, C. Mercer and E. O'Neill, eds. Oxford: Oxford University Press, 161–82.

Bennett, Jonathan and Remnant, Peter. 1978. "How Matter Might at First Be Made." In *New Essays on Rationalism and Empiricism*, Charles Jarrett, John King-Farlow, and F. J. Pelletier, eds. Guelph, Ont.: Canadian Association for Publishing in Philosophy (Canadian Journal of Philosophy Supplementary volume 4), 1–11.

Bergmann, Gustav. 1967. *Realism*, Madison, Wisconsin: University of Wisconsin Press.

Berkeley, George. 1975. *Philosophical Works*, M. R. Ayers ed. London: J. M. Dent.

Berlin, Isaiah. 1953. *The Hedgehog and the Fox: An Essay on Tolstoy's View of History*, New York: Simon & Schuster.

Bolton, Martha Brandt. 1976. "Substances, Substrata and Names of Substances in Locke's *Essay.*" *Philosophical Review* 85, 488–513.

Bolton, Martha. 1994. "Locke on Identity: The Scheme of Simple and Compound Things." In *Individuation and Identity in Early Modern Philosophy*, K. Barber and J. Gracia, eds. Albany: SUNY Press, 103–31.

Bolton, Martha. 2001. "John Locke" in *The Blackwell Guide to the Modern Philosophers*, Steven Emmanuel, ed. Oxford: Blackwell Publishing Ltd., 101–26.

Boyd, Richard. 1988. "How to Be a Moral Realist," in *Essays on Moral Realism*, G. Sayre-McCord, ed. Ithaca: Cornell University Press, 181–228.

Boyle, Robert. 1664. *Experiments and Considerations Touching Colours*. London: Printed for Henry Herringman at the Anchor in the Lower walk of the New Exchange.

Boyle, Robert. 1676. *Experiments and Notes about the Mechanical Production of Magnetism*. London: Printed by E. Flesher for R. Davis, Bookseller in Oxford.

Boyle, Robert. 1991. *Selected Philosophical Papers of Robert Boyle*, M. A. Stewart ed. Indianapolis: Hackett Publishing Co.

Brand, Myles. 1968. "Danto on Basic Actions." *Nous* 2, 187–90.

Brand, Myles. 1971. "The Language of Not Doing." *American Philosophical Quarterly* 8, 45–53.

Brogan, A. P. 1959. "John Locke and Utilitarianism." *Ethics* 69, 79–93.

Brown, Stuart and Fox, N.J. 2006. *Historical Dictionary of Leibniz's Philosophy*, Lanham, MD: Scarecrow Press.

Burns, Norman. 1972. *Christian Mortalism from Byndale to Milton*, Cambridge, MA: Harvard University Press.

Butler, Joseph. 1736. *The Analogy of Religion, Natural and Revealed, to the Constitution and Course of Nature. To Which are Added two Brief Dissertations: 1. Of Personal Identity. II. Of the Nature of Virtue.* London: Printed for James, John and Paul Knapton, at the Crown in Ludgate Street.

Campbell, John. 1980. "Locke on Qualities." *Canadian Journal of Philosophy* 10, 567–85.

Campbell, Keith. 1990. *Abstract Particulars*, Oxford: Basil Blackwell Ltd.

Chappell, Vere. 1989. "Locke and Relative Identity." *History of Philosophy Quarterly* 6, 69–83.

Chappell, Vere. 1990. "Locke on the Ontology of Matter, Living Things and Persons." *Philosophical Studies* 60, 19–32.

Chappell, Vere. 1994a. "Locke on Freedom of the Will." In *Locke's Philosophy: Content and Context*. G. A. J. Rogers, ed. Oxford: Oxford University Press, 101–21.

Chappell, Vere. 1994b. "Locke on the Intellectual Basis of Sin." *Journal of the History of Philosophy* 32, 197–207.

Chappell, Vere. 1998. "Locke on the Suspension of Desire." *Locke Newsletter* 29, 23–38.

Chappell, Vere. 2000. "Locke on the Suspension of Desire" (revised version). In *John Locke: An Essay Concerning Human Understanding in Focus*. G. Fuller, R. Stecker, and J. Wright, eds. London: Routledge, 236–48.

Chisholm, Roderick. 1966. "Freedom and Action." In *Freedom and Determinism*. Keith Lehrer, ed. Atlantic Highlands, NJ: Humanities Press, 11–44.

Clagett, Marshall. 1959. *The Science of Mechanics in the Middle Ages*. Madison: University of Wisconsin Press.

Cohen, Marc. 2009. "Aristotle's Metaphysics", *The Stanford Encyclopedia of Philosophy (Spring 2009 Edition)*, Edward N. Zalta (ed.), URL = <http://plato.stanford.edu/archives/spr2009/entries/aristotle-metaphysics/>.

Colman, John. 1983. *John Locke's Moral Philosophy*. Edinburgh: Edinburgh University Press.

Conn, Christopher. 1999. "Two Arguments for Lockean Four-Dimensionalism." *British Journal for the History of Philosophy* 7, 429–46.

Conn, Christopher. 2003. *Locke on Essence and Identity*. Dordrecht: Kluwer Academic Publishers.

Costa, Michael. 1983. "What Cartesian Ideas are Not." *Journal of the History of Philosophy* 21, 537–49.

Cottingham, John. 1985. "Cartesian Trialism." *Mind* 94, 218–30.

Cummins, Robert. 1975. "Two Troublesome Claims about Qualities in Locke's *Essay*." *Philosophical Review* 84, 401–18.

Curley, Edwin. 1972. "Locke, Boyle, and the Distinction Between Primary and Secondary Qualities." *Philosophical Review* 81, 438–64.

Dalí, Salvador. 1942. *The Secret Life of Salvador Dalí*. H. Chevalier trans. New York: Dial Press.

Daly, Chris. 1994. "Tropes." *Proceedings of the Aristotelian Society* 94, 253–61.

Dancy, Jonathan, ed.. 1997. *Reading Parfit*. Oxford: Blackwell Publishers.

Danto, Arthur. 1965. "Basic Actions." *American Philosophical Quarterly* 2, 141–48.

Darwall, Stephen. 1995. *The British Moralists and the Internal "Ought"*. Cambridge: Cambridge University Press.

Davidson, Donald. 1963. "Actions, Reasons, and Causes." *Journal of Philosophy* 60, 685–700.

Della Rocca, Michael. 1999. "If a Body Meet a Body: Descartes on Body–Body Causation." In *New Essays on the Rationalists*, R. Gennaro and C. Huenemann, eds. Oxford: Oxford University Press, 48–81.

Dennett, Daniel. 1984. *Elbow Room: The Varieties of Free Will Worth Wanting*. Cambridge, Mass.: MIT Press.

Dennett, Daniel. 2003. *Freedom Evolves*. New York: Viking.

Descartes, René. 1983. *Principles of Philosophy*, V. Miller and R. Miller eds. and trans. Dordrecht: D. Reidel Publishing Company.

Descartes, René. 1985. *The Philosophical Writings of Descartes*, 2 vols. J. Cottingham, R. Stoothoff, and D. Murdoch eds. and trans., Cambridge: Cambridge University Press.

Descartes, René. 1991. *The Philosophical Writings of Descartes*, vol. 3, J. Cottingham, R. Stoothoff, D. Murdoch, and A. Kenny, trans. Cambridge: Cambridge University Press.

Deutsch, Harry, 2008. "Relative Identity", *The Stanford Encyclopedia of Philosophy (Winter 2008 Edition)*, Edward N. Zalta (ed.), <http://plato.stanford.edu/archives/win2008/entries/identity-relative/>.

Digby, Kenelm. 1665a. "Of Bodies." In *Two Treatises*. London: Printed for John Williams, and are to be sold at the Crown in S. Paul's Church-yard.

Digby, Kenelm. 1665b. "Of Man's Soule." In *Two Treatises*. London: Printed for John Williams, and are to be sold at the Crown in S. Paul's Church-yard.

Downing, Lisa. 1998. "The Status of Mechanism in Locke's *Essay*." *Philosophical Review* 107, 381–414.

Downing, Lisa. 2007. "Locke's Ontology." In *The Cambridge Companion to Locke's Essay Concerning Human Understanding*, L. Newman, ed. Cambridge: Cambridge University Press, 352–80.

Ehring, Douglas. 1997. *Causation and Persistence*. New York: Oxford University Press.

Eklund, Jon. 1975. *The Incompleat Chymist*. Washington, DC: Smithsonian Institute Press.

Feynman, R., R. Leighton, and M. Sands. 1989. *The Feynman Lectures on Physics: Commemorative Issue*, vol. 1. Reading, Mass.: Addison-Wesley.

Flew, Antony. 1951. "Locke and the Problem of Personal Identity." *Philosophy* 26, 53–68.

Fox Bourne, H. R. 1876. *The Life of John Locke*, 2 vols. New York: Harper & Bros.

Freddoso, Alfred. 1991. "God's General Concurrence with Secondary Causes: Why Conservation is Not Enough." *Philosophical Perspectives* 5, 553–85.

Freddoso, Alfred. 1994. "God's General Concurrence with Secondary Causes: Pitfalls and Prospects." *American Catholic Philosophical Quarterly* 52, 131–56.

Garber, Daniel. 1993. "Descartes and Occasionalism." In *Causation in Early Modern Philosophy: Cartesianism, Occasionalism, and Preestablished Harmony*, S. Nadler, ed. University Park, PA: Penn State Press, 9–26.

Garber, Daniel and Ayers, Michael, eds. 1998. *The Cambridge History of Seventeenth-Century Philosophy*, Cambridge: Cambridge University Press.

Garrett, Don. 2003. "Locke on Personal Identity, Consciousness, and 'fatal errors'." *Philosophical Topics* 31, 95–125.

Geach, Peter. 1968. *Reference and Generality*, Ithaca, NY: Cornell University Press.

Gibson, James. 1917. *Locke's Theory of Knowledge and Its Historical Relations*. Cambridge: Cambridge University Press.

Ginet, Carl. 1990. *On Action*. Cambridge: Cambridge University Press.

Glanvill, Joseph. 1765. *Essays on Several Important Subjects in Philosophy and Religion*, London: Printed by J. D. for John Baker at the Three Pidgeons.

Goldman, Alvin. 1970. *A Theory of Human Action*. Englewood Cliffs, NJ: Prentice-Hall.

Goldman, Alvin. 1976. "The Volitional Theory Revisited." *Action Theory*. M. Brand and D. Walton, eds. Dordrecht: D. Reidel, 67–85.

Green, O. H. 1980. "Killing and Letting Die." *American Philosophical Quarterly* 17, 195–204.

Green, Thomas Hill. 1885. *Works of Thomas Hill Green*, vol. 1, R. L. Nettleship ed. London: Longmans, Green and Co.

Griffin, Nicholas. 1977. *Relative Identity*, Oxford: Oxford University Press.

Guyer, Paul. 1994. "Locke's Philosophy of Language." *The Cambridge Companion to Locke*, V. Chappell ed. Cambridge: Cambridge University Press, 115–45.

Hall, Roland. 1975. "John Locke's New Words and Uses." *Notes and Queries* 220, 548–57.

Hall, Roland. 1996. "Locke's Apologies in the Essay." *Locke Newsletter* 27, 131–8.

Hardie, W. F. R. 1971. "Willing and Acting." *Philosophical Quarterly* 21, 193–206.

Hardin, C. L. 1983. "Colors, Normal Observers, and Standard Conditions." *Journal of Philosophy* 80, 806–13.

Hardin, C. L. 1984. "Are Scientific Objects Coloured?" *Mind* 93, 491–500.

Hardin, C. L. 1988. *Color for Philosophers*. Indianapolis: Hackett.

Harman, Gilbert. 1976. "Practical Reasoning." *Review of Metaphysics* 29, 431–63.

Hatfield, Gary. 1994. "The Cognitive Faculties." In *The Cambridge History of Seventeenth Century Philosophy*, vol. 2, M. Ayers and D. Garber, eds. Cambridge: Cambridge University Press, 953–1002.

Helm, Paul. 1979. "Locke's Theory of Personal Identity." *Philosophy* 54, 173–85.

Heyd, Thomas. 1994. "Locke's Arguments for the Resemblance Thesis Revisited." *Locke Newsletter* 25, 13–28.

Hill, Benjamin. 2004. "'Resemblance' and Locke's Primary–Secondary Quality Distinction." *Locke Studies* 4, 89–122.

Hirsch, Eli. 1976. "Physical Identity." *Philosophical Review* 85, 357–89.

Hirsch, Eli. 1982. *The Concept of Identity*. Oxford: Oxford University Press.

Hirsch, Eli. 1997. "Basic Objects: A Reply to Xu." *Language & Mind* 12, 406–12.

Hobbes, Thomas. 1991. *Leviathan*, R. Tuck ed. Cambridge: Cambridge University Press.

Hoffman, Joshua. 1980. "Locke on Whether a Thing Can Have Two Beginnings of Existence." *Ratio* 22, 106–11.

Honoré, A. M. 1964. "Can and Can't." *Mind* 73, 463–79.

Hornsby, Jennifer. 1980. *Actions*. London: Routledge.

Jackson, Reginald. 1929. "Locke's Distinction Between Primary and Secondary Qualities." *Mind* 38, 56–76.

Jacobs, Struan. 1994. "Laws of Nature, Corpuscles, and Concourse: Non-occasionalist Tendencies in the Natural Philosophy of Robert Boyle." *Journal of Philosophical Research* 19, 373–93.

Jacovides, Michael. 1999. "Locke's Resemblance Theses." *Philosophical Review* 108, 461–96.

Jacovides, Michael. 2003. "Locke's Construction of the Idea of Power." *Studies in the History and Philosophy of Science* 34, 329–50.

Jacovides, Michael. 2007. "Locke's Distinctions between Primary and Secondary Qualities." In *The Cambridge Companion to Locke's "Essay Concerning Human Understanding"*, L. Newman, ed. Cambridge: Cambridge University Press, 101–29.

Jacovides, Michael. 2008. "Lockean Fluids." *Contemporary Perspectives on Early Modern Philosophy*, P. Hoffman, D. Owen and G. Yaffe, eds. Peterborough, Ontario: Broadview Press, 215–29.

Jolley, Nicholas. 1990. *The Light of the Soul*, Oxford: Oxford University Press.

Jolley, Nicholas. 1999. *Locke: His Philosophical Thought*, Oxford: Oxford University Press.

Jones, Jan-Erik. "Locke vs. Boyle: The Real Essence of Corpuscular Species." *British Journal for the History of Philosophy* 15, 659–84.

Kant, Immanuel. 1977. *Prolegomena to Any Future Metaphysics*. J. Ellington ed. and trans. Indianapolis: Hackett.

Kaufman, Dan. 2007. "Locke on Individuation and the Corpuscular Basis of Kinds." *Philosophy and Phenomenological Research* 75, 499–534.

Kim, Jaegwon. 1984. "Concepts of Supervenience." *Philosophy and Phenomenological Research* 65, 153–76.

King, Peter. 1830. *The Life of John Locke*, 2 vols. London: Henry Colburn and Richard Bentley.

Kistler, Max. 1998. "Reducing Causality to Transmission." *Erkenntnis* 48, 1–24.

Kornblith, Hilary. 1993. *Inductive Inference and Its Natural Ground*, Cambridge, MA: MIT Press.

Langton, Rae. 2000. "Locke's Relations and God's Good Pleasure." *Proceedings of the Aristotelian Society* (new series) 100, 75–91.

Langton, Rae and Lewis, David. 1998. "Defining 'Intrinsic'." *Philosophy and Phenomenological Research* 58, 333–45.

Langtry, Bruce. 1975. "Locke and the Relativization of Identity." *Philosophical Studies* 27, 401–9.

LaPorte, Joseph. 2004. *Natural Kinds and Conceptual Change*. Cambridge: Cambridge University Press.

Laycock, Henry. 1975. "Theories of Matter." *Synthese* 31, 411–42. Also in *Mass Terms: Some Philosophical Problems*, F. J. Pelletier, ed. Dordrecht: D. Reidel Publishing Company.

Lee, Henry. 1702. *Anti-Scepticism: or, Notes Upon each Chapter of Mr. Lock's Essay Concerning Humane Understanding*. London: Printed for R. Clavel and C. Harper, at the Peacock in S. Paul's Church-yard, etc.

Leibniz, G. W. 1981. *New Essays on Human Understanding*, P. Remnant and J. Bennett trans. Cambridge: Cambridge University Press.

Lindberg, David. 1976. *Theories of Vision from Al-Kindi to Kepler*. Chicago: University of Chicago Press.

Locke, John. 1690/1975. *An Essay Concerning Human Understanding*, P. H. Nidditch ed. Oxford: Oxford University Press.

Locke, John. 1695. *The Reasonableness of Christianity, as Delivered in the Scriptures*. London: Printed for Awnsham and John Churchil, at the Black Swan in Pater-Noster Row.

Locke, John. 1697. *A Letter to the Right Reverend Edward Ld Bishop of Worcester*. London: Printed by H. Clark, for A. and J. Churchill, at the Black Swan in Pater-noster Row.

Locke, John. 1720. *A Collection of Several Pieces of Mr. John Locke, Never before Printed, or Not Extant in His Works*, Pierre Desmaizeaux, ed. London: Printed by J. Bettenham for R. Francklin.

Locke, John. 1823. *The Works of John Locke,* 11th ed., London: Thomas Tegg.

Locke, John. 1954. *Essays on the Laws of Nature*. W. von Leyden ed. Oxford: Clarendon Press.

Locke, John. 1976–1989. *The Correspondence of John Locke*, E. S. DeBeer ed. Oxford: Oxford University Press.

Locke, John. 1987. *A Paraphrase and Notes on the Epistles of St Paul to the Galatians, 1 and 2 Corinthians, Romans, Ephesians*, 2 vols, Arthur W. Wainwright ed. Oxford: Oxford University Press.

Locke, John. 1990. *Drafts for the Essay Concerning Human Understanding, and Other Philosophical Writings*, vol. 1, P. H. Nidditch and G. A. J. Rogers eds. Oxford: Oxford University Press.

Locke, John. 1999. *The Reasonableness of Christianity*, ed. John Higgins-Biddle. Oxford: Oxford University Press.

Lohr, Charles. 1976. "Renaissance Latin Aristotle Commentaries: Authors D–F." *Renaissance Quarterly* 29, 714–45.

LoLordo, Antonia. 2010. "Person, Substance, Mode and 'the *moral Man*' in Locke's Philosophy." *Canadian Journal of Philosophy* 40, 643–68.

Lowe, E. J. 1995. *Locke on Human Understanding*. London: Routledge.

Lowe, E. J. 1986. "Necessity and the Will in Locke's Theory of Action." *History of Philosophy Quarterly* 3, 149–63.

Lowe, E. J. 2005. *Locke*, London: Routledge.

Lowe, E. J. 2009. "Ontological Dependence." *Stanford Encyclopedia of Philosophy*. <http://plato.stanford.edu/entries/dependence-ontological/>.

MacAdam, D. L. 1985. The Physical Basis of Color Specification. In *Readings on Color*, vol. 2, Alex Byrne and David Hilbert, eds. Cambridge: MIT Press, 33–63.

McCann, Edwin. 1985. "Lockean Mechanism." In *Philosophy, its History and Historiography*, A. J. Holland ed. Dordrecht: Reidel/Kluwer, 209–31.

McCann, Edwin. 1987. "Locke on Identity: Matter, Life and Consciousness." *Archiv für Geschichte der Philosophie* 69, 54–77.

McCann, Edwin. 1994. "Locke's Philosophy of Body." In *The Cambridge Companion to Locke*, V. Chappell ed. Cambridge: Cambridge University Press, 56–88.

McCann, Edwin. 2001. "Locke's Theory of Substance Under Attack!" *Philosophical Studies* 106, 87–105.

McCann, Edwin. 2007. "Locke on Substance." in *The Cambridge Companion to Locke's "Essay Concerning Human Understanding"*, L. Newman, ed., Cambridge: Cambridge University Press.

McCracken, Charles. 1983. *Malebranche and British Philosophy*. Oxford: Oxford University Press.

McGuire, J. E. 1972. "Boyle's Conception of Nature." *Journal of the History of Ideas* 33, 523–42.

Macintosh, John. 1976. "Primary and Secondary Qualities." *Studia Leibnitiana* 8, 88–104.

MacIntosh, J. J. 1983. "Perception and Imagination in Descartes, Boyle and Hooke." *Canadian Journal of Philosophy* 13, 327–52.

Mackie, J. L. 1965. "Causes and Conditions." *American Philosophical Quarterly* 2, 245–64.

Mackie, J. L. 1976. *Problems From Locke*, Oxford: Oxford University Press.

Magri, Tito. 2000. "Locke, Suspension of Desire, and the Remote Good." *British Journal of the History of Philosophy* 8, 55–70.

Malebranche, Nicholas. 1980a. *The Search After Truth*, trans. by T. Lennon and P. Olscamp. Columbus: Ohio State University Press.

Malebranche, Nicholas. 1980b. *Dialogues on Metaphysics*, W. Doney trans. New York: Abaris Books.

Mandelbaum, Maurice. 1964. *Philosophy, Science and Sense Perception*, Baltimore: Johns Hopkins Press.

Martin, C. B. 1980. "Substance Substantiated." *Australasian Journal of Philosophy* 58, 3–10.

Mattern, Ruth. 1981. "Locke on Power and Causation: Excerpts from the 1685 Draft of the Essay." *Philosophy Research Archives* 7, no. 1357. [microfilm collection not published in print, no pagination.]

Maull, Nancy. 1978. "Cartesian Optics and the Geometrization of Nature." *Review of Metaphysics* 32, 253–73.

Mayne, Zachary. 1728. *Two Dissertations Concerning Sense, and the Imagination.* London: Printed for J. Tonson in the Strand.

Mertz, D. W. 1996. *Moderate Realism and Its Logic,* New Haven: Yale University Press.

Michael, Emily and Michael, Fred. 1989. "Corporeal Ideas in Seventeenth-Century Psychology." *Journal of the History of Ideas* 50, 31–48.

Milanich, Patricia. 1983. "Allowing, Refraining, and Failing: The Structure of Omissions." *Philosophical Studies* 45, 57–67.

Mill, John Stuart. 1973. *A System of Logic.* J. M. Robson ed. Toronto: University of Toronto Press and London: Routledge.

Moore, Robert. 1979. "Refraining." *Philosophical Studies* 36, 407–24.

Moreland, J. P. 1998. "Theories of Individuation: A Reconsideration of Bare Particulars." *Pacific Philosophical Quarterly* 79, 251–63.

Mumford, Stephen. 1998. *Dispositions.* Oxford: Oxford University Press.

Nadler, Steven. 1992. *Malebranche and Ideas.* Oxford: Oxford University Press.

Nadler, Steven. 1994. "Descartes and Occasional Causation." *British Journal for the History of Philosophy* 2, 35–54.

Nassau, Kurt. 1985. "The Causes of Color." In *Readings on Color,* vol. 2. Alex Byrne and David Hilbert, ed. Cambridge: MIT Press, 3–39.

Newman, Lex. 2000. "Locke on the Idea of Substratum." *Pacific Philosophical Quarterly* 81, 291–324.

Norris, John. 1690. *Cursory Reflections upon a Book call'd An Essay concerning Human Understanding. Appended to Christian Blessedness.* London: Printed for S. Manship at the Black Bull.

Norris, John. 1704. *An Essay Towards the Theory of the Ideal or Intelligible World.* London: Printed for S. Manship, at the Ship in Cornhill, near the Royal-Exchange; and W. Hawes, at the Rose in Ludgate-Street near the West-End of St. Paul's Church.

O'Connor, D. J. 1952. *John Locke.* London: Penguin Books.

Odegard, Douglas. 1969. "Locke and Substance." *Dialogue: Canadian Philosophical Review* 8, 243–55.

Odegard, Douglas. 1988. "Volition and Action." *American Philosophical Quarterly* 25, 141–51.

Olson, Eric. 1997. *The Human Animal: Personal Identity Without Psychology.* Oxford: Oxford University Press.

O'Shaughnessy, Brian. 1973. "Trying (As the Mental 'Pineal Gland')." *Journal of Philosophy* 70, 365–86.

Ott, Walter. 2009. *Causation and Laws of Nature in Early Modern Philosophy*. Oxford: Oxford University Press.

Owen, David. 1991. "Locke on Real Essence." *History of Philosophy Quarterly* 8, 105–18.

Owen, David. 2007. "Locke on Judgment." In *The Cambridge Companion to Locke's Essay*, Lex Newman ed. Cambridge: Cambridge University Press, 406–35.

Parfit, Derek. 1984. *Reasons and Persons*. Oxford: Clarendon Press.

Pasnau, Robert. 1997. *Theories of Cognition in the Later Middle Ages*. Cambridge: Cambridge University Press.

Pasnau, Robert. 2011. *Metaphysical Themes 1274–1671*. Oxford: Clarendon Press.

Pelletier, F. J., ed. 1979. *Mass Terms: Some Philosophical Problems*. Dordrecht: D. Reidel Publishing Company.

Pessin, Andrew. 2003. "Descartes's Nomic Concurrentism: Finite Causation and Divine Concurrence." *Journal of the History of Philosophy* 41, 25–49.

Pessin, Andrew. 2004. "Malebranche on Ideas." *Canadian Journal of Philosophy* 34, 241–86.

Phemister, Pauline. 1990. "Real Essences in Particular." *Locke Newsletter* 21, 27–55.

Platt, Andrew. 2011a. "Divine Activity and Motive Power in Descartes's Physics, Part 1." *British Journal for the History of Philosophy* 19, 623–46.

Platt, Andrew. 2011b. "Divine Activity and Motive Power in Descartes's Physics, Part 2." *British Journal for the History of Philosophy* 19, 849–71.

Porphyry. 2003. *Introduction*, Jonathan Barnes trans. and ed. Oxford: Clarendon Press.

Prichard, H. A. 1949. *Moral Obligation*. Oxford: Clarendon Press.

Radner, Dasie. 1978. *Malebranche: A Study of a Cartesian System*. Assen: Van Gorcum.

Rea, Michael, ed. 1997. *Material Constitution: A Reader*. Lanham: Rowman & Littlefield Publishers, Inc.

Rickless, Samuel. 1997. "Locke on Primary and Secondary Qualities." *Pacific Philosophical Quarterly* 78, 297–319.

Reid, Thomas. 1983. *Inquiry and Essays*, R. Beanblossom and K. Lehrer eds. Indianapolis: Hackett Publishing Co.

Rozemond, Marleen and Yaffe, Gideon. 2004. "Peach Trees, Gravity and God: Mechanism in Locke," *British Journal for the History of Philosophy* 12, 387–412.

Ryle, Gilbert. 1932/1971. "John Locke on the Human Understanding," in *Collected Papers*, vol. 1. London: Hutchison & Co.

Ryle, Gilbert. 1949. *The Concept of Mind*. London: Hutchinson & Co.

Ryle, Gilbert. 1979. "Negative 'Actions'." *On Thinking*. K. Kolenda ed. Oxford: Blackwell.

Searle, John. 1983. *Intentionality*, Cambridge: Cambridge University Press.

Schmaltz, Tad. 2008. *Descartes on Causation*. Oxford: Oxford University Press.

Schouls, Peter. 1992. *Reasoned Freedom*. Ithaca: Cornell University Press.

Sergeant, John. 1697. *Solid Philosophy Asserted Against the Fancies of the Ideists*. London: Printed for Roger Clavil at the Peacock, etc.

Sergeant, John. 1697/1984. *Solid Philosophy Asserted Against the Fancies of the Ideists*. New York: Garland Publishing, Inc. (A reprint of Locke's personal copy of Sergeant 1697, with his handwritten marginalia.)

Shanahan, Timothy. 1988. "God and Nature in the Thought of Robert Boyle." *Journal of the History of Philosophy* 26, 547–69.

Shoemaker, Sydney. 1963. *Self-Knowledge and Self-Identity*. Ithaca: Cornell University Press.

Shoemaker, Sydney. 1980. "Causality and Properties" reprinted in Shoemaker 1984.

Shoemaker, Sydney. 1984. *Identity, Cause and Mind*. Cambridge: Cambridge University Press.

Shoemaker, Sydney. 1990. "Qualities and Qualia: What's in the Mind?" *Philosophy and Phenomenological Research* 50, supp.: 109–131.

Shoemaker, Sydney. 1994. "Phenomenal Character." *Noûs* 28, 21–38.

Sidelle, Alan. 1989. *Necessity, Essence and Individuation: A Defense of Conventionalism*. Ithaca: Cornell University Press.

Sidelle, Alan. 1991. "Formed Matter Without Objects: A Reply to Denkel." *Dialogue* 30, 163–71.

Simmons, Alison. 1994. "Explaining Sense Perception: A Scholastic Challenge," *Philosophical Studies* 73, 257–75.

Simmons, Alison. 2003. "Descartes on the Cognitive Structure of Sensory Experience," *Philosophy and Phenomenological Research* 67, 549–79.

Sinnott-Armstrong, Walter and Sparrow, David. 2002. "A Light Theory of Color." *Philosophical Studies* 110, 267–84.

Smith, A. D. 1988. "Agency and the Essence of Actions," *Philosophical Quarterly* 38, 401–21.

Smith, A. D. 1990. "Of Primary and Secondary Qualities." *Philosophical Review* 99, 221–54.

Solomon, Robert and Higgins, Kathleen. 1996. *A Short History of Philosophy*. Oxford: Oxford University Press.

Sorabji, Richard. 1988. *Matter, Space and Motion: Theories in Antiquity and their Sequel*. Ithaca, NY: Cornell University Press.

Spellman, William M. 1994. "Between Death and Judgment: Conflicting Images of the Afterlife in Late Seventeenth-Century Eulogies." *Harvard Theological Review* 87, 49–65.

Spinoza, Benedictus de. 1985. *The Collected Works of Spinoza*, vol. 1, E. Curley trans. and ed. Princeton, NJ: Princeton University Press.

Stillingfleet, Edward. 1697. *A Discourse in Vindication of the Doctrine of the Trinity*. London: Printed by J.H. for Henry Mortlock at the Phœnix in S. Paul's Church-yard.

Stillingfleet, Edward. 1698. *The Bishop of Worcester's Answer to Mr. Locke's Second Letter*, London: Printed by J.H. for Henry Mortlock at the Phœnix in St. Paul's Church-Yard.

Stjernberg, Fredrik. 2003. "An Argument Against the Trope Theory." *Erkenntnis* 59, 37–46.

Strawson, Galen. 2011. *Locke on Personal Identity: Consciousness and Concernment*, Princeton: Princeton University Press.

Strawson, P. F. 1959. *Individuals*, London: Methuen.

Stuart, Matthew. 1996. "Locke's Geometrical Analogy." *History of Philosophy Quarterly* 13, 451–67.

Stuart, Matthew. 1998. "Locke on Superaddition and Mechanism," *British Journal for the History of Philosophy* 6: 351–79.

Stuart, Matthew. 2008. "Lockean Operations." *British Journal for the History of Philosophy* 18, 511–33.

Stuart, Matthew. 2010. "Having Locke's Ideas." *Journal of the History of Philosophy* 48, 35–59.

Suarez, Francisco. 1994. *On Efficient Causality*, A. Freddoso trans. New Haven: Yale University Press.

Tachau, Katherine. 1988. *Vision and Certitude in the Age of Ockham*. Leiden: E. J. Brill.

Thiel, Udo. 1998. "Individuation." In *The Cambridge History of Seventeenth-Century Philosophy*, Daniel Garber and Michael Ayers. eds. Cambridge: Cambridge University Press.

Thomson, Judith. 1997 "People and Their Bodies." In *Reading Parfit*, Jonathan Dancy, ed. Oxford: Blackwell Publishers.

Uzgalis, William. 1990. "Relative Identity and Locke's Principle of Individuation." *History of Philosophy Quarterly* 7, 283–97.

Vailati, Ezio. 1990. "Leibniz on Locke on Weakness of Will." *Journal of the History of Philosophy* 28, 213–28.

Van Inwagen, Peter. 1990. *Material Beings*. Ithaca: Cornell University Press.

Wiggins, David. 2001. *Sameness and Substance Renewed*, Cambridge: Cambridge University Press.

Williams, Donald C. 1953. "The Elements of Being." *Review of Metaphysics* 7, 3–18, 171–92.

Wilson, Margaret. 1979. "Superadded Properties: The Limits of Mechanism in Locke," *American Philosophical Quarterly* 16, 143–50.

Wilson, Margaret. 1992. "Descartes on the Perception of Primary Qualities," in *Essays on the Philosophy and Science of René Descartes*, Stephen Voss, ed. Oxford: Oxford University Press, 162–76.

Wilson, Robert. 2002. "Locke's Primary Qualities." *Journal of the History of Philosophy* 40, 201–28.

Winkler, Kenneth. 1991. "Locke on Personal Identity." *Journal of the History of Philosophy* 29, 201–26.

Winkler, Kenneth. 1992. "Ideas, Sentiments and Qualities." In *Minds, Ideas, and Objects*, ed. P. Cummins and G. Zoeller. Atascadero, CA: Ridgeview Publishing Co. 151–65.

Winkler, Kenneth. Forthcoming. "Locke on Essence and the Social Construction of Kinds." To appear in *The Blackwell Companion to Locke*, ed. Matthew Stuart, London: Wiley-Blackwell.

Woolhouse, R. S. 1971. *Locke's Philosophy of Science and Knowledge*. New York: Barnes & Noble.

Woolhouse, R. S. 1983. *Locke*. Minneapolis: University of Minnesota Press.

Woozley, A. D. 1964. "Introduction" In *An Essay Concerning Human Understanding*, A. D. Woozley ed. and abridged. London: W. Collins.

Xu, Fei. 1997. "From Lot's Wife to a Pillar of Salt: Evidence that *Physical Object* is a Sortal Concept." *Mind and Language* 12, 365–92.

Yaffe, Gideon. 2000. *Liberty Worth the Name: Locke on Free Agency*. Princeton: Princeton University Press.

Yaffe, Gideon. 2001. "Locke on Refraining, Suspending and the Freedom of the Will." *History of Philosophy Quarterly* 18, 373–91.

Yaffe, Gideon. 2007. "Locke on Ideas of Identity and Diversity." In *The Cambridge Companion to Locke's "Essay Concerning Human Understanding"*, L. Newman, ed., Cambridge: Cambridge University Press, 192–230.

Yolton, John. 1970. *Locke and the Compass of Human Understanding*, Cambridge: Cambridge University Press.

Index

Index Locorum